Cognition

Cognition

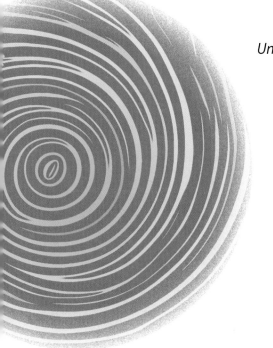

Marvin M. Chun
Yale University

Steven B. Most
University of New South Wales, Sydney

OXFORD
UNIVERSITY PRESS

NEW YORK   OXFORD
OXFORD UNIVERSITY PRESS

Oxford University Press is a department of the University of Oxford. It furthers the University's objective of excellence in research, scholarship, and education by publishing worldwide. Oxford is a registered trade mark of Oxford University Press in the UK and certain other countries.

Published in the United States of America by Oxford University Press
198 Madison Avenue, New York, NY 10016, United States of America.

ACCESSIBLE COLOR CONTENT   Every opportunity has been taken to ensure that the content herein is fully accessible to those who have difficulty perceiving color. Exceptions are cases where the colors provided are expressly required because of the purpose of the illustration.

NOTICE OF TRADEMARKS   Throughout this book trademark names have been used, and in some instances, depicted. In lieu of appending the trademark symbol to each occurrence, the authors and publisher state that these trademarks are used in an editorial fashion, to the benefit of the trademark owners, and with no intent to infringe upon the trademarks.

Library of Congress Cataloging-in-Publication Data

Names: Chun, Marvin M., author. | Most, Steven B., author.

Title: Cognition / Marvin M. Chun, Yale University, Steven B. Most, The University of New South Wales, Sydney.

Description: New York : Oxford University Press, 2021. | Includes bibliographical references and index. |
Summary: "Chun and Most's *Cognition* brings new, modern vitality to course materials by presenting exciting findings from cognitive psychology in a way that students can easily grasp. Highlighting everyday-life applications, *Cognition* motivates students to share in the excitement of cognitive psychology through highly relevant examples, discussions, and demonstrations. Its engaging prose and pedagogical features, such as "Think for Yourself" and "See for Yourself," immerse students in the process of scientific discovery. This comprehensive text presents both classic and contemporary research, emphasizing conceptual understanding and lifelong discovery. In addition, the authors integrate exciting new topic areas such as emotion and highlight essential connections to social, clinical, and developmental psychology."
--Provided by publisher.

Identifiers: LCCN 2021009441 (print) | LCCN 2021009442 (ebook) | ISBN 9780199950638 (hardback) | ISBN 9780190878733 | ISBN 9780190878726 (epub)

Subjects: LCSH: Cognition. | Perception. | Memory. | Developmental psychobiology.

Classification: LCC BF311 .C53918 2021 (print) | LCC BF311 (ebook) | DDC 153--dc23

LC record available at https://lccn.loc.gov/2021009441

LC ebook record available at https://lccn.loc.gov/2021009442

Printing number: 9 8 7 6 5 4 3 2 1
Printed by LSC Communications, United States of America

For our families, who sustain us;
for our mentors and colleagues, who teach us;
and for the students we seek to inspire.
MMC and SBM

Brief Table of Contents

Contents

About the Authors

Marvin M. Chun is the Richard M. Colgate Professor of Psychology at Yale University, with secondary appointments in the Cognitive Science Program and the Yale School of Medicine Department of Neuroscience. He received his PhD in Brain and Cognitive Sciences from the Massachusetts Institute of Technology, where he won a graduate teaching award, followed by postdoctoral training at Harvard University. Professor Chun leads a cognitive neuroscience laboratory that uses functional brain imaging and machine learning to decode and predict how people see, attend, remember, and perform optimally. His research has been honored with a Troland Award from the U.S. National Academy of Sciences, an American Psychological Association Distinguished Scientific Award for an Early Career Contribution to Psychology in the area of cognition and human learning, and a Samsung Ho-Am Prize in Science (South Korea). His teaching has been recognized with both the Lex Hixon '63 Prize for Teaching Excellence in the Social Sciences and the Phi Beta Kappa William Clyde DeVane Medal for Distinguished Scholarship and Teaching in Yale College.

Steven B. Most is Associate Professor of Psychology at the University of New South Wales in Sydney, Australia (UNSW Sydney), with an affiliate appointment in the Department of Psychological and Brain Sciences at the University of Delaware. He received his BA in psychology from Brandeis University and PhD in psychology from Harvard University, where he won graduate teaching awards, followed by postdoctoral training at Vanderbilt and Yale Universities. Dr. Most leads the Motivated Attention and Perception Lab at UNSW Sydney, where his team uses behavioral and physiological measures to understand how attention, motivation, and emotion shape what people see, remember, and do, as well as how cognition affects safety and well-being in the real world (e.g., road safety). Dr. Most's research has been recognized through fellowships and awards from the National Institutes of Health, the Australian Research Council, and the New York Academy of Sciences, and with an appointment as Fellow of the Association for Psychological Science. His teaching and mentoring have been recognized with the Alpha Lambda Delta Excellence in Teaching Award at the University of Delaware and both a Postgraduate Supervisor Award and an Outstanding Postgraduate Supervisor Award at UNSW Sydney.

Before writing *Cognition*, Professors Chun and Most collaborated on research examining how emotional stimuli capture attention.

Preface

"Seven minutes of terror." That's how NASA engineers described the wait as the Mars rover *Perseverance* made its descent in February 2021. To introduce our text, let's begin by considering what went into this suspenseful, historic moment.

The abilities to solve problems, visualize, predict obstacles, communicate with team members, and develop creative solutions were vital to the success of the mission—and all are central features of cognition. More broadly, at the core of cognitive psychology are the topics of perception, attention, learning, memory, language, reasoning, and decision making, all well represented in our book.

In a way, the rover itself helps illustrate what "cognition" means, relying on an artificial intelligence that acts like the human mind. As it entered Mars's atmosphere, the rover took in information from the environment, manipulated this information, and adjusted its actions accordingly. It did so while hurtling 13,000 miles per hour, reaching temperatures of 1,600 degrees Fahrenheit. The jaw-dropping images the rover has sent back are possible because the onboard computers format them into nonvisual signals that can be transmitted back to Earth, where they are reconstructed into visual form. This process of encoding, reformatting, and reconstructing information is analogous to what our minds do each time we take in the world around us or draw on our memory. Cognitive psychology is the study of what the mind is and what it does.

Throughout this book, we remind readers of the big picture, using anecdotes and current events to show how cognitive psychology helps us understand the way people act every day. As part of presenting the broader scope, we cover topic areas such as emotion and draw essential connections to social, clinical, and developmental psychology. Understanding the role of cognition in psychology will improve human lives and society, and it can also make machines more intelligent and useful. Our hope is to inspire new generations of students to share in our excitement about this fascinating field.

Approach

Cognition presents exciting findings from contemporary cognitive psychology in a way that students can easily grasp. Highlighting everyday-life applications, *Cognition* invites students to participate in the process of science through activities, videos, and demonstrations. An overarching goal is for students to come away with an appre-

Courtesy of NASA/JPL-Caltech

An illustration of NASA's *Perseverance* rover touching down on Mars in 2021.

© NASA Photo/Alamy Stock Photo

The cheering team upon receiving confirmation of successful touchdown on the surface of Mars.

ciation of the scope and nature of cognitive psychology. We cover how cognitive scientists test hypotheses about the workings of the mind, how cognitive psychology applies to everyday life, and how this field connects with other disciplines and areas of psychology. Like many teachers of cognition, we are active researchers who study cognition. We want students to discover a vibrant, dynamic, challenging field of study and to form their own questions.

This book's combination of characteristics helps make it unique, enhancing the learning and teaching experience alike:

An integration of neuroscience. Over recent decades, rapid advances in neuroscience have informed every branch of psychology. This synthesis has had profound consequences for our understanding of cognition. By combining powerful neuroimaging techniques with established cognitive measures, researchers have blurred the line between what it means to be a cognitive psychologist and what it means to be a cognitive *neuroscientist*. In short, the emergence of *cognitive neuroscience* marked a fundamental shift in the field, as this book reflects. Each chapter weaves in a discussion of neural underpinnings, but only when relevant to behavior. For example, the fact that brain injuries can selectively impair some memory behaviors but not others suggests that there are different memory types and systems. Similarly, functional brain imaging has helped inform debates about the nature of mental representation, such as the relation between perception and mental imagery.

An integration of emotion. Emotion affects nearly all aspects of cognitive processing, from attention and memory to reasoning and decision making. Yet the field of cognition has traditionally steered away from considerations of emotion; it is only in the last few decades that emotion has become increasingly recognized as an integral aspect of information processing. Reflecting the pervasiveness of emotion's influence, we incorporate discussions of emotion throughout the book.

An integration of real-world examples. Throughout this book, we incorporate compelling real-life news stories, anecdotes, and demonstrations, all of which make the text engaging and accessible. For example, to introduce students to the relevance and scope of cognitive psychology, the text opens with the dramatic true story of a pilot who landed his plane in New York City's Hudson River. Chapter 6, Everyday Memory, begins with a difficult case of mistaken eyewitness testimony. Chapter 8, Language and Communication, begins with young couples in Coahulia, Mexico, who communicate via whistling in the night. In addition to including real examples, chapters incorporate videos and demonstrations that help bring the material to life.

Links to social, clinical, and developmental psychology. Rather than being islands unto themselves, these subareas inform our understanding of cognition. Throughout the chapters, this book highlights links between cognitive principles and their social, clinical, and developmental implications and extensions.

Organization

The book is organized for ease of teaching in one semester or in one to two quarters. For a semester-long course, each of the twelve chapters can correspond to a week.

Chapter 1, What Is Cognitive Psychology?, describes the types of questions cognitive psychologists ask, explains how the field developed, and highlights connections to other areas of psychology.

Chapter 2, Cognitive Neuroscience, helps students understand the tight link between brain and behavior. Supporting the interdisciplinary thread that runs throughout the book, this chapter also provides an overview of cognitive neuroscience methods, focusing on their strengths and weaknesses.

Chapter 3, Perception and Mental Imagery, explores ways in which perception is something we construct and how it is a combination of sensory stimulation and the mind's detective work. We provide a multitude of engaging examples (e.g., the dress photo that went viral) to help students make the connection between perception and mental imagery.

We cover the study of attention across both Chapter 4, External Attention, and Chapter 5, Cognitive Control and Working Memory. This organization allows us to discuss in depth how attention can be directed both outwardly and inwardly, as well as factors that affect selection and attention in different cases.

We discuss the rich topic of memory across the next two chapters. Chapter 6, Everyday Memory, covers strategies for improving memory and also shows how memories can be distorted in everyday life. Chapter 7, Memory Systems, provides an overview of different types of memory and the brain systems supporting them.

Chapter 8, Language and Communication, offers comprehensive yet succinct coverage of the fascinating topic of language, including its defining qualities, the work of Noam Chomsky, phonemes and morphemes, language development in children, communication challenges, and the Sapir-Whorf hypothesis.

This text covers high-level cognition in detail. Chapter 9, Judgment and Decision Making, prompts students to consider the differences between different types of decision making and how various factors can affect each type. The chapter ends with insights from the field of neuroeconomics based on brain imaging studies. Chapter 10, Reasoning and Problem Solving, looks at everyday examples of delay discounting; different forms of deductive reasoning, inductive reasoning, and confirmation bias; Bayesian reasoning; different problem-solving techniques and factors that contribute to creativity; and the role of theory of mind and trust in social reasoning.

Chapter 11, Knowledge, Intelligence, and Cognitive Development, covers how categories are defined and represented, discusses subtleties in the meaning of intelligence, and outlines how cognitive capacities develop across childhood.

Chapter 12, Social Cognition, is especially innovative and is unique among texts for this course. It emphasizes how social cognition connects with other areas of cognitive psychology; considers evidence of human sensitivity to social information; examines research on stereotypes, prejudice, and in-groups and out-groups; and discusses how motivated reasoning can impede civility, cooperation, and understanding.

Features

Cognition motivates students to share in the excitement of cognitive psychology through highly relevant examples, demonstrations, and features, including the following:

- Thirty-seven **Discovery Labs** offer a wide variety of interactive experiments, exercises, and animations designed to help students understand important concepts and principles. These labs bring cognition topics to life, allowing students to act as researchers and test subjects in simulated experimental trials. Discovery Labs are incorporated into each chapter as the relevant topics are discussed.

- **See for Yourself** demonstrations describe an activity or mental trick students can easily do themselves to see cognition in action. For example, Chapter 3 illustrates compelling visual demonstrations and illusions, and Chapter 9 challenges the reader with decision-making and judgment tasks.

- **Think for Yourself** features provide an in-depth look at interesting subjects relevant to the chapter content. Examples include whether Google is hurting your memory, how poverty impairs decision making, and the role of emotions in making moral judgments.

- **Research Focus** boxes highlight cutting-edge research studies, explaining methodology and results. For example, Chapter 9 looks at research on decision making in monkeys and humans, which demonstrates that some biases in decision making are shared across different species.

- **Checkpoint Questions** at the end of each major section help students test their understanding as they progress through a chapter.

Enhanced E-book

An enhanced e-book offers interactive multimedia content integrated with the text and is ideal for self-study. Chapters include the following:

- Video clips to engage students in learning about cognition
- Access to the relevant Discovery Labs
- Flashcards to help students master new vocabulary
- Multiple-choice self-quizzes at the end of each major section

Oxford Learning Link

Simple, accessible, and user-friendly, Oxford Learning Link at www.oup.com/he/chun1e is the hub for a wealth of engaging, digital learning tools and resources, including:

- Test bank
- Discovery Labs and quizzes
- Video clips and quizzes
- PowerPoints
- Instructor's manual
- Chapter quizzes

In addition, **Oxford Learning Link Direct** brings all the high-quality digital teaching and learning tools for *Cognition* right to your local **learning management system**. Instructors and administrators can easily download the Learning Link Direct cartridge from Oxford Learning Link.

Oxford Learning Cloud

Ideal for instructors who do not use their school's designated learning management system, Oxford Learning Cloud delivers engaging learning tools in an easy-to-use, mobile-friendly, cloud-based courseware platform. Learning Cloud offers prebuilt courses that instructors can either use off the shelf or customize to fit their needs. A built-in gradebook allows instructors to see quickly and easily how the class and individual students are performing.

Features Contents

Acknowledgments

If this textbook were a research article for a journal (our usual publication outlet), we would get to properly recognize the contributions of more than a dozen authors, all of whom brought essential and diverse expertise to this book. The team at Oxford University Press has been extraordinary, led by Joan Kalkut, Senior Editor of Higher Education at the press. Joan supervised all aspects of this project, and her steady hand is what ensured its successful completion. Prior to that, we are grateful to Jane Potter for approaching us to write this book and for guiding it through the first draft. Throughout the writing process, Senior Development Editors Lauren Mine and Marian Provenzano provided extensive edits and suggestions that improved our drafts immensely—we wish we could write all our papers with them. Media Editors Lauren Elfers and Suzanne Carter oversaw key aspects of the complex digital package. The production stage of the book was exciting for us, and we are thrilled with the overall look of the book and its figures. For all this, we thank the leadership of Linnea Duley, Production Editor; Tracy Marton, Senior Production Editor; Joan Gemme, Production Manager; Donna DiCarlo, Production Specialist and Book Designer; Mark Siddall, Photo Research Editor; Michele Beckta, Permissions Supervisor; Sandy Cooke and Cailen Swain, Permissions Managers; and Liz Pierson, Copy Editor. For marketing, we are grateful to Joan Lewis-Milne, Marketing Manager, and to Ashendri Wickremasinghe, Marketing Assistant. Everyone was so encouraging, responsive, and patient—this book reflects their professional expertise and warm spirits.

Our sincere thanks to Wil Cunningham, University of Toronto, and Roberta Golinkoff, University of Delaware. We also received helpful suggestions from Marilynn Brewer, UNSW Sydney; Kim Curby, Macquarie University; Dan Grodner, Swarthmore College; Eric Hehman, McGill University; and Marcus Taft, UNSW Sydney.

The Discovery Labs were created by Carolyn Ensley of Wilfrid Laurier University. Our thanks to Tim Ellmore of City University of New York for creating accessible versions and quizzes for these labs, as well as quizzes for the videos incorporated throughout the book. We are grateful to Michael Chen of California State University, Los Angeles, for writing the e-book review quizzes and chapter exams; to Shahram Ghiasinejad of University of Central Florida for writing the chapter quizzes; to David Holtzman of Rochester Institute of Technology and Xavier University School of Medicine, Aruba, for creating the test bank and lecture PowerPoints; and to Christie Chung of Mills College for writing the instructor's manual.

We are grateful to the members of our Editorial Advisory Board for their thoughtful feedback:

Timothy Ellmore, *City University of New York*
Shahram Ghiasinejad, *University of Central Florida*
Jeffery Gray, *Charleston Southern University*
Arturo Hernandez, *University of Houston*
Louisa Slowiaczek, *Bowdoin College*
Andreas Wilke, *Clarkson University*

Finally, we sincerely appreciate the comments of all the thoughtful reviewers commissioned by Oxford University Press:

Aisha Adams, *Columbus State University*
Erik Altmann, *Michigan State University*
Pamela Ansberg, *Metropolitan State University of Denver*
Stephen Baker, *Saint Francis University*
Kristy Biolsi, *St. Francis College*
Hiram Brownell, *Boston College*
Kit W. Cho, *University of Houston-Downtown*
Christie Chung, *Mills College*
David Cipolloni, *Bethune-Cookman University*
Luis Cordon, *Eastern Connecticut State University*
Natalie Costa, *University of New Orleans*
Lauren Coursey, *University of Texas at Arlington*
Baine Craft, *Seattle Pacific University*
Wil Cunningham, *University of Toronto*
Rebecca Deason, *Texas State University*
Mike Dodd, *University of Nebraska–Lincoln*
Stephen Dopkins, *George Washington University*
Jamie Edgin, *The University of Arizona*
Arne Ekstrom, *The University of Arizona*

Sarah Elliott, *Roosevelt University*

Stephani Foraker, *State University of New York, Buffalo State College*

Anne Gilman, *Bennington College*

Roberta Golinkoff, *University of Delaware*

Keith Gora, *Bemidji State University*

Jeffery Gray, *Charleston Southern University*

Kim Guenther, *Hamline University*

Andrea R. Halpern, *Bucknell University*

Sebastien Hélie, *Purdue University*

Linda A. Henkel, *Fairfield University*

Roberto Heredia, *Texas A&M International University*

Arturo Hernandez, *University of Houston*

Debora Herold, *Indiana University–Purdue University Indianapolis*

Julie Higgins, *Manhattanville College*

Robert Hines, *University of Arkansas, Little Rock*

James Hoeffner, *University of Michigan*

James Hoelzle, *Marquette University*

McNeel Jantzen, *Western Washington University*

Jerwen Jou, *University of Texas Rio Grande Valley*

Albert Kim, *University of Colorado*

Heather Kleider-Offutt, *Georgia State University*

Nate Kornell, *Williams College*

Roger Kreuz, *University of Memphis*

Cara Laney, *College of Idaho*

Mervin Matthew, *University of Mississippi*

Conor McLennan, *Cleveland State University*

Mary Michael, *University of North Carolina at Charlotte*

Steve Mitroff, *George Washington University*

Ben Motz, *Indiana University, Bloomington*

Janet Nicol, *University of Arizona*

Matthew Nordlund, *Cleveland State University*

Daniel Oppenheimer, *Carnegie Mellon University*

Laura O'Toole, *City University of New York, Hunter College*

Anna Papafragou, *University of Pennsylvania*

Matthew J. Pastizzo, *State University of New York, Geneseo*

Luiz Pessoa, *University of Maryland, College Park*

Mary Potter, *Massachusetts Institute of Technology*

Jennifer Queen, *Rollins College*

Paul Quinn, *University of Delaware*

Kristin Ritchey, *Ball State University*

Shannon Robertson, *Jacksonville State University*

Jennifer Roth, *Carlow University*

Jeff Sandoz, *Troy University*

Daniel Schacter, *Harvard University*

Pamela Joyce Shapiro, *Temple University, Ambler*

Tatiana Schnur, *Baylor College of Medicine*

Bennett Schwartz, *Florida International University*

Robert Slevc, *University of Maryland, College Park*

Colleen Stevenson, *Muskingum University*

Greg Stone, *Arizona State University*

Evelina Tapia, *University of Illinois at Urbana-Champaign*

Jason Trent, *Hood College*

Lisa VanWormer, *St. Norbert College*

Audrey Weil, *Washington College*

Miko Wilford, *University of Massachusetts, Lowell*

Erica Wohldmann, *California State University, Northridge*

Maryjane Wraga, *Smith College*

Abdolhossein Abdollahy Zarandi, *University of Texas at El Paso*

What Is Cognitive Psychology?

1

In January 2009, two minutes after taking off from New York's LaGuardia Airport, US Airways Flight 1549 slammed into a flock of birds. The engines lost power. Amid the alarm and confusion, and with too little time to return to the airport, the pilot, Chesley "Sully" Sullenberger, made the call to land the plane in the Hudson River. Miraculously, everyone survived. Captain Sullenberger's name became synonymous with cool, collected competence, the result of rigorous training, and—many would say—heroism. What does this story have to do with cognitive psychology?

Think about everything that had to happen in the three minutes before the plane came to rest in the frigid water (or watch the 2016 movie *Sully*, starring Tom Hanks). Despite the panic, Sullenberger had to focus only on the information relevant for a safe landing; he had to make critical decisions and act fast. This was possible only because of the relative automaticity that comes with extensive training. He also had to remember plans of action for emergency situations. And he had to do all this in a high-pressure context, regulating and putting aside any rising feelings of terror. In other words, all

Chris McGrath/Getty Images

The safe landing of Flight 1549 was hailed as "the Miracle on the Hudson." Because of Captain Sullenberger's quick assessment of the situation and skill, all passengers and crew on the flight survived the emergency landing in the river.

LEARNING OBJECTIVES

1.1 Describe the types of topics cognitive psychologists investigate.

1.2 Describe the precursors to the field of cognitive psychology as a science.

1.3 Discuss the emergence of the Cognitive Revolution and the developments that followed.

1.4 Explain how cognitive psychology connects with other areas of research, both within and outside psychology.

passengers and crew of Flight 1549 survived partly because of a complex coordination of attention, memory, expertise, decision making, and self-control. These are topics at the heart of cognitive psychology.

1.1 The Study of Cognition

People have wondered how the mind works for thousands of years. **Cognitive psychology** is the scientific study of how the mind encodes, stores, and uses information—in other words, it is the study of **cognition**. Although questions of cognition sat on the fringes of mainstream psychology 70 years ago, they now permeate nearly every corner of the field. The resurgence of the study of cognition came about from multiple fields—including psychology, computer science, neuroscience, and more. These fields converged on the notion that information processing itself can be a fruitful focus of study.

Cognitive psychology is relevant not only to such rare and dramatic cases as the Sullenberger story. It is the study of how we process information in everyday life, whether we are navigating traffic, studying for an exam, or deciding to end a long-term romantic relationship. It helps us understand how a football quarterback can track multiple teammates at once, how a radiologist can make diagnoses from X-rays that most of us can't interpret, why eyewitnesses so often give unreliable testimony (and what to do about it), and why even the most experienced financial investors are apt to make bad decisions. In short, the study of cognitive psychology pertains to almost everything we do.

Since the first modern cognitive psychology textbook was published in 1967, the scope of the field has grown, including topics such as perception, attention, memory, reasoning, and decision making, among other aspects of information processing. Approaches to cognitive psychology range from highly controlled experiments that isolate mental processes within the lab to broader studies that aim to understand how cognitive processes operate in the real world. The results of these efforts continually inform our understanding of social interactions, emotion, and mental health.

The human capacity for wonder knows no bounds. Who hasn't wondered about the origin of the stars, the possibility of life on other planets, or the mysterious species that might roam undiscovered on the ocean floor? For those inclined to look inward, the workings of the mind have been a source of similar fascination. Cognitive psychology aims to use objective measures of behavior to scientifically test and build an understanding of how the mind works. Appropriately, the word "cognitive" comes from the Latin *cognosco*, "to know." Put simply, cognitive psychology seeks to understand how we come to know about the world and how we use that knowledge to make our way through it. **SEE FOR YOURSELF 1.1**, **1.2**, and **1.3** provide examples of what cognitive psychologists examine when they investigate how we encode, store, and use information.

▶ **See for Yourself 1.1**

Encoding Information: Selective Attention

Despite deeply held intuitions, seeing is not just a matter of opening our eyes. Instead, the mind selects only portions of information and constructs what we mistakenly believe to be a faithful and complete perception of the world around us.

Look up and watch the "Selective Attention Test" by Dan Simons, available on YouTube, as an example.

As you can see, encoding (in this case through vision) is just as much a matter of what your mind can keep track of as it is a matter of how you use your eyes. We will discuss the striking phenomenon of inattentional blindness in Chapter 4.

► **See for Yourself 1.2**

Storing Information: Can We Trust Our Memories?

How much can we trust our memories? To what degree are they faithfully stored recordings of what we've experienced? Not so much, it turns out. Memory is so suggestible that even very vivid recollections may contain false information—things we are sure we experienced but in fact never did. How easy is it to experience a false memory? In Chapter 6 you will learn about an easy way to induce false memories in the lab. In the meantime, watch famed memory researcher Elizabeth Loftus discuss her groundbreaking research on false memories in her widely watched TED talk, entitled "How reliable is your memory?" and viewable on YouTube.

► **See for Yourself 1.3**

Using Information: Making Moral Decisions

Do you think we can make all decisions by rationally weighing the pros and cons of each option? Well, what would you do in the following scenario, known as the Trolley Problem?

You are walking near train tracks when you notice a runaway trolley racing toward five people who can't move out of the way in time. You happen to be standing next to a lever that will switch the train onto a different track, thereby saving all five people. Unfortunately, there is a sixth person trapped on the alternative track who will be killed if you move the lever. What do you do? Do you throw the lever, saving five people but killing one? Or do you do nothing, sparing the one person's life while allowing the five others to be killed?

(Based on Foot, 1967; Thomson, 1976.)

This is not an easy decision. But many people choose to throw the lever. After all, as tragic as either outcome would be, surely five deaths are worse than one. But what would you do in the following, slightly different scenario?

You are standing on a bridge over train tracks when you notice a runaway trolley racing toward five people who can't move out of the way in time. You are standing next to a very big man, and you realize that if you were to push him off the bridge and in front of the trolley, his weight would be enough to stop it, thereby saving five people but killing him. What do you do? Do you push the man off the bridge, saving five people but killing one? Or do you do nothing, sparing the one person's life while allowing the five others to be killed?

(Based on Foot, 1967; Thomson, 1976.)

Notice here that the trade-off in terms of number of people saved is the same. And in both scenarios, you are faced with the same decision of action versus inaction. Yet if you are like most people, you probably find that the second scenario presents a more difficult ethical dilemma. Why? This is a type of question that cognitive psychologists who study decision making and moral reasoning try to answer. We will discuss this work in Chapters 9 and 12.

The Mind as an Information Processor

What does it mean to understand the mind as an information-processor? This seems like a vague way to define cognitive psychology. After all, the word "information" can refer to almost anything—a thermometer provides information about temperature, a scowl provides information about someone's emotional state, and hunger pangs provide information about needing food. Mental life is all about information, whether you are reading a map, following the plot of a movie, or gossiping over lunch. Information permeates not only the social world but also fields such as economics, medicine, law, history, computer science, art, and drama. And many psychological disorders are characterized by abnormalities in how information is processed.

More specifically, cognitive psychology largely tries to understand the rules and systematic **processes** by which the mind handles information—how it encodes, transforms, stores, interprets, and acts on it. Often (but not always), this is independent of what that information means. To use an analogy, digital photographs of a thermometer, a party, and a landscape could be created through the same processing steps even though they are images of different things. If you wanted to learn how a digital camera works, you would try to understand these processes without regard to what the pictures show.

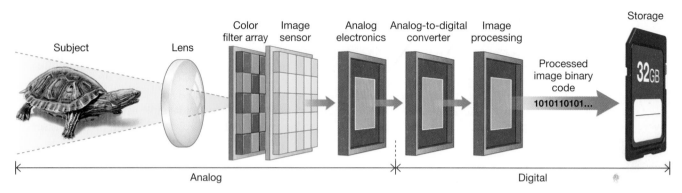

FIGURE 1.1 Turning light into a digital file   The relationship between representations and processes in cognitive psychology can be compared to the steps through which a digital camera creates images. In this figure, the turtle is what is being *represented* in the image. The rest of the figure illustrates the *processes* through which this representation is encoded through a sensor, then converted from analogue to digital format, and stored for later reconstruction by computer software.

A complementary focus is on the nature of mental **representations**, roughly defined as encoded and stored information about the environment. Such representations are distinct from, but intertwined with, the **computations**—that is, the processing steps—performed on them. Mental representations can be transformed, stored, and reconstructed in ways that maintain the meaning of the information (**FIGURE 1.1**). The processes work the same regardless of what the image is, and can be understood separately from understanding the representation.

To illustrate how cognitive processes and representations are intertwined, consider money as an analogy. Money is a representation of both our limited resources and the degree of value we place on things. If you had five million dollars, you could transform or store that amount in many different ways (processes) without changing the representation of your net worth. For example, if you deposited the money in a bank account, you would transform the physical cash into a digital record of that amount. Other processes may change the representation of your net worth. For example, you could make a strategic investment that transforms five million dollars into eight million dollars. Or you could exchange a portion of the money for something that cannot be represented by a mere dollar amount, such as the experience of a mountain expedition or the knowledge you might gain from this book. Analogous to financial transactions, cognitive psychology seeks to understand how information about the world is represented in the mind; how the representational formats change through the course of encoding, storage, and application; and how such processes may even change our understanding of what we're mentally representing in the first place (e.g., how our memories can change over time, depending on how we store and retrieve them).

An Explanation of Cognition at Multiple Levels

Another important idea in cognitive psychology, put forth by the influential cognitive scientist David Marr (1982), is that it is useful to understand cognition at multiple levels of analysis. According to this notion, understanding the *function* of a mental process is quite different from understanding the *information transformations* that support that function, and both of these are different from understanding the neural processes involved. In Marr's terms, perception and cognition can be probed at three different levels: *computational*, *algorithmic*, and *implementational*.

The **computational level of analysis** seeks to understand *what* the mind is trying to compute and *why*. As an analogy, consider cruise control, which keeps a car's speed constant (say, 65 mph). In this case, the car's computer serves as a metaphor for the mind. *What* it is trying to compute is the car's speed relative to the target speed; *why* it is computing this is to help you stay safe and avoid a speeding ticket. Similarly, at the computational level of analysis, cognitive psychologists are interested in understanding what information the mind is trying to process and for what purpose. For example, when figuring out how to design a kindergarten lesson plan it is useful to keep in mind what children are trying to learn and why (e.g., how letters combine to form words, so that the children can become independent readers).

This excerpt from a recent journal article provides an example of how cognitive psychologists can try to understand the computational demands of reading. To set the scene, consider the challenges posed by this simple, two-sentence text: "Denise was stuck in a traffic jam. She was worried what her boss would say." What do we need to do to understand this text?

- First and foremost, we must identify the *individual words*. This task in itself is hugely challenging, requiring us to distinguish a word such as "jam" from all the similar-looking words it could be, such as "jar" or "ham." We must have a means of identifying words that may be unfamiliar, such as "Denise," and of analyzing words that appear in a complex form, such as "worried." Words are the building blocks of comprehension.

- Then, it's not just a matter of identifying words. Their *meanings* need to be activated, appropriate for the *context*. Thus, we must understand "jam" with respect to traffic, not the fruit preserve.

- We need to make *causal connections* within and across sentences to understand that "she" and "her" in the second sentence refer to "Denise" in the first sentence.

(From A. Castles et al. 2018. *Psychol Sci Public Interest* 19: 5–51.)

The **algorithmic level of analysis** aims to understand the rules, mechanisms, and representations the mind uses. In the cruise control analogy, this is akin to asking how the car's computer measures the car's speed and what calculations it performs to match the target speed. For example, does it track the car's speed via the number of wheel rotations per second, or via the rate of change in position as measured by GPS? Similarly, imagine a cognitive psychologist who wants to study mechanisms that affect how we process written text. At the algorithmic level, the researcher might measure eye movements to see how our familiarity with different words (e.g., the frequency with which they appear) guides the way we pay attention to words as we read them (Rayner & Raney, 1996; Reingold et al., 2012).

Many cognitive psychologists pursue questions at the computational and algorithmic levels of analysis without probing the underlying neural processes involved. However, it is often useful to know what happens in the brain to enable cognition. The **implementational level of analysis** seeks to understand the "hardware"—that is, the brain—that physically enables the processes of human cognition. In many cases, understanding the neural implementation of cognitive processes helps inform our understanding of the computational and algorithmic processes. A researcher who wants to understand reading at the implementational level might focus on a region known as the "visual word form area," which is typically found in the left hemisphere of the brain and is particularly active when people view written words. Researchers have found that this region becomes increasingly selective for written words as children learn to read (Dehaene-Lambertz et al., 2018).

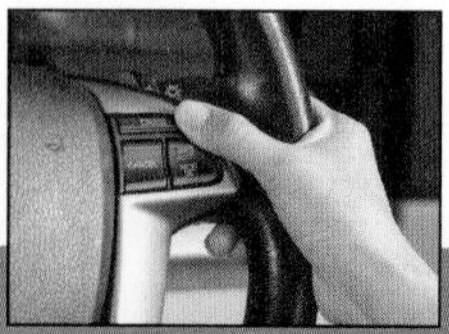

Levels of analysis	Cruise control	Reading
Computational	What is cruise control trying to compute and why?	What skills are involved in reading development?
Algorithmic	How does cruise control keep track of and adjust the car's speed?	How do changes in attention to words support reading development?
Implementational	What circuits enable the onboard computer to adjust the car's speed?	What areas of the brain become more involved as children become better readers?

FIGURE 1.2 Marr's three levels of analysis Questions that could be asked at the computational, algorithmic, and implementational levels by engineers trying to understand cruise control and by psychologists trying to understand reading development. Analyses at the computational level seek to understand the functions and purpose of a process. Analyses at the algorithmic level seek to understand the rules and mechanisms that enable a function to occur. Analyses at the implementational level seek to understand how such algorithms are physically accomplished.

These three levels of analysis complement each other (**FIGURE 1.2**), and a complete understanding of any given phenomenon can't be achieved through any one level in isolation. For example, even the most detailed and accurate understanding of the visual system's neural wiring (implementational) can't provide full insight into the mental "rules" (algorithmic) by which raw visual sensation is transformed into conscious visual experience.

► CHECKPOINT 1.1

1. What questions lie at the heart of cognitive psychology?
2. In cognitive psychology, what is the difference between processes and representations, and how do they relate to each other?
3. What are the computational, algorithmic, and implementational levels of analysis?

1.2 Precursors to Cognitive Psychology

Read nearly any introduction to cognitive psychology, and you'll encounter the startling claim that the field emerged sometime during the 1950s and 1960s. This claim is startling because scholars have been theorizing about cognition for thousands of years. Why aren't the early contemplations of Socrates (469–399 BCE) and Plato (428–347 BCE) about the origins of knowledge, or the musings of Aristotle (384–322 BCE) about the nature of perception, considered the start of cognitive psychology? One temptingly simple answer might be that it was the shift to experimental testing that demarcated the emergence of the new field of cognitive psychology, but this would be incorrect. Indeed, many scientists had conducted rigorous experiments that helped lay the foundation for modern cognitive psychology in the nineteenth century and the early part of the twentieth century, before what is often regarded as the birth of cognitive psychology.

Ancient Beginnings

In some respects, cognitive "psychologists"—or at least those who thought deeply about the nature of cognition—predated the field of cognitive psychology by many centuries. Questions about human cognition stretch back at least as far as the time of the ancient Greeks. Plato, for example, explored the nature of knowledge in his classic dialogue *The Meno* (402 BCE), a discussion between Socrates, a distinguished visitor named Menon, and a boy who was one of Menon's slaves. The discussion focused on the nature of knowledge: does each of us come into the world as a "blank slate" and learn everything from scratch, or is there some form of knowledge that we possess even as we draw our first breath? In the dialogue, Socrates attempted to demonstrate through a discussion with the slave boy that some knowledge is innate. Although the boy initially answered a geometry question incorrectly, he eventually arrived at the right answer after Socrates guided him through a series of questions that did not in themselves divulge the solution. To Plato and Socrates, the fact that the boy was able to arrive at the solution simply through guided questions suggested that he possessed innate knowledge and that Socrates's series of questions merely enabled the boy to gain access to this innate knowledge.

The School of Athens, a fresco painted by the Italian Renaissance artist Raphael between 1509 and 1511. It depicts major figures of classical wisdom and science, including Socrates and Plato.

The connection between such ancient thought and the modern field of cognitive psychology is underscored by the fact that modern research continues to test—and in some cases support—Socrates's and Plato's intuitions. For example, to some people the notion that we are born with innate knowledge might sound far-fetched, but a vigorous literature on cognitive development has suggested that infants may come into the world with a rudimentary understanding of physics (e.g., Baillargeon, 1987; Spelke et al., 1992) and numbers (Wynn, 1992).

In one late-twentieth-century seminal study (Wynn, 1992), 5-month-old infants saw a toy that was placed behind a barrier and then saw a second toy placed behind the barrier (see Chapter 11). The barrier was then removed to reveal either one toy or two toys. Infants looked longer when only one toy was revealed, as if puzzled not to see the second toy alongside it. Such evidence has suggested that infants do have some innate mathematical abilities, consistent with what Plato and Socrates claimed long ago.

Although Plato and Socrates shared with today's cognitive psychologists a passion for understanding the nature and origins of knowledge, they were not cognitive psychologists themselves. Their approach was rooted in philosophy, the application of logic and reason toward the revelation of truth. Nevertheless, it is striking that more than 2,000 years ago, they and their followers anticipated many of the questions that cognitive psychologists ask today.

Psychological Science Before the Cognitive Revolution

Because people we would today recognize as cognitive scientists or theorists existed long before the emergence of cognitive psychology as a field, it is important to have some context about the state of psychological science leading to the 1950s and 1960s. The mid-twentieth century earned its status as a revolutionary period in the history of cognitive psychology—the so-called **Cognitive Revolution**—for several reasons:

- First, although experimentalists had empirically investigated cognitively oriented questions a century earlier, they did not consider themselves psychologists per se, as the field of scientific psychology had not yet been formalized.

- Second, although the field of scientific psychology is often regarded as having been formally established when Wilhelm Wundt opened his psychology lab in Leipzig, Germany, in 1879, many of the methods and approaches used in the field differed markedly from those that characterize the field today. For example, one method adopted by many early psychologists was **introspection**, whereby psychologists attempted to carefully observe their own mental experiences. By today's standards, such an approach is too subjective to serve as the foundation for a science of the mind. When the Cognitive Revolution arrived in the mid-twentieth century, it was made possible by more rigorous and objective methods.

- Third, the Cognitive Revolution emerged at a time in which many psychologists had turned their backs on attempts to understand the inner workings of the mind. By the second decade of the twentieth century, many had grown impatient with the subjective, unreliable methods then popular for studying the mind, and they argued that a true science could move forward only on the basis of outwardly observable behavior. Calling themselves "behaviorists," these psychologists—particularly in the United States—shifted their efforts toward recording outwardly observable actions, eschewing terms and concepts that referred to the mind. Their movement, **Behaviorism**, achieved a high degree of experimental rigor and led to lasting insights into how experience changes behavior. However, the movement's focus on only outwardly observable behavior meant there was little impetus to probe mental mechanisms.

- Fourth, eventual frustration with Behaviorism grew as advances in other fields were providing new tools and models for thinking about cognition. This last convergence of factors formed the crucible of the Cognitive Revolution. The following sections address each of these factors.

Cognitively Oriented Researchers

Before the field of scientific psychology was formalized, cognitively oriented experimentalists largely considered themselves physiologists. Many were interested in how nerve impulses conveyed externally generated stimulation in a way that gave rise to conscious experience.

WEBER AND HIS FORMULA   At the University of Leipzig in the 1830s, the German physician Ernst Weber embarked on a series of studies on how changes in external stimulation lead to changes in what the mind perceives. In the typical experiment, he asked participants to judge whether the lengths of two lines, or the brightness of two lights, or the pitches of two tones were identical or ever so slightly different—that is, he tested how much stimuli needed to differ to give rise to a **just-noticeable difference**. He noted that a person's ability to detect differences between the stimuli varied depending on the magnitude of their initial intensity: the brighter the initial light or the longer the initial line, the greater the change necessary for a participant to notice it. His formula describing this relationship came to be known as **Weber's Law**—the first precise formula specifying the relationship between a physical aspect of the environment and the mind's ability to perceive it.

FECHNER AND THE INTRODUCTION OF PSYCHOPHYSICS   In the 1850s, the German scientist Gustav Fechner built on Weber's work by incorporating the method of just-noticeable differences into an overarching attempt to reveal laws governing the relationship between the intensity of external stimulation and perceptual experience. In the process, he formulated the principle that the intensity of subjective experience of a stimulus increases in proportion to the stimulus's intensity: **Fechner's Law**. In demonstrating the broad feasibility of using physical events to measure mental processes, Fechner established the field of **psychophysics**—the study of the relationship between physical stimuli and mental experience—which continues to play a major role in cognitive psychology research to this day.

VON HELMHOLTZ AND NERVE PHYSIOLOGY　In the 1850s and 1860s, another German scientist, Hermann von Helmholtz, conducted influential work on nerve physiology that would have important implications for psychology. Starting with earlier observations that different types of nerves conveyed different types of information (e.g., auditory vs. visual vs. tactile), he hypothesized that color vision arises via the combined activity of separate nerve fibers that respond to each of the primary colors (a roughly accurate account). Helmholtz further suggested that the mind must actively engage in relatively automatic **unconscious inference**, in which the mind makes "best guesses" in order to turn sensory impulses into percepts of the external world. (A similar conclusion was drawn by the Arab scholar Ibn al-Haytham nearly 1,000 years earlier, but this insight of his did not become widely known in the West; e.g., Howard, 1996.)

In another major contribution to the field, Helmholtz discovered that he could measure the speed of nerve impulses by stimulating nerves at varying distances from a muscle and observing the delay before the muscle contracted. In doing so, he laid the groundwork for later use of reaction times as an important tool in cognitive psychology (**SEE FOR YOURSELF 1.4**).

Michel Bakni/CC BY-SA 4.0

10th-century scholar Ibn al-Haytham is also known as the father of modern optics due to his sophisticated theories of vision and adherence to scientific methods. Like Helmholtz nearly 1,000 years later, he noted that because the projection of light into the eyes is not sufficient to support 3-D perceptions of our surroundings, "seeing" involves the mind making unconscious inferences of the physical world.

▶ **See for Yourself 1.4**

In Helmholtz's Footsteps: Measuring the Speed of Nerve Impulses

One of Helmholtz's contributions to cognitive psychology was the measurement of the speed of nerve impulses. With his concrete demonstration that the speed of nerve impulses was constrained by physical laws, it became less of a leap to suggest that the speed of mental functions—carried out by the brain's vast network of nerves, called neurons—could also be measured. This revelation opened the door for the recording of reaction times to tap into cognitive processes.

If you are studying in a group, you can easily get a rough sense of how fast nerve impulses travel. You'll need several people (ideally ten or more, but you can try it with fewer) and a stopwatch:

1. Stand in a circle, with each of you grasping the ankle of the person to your right.

2. If you are holding the stopwatch, start it at the same time that you squeeze the ankle of the person next to you.

3. Each person in the circle should squeeze the next person's ankle as soon as they feel their own ankle squeezed.

4. Stop the stopwatch as soon as this chain comes back to you and you feel your own ankle squeezed.

5. After doing some practice rounds, do this about three times and take the average of the time it takes for the squeezes to come back to you.

6. Now do the exact same thing again, but this time everyone should squeeze their neighbor's shoulder instead of ankle.

You should find that the "shoulder squeezes" take less time to come back around to you than the "ankle squeezes." This result occurs because the nerve impulses have to travel farther to your brain when the starting point is your ankle than when it is your shoulder. In fact, if you take the difference in time between the ankle and shoulder versions (e.g., 120 ms) and the sum of distances from ankle to shoulder within your group (e.g., 1.5 m × 6 people = 9 m), you should be able to derive (very roughly) the speed of nerve transmission from ankle to shoulder (e.g., 9 m/120 ms = 75 m/s).

Source: P. Rozin and J. Jonides. 1977. *Teach Psychol* 4: 91–94.

DONDERS AND HIS SUBTRACTION METHOD　Inspired by Helmholtz's measurements of the speed of nerve transmission, in the 1860s Dutch ophthalmologist Franciscus Cornelius Donders hypothesized that the speed of higher mental processes could be similarly measured (the brain, after all, is composed of billions of nerves, called neurons). Donders reasoned that the time course of different mental processes could be isolated by measuring the difference in reaction times for tasks of varying complexity. For example, when participants were told simply to repeat a nonsense sound immediately upon hearing it, their reaction time was shorter when they knew in advance what the sound would be than when they did not. In both cases, participants had to discriminate what they heard, but only the latter case involved choosing a correct response. By taking the difference between these reaction times, a clever experimenter could isolate the time courses involved in mentally discriminating a stimulus and in choosing an appropriate response.

Although Donders's insights have informed many cognitive research approaches to this day, they have limitations as well. One limitation is that this approach assumes that cognitive processes unfold serially (i.e., one after the other) and that the duration of one process is unaffected by the addition of a second task. Even if such assumptions are flawed, variations on Donders's subtraction method can be useful for gaining insights about processing stages (e.g., Sternberg, 1969).

The Pioneering Psychologists

In 1979 psychologists across the world came together to celebrate the 100th birthday of scientific psychology, and the American Psychological Association sponsored a special series of symposia titled "A Century of Psychology as Science" (Leary, 1980). What was it that had happened a century earlier? It was in 1879 that Wilhelm Wundt and two of his students at the University of Leipzig ran what is commonly referred to as the first psychology experiment. As psychology experiments go, it was simple. The setup included a brass chronoscope (a device for measuring short time intervals) attached to a telegraph key, sitting on a table next to an elevated arm from which a ball could fall onto a platform. Participants were instructed to press the telegraph key immediately upon hearing the ball hit the platform. The chronoscope measured the time that elapsed between the release of the ball and the press of the key, and the data supported student Max Friedrich's PhD dissertation, titled "On the Duration of Apperception for Simple and Complex Visual Stimuli." It was the world's first PhD dissertation on experimental psychology.

WUNDT, STRUCTURALISM, AND INTROSPECTION   Many of the questions that Wundt and his students explored were "cognitive" in nature. For example, one of their primary missions was to understand how raw physical sensations are transformed into the contents of conscious experience. Their approach was different from that of most modern cognitive psychologists. For example, inspired by physicists' success in identifying elements that served as basic building blocks of matter, Wundt and his followers sought to uncover the most elemental building blocks of consciousness. This emphasis on the structural components of mental life gave the movement a name: **Structuralism**. In some cases, such investigations took the form of reaction time tests, under the assumption that the fastest reaction times would be associated with the most elemental units of experience.

Another approach that Wundt championed—to such a degree that (perhaps somewhat unfairly) his name became nearly synonymous with the method—was introspection, an approach wherein investigators looked carefully inward to observe their own experience of a stimulus as the experience unfolded. Wundt believed that introspection could provide insight into the nature of consciousness. However, quite aware of the pitfalls and subjectivity of such an approach, Wundt argued that one's inward observations could yield true insights only in certain cases and only when the observer had been rigorously and properly trained.

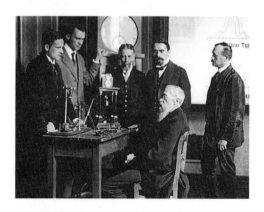

Wilhelm Wundt, seated in front of a brass chronoscope and surrounded by his colleagues. Wundt is often regarded as the founder of the world's first lab dedicated to scientific psychology.

EBBINGHAUS: PIONEER OF MEMORY RESEARCH   A contemporary of Wundt's who also became famous for his use of rigorous experimentation was the German scientist Hermann Ebbinghaus, a pioneer of memory research. Whereas Wundt believed that higher mental functions such as memory could not be measured and understood through experimentation (he limited his experimental work largely to aspects of sensation and perception), Ebbinghaus believed otherwise. Inspired by the rigor and precision exemplified by Fechner's earlier work on psychophysics, Ebbinghaus aimed to apply similar experimental control to understanding memory and forgetting. In contrast to most cognitive psychologists today—who typically test many participants in the course of an experiment—Ebbinghaus ran his experiments using only himself as a participant. In one of his studies, he carefully recited "nonsense syllables" (syllables with no meaningful content, such as "dax") 15,000 times, all with the same tone of voice and at regular intervals. Through such efforts, Ebbinghaus (1885) provided the world with lasting insights into the role of repetition in memory and the rate at which forgetting occurs, known as the **forgetting curve** (see Chapter 6).

A SHIFT AWAY FROM WUNDT'S STRUCTURALISM   For a while, Wundt was a leading light in psychology. Students traveled from far and wide to study with him, and on leaving they carried his influence as they set up their own psychology labs around the world. In time, though, the field began to reject at least two aspects of Wundt's work.

First, some scholars rebelled against what they perceived to be the most fundamental tenet of Structuralism: the notion that conscious experience could be usefully understood through an examination of its basic building blocks. Some aligned themselves with the **Gestalt movement**, which promoted the idea that even if we could observe such basic elements, such an approach could not provide insights into the nature of conscious experience (**FIGURE 1.3**). For example, even the most detailed characterization of each note in a Mozart sonata would not grant us the ability to understand the piece as a whole, and we could hypothetically take many of those same notes and reassemble them into a very different piece by Beethoven. The familiar phrase "the whole is other than the sum of its parts" finds its origins in the rallying cry of this movement.

Meanwhile, in the United States, psychologist and philosopher William James decried what he perceived as the irrelevance of a structuralist approach to mental processes in the real world. Inspired in part by Darwin's theory of evolution and its accompanying emphasis on the adaptiveness of physical traits, James argued that the appropriate focus of a scientific psychology should be on the *functions* of the mind. That is, he was interested in what enabled an organism to engage with and successfully navigate the challenges of its environment. The movement that aligned itself with James's focus on psychological functions became known as **Functionalism**. In introductions to the history of psychology, the functionalist perspective—with its emphasis on the utility of mental processes—is often contrasted with Structuralism, with its elemental emphasis on the building blocks of conscious experience.

A second reason for the eventual waning of Wundt's influence was the widespread rejection of introspection as a valid research tool. As we already noted, Wundt had been cautious in his advocacy and use of introspection. However, many of his followers were less reserved in their enthusiasm for the method, and the movement that Wundt inspired began to be viewed as too highly subjective for a young field that was striving to become a science. Furthermore, even when investigators had been rigorously trained in introspection, it soon became apparent that different labs were producing different

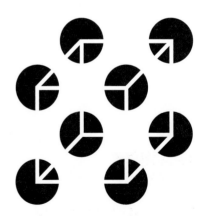

FIGURE 1.3 A Necker cube Gestalt psychologists argued against Structuralism, noting that conscious experience can't be understood as the sum of more basic perceptual elements. In this figure, for example, even the most detailed description of the individual elements would not describe the cube that many people see when looking at this display. According to the Gestalt psychologists, the "whole" that we experience is more than the sum of its parts. (After D. R. Bradley et al. 1976. *Nature* 261: 77–78.)

results when relying on it. Indeed, it was partly frustration with the field's subjective and nonreplicable flavor that led to the rise of Behaviorism.

The Rise of Behaviorism

A few decades after the time of Wundt's peak influence, a new generation of experimental psychologists began to redouble efforts to transform psychology into a truly objective science. Many of these psychologists had grown wary, impatient, and somewhat contemptuous of the methods and goals championed by Wundt and his students. The bold new movement of Behaviorism argued that outwardly observable behavior was the most appropriate topic of research, to the general exclusion of relatively unobservable internal mental processes.

The American scientist John Watson, generally considered the founder of Behaviorism, is often regarded as the epitome of an anti-cognitive psychologist. In his view, laid out in his classic 1913 manifesto *Psychology as the Behaviorist Views It*, the main obstacle to a scientific psychology was the subjective nature of the introspective approach popular at the time. Watson argued that a true science of psychology had to be achieved through the use of purely objective measures, which could be guaranteed only if investigations were limited to manipulating and measuring observable environmental conditions and observable behavior. Adherents to this perspective argued that the inner workings of the mind could not be the focus of an objective science. One consequence was that mainstream psychological work was increasingly conducted on non-human animals—a consequence that was in line with Watson's assertion that "the behaviorist, in his efforts to get a unitary scheme of animal response, recognizes no dividing line between man and brute" (Watson, 1913, p. 158). As behaviorists came to dominate psychology, research on cognition fell to the wayside. Topics that had initially been framed in terms of the mind were reframed in terms of behavior. Thus, "perception" became the study of "discrimination," "memory" became the study of "learning," and "language" became the study of "verbal behavior" (Miller, 2003).

Today, we often treat learning and memory as overlapping concepts; for example, students who are tested on what they learned in school are asked to consciously recollect information from class. However, in its role as a core principle of Behaviorism, "learning" referred not to internal representations of the past, but to observable changes in behavior that resulted from repeatedly paired associations. These associations were either between external stimuli, as in the case of **classical conditioning**, or between an organism's actions and desired or undesired outcomes, as in the case of **operant conditioning**.

Whereas classical conditioning involved the pairing of sets of external stimuli, operant conditioning—epitomized by the work of B. F. Skinner—involved the pairing of pleasant or aversive outcomes with an organism's own actions (**FIGURE 1.4**). Rewarding outcomes that increased the likelihood that an action would be repeated were called **reinforcers**. (If you've ever trained a dog to come, sit, and stay through the use of treats, you've employed reinforcers and principles of operant conditioning.) Conversely, aversive outcomes that decreased the likelihood that an action would be repeated were called

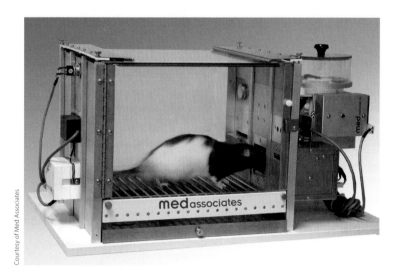

Courtesy of Med Associates

FIGURE 1.4 Operant conditioning   Animals in a Skinner box can learn to press a lever to gain food pellets or to avoid footshock, a form of learning called operant conditioning.

punishments. (Electric shocks are an example of a punishment; please don't use them while training your dog.)

Many behaviorists believed that all behavior could be explained by an organism's history of experiencing paired associations. This was an exciting idea because it raised the possibility that any and all of the world's problematic behaviors could be solved through exposures to the right combinations of paired associations. Skinner, for example, believed deeply that many of the world's problems could be solved if only society could understand and reengineer systems of reinforcers and punishments that were already in place. He even wrote a utopian novel, *Walden Two* (1948), describing what such an engineered society might look like. (As a matter of taste, some readers might consider *Walden Two* to be a dystopian novel; read it for yourself and see what you think.) Heightening the perceived feasibility of such an approach, the behaviorist movement was responsible for some of the field's most robust and replicable methods and insights, and it introduced a new standard of experimental rigor and objectivity. These contributions were lasting, and when psychology's focus returned to internal mental processes during the Cognitive Revolution, the field was stronger for them. The currently flourishing field of **behavioral neuroscience**, which uses animal models to understand neural mechanisms underpinning normal and abnormal psychological processes, owes much to the behaviorist work that came before.

Behaviorism held particular sway in the United States, where Functionalism —inspired by the work of William James—had been popular. The functionalist emphasis on the adaptiveness of psychological processes made for a natural precursor to Behaviorism and its focus on the shaping of behavior through rewarding and aversive associations and cues in the environment. The United States may also have been receptive to Behaviorism because its emphasis on the role of the environment meshed well with prevalent egalitarian sentiments (e.g., the ideal that differences among people could be accounted for purely by their environment). John Watson's famous 1930 statement would have resonated with such sentiments:

> *Give me a dozen healthy infants, well-formed, and my own specified world to bring them up in and I'll guarantee to take any one at random and train him to become any type of specialist I might select—doctor, lawyer, artist, merchant-chief and, yes, even beggar-man and thief, regardless of his talents, penchants, tendencies, abilities, vocations, and race of his ancestors.*
>
> (From J. B. Watson. 2009. *Behaviorism*. Seventh Printing.
> Transaction Publishers: New Brunswick, NJ.)

As prominent and influential as the movement was, the dominance of Behaviorism was not to last. Much of its power stemmed from the overarching belief that it represented the only scientifically viable path for understanding all of human behavior. However, the limitations of the approach grew increasingly apparent in the face of observations and findings that could not be explained without taking into account internal mental processes. Against this backdrop, the Cognitive Revolution burst onto the scene.

➤ CHECKPOINT 1.2

1. What were some ways cognitive questions were being asked prior to the Cognitive Revolution?

2. Why were questions of cognition generally sidelined with the emergence of Behaviorism?

1.3 The Cognitive Revolution

The 1950s and 1960s were a time of such rapid and radical shifts in approaches to cognition that this period is frequently referred to as the **Cognitive Revolution**. The term "cognitive psychology" became widely used following the publication of psychologist Ulric Neisser's 1967 book of the same name, which provided the first comprehensive overview of the emerging field. (An earlier book with the same title, published in 1939, anticipated some of the ideas that would flourish during the Cognitive Revolution, but it did not find as receptive an audience and was not as impactful.) (Moore, 1939; see Surprenant & Neath, 1997.)

In the mid-twentieth century, several factors combined to catalyze the issuing forth of a rich new research endeavor that we know today as the field of cognitive psychology. A thorough discussion of these factors would easily occupy a full book. (Howard Gardner's 1985 book *The Mind's New Science* is devoted to just such an analysis.) These factors originated both from within psychology, where it grew increasingly apparent that the tenets of Behaviorism were ill equipped to illuminate psychological phenomena at the core of experience, and from outside psychology, where advances in other fields, such as computer science, artificial intelligence, linguistics, and neuroscience, were providing new tools and models for thinking about cognition.

Converging Strands of the Revolution

Little by little, led either against their will by their own data or driven by a desire to understand the inner workings of the mind, psychologists strained against the limits of what were then considered the boundaries of a "respectable" scientific psychology.

CHOMSKY AND VERBAL BEHAVIOR   Many psychologists believed that Behaviorism's limitations were exposed when Skinner, in his 1957 book *Verbal Behavior*, tried to describe children's language development as resulting from reinforcement learning. His ideas were met with a powerful critique by the young linguist Noam Chomsky (1959). Chomsky argued that children learn language too effortlessly to be accounted for by behaviorist principles and in situations where there is limited opportunity for reinforcement (e.g., such as when young children from immigrant families learn their adopted language more rapidly than their parents do). In highlighting aspects of language development that could not be explained by behaviorist principles, and by shifting focus toward mental processes that underlie language acquisition, Chomsky tore at the edges of the behaviorist movement. The time was ripe for shifting experimental psychology's attention back to matters of the mind.

TOLMAN AND COGNITIVE MAPS   Accomplished behaviorist Edward Tolman found patterns in his data that seemingly could not be explained without reference to mental representation. As detailed in a paper he published in 1930, he and his team ran three groups of rats through mazes. One group received rewards each time they successfully completed a maze. A second group received no rewards. A third group went unrewarded for the first 10 days but then began to receive rewards when completing the maze. As expected, the rewarded group learned the maze fastest, whereas the other two groups initially wandered aimlessly. However, when rats in the third group began to receive rewards, they then learned the maze faster than the first group had. This evidence suggested that during those first 10 days, the rats had been building up some sort of knowledge or representation of the space, even in the absence of rewards.

Additional striking findings were yet to come. A few years later, Tolman's team placed rats in cross-shaped mazes, with arms labeled north, south, east, and west. When a rat was placed in the south end-point, with a reward placed at the east end-point, the rat would be rewarded for turning right. Once such learning was established, however, a rat placed in the north end-point exhibited the behavior of turning left. In other words, the rats appeared to have developed **cognitive maps** of their environments rather than simply executing the motor responses that had previously been linked to reward (as would have been predicted by behaviorist accounts of learning; Tolman, 1948).

SHANNON AND INFORMATION THEORY   Meanwhile, some psychologists hoped to extend the objectivity of Behaviorism to explorations of mental processes, and they drew inspiration from advances in other, related fields.

A watershed moment was the 1948 publication of a paper by the young American electrical engineer and mathematician Claude Shannon, titled "A Mathematical Theory of Communication." A researcher at Bell Telephone Laboratories, Shannon was interested in how to optimize the transmission of information from a source to a receiver, taking into account the capacity limits (e.g., bandwidth) of the transmission channels and any resulting distortion that could compromise the fidelity of the message at the other end. In his paper, Shannon demonstrated that the nature and processing of "information" itself could be studied and analyzed without necessary consideration of the actual content of a message. He instead focused on how messages from one source could be recoded into easily transmittable binary units (think of the 1's and 0's that serve as the foundation for computer languages), sent through channels that might vary in their capacity and degree of distortion, and be recoded by a receiving agent according to rules and algorithms that enabled reconstruction of the original message. This approach laid the foundation for the cross-disciplinary field of **information theory**, which focuses on the processes by which information can be coded, stored, transmitted, and reconstructed. Importantly for cognitive psychology, the success of Shannon's approach demonstrated that information processing—and not just outwardly observable behavior—could truly serve as a fruitful topic of investigation.

TURING, SIMON, NEWELL, AND ARTIFICIAL INTELLIGENCE   This new information-processing approach—focusing on the rules and algorithms that encode, store, transform, and apply information—represented a departure from the concerns of earlier psychologists such as Wundt, who had focused on the *contents* of consciousness, and the impact of this new perspective was bolstered by the fact that several of Shannon's contemporaries were similarly demonstrating the value of a computational approach to the mind. The British mathematician Alan Turing, for example, had earlier shown how a relatively simple algorithm could be used to carry out any possible calculation. The algorithm would be instantiated by a hypothetical machine—now called a **Turing machine** in his honor—that would consist of a long piece of tape divided into sequential cells, each of which could contain a single symbol or no symbol. The machine itself could perform one of only four different actions upon encountering each cell. It could:

1. move the tape one cell to the right,
2. move the tape one cell to the left,
3. delete the symbol in a cell, or
4. write a new symbol in the cell.

The machine's action upon encountering each cell was determined by a set of instructions (e.g., a rudimentary program) called a machine table. Turing's insight was that this exceeding small set of operations could be used to implement any conceivable calculation, given a sufficiently long piece of tape.

As an engineer and mathematician at Bell Telephone Laboratories, Claude Shannon focused on the accurate recoding, transmission, and reconstruction of information.

Turing's concept was abstract, and he never actually built a Turing machine, but his concept served to focus attention on the steps that—in humans—might underlie cognitive information processing. To early pioneers of cognitive psychology, Turing's work appeared to provide a plausible model of how information might be processed by the mind. This potential became even more relevant when Herbert Simon and Allen Newell stunned colleagues by programming simple vacuum-tube computers to prove various theorems. From a modern-day perspective, the computers were primitive: in 1956, Simon and Newell's first demonstration, dubbed Logic Theorist, could perform only a limited number of strictly defined computations, and it took somewhere between 1 and 15 minutes to do so. But advances came rapidly: in 1957, they and their colleague Clifford Shaw developed the General Problem Solver, which could solve geometric theorems and arithmetic-based puzzles and even play chess.

The age of "artificial intelligence" had begun, and it soon became apparent that psychologists and computer scientists had much to learn from each other. **Computational modeling** refers to the use of computers and mathematical functions to constrain and predict aspects of human cognition, and it is a means to make theoretical models more precise and explicit than could be achieved through verbal descriptions alone. To this day, it serves as an important tool through which psychologists make predictions and seek to understand cognitive processes.

Influence of the Information-Processing Approach on Psychology

Increasingly, the information-processing approach permeated the work of psychologists of the day. In the United States, George Miller sought to understand memory by focusing explicitly on the amount of information that people could store, as well as how to conceptualize and quantify such information. This work gave rise to the notion that people can remember "7 plus or minus 2" bits of information ("My problem is that I have been persecuted by an integer," Miller began.) (Miller, 1956, p. 81). Such work then converged in spirit with other threads of cognitively oriented research.

In the United Kingdom, famed psychologist Donald Broadbent (1958) built a filter model of attention that emphasized the flow of information as it passed through a selection process (**FIGURE 1.5**). This model was modified by Anne Treisman only a couple of years later, with her "attentuation model" of attention accounting for findings that ignored information was not always completed filtered from awareness (Treisman, 1960). At the University of Cambridge, Sir Frederic Charles Bartlett conducted seminal work on memory. In

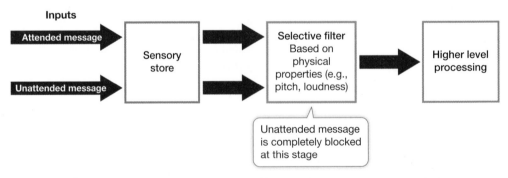

FIGURE 1.5 Donald Broadbent's filter model of attention   The model emphasizes the flow of information as it passes through a selection process. (Adaptation of image by Kyle.Farr/ Wikipedia CC BY-SA 3.0, based on D. E. Broadbent. 1958. *Perception and Communication*, p. 299. Pergamon Press: New York.)

Switzerland, the famous developmental psychologist Jean Piaget pioneered new understanding of how children's representations, concepts, and cognitive abilities changed with age. Behind the Iron Curtain in the Soviet Union, Lev Vygotsky explored the link between children's social and cognitive development, and Alexander Luria probed relationships between cognitive and neural functions. In the United States, Eleanor Rosch conducted pioneering studies of how people categorize the world, and Eleanor Gibson pioneered research on perceptual learning and how people extract information from their environments in order to guide their actions.

Notably, in the United States an undercurrent of cognitive research had continued apace, though sometimes apart from the mainstream establishment and often within the traditions of social psychology. At Harvard University, for example, social psychologist Jerome Bruner published with his colleagues the classic *A Study of Thinking* (1956), which gave serious consideration to the notion of cognitive strategies. Just a few years earlier, Bruner and his colleagues had jump-started an exciting (but arguably flawed) movement known as the New Look, which explored the ways that aspects often studied by social psychologists, such as motivations and emotions, could shape conscious perception itself (Bruner & Goodman, 1947; but see Firestone & Scholl, 2016, and Pylyshyn, 1999, for critical treatments both of the New Look and its modern variations).

Eleanor Gibson considered perceptual development to be fundamental for cognitive development. She conducted pioneering research on how people learn to perceive the world, as well as on reading.

The "Big Bang" of Cognitive Psychology: The Symposium on Information Theory

It was at this point that a pivotal event occurred. In 1956, at the Massachusetts Institute of Technology, a Symposium on Information Theory brought together (among others) George Miller, Noam Chomsky, Allen Newell, and Herbert Simon, each of whom gave talks on their work—which seemed, on the face of it, to represent work in different disciplines. But as George Miller would later recall,

> I left the symposium with a conviction, more intuitive than rational, that experimental psychology, theoretical linguistics, and the computer simulation of cognitive processes were all pieces from a larger whole and that the future would see a progressive elaboration and coordination of their shared concerns.
>
> (From G. A. Miller. 2003. *Trends Cogn Sci* 7: 141–144.)

Miller, Newell, and Simon have all pinpointed this event—and the year 1956—as the "Big Bang" of cognitive psychology, unleashing a flourishing of cognitively oriented research of which vibrations can still be felt today.

➤ CHECKPOINT 1.3

1. What factors led to a refocusing on cognition in the mid-twentieth century?
2. Who were some key figures of the Cognitive Revolution, and what were their accomplishments?
3. What was the influence of the information-processing approach on psychology?

1.4 Cognitive Psychology in Relation to Other Areas

The breadth of questions probed by cognitive psychologists introduces a challenge: How does one define the boundaries of cognitive psychology, such that it is a discipline apart from other areas of psychology? Where does "cognitive" psychology end and "social" or "clinical" psychology begin? The answer is not

In addition to receiving a Nobel Prize, psychologist Daniel Kahneman received the Presidential Medal of Freedom for his groundbreaking research on human reason and decision making, given to individuals who have made especially meritorious contributions to the security or national interests of the United States, to world peace, or to cultural or other significant public or private endeavors.

always clear. Although it may be tempting to define cognitive psychology by the topics it covers—for example, attention, memory, and decision making—these are topics that are also explored in social and clinical psychology. A better answer may be that cognitive psychology is unique in the degree to which it explores these topics with a mission to understand how the information itself is absorbed, transformed, and used. In contrast, social and clinical psychologists may be more interested in how these processes help us understand interpersonal interactions and mental health, respectively. For example, social psychologists are also often interested in how people attend to and remember social cues such as facial expressions. (We discuss the fascinating emergent field of social cognition in more detail in Chapter 12.) And clinical psychologists often try to understand how atypical attention and memory processes contribute to anxiety and depression.

Just as the lines are fuzzy between cognitive psychology and other areas of psychology, the lines are also fuzzy between cognitive psychology and fields that many students might initially assume are completely separate. In 2002, eminent cognitive psychologist Daniel Kahneman was awarded the Nobel Prize not in Psychology—there is no Nobel Prize in Psychology (yet)—but in Economic Sciences. The award was in recognition of the profound degree to which Kahneman's work on judgment and decision making (in collaboration with his colleague Amos Tversky) altered economists' fundamental assumptions about how people make economic decisions. (We will discuss this work in Chapter 9.) The interface between cognitive psychology and other fields is also evident in the burgeoning, overlapping fields of cognitive science and cognitive neuroscience.

Cognitive Science and Cognitive Neuroscience

As briefly described earlier, in the mid-twentieth century scholars specializing in cognitive psychology, computer science, neuroscience, philosophy, linguistics, and anthropology came to view each other as partners in the quest to understand the mind. **Cognitive science** emerged as a formal effort to synthesize insights across such disciplines. As cognitive psychologist George Miller explained in his firsthand account of the emergence of cognitive science, each discipline "by historical accident, had inherited a particular way of looking at cognition and each had progressed far enough to recognize that the solution to some of its problems depended crucially on the solution of problems traditionally allocated to other disciplines" (Miller, 2003, p. 143.)

For example, concepts developed by computer scientists became central to the modeling of brain functions; the intersection of linguistics and psychology gave rise to the now thriving area of psycholinguistics; and insights from anthropology and neuroscience shed light on cultural and biological constraints on how cognition could work. To this day, these links have continued to grow stronger and richer, with cognitive scientists freely referencing and merging insights across such interrelated disciplines (**FIGURE 1.6**). Traditionally, cognitive psychologists can be regarded as the subset of cognitive scientists who principally use behavior to understand mental processes, usually within the context of experiments.

Among the most successful and exciting of the links among the subfields of cognitive science was that between cognitive psychology and neuroscience—a merger that is now known as **cognitive neuroscience**. The power of cognitive experiments to reveal and isolate relatively specific cognitive processes, combined with the rapidly advancing technology to observe and

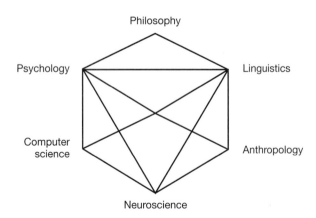

FIGURE 1.6 Cognitive science in the mid-twentieth century A schematic diagram of links between fields that traditionally make up cognitive science, and which were in existence at the time of the Cognitive Revolution. (Sloan Foundation. 1978. Cognitive Science, 1978. Report of the State of the Art Committee to the Advisors of The Alfred P. Sloan Foundation. New York.)

measure the brain in action, led to such an integrated partnership that today it would hardly make sense to have a cognitive psychology textbook that does not incorporate neuroscience. Chapter 2 is dedicated to an overview of cognitive neuroscience techniques and their role in understanding cognition. Subsequent chapters of this book will draw on both cognitive psychology experiments and cognitive neuroscience experiments.

Emotion in Cognitive Psychology

Emotions play a powerful role in our experience of the world and our behavior, but historically the field of cognitive psychology has treated emotion with some trepidation. Considerations of emotion have often existed only at the field's fringes. One reason may be, as Neisser (1967) pointed out, that with most cognitive phenomena, researchers rely on using a stimulus with easily verified properties as an objective starting point. Thus, by comparing what a stimulus is objectively like with how people perceive and remember it, researchers can try to understand what transformations and computations were involved in cognitively processing it. In contrast, it is more difficult to agree on an objective description of emotional experience.

For example, imagine that a researcher wants to understand how sadness changes the way we pay attention. To get at this question, the researcher might try to induce sadness by having participants watch sad film clips, but how can the researcher know that a particular film produces the same emotional state in everyone? In addition, emotions are characterized by a range of responses, from changes in physiological responses to changes in subjective feelings, and these do not always occur together. Such complications make it difficult for researchers to ensure that any emotional event or stimulus gives rise to the same cascade of changes in each experiment participant.

The variability and unpredictability of people's emotional reactions mean that emotion has sometimes been considered "noise"—something that obscures objective and precise measurements. However, implicit in this perspective is the notion that cognition can be regarded as distinct from emotion, whereas in truth cognition and emotion may not be so easily disentangled. For a time, the presumed distinction between cognition and emotion inspired debates over the relationship between them. One prominent debate centered on whether cognitive interpretations and appraisals typically precede an emotional response (the **cognitive primacy hypothesis**; e.g., Lazarus, 1984) or whether emotion typically precedes cognition (the **affective primacy hypothesis**; e.g., Zajonc, 1980).

In recent years, research has begun to suggest that the division between emotion and cognition is murky. Some of this work comes from the realm of neuroscience, where distinguishing brain areas involved in emotion from those involved in cognition has proven trickier than once supposed. For example, whereas strong versions of the cognitive primacy hypothesis might suggest that a stimulus must be perceived and interpreted prior to evoking an emotional reaction, newer research has found that emotion helps shape activity even in very early visual areas of the brain (Stolarova et al., 2006). Such findings and suggestions have cast doubt on notions that perception and emotion proceed one after the other. With researchers increasingly discovering neural regions that appear to be involved in both emotional and cognitive processing, it has become unlikely that the brain (and mind) can be subdivided into cognitive functions and emotional functions. Rather, it has been suggested that cognition and emotion form "functionally integrated systems" that profoundly and continuously shape each other (Pessoa, 2015).

Thus, emotion has a home in the study of cognitive psychology. After all, if we have "a bad feeling" about something, doesn't this count as information that helps us make sense of a situation? In cases such as this, emotion serves as critical information for us to process alongside other aspects of our environment. Consider, for example, what is known as the **somatic marker hypothesis**, which suggests that people learn to link their physiological responses (corresponding to their emotional reactions) to outcomes associated with their actions, and that these learned associations begin to guide subsequent decision making even when people can't quite put their finger on the reasons for their decisions (Bechara, 2004; Damasio, 1994; but see Dunn et al., 2006). That is, our internally generated, emotion-driven bodily sensations (or mental representations of them) become information that is integrated into and guides our interpretations and evaluations of the world around us.

The link between cognition and emotion has been suggested to be so tight that some psychologists have suggested that emotion *is* cognition (Duncan & Barrett, 2007). According to the **theory of constructed emotion**, the experience of emotion itself does not stem from unique, isolated processes but is an experience that we construct based on external cues, bodily cues, and our existing concepts and categories (Barrett, 2006; Russell, 2003). In this way, our experience of emotion may have much in common with our perceptual experience of the external world (see Chapter 3). Complementing the view that emotion is a form of cognition, a wealth of evidence suggests that when normal emotions are disrupted, core aspects of cognition also fail (e.g., Damasio, 1994). With the line between cognition and emotion growing ever blurrier, emotion has increasingly found itself welcomed—sometimes with great enthusiasm, sometimes with less—into the fold of cognitive psychology.

The Legacy of the Cognitive Revolution

We can appreciate the degree to which cognitive research flourished between the dawn of the Cognitive Revolution and today by comparing the contents of the first modern cognitive psychology textbook (Neisser's 1967 *Cognitive Psychology*) with those of a cognitive psychology textbook today. The 1967 textbook devoted numerous chapters to visual and auditory processing and only one chapter to memory and reasoning. By contrast, the textbook you are currently holding is typical of many modern ones in that its pages are swelled with research on memory, reasoning, language, decision making, and other higher-order processes.

LIMITATIONS OF THE INFORMATION-PROCESSING APPROACH Along with the many successes of cognitive psychology, it is important to note pitfalls that have been frustrating even to some of the field's founding leaders. The fruitfulness of the information-processing approach and the zeal it inspired came with a cost, at least at first. The ability to make minor (but measurable) tweaks in the lab and to observe how they changed mental processes—which for so long had been unobservable—was intoxicating, but leaders such as Jerome Bruner and Ulric Neisser worried that psychologists who sequestered their experiments in the recesses of university corridors ran the risk of losing touch with the relevance of cognition in everyday life. Within a decade or so of the Cognitive Revolution, these leaders independently came to criticize the field they had helped found.

Bruner argued that an overemphasis on information-processing computations failed to capture the importance of how "meaning" shapes cognition. Cognition in the real world, Bruner argued, must contend with the meanings that our daily activities and interactions have for us, and he worried that by prioritizing computational processes of cognition the field was sacrificing its power to explain cognition as it actually occurs (Bruner, 1990). Neisser produced a similar criticism in his book *Cognition and Reality* (1976).

In some respects, such criticisms still resonate, but one can also find many instances today in which researchers attempt to connect research on cognitive processes with their implications and functions in the real world, both for other areas of psychology and for other fields of research. Entire academic journals and societies now exist to support such endeavors, such as the *Journal of Experimental Psychology: Applied*; *Psychological Science in the Public Interest*; and the Society for Applied Research in Memory and Cognition. Connections between cognitive psychology, other research areas, and the real world are described throughout this textbook, and Chapter 12 surveys an area of the field dedicated to understanding how cognition is affected by social meaning.

➤ CHECKPOINT 1.4

1. How does cognitive psychology fit in and connect with the broader field of cognitive science?
2. Why might it be important to consider the role of emotion in human cognition? Why, historically, has this approach been difficult to use?
3. What have been considered to be the limitations of the information-processing approach on psychology?

Chapter Summary

1.1 Describe the types of topics cognitive psychologists investigate.

Cognitive psychology is the scientific study of how the mind encodes, stores, and uses information. Investigated topics generally include perception, attention, memory, language, categorization, reasoning, and decision making. Of course, these are topics that are often of interest to psychologists from other corners of the field as well (e.g., social psychology). One way cognitive psychology distinguishes itself is in its focus on trying to understand how information gets represented in the mind and the processes that allow this to happen.

Q: It is a testament to the success of cognitive psychology that its insights now permeate and inform nearly every corner of the field. Describe examples of topics that are investigated by cognitive psychologists. Suggest questions that a researcher might ask at the computational, algorithmic, and implementational levels when trying to understand reading.

1.2 Describe the precursors to the field of cognitive psychology as a science.

Questions about cognition have been asked for thousands of years, but the science of cognitive psychology was formalized only in the mid-twentieth century, during what is now called the Cognitive Revolution. Its late emergence as a field reflected the difficulty of applying scientific methods to observe the mind. Some early pioneers did seek to understand how physical sensations translated into conscious experience, but psychology did not view itself as its own scientific discipline until the late 1800s. Within a handful of decades the desire for a truly objective science of behavior had led many psychologists to push aside questions of mental activity in order to focus only on outwardly observable behavior, or Behaviorism.

Q: Some cognitively oriented researchers considered themselves physiologists prior to the recognition of psychology as a scientific field. Describe examples of research done by such physiologists that demonstrated that aspects of the mind could be measured.

1.3 Discuss the emergence of the Cognitive Revolution and the developments that followed.

In the 1950s and 1960s, psychologists who had maintained keen interest in cognition were inspired by converging insights from fields such as artificial intelligence, linguistics, and engineering. In the years that followed, the initially narrow array of topics explored by cognitive psychologists blossomed into a field of broad scope. In nearly all cases, understanding has been enriched by bridging cognitive psychology with neuroscience, leading to the success of cognitive neuroscience.

Q: The pivotal moment for cognitive psychology was its 1954 "Big Bang": The Symposium on Information Theory. Discuss some key figures of this Cognitive Revolution and describe their work. What was the influence of the information-processing approach on psychology?

1.4 Explain how cognitive psychology connects with other areas of research, both within and outside psychology.

Because cognitive psychology specializes in understanding mental processes at the heart of how people encode, store, and use information, it connects with nearly all aspects of human experience. Areas of psychology such as social and clinical psychology have shown how understanding of cognition helps us understand social relationships and clinical disorders. Similarly, fields such as economics have had to adjust to what cognitive psychology has revealed about human reasoning. At the same time that cognitive psychology has influenced other fields, disciplines such as computer science, philosophy, linguistics, neuroscience, and anthropology have helped shape the field of cognitive psychology.

Q: Describe examples of work from the fields of psychology, linguistics, engineering, and artificial intelligence that converged to help inspire the Cognitive Revolution.

Key Terms

affective primacy hypothesis
algorithmic level of analysis
behavioral neuroscience
Behaviorism
classical conditioning
cognitive map
cognitive neuroscience
cognitive primacy hypothesis
cognitive psychology
Cognitive Revolution
cognitive science
computational level of analysis
computational modeling
Fechner's Law
forgetting curve
Functionalism
Gestalt movement

implementational level of analysis
information theory
introspection
just-noticeable difference
operant conditioning
processes
psychophysics
punishments
reinforcers
representations
somatic marker hypothesis
Structuralism
theory of constructed emotion
Turing machine
unconscious inference
Weber's Law

Critical Thinking Questions

1. Consider the real-life scenario that opened this chapter, the landing of US Airways Flight 1549 on New York's Hudson River ("the Miracle on the Hudson"). It is important to understand what went right in this situation so that flight crews in the future will also be able to guide their plane to a safe landing, should anything similar occur. How might a cognitive psychologist contribute to such understanding? How might the questions asked by a cognitive psychologist differ from or overlap with those asked by a social psychologist trying to understand what went right?

2. Famed psychologist Hermann Ebbinghaus once remarked that "psychology has a long past, but only a short history." How might such a statement apply specifically to cognitive psychology? For example, why is the field often said to have emerged in the mid-twentieth century when questions about cognition date back thousands of years?

3. Think of a job or field of study that seems far removed from cognitive psychology. Then see if you can come up with ways that cognitive psychology can connect, inform, or contribute insight to it. For example, as seemingly far removed as, say, chemistry might be, think about what questions cognitive psychologists might ask about chemists themselves.

Suggested Readings

Gardner, H. (1985). *The Mind's New Science: A History of the Cognitive Revolution*. New York: Basic Books.

Hatfield, G. (2002). Psychology, philosophy, and cognitive science: Reflections on the history and philosophy of experimental psychology. *Mind & Language, 17*, 207–232.

Hunt, M. (1993). *The Story of Psychology*. New York: Anchor Books.

Miller, G. A. (2003). The cognitive revolution: A historical perspective. *Trends in Cognitive Sciences, 7*, 141–144.

Cognitive Neuroscience

2

A distinguished neurologist and writer, the late Dr. Oliver Sacks was one of the world's most astute observers of human behavior. Yet because of a brain condition, Dr. Sacks could barely recognize the faces of the people around him. In a publisher's office where he was scheduled to meet his assistant of six years, he failed to recognize her sitting in the reception room. On another occasion, he was unable to acknowledge an acquaintance in his apartment building lobby until the doorman greeted that person by name. And there were more extreme instances: he described an incident wherein he apologized for almost bumping into someone, only to realize that the person was his own reflection in the mirror. Because of this difficulty, Dr. Sacks was labeled with "shyness," "reclusiveness," "eccentricity," and even "Asperger's syndrome." His difficulty with faces caused huge embarrassment, requiring awkward solutions such as asking close friends to wear name tags at his own birthday parties (Sacks, 2010).

Oliver Sacks was a tremendously intelligent man, with normal corrected eyesight. Like other patients with his condition, known as face blindness, or **prosopagnosia**, Dr. Sacks was not blind—he could recognize non-face objects such as pens and cups just fine. His difficulty was specifically restricted to faces. The highly selective nature of prosopagnosia suggests that the ability to distinguish faces is separate from everyday vision. Face processing may even have its own **module**, a specialized mechanism in the brain that performs a specific function.

By some estimates, 2% of the general population has some degree of prosopagnosia (Kennerknecht et al., 2006). Many of these individuals function very well in society in spite of their inability to recognize faces. Other famous people with prosopagnosia apparently include primatologist Jane Goodall, actor Brad Pitt (Duchaine, 2015), and portrait artist Chuck Close (Sacks, 2010).

If there is a module for face processing in the brain, what other modules might exist, and how can we study them? How does investigating brain function enhance our understanding of the mind and behavior?

Neurologist Dr. Oliver Sacks

2.1 The Neural Basis of Cognition

These days, few people believe that we think or feel using our heart or liver. Yet in one survey, a majority of undergraduate students agreed with the idea that mind and brain are separate (Demertzi et al., 2009). This raises the question, What is the mind? The *Oxford English Dictionary* defines the mind as "The element of a person that enables them to be aware of the world and their experiences, to think, and to feel; the faculty of consciousness and thought." This definition may seem straightforward, but then, where is the mind, if not in the brain? And you can ask further questions, such as, "Does a computer have a mind?" "Does a worm have a mind?" "Are the mind and the soul one and the same?"

The idea of a separate, nonphysical mind is known as **dualism** and is credited to the seventeenth-century philosopher René Descartes. Dualists believe that the mind exists outside of the brain and body, both receiving information from the brain and directing the body via the brain. Thus, dualism distinguishes between the physical world, where the brain resides, and a nonphysical world, where minds and souls operate (**THINK FOR YOURSELF 2.1**).

► **Think for Yourself 2.1**

Dualism and "My Brain Made Me Do It"

In a charming little town in England, a tragedy occurred: a driver named Peter failed to stop at a road junction, and after narrowly missing two cyclists, his car vaulted straight into a wall, killing a friend who was a passenger (Robson, 2013). Was Peter guilty of murder? If Peter had been driving under the influence, people undoubtedly would have condemned him as responsible for his friend's death. But Peter had suffered an epileptic seizure, rendering him momentarily unconscious so that he lost control of the vehicle. Because he was taking medication, which usually controlled his epilepsy in a reliable way and legally allowed him to drive, Peter was absolved of wrongdoing by the court and the victim's family. This much seems fairly uncontroversial.

But what about Charles Whitman, who in 1966 killed 13 people and wounded 32 more from a perch in the University of Texas Tower in Austin? Before going on his shooting spree and committing suicide, he wrote a note about his "overwhelming violent impulses," which on the morning of the mass shooting also

My brain made me do it. How responsible was the driver for this car accident?

Think for Yourself   (continued)

led him to kill his mother, and his wife in her sleep. Tragic stories such as this are alarmingly common. In the case of Charles Whitman, however, he suspected that something was wrong with his brain and requested an autopsy in his suicide note. The autopsy revealed a tumor compressing a brain region called the amygdala, well known to be involved in emotion regulation. Could this brain abnormality have triggered Whitman's unspeakable violence? And if so, does knowing about this biological explanation change *your* feelings about his murderous acts? Does it reduce Whitman's criminal responsibility? What is the distinction between a death caused by someone else's epileptic seizure, and one caused by someone else's ill-placed tumor? Does a philosophy of materialism that equates the mind and brain put these two cases in the same category of culpability? The fact that some brains have biological abnormalities means that not everyone is equally likely to make socially appropriate choices. Or does the instinctive desire to make individuals culpable for their actions push us back toward dualism, separating the state of mind known as *mens rea* (guilty mind) from the biological "brain states" that produce behavior?

Modern psychology and neuroscience, however, take the position of **materialism**, which treats the mind as entirely a product of the brain. In other words, all cognition has a neural basis; there is no mind without the brain. According to Donald Hebb, one of the most influential neuroscientists of the twentieth century, "behavior and neural function are perfectly correlated...one is completely caused by the other" (Hebb, 1949). The tight relation between mind and body makes it essential to understand how the brain supports cognition.

The examples in Think for Yourself 2.1 strain the foundations of legal systems that must determine whether individuals are blameworthy, assuming that most people use free will to make rational, appropriate decisions (Eagleman, 2011). However, it is not scientifically sound to ask whether a behavior is a person's fault or his brain's fault. There is no way to tease apart one's choices and one's neural circuitry, genetic predispositions, and even environmental influences, such as having been abused as a child. Thus, neuroethicists—scholars who consider the implications of cognitive neuroscience on ethical issues such as criminal responsibility—believe the judicial focus should change from "Who is to blame?" to a more forward-looking "What to do with the accused?" (Eagleman, 2011; Gazzaniga, 2005b; Greene & Cohen, 2004). For violent offenders, incarceration is necessary to protect broader society, but it can be rehabilitative rather than punitive. In the case of epileptic patient Peter Murdoch, given the tragic evidence that his medication was fallible, his license to drive was revoked.

Cognitive neuroscience is the interdisciplinary study of the neural mechanisms of cognition and behavior (Eagleman & Downar, 2015). Its goals are the same as those of cognitive psychology—namely, to better understand how we perceive, think, learn, communicate, and control action—but with a focus on the role of brain mechanisms. While it is certainly possible to study cognitive psychology without considering the underlying brain systems, such an approach would lack a powerful and insightful element. A growing list of clinical problems or behavioral disorders—ranging from memory loss and dementia, attentional deficits, and thinking and decision-making problems (common to schizophrenia) to emotional and social difficulties such as depression, anxiety, antisocial behaviors, and autism—is linked to brain disorders.

The human brain is among the most complex physical and computational devices in the universe, enabling all of our perceptions, thoughts, and emotions. The brain allows us to constantly learn about, adapt to, and enact change on the environment. It contains almost 100 billion neurons, which are cells that serve as little computers. Each neuron is embedded in a massively interconnected network, like people in social media networks, and receives input from the external environment or from other neurons. Within this extraordinarily rich network of about 100 trillion connections, neural signals transform information from the environment and past experience into thought, emotion, action, and consciousness.

This tremendous mental complexity has enabled countless examples of human genius and accomplishment, from Greek philosophy to Islamic art to the Mars rover. No less remarkable are the everyday abilities most of us take for granted, such as speaking and driving. Even in the twenty-first century, computers do not come close to doing what the human brain can do. They can neither communicate as well as a four-year-old nor drive cars as reliably as a teenager—at least not yet. We are on the cusp of an autonomous (self-driving) vehicle revolution, which we will discuss in more detail in Chapter 3.

The primary task of cognitive neuroscience is to link this physiological and computational complexity to behavior and the mind, from how people respond to visual signals, to the nature of consciousness. Studying the brain advances our understanding of cognition.

➤ CHECKPOINT 2.1

1. What is the difference between dualism and materialism?
2. What is cognitive neuroscience? How is it similar to and different from cognitive psychology? How does neuroscience inform the understanding of the mind?

2.2 The Basics of Brain Structure and Function

If the 100 billion neurons in each person's head were as disconnected as grains of sand on a beach, the brain would be impossible to study. Fortunately, the brain can be organized into meaningful systems and subsystems.

Functional Specialization

Different parts of the brain serve different functions, such as the ability to perceive faces or motion. Thus, cases such as prosopagnosia highlight a fundamental feature of brain organization and function. **Functional specialization** is the principle that different brain areas serve different perceptual and cognitive skills. For example, malfunction in a specific part of the brain called the fusiform gyrus leads to prosopagnosia. As you'll see in Chapter 7, removal of a brain structure called the hippocampus produces memory loss. Later in this chapter, you'll learn how damage to Broca's area in the brain leads to an inability to speak, but the ability to comprehend language is preserved unless Wernicke's area is compromised.

Although functional specialization means that different brain areas perform different roles, all the modules must work together to enable even the simplest act, such as turning on a light switch. Thus, we must understand not only the individual parts but how the parts work together. It may be helpful to think about the brain as a big, complex company. Neurons are its employees, organized into different divisions with purposes ranging from marketing to finance to research and development. Within offices and divisions, workers communicate and collaborate, and the company as a whole relies on the different parts of the company cooperating well with each other. With this analogy in mind, let's consider neurons and brain organization.

Actor Brad Pitt, like neurologist Oliver Sacks, reports having prosopagnosia.

Neurons and Glial Cells

Neurons are cells in the nervous system. Each one is a little computer (or employee) that receives input, and then makes a decision about whether to pass on a signal to other neurons in a network. It is like a member in a game of telephone.

The neuron's three major anatomical components are the **dendrites**, the **soma** (**cell body**), and the **axon**. The dendrites are like branches of a tree, receiving input from sensory receptors or other neurons. The cell body also receives input and provides the metabolic machinery for the neuron. The axon transmits signals to other neurons. If the input from the dendrites and cell body exceeds a threshold, which corresponds to a decision to fire, an electrical signal called an **action potential** is generated down the length of the axon. Action potentials occur in an "all-or-nothing" fashion—the neuron either fires to influence other neurons or does not. The electrical signal triggers the release of chemicals called **neurotransmitters** at the end of the axon, which is how neurons communicate with other networked neurons (**FIGURE 2.1**).

At the core of the human brain's activity are about 100 trillion connections between individual neurons. Although neurons are not physically connected to each other, they communicate via neurotransmitters across gaps called **synapses**. The **presynaptic** (sending) neuron can either facilitate or inhibit the firing of the **postsynaptic** (receiving) neuron, depending on the type of neurotransmitter that is released. Connections between neurons are **plastic**, meaning that their strength can change with learning and experience. Specifically, learning can make it more likely or less likely that signals will transmit from one neuron to another, which is the foundation of memory. **Glial cells** are even more numerous than neurons and provide both structural and functional support to the neurons. Try the Discovery Lab to see synaptic transmission in action.

▶ DISCOVERY LAB
Synaptic Transmission

The Global Organization of the Brain

Some neurons receive input from sensory receptors to convey information from the environment to the brain. Others control motor output for action or speech. The majority of neurons communicate with each other to form networks that enable language, reasoning, perception, learning, and action. There is a precise and elegant organization to the brain that is fairly universal across humans.

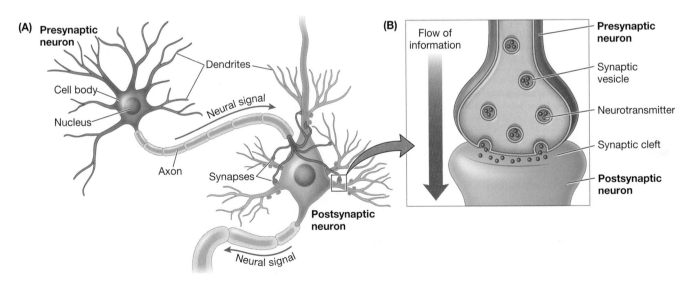

FIGURE 2.1 Schematic of two neurons and a synapse **(A)** The presynaptic neuron sends an action potential (the neural signal) down the axon to the dendrites of the postsynaptic neuron. **(B)** The electrical signal from the presynaptic neuron is transformed into chemical signals (neurotransmitters) that travel across the synaptic cleft to influence the activity of the postsynaptic neuron. (After S. M. Breedlove and N. V. Watson. 2019. *Behavioral Neuroscience*, 9th Edition. Oxford University Press/Sinauer: Sunderland, MA.)

This book on cognitive psychology will not require you to memorize a detailed map of the brain, but it is useful to have a sense of its broad organization, just as you know the locations of North and South America, Europe, Africa, Asia, Australia, and Antarctica on a globe.

The most prominent feature of the brain's anatomy is that it is organized into two halves called the left and right **hemispheres**. Structurally they are somewhat symmetrical, while functionally they have both common and unique roles. A major functional difference is that the left hemisphere processes sensory and motor functions for the right side of the body, while the right hemisphere controls the left side of the body. To a lesser degree, language functions are somewhat stronger in the left hemisphere, while visuospatial tasks are a little more concentrated in the right hemisphere (Gazzaniga, 2005a). However, functional differences between the hemispheres have been exaggerated in the popular media—contrary to popular belief, these differences are not strong enough to categorize people as primarily left-brain or right-brain. Both hemispheres interact heavily via a massive interconnection between the two hemispheres called the **corpus callosum**, which is a large bundle of neural fibers (axons) forming an information highway. Interesting differences emerge when the corpus callosum is severed, as in **split-brain** patients (**RESEARCH FOCUS 2.1**).

RESEARCH FOCUS 2.1

Split-Brain Patients

Is having two brain hemispheres like having two brains? Hearing a gifted pianist play a piece by Chopin, with different melodies emanating from the left and right hands, makes you appreciate how each hemisphere seems to have its own mind. Each controls the precise and complex fingering of the hand on the opposite side of the body, seemingly independent of the other. Yet the two hemispheres are in harmonious concert, and we can ask how each hemisphere operates and to what extent the two hemispheres work independently or in unison.

The left and right hemispheres are connected by a massive bundle of neural fibers called the *corpus callosum* (see Section 2.2). There was a time when physicians would sever that bundle of wiring in order to control severe cases of epilepsy. This procedure was effective in reducing debilitating seizures, and at first it seemed to leave perceptual and cognitive functions intact. Indeed, one such split-brain patient, W.J., appeared unaffected and charming, with a sharp sense of humor, according to the distinguished cognitive neuroscientist Michael Gazzaniga (Gazzaniga et al., 2018).

However, Gazzaniga tested W.J. more carefully and discovered a remarkable pattern of deficits (Gazzaniga, 2000; Gazzaniga, 2005a). Each hemisphere was able to do things the other hemisphere could not do, as if of a different mind. W.J. could name and describe objects presented to his left hemisphere. But when these items were presented to his right hemisphere, he claimed that he saw nothing. In contrast, his right hemisphere was good at directing the left hand to perform spatial tasks such as arranging a pattern of colored blocks, while the left hemisphere, controlling the right hand, could not do these same tasks. When he attempted the spatial task with both hands at the same time, the left hemisphere, controlling the right hand, appeared to confuse the spatially adept right hemisphere. These conflicts do not arise for other people because of left–right hemisphere coordination via the corpus callosum. Given the results of Gazzaniga's tests, it is not surprising that such split-brain surgical procedures are extremely rare now.

The symmetrical hemispheric organization of the brain mirrors the symmetry of our body. Two legs enable walking and running. Having two hands allows us to manipulate objects more easily. Having two ears helps us localize the source of sounds. It is biologically fitting to have separate hemispheres process input from the sensory organs or control the muscle movements on each side of the symmetrical body.

But what about cognitive functions? Why aren't these equally distributed or redundantly processed across the two hemispheres? The strongest hypothesis is based on processing efficiency. It takes time for information to travel across hemispheres. For complex skills such as language use, a faster response is advantageous. Of course, some degree of coordination and interhemispheric transfer is necessary, but within-hemisphere processing improves efficiency in performing complex cognitive tasks.

Under precise experimental conditions or when testing rare split-brain patients, hemispheric specialization can be detected. The left hemisphere is adept at language processing and analytic skills, while the right hemisphere is more reliably involved in tasks requiring spatial manipulation or attention. Despite such specialization, it is important to note that the two hemispheres interact too extensively to be simplified by popular attempts to characterize people as being either "left-brain" (logical and analytic) or "right-brain" (intuitive and creative).

The outer layer of each hemisphere is a thin, folded sheet of neurons, called the **cerebral cortex** (from the Latin for "tree bark"). The cortex has grooves (sulci) and bumps (gyri), increasing the surface area that can fit inside the skull, like crumpled paper. Each hemisphere can be further divided into four zones, or **lobes.**

Each lobe contains many different types of neural systems, and again, the entire brain must work together to perform any action. That said, some general points can be made about the different lobes, and for basic brain anatomy, you should know the locations and general functions of the four lobes and the cerebellum (**FIGURE 2.2**). The **occipital lobe** is devoted to visual perception. The cerebellum has classically been linked with control of fine motor movements, but more recent research revealed that it is involved in the coordination of complex thought as well (e.g., Schmahmann et al., 2019). The **temporal lobe** is important for complex perception, memory, and language. The **frontal lobe** is involved in thinking, planning, and decision making, while the **parietal lobe** is important for controlling action. The frontal and parietal lobes are close partners in leading many complex cognitive operations such as memory, attention, and decision making.

In sum, different parts of the brain perform different functions (functional specialization), with cognition depending on the coordination of these different parts. Like an orchestra, different sections play different instruments, and out of the harmonious interplay emerges the music of mind and behavior.

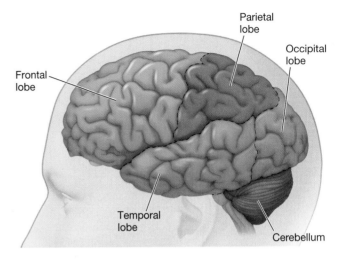

FIGURE 2.2 The four lobes of the brain   The four lobes of the brain are mirrored in each hemisphere: the frontal lobe (green), parietal lobe (purple), temporal lobe (blue), and occipital lobe (orange). The cerebellum (brown) is not considered a lobe. (After S. M. Breedlove and N. V. Watson. 2019. *Behavioral Neuroscience,* 9th Edition. Oxford University Press/Sinauer: Sunderland, MA.)

> ➤ CHECKPOINT 2.2

1. What is functional specialization? Give some examples.
2. What are the three major components of neurons and their functions?
3. Which aspect of neural activity is electrical and which is chemical?
4. What are the main functions of glial cells?
5. Draw from memory where the four lobes and the cerebellum are located; summarize each of their functions.

2.3 Neuroscience Methods

How do cognitive neuroscientists study the brain? To help illustrate the broad variety of neuroscience methods, let's take the example of studying prosopagnosia, which opened the chapter. Recall that this is a deficit in face recognition, leading many neurologists and neuropsychologists to hypothesize that a specific region (module) of the brain is devoted to face processing, separate from the brain regions used for everyday object perception, which remain intact in prosopagnosic patients since they can recognize common objects. However, the specific brain damage leading to prosopagnosia is quite rare, so the ability to test and understand this hypothesis has been limited.

Fortunately, modern technology and scientific ingenuity have given us tools to better understand basic functions such as face recognition. In this section we consider a variety of methods in the context of face perception. As you will see, each method has both advantages and limitations. First, the methods differ in their **spatial resolution**—their ability to pinpoint *where* neural activity occurs. Some methods are spatially precise at the level of neurons (offering a resolution as high as 0.001 mm for recording from single cells), whereas other methods can localize function only to relatively large brain areas (as low as 5 cm resolution for

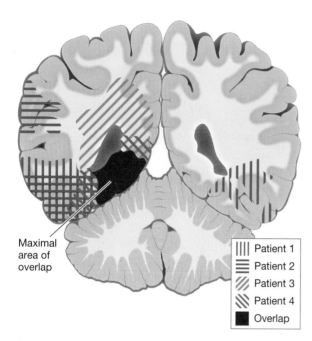

||||	Patient 1
≡≡≡	Patient 2
////	Patient 3
\\\\	Patient 4
■	Overlap

FIGURE 2.3 A cross section of the brain shows the lesioned areas of four patients with prosopagnosia The maximal area of overlap (solid color) includes the fusiform face area, important for face processing. (From J. J. S. Barton et al. 2002. *Neurology* 58: 71–78.)

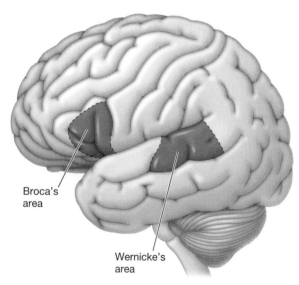

FIGURE 2.4 Brain areas important for conversation Lesions in the area of the left frontal lobe called Broca's area interfere with speech production; injury to an area called Wernicke's area interferes with language comprehension. (After S. M. Breedlove and N. V. Watson. 2019. *Behavioral Neuroscience*, 9th Edition. Oxford University Press/Sinauer: Sunderland, MA.)

electroencephalography, or EEG). Second, the methods differ in their **temporal resolution**—their ability to pinpoint *when* neural activity occurs. The most temporally precise methods measure neuronal firing in milliseconds, while other methods are limited to inferring neural activity over the course of seconds or longer. Finally, the methods differ greatly in their **invasiveness**—their impact on the individual whose brain is being studied—which determines how practically and broadly scientists can use them. Invasive methods include implanting electrodes (sensors), which requires opening the skull with surgery. Noninvasive methods can be as straightforward as observing an individual doing a task on a computer.

Neuropsychology

Neuropsychology studies the behavioral consequences of brain damage. Often this damage is from natural causes such as stroke or illness, but it can also be from unnatural causes such as surgery or trauma. When a patient presents him- or herself with a deficit such as face blindness, neurologists will look for damage in the brain, which can be plotted on a map of the brain. When several patients are plotted, the neurologist can ask if there is overlap across the patients with common face blindness disorders (**FIGURE 2.3**). The overlapping area of damage becomes a candidate as the brain area important for the function that was impaired.

Understanding the brain is important to help patients who suffer memory, attention, thinking, and emotional problems due to brain damage. The task of mapping brain mechanisms to behavior is possible because of functional specialization, a principle that early neuropsychology helped illuminate. In the mid-1800s, neurologist Paul Broca described a patient who could not speak but who could nevertheless understand language. Broca was later able to link this selective speech deficit to a small area of damage in the left frontal lobe, now known as **Broca's area** (**FIGURE 2.4**). Intriguingly, a few years later Carl Wernicke discovered a patient who had the opposite problem: the patient could speak but could not comprehend language. This condition was associated with damage in the left temporal lobe, in a location now termed **Wernicke's area** (see Figure 2.4). Although cognitive problems are usually not so specific, these links between brain damage and selective deficits greatly advanced our understanding of the brain and allowed investigators to infer functional specialization. Thus, neuropsychology provided early evidence in support of materialism over dualism.

Brain damage is sadly common, especially as a result of stroke, a leading cause of death and disability in the United States. During a stroke, blood supply to a brain area is interrupted or severely reduced, depriving neurons of oxygen and nutrients and causing them to die. Depending on the area that is damaged, patients may lose their ability to speak, become paralyzed, or even lose consciousness for a long time. Brain trauma from car accidents is another frequent cause of brain damage. More subtle and less well understood are the potential effects of chronic head injury and concussions (**RESEARCH FOCUS 2.2**).

RESEARCH FOCUS 2.2

Concussions and Chronic Brain Injury

Former professional American football player Romney Jenkins dodged a bullet—for real. Suffering from major depression, anger, and cognitive problems, he put a gun to his head for a game of Russian roulette, pulling the trigger one click at a time. Fortunately for him, when the bullet fired, it missed, making him realize that "it wasn't time to go." Other former National Football League (NFL) players have not been so lucky, and confirmed suicides among veteran athletes number over a dozen (Smith, 2014).

Romney was diagnosed with chronic traumatic encephalopathy (CTE), which causes symptoms of dementia, depression, anxiety, attention deficits, and memory problems. CTE is associated with repeated concussions, and researchers are actively studying its effect on the brain and behavior. Can these problems be linked to brain abnormalities?

Magnetic resonance imaging (MRI) has revealed that the brains of college football players, especially those who have suffered concussions, are different from the brains of students who did not play football or other sports that risk head injury, such as hockey. The football players showed 16% less volume in the hippocampus, a structure important for memory. Players who suffered a concussion showed up to 25% less hippocampal volume. And even without a documented history of concussions, the more seasons a student played football, the smaller the hippocampal volume (Singh et al., 2014).

These findings raise serious concerns, but more research is needed. Correlation does not equal causation. For example, it's logically possible that students with smaller hippocampal volume may be drawn to play football. Furthermore, the impact on cognition is not clear: hippocampal volume and thinking skills did not correlate strongly (Singh et al., 2014). Yet it remains possible that a larger study may reveal an association between hippocampal volume and cognitive ability.

Thus, it will be important to track the effects of chronic brain injury on cognition, emotion, and brain integrity. In other studies, smaller hippocampal volume links to a higher likelihood of suffering from post-traumatic stress disorder (Gilbertson et al., 2002). And dementia and other neurological diseases such as seizures are more common in former NFL players than in the general population, making it difficult for them to work and to pay for mounting medical bills. In order "to compensate victims, pay for medical exams, and underwrite research," the NFL reached a settlement over concussion-related brain injuries among its players (Associated Press, 2013; NFL Concussion Settlement, 2021).

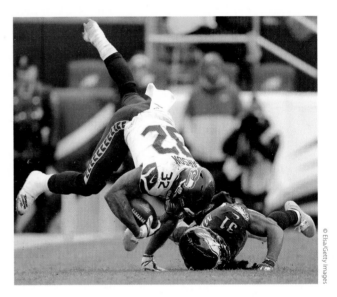

What are the long-term effects of repeated hits to the head?

A primary advantage of neuropsychology is that it allows researchers and physicians to identify brain regions required for specific functions. In the case of prosopagnosia, fusiform gyrus damage can result in face blindness, leading researchers to conclude that the fusiform gyrus is necessary for face recognition. This kind of information can help clinicians when treating other patients. For example, when neurosurgeons detect a brain tumor, they must estimate how removal of the tumor and some brain tissue around it may impact the patient's ability to think and behave normally. In many cases, behavioral and cognitive problems are what allow physicians to suspect the presence of a tumor in the first place.

However, for at least three reasons, neuropsychology alone cannot fully advance the scientific study of the brain. First, brain lesions are imprecise and generally affect more than one region. Thus, the chance that brain damage will be well defined or consistent across patients is low, making it difficult to systematically associate patterns of brain damage with specific functions such as face discrimination. Second, any studies conducted with patients who have brain damage are not easy to compare with studies of control individuals, because brain damage usually impairs several functions. Third, clinicians obviously must prioritize treating patients rather than testing them for scientific gain. Because of these limitations of neuropsychology, scientists need other methods to study brain function.

Electrophysiology

Neural activity is electrical. As noted earlier, a neuron receives input from other neurons across hundreds of thousands of synapses on its dendrites, and this collective input helps determine whether the neuron will or will not transmit a signal to other neurons down its axon and across synapses. The signals are transmitted in the form of action potentials, so measurements of action potentials directly reveal whether a neuron is active.

SINGLE-CELL ELECTRODE RECORDINGS   Typically in animal subjects, but also in people, cognitive neuroscientists can measure action potentials by placing thin electrodes—needlelike probes that measure electrical activity—into a network of neurons in a region of interest. Just as a microphone will pick up multiple voices at a cocktail party, the electrode will pick up signals from multiple neurons, from which computer algorithms can isolate individual signals. The ability to directly measure electrical activity from neurons using electrodes—the field of **electrophysiology**—has greatly advanced our understanding of the brain.

Because action potentials are binary (all-or-nothing) and brief, like a clap, a neuron's activity can be quantified as its firing rate (**FIGURE 2.5**). For example, a neuron that fires at a rate of 20 times per second is more active than one that fires 3 times per second.

The goal of electrophysiology research is to find experimental manipulations that *change the firing rate of a neuron*, thereby demonstrating the neuron's function. Neurons are active even in the absence of an explicit task or stimulation; the rate of this neural activity is known as the baseline firing rate. The firing rate will change in comparison with the baseline when the neuron is responsive to a stimulus being shown (e.g., a face) or involved in a task or action (e.g., moving a finger). For example, to study the function of a visual neuron, a cognitive neuroscientist could first place an electrode in a brain region hypothesized to be important for visual processing. The next step would be to measure

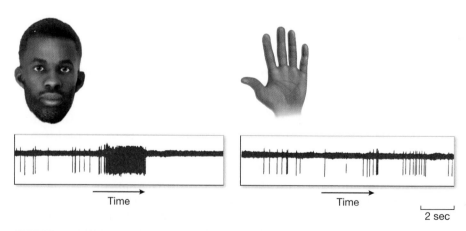

FIGURE 2.5 Neuronal activity   The graphs show neuronal action potentials over time in response to a face (left) or to a control stimulus, a hand (right). Each vertical notch represents an action potential, showing that the neuron is more actively responding to the face than to the hand. (From C. Bruce et al. 1981. *J Neurophysiol* 46: 369–384.)

the neuron's baseline firing rate while the animal subject is looking at nothing. Finally, the researcher would present various kinds of stimuli to see which of them make the neuron fire differently from baseline. Nobel Prize Laureates David Hubel and Torsten Wiesel discovered that neurons in the **primary visual cortex**, an area in the occipital lobe that receives visual information from the eyes, changed their firing rate in response to visual stimuli with spotlike or edgelike features (Hubel & Wiesel, 1962, 1968).

Not all visual neurons have the same function; they are further specialized to specific stimulus categories such as faces. The most important property of brain cells is their selectivity—the fact that they respond more robustly to certain kinds of stimuli or tasks. For example, to establish that a neuron is selective to face stimuli, a researcher must show that the neuron does not respond as strongly to other kinds of stimuli (controls). A neuron that responds similarly to other visual stimuli, such as non-face body parts, is not face selective. Another common control stimulus that researchers use to demonstrate selectivity is scrambled images, as shown in **FIGURE 2.6** (Kanwisher et al., 1997). Face cells—neurons that seem to be specialized for face recognition—do not respond to such scrambled features as strongly. This finding indicates that the cells are responding not just to face parts but to the coherent configuration of parts. Interestingly, face cells in monkeys will respond as strongly to a human face as to a monkey face, suggesting that these neurons categorize human faces together with monkey faces (Desimone et al., 1984; Perrett et al., 1982). Claims for selectivity are only as good as the control stimuli tested. Establishing selectivity compared with valid controls is important not just for electrophysiology but also for other neuroscience methods such as functional brain imaging, discussed later in this chapter.

An advantage of single-cell electrode recording is clearly both its spatial and temporal precision. By measuring the activity of single neurons, researchers can study the basic unit of processing in the brain. This method offers the highest possible spatial resolution. Temporal precision is also exquisite in single-cell recording, since this method allows neuronal firing to be measured the instant it happens, at the millisecond resolution of action potentials.

The disadvantages and limitations of single-cell electrophysiology are also obvious. Inserting electrodes into the brain is highly invasive. Although enormous efforts make these procedures as safe and comfortable as possible (brain tissue itself is insensitive to pain), these types of experiments cannot be conducted in humans for scientific research purposes alone; there must be a clinical reason to help the individual.

ELECTROCORTICOGRAPHY (ECoG) The benefits of new knowledge, as great as they may be, do not outweigh the potential risks involved in performing surgery to insert electrodes into the human brain. However, sometimes surgery is inevitable. In clinical conditions such as severe epilepsy, electrode implantation can help localize the sources of seizures, as targets for removal. These **intracranial recordings**, or **electrocorticography** (**ECoG**), can also produce scientific benefits. While recording for abnormal brain activity, clinicians are also keen to preserve function, so that they do not remove brain tissue that underlies language or memory, for example.

Intracranial recordings revealed highly selective face neurons in the human brain (Allison et al., 1999). One patient had a neuron that was active for pictures

Intact Faces

Scrambled Faces

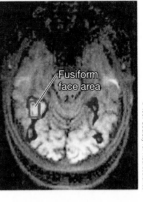

FIGURE 2.6 The fusiform face area Fusiform face area activity is higher for intact faces than for scrambled faces (yellow region outlined with the green box on the brain as measured by fMRI).

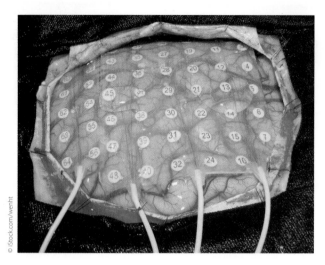

FIGURE 2.7 Intracranial electrodes on the surface of an exposed human brain

of the actress Jennifer Aniston and not responsive to other famous faces or places. Moreover, the cell was suppressed (did not fire) when Jennifer Aniston was in a picture with her then-husband, actor Brad Pitt—and this was even before they divorced (Quiroga et al., 2005). Different electrodes in visual cortex responded to other types of stimuli, such as non-face objects and words (Nobre et al., 1994).

Intracranial electrode studies have all the advantages of single-cell electrophysiology—namely, high spatial and temporal resolution. The disadvantages are similar too: the method is invasive. **FIGURE 2.7** shows a brain with electrodes placed directly on its cortical surface. Another disadvantage is the obvious fact that the placement of electrodes is clinically determined rather than guided by research hypotheses. A third limitation is that ECoG recordings are from individuals who tend to be heavily medicated to control their epileptic seizures. These patients have abnormal brain activity due to their epilepsy, so their brains likely operate differently from those of control individuals. These factors reduce the ability to generalize results from the brains of people who have epilepsy to healthy brains.

ELECTROENCEPHALOGRAPHY (EEG)   A popular, less invasive way to measure electrical activity is by placing electrodes on an individual's scalp. The aggregate activity of millions to billions of active neurons transmits throughout the head and can be detected on the scalp. It is like listening to the reactions of a crowd from outside a sports arena. You may not be able to tell exactly what's going on, but you can get a rough sense of when something exciting or disappointing is happening. For the arena of the brain, **electroencephalography** (**EEG**) uses electrodes on the scalp to detect and amplify global electrical activity. EEG is widely used in clinical settings because different states of consciousness and sleep produce different EEG patterns that can be reliably measured (**FIGURE 2.8**). EEG can easily assess clinical conditions such as epilepsy that are accompanied by a transient loss of consciousness. During such seizures, EEG reveals large oscillations in brain waves.

In the laboratory, EEG can measure perceptual and cognitive function in an individual performing a task. Although EEG is limited in spatial precision, it produces systematic signals that inform properly designed studies

FIGURE 2.8 **Levels of consciousness change across different sleep stages** EEG signal patterns change according to levels of consciousness, which vary across stages of sleep. NREM, non-rapid-eye-movement sleep; REM, rapid-eye-movement sleep. (From P. Bryant et al. 2004. *Nat Rev Immunol* 4: 457–467.)

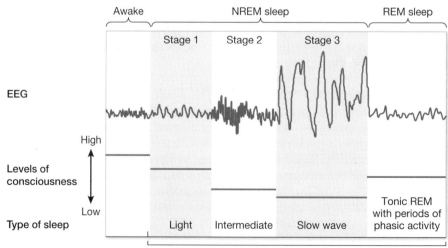

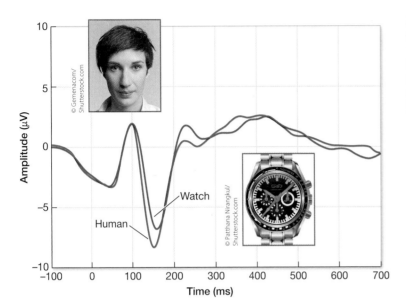

FIGURE 2.9 The EEG component N170 is sensitive to faces The EEG component called the N170 occurs about 170 ms after the appearance of a stimulus, and as shown by the difference between the signals at around 170 ms, it is selectively larger for face stimuli than for non-face stimuli. (From https://www.mada.org.il/brain/question-e.html, with permission from Elana Zion-Golumbic.)

of functional specificity. The EEG pattern in response to a stimulus or task is called an **event-related potential** (**ERP**). For example, when recording from individuals viewing several different kinds of objects, EEG reveals a different pattern for face stimuli than for other visual stimuli. This face-selective ERP is called the N170 because it occurs about 170 ms after stimulus onset, and because its electrical polarity is negative (**FIGURE 2.9**) (Bentin et al., 1996).

The N170 example highlights a major methodological advantage of the EEG signal, which is its high temporal precision: EEG directly pools the electrical signals of neurons. In other words, it has high temporal resolution, akin to measuring a 100-m dash running time in milliseconds rather than seconds. A second advantage of EEG is that it is inexpensive compared with other neuroimaging methods such as fMRI (discussed in the next section), so its clinical use is widespread. Third, it is noninvasive and relatively convenient because it only involves placing electrodes on the scalp. This may require shampooing afterward (because of the conductive gel), but it poses no risk. In fact, EEG is so safe that it can be used to record brain signals from babies, who, as a plus, often do not have much hair to get in the way of the electrodes.

As noted earlier, EEG has poor spatial resolution because it sums activity across the entire brain, and signals from different areas mingle with each other in ways that are difficult to decipher. Although it is usually possible to distinguish whether activity is occurring in the front (anterior) versus back (posterior) of the brain, or left versus right hemisphere, many research questions require more anatomical precision. This disadvantage has opened the path for other methods, such as fMRI.

Functional Magnetic Resonance Imaging (fMRI)

A common scene in science fiction movies involves putting people in brain scanners to read their thoughts and dreams. What is hype, what is current reality, and what is feasible in the near future? Remarkably, under certain conditions using functional magnetic resonance imaging (fMRI), researchers can now roughly recreate what type of movie a person is viewing while in a brain scanner (Nishimoto et al., 2011). From brain activity, researchers can even decode which face a person is seeing—not perfectly, but at better than chance levels (Cowen et al., 2014) (**FIGURE 2.10**).

Functional brain imaging uses medical technologies to noninvasively study brain activity. Originally developed for clinical purposes, medical imaging

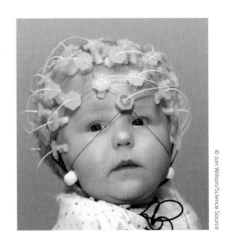

EEG electrodes record the brain's electrical activity from the scalp. It is sufficiently noninvasive to use on babies.

(A)

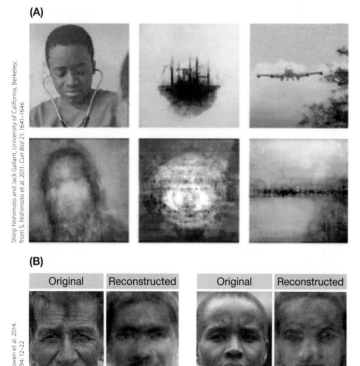

Shinji Nishimoto and Jack Gallant, University of California, Berkeley; from S. Nishimoto et al. 2011. *Curr Biol* 21: 1641–1646

(B)

| Original | Reconstructed | Original | Reconstructed |

From A. S. Cowen et al. 2014. *NeuroImage* 94: 12–22

FIGURE 2.10 Brain decoding with fMRI   **(A)** The top row shows clips from videos shown to observers in MRI scanners. Based on decoding MRI measurements collected while participants viewed these images, the bottom row shows what computer algorithms guessed that the participant was viewing. **(B)** Original faces are what participants viewed in the scanner, while reconstructed faces were generated by computer algorithms that decoded brain responses to draw a best guess of which face the participant was viewing.

© iStock.com/JohnnyGreig

An MRI scanner that is commonly used to study brain activity. After setup, the participant is slid into the MRI bore (tube).

provides detailed views of internal body structures and abnormalities ranging from fractures to tumors.

Among several imaging techniques such as X-rays, computerized tomography (CT) scans, and positron emission tomography (PET), we will focus on **magnetic resonance imaging** (**MRI**), which is the most widely used technique for studying cognition. MRI was initially developed to provide detailed images of internal organs and other soft tissues, such as the brain. Most MRI machines are shaped like tubes, in which a person, animal, or nonmagnetic object can be placed for scanning.

The name of this technique derives from its use of a powerful magnetic field and brief radio pulses. While the principles of MRI are beyond the scope of this book, the basic thing to know is that different brain structures and tissues have different magnetic properties. The MRI scanner is able to detect these differences in any three-dimensional volume, and by assigning different shades of gray, it can transform numerical values into two-dimensional images, taken as layered slices through the brain volume. Physicians then use the exquisite structural pictures from MRI technology to help identify abnormalities in patients.

MRI machines were initially used for structural imaging, which does not reveal mental function. But after about a decade of active clinical use to reveal structural abnormalities (e.g., cartilage problems, tumors), a revolutionary discovery was announced in 1990. Ogawa et al. (1990) modified structural MRI in a way that allowed researchers to infer brain function—hence the term **functional magnetic resonance imaging** (**fMRI**). fMRI measures and localizes blood oxygen levels throughout the brain. Because blood oxygen levels increase in active brain areas, this **blood-oxygen-level-dependent** (**BOLD**) signal can be used to infer brain activity.

As an example, neurons in the occipital cortex are more active when a visual stimulus appears on a screen than when the screen is dark. Increased activity means that neurons are firing more action potentials. This neural activity consumes energy and oxygen, which are supplied through the bloodstream. In particular, hemoglobin molecules deliver oxygen to all cells, and oxygenated hemoglobin becomes concentrated in active brain regions, like students swarming to free pizza. Importantly, oxygenated hemoglobin has different magnetic properties than deoxygenated hemoglobin. fMRI detects and localizes these differences in magnetic properties, determining where in the brain oxygenated hemoglobin is increasing in concentration—the BOLD contrast signal. It is this signal that allows researchers to infer which brain areas are more active while a task is being performed. During visual stimulation, the BOLD signal increases in the occipital cortex. This signal can be plotted on anatomical images of the brain to identify which regions are more active.

The first decade of fMRI research, the 1990s, saw furious efforts to map the different functions of the brain. One of the most widely studied subsystems in cognitive neuroscience is the processing of faces compared with the visual processing of scenes (Aguirre et al., 1996; Epstein & Kanwisher, 1998; Kanwisher et al., 1997; Puce et al., 1995) (**FIGURE 2.11**). In these studies, participants were scanned while viewing sequences of faces versus sequences of scenes. Because both tasks involve visual stimulation, broad swathes of visual cortex become active in response to both. The **fMRI subtraction method**, however, allows for comparison of the patterns of brain activity for two categories of stimuli. When you apply this method, activity in early visual cortex, which is common to both face and scene processing, drops out, and category-specific activity remains. Activity higher for faces alone reveals the brain regions important for face processing, which falls in the right fusiform gyrus, known as the fusiform face area (FFA) (Kanwisher et al., 1997). Activity higher for scenes alone is in a separate region in the parahippocampal gyrus (the parahippocampal place area, or PPA) (Epstein & Kanwisher, 1998).

The FFA and PPA are examples of **functional brain mapping**, the task of localizing cognitive and perceptual functions to specific brain regions. Functional brain mapping has obvious clinical benefits, allowing neurosurgeons and neurologists to understand or predict what may happen when a brain area is damaged or removed. But why should cognitive psychologists care about brain mapping? To be skeptical, one could argue that knowing where functions are located in the brain does not directly tell us how the mind works. We do not need brain imaging to know that face perception happens somewhere between the two ears; what good is more precise localization to the fusiform gyrus? Isn't it sufficient to study behavior alone?

Throughout this book, you'll see how brain imaging and functional mapping greatly advance our understanding of the mind and behavior. Brain imaging data are extremely useful in testing hypotheses about how the mind works. Localization or mapping brain function is just the first, fundamental step to understanding a complex behavior such as face perception. Brain mapping establishes **regions of interest (ROIs)** for further testing of brain and cognitive function. A region of interest is a brain area designated by an investigator to be the focus of study. Using the face area as an example of an ROI, fMRI can illuminate our understanding of autism spectrum disorder (ASD), including Asperger's syndrome, as this developmental disorder includes difficulty in social interaction and face recognition. Is ASD a high-level social deficit, or does it affect basic processes such as the ability to discriminate faces? Do individuals with ASD have less well developed face areas in the brain? Studies asking these questions have revealed that the face areas of individuals with ASD show less activity in response to faces than do the face areas of control individuals (Schultz et al., 2000). These studies can motivate interventions to directly train face and facial emotion recognition skills in individuals with ASD (Golan & Baron-Cohen, 2006; Tanaka et al., 2010).

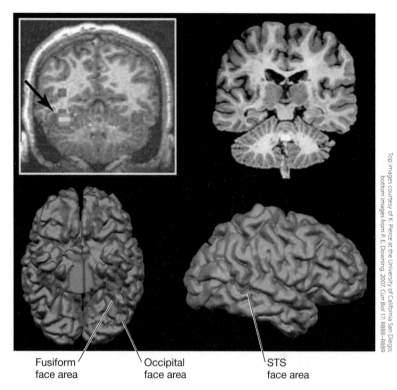

Top images courtesy of K. Pierce at the University of California San Diego; bottom images from P. E. Downing 2007. *Curr Biol* 17: R888–R889

Fusiform face area   Occipital face area   STS face area

FIGURE 2.11 Different ways to show the areas fMRI reveals face areas around the human brain, marked in yellow-red throughout the four images. MRI images (top row) are two-dimensional but can be reconstructed as three-dimensional models (bottom row). The top left image is an MRI image from a coronal slice through the brain; the top right image is from a postmortem brain. The bottom left image is a view from the bottom of the brain; the bottom right image is from the right side of the brain. The three-dimensional models also show other face-sensitive brain regions, such as the occipital face area and the superior temporal sulcus (STS) face area. Note the images are shown as radiological reverse.

As a tool to study the mind and brain, fMRI has several advantages. It offers significantly better spatial resolution than any other noninvasive method to study brain activity. EEG has inherent limitations in its spatial precision relative to fMRI. Another advantage is that fMRI does not require placing electrodes into the brain or even on the scalp, so it is less invasive.

The primary disadvantage is that unlike electrophysiological methods that directly measure neural activity, fMRI measurements are indirect—they infer activity based on increased measurements of oxygenated hemoglobin to a brain area. Hence, the accuracy of fMRI is limited by the blood vasculature in two ways. First, the spatial resolution of fMRI is limited; currently the best methods are about 1 mm × 1 mm × 1 mm, and more commonly 3 mm × 3 mm × 3 mm because the larger resolution makes fMRI signals easier to measure (Huettel et al., 2014). This is still sufficiently precise for many purposes, and better than EEG, but far worse than the resolution of single-neuron recording. Second, temporal resolution is poorer for fMRI than for electrophysiological methods. EEG lacks spatial resolution but boasts millisecond precision. fMRI cannot offer such precision because it relies on the rise and fall of oxygenated hemoglobin levels, which happen far more slowly (over seconds) than electrical currents in the brain (milliseconds). Finally, although fMRI is relatively noninvasive, there are important safety measures to take. Participants cannot have any metal in their bodies because of the scanner's high magnetic field. Also, participants should not be claustrophobic because most scanners require them to lie inside a confined tube.

Another important limitation—which is not specific to fMRI but is relevant to interpreting any kind of brain activity—is the need to avoid **reverse inference**, which is when you illogically infer a mental process (cognitive or emotional) from the activation of a particular brain region (Poldrack, 2006). For example, if you observe that the FFA is active, you might infer that the individual was viewing faces. However, logically speaking, you can't be certain about this. In reasoning, when you observe that A causes B, you cannot infer that B causes A. Spraying water (A) directly on someone will cause them to become wet (B) with 100% certainty. However, just because you see that someone is wet (B) does not mean that you can infer with 100% certainty that someone sprayed water on them (A)—there are many reasons the person could be wet (rainstorm, having just finished a shower, falling in a pool, etc.). Likewise, in neuroimaging we know that viewing human faces (A) will cause the FFA to become active (B). However, we cannot infer with certainty that activity in the FFA (B) means that the observer viewed human faces (A). As alternative explanations, the observer may have been thinking about faces, or the observer may have viewed animal faces, or other stimuli that activate the face area to a lesser extent.

Nevertheless, this does not mean we should abandon the use of fMRI for trying to decode the mind. It simply highlights the need for caution in interpreting such data, whether in journals or in the media. Statistical methods can help make reverse inferences more accurate, especially if you can catalog a large number of studies mapping different functions to different brain areas. Doing so allows you to estimate the strength of the inferences you want to make (Poldrack, 2006). New imaging analysis methods can further enhance the precision and our confidence in reverse inferences (Norman et al., 2006).

Brain Stimulation

An important caution in psychology and neuroscience is to avoid the **correlation and causation problem,** which is when people confuse a correlation as a cause and effect. Making this mistake is especially tempting in neuroscience. For face perception, it is highly compelling to see the face area become active in fMRI images, to see the N170 in EEG waveforms, or even to see a Jennifer Aniston cell become active with electrodes implanted in the head. However, none of these findings can prove that such activity is logically *necessary* for face perception. Instead, such face activity, no matter how selective, simply correlates with face perception. As an analogy, the LED light indicator on your TV or computer screen will correlate perfectly with whether your screen is powered on, but that doesn't mean that the signal causes your device to turn on, or that a malfunction of the power light will prevent your screen from turning on. Similarly, just because the face area is active while viewing faces does not logically dictate that the face area is necessary for face perception. To demonstrate necessity, you need to show that blocking face area activity will disrupt face perception.

By experimentally stimulating or blocking neurons in a particular brain region, it is possible to demonstrate the necessity of that region for a behavior. Accordingly, neuroscientists have developed **brain stimulation** methods—ways to stimulate or disrupt brain activity to study causal effects on perceptual and cognitive function.

TRANSCRANIAL MAGNETIC STIMULATION (TMS)   TMS is a method to temporarily disrupt brain activity using focal magnetic pulses targeted over different areas of the scalp. With proper supervision and training, TMS is a generally safe method for temporarily stimulating or interrupting brain activity (Rossi et al., 2009). As shown in **FIGURE 2.12**, a coil is placed at strategic locations around an individual's head. Based on Faraday's principles of magnetic induction, a pulse of powerful electrical current running through the coil induces a directional magnetic field. This field easily passes through the skull, influencing neural activity in the region under the coil. TMS over visual cortex can generate phosphenes, the perceptual sensation of visual speckles, while TMS over motor cortex can cause muscles to twitch.

TMS can temporarily and safely disrupt neural processing, helping determine whether a brain region is important for a particular brain function. Such TMS-induced "virtual lesions" (Pascual-Leone, 1999) can help establish whether a brain region plays a causal role, getting around limitations of correlation-based methods such as fMRI. Based on fMRI localization of separate brain regions for the processing of faces, bodies, and objects, TMS over the right hemisphere occipital face area impairs visual processing of faces but not of objects or bodies, while TMS over the right fusiform face area impairs processing of bodies but not of objects or faces. Finally, TMS over the lateral occipital areas impairs recognition of objects but not of faces or bodies (Pitcher et al., 2009). These findings show that separate brain areas are not just differentially active during viewing of faces, bodies, and objects, but that these areas play a causal role in perceiving these different categories.

An advantage of TMS, in addition to its ability to help establish causality, is its temporal precision. For example, the timing of the TMS pulse to visual cortex is crucial to whether or not a behavior is impaired. This is consistent with our understanding of the timing by which a visual stimulus arriving in the retina gets processed through the visual hierarchy. Another advantage of TMS is that it can provide clinical benefits (such as deep brain stimulation) for some disorders such as drug-resistant depression (Pascual-Leone et al., 1996).

Limitations of TMS include its spatial precision and reach. The foci of TMS disruption are not well defined (Pascual-Leone et al., 2000), although the spatial extent can be limited to just a few millimeters, small enough to stimulate individual fingers from primary motor cortex (Ro et al., 1998). Also, because TMS is induced above the scalp, it can disrupt activity only within about 3 cm of the scalp, but not deeper structures. Finally, some forms of TMS, based on

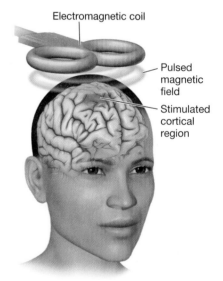

Electromagnetic coil

Pulsed magnetic field

Stimulated cortical region

FIGURE 2.12 A schematic of transcranial magnetic stiumulation (TMS) When an electric current runs through the figure-eight-shaped coil above the head, a powerful magnetic field is generated and passes safely through the skull to stimulate and disrupt cortical activity within about 3 cm below the coil, depicted in red. (From S. M. Breedlove and N. V. Watson. 2019. *Behavioral Neuroscience*, 9th Edition. Oxford University Press/Sinauer: Sunderland, MA.)

Courtesy of Focus

Transcranial direct current stimulation (tDCS)

how frequently magnetic pulses are delivered, can cause discomfort or even raise a small risk of seizures. Clinicians follow rigorous guidelines to minimize these negative effects (Pascual-Leone et al., 2000; Rossi et al., 2009).

TRANSCRANIAL DIRECT CURRENT STIMULATION (tDCS)

Can you jump-start your brain like you would a weak car battery? **Transcranial direct current stimulation** (tDCS) involves applying a weak electrical current across the skull to modify brain activity (Nitsche et al., 2008). tDCS does not cause underlying neurons to fire, but rather increases or decreases the likelihood that they will fire. Like a battery, tDCS delivers a current that flows from a negative electrode on the scalp to a positive one. The orientation of this current flow and the placement of the electrodes affect how tDCS will modulate brain activity. The method is considered safe and noninvasive because electrodes are on the scalp and the levels of electrical currents are minimal.

Changing the likelihood that neurons will fire may promote learning. An early study demonstrated that tDCS over motor cortex can improve the ability to learn a sequence of motor responses, akin to playing a sequence of notes on a piano. As a control to show its specificity, tDCS over other areas of the brain did not produce these motor learning benefits (Nitsche et al., 2003). Conversely, tDCS over dorsolaterial prefrontal cortex improved the ability to briefly remember and manipulate information (working memory; see Chapter 5), while tDCS over motor cortex did not (Fregni et al., 2005). More research is needed, however, so hold off on wearing a tDCS cap before an exam.

Genetics and Cognitive Neuroscience

Each of us is a product of our genes and our environment. **Genes** are heritable codes in almost every cell of our bodies (i.e., they are transmissible from parent to offspring), and they dictate how our bodies develop and function. Genes are defined as sections on a strand of **DNA** (**deoxyribonucleic acid**), which is a molecule shaped like a twisted ladder, known as a double-helix configuration. Long strands of DNA form **chromosomes**. Humans have 23 pairs of chromosomes, and each pair contains one chromosome from the mother and one from the father. These genetic instructions are what everyone inherits from their biological parents. If genes are like recipes, DNA is like a cookbook, and chromosomes are like a collection of cookbooks copied from your parents' collection. To continue the analogy, cells follow the gene "recipes" to make proteins, which give cells their structure and function.

A **genotype** refers to the entire set of genes that an organism carries, while a **phenotype** is all of an organism's observable traits resulting from the interaction of its genotype with its environment. Traits can be physical, such as eye color, hair color, skin tone, and height, as well as behavioral, such as our temperament, working memory capacity, or ability to learn a language. Some fun examples of heritable phenotypes include whether you are able to bend your thumb backward, whether your earlobes are attached or dangle freely, and whether you can roll your tongue.

More significant (though less obvious) phenotypes include our susceptibility to physical or mental illness. Most phenotypes are not determined by one gene but by multiple genes. For example, there does not appear to be a single gene that determines height, even though height is a heritable trait. In sum,

© srulik/Shutterstock.com

A person rolling her tongue. Try it. Not everyone can do this. You need to have inherited this phenotype.

linking phenotypes to genotypes is not easy, and the computational challenges of this task are conceptually similar to those of linking cognition and behavior to brain areas.

BEHAVIORAL GENETICS   **Behavioral genetics** is the field that attempts to link behavior (phenotypes) and genes (genotypes). To the extent that some cognitive functions, such as intelligence and executive function, are heritable (Friedman et al., 2008; Toga & Thompson, 2005), genetics should be considered in cognitive psychology and neuroscience (Plomin et al., 1994). A common example is the study of identical twins separated at birth. Despite being raised in different environments, these identical twins show a strong correlation in intelligence. Again, this does not mean that genes determine intelligence but rather that they are an important factor.

Understanding the interaction between genes and environment is crucial for isolating genetic influences. Genes are instructions that are not followed automatically in a vacuum but in a way that depends on other genes and the environment. For example, rat offspring that received more maternal behaviors such as licking and grooming responded better to stress as adults. Essentially, maternal behaviors changed how genes were expressed in the pups (Weaver et al., 2004). In other words, the environment influences how genes operate without changing the genes themselves. The field that studies such external factors affecting the genome is called **epigenetics**.

Behavioral genetics helps link human cognitive psychology with powerful scientific advances that are usually developed first in animal models. The genome sequences for the fruit fly and mouse have been fully mapped, and modern advances allow for manipulations of specific genes. Typically, this manipulation involves rendering a gene absent or unexpressed—a technique known as **knock-out**. Then the effects of these genetic knock-out strains can be linked to different behaviors ranging from memory impairment to the generation of false memories, which are memories of events that never happened (Ramirez et al., 2013).

Comparing Methods

In this chapter we have explored the dazzling array of methods that psychologists and neuroscientists have in their tool chest to study mind, brain, and behavior. We have highlighted each method's strengths and weaknesses, and in **FIGURE 2.13** we summarize them in direct comparison. The figure is informative in that it organizes the methods according to spatial resolution, from synapses to the entire brain, and temporal resolution, from milliseconds to years. In addition, filler colors indicate how invasive each technique is relative to others. Modern technology aims to make the spatial resolution finer and temporal resolution faster (these techniques would be in the bottom left of the figure's coordinate plane) and to make the methods safer and less invasive. Many cognitive neuroscience researchers have expertise in both fMRI and EEG to use each method's strengths. Both the global and microscopic levels are useful. That is, we need to understand both the forest and the trees.

These tools to investigate brain function, especially in humans, have revolutionized our understanding of the mind, just as telescopes changed our understanding of our place in the universe, and just as microscopes advanced the study of microbiology and disease. No longer limited to studying patients with brain damage or using invasive recording methods, neuroscientists have now gained unprecedented insight into how the brain works. By cleverly using the strengths of each of these methods in combination with measures of behavior, neuroscientists and cognitive psychologists alike can expect more exciting discoveries over the next few decades.

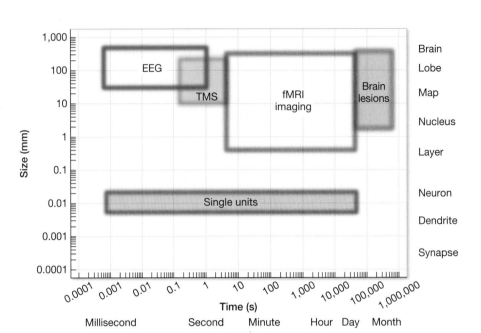

FIGURE 2.13 Different ways to study the brain   Different methods (distinguished by color) to study the brain plotted according to their spatial resolution (more precise along the lower *y*-axis), and temporal resolution (more precise along the lower *x*-axis). Open regions are less invasive, while filled regions are invasive. (After T. J. Sejnowski et al. 2014. *Nat Neurosci* 17: 1440–1441.)

➤ CHECKPOINT 2.3

1. What is neuropsychology? What is its primary advantage over other methods, and what are its limitations?
2. What is a neuronal firing rate, and why do we study its change? How do you demonstrate the selectivity of a neuron, such as in response to faces?
3. What are the advantages and disadvantages of fMRI and EEG relative to each other?
4. What is the correlation and causation problem in neuroscience, and what methods are available to overcome it?
5. In comparing the strengths and weaknesses of each cognitive neuroscience research method, what are the three dimensions to consider?

Chapter Summary

2.1 Discuss the tight link between brain and behavior.

Cognitive neuroscience is the interdisciplinary study of how the brain supports our ability to perceive, think, learn, communicate, and control behavior. The field assumes materialism, which views the mind to be a product of the brain, as opposed to dualism, which considers the mind to be separate from the brain. One example of the tight relationship between brain and behavior is when patients with brain damage (to specific regions involved in face perception) show impairments in face recognition.

Q: Why should cognitive psychologists care about how the brain works? Cite one type of evidence showing the tight link between the mind and the brain.

2.2 Describe basic principles of brain structure and functional specialization.

The fundamental unit of the brain is the neuron, a cell in the nervous system that receives input from other neurons and decides whether to signal output to other neurons. The brain is a rich network of about 100 billion neurons, which are connected via synapses, across which neurons communicate with each other using chemicals called neurotransmitters. These heavily interconnected neurons form networks within a brain area, which are also networked with other brain areas. They are organized into different systems across the brain, and many of these systems have specialized functions. At the largest scale, the brain's anatomy is organized into left and right hemispheres, which communicate across a large bundle of neural fibers called the corpus callosum. Each hemisphere can be further divided into the occipital, temporal, parietal, and frontal lobes.

Q: Starting with neurons and synapses, think about how they are organized into networks, areas, lobes, and hemispheres. What is their function? How do the hemispheres communicate with each other?

2.3 Explain and compare the different neuroscience methods, noting their advantages and limitations.

Safely protected by the skull, the brain is difficult to study. Neuroscientists have had to rely on a variety of clever techniques, each with strengths and limitations, especially with regard to spatial precision (whole brain to single neurons), temporal precision (years to milliseconds), and invasiveness (brain lesions and surgery to brain imaging and behavioral measurements). Neuropsychology studies the effects of brain damage. Electrophysiology measures action potentials, that is, electrical activity from neurons, either from single cells or from an aggregate of cells. fMRI uses MRI to infer neural activity from different brain areas. Brain stimulation techniques allow for the manipulation or disruption of brain activity.

Q: Compare the different ways scientists study the brain and what each method can reveal. Consider how functional specialization and stimulus selectivity are important for most of these methods. Each method has strengths and weaknesses, which should be evaluated in terms of spatial precision, temporal precision, and invasiveness. What are the trade-offs of each method?

Key Terms

action potential
axon
behavioral genetics
blood-oxygen-level-dependent (BOLD)
brain stimulation
Broca's area
cerebellum
cerebral cortex
chromosome
cognitive neuroscience
corpus callosum
correlation and causation problem
dendrite
DNA (deoxyribonucleic acid)
dualism
electrocorticography (ECoG) (intracranial recording)
electroencephalography (EEG)
electrophysiology
epigenetics
event-related potential (ERP)

fMRI subtraction method
frontal lobe
functional brain imaging
functional brain mapping
functional magnetic resonance imaging (fMRI)
functional specialization
gene
genotype
glial cell
hemisphere
invasiveness
knock-out
lobe
magnetic resonance imaging (MRI)
materialism
module
neuron
neuropsychology
neurotransmitter
occipital lobe

parietal lobe
phenotype
plastic
postsynaptic
presynaptic
primary visual cortex
prosopagnosia
region of interest (ROI)
reverse inference
soma (cell body)
spatial resolution
split-brain
synapse
temporal lobe
temporal resolution
transcranial direct current stimulation (tDCS)
transcranial magnetic stimulation (TMS)
Wernicke's area

Critical Thinking Questions

1. If we could make a computer as precise and complex as a brain, could we upload the mind into a computer? How would the lack of a physical body affect such a mind?

2. What would be an ideal future method to study the brain, integrating the strengths of all the methods? That is, if you were to tell an engineer to develop a dream technology, what features would it need to have?

3. As brain imaging technologies continue to improve, what would be some useful new applications? What ethical issues might they raise?

Discovery Lab

oup.com/he/chun1e

Synaptic Transmission

In this demonstration, students discover the process by which neurons communicate across synapses. After students see an animation, they are asked to complete several labeling activities. Approximate completion time: 10 minutes.

Suggested Readings

Eagleman, D. (2011). *Incognito: The Secret Lives of the Brain*. New York: Vintage Books.

Gazzaniga, M. S. (2011). *Who's in Charge?: Free Will and the Science of the Brain*. New York: HarperCollins.

Sacks, O. (1998). *The Man Who Mistook His Wife for a Hat*. New York: Touchstone.

Perception and Mental Imagery

3

More than 50 years ago, in 1969, the United States landed astronauts on the moon. In the most literal sense, the sky was no longer the limit. What was next? Jet packs? Moon colonies? Robot overlords? With that monumental technological achievement now in the rearview mirror, it is reasonable to wonder why it's taken half a century for self-driving cars—only recently—to be approved for public road testing. This may sound surprising, but from an engineering perspective, it's easier to keep a 747 jetliner on its flight path than to navigate a Lexus down the tame streets of Palo Alto, California.

The challenge for self-driving cars is not mechanical—they have no problem moving forward, changing direction, or stopping. The problem is **perception**: the ability to recognize and interpret information from the senses. To navigate successfully, drivers must be able to perceive and predict the road ahead, potential obstacles (such as other vehicles and pedestrians), and traffic signs and signals. People rely so heavily on vision to accomplish this perceptual task that we tend to take it for granted. Self-driving cars also use vision, but because of the challenges we'll describe, they require supplemental radar, ultrasonic sensors, or laser scanning systems.

© James Schwabel/Alamy Stock Photo

We tend to take for granted our ability to perceive and make sense out of complex scenes. Despite years of advances in computer engineering, self-driving cars have much more difficulty parsing a scene like this.

LEARNING OBJECTIVES

3.1 Explain why visual perception is a construction and why it is so challenging.

3.2 Describe how perception is a combination of sensory stimulation and the mind's detective work.

3.3 Describe the relation between perception and mental imagery.

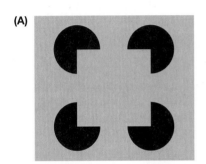

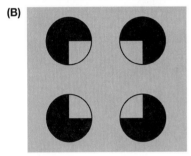

FIGURE 3.1 Modal and amodal completion **(A)** When the gaps in the circles are aligned this way, you may perceive a light square overlaid on the circles, even though there isn't one there. It may even look like the interior of the square is lighter than the exterior background, but it is not. This image depicts *modal completion* (where the perceived edges of the square are camouflaged against the background). **(B)** You may similarly perceive a complete square here, this time glimpsed through four circular holes in the page, but again, the square is not there. This image depicts *amodal completion* (where you subjectively perceive an item despite it being partially blocked). In both images, you see what you see because your mind completes the picture for you. (After B. Spehar and V. A. Halim. 2016. *Vis Res* 126: 97–108.)

Without these, even highly advanced cars cannot implement basic visual tasks that many of us take for granted. This became tragically clear in May 2016, when a Florida driver was killed because his car's preliminary autopilot system, relying on vision alone, failed to detect a white semitrailer turning across the road ahead, perhaps mistaking it for the sky (*New York Times*, July 12, 2016).

This chapter introduces a theme that runs throughout the entire book: perception, categorization, memory, and knowledge are all tightly integrated. Although it's easy to assume that perception is something that the eyes do (in the case of vision), perception also involves the ability to group and sort various objects in accordance with their common features—the ability, for example, to recognize that all the images in a photo are of cats and not dogs. Such knowledge also supports future memory retrieval and mental imagery (the ability to imagine objects in the absence of any visual input). Thus, we will detail how perception not only interprets information coming through the senses, but also how it provides the basis for how we think about and remember such information.

All modalities of perception are important, but we will continue to focus on vision because it is the most dominant, best understood, and easiest to demonstrate in a textbook. However, we encourage you to study the other modalities in a perception course.

3.1 Perception as a Construction of the Mind

The challenges of designing machines that "see" highlight an often underappreciated aspect of perception: perception is the result of the mind's detective work. The very act of perceiving involves making sense of the raw stimulation conveyed by our senses (Gregory, 1966). From this raw stimulation, we piece together a coherent, stable, mental representation that we experience as perception. In many cases, our minds fill in missing pieces of the scene without us even realizing it. (Indeed, each of our eyes has a **blind spot** toward the outside edges of our vision, where the optic nerve passes through to convey visual signals to the brain. We don't notice this gap in our visual experience of the world because our minds fill in the missing information.) This is what is meant when we speak of perception as a construction. It is like perceiving the whole picture when you have access to only a few pieces of a puzzle (but see Gibson, 1979).

Consider **FIGURE 3.1A**, which depicts a light square with black disks sitting behind each of its corners. Or does it? Even though it may seem obvious that there is a square in this picture, it's just an illusion. There is only a set of four black circles with missing slices. We perceive the square when our mind puts together clues to suggest that there *should* be a square there. Some people may even perceive the illusory square to be brighter or closer than the surrounding background (it's not). A similarly compelling example can be found in **FIGURE 3.1B**, but this time you might perceive a square that lies farther away than the page, as if viewed through four circular holes. In both cases, the mind uses available clues to complete the picture. The first case—where your view of the illusory object is not obstructed, and where there is no objective boundary between the illusory object and the background—is known as **modal completion**. The second case, where you seem to perceive an object despite an apparently obstructed view, is known as **amodal completion** (discussed later in this chapter). In short, perception is a *cognitive* act. In this chapter we cover a range of cognitive processes that contribute to perception. The body of research on these processes is known as **visual cognition**.

Because we tend to be unaware of the cognitive processes that help us construct our perceptions, people are often taken by surprise when they find that such "visual cognitive" processes can cause us to literally see the world differently from each other. In some cases, such as in "the dress" in **SEE FOR YOURSELF 3.1**, this surprise is so great that it creates viral sensations that sweep the globe.

▶ **See for Yourself 3.1**

"The Dress" and the Constructive Nature of Perception

In 2015, a simple photograph of a dress became a viral online sensation because people just couldn't agree on what color it was. About 60% of viewers see the dress as blue and black, whereas 30% see it as white and gold (and another 10% see it as blue and brown). Only 10% of people can switch between the color combinations (Lafer-Sousa et al., 2015). Here's the fascinating thing: when viewing the picture of the dress, everyone's eyes are receiving the same information. So why do so many people disagree about what they're looking at? It's because perception is an experience that our minds construct, based on several factors beyond pure sensory stimulation.

It turns out that—whether we realize it or not—we follow rules and heuristics that shape what we see. For example, our minds make assumptions about the lighting conditions illuminating a scene. This makes sense, as objects will reflect different wavelengths of light back to our eye if illuminated directly by the sun than if illuminated by an interior lightbulb (or even if viewed outside at noon versus at dusk). Unconsciously analyzing evidence about what the lighting source might be allows us to perceive objects as a stable color as we bring them, say, from outside to inside. In one study, more than 13,000 people participated in an online survey in which they were asked what colors they perceived the dress to be and whether they assumed that the dress was situated in a shadow or not. Those who assumed that it sat within a shadow were

Courtesy of Cecilia Bleasdale

more likely to perceive it as white (Wallisch, 2017; also see Chetverikov & Ivanchei, 2016; Lafer-Sousa et al., 2015). According to New York University researcher Pascal Wallisch, "Shadows are blue, so we mentally subtract the blue light in order to view the image, which then appears in bright colors—gold and white. However, artificial light tends to be yellowish, so if we see it brightened in this fashion, we factor out this color, leaving us with a dress that we see as black and blue" (P. Wallisch as quoted in S. Wong. 2017).

In other words, our visual systems are constantly constructing our perception of the world—based on clues and assumptions that extend beyond the raw stimulation received by our senses—all in the blink of an eye and without us even realizing it.

"Bottom-Up" and "Top-Down" Influences on Perception

Perception brings the world into the mind via the five senses. This perceptual understanding is not like a video feed or a photograph, but is more like a story based on incomplete information. The perceptions that our minds construct are based on physical reality, but significant interpretation is required. Compared with objective facts, such as agreed-upon official measurements of a soccer goal, subjective interpretation can differ from one moment to another and from one person to another—the soccer goal may "look" larger or smaller depending on the context.

What you consciously perceive is heavily shaped by what your mind chooses to see, hear, taste, feel, or smell. Some philosophers have appreciated this problem deeply. The Irish philosopher George Berkeley (1685–1753), for example, famously argued that "To be is to be perceived," meaning that an object doesn't exist if your mind doesn't perceive it (Berkeley, 1710). A different approach is to ask, "Do we all see an object in the same way?" The famous dress discussed in See for Yourself 3.1 demonstrates that, even when looking at the same object, different people may see different things.

Perception depends on both bottom-up and top-down information. **Bottom-up information** is the sensory input, such as an image coming through the eyes and falling on the **retina** (the light-sensitive part of our eyes), or sounds impinging on the ears, stimulating the cochlea. In vision, light reflected by objects in the world passes through our eyes and stimulates a collection of more than 100 million **photoreceptors** on the retina at the back of each eye (**FIGURE 3.2**). The center of the retina, known as the **fovea**, contains densely packed photoreceptors known as **cones**, which are differentially sensitive to wavelengths corresponding

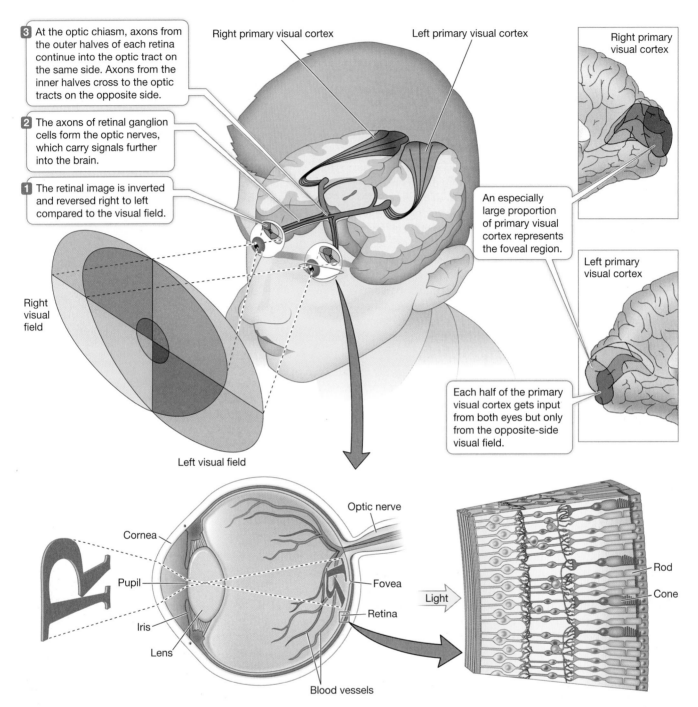

3 At the optic chiasm, axons from the outer halves of each retina continue into the optic tract on the same side. Axons from the inner halves cross to the optic tracts on the opposite side.

2 The axons of retinal ganglion cells form the optic nerves, which carry signals further into the brain.

1 The retinal image is inverted and reversed right to left compared to the visual field.

Right primary visual cortex

Left primary visual cortex

Right primary visual cortex

An especially large proportion of primary visual cortex represents the foveal region.

Left primary visual cortex

Each half of the primary visual cortex gets input from both eyes but only from the opposite-side visual field.

Right visual field

Left visual field

Cornea

Pupil

Iris

Lens

Blood vessels

Optic nerve

Fovea

Retina

Light

Rod

Cone

FIGURE 3.2 A rough anatomy of the visual system   Light passes through the eye and falls on photoreceptors (rods and cones) in the retina, at the back of the eye. Signals corresponding to the left visual field (of both eyes) travel to the right primary visual cortex, and those corresponding to the right visual field (of both eyes) travel to the left primary visual cortex. Visual information falling on the fovea—the central portion of each retina—is processed by a larger portion of the primary visual cortex than information falling on the rest of the retina, which is one reason why we see things in decreasing detail as they move to the periphery of our vision. (After S. M. Breedlove and N. V. Watson. 2010. *Biological Psychology: An Introduction to Behavioral, Cognitive, and Clinical Neuroscience,* 6th ed., Oxford University Press/Sinauer: Sunderland, MA; J. Wolfe et al. 2018. *Sensation and Perception,* 5th ed., Oxford University Press/Sinauer: Sunderland, MA.)

to different colors. The retina also contains extremely light-sensitive photoreceptors known as **rods**, which come in handy when light is very dim but which do not distinguish among colors. Such input for perception—the stimulation of the sensory receptors—is called **sensation**. These physical signals from the environment are translated into neural signals that the brain can use in a process called **transduction**. Through this process, signals are projected all the way to the **primary visual cortex**, at the very back of the brain (see Figure 3.2). The primary visual cortex is specialized for the most rudimentary visual processing, such as determining the orientations and spatial frequencies of light and dark patches in the visual world (e.g., De Valois & De Valois, 1988; Hubel & Wiesel, 1959). From there, signals are sent forward in the brain via different pathways, where visual processing becomes increasingly more sophisticated. This hierarchical account of the flow of visual information processing is often referred to as a **feedforward** system (e.g., see Felleman & Van Essen, 1991). Finally, perceptual systems in the brain interpret this sensory information to guide thought and action.

Ultimately, what we perceive results from a combination of bottom-up information and **top-down information**—the knowledge and expectations that influence and enhance our interpretation of sensory input. **SEE FOR YOURSELF 3.2** gives examples of bottom-up and top-down information. The role of top-down information in shaping what we see may be made possible by the fact that the flow of visual information processing in the brain isn't only feedforward: there are also reciprocal, feedback (or reentrant) connections that enable brain areas responsible for relatively sophisticated processing to modulate activity of hierarchically earlier stages of visual processing (e.g., Bullier, 2001). Such reentrant connections can play a significant role in shaping what we see, as in the Discovery Lab on top-down processing of color information. This is important, as information derived from initial feedforward processing may be coarse and consistent with multiple interpretations of what lies before us; one account suggests that feedback (reentrant) processing can resolve such ambiguity by comparing this coarse feedforward signal with a narrower range of likely representations that match the stimulus (Di Lollo et al., 2000).

▶ DISCOVERY LAB
Top-Down Processing of Color Information

▶ **See for Yourself 3.2**

The Necker Cube and Ambiguous Figures

What do you see?

Ambiguous figures highlight the interplay between bottom-up and top-down information, as shown in **FIGURE A**. Bottom-up information is important. Obviously, when viewing the Necker Cube (Part 1), no one is seeing circles. However, the interpretation varies depending on what's going on inside the observer's head. With some effort, you can even change what you see voluntarily. For example, you might find that you can make yourself see the square at the bottom right of the Necker Cube as being the side closest to you (as in Part 2), and you can alternatively make yourself see the square at the top left look like it is closest to you (as in Part 3). Examples of such ambiguous figures extend beyond simple examples like the Necker Cube. In Part 4, for example, you can see the head of either a duck or a rabbit.

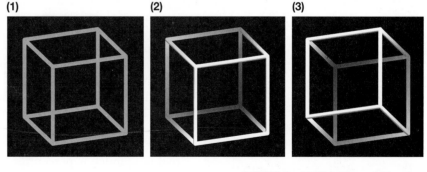

FIGURE A **(1)** Which face of this cube looks closest to you? You can see the front face as bounded by the rightmost edge or by the leftmost edge, as disambiguated in **(2)** and **(3)**, respectively. **(4)** This ambiguous image can be seen as either a duck or a rabbit. (1–3 after J. Kornmeier and M. Bach. 2004. *Psychophysiology* 41: 1–8.)

FIGURE 3.3 Context shapes perception
Read the row from left to right (starting with A), then the column from top to bottom (starting with 12). How does the center character change? (After J. S. Bruner and A. L. Minturn. 1955. *J Gen Psychol* 53: 21–28.)

CONTEXT SHAPES PERCEPTION Top-down information facilitates object recognition in several ways. First, knowledge of context can help us choose an interpretation for an ambiguous image (as in See for Yourself 3.1). For example, in **FIGURE 3.3** quickly try to identify the item in the center of the array. If you look first at the row that starts with "A," you might see the central item as "B," but if you look first at the column that starts with "12" you might see the central item as "13." Even though your eyes receive the same visual information in both cases, the way you see it depends on how you process the context.

EXPERIENCE SHAPES PERCEPTION Our experiences in the world also affect how we see things. The illusion produced in **FIGURE 3.4** occurs because experience tells us that objects are illuminated from above, and we interpret their shadows and corresponding shapes accordingly. Shadows are such powerful cues for depth and spatial relations that, by manipulating these features, we can make objects appear to hover in midair (**FIGURE 3.5**).

Thus, perception is a construction. We do not simply see what's out there in the world; we make educated guesses based on visual clues. The German physicist Hermann von Helmholtz (1821–1894) described this process as **unconscious inference**. Because retinal input is ambiguous, we combine bottom-up and top-down information to make the interpretation that is most likely to reflect reality. The process is rapid, unconscious, and fairly automatic.

THE VISUAL BRAIN MAKES PREDICTIONS In addition to making inferences about retinal input that has already been received by the eyes, the visual brain also seems to operate by making predictions about what input the eyes are *about to receive* (Press et al., 2020). This is known as **predictive coding**. Predictive coding theories envision the brain as a constant generator of expectations about the world (Clark, 2013; Dayan et al., 1995), with ongoing comparison of such expectations with bottom-up information coming through the eyes (O'Callaghan et al., 2017). Because raw sensory input alone can be consistent with several competing perceptual interpretations, one suggestion is that we are able to settle on and see only one resulting percept because predictions and expectations serve to guide the competition in favor of the most likely interpretation (Trapp & Bar, 2015). The context in which perception takes place can serve as a source of perceptual predictions, and indeed, objects appear to be more quickly and accurately recognized when they are paired with scenes in which they might typically be found, as depicted in **FIGURE 3.6** (Bar, 2004; Biederman, 1981; Biederman et al., 1982; Palmer, 1975; but see Hollingworth & Henderson, 1998).

Is Perception "Cognitively Penetrable"?

Just how much is perception shaped by cognition? It's one thing to suggest that perception requires the mind to engage in some cognition-like computations; it's a step further to suggest that perception can be influenced by whatever desires or beliefs we may hold.

Although there is general consensus that perception involves a range of complex computations and rules that are "cognition-like," there is considerably less agreement about whether cognitive processes that seem far removed from perception—like our beliefs, knowledge, or motivations—can permeate and change our perceptual experience. Some researchers have argued that beliefs, knowledge, and motivations *can* change perception. For example, researchers have reported that participants wearing a heavy backpack tend

FIGURE 3.4 Experience shapes perception
Which circles look like bumps rising up, and which look like dimples? What happens when you look at the image from other angles or rotations?

to overestimate distances relative to participants not wearing a heavy backpack (Proffitt et al., 2003); that people who are out of shape or tired overestimate the steepness of slopes (Bhalla & Proffitt, 1999); and that things people want (e.g., chocolate) are perceived as being closer than things people don't want (e.g., feces) (Balcetis & Dunning, 2010). Such reports follow in the tradition of a historical movement known as the New Look, a movement that was sparked by a 1947 paper titled "Value and need as organizing factors in perception" (Bruner & Goodman, 1947), which reported both that children estimated coins to be larger than identically sized cardboard discs and that this effect was particularly pronounced among children from poor families (the claim being that things look larger when they are perceived as more valuable).

However, some scholars have argued that such claims are based on studies with flawed methodology and on mistakes such as confusing perception itself with people's *judgments* about what they have seen (Erdelyi, 1974; Firestone & Scholl, 2016). For example, could it be that experiment participants who wear and who don't wear heavy backpacks actually *see* the same-sized gap in space between themselves and a destination, but that

FIGURE 3.5 The boat looks like it's hovering above the water's surface If you cover the shadow of the boat with your finger, the boat appears to be floating as normal.

those who wear a heavy backpack simply adjust their estimation of distance only after they have processed the visual information? Those who argue that perceptual processing proceeds without influence from "high-level" cognition—for example, beliefs, knowledge, or motivation—suggest that perception is **cognitively impenetrable** (Pylyshyn, 1999). Determining whether perception is cognitively penetrable or impenetrable is a thorny issue, as we discuss further in **SEE FOR YOURSELF 3.3**.

FIGURE 3.6 The brain generates perceptual predictions based on context Whether you ultimately see a hairdryer or an electric drill in these pictures depends partly on how you interpret the context in which they appear (bathroom on the left; workshop on the right). These pictures look blurry because they provide "low spatial frequency" information, which is processed very quickly in the brain but can give rise to competing perceptual representations. The brain generates perceptual predictions based (in part) on context, which helps resolve the otherwise ambiguous information conveyed through your senses.

► See for Yourself 3.3

Is Perception Cognitively Penetrable or Impenetrable?

If you and your friend believe different things, will your different beliefs lead you literally to see the world differently from each other? If so, then perception can be said to be "cognitively penetrable." If beliefs *don't* affect perception, then perception might be said to be "cognitively impenetrable" (see the main text).

Visual illusions are sometimes used to support the notion that perception is cognitively impenetrable. Consider the *rotating snakes* illusion created by Akiyoshi Kitaoka (**FIGURE A**). You may *know* that the image is static and non-moving on the page, but nothing about your knowledge or beliefs changes the degree to which you "see" motion in the picture. Perception is cognitively impenetrable!

Or is it? Even those who argue that perception is cognitively impenetrable will generally acknowledge that perception involves cognitive acts such as inference and problem solving. Consider, for example, the image of the otters in **FIGURE B**. The two otters in the picture are exactly the same size: they both cast the same size image on your retina. But even if you prove this to yourself by cutting out one otter and placing it on top of the other, you almost can't help but see the top otter as larger than the bottom otter. As with the rotating snakes illusion, this could again be seen as evidence for the cognitive impenetrability of perception.

But wait a second. The reason the top otter appears to be larger is because cues within the picture (such as linear perspective and the sizes of the otters relative to the architecture) lead the visual system to interpret it as being farther away than the bottom otter. And if two otters cast the same retinal image, the one that is interpreted as being farther away must be seen as larger. Obviously, there is a fair degree of problem solving and construction going on here (also see "the dress" example discussed in See For Yourself 3.1). So is perception cognitively penetrable or not?

The debate surrounding cognitive penetrability of perception is not over whether or not some cognition-like processes are involved in perception. Instead, many of those who claim that perception is cognitively impenetrable would argue that the computations that *are* involved in constructing perception are walled off from other aspects of cognition—such as beliefs, knowledge, and motivations—that comprise what is often called "high-level" cognition. Others disagree, noting that the brain is not wired in a way that clearly distinguishes between perceptual and cognitive systems (Beck & Clevenger, 2016; Hackel et al., 2016; Miskovic et al., 2016; O'Callaghan et al., 2016; Vinson et al., 2016). As with many debates in the literature, much of the disagreement may be semantic, with no clear agreement on where the line should be drawn between what we consider to be "perception" and what we consider to be "cognition."

FIGURE A   For most people, it is impossible *not* to see movement in the rotating snakes illusion, even though they know that the picture is stationary.

FIGURE B   Illusions such as this simultaneously demonstrate that our perception involves a fair degree of problem solving *and* that perception can be impervious to the influence of high-level knowledge.

➤ **CHECKPOINT 3.1**

1. What is the distinction between top-down and bottom-up processing?

2. What does it mean to say that perception is a "construction of the mind"?

3.2 Challenges of Perception: It's Not Easy Being Seen

To get a better handle on perception, let's consider the challenges that make it difficult. In 1966, researchers at the famous MIT Computer Science and Artificial Intelligence Laboratory connected cameras to computers to examine how artificial intelligence could interpret and extract salient information from the digital images. They thought this study would be easy, but everyone grossly underestimated the project's difficulty. It is a sobering fact that, while the entire global financial system runs on computers, we still can't make a digital recognition system that matches the ability of a young child to visually navigate and recognize everyday objects. Explore some of these perception challenges a bit further in **THINK FOR YOURSELF 3.1**.

➤ **Think for Yourself 3.1**

Project Prakash

If you were suddenly able to see after being blind your entire life, what would the world look like to you? You know what a fork is, but could you recognize one by sight? You know who your mother is, but could you distinguish her face from that of your father?

Some infants are born with cataracts, a clouding of the lens that admits light into the eye. This defect makes vision blurry to the point of functional blindness. In India, countless families cannot afford the surgery required to remove the cataracts. Many children are thus deprived of sight and of an education, sentencing them to a life of poverty and marginalization. Vision scientist Pawan Sinha noticed this crisis and started Project Prakash (*Prakash* is Sanskrit for "light") to provide corrective surgery to children born with treatable cataracts. While humanitarian in purpose, this project also provides a unique opportunity to answer the question about how much of vision depends on training and development (Winerman, 2012).

More than 300 years ago, the writer William Molyneux asked philosopher John Locke, "Must a person learn to see?" (Molyneux, 1688). If a blind person can distinguish a cube from a sphere by touch, would he or she be able to distinguish the two objects by sight alone after gaining vision? Children in Project Prakash seem to provide an answer to this question. Upon removal of their cataracts, they cannot immediately make the transfer from touch to sight. However, Sinha found that they can learn to do so rapidly. This was surprising because people thought that the brain becomes less adaptable, or "plastic," with aging. Animal research in particular suggests that, once a critical period of brain development has passed, sight-deprived organisms exhibit permanent disabilities in gaining normal visual function. Yet Sinha and colleagues have shown that older children experience improvements in their ability to see contrast (difference between light and dark areas). Even children deprived of sight for 10–14 years can recover much of their visual function for tasks such as matching shapes or counting the number of overlapping objects, which runs contrary to what researchers thought. Thus, at least in humans, the visual system can continue to learn and develop.

Courtesy of Steve Most

FIGURE 3.7 A dignified example of object segmentation   In this photo of one of the authors' dog, it seems easy for us to segment the dog from the table from the laptop from the mug from the barbecue.

Perceiving Objects and Their Context

For vision, one fundamental challenge is **object segmentation**—that is, visually assigning the elements of a scene to separate objects and backgrounds. To recognize objects and their locations, you need to separate them from the background. Sometimes this seems easy to us. For example, in **FIGURE 3.7**, it is easy to see that a dog sits in front of an open laptop and coffee mug, which are on a table that extends into the background toward a barbecue grill and some trees. In fact, it seems so easy that we fail to appreciate how complex this process is. We take for granted that objects look distinct from each other, but such bottom-up cues are insufficient for a computer (**FIGURE 3.8**). In the real world, objects often do not have clear boundaries outlining their shape, a fact that animals exploit to camouflage themselves from predators (**FIGURE 3.9**).

FIGURE-GROUND ORGANIZATION   Even when the boundary between an object and its background is clear, it's not always evident which side of the boundary belongs to the object (or figure) and which side of the boundary belongs to the background (or ground). This aspect of object segmentation is known as the problem of **figure-ground organization** (e.g., Peterson & Gibson, 1994; Rubin, 1921). The most famous demonstration of this ambiguity is known as the *Rubin vase* (named after the early twentieth-century Danish psychologist Edgar Rubin), a version of which can be seen in **FIGURE 3.10**. Depending on which part of the picture people see as the figure, they might see a single vase or two faces looking at each other. One reason this determination is somewhat ambiguous is because each "face" is separated from the "vase" by a shared boundary or contour.

So how do people decide which side of a shared boundary is the figure and which is the ground? According to current models of figure-ground organization, the sides falling on either side of a shared boundary activate representations that compete with each other for "figure" status, with the winning representation inhibiting neural activity corresponding to the losing representation (e.g., Grossberg, 1994).

From Y. Ostrovsky et al. 2009. Psychol Sci 20: 1484–1491

FIGURE 3.8 The complexity of object segmentation   The boundaries of objects in the real image in the left-hand panel may seem simple, as suggested by the middle panel. But as the right-hand panel shows, the boundaries are much more complex (and hopeless) when analyzed by a computer.

FIGURE 3.9 Blending in through camouflage   Camouflage makes it difficult to distinguish an object or animal from its background, something that nature often takes advantage of. Try to find the animal hidden in each image.

Researchers have discovered that in order to resolve this competition, the mind follows a handful of rules (Peterson & Kimchi, 2013). For example, imagine a picture containing one uniformly black region and one uniformly white region, separated by a shared boundary or contour. **FIGURE 3.11** illustrates some "rules" that the mind appears to follow in order to determine which region is figure and which is ground, assuming all other things being equal. For example, if one of those regions is completely surrounded by the other, the surrounded region will be perceived as the figure (the rule of *enclosure*). If one of the regions is more symmetrical than the other, then the symmetrical region will tend to be perceived as the figure (the rule of *symmetry*). If the shape of the contour is such that the region on one side of it bulges out (i.e., it is *convex*)

FIGURE 3.10 A version of a classic Rubin vase   Do you see a vase or two faces? It depends on what you see as "figure" and what you see as "ground." (From J. M. Wolfe et al. 2017. *Sensation & Perception*, 5th ed. Oxford University Press/Sinauer: Sunderland, MA.)

Enclosure

Symmetry

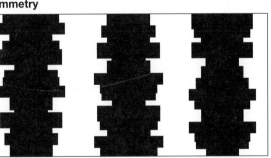

Convexity

FIGURE 3.11 Examples of enclosure, symmetry, and convexity   In the top left panel, the black region is seen as the figure because it is completely surrounded by the white region. In the top right panel, the black regions are seen as figures because they are more symmetrical than the white regions. In the bottom right panel, the black regions are seen as figures because they are convex (they bulge outward) rather than concave. (After http://www.scholarpedia.org/article/Figure-ground_perception.)

FIGURE 3.12 **Experience and meaning aid object segmentation** In this example, it is easy to decide which side of the border is the figure (the silhouette of the woman) and which is the ground because the one side resembles a meaningful item. This nicely demonstrates how a lifetime of experience and learning helps shape what we see. (From M. A. Peterson et al. 1998. *Psychobiology* 26: 357–370.)

and the other side caves in (i.e., it is *concave*), the convex side will tend to be perceived as the figure (the rule of *convexity*) (Kanizsa & Gerbino, 1976).

The way we organize a scene into figures and grounds (i.e., objects and backgrounds) also appears to be shaped by our previous experience. For example, the degree to which we perceive one side of the boundary to be meaningful plays a strong role in figure-ground organization, with people assigning "figure" status to the meaningful side of the boundary (the rule of *meaningfulness*) (Peterson & Gibson, 1991; Peterson et al., 1991) (**FIGURE 3.12**).

Intriguingly, in line with the notion that figure-ground organization involves competition between representations that inhibit neural activity elicited by each other, evidence suggests that in populations characterized by weaker inhibitory processes—such as older adults—the process of organizing figure-ground relationships is less efficient (Anderson et al., 2016).

SEEING DESPITE BLOCKED VIEWS Another challenge we encounter when trying to make sense of a visual scene is **occlusion**, which refers to the fact that our views of objects are often partially blocked by other objects. The brain needs to "fill in," or infer, the missing information, a process known as amodal completion (a concept we introduced early in Section 3.1). In Figure 3.1B we perceive that there is a whole square lying behind circular holes rather than simply four black circles with missing wedges, because the visual system rejects the unlikely alternative that the circles' orientations happen to accidentally line up perfectly with what would be four corners of an imaginary square. (The term "amodal" reflects the fact that the stimulus we ultimately perceive does not correspond to information available to any sensory modality.) When we interpret image fragments, we try to come up with the most plausible explanation. One related phenomenon may be something known as **boundary extension**, where people tend to remember pictures as having extended beyond their edges, as if their minds fill in a little bit of what the scene would have looked like had it not been cut off at its border (Intraub & Richardson, 1989). Although this is often described as a memory effect, it has been found to emerge within 1/20th of a second after viewing a picture, raising the possibility that it stems from how people fill in the edges of a scene during perception (Intraub & Dickinson, 2008).

In the real world, we engage in amodal completion so effectively that we often don't realize that our views are obscured at all. In **FIGURE 3.13**, for example, you may perceive a partially obscured fire truck in each of the left-hand panels, but you may not realize just *how much* of the fire truck is truly obscured. As you can see in the right-hand panels, very little of the fire truck is actually visible at any one time. Note that the left-hand panels are actually still frames from a movie. In the actual movie, the fire truck moves through the scene—similar to the types of dynamic occlusions we encounter in the real world. Under such conditions, different portions of the fire truck are visible at any given moment, and people appear to "stitch" them together, yielding increased effectiveness of amodal completion and the subjective feeling of perceiving the whole vehicle (Palmer et al., 2006). In some cases, amodal completion that

Movie frames   Visible regions

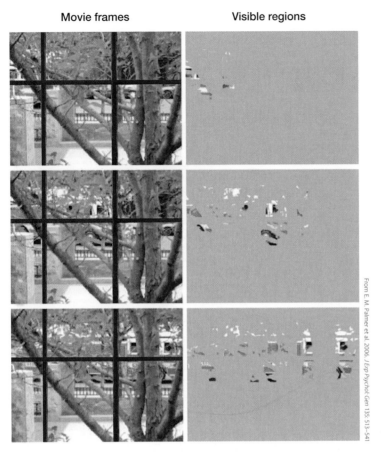

From E. M. Palmer et al. 2006. *J Exp Psychol Gen* 135: 513–541

FIGURE 3.13 Amodal completion enables us to see more than meets the eyes   The left-hand panels show obstructed views of a fire truck in a movie. Although you can tell that your view of the truck is obstructed, you might be surprised by just how little of it is visible in any given frame (revealed by the right-hand panels). Amodal completion lets us have a richer perception of the world than is actually available to our eyes.

occurs because of occlusion allows you to mentally connect fragments of information better than when there is no occlusion. **SEE FOR YOURSELF 3.4** provides an example of this.

▶ **See for Yourself 3.4**

Fragments of a Letter

These shapes look random, but they are the fragments of the same letter repeated multiple times. What letter is it? This is a case where having an obvious occlusion (which is absent here) would allow you to connect the fragments via amodal completion. (See the image on the following page for the answer.) (After A. S. Bregman. 1981. In M. Kubovy and J. Pomerantz. [eds.] *Perceptual Organization*. Hillsdale, NJ: Routledge, pp. 99–118.)

(Continued)

When an obvious occlusion is added (i.e., the black squiggly region), your powers of amodal completion kick into gear, enabling you to connect the fragments to see the letter B in several orientations. (After A. S. Bregman. 1981. In M. Kubovy and J. Pomerantz. [eds.] *Perceptual Organization*. Hillsdale, NJ: Routledge, pp. 99–118.)

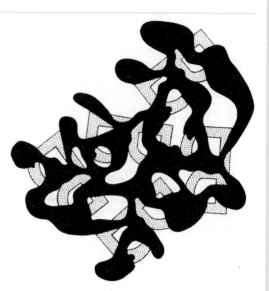

Although such processes of amodal completion often allow us to perceive things that are obstructed from our view, sometimes our minds complete the picture in a way that doesn't correspond to reality (**FIGURE 3.14**). You can experience this for yourself through pictures of "amodal nudity," which appear to be somewhat of an Internet sensation. In images of amodal nudity, people's clothes are hidden behind occlusion, leading many viewers to perceive them as naked (Bonnet, 2013; Hill, 2013)!

© iStock.com/AmpH

FIGURE 3.14 Amodal nudity   On the left is a man in a bathing suit. Amodal completion causes many people to perceive him as nude in the picture on the right. Sometimes, our minds fill in the blanks incorrectly.

Perceiving a Three-Dimensional World

Another basic challenge to vision is the **inverse projection** problem. This refers to the fact that we live in a three-dimensional (3-D) world, but the input to our eyes is two-dimensional (2-D). Like the sensor in a camera, the retina in each eye is flat. The sheet of photoreceptors on the retina converts images to neural signals that the brain must reconstruct into a 3-D representation that allows us to determine the distance and layout of objects and obstacles. The same 2-D image can be produced by a multitude of different 3-D objects. In other words, we cannot tell from a given 2-D retinal image what 3-D object is out there in the physical world. The bottom-up image is incomplete; to disambiguate it, the perceptual system must bring top-down information to bear. **FIGURE 3.15** examines this concept further.

(A)

From S. Nundy et al. 2000. *Proc Natl Acad Sci USA* 97: 5592–5597. © 2000 National Academy of Sciences, U.S.A.

(B)

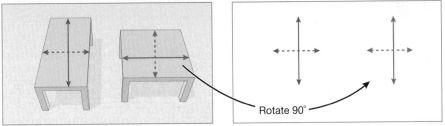

Rotate 90°

(After D. Purves and R. B. Lotto. 2011. *Why We See What We Do Redux: A Wholly Empirical Theory of Vision.* Oxford University Press/Sinauer: Sunderland, MA, based on R. N. Shepard. 1990. *Mind Sights: Original Visual Illusions, Ambiguities, and Other Anomalies, with a Commentary on the Play of Mind in Perception and Art.* W. H. Freeman/Times Books/Henry Holt & Co.)

FIGURE 3.15 The inverse projection problem **(A)** It is challenging to reconstruct a perception of the correct 3-D object (e.g., the yellow angled objects) when any number of items could have cast the same 2-D projection. **(B)** The blue table looks longer than the red table is wide. As shown below, however, when the red table is rotated 90 degrees, it is apparent that the dimensions of the two surfaces are identical (although the angles at the corners differ). The apparent discrepancy arises because of how people use perspective to infer 3-D shape from 2-D images—the inverse projection problem.

Gustave Caillebotte (1848–1894)

FIGURE 3.16 Monocular depth cues Gustave Caillebotte's 1877 painting *Rue de Paris, temps de pluie* (*Paris Street; Rainy Day*) makes striking use of several monocular depth cues. It currently hangs in the Art Institute of Chicago.

DISCOVERY LAB
Ponzo Illusion

© Leon Keer/www.leonkeer.com

FIGURE 3.17 Using monocular depth cues to create 3-D illusions Pavement artists such as Leon Keer sometimes use monocular depth cues to stunning effect, as in this creation, *Fake News*, which is drawn on a flat horizontal surface. Illusions such as this only work if you look at them from precisely the right viewpoint, so that the depth cues line up just right.

VISUAL CUES UNDERLYING PERCEPTION OF A 3-D WORLD
When it comes to solving the inverse projection problem, there are several "hints," or cues, that the visual system uses. One, for example, stems from the fact that your two eyes occupy different places on your head. This means that each eye gets a slightly different view than the other. The closer something is to you, the greater the difference between what your two eyes see, a phenomenon known as **binocular disparity**. Cues that require both eyes to be effective are known as **binocular depth cues**. You can demonstrate binocular disparity for yourself: simply close one eye and hold up a finger so that it blocks the view of an object a few feet away. Then close that eye and open your other eye, and you may find that your view of the object is no longer blocked. Each of your eyes gets a different view of the scene. Your mind computes the difference between the two views of any given object, and this helps you see how close something is to you.

MONOCULAR DEPTH CUES Even if your two eyes have roughly the same view (for example, when you're looking at a flat photograph in front of you), there are cues that your mind uses to construct a 3-D understanding of the 2-D image cast on your retinae. These are known as **monocular depth cues**, which can be explored in the Discovery Lab on the Ponzo illusion. Consider, for example, the painting in **FIGURE 3.16**, *Paris Street; Rainy Day* by the French artist Gustave Caillebotte, which hangs in the Art Institute of Chicago and makes striking use of several monocular depth cues. **Linear perspective**, for example, refers to the way parallel lines appear to move closer together and converge on a single point (a *vanishing point*) as they recede into the distance; this can be seen in the building at the painting's upper left. **Texture gradient** refers to the way textural elements that are presumably of similar size appear to get smaller and more densely packed together as they recede into the distance; this can be seen in the street's cobblestones. "Pavement artists" sometimes make use of such cues to create powerful depth illusions, as in **FIGURE 3.17**.

OBJECT AND SIZE CONSTANCY The cues the mind uses to solve the inverse projection problem can be sophisticated. For example, biological vision manifests two capacities essential to visual recognition: object constancy and size constancy. **Object constancy** refers to the fact that although the same object looks very different on the retina depending on its orientation (indeed, try rotating a book around in your hand), people are good at recognizing objects despite their orientation. **Size constancy** refers to the fact that the perceived sizes of objects are remarkably stable despite radical differences in their image size on the retina. Physics dictates that the farther an object is from an observer, the smaller its image will be on his or her retina (**FIGURE 3.18**). Yet we do not perceive objects shrinking as they move farther away. Instead, we use the apparent size as a cue to help determine its distance. This is evident once again in the painting *Paris Street; Rainy Day*: the people in the background are painted much smaller than the people in the foreground. But experience tells us that they are probably more or less the same size, so our minds use the smaller retinal image they cast to infer that they must be farther away.

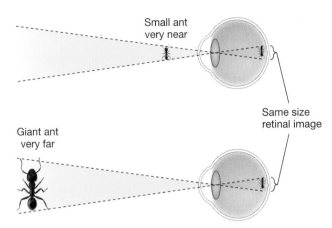

FIGURE 3.18 Trade-off between size and distance The sizes of the images that these two ants cast on the retina are the same because of the different distances that the ants are from the perceiver. The size of a retinal image that is cast by a normal-sized ant close up might be cause for alarm if the ant is actually far away. The image on the right is from Warner Brothers' 1954 sci-fi horror movie *Them!* (Eye illustration after J. Wolfe et al. 2020. *Sensation and Perception*, 6th ed. Oxford University Press/Sinauer: Sunderland, MA.)

Color and Lightness Constancy

Note that size constancy contributes to a perception of depth because our visual systems factor in "knowledge" of how the sizes of things typically compare with each other. There are many other examples of how the mind appears to apply implicit understanding of physics when constructing what we see. For example, if we were to take two paint chips of the same color, place one in a patch of sun and the other in a patch of shade, they would reflect different wavelengths of light and therefore activate different collections of cones in our retinae. But we will often perceive them as being the same color because our minds factor in the different lighting conditions that illuminate them. It can also work in reverse: two patches that reflect the exact same wavelengths of light will appear to us to be different colors if they appear to be falling under different illumination conditions (e.g., one in the light and one in shade). When our visual system factors in differences in illumination when shaping our color perception, the effect is known as **color constancy**. Our minds similarly factor in illumination conditions when perceiving the brightness of things, an effect known as **lightness constancy**. It may sound subtle, but the effects are striking, as can be seen in the illusions in **FIGURES 3.19** and **3.20**. These are powerful examples of how perception is

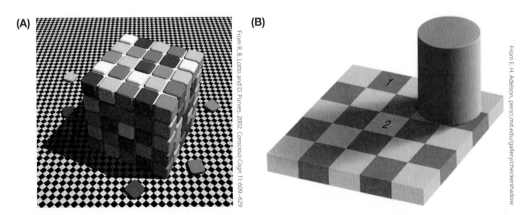

FIGURE 3.19 Color constancy and lightness constancy **(A)** This illusion provides a striking example of color constancy. It may appear that the center square on the top side is brown, and that the center square on the shaded side is orange, but they are the exact same color! You just see it differently because you perceive the top side as being under bright light and the shaded side as being in, well, shade. You can prove this to yourself by covering up the squares between them with your fingers. **(B)** This illlusion provides an equally striking example of

lightness constancy. Believe it or not, the square with a 1 on it and the square with a 2 on it are the exact same shade of gray. Your mind just applies logic: because square 2 falls within the cylinder's shadow, your mind assumes that it must have less light to reflect back to you. Yet it activates your photoreceptors to the same degree as square 1. Logically, then, your mind assumes that square 2 must be brighter from the start, and that's what you see. Once again, you can prove this to yourself by using your fingers to cover the squares in between them.

From B. A. Anderson and J. Winawer. 2005. *Nature* 434: 79–83

FIGURE 3.20 Lightness perception is shaped by how we segment a scene This powerful illusion provides another example of how our perception of lightness is influenced by how we mentally segment a scene. Believe it or not, the chess pieces on the top and bottom are *exactly the same!* In the top row, however, we perceive the bright patches as belonging to the pieces themselves, and the dark patches as clouds that obscure them here and there. In contrast, in the bottom row it's the bright patches we interpret as belonging to the clouds, and the dark patches that we interpret as belonging to the pieces. Thus, how we perceive lightness does not depend just on the raw stimulation received by our eyes.

constructed not merely from retinal stimulation, but from our mind's ability to fit the multiple elements of a visual scene together in a way that makes sense.

Object Recognition

Even if objects were presented in isolation, segregated from their backgrounds and other parts of a scene, object recognition would remain difficult because of variation in shape, orientation, and lighting conditions. Only when images are standardized, as in the barcodes you scan at the supermarket checkout, are machines able to process them easily. Misalign a small part of a barcode, and the machine will no longer be able to process it. So how is it that we are so good at recognizing things despite variations across typefaces or viewpoints and orientations for everyday objects, such as flowers? The challenge is how to match these different images to recognize an object for what it is. Understanding how our brains do this may provide researchers with hints about how to build machines that perceive objects more like humans do.

Our ability to match perceptual images with stored representations is achieved by several areas in the brain, each of which performs a specific function. Here we distinguish between low-level (early) vision and high-level (late) vision. The early stages of vision are devoted to detecting an object's basic features, such as orientation, color, and motion. Higher-level vision analyzes and combines these features to recognize objects, faces, and scenes. **SEE FOR YOURSELF 3.5** describes how our ability to recognize faces may involve a combination of low- and high-level vision.

► **See for Yourself 3.5**

Matching Perceptual Images with Stored Representations

We are generally good at recognizing people and objects despite variations in lighting conditions and angles. In many cases, our ability to do this is driven by our ability to match what we see against stored representations. You can experience this yourself when trying to decide whether two photos are of the same person. When the two photos are of a highly familiar person, the task is easy. But when the photos are of someone you've never seen before, the task becomes much harder. Do the two unfamiliar faces on the left in **FIGURE A** belong to the same person? How about the two faces on the right?

If you're even passingly familiar with American politics, you probably had no trouble recognizing that the two photos on the right are of the same person (Hillary Clinton), despite the differ-

ence in photo quality, lighting conditions, and facial expressions. But did you realize that the two faces on the left are also of the same person? It's harder to recognize this when we have no stored representation to match the faces to. Next time you go through passport control at an airport, consider how hard it is for the agents to match your face against the photo in your passport (White et al., 2014)!

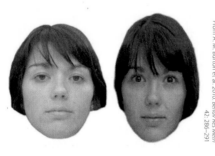

From A. M. Burton et al. 2010. *Behav Res Meth* 42: 286–291

FIGURE A The image pair on the left is an item from the Glasgow Face Matching Test.

impaired early vision

(A) Apperceptive agnosia

Model   Copy

(B) Associative agnosia

Model   Copy

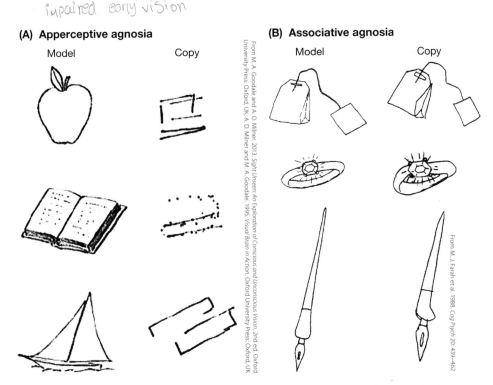

FIGURE 3.21 Apperceptive and associative agnosia   **(A)** In individuals with impaired early vision, agnosia can involve difficulty processing the visual forms of objects, as demonstrated in the attempts to copy the drawings in the left-hand panel (apperceptive agnosia). **(B)** With associative agnosia, the ability to process visual forms appears to be intact, as demonstrated by the drawings in the right-hand panel. Associative agnosia appears to involve later stages of recognition and categorization.

AGNOSIA: TROUBLE RECOGNIZING OBJECTS   Early and late stages of vision can be distinguished by the effects of brain damage, which causes **agnosia**, the inability to recognize objects. People with agnosia are not blind and do not seem to be missing the relevant mental representations, but they lack the ability to match images to their correct categories and labels. For example, an individual who fails to recognize a visually presented cup may be able to name it when given the opportunity to feel the object (Farah, 1990).

There are two main types of agnosia—one caused by damage to the early visual system and one by damage to the late visual system. Damage of either type will result in object recognition difficulties. With **apperceptive agnosia**, individuals seem to have impaired early vision, because they cannot perform even the simplest visual feature tasks; they are unable even to copy images (**FIGURE 3.21A**). With **associative agnosia**, early vision (perception) seems intact, as individuals can copy what they see (albeit slavishly) (**FIGURE 3.21B**). For people with associative agnosia, the inability to name objects is attributed to a later stage of recognition and categorization.

VIEW-BASED AND STRUCTURAL APPROACHES TO OBJECT RECOGNITION
How the brain uses features to recognize objects is still poorly understood. There are several issues to consider in developing a model of object recognition. Classically, two primary approaches have dominated the study of object recognition. The **view-based approach** claims that we match images to representations that are like two-dimensional pictures or "templates" (Poggio & Edelman, 1990; Ullman & Basri, 1991). Here, a **template** is a representation that fully describes the shape of an object; imagine, for example, a toy with

(A)

(B)

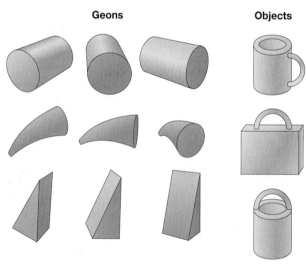

Courtesy of M. H. Siddall

FIGURE 3.22 Template matching **(A)** When numerals are designed to maximize differences among them in a standardized way, it makes it easier for computers to recognize and distinguish the letters using templates. **(B)** Template matching may not be as effective for natural images (such as this sneaker), which we might encounter—and which look different—from any number of angles.

differently shaped holes that allow only blocks of that shape to drop through. Analogously, template matching involves recognizing objects by matching the image you see to stored representations or standards. Template models of vision are simple and efficient, and they work well for prescribed domains—for example, the numerals on bank checks are standardized and recognized by computers using templates (**FIGURE 3.22A**). Although simple in theory, template matching is difficult for natural images, which have greater variation and noise (**FIGURE 3.22B**). What counts as a match, and how much noise or deviation can a matching process tolerate?

Another approach that has played a key role in object recognition is based on **structural descriptions**, which are models that represent objects as sets of three-dimensional parts standing in spatial relationships to each other (Biederman, 1987; Marr & Nishihara, 1978). These models have a vocabulary of volumetric parts that can be analyzed quickly regardless of their orientation. Historically, one of the most prominent models is Biederman's **recognition by components**. Biederman proposed that there is an alphabet of about 36 or fewer basic shapes, or **geons** (**FIGURE 3.23**). According to this account, different combinations of geons allow for representation of different objects, and it has been estimated that combinations of up to three geons can yield about 154 million distinct structures (Biederman, 1987). For any three-dimensional object, a "recipe" called a *structural description* specifies how the different geons should be arranged. According to this account, visual recognition of objects occurs when visual input is matched against these structural descriptions.

We noted earlier that an impressive feature of object recognition is that we can recognize and categorize objects when viewing them from a range of angles. How do we do this? The view-based approach proposes that we store multiple representations corresponding to multiple views (or templates) of the same object, allowing us to quickly match an incoming object to the corresponding representation (this is sometimes known as the **multiple-trace memory model**, as described in Hintzman, 1986; Hintzman et al., 1992; O'Toole 2005). In contrast, the structural description approaches typically have one model per object that specifies how its parts relate to each other. Because the model provides "recipes" for how the parts fit together, the three-dimensional mental models that result allow for a match regardless of orientation.

How does a person even begin to test how these approaches—view-based and structural description—hold up against each other? If you think about it, they predict different things under different conditions. For example, view-based and structural description approaches make different predictions about how quickly an object can be recognized when viewed across different viewpoints. View-based approaches predict that the more an object is rotated away from the learned view, the more slowly people will be to recognize it (Edelmen & Bulthoff, 1992; Tarr & Pinker, 1990). In contrast, structural description approaches are more tolerant (less sensitive) to such

Geons   **Objects**

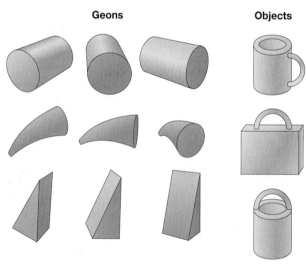

FIGURE 3.23 Examples of geons From the three geons on the left, a great range of objects can be made. (From J. M. Wolfe et al. 2017. *Sensation & Perception*, 5th ed. Oxford University Press/Sinauer: Sunderland, MA. Based on I. Biederman. 1987. *Psych Rev* 94: 115–147.)

rotations (Biederman & Bar, 1999, 2000). That said, the line separating viewpoint models from structural description models can be hazy: viewpoint models can be made to be more viewpoint-independent, and structural description models can be made to be viewpoint-dependent. Thus, while the debate has been historically informative, the options are no longer considered to be exclusive (Hummel, 2013; Tarr & Bülthoff, 1998). Instead, one can ask whether shape is represented as two-dimensional pictures or three-dimensional volumes. The answer seems to be both, with some objects being the former and others the latter (Liu et al., 1995).

HOLISTIC PERCEPTION OF OBJECTS AND FACES   Another debate concerns the extent to which object recognition involves **holistic perception**, meaning that we process a whole object at once, including the relations of the individual parts to each other. Do we recognize a motorcycle after recognizing its individual parts: two wheels, handlebar, and a seat? Or is there a template in the mind that is holistically activated by an entire motorcycle or its image? Likewise, do we recognize the letter Q as an O with a tail, or is there just a separate representation for the entire shape of Q?

Some evidence suggests that experience helps shape the degree to which object recognition is holistic. For example, in one experiment, people saw alternating faces and cars appear on the screen one at a time. For each presentation, they reported whether a target half of the face or car (i.e., the top or bottom) was identical to the same half of the previous face or car. Most important, the nontarget half could also be the same as or different than in the item that preceded it, and judgment for the nontarget half could be congruent or incongruent with the judgment for the target half. When people responded to a face, they were worse when the judgment for the nontarget half was incongruent with the judgment for the target half, suggesting that people couldn't help processing the whole face at once (Gauthier et al., 2003). **FIGURE 3.24** shows an example of this process. These results are consistent with a wealth of data suggesting that faces are processed holistically (McKone et al., 2007; Richler & Gauthier, 2014; Tanaka & Farah, 1993).

Interestingly, the same holistic processing appeared to emerge when people responded to a car—but this occurred only among car experts. The researchers concluded that as a person gains expertise in recognizing particular objects, their visual processing of those objects becomes holistic (**RESEARCH FOCUS 3.1**). One suggestion is that when people become visual experts, they begin to recruit parts of the brain typically involved in face recognition (e.g., the fusiform face

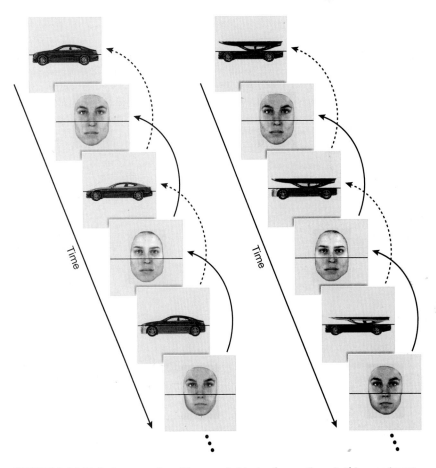

FIGURE 3.24 Holistic processing of faces and objects of expertise   In this experiment, participants saw interweaved faces and cars and had to judge whether the top half or bottom half of each item was identical to the preceding car or face (the curved arrows connect each presentation of a car or face to the preceding one). (After I. Gauthier et al. 2003. *Nat Neurosci* 6: 428–432.)

area, or FFA; see Research Focus 3.1) when visually processing the objects of their expertise. Evidence suggests that visual expertise—gained through experience—is linked with holistic visual processing across a range of visual stimuli, including Chinese characters (Wong et al., 2012), fingerprints (Vogelsang et al., 2017), and musical notes (Wong & Gauthier, 2012). Some evidence suggests that holistic processing can be modulated by how people learn to use cues to group features together (Chua et al., 2015; Curby & Entenman, 2016).

RESEARCH FOCUS 3.1

Birding

The ability to discriminate faces improves with experience and develops over time, maturing after adolescence (Diamond & Carey, 1986), which explains why it's easier to recognize right-side-up faces or faces from the race with which you are most familiar (the *other race face effect*). Nonetheless, distinguishing faces is complex. Faces are all more similar to each other than everyday objects are, and many of the differences among faces are in subtle feature or configuration changes, such as the width of one's nose or the spacing between one's eyes. Specialized brain machinery has evolved to process these differences as quickly as possible, given the social importance of face recognition.

These considerations led some researchers to wonder if face areas must be solely devoted to face processing or if they're just special machinery for any form of categorization that requires perceptual expertise. Consider Noah Strycker. In an informal competition called the Big Year, in which birders compete to see as many birds as possible within a calendar year, Strycker recorded a world-record 6,042 species in 2015 (the record has since been beaten) (Lund, 2016). What gives such birders the perceptual skill to detect subtle differences that ordinary people cannot notice?

Isabel Gauthier proposed that the fusiform face area (FFA) of the brain can be used for non-face stimuli for which a person has considerable expertise. To test this hypothesis, Gauthier and colleagues (2000) recruited bird experts and car experts from local birding and automotive clubs. They tested these experts on face stimuli, bird stimuli, and car stimuli. The experts were tested on objects with which they had expertise (birders viewing birds; car experts viewing cars) and on objects in which they did not

(birders viewing cars; car experts viewing birds). The researchers first demonstrated face areas in all participants (although for some inexplicable reason, car experts had smaller face areas). Then they probed the face area for how it responded to birds and cars. The face area was active when birders viewed birds and when car experts viewed cars, but not when birders viewed cars or when car experts viewed birds. This demonstrates that the face area processes objects in which people have considerable expertise (**FIGURE A**).

However, the face area does not respond to all types of expertise. For example, most people are expert readers in their native language, but printed words activate a separate brain region known as the visual word form area, not the face area. Also, it remains possible that clusters of neurons in the face area, smaller than can be detected with fMRI, are selectively devoted to faces (Kanwisher & Yovel, 2006; Tsao et al., 2006).

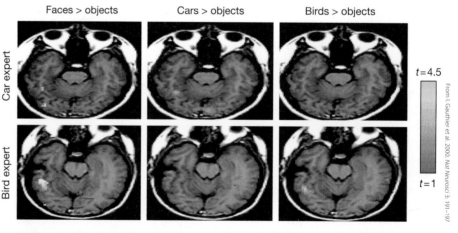

FIGURE A Results of brain imaging of car experts and bird experts looking at faces, cars, and birds, while being scanned using fMRI Face areas are defined in the left column for both car experts (top row) and bird experts (bottom row). In car experts, the face area is particularly active when viewing cars but not birds, and in bird experts, when viewing birds but not cars. The red, orange, and yellow spots overlaid on the brain images indicate regions that are more active in the comparisons listed along the top of the figure (for example, the spots in the left-hand images correspond to regions that are more active when viewing faces than when viewing various familiar objects). The *t* scale on the right refers to the strength of the neural activity associated with a given condition (relative to its comparison condition).

From a clinical psychology perspective, it is noteworthy that disorders that involve difficulty processing faces—such as autism and schizophrenia—have been linked with diminished holistic processing of faces (Gauthier et al., 2009; Watson, 2013). If it's true that holistic processing develops because of how people *learn* to group features together (a proposition that is highly debated in itself), this raises the exciting possibility that some debilitating aspects of such disorders might be countered through targeted training (Tanaka et al., 2010).

VISION AS A LEARNING PROBLEM   Modern research tends to treat vision as a learning problem. **Deep learning** is a form of artificial intelligence that uses deep **neural nets**—brainlike algorithms that analyze images in multiple steps—to process, categorize, and label natural images (LeCun et al., 2015). The first stage processes the raw image, while subsequent layers extract more abstract features that make recognition more robust across image changes and noise. The final layer, or output, can be a categorization label, allowing the algorithm to name a cat image as a cat. With enough training, the system learns the mapping between images and their category labels. Using such artificial intelligence based on deep learning, photo album software now allows you to group images or search for specific ones with words (Vinyals et al., 2014).

What, Where, and How

Perception allows you to determine both what is around you and where it is in a given space. Although it may seem like seeing something also involves seeing *where* it is spatially in relation to other things, the brain actually has two separate pathways, or mechanisms, for computing information about "what" and "where." The two pathways are tightly integrated, such that the *what* pathway contains some location information and the *where* pathway contains some object information. But because of specialization, these pathways can be dissociated (**FIGURE 3.25**). When asked to focus on objects, your ventral cortex (toward the bottom of the brain) is more active; when performing a location task on similar types of stimuli, your dorsal cortex (the parietal cortex, toward the top of the brain) is more active. This mirrors earlier work done with animals (Mishkin et al., 1983).

THE PERCEPTION PATHWAY AND THE ACTION PATHWAY   Rather than a what/where distinction, Goodale and Milner (1992) proposed a perception pathway and an action pathway. The **perception pathway** allows us to determine what is located where, while the **action pathway** uses perceptual information to guide ongoing actions, such as picking up a cup of tea or catching a baseball. In a classic experiment, a patient with agnosia who had damage to her lateral occipital cortex (often considered to be part of the ventral "what" pathway; James et al., 2003) was unable to report the orientation of a slot when trying to match it with her hand from a distance (**FIGURE 3.26**). However, she could easily place a card into a slot, a task that required her to position the card to match the slot's narrow orientation. This is striking because the latter task required using perception to analyze the orientation of the slot as well, suggesting that perception and action use information differently. Visual information may influence action (motor control) directly without going through the recognition pathway. For example, frogs don't hunt by trying to recognize the shape of their prey. Instead, they simply lash out their tongues whenever they detect flylike movement.

Object discrimination task

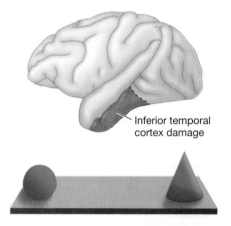

Inferior temporal cortex damage

Landmark discrimination task

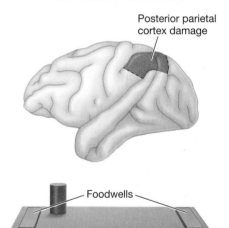

Posterior parietal cortex damage

Foodwells

FIGURE 3.25 Object and landmark discrimination   In the object discrimination task, monkeys were familiarized with one of the objects and then were rewarded for selecting the unfamiliar object. Monkeys with damage to the inferior temporal cortex (depicted on the bottom of the brain) were impaired on this task. In the landmark discrimination task, monkeys were rewarded for choosing the covered foodwell that was closest to the tall cylinder (Mishkin et al., 1983). Monkeys had difficulty with this task if they had bilateral damage to the posterior parietal cortex (depicted at the top of the brain). (From M. Mishkin et al. 1983. *Trends Neurosci* 6: 414–417.)

FIGURE 3.26 Perception and action pathways The top image shows the perception task in which an individual with agnosia had trouble indicating the slot's orientation when trying to match it with her hand from a distance. The bottom image shows how this same individual was able to match the slot's orientation when trying to slip a card through it (as if posting a letter). The action pathway can use perceptual information to guide motor behaviors. (After M. A. Goodale et al. 1991. *Nature* 349: 154–156.)

➤ **CHECKPOINT 3.2**

1. Think of examples that illustrate the challenges of object segmentation, occlusion, and inverse projections in everyday vision.
2. What are the different types of visual constancy that perception achieves?
3. What is the distinction between apperceptive and associative agnosia?
4. Define and contrast view-based approaches and structural description approaches to object recognition.
5. What is the evidence distinguishing what and where pathways? What evidence suggests that the what/where distinction might be better thought of as a perception/action distinction?

3.3 Mental Imagery

The questions in **SEE FOR YOURSELF 3.6** benefit from **mental imagery**, which is the act of forming a percept in mind without sensory input (Pearson et al., 2015). Mental imagery is important for all kinds of activities, such as giving directions to other people, determining if a top at the store would go well with a pair of pants at home, visualizing your performance before an athletic competition, or coming up with novel solutions for problems. While developing his theory of relativity, Albert Einstein famously imagined traveling on a beam of light. Strikingly, some people appear to have an inability to engage in mental imagery, a phenomenon called **aphantasia** (Keogh & Pearson, 2018; Zeman et al., 2010). People with aphantasia report not being able to generate images in their minds.

▶ **See for Yourself 3.6**

Your Mind's Eye

1. Imagine the letter *D*, rotate it 90 degrees to the left, and place a *J* on the bottom. What object do you see?
2. What symbol is on Captain America's chest?
3. What colors are in the McDonald's logo?
4. Read the following words:

rain	chimney	pencil	question
verdict	clue	utensil	butter
bliss	house	nose	noun
soul	boulder	pendant	foot
opinion	hour	luck	area
officers	beard	stairs	instance

Wait five minutes and recall the word list.

(Item #1 from R. A. Finke at al. 1989. *Cogn Sci* 13: 51–78.)

Mental imagery also aids memory. People are better at remembering concrete nouns than abstract nouns. Concrete nouns can be visualized, allowing for more elaborative processing that improves memory. The memory strategy called method of loci—which we discuss in Chapter 6—involves mental imagery: in order to use this method to remember a list of objects, one might imagine themselves walking through an imaginary room and encountering each object at a different location in the room. The visualization of each object at an imagined location has been shown to enhance memory of the objects.

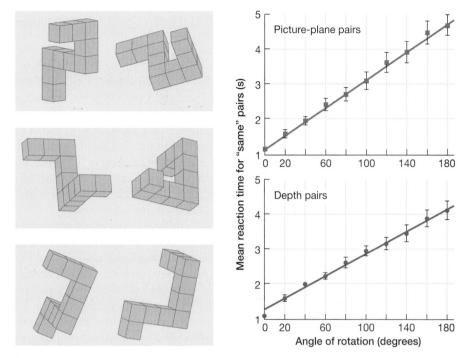

FIGURE 3.27 Mental rotation In a classic study, Shepard and Metzler demonstrated that the time it took to compare rotated views of an object (i.e., are they the same or different?) increased linearly as a function of how much the views were rotations of each other, both when the items were rotated in depth (depth pairs) and rotated in way that didn't change what parts were visible to the viewer (picture-plane pairs). This suggests that people visualize rotating objects in mind as if they were rotating them physically. (After R. N. Shepard and J. Metzler. 1971. *Science* 171: 701–703.)

MENTAL ROTATION Mental imagery is important for interacting with objects in the real world. For example, imagine yourself assembling a set of shelves from Ikea—not only will you need to rotate the pieces around in your hands, but you will also need to keep track of whether you have the pieces in the correct orientation relative to the instructions. Mental imagery is important for comparing and matching rotated images, something known as **mental rotation**. As **FIGURE 3.27** shows, the time it takes to mentally rotate and match two objects is directly proportional to the amount of rotation that separates the objects. It is as if one were turning one of the objects at a fixed speed with one's mind, just as they might with their hands (Shepard & Metzler, 1971). Beyond being useful for assembling furniture, mental rotation may be useful for certain jobs in fields such as architecture, engineering, and the sciences. See the Discovery Lab for more on mental rotation.

 DISCOVERY LAB
Mental Rotation

DEPICTIVE VERSUS PROPOSITIONAL EXPLANATIONS OF MENTAL IMAGERY
How does the mind perform mental imagery? The answer depends, in general, on how similar mental imagery is to perception and, in particular, on the extent to which mental imagery engages specifically perceptual machinery. The central participants in this debate are Stephen Kosslyn and Zenon Pylyshyn. Kosslyn's view is **depictive** and suggests that the brain represents mental images like it represents real images coming through the eyes. Pylyshyn's view is **propositional** and suggests that mental images are held in a post-perceptual, abstract way, more like a linguistic description than a picture. Whereas a color-highlighted route on a map is depictive, verbal directions to a destination are propositional.

FIGURE 3.28 Mental scanning Study this map of a fictional island and remember the locations of the hut, tree, rock, lake, sand, and grass. Using this map, Kosslyn and colleagues found that the time it took to scan memory for the spatial relationships between objects on the island corresponded to their actual physical distance on the map. (After S. M. Kosslyn et al. 1978. *J Exp Psychol* 4: 47–60.)

Kosslyn (1973) argues that mental imagery is like perception, and he provides several demonstrations to this effect. For example, after briefly showing participants a map (**FIGURE 3.28**), he would give them an instruction such as, "Without looking back at the map, determine whether the hut and the lake are closer than the hut and the tree." This task requires **mental scanning**, which is the process of mentally moving from one point in an image to another. The time it takes to travel or scan this distance is proportional to the distance between the objects, much like the time for mental rotation is proportional to the objects' angular separation. This similarity suggests that imagery is like perception (also see Kosslyn, 1976). In sum, mental images seem to contain spatial relationships.

In contrast, Pylyshyn (1973) contends that people are simply "simulating" perception but do not actually use visual imagery. He describes imagery as an **epiphenomenon**—something that occurs together with a process of interest but is not central for its function. For example, your laptop has an indicator that may reveal the current Wi-Fi signal strength, but the screen icon is not necessary for receiving and transmitting signals; chips inside the computer provide connectivity. According to Pylyshyn, all that Kosslyn's behavioral evidence shows is that people simulate perception in their mental imagery; it does not show that they are actively engaged in perceptual processing.

CONVERGING EVIDENCE FROM COGNITIVE NEUROSCIENCE AND WORK WITH PATIENTS You can see that the debate about depictive versus propositional explanations of mental imagery is difficult to resolve with behavioral data alone. However, the imagery question is one of the most prominent tests for the cognitive neuroscience approach to studying the mind. Kosslyn has a very concrete prediction about how mental imagery works and what the corresponding neuroimaging data should reveal. Given (a) Kosslyn's suggestion that mental imagery engages perceptual mechanisms and (b) that brain imaging methods and neuropsychological evidence can reveal the activity of perceptual brain areas, cognitive neuroscience offered a way to directly test Kosslyn's predictions. The key prediction is that machinery used for everyday perception is also used in mental imagery (Behrmann, 2000; Farah, 1988, 1989; Ishai & Sagi, 1995; Kosslyn, 1994). We can consider both patient work and brain imaging research.

If imagery is dependent on perceptual mechanisms, individuals with impairments in visual perception should have similar impairments in mental imagery. Indeed, individuals with color-vision impairments also show impairments in reporting the colors of common objects from memory (De Renzi & Spinnler, 1967; De Vreese, 1991). For example, individuals with occipital lobe damage in one hemisphere are not only impaired in visually perceiving but also in imagining (Butter et al., 1997; Farah et al., 1992). In one study, such individuals saw an array of dots on a computer screen; after the dots disappeared, an arrow appeared and the individuals had to judge—using only their mental imagery—whether the arrow was pointing to the location of one of the dots in the preceding array. When the arrow pointed to the side of the array that would normally have been processed by the damaged part of the occipital cortex, the individuals made more errors than when the arrow pointed to the other side (Butter et al., 1997). This is consistent with a key feature of the occipital cortex, which is that it is **topographic**—items adjacent in visual space

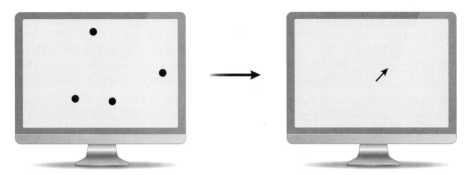

FIGURE 3.29 A task to measure mental imagery After an array of dots appeared and disappeared, individuals with damage to their occipital cortex were asked to judge whether a subsequent arrow was pointing to one of the dot locations. They could do this only by reconstructing a mental image of the dot array. When the arrow pointed to a location that would normally be processed by the damaged portion of the occipital cortex, the individuals made more errors than when the arrow pointed elsewhere. (After C. M. Butter et al. 1997. *Brain* 120: 217–228.)

are represented by neurons that are close to each other in the cortex. In other words, the occipital cortex is like a map that reveals activity in the visual world, just like a weather map on your phone or computer can represent where rain is falling in the regions around you. Accordingly, when a particular section of the occipital cortex is damaged, the ability to "see" parts of the visual world that map onto that region will be compromised. By testing individuals with damage to select regions of the occipital cortex, researchers have found evidence that mental imagery is similarly impaired in a location-specific way (**FIGURE 3.29**).

IMAGERY AND SPATIAL NEGLECT Spatial deficits can also be observed among individuals with **spatial neglect**, who cannot visually attend to objects on one side of their visual fields (for more on spatial neglect, see Chapter 4). For example, if facing the Piazza del Duomo in Milan from the vantage point shown in the **FIGURE 3.30**, left-neglect individuals will be able to describe aspects of the scene on the right-hand side only. Because this piazza is so famous, Italian neuropsychologists were able to ask citizens to describe it from memory, using questions that require imagery. But most clever about this experiment is that the individuals were asked to stand on the opposite side of the piazza—in their mind's eye—so that buildings on the right of the picture were on the individuals' left, and vice versa. When they did so, individuals were able to report what was previously unreportable in the neglected field (Bisiach & Luzzatti, 1978).

Levine and colleagues (1985) showed that dissociations between "what" and "where" in mental imagery mimic the what/where dissociations found in perceptual abilities. One individual did poorly on spatial tasks while another did poorly on object tasks, and their visual imagery performance corresponded with their visual perceptual performance.

Brain imaging further reinforced Kosslyn's view that imagery and perception share neurological machinery (e.g., Dijkstra et al., 2019). Imagining a face activates the brain area that

FIGURE 3.30 A view of the Piazza del Duomo in Milan, Italy Because this piazza is so famous, Italian neuropsychologists were able to ask participants to imagine it from the opposite side. The results revealed that spatial neglect persists in mental imagery.

is typically stimulated by viewing faces, whereas imagining a scene triggers the brain area that is typically activated by viewing scenes (O'Craven & Kanwisher, 2000). Furthermore, visual areas that are topographic show larger activity for mental imagery of larger objects, as if they were stimulating larger areas of cortex (Kosslyn et al., 1993, 1995, 1999). Area MT—an area of the visual system that is responsible for perceiving motion—is active during imagery of motion (Goebel et al., 1998). Moreover, using transcranial magnetic stimulation (TMS) to disrupt visual area activity disrupts visual imagery (Kosslyn et al., 1999). Single neurons that are active during perception of images are also selectively active when those previously viewed stimuli are imagined (Kreiman et al., 2000).

In sum, most researchers believe that perception and imagery share common representations in the brain, supporting Kosslyn's depictive theory of mental imagery, even as nuanced debate continues (e.g., Bartolomeo et al., 2020; Pearson, 2019). For more on mental imagery, read **THINK FOR YOURSELF 3.2**.

▶ **Think for Yourself 3.2**

Mental Imagery and Mental Illness

Many mental disorders such as post-traumatic stress disorder (PTSD) and anxiety involve highly intrusive emotional imagery. How real does imagery feel to patients, and to what extent do they think that imagined events will occur in real life? With its powerful sensory-perceptual features, mental imagery elicits stronger emotions than verbal thinking does (Holmes & Mathews, 2005). Images are rated as more real (Mathews et al., 2013) and thus affect patients' behavior more, such as hallucinations in schizophrenia and Parkinson's disease. The sensory strength of voluntary imagery correlates with the strength of hallucination (Shine et al., 2015). The more people engage in imagining a future event, the more they think it likely to happen, further heightening their anxiety (Raune, 2005; Szpunar & Schacter, 2013). In mental illness, imagining suicidal acts is associated with an increased risk of suicide (Crane et al., 2012).

Alternately, learning to imagine positive future events may help with depression. To treat phobias, imaginary exposure helps people habituate in order to lower anxiety levels—if such therapy works, imaginary exposure to snakes can make one less afraid of snakes. Imagination-focused therapy is helpful for PTSD and social phobia. Because perception shares machinery with imagery, performing a visually demanding task may help reduce imagery, especially negative imagery. As one innovative procedure, playing a video game such as Tetris soon after an experimental trauma within the time frame of memory consolidation can reduce the later frequency of intrusive images (Holmes et al., 2010). The idea is that playing the video game distracts people from rehearsing the trauma in their minds, leading to weaker and less vivid emotional memories.

▶ **CHECKPOINT 3.3**

1. What is the mental rotation test, and how does performance change as a function of the angle of rotation?
2. Define and contrast the depictive view and the propositional view of mental imagery.
3. What is the neuropsychological patient evidence supporting a tight relation between mental imagery and perception?
4. What is the brain imaging evidence supporting a tight relation between mental imagery and perception?

Chapter Summary

3.1 Explain why visual perception is a construction and why it is so challenging.

Although it happens so quickly and automatically that we are not aware of it, our minds are constantly assembling a puzzle from the pieces provided by the environment. Our views of objects are often incomplete because they lie behind other objects and are obscured from view; yet this doesn't stop us from seeing them as whole objects. (Indeed, our minds fill in whole regions of missing information, such as the "blind spot" that corresponds to the gap in photoreceptors in our eyes, where the optic nerve passes through our retinae). Items that are otherwise identical to each other cast images on our retinae that are of different sizes (because they are different distances away from us) and of different colors and brightness (because they are illuminated by different sources), and yet we are able to perceive them as being identical. The *inverse projection problem* refers to the fact that our minds need to build a three-dimensional experience of the world from the mere two-dimensional projections cast on our eyes. These are just some of the challenges that are involved in perception, and which our minds constantly solve with great efficiency in order to *construct* what we perceive. In some cases, our minds arrive at incorrect interpretations, which can yield illusions that give us clues about the rules that the mind uses to construct perception.

Q: Take a few moments to look around you and notice where there might be incomplete or potentially misleading visual information. For example, are there chairs that are partially blocked by other chairs? Or do you see two people, one who is farther away and who thus casts a much smaller image onto your eyes? Why are such instances of incomplete or misleading information not constantly confusing us? Looking back on what you read in this chapter, what rules and processes have you learned about that are helping you make sense of this scene?

3.2 Describe how perception is a combination of sensory stimulation and the mind's detective work.

Perception arises from how our minds make sense of sensory stimulation. For example, our minds use depth cues to build a perception of three-dimensional space. Some types of cues work because they engage both eyes at once. For example, *binocular disparity* gives you a sense of depth because each eye gets a slightly different view. The closer something is to you, the greater the difference between the views that your left and right eyes get. Other types of cues—known as *monocular depth cues*—work even if you are viewing something with one eye. Monocular depth cues include things such as linear perspective, texture gradient, and relative size, and are the kinds of things that skilled painters use to make a scene on a two-dimensional canvas look like it extends back through the wall.

Q: Look at any picture, painting, or photograph: what monocular depth cues do you see that give it a sense of depth? If you were to present two copies of this picture to someone at once—one to each eye—how would you adjust the positions of things in the picture in order to provide an even more powerful sense of depth?

3.3 Describe the relation between perception and mental imagery.

When it comes to vision, perception amounts to images constructed in our minds on the basis of clues in the external environment. But we are also able to construct similar images in our minds without immediate input from the environment, and this is called mental imagery. A central question in the study of mental imagery is, To what degree does it involve the same processes as perception itself? Evidence from both behavioral testing and from neuroimaging suggests that the processes of perception and mental imagery overlap. For example, when people scanned through their mental image of a map that they had previously studied, it took them longer to compare places on the map that had been far apart than places that had been close together, as if they were moving their mind's eye across the image. Damage to regions of the occipital cortex that impairs perception of the corresponding part of the visual field also seems to impair mental imagery corresponding to that part of the visual field.

Q: How vivid are your mental images compared with your perceptual experience of the world? People differ in how vividly they can build mental images (and some people report not being able to build mental images at all, known as aphantasia). For example, people score differently on a measure known as the *Vividness of Visual Imagery Questionnaire* (Marks, 1973). Try some of these adapted questions for yourself and compare your answers with those of your friends: on a scale of 1 (no image at all) to 5 (very clear image, almost as if looking at it), how well are you able to imagine the following features of a friend you often see? (1) The exact shape of face, head, shoulders, and body, (2) the way they typically hold their head and body, (3) the precise way they carry themselves when walking, (4) the colors of the clothes they often wear. Similarly, rate how vividly you can picture the following when imagining a country scene with trees, mountains, and a lake: (5) the shape and color of the lake, (6) the shapes and colors of the trees, and (7) a strong breeze blowing through the trees and creating ripples in the water.

Key Terms

agnosia
action pathway
amodal completion
aphantasia
apperceptive agnosia
associative agnosia
binocular depth cues
binocular disparity
blind spot
bottom-up information
boundary extension
cognitively impenetrable
color constancy
cones
deep learning
depictive
epiphenomenon
feedforward
figure-ground organization

fovea
geons
holistic perception
mental imagery
inverse projection
lightness constancy
linear perspective
mental imagery
mental rotation
mental scanning
modal completion
monocular depth cues
multiple-trace memory model
neural nets
object constancy
object segmentation
occlusion
perception
perception pathway

photoreceptors
predictive coding
primary visual cortex
propositional
recognition by components
retina
rods
sensation
size constancy
spatial neglect
structural descriptions
template
texture gradient
top-down information
topographic
transduction
unconscious inference
view-based approach
visual cognition

Critical Thinking Questions

1. If perception is a construction of the mind, does this mean that people who witness the same scene are likely to perceive it completely differently? What are some implications for eyewitness testimony?

2. Imagine that you have been invited to visit the International Space Station, which orbits Earth. While there, you notice an object on a shelf that you do not recognize. Of course, you might not be expected to recognize a specialized piece of equipment that you have never seen before. But now imagine that you have the same experience with an object back at home. You might be able to draw it, but you cannot name it or describe its function. What kind of agnosia might this resemble? What do you think is going on?

3. For which of your daily activities is it more important to know where something is than what something is? For which daily activities is it more important to know what something is? When is it more crucial to use visual information to guide your actions than to recognize objects?

Discovery Labs

oup.com/he/chun1e

Top-Down Processing of Color Information

In this activity, students explore how expectations can influence color perception, as opposed to color being the product of activation of wave-length specific cells in the retina. Students are presented with several images and asked about which colors in the image are darker or lighter. Approximate completion time: 20 minutes.

Ponzo Illusion

Students explore monocular cues of human depth perception in this classic experiment. Participants are asked to make line B the same size as line A in a series of trials. Approximate completion time: 15 minutes.

Mental Rotation

Students explore the issue of differences in vividness of visual imagery by using a mental rotation paradigm. Participants are shown two images of objects in different rotated positions and must quickly determine if they are the same object. Approximate completion time: 25 minutes.

Suggested Readings

Farah, M. J. (2004). *Visual Agnosia*. Cambridge, MA: MIT Press.

Hoffman, D. D. (1998). *Visual Intelligence: How We Create What We See*. New York: W. W. Norton.

Lotto, B. (2017). *Deviate: The Science of Seeing Differently*. London: Weidenfield & Nicolson.

Pearson, J., Naselaris, T., Holmes, E. A., & Kosslyn, S. M. (2015). Mental imagery: Functional mechanisms and clinical applications. *Trends in Cognitive Sciences, 19,* 590–602.

Wolfe, J., Kluender, K., Levi, D., Bartoshuk, L., Herz, R., Klatzky, R., & Merfeld, D. (2020). *Sensation & Perception*. 6th Edition. Sunderland, MA: Oxford University Press/Sinauer.

External Attention

4

Within two weeks of opening in Oklahoma City, a Hustler Hollywood store made headlines. Eight cars had crashed in separate incidents outside the purveyor of adult toys, novelties, apparel, and erotica. Some drivers blamed the accidents on the store's risqué window display, claiming they were too distracted to keep their eyes on the road (Detling, 2014).

This anecdote raises important questions about attention. For example, to what extent is our attention within our control? Could drivers have attended to the road and the window display at the same time? Would attending to the window display affect drivers' awareness of other cars on the road? These are the kinds of questions we will address in the following pages.

But let's start with the most basic question: What is attention?

© Richard B. Levine/Alamy Stock Photo

Does the attention-grabbing nature of sexy billboards make them hazards on the roadway?

4.1 What Is Attention?

The American philosopher and psychologist William James famously stated in 1890 that "everyone knows what attention is." To him, it meant:

> *taking possession by the mind in clear and vivid form, of one out of what seem several simultaneously possible objects or trains of thought. Focalization, concentration, of consciousness are of its essence. It implies withdrawal from some things in order to deal effectively with others.*

(W. James. 1890. *The Principles of Psychology, Volume I.*
Henry Holt and Company: New York.)

To a degree, James's description is as true to our understanding today as it was more than a century ago. However, decades of research have given us a richer understanding of the cognitive and neural mechanisms at work. Cognitive psychologists have come to understand that what we call "attention" is not one unified phenomenon.

Attention refers to a family of cognitive mechanisms that combine to help us select, modulate, and sustain focus on information that might be most relevant for behavior (Chun et al., 2011). Our ability to process information is **capacity-limited**, meaning we can handle only small amounts of information at a time. Attention functions as an essential gatekeeper. Because the amount of information available to us in any given moment exceeds our ability to process it, stimuli compete for our processing resources. Attention allows us to select and prioritize some information over other information. **THINK FOR YOURSELF 4.1** provides a fascinating example of how selection of some information for enhanced processing entails less processing of other information.

▶ **Think for Yourself 4.1**

Apollo Robbins: Master of Attention

Apollo Robbins is a thief. Just ask the Secret Service agents he pickpocketed while they were protecting former U.S. president Jimmy Carter. Fortunately, Robbins uses his talent to educate and entertain. His primary tool for picking pockets is his masterful manipulation of attention. By getting people to attend where and when he wants—both to things happening around them and to images in their mind—he is able to surreptitiously take a wallet from a pocket or a watch off a wrist.

Watch the short, entertaining, and insightful TED talk by Robbins entitled "The Art of Misdirection," in which he discusses how he manipulates internal and external attention in the art of the steal. As you read this chapter and Chapter 5, think about how the material either does or does not converge with Robbins's explanation of attention.

Apollo Robbins manipulates attention in his pickpocketing performances.

External versus Internal Attention

Attention can be directed outwardly, to the world around us. It can also be directed inwardly, toward our thoughts, feelings, task rules, potential responses, and items in memory (Chun et al., 2011; Panichello & Buschman, 2021). In this chapter we explore discoveries about **external attention**—how we attend outwardly, or select and modulate (adjust the influence of) sensory information. In Chapter 5 we will explore *internal attention*—how we select, modulate, and maintain internally generated information. It is important to note that the division between external and internal attention is not clear and rigid. It is simply a useful way to break down the complicated array of attention phenomena. In many respects, internal attention and external attention are closely related and can influence each other, as discussed in **RESEARCH FOCUS 4.1** (also see Ruff et al., 2007). One example might be daydreaming while sitting in class: paying too much attention to your own thoughts can interfere with your ability to follow your professor's lecture.

Daydreaming during class can be a case of internal attention interfering with external attention.

RESEARCH FOCUS 4.1

Working Memory and the Connection between External and Internal Attention

Try this: close your eyes, turn your head to the side, and open and shut your eyes just once, very quickly. How many details can you vividly remember from the brief time that your eyes were open? If you are in a familiar setting or someplace where you can predict your surroundings, it's easy enough to reconstruct the contents of the scene. For example, on a train, you know there should be seats running down both sides of an aisle. But in the laboratory, researchers have created experiments that strip away the contributions of familiarity and high-level knowledge. These experiments reveal the rawer limits of working memory capacity.

Working memory refers to our ability to keep selected information consciously in mind—to maintain and manipulate it even when the source of the information is no longer physically present. It is thus closely related to internal attention. In fact, it appears that the amount of information we are able to hold in working memory may be linked to how well we direct external attention.

In one study, researchers used event-related potentials (ERPs; see Chapter 2) to explore this relationship. Previous research had demonstrated that an ERP waveform known as the contralateral delay activity (CDA) is sensitive to the number of items in working memory. The amplitude of CDA increases with the number of items held in mind, but it levels off as the number of items held in working memory reaches each person's limit (i.e., working memory capacity) (Vogel & Machizawa, 2004). In follow-up studies, researchers asked participants to remember the orientations of either two or four blue bars or, in a critical condition, the orientations of two blue bars while ignoring the orientations of two red bars. As shown in **FIGURE A**, CDA amplitude in the critical condition among participants who had scored high in working memory capacity was similar to when there were two blue bars alone. But for those who had scored low in working memory capacity, CDA amplitude was similar to when there were *four* blue bars. In other words, participants who had exhibited higher working memory capacity were better at ignoring the irrelevant red information. The researchers concluded that control over external attention appears to be linked to working memory capacity (Vogel et al., 2005).

We will cover working memory in more depth in Chapter 5. For now, note how such findings suggest strong links between internal attention and external attention, and how the line between them can be blurry.

(Continued)

RESEARCH FOCUS 4.1 (continued)

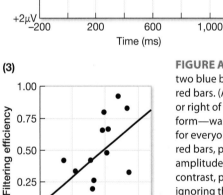

(1)

Cue	Memory array	Retention interval	Test array
200 ms	100 ms	900 ms	2,000 ms

(2)

High capacity

Four items

Two items

Two items with
two distractors

Low capacity

Four items

Two items

Two items with
two distractors

(3)

FIGURE A **(1)** Participants tried to remember the orientations of two blue bars, four blue bars, or two blue bars *while ignoring* two red bars. (An arrow indicated whether the targets were to the left or right of fixation.) **(2)** The amplitude of the CDA—an ERP wave-form—was larger when remembering four than two blue bars for everyone. When remembering two blue bars while ignoring red bars, people with high working memory capacity had a CDA amplitude similar to when remembering two blue bars alone. In contrast, people with low working memory capacity had trouble ignoring the red bars, leading to a CDA amplitude similar to when remembering four blue bars alone. **(3)** The researchers concluded that high working memory capacity seems to be linked to an ability to direct external attention where we want it to go. (After E. K. Vogel et al. 2005. *Nature* 423: 500–503.)

Covert versus Overt Attention

One tool researchers sometimes use in studying attention is **eye tracking**, whereby cameras record where participants are looking (Hoffman & Subramaniam, 1995). Because the light-sensitive part of our eyes (the retina) has relatively low acuity except at its center (the fovea), we need to move our eyes around (about 150,000 to 250,000 times per day; Itti & Koch, 2001) to piece together a high-resolution understanding of what lies before us. Studies have found links between **saccades** (eye movements) and attention. The act of mentally programming a saccade to a particular location seems to cue attention to that location, even before the eyes have started to move (e.g., Kowler et al., 1995; Sheliga et al., 1994). What's more, many of the neural regions associated with eye movements—such as the superior colliculus, pulvinar, intraparietal and postcentral sulci, and frontal eye field—overlap with those involved in shifts of attention (Corbetta et al., 1998; Nobre et al., 2000).

A classic study by Alfred Yarbus (1967) was one of the first to demonstrate the role of saccades in attention. When participants looked at the face in **FIGURE 4.1**, their eyes moved as shown in the map to the right of the

Eye trackers are useful tools in attention research.

face. The eye-tracking data revealed that people looked mostly at the eyes, mouth, and nose. This makes sense, as these are often the most informative features and were likely what people were attending to. Tools such as eye-tracking, which measure outwardly observable signs of where people are paying attention, are said to measure **overt attention** (the word "overt" refers to things that are plainly apparent).

Eye tracking has led to important insights. For example, children with autism tend to focus less on the eyes, which can give important social cues, than do children without autism (Klin et al., 2002). What's more, among infants as young as 6 months old, eye-tracking measures of attention to facial features may be predictive of an autism diagnosis (Jones & Klin, 2013).

Although eye tracking is a useful tool, attention is a function of the *mind*, not just of the eyes. Where people look often matches where they direct attention, but this is not always the case. For example, it is possible to look one place while directing visual attention somewhere else. You can see this for yourself by holding your hands out in front of you, then looking at your right hand while wiggling the fingers on your left. You'll find that you are capable of looking to your right while attending to your left. This is called **covert attention** because, in such cases, you are able to direct attention in a way that could not be discerned by someone watching you.

Note that when you selectively attend to auditory or olfactory information, you often do so covertly. For example, if you eavesdrop on a conversation in a coffee shop, you are able to do so without moving your ears. Of course, there are ways you could also attend overtly to these types of stimuli—for example, by tilting your head to hear someone better, or bending down to sniff a flower.

Understanding the distinction between overt and covert attention is important for safety. For example, pedestrians often believe that if a driver is looking at them as they cross the street, it is safe to assume that the driver is attending to them and will see them. But it is important not to assume that overt signs always indicate where or how someone is paying attention. Consider the video from See for Yourself 1.1 (in Chapter 1), in which many viewers fail to notice the person in a gorilla suit walking through the group of basketball players. Eye-tracking studies have shown that people fail to see the gorilla even if they're looking right at it (Memmert, 2006). In other words, viewers' attention contrasts with their overt behavior. The incorrect confusing of overt measures with covert attention has affected real-world policies. For example, in Australia one town experimented with placing advertisements on road surfaces rather than on billboards. The assumption was that such ads should be safer because drivers would not need to move their eyes from the road to see them. However, because attention can be decoupled from where people are looking, this is not necessarily so. Much also depends on the type of attention in question; **SEE FOR YOURSELF 4.1** presents an example of how your eyes and your attention can go to different places.

Three of attention's overarching functions include *selection*, *modulation*, and *vigilance*. In this chapter we outline these functions as they relate to external attention. We begin by examining different ways of engaging in attentional selection.

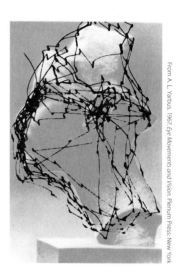

FIGURE 4.1 What is the strange pattern of lines and dots to the right? It shows how people moved their eyes while looking at the face on the left (a bust of the famous Queen Nefertiti of Ancient Egypt). The lines are the paths along which the eyes moved, and the dots represent eye fixations.

Are ads on road surfaces safer than roadside billboards? Perhaps not: looking in a particular direction does not guarantee attention to everything that's there.

► **See for Yourself 4.1**

Multiple-Object Tracking and Covert Attention

Using covert attention, you can attend visually to something you are not looking at. See for yourself by trying out *multiple-object tracking*, a widely used technique for assessing sustained, often covert attention (e.g., Fougnie et al., 2018; Scholl & Pylyshyn, 1999; Tran & Hoffman, 2016).

The task typically involves keeping track of several identical items that move among other identical items on a computer screen. At the end of each trial, participants are asked which items were the targets. Because all the items are identical, participants must attend to them constantly to complete the task. It turns out that people are typically able to track about four items correctly (Pylyshyn & Storm, 1988), even though it would be impossible for them to follow that many using only their eyes (most of us have fewer than four eyes).

You may be able to think of situations in everyday life that involve some form of multiple-object tracking. For example, a football quarterback must keep track of his teammates as they run down the field. Parents need to keep track of their children in a crowd. Even just crossing the street can involve tracking multiple cars, cyclists, and pedestrians.

Crossing the street can be an exercise in multiple-object tracking.

A collection of multiple-object tracking demonstrations (complete with further explanation) can be found on Oxford Learning Link.

► CHECKPOINT 4.1

1. What is the distinction between internal and external attention? Are they completely unrelated to each other?

2. Can you always tell where people are paying attention? Why or why not? What is the difference between covert and overt attention? Provide an example of each.

4.2 Selection: A Core Function of Attention

If you've ever walked through New York City's Times Square, you know what it is like to be bombarded with sensory information such as traffic, flashing lights, images, and advertisements. Because our processing capacity is limited, all this information competes for priority. A critical part of attention, then, is **selection**, or singling out certain pieces of information among many.

We are bombarded with more sensory information than we can process.

For a visitor to New York's Times Square, a challenge might be to find a particular storefront amid a barrage of irrelevant stimuli. But this mission might conflict with an advertiser's mission to have their ad beat out all other competing stimuli. Such competing demands can reflect a tension between **voluntary attention** (the effort to select goal-relevant information) and **reflexive attention** (attending to a particular stimulus because it has seized your attention, instead of you actively choosing to attend to it).

The tension between voluntary and reflexive attention also occurs in other sensory modalities besides vision. For example, imagine trying to listen to a friend at a crowded party despite the loud voices of other people nearby. In this case you would be directing voluntary attention to your friend's voice even as other people's festive whoops and hollers might grab your attention reflexively. To experience—right now—how attention shapes your awareness of a moment, try this simple exercise: If you are sitting down reading this book, try selecting different bits of tactile information. First focus on the feeling and weight of the book in your hands, and then focus on the feeling of the seat beneath you. By doing so, you can change your conscious experience of the moment.

People are able to selectively attend on the basis of various characteristics. For example, you can focus on sounds in the environment and ignore sights. Within a particular sensory modality, people also are capable of selecting on the basis of location (spatial attention), features (feature-based attention), or time (temporal attention), among other aspects.

Spatial Attention

Where's Waldo? (also called *Where's Wally?* in some parts of the world) is a popular children's book series in which readers are challenged to find the title character—who is always dressed in a red-and-white striped shirt—hidden within a crowded scene. You may have owned one of these books yourself. If so, think about your strategy for finding Waldo. Did you move your attention around the page, sampling first one location, then the next? If so, you were using spatial attention. **Spatial attention**—the ability to attend to regions in space—has been likened to a spotlight that illuminates and raises the profile of whatever falls within its focus (Posner, 1980).

It is worth taking a moment to wonder how such a spotlight of attention might work. For example, does attention simply enhance information at a particular location, or does attention suppress information that is not at that location? Evidence suggests both. For example, when people attend to a particular location, their ability to process other information very nearby is worse than their ability to process information a little farther away (**FIGURE 4.2**). That is, while attention facilitates processing at the attended location, it may also dampen processing of adjacent stimuli (e.g., Cutzu & Tsotsos, 2003; also see McCarley & Mounts, 2007; Mounts, 2000). It makes sense that this can help you focus on what you want to attend to: stimuli adjacent to your target are particularly likely to be a source of interference, so it can be helpful to reduce processing of such stimuli.

Complementing the metaphor of attention as a spotlight, some evidence suggests that spatial attention can act like a zoom lens (Eriksen & St. James, 1986; Goodhew et al., 2017). That is, given a particular location of interest, it is possible to focus on a small region in high detail or zoom out to take in a wider region at lower resolution. Evidence from fMRI studies supports this notion: when people were instructed to pay attention to a larger spread of potential target locations, the spread of corresponding neural activation in the visual system increased, but the level of neural activity within given subregions of that spread decreased (Müller et al., 2003). This is consistent with the notion that attentional resolution decreases as attentional breadth increases.

POSNER CUEING TASK   One of the most widely used tasks for revealing the movement of attention in space is the **Posner cueing task** (**FIGURE 4.3**), named after its creator, Michael Posner.

Like in a *Where's Waldo?* game, finding the fellow in the grey cap (inset) can be an exercise in deploying spatial and feature-based attention.

FIGURE 4.2 **Attention enhances target information partly by suppressing surrounding information**   Here, the sharply rendered kitten is the attended item and the blurry kittens are the unattended items. The more opaque white region around the target illustrates additional suppression of information surrounding the target.

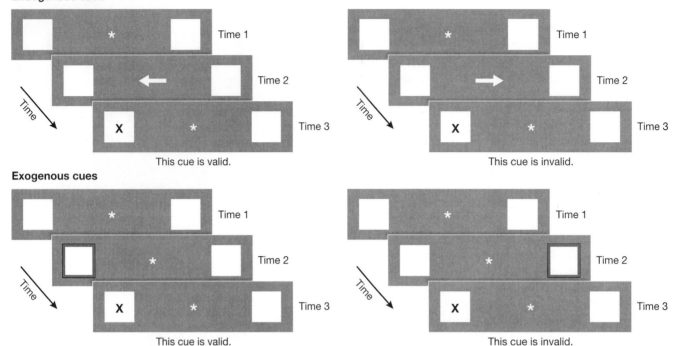

FIGURE 4.3 Example of a Posner cueing task   "Valid" and "invalid" versions of both endogenous and exogenous cues are shown. Valid cues direct attention to the location of the subsequent target, whereas invalid cues direct attention to the opposite location. Endogenous cues engage voluntary attention and often need to be interpreted symbolically, whereas exogenous cues often grab attention by appearing at one of the potential target locations. (From J. M. Wolfe et al. 2017. *Sensation & Perception*, 5th Edition. Oxford University Press/Sinauer: Sunderland, MA. Based on M. I. Posner. 1980. *Q J Exp Psychol* 32: 3–25.)

DISCOVERY LAB
Spatial Cueing

It looks like this: imagine you are sitting at a computer, watching the monitor and trying to respond as fast as you can to a target that will appear at any moment. You don't know where the target will appear, but about a half-second before it does, an arrow appears and points to the target location. If you think this cue will help you respond to the target faster, you are correct. Upon seeing the cue, you can move your spatial attention voluntarily to the correct location so that you are more prepared to attend to it. The benefits of such cueing have been demonstrated many times. Studies show that people are faster and more accurate at responding to a target when a cue predicts the target location (Posner, 1980; Posner et al., 1980). Demonstrations like this have been used to establish fundamental insights about attention and its neurological basis. Work like this earned Posner the National Medal of Science in 2009, one of the highest scientific honors in the United States. See the Discovery Lab on spatial cueing to learn more.

ENDOGENOUS VERSUS EXOGENOUS CUES   To understand what happens when we shift attention voluntarily versus involuntarily, two different types of cues are typically used in a Posner cueing task. An **endogenous** (or **central**) **cue** engages voluntary attention and can appear in between the potential target locations and indicate symbolically where the target is likely to appear. An **exogenous** (or **peripheral**) **cue** engages reflexive attention and can appear at one of the target locations instead of in between them. Both endogenous and exogenous cues can be either *valid* or *invalid*—meaning they either correctly or incorrectly indicate the target location. Whereas valid cues lead to faster responses, invalid cues lead to slower responses. This difference in speed is typically used as an index of the movement of attention in space.

Michael Posner receives the National Medal of Science in 2009.

Do endogenously and exogenously cued attention reflect two different attention processes, or are they aspects of a single attentional resource? There is reason to think they reflect different attentional mechanisms. For example, different neural regions seem to be involved in voluntary and reflexive attention (**FIGURE 4.4**) (Corbetta & Shulman, 2002).

Further evidence that endogenous and exogenous attention reflect different selection mechanisms comes from studies of their time courses. For example, reflexive attentional shifts tend to be **transient**: the benefits of reflexively processing stimuli at a location peak after about 150 ms (Müller & Rabbitt, 1989; Nakayama & Mackeben, 1989). After that peak, the benefits diminish. In fact, these brief benefits are followed by a short period when processing at this location is actually suppressed, a phenomenon known as an **inhibition of return** (because attention is briefly inhibited from returning to that spot; Klein, 2000; Posner & Cohen, 1984). What could possibly be the advantage of inhibition of return? One hypothesis is that such a mechanism aids our ability to find things. As an example, imagine trying to find your friend in a crowd. In this case, you will likely find your friend faster if some mechanism helps you avoid checking the same place over and over again (Klein, 1988; Klein & MacInnes, 1999; Tipper et al., 1999; but see Horowitz & Wolfe, 1998).

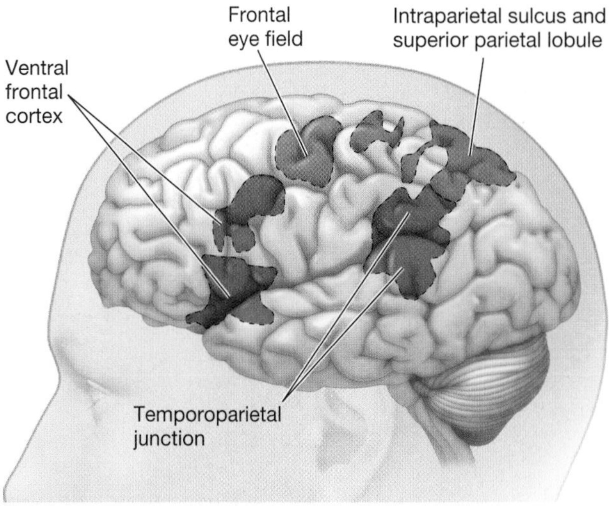

FIGURE 4.4 Neural systems involved in voluntary and reflexive attention   Areas along the dorsal (top) portion of the brain have been implicated in voluntary shifts of attention. These areas include the intraparietal sulcus and superior parietal lobule and the frontal eye field. A network alongside the ventral (lower) side of the brain has been implicated in reflexive shifts of attention. These include the temporoparietal junction, located along the inferior parietal lobule and superior temporal gyrus, and the ventral frontal cortex, located along the inferior frontal gyrus and middle frontal gyrus. (After S. M. Breedlove and N. V. Watson. 2019. *Behavioral Neuroscience*, 9th Edition. Oxford University Press/Sinauer: Sunderland, MA.)

Feature-Based Attention

Moving your attention around the page (like a spotlight) isn't the only way to find what you're looking for. If you're searching through a crowd for a friend who told you they'd be wearing a red-and-white striped shirt, another good strategy is to search for patches of red while ignoring anything in a different color. If you do this, you are using **feature-based attention**, the ability to attend to or filter out information based on features like color, shape, or motion. Neuroimaging studies have found evidence for a neural distinction between feature-based attention and spatial attention (Harris et al., 2017), and feature-based tuning of attention often occurs even when we're preparing to search for a target that hasn't appeared yet (e.g., Bundesen, 1990; Duncan & Humphreys, 1989; Folk et al., 1992; Liu et al., 2003; Serences & Boynton, 2007; Wolfe, 1994). Feature-based attention appears to increase activity in neural regions sensitive to the target feature across the visual field, even in the absence of sensory stimulation (Serences & Boynton, 2007). When attention is tuned to prioritize a feature, visual neurons responsive to that feature exhibit heightened sensitivity. Meanwhile, neurons that are not responsive to that feature exhibit suppressed sensitivity (Boynton, 2005; Corbetta et al., 1991; Martinez-Trujillo & Treue, 2004; Treue & Martinez-Trujillo, 1999; Treue & Maunsell, 1996). When people tune their attention for particular features, those features are more likely to reach awareness, as we'll see later in the chapter.

Temporal Attention

Have you ever held a stopwatch and tested how quickly you could press the start and stop buttons in succession? No matter how fast you get with practice, there will always be a threshold—maybe about 50 ms or so—that you can't get below. The same appears to be true for **temporal attention**, which refers to our ability to pay attention to points in time. For example, the **attentional blink** is an effect

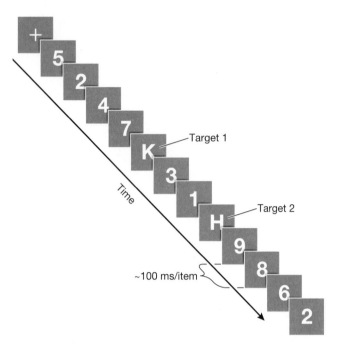

FIGURE 4.5 Part of an attentional blink task   Here, items flash by at a rate of ten per second. On each trial participants try to report the two letters embedded among the digits. People are typically bad at reporting the second target if it appears within about a half-second of the first target. (After S. Martens and B. Wyble. 2010. *Neurosci Biobehav Rev* 34: 947–957. Based on M. C. Chun and M. C. Potter. 1995. *J Exp Psychol Human* 21: 109–127.)

in which the second of two targets in rapid succession of items is more difficult to detect than the first (**FIGURE 4.5**) (Chun & Potter, 1995; Dux & Marois, 2009; Olivers & Meeter, 2008; Raymond et al., 1992). Even though people are able to process visual stimuli at very fast speeds (Holcombe, 2009; Potter et al., 2014), when they view rapid sequences of items they have trouble reporting the second target if it appears within about a half-second of the first (Broadbent & Broadbent, 1987; Weichselgartner & Sperling, 1987). We describe the attentional blink in more depth later in the chapter, where we discuss what it tells us about the relationship between attention and awareness. Evidence suggests that temporal properties of attention play an important role in shaping what we become aware of. For example, it has been found that awareness of stimuli can be modulated by whether or not the stimuli are presented in sync with rhythmic fluctuations of activity in the brain (known as "alpha oscillations"; Mathewson et al., 2012). One intriguing implication of such findings may be that our experience of the world comes in waves rather than as one continuous flow.

Object-Based Attention

Imagine you are reading this textbook in the library, when all of a sudden you hear a voice—"Hello!"—behind you. Your attention shifts from these pages to your friend who has just stopped by. But what does it mean to attend to your friend? If you turned your attention to the location of the voice, does that mean you are now visually attending only to your friend's mouth, or perhaps whole head? Or do you automatically attend to rest of your friend as well? **Object-based attention** is selective attention to an object rather than to a point in space (O'Craven et al., 1999). Evidence suggests that objects themselves can sometimes be a unit of attention—meaning that attention to one part of the object entails attention to the whole object (Duncan, 1984; Lamy & Egeth, 2002; Scholl, 2001; Shomstein & Behrmann, 2008).

In a classic demonstration of this principle, participants responded quickly to a target that could appear at one of four locations on a computer screen (Egly et al., 1994; see also Moore et al., 1998). The four locations sat on the corners of an imaginary square, so that the vertical and horizontal distances between them were equal. Just before the target appeared, one of the locations was cued with a flash. In a critical manipulation, each of two rectangles enveloped two of the potential target locations (**FIGURE 4.6**). In this experiment, response times to a valid cue were not of primary interest. Instead, the researchers were interested in the difference

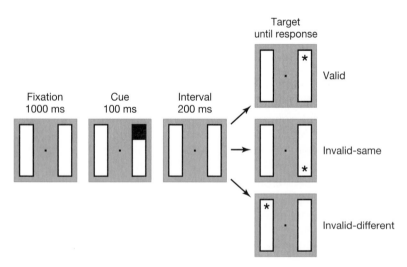

FIGURE 4.6 Example of three cue-target conditions from an object-based attention experiment   After a 100-ms cue, a target could appear at the same location as the cue (valid), at a different location but on the same object (invalid-same), or at a different location on a different object (invalid-different). Response time is slower in the invalid-different than in the invalid-same condition, even though both targets are the same distance from the cued location. Thus, attention appears to spread more easily within objects than between them. (From K. S. Pilz et al. 2012. *PLOS ONE* 7: e30693/CC BY 4.0.)

in response times to two invalid cue conditions: one where the cue and target were enveloped within the same object (i.e., rectangle) and one where the cue and target were enveloped by different objects. The researchers found that invalid cues slowed response time more when they appeared on the opposite rectangle than on the same rectangle as the target, suggesting that visual attention is influenced by how we parse the world. Rather than being limited simply to selecting coordinates in space, people appear to be capable of selecting cohesive objects as a unit of attention.

Additional evidence for object-based attention comes from studies of brain lesions. Patients with damage to the right side of the brain often exhibit what is known as **spatial neglect**, in which they fail to process stimuli that fall within their left visual field (**FIGURE 4.7**). Adding complexity to this phenomenon, some patients fail to process the left sides of all objects, even those that are situated in their right visual field. This finding indicates that spatial neglect can sometimes be manifested as a failure to attend to the left sides of individual objects ("object-based neglect"; Arguin & Bub, 1993; Driver & Halligan, 1991). Such findings support the notion that, among normally functioning participants, attention can select whole objects.

Biased Competition

In recent years, one of the most influential and empirically supported models of attention has been the **biased competition model of attention**. According to this account, stimuli in a cluttered visual environment compete with each other to drive the responses of neurons in the visual system (Desimone, 1998; Desimone & Duncan, 1995). You might think of it as a competition among stimuli for neural "real estate." Within the visual system, each neuron tends to respond optimally to stimuli falling within a specific part of the visual world (or "visual field"). A given neuron's preferred region of the visual field is known as that neuron's **receptive field**, and the competition among stimuli is particularly fierce when they fall within the same receptive field. When stimuli appear simultaneously but lie far enough apart in the visual field, they may evoke activity in minimally overlapping neuron populations, and there will be little competition among them. However, the smaller the distance among the stimuli, the greater the overlap in the neuron populations that are activated, leading to increased competition among the neural representations. In this situation, selective attention *biases* the competition in favor of one stimulus over the others. This competition can be biased by what's called **bottom-up selection**—which is driven by the salience of the physical features—or by what's known as **top-down selection**—in favor of items that are goal-relevant (Beck & Kastner, 2009; Desimone, 1998; Desimone & Duncan, 1995). Data consistent with an "arousal-biased competition" theory suggest that such biasing of competition may be amplified when people experience emotional arousal (Mather & Sutherland, 2011).

Recordings of neural activity have provided evidence consistent with the biased competition account. For example, work by researchers such as Diane Beck and Sabine Kastner has shown that visual cortical neurons that are highly responsive to one stimulus become less responsive when other, competing stimuli simultaneously occupy the neurons' receptive fields (Beck & Kastner, 2007). In this situation, attention to one of the stimuli leads to a neural response similar to that observed when the attended item appears alone (e.g., Chelazzi et al., 2001). Competition for neural processing has been found to occur throughout the visual cortex. Meanwhile, signals that bias this competition have been found to flow from networks of areas in the frontal and parietal cortex, which have been linked with attentional control (Kastner & Ungerleider, 2000; also see Cosman et al., 2018).

From M. Grabowecky et al. 1993 *J Cogn Neurosci* 5 288–302

FIGURE 4.7 Drawings by patients with spatial neglect The clock contains only the numbers on the right side, just as only the lines on the right side have been crossed off. Patients with spatial neglect often fail to process stimuli that fall within their left visual field.

The biased competition model of attention has generated much supporting data. In the process, the basic assumptions of the model have been fine-tuned and subtle variations of the model have emerged (e.g., Franconeri et al., 2013; Lee & Maunsell, 2009; Reynolds & Heeger, 2009; Treue & Martinez-Trujillo, 1999). For example, one closely related model builds on evidence that aspects of the environment are represented in the brain via broadly distributed networks of neural activation. This distributed property means that any one cluster of neurons can actively support several different representations. By virtue of this, the presence of multiple stimuli can lead to ambiguity about which mental representations accurately reflect the external world when neural clusters are activated. Attention, in this case, is thought to help resolve this ambiguity. This is known as the **ambiguity resolution theory of visual selective attention** (Luck et al., 1997).

➤ **CHECKPOINT 4.2**

1. Describe different ways that attention can select information from the world (e.g., spatial, feature-based, etc.).
2. How have researchers distinguished between voluntary and reflexive attention?
3. What is the biased competition model of attention?

4.3 Processing Before Selection versus After Selection

One of the biggest questions driving attention research over the last half century is this: At what point in the flow of information processing does attention do its selecting? What is our experience of the world like prior to attentional selection?

Early versus Late Selection

This question of when attention does its selecting has important implications because it suggests that, until attention has played its role, we are potentially processing everything at some level. If attention involves what we call **late selection**, then we may even process the meaning of everything around us before we select what will gain entry to heightened awareness. **Early selection**, by contrast, suggests that we attentionally select stimuli on the basis of physical features such as color, pitch, or location, and that we register their meaning only after we have selected them. The question of whether attention involves late versus early selection was a prominent issue for much of the history of modern attention research. Eventually this work produced evidence that attention can operate at many points during information processing.

To whatever extent we process information before attentionally selecting it, this is known as **preattentive processing**. One school of thought suggests that during preattentive processing, stimuli are analyzed via **parallel processing**. In other words, we take in stimuli quickly and all at once. In contrast, as items get attentionally selected, analysis of them proceeds via **serial processing** —that is, more slowly, one bit at a time (e.g., Egeth, 1966). Understanding of what kinds of stimuli we are able to process quickly "in parallel", versus more slowly and "serially", has implications for the real world: for example, consider drivers who arrive at a busy intersection and need to react to pedestrians, other vehicles, and

DISCOVERY LAB
Visual Search

Simple feature search

Find the white square among the black circles.

Conjunction search

Find the white square among the white circles and black squares.

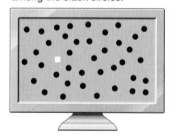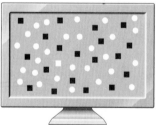

FIGURE 4.8 Examples of visual search tasks   In the display on the left, the target can be found quickly because it is defined by a simple feature ("feature search"). In the display on the right, it takes more time to find the target because it is defined by a conjunction of features (color and identity). (After S. M. Breedlove and N. V. Watson. 2019. *Behavioral Neuroscience*, 9th Edition. Oxford University Press/Sinauer: Sunderland, MA. Based on A. M. Treisman and G. Gelade. 1980. *Cogn Psychol* 12: 97–136.)

the colors of stoplights. Potentially, the more quickly that drivers can processes such information, the less their chances of getting into an accident.

Research has tried to capture the distinction between parallel and serial processing and their interaction (e.g., Buetti et al., 2016; Wolfe, 1994, 2007; Woodman & Luck, 2003). In what is known as a **visual search task**, participants look for a target embedded in an array of nontargets (**FIGURE 4.8**). See the Discovery Lab on visual search to learn more. When the target is characterized by a distinctive feature—for example, a red target among green nontargets—it is said to "**pop out**": detection is quick regardless of the search array's size. This finding is taken as evidence of parallel processing. In contrast, when the target is characterized by a **conjunction** of features—say, a red circle among red squares and blue circles, meaning that people can't find it on the basis of just color or just shape—search time increases as the search array gets larger (**FIGURE 4.9**).

Notably, some researchers have argued that it is often difficult to distinguish parallel and serial processing from each other. For example, it may be possible for parallel processing mechanisms to mimic patterns of data that one would expect from serial processing mechanism (and vice versa; Townsend & Wenger, 2004). It has also been argued that the terms "parallel" and "serial" processing are too bold and misleading: that rather than a categorical distinction between these two types of processing, they are better characterized as falling along a spectrum of "efficient" and "inefficient" processing (Wolfe, 1998; also see Kristjánsson, 2015). Ultimately, debates such as these are motivated by a desire to understand the mental architecture that enables us to perceive and react to the world around us.

FEATURE INTEGRATION THEORY Studies using visual search tasks have led to important findings about preattentive processing. One suggestion is that during preattentive processing we experience the world as a jumble of simple features that are not bound together into cohesive objects. For example, instead of seeing yellow bananas, purple grapes, and green apples on a grocery shelf, we might experience splashes of yellow, green, and purple and generally round or oblong shapes, without being able to say which colors belong to which shapes. Focusing attention on an object binds these features together, allowing us to perceive a meaningful object. This notion, pioneered by Anne Treisman, is known as **feature integration theory** (Treisman & Gelade, 1980).

Feature integration theory addresses a profound question about perception. Visual features such as color, shape, and motion are processed in different regions of the brain. How do we make sense of the nearly infinite number of ways that such features can be combined? This is known as the **binding problem**. According to feature integration theory, such features are correctly bound to each other only as needed, through the allocation of attention.

Support for feature integration theory comes from a phenomenon known as **illusory conjunctions**, the incorrect combining of the features in front of us (**FIGURE 4.10**). For example, in one study by Treisman and Schmidt (1982), participants viewed briefly flashed arrays of four letters and were instructed to (1) report the identities of two digits that flanked the array, and (2) report the colors and positions of the letters in the array. The researchers found that people's errors tended to reflect the incorrect combining of features that had been present in the display (e.g., a letter that had been present but in the color of a different letter that had been present) more than the combining of a present feature with one that had not been present in the display. Such findings are consistent with the notion that although we are able to process features prior to attentional selection, we need attention to combine them accurately.

DICHOTIC LISTENING You may have noticed that, so far, most of our discussion has been limited to visual attention. Indeed, much contemporary attention

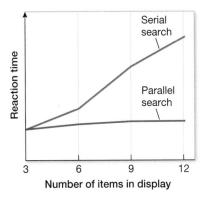

FIGURE 4.9 Example of a serial search slope versus a parallel search slope When people search through potential target items one by one (serially), the time it takes to find the target increases with the number of items in the display. When people process items in parallel, search time is roughly consistent regardless of the number of display items.

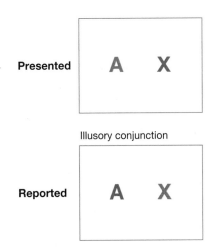

FIGURE 4.10 Example of an illusory conjunction When attention is distracted, people often bind colors to the wrong objects. For example, when presented with a red A and a blue X, a person might report the A as blue and the X as red. (From L. C. Robertson. 2003. *Nat Rev Neurosci* 4: 93–102.)

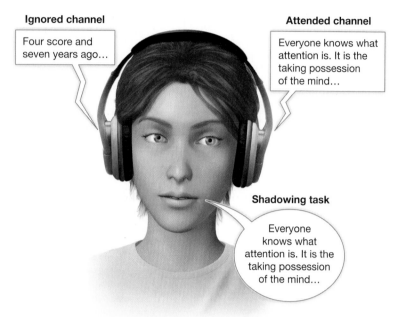

Ignored channel

Four score and seven years ago...

Attended channel

Everyone knows what attention is. It is the taking possession of the mind...

Shadowing task

Everyone knows what attention is. It is the taking possession of the mind...

FIGURE 4.11 Example of a dichotic listening task People attend to (and sometimes repeat) a message in one ear while ignoring the message in the other ear. Researchers then test what people processed from the ignored message. (Excerpts from Lincoln's Gettysburg Address, November 19, 1863, and W. James. 1890. *The Principles of Psychology*, Volume 1. Henry Holt and Company: New York.)

research uses visual presentations. As it turns out, though, some of the earliest studies on attention involved listening.

Such studies employed a technique called **dichotic listening**, in which participants listen to two different messages played simultaneously over headphones (**FIGURE 4.11**). One central question addressed by dichotic listening studies was: What happened to information that was unattended? For example, if participants attended to the message played to the right ear, what would they be able to report about the message played to the left ear? In order to test this question, researchers had to ensure that participants were truly attending to the assigned message. To do this, they would often ask participants to repeat the message out loud as it played, a technique called **shadowing** (see Figure 4.11).

A finding that emerged from this research was that people were barely able to report anything about the unattended message. People's ability to attend to one message while ignoring the other has been likened to they way that people can attend to one person's speech at a loud party; this is known as the **cocktail party problem**. Participants could report that there *was* a message presented to the opposite ear, but they couldn't report its meaning, and they even failed to notice when the language changed from English to German (Cherry, 1953). However, people were able to report things about the physical properties of the stimuli. For example, they noticed when the speaker switched gender or pitch or when the voice was replaced by a 400-Hz tone.

BROADBENT'S FILTER MODEL   Based on such evidence, Donald Broadbent (1958) suggested that information is attended or ignored based on "early" stimulus characteristics (e.g., pitch or loudness), before the semantic meaning of the information is processed. His **filter model of attention**, which aimed to describe the flow of information processing pre- and post-attention (see Figure 1.5), became widely influential and is notable for several reasons. One major reason is that it was one of the first applications of information theory to mental phenomena, in that it focused on the transmission of information itself through several stages of processing.

Broadbent's filter model of attention was also notable for attempting to pinpoint the stage of processing at which information gets selected. In particular, in positing that information gets selected based on physical properties prior to the semantic processing of meaning, Broadbent proposed an "early selection" account of attention. This set the stage for what would become a driving question of attention research for the next several decades.

As is the way in science, challenges to Broadbent's theory arose almost as soon as it was published. In one classic example, words with particularly relevant meaning—such as a participant's own name—*were* noticed when presented to the unattended ear (Moray, 1959; also see Wood & Cowan, 1995). (Note, though, that this effect is not quite as overwhelming as is often assumed:

According to feature integration theory, our experience of a fruit stand is simply as a jumble of unbound colors and shapes, which become bound together only when we direct attention their way.

although noticing rates went up when the unattended message contained the participant's name, a majority of people still failed to notice it; Pashler, 1998.) To some theorists, findings such as this suggested that people must process the semantic meaning of items even when they aren't attending to them. After all, how could the meaning of the unattended word influence noticing of it unless the meaning was processed prior to selection? Thus, psychologists such as Deutsch and Deutsch (1963) argued that attention is characterized by late selection.

TREISMAN'S ATTENUATOR MODEL   In one early attempt to reconcile evidence for early selection and late selection, Anne Treisman (1960) suggested that attentional selection initially occurs based on early, physical properties but does not eliminate processing of unattended information. Rather, the strength of the unattended signal gets dampened, even as the attended information is fully processed. This account suggested a reason why particularly meaningful stimuli—such as one's own name—are often perceived even when appearing within an unattended stream of information. According to this account, known as Treisman's **attenuator model of attention**, meaningful information needs to meet a lower threshold of processing in order to reach awareness. Thus, whereas most of what a person says from across a noisy room might fail to reach threshold, if the person says your name you will be more likely to hear it.

In the filter model of attention, attention acts like a bouncer at a nightclub. Many stimuli compete for access to awareness, and attention selects which get in and which get stopped at the door. (Thanks to Andrew Leber for this analogy. Also see Awh & Vogel, 2008.)

Evidence for a Flexible Locus of Selection

Current research suggests that the locus of attentional selection is flexible. Nilli Lavie's **load theory** of attention has been particularly influential (Lavie, 1995). According to this account, much depends on how demanding the attended task is. If the attended task is very demanding ("high load"), then attentional resources will largely be occupied, with few spare attentional resources for processing of unattended information. In this case, "unattended" information will be filtered out at an early stage of processing and will neither reach awareness nor interfere with the attended task. However, if the attended task is very easy ("low load"), it may occupy few attentional resources, allowing attention to "spill over" onto other items. In this case, unattended information is likely to be analyzed to a greater extent and will be more likely to reach awareness and interfere with the task at hand.

Importantly, the consequences of high versus low load seem to depend on the nature of the load itself. For instance, if load is high because the perceptual demands are difficult (e.g., finding a target in a noisy display), this is known as high **perceptual load** and processing of nontarget information is diminished (**FIGURE 4.12**). However, if load is high because a task taxes working memory, this is known as **working memory load** and processing of nontarget information appears to increase (de Fockert et al., 2001). This is consistent with notions that working memory and selective attention are intimately linked, with working memory playing a role in inhibiting distraction (see Research Focus 4.1).

The distinct effects of these different types of load have been found to be reflected in brain activity. For example, in one study people attended to faces that appeared one at a time, each one centrally superimposed atop a larger indoor or outdoor scene. Participants performed one of three tasks: they either (1) pressed a button each time a face was the same as the one before it (baseline condition), (2) pressed a button each time a face was the same as the one before it, but with degraded, hard-to-see versions of the faces (perceptual load condition), or (3) pressed a button each time a face was the same as the one that had appeared two items ago (working memory load condition, because here participants needed to constantly update two representations in

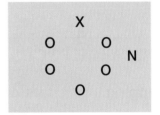

Low Load

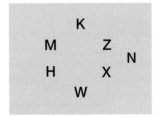

High Load

FIGURE 4.12 Example of a perceptual load manipulation   It is harder to find the X under high load than under low load. Because the task of finding the X requires less attentional effort in the low load condition, the task-irrelevant N is more likely to also be processed and cause distraction. (After N. Lavie and S. Cox. 1997. *Psychol Sci* 8: 395–398.)

mind). As participants engaged in these tasks, the researchers used fMRI to measure activity in a brain region known as the parahippocamal place area (PPA), which is especially responsive to pictures of scenes. They found that neural activity in response to the scenes (which were task-irrelevant) was lowest in the perceptual load condition and highest in the working memory load condition, supporting the notion that people's ability to filter out irrelevant stimuli is best under perceptual load and worst under working memory load (Yi et al., 2004). Such findings illustrate how neuroimaging can be used to understand cognitive mechanisms.

➤ CHECKPOINT 4.3

1. How do late selection and early selection accounts of attention differ? How do load theory (perceptual load & working memory load) and Treisman's attenuator model fit in with or modify this distinction? What evidence supports these different accounts?

2. What is preattentive processing, and what might our experience of the world be like during this stage of processing?

4.4 Modulation and Vigilance

As mentioned earlier in this chapter, selection of information is a core function of attention, but attention performs other functions as well (**RESEARCH FOCUS 4.2**)—even in the absence of competing stimuli (a rare situation in which selection is not as crucial). For example, attention can change the way we perceive a stimulus, a function known as **modulation**. A state of heightened attentional anticipation—or **vigilance**—can enable us to better respond to stimuli before they appear.

RESEARCH FOCUS 4.2

Tapping into Attentional Networks

Research has suggested differences among neural networks implicated in stimulus selection (*orienting*), temporal readiness to select information (*alerting*; related to the vigilance function of attention described in this chapter), and the operation of *executive* attention. Executive attention (which we will cover in Chapter 5) refers broadly to the ability to monitor and adjust competing demands.

This existence of distinct attentional networks is relevant to investigators who wish to understand individual differences in how—and how *well*—people pay attention. Some people might be above average on some attentional measures but below average on others. But how can we isolate and measure the effectiveness of each of these networks and compare them across individuals?

The attentional network task (ANT) is one method that researchers have developed to tap into the three networks within the context of a single experimental session (**FIGURE A**). In this task, participants report as quickly as possible whether an arrow is pointing to the right or left. The arrow is flanked

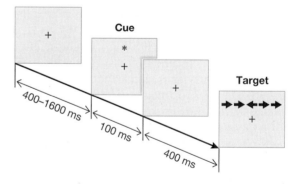

FIGURE A **Sample trial of the attentional network task** In this case, the preceding cue is spatially informative, as it appears in the location of the upcoming target. The trial is also an example of an incongruent trial, as the target arrow (fourth in the row of five) is flanked by arrows that point in the opposite direction of the target itself. (After J. Fan et al. 2002. *J Cogn Neurosci* 14: 340–347.)

(Continued)

---

on both sides either by other arrows that point in the same direction as the target ("congruent") or by arrows that point in the opposite direction ("incongruent"). What's more, just before an arrow appears, a cue can appear, which does or doesn't indicate where the arrow will appear.

ORIENTING To index how well people can orient their attention in space, response time after a spatially informative cue is subtracted from response time when no spatially informative cue appears. The resulting difference reflects the benefit of knowing *where* the target will appear.

ALERTING To index how effectively people are able to prepare in anticipation of a target, response time after a spatially noninformative cue is subtracted from response time when no cue appears at all. The resulting difference reflects the benefit of knowing *when* the target is about to appear.

EXECUTIVE To index how well people are able to resolve interference from mutually conflicting pieces of information, response times in congruent trials are subtracted from response times in incongruent trials. Typically, response times are longer in incongruent trials, as people need to filter out the conflicting information (see the figure).

Modulation

Attention increases our perceptual sensitivity, providing benefits to how well, fast, and accurately we can perceive something. For example, attention has been found to enhance the spatial resolution with which we perceive objects (Anton-Erxleben & Carrasco, 2013), sensitivity to temporal and motion properties (Anton-Erxleben et al., 2013; Montagna & Carrasco, 2006; Spering & Carrasco, 2012), and contrast (Barbot et al., 2011; Rolfs & Carrasco, 2012), among other attributes.

In one study, participants were presented with two visual stimuli known as **Gabor patches** (**FIGURE 4.13**). On each trial, the participants were asked to determine which Gabor patch had the highest contrast between the dark and light stripes and to report whether that patch was tilted to the right or left. The patches were preceded by an attention-grabbing cue that flashed either in between them or at one of the patch locations. The purpose of this cue was to manipulate where people were allocating their attention. When the cue flashed in between the two patches (thus failing to bring attention to either patch), participants showed no bias in reporting the tilt of one patch over the other. However, when the cue flashed at one of the patches, participants tended to perceive that patch as having higher contrast, as reflected in a bias to report the tilt of the patch at the flashed location (Carrasco et al., 2004). Thus, spatial attention modulated how people perceived the visual qualities (i.e., contrast) of a stimulus.

Vigilance

Imagine that you are a sprinter waiting for the sound of a starting pistol in a big race. If you are given no countdown, you might find yourself in a state of uncertain anticipation, unsure of when to burst from the starting line. However, if you are given a countdown—"3, 2, 1, GO!"—you will be better prepared to propel yourself into the race with optimal explosive force. In similar fashion, when given information about when a stimulus will appear, people are able to prepare themselves to allocate attention in time. For example, when given a cue that indicates that a target is about to appear, people are faster to respond to the target than when they are given no such warning (Fan et al., 2002).

Many tests of attentional vigilance ask people to engage in what's known as a **continuous performance task**, in which they are required to stay "on task" for a prolonged period of time. For example, in one version people view letters that appear one at a time and need to press a key each time the letter *X* follows the letter *A* (Rosvold et al., 1956). Such tasks are sensitive to a variety of types of brain damage and have been widely used by neuropsychologists. As it turns out, even just missing out on a bit of sleep can impair one's ability to

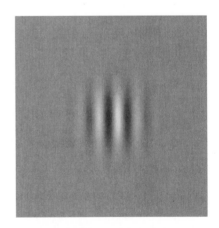

FIGURE 4.13 Example of a Gabor patch A Gabor patch is a widely used stimulus in vision research that takes the form of a circular area containing undulating dark and light stripes. The undulation is determined by a sinusoidal function that can vary in amplitude, which affects the contrast between the dark and light stripes. It can also vary in frequency, which determines the width of the stripes and the suddenness of the transition between them. Thus, Gabor patches are ideal for probing several perceptual qualities. (From J. M. Wolfe et al. 2017. *Sensation & Perception*, 5th Edition. Oxford University Press/Sinauer: Sunderland, MA.)

stay vigilantly on task (Lim & Dinges, 2008). Understanding factors that enable people to stay vigilant during such tasks has real-world importance. Consider baggage screeners at airports, who must stay alert for dangerous or banned objects even though they encounter such objects relatively rarely. By analyzing millions of trials of a gamified smartphone application (Airport Scanner), one research group found that people were extremely poor at detecting targets that appeared very rarely (Mitroff & Biggs, 2014).

➤ CHECKPOINT 4.4

1. How are modulation and vigilance functions of attention different from the selection function of attention?
2. What evidence suggests that attention modulates our perceptions?
3. How are measures of attentional vigilance relevant to the real world?

4.5 Attention and Awareness

On the evening of September 23, 2013, a university student was disembarking from a crowded San Francisco commuter train when he became a victim of random violence, shot from behind by a gunman who had waved his gun several times among the crowd. Why did none of the other passengers intervene or at least shout a warning? According to the district attorney, nobody had even noticed the gun because they were engrossed in reading and texting on their phones (Kearney, 2013).

Inattentional Blindness

Although we all know our phones can distract us, the degree to which this happens can be shocking. Attentional preoccupation often causes us to miss the most obvious things. How often have you looked over to the car in the next lane, only to see the driver texting? (And how often have you been the one texting while driving?) Most likely, the driver was not intentionally indifferent to safety. Rather, people tend not to fully appreciate the degree to which their awareness relies on attention.

Look up and watch the famous video "The Monkey Business Illusion" (Simons, 2010), which is a follow-up to the video mentioned in See for Yourself 1.1. This video demonstrates **inattentional blindness**, a phenomenon in which people fail to notice an unexpected item right in front of their eyes when their attention is preoccupied. Variations of this phenomenon were reported by Ulric Neisser and his colleagues as early as the 1970s, when the phenomenon was simply referred to as "selective looking" (Becklen & Cervone, 1983; Neisser & Dube, 1978, cited in Neisser, 1979).

To anyone not counting the passes in the video, the gorilla is plainly visible, but many people fail to see it when they're counting the passes. What's remarkable about the demonstration in the video mentioned above is that it tends to work even when people know about the original gorilla video. This is because inattentional blindness is influenced by our expectations: if you expected a gorilla, you probably saw the gorilla, but you might still have missed the player who left the game or the changing color of the curtain.

A striking aspect of inattentional blindness is that it involves people failing to see things that appear *right where they are looking* (Beanland & Pammer, 2010; Koivisto et al., 2004; Memmert, 2006). Thus, inattentional blindness reveals that despite what the eyes register, the things that we become aware of depend on which aspects of visual information we select for further processing—in other words, what we attend to.

What distractions keep you from seeing things around you every day?

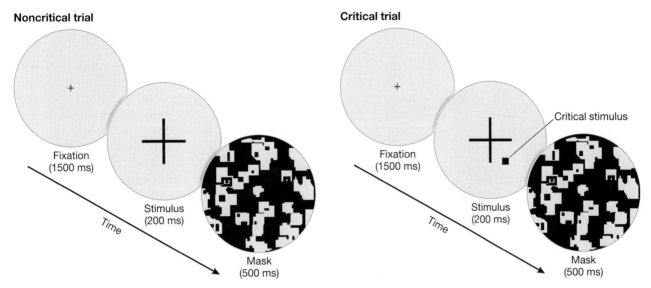

FIGURE 4.14 Two inattentional blindness trials from Mack and Rock (1998) On each trial, participants reported whether the horizontal or vertical aspect of a briefly presented cross was longer. On a critical trial, an unexpected item appeared in one of the cross's quadrants. Consistently, about 25% of people failed to notice it. (After A. Mack and I. Rock. 1998. *Inattentional Blindness*. MIT Press: Cambridge, MA.)

The term "inattentional blindness" was coined by perception researchers Arien Mack and Irvin Rock (1998), who embarked on an ambitious series of experiments that tested hundreds of participants in order to understand whether some kinds of stimuli were more likely to capture awareness than others. On each of several trials, a cross appeared for 200 ms, and participants indicated whether the horizontal or vertical part of the cross was longest. This task was designed to preoccupy attention. On a "critical trial," an additional object unexpectedly appeared in one of the cross's quadrants, also for 200 ms, and participants were then probed for their awareness of it (**FIGURE 4.14**). The researchers found that even when the unexpected object was brightly colored or appeared close to where participants were fixating, participants experienced a high degree of inattentional blindness. Particularly meaningful stimuli, such as an iconic smiley face, were more likely to be noticed, although even they were not noticed all the time. The researchers concluded that conscious perception relies on the availability of attention. Stimuli that are not attended will not reach awareness.

As you might imagine, inattentional blindness has consequences for health and safety in the real world. It is not unusual, for example, for traffic accidents to occur because drivers failed to notice another vehicle or pedestrian, despite looking right at them. This type of incident is so common that it has its own name in the traffic safety literature: "looked-but-failed-to-see" accidents. (In Australia they are sometimes known as SMIDSY accidents, "Sorry, mate, I didn't see you.") In a study that highlighted the relevance of inattentional blindness in the health system, 83% of radiologists tasked with detecting small nodules in lung scans failed to notice something as striking as a photo of a gorilla placed in the scan—even though it was 48 times as large as the nodules being searched for (Drew et al., 2013)!

THE ROLE OF FEATURE-BASED ATTENTION IN INATTENTIONAL
BLINDNESS One approach to inattentional blindness has been to combine the dynamic and prolonged qualities of video-based studies (e.g., the gorilla video) with the control afforded by computerized series of experiments. In one such experiment, participants kept track of four white shapes

Forget the "elephant in the room." Who could miss the gorilla in the room? Lots of people, it turns out, at least when their attention is preoccupied by counting the passes made by the players. Still frame from the classic inattentional blindness video by Simons & Chabris (1999).

From D. J. Simons and C. F. Chabris, 1999. *Perception* 28: 1059

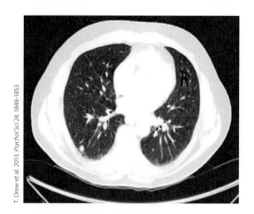

T. Drew et al. 2013. *Psychol Sci* 24: 1848–1853

Radiologists who were tasked with detecting nodules in lung scans failed to notice the gorilla in the upper right, even though it was much larger than the nodules they were looking for. Inattentional blindness can occur even among the experts we trust to look after our health and safety.

DISCOVERY LAB
Change Blindness

that moved around a computerized display, all the while ignoring four black shapes, and counted the number of times the white shapes touched the display edges. On a critical trial, a novel white, black, or gray shape entered and traveled across the display. When probed, hardly anyone noticed the black shape, almost everyone noticed the white shape, and noticing of the gray shape fell in between (Most et al., 2001). When people tracked the four black shapes rather than the four white shapes, this pattern reversed, suggesting that unexpected objects are most likely to be noticed when they contain features that people have tuned attention to prioritize. The real-world implications for this were highlighted by a study in which people "drove" through a virtual reality cityscape while looking for a road sign of a particular color. When a motorcycle veered into their path, people were less likely to collide with it when its color matched that of the road sign they were looking for (Most & Astur, 2007).

Change Blindness

Change blindness refers to the failure to notice large changes from one view to the next, and it reflects another, related failure of awareness in the absence of attention. If you've ever ordered a meal from one waiter at a restaurant and then failed to notice that it was a different waiter who brought you the bill, then you've experienced the phenomenon: people are bad at noticing even obvious changes. Change blindness differs from inattentional blindness in an important way: whereas inattentional blindness refers to a failure to notice a stimulus at all, evidence suggests that change blindness can sometimes occur not because people fail to notice a stimulus, but because people fail to compare two views of a stimulus in memory. For example, in one experiment people saw an array of objects, which disappeared and was then replaced by a new array, in which one of the objects may or may not have changed (Mitroff et al., 2004). People were then asked to select items that had been in the pre-change array and items that had been in the post-change array. The data showed that when a change had occurred, people were often able to recognize both the pre-change and post-change critical items even when they did not notice that a change had occurred. For more on change blindness, check out **SEE FOR YOURSELF 4.2.**

► See for Yourself 4.2

Change Blindness

If you are viewing a picture on a computer screen and suddenly a new object appears in the picture, you would likely notice it because the sudden onset of the new object (a "transient" signal) would draw attention to itself. However, any manipulation that masks the transient signal associated with the object's onset would make it harder for you to notice the change (e.g., O'Regan et al., 1999). For example, try the Discovery Lab on change blindness.

If you're like most people, it probably took you a while to find some of the recurring changes (if you were able to spot them at all). This is because, in several of these examples, the change happened every time the two versions of the picture were separated by a very brief flicker. In the examples where there was no flicker, you probably were able to find the change more quickly.

Although change blindness demonstrations are striking and fun, it is fair to wonder whether they tell us much about attention and perception in everyday life. After all, the demonstrations in See for Yourself 4.2 involve mere computerized displays. It is easy to assume that we'd notice big changes that happen in front of our eyes in the real world. However, experiments have shown that this is not the case. For example, in one study, an experimenter would stop a stranger on the university campus and ask for directions. Midway through the conversation, two people carrying a door would rudely walk between the conversationalists, blocking their view of each other. As the door carriers passed, the experimenter who had asked for directions would walk away behind the door and one of the initial door carriers would stay behind to continue the conversation. When queried, a whopping 53% of the strangers failed to notice that the person they were talking to had changed (Simons & Levin, 1998). You can see footage from this experiment by looking up the "Door Study" by Daniel Simons and Daniel Levin on YouTube.

In an interesting and informative twist on this experiment, the people who did notice the change were roughly the same age as the experimenters, whereas those who missed the change were somewhat older. However, when the researchers repeated the experiment while dressed as construction workers, the proportion of same-age participants who noticed the change dropped to 33% (Simons & Levin, 1998). This suggests that our likelihood of noticing a change depends on what aspects of a person's appearance we attend to: when confronted with an apparent out-group member (e.g., a professor approached by a student), participants may only have encoded their features enough to classify them as a belonging to another social group. However, when confronted with an apparent in-group member, participants may have encoded their individuating features.

Attentional Blink

Another method that researchers use to explore the relationship between attention and awareness is to push attention to its temporal limits. In essence, doing so increases the difficulty of attending to some stimuli because they appear too soon after other stimuli. The attentional blink, described earlier in Section 4.2, is a commonly used task for this purpose. In this task, participants try to find two targets in a very rapid sequence of items, known as a **rapid serial visual presentation task** (or "RSVP task"; Potter, 1984), and they typically have difficulty reporting the second target if it appears too soon after the first target. Attention, it appears, needs a "resetting period" before a second item can be brought to conscious awareness. See the Discovery Lab on the attentional blink to learn more.

DISCOVERY LAB
Attentional Blink

What factors underlie the phenomenon of the attentional blink? Several have been proposed to explain it. One account suggests that people have difficulty reporting the second target in a rapid sequence because of difficulty retrieving it from short-term memory (Shapiro & Raymond, 1994). Another account, known as the "two-stage model" of the attentional blink (Chun & Potter, 1995), suggests that all items are identified at an early stage of perceptual processing, but that the information quickly deteriorates and becomes inaccessible unless it is quickly consolidated (i.e., solidified) in visual short-term memory (also see Potter, 1976). (The process of consolidation is something like trying to remember a dream as you wake up; if you can't catch it and solidify your memory of the dream, it quickly fades and is forgotten.) Evidence that stimuli are identified at an early stage of processing, even when they fail to reach awareness, comes from studies that employ neuroimaging. For example, when people fail to see the second target word in an attentional blink task, neural signatures indicative of word processing are still observable (e.g., Vogel et al., 1998; also see Marois et al., 2004).

Explicit versus Implicit Attention

Phenomena such as inattentional blindness, change blindness, and the attentional blink vividly demonstrate the central role of attention in shaping awareness. But as you may have already noticed in this chapter, some measures of attention don't rely on people's conscious report of what they've seen or heard. In fact, many of our most fundamental insights about attention come from studies that have employed measures such as response time. Measures that probe people's conscious awareness can be categorized as tapping into **explicit attention**, whereas those that rely on nonconscious measures such as response time or eye movements can be categorized as tapping into **implicit attention** (Simons, 2000). This distinction is more than simply methodological, as studies have shown that it is possible to attend to something implicitly without becoming aware of it (e.g., Hsieh et al., 2011; Koch & Tsuchiya, 2007; Jiang et al., 2006). One striking demonstration of this comes from neuropsychological patients experiencing **blindsight**: a condition in which patients who have suffered damage to their visual cortex (e.g., through stroke) are sometimes able to respond to and localize visual stimuli that they report not being able to see (Weiskrantz, 1986). It has been found that cues presented to such impaired visual regions cause such patients to respond faster to subsequent stimuli, even though they could not report the cues (Kentridge et al., 1999, 2004). In other words, the cues captured attention implicitly without capturing awareness. Attention may be necessary for awareness, but at least some aspects of attention are not sufficient.

When we combine findings that attention appears necessary for awareness and findings that we are only able to attend to about four items at a time (see See for Yourself 4.1), we arrive at a deep and perplexing question that lies at the heart of attention and perception research: Given these constraints, how is it that we experience a richly detailed world? For example, if you happen to be sitting in a library at the moment, you might perceive yourself to be surrounded by many bookshelves, tables, chairs, and people. Perhaps you are also aware of a view out the window or signs and artwork on the walls. How is such a rich perception possible if you can attend to—and presumably be aware of—only four items at a time?

Part of the answer involves the complex relationship between perception and memory. In many ways, our perception of the world at any given moment is a construction of the mind, which "stitches together" immediate sensory information with information from immediately preceding views. It also appears that we are able to rapidly process the **gist**—the overall idea—of a scene more quickly than we can process a scene's details, and this gist information helps give us the sense of a richly perceived world (e.g., Greene & Oliva, 2009; Wolfe et al., 2011).

➤ CHECKPOINT 4.5

1. Describe at least one way that inattentional blindness and change blindness differ from each other.
2. What is one piece of evidence suggesting that attention and awareness may not be the same thing?
3. If we can be aware of only a few things at a time, why do we often feel like we experience a richly detailed world in any given moment?

4.6 Are We in Control of Our Attention?

"Pay attention!"

If you've ever said that to someone, or if someone has ever demanded that of you, you might be struck by the assumption that we are always in control of how we direct attention. Think also about the anecdote that opened this chapter, where drivers appeared to have attended to the risqué window display rather than to the road in front of them. We discussed the difference between voluntary attention (engaged by endogenous cues) and reflexive attention (engaged by exogenous cues) earlier, although the line between these two types of attention is fuzzy (Awh et al., 2012). One active area of attention research, known as **attentional capture**, focuses on understanding the kinds of stimuli that can draw our attention reflexively (Folk & Gibson, 2001; Theeuwes, 1992; Yantis & Jonides, 1984). Experience and learning also shape how we direct attention, as do our emotional responses to aspects of the environment.

Evidence suggests that we tend to reflexively look where others are looking.

Attentional Capture

Earlier, when we discussed the Posner cueing task, we highlighted a distinction between endogenous and exogenous cues. If you recall, an endogenous cue does not appear at the location of a subsequent target, but instead indicates symbolically where the target is likely to appear. The degree to which this type of attention shift is voluntary seems to depend on the nature of the cue, though. For example, in many cases arrows (or the words "left" or "right") seem to elicit voluntary shifts, whereas evidence suggests that a pair of eyes looking in one direction or the other causes people to shift attention automatically (Driver et al., 1999; Friesen & Kingstone, 1998).

In contrast, an exogenous cue is one that flashes on the screen at the location of the upcoming target, and this type of cues seems to grab attention even when a person doesn't want it to. Exogenous cues aren't all equal in their power to grab attention. Some types of cues appear to be more effective than others.

Why should some stimuli grab attention more than others? One suggestion is that very early in processing, the visual system computes the relative differences between visual signals across the visual field and forms a topographical representation known as a **saliency map** (Koch & Ullman, 1985). According to this notion, aspects computed to have particularly high "salience" (i.e., are very different from the surrounding aspects) capture attention automatically.

For example, in one experimental task (known as the "additional singleton" task), people search for a unique target in an array of distractors and report the orientation of a line embedded within the target (**FIGURE 4.15**). In a display of blue circles, participants report on the line contained only within the blue diamond (e.g., Theeuwes, 1992, 1994). On some of the trials, an additional unique property is present—for example, one of the distractor diamonds might be unique in color—whereas other trials contain no unique property. In the presence of a salient, unique distractor, response time in the primary search task is slowed compared with response time in trials containing no unique distractor (Theeuwes, 1992, 1994). The power of such unique distractors to capture attention has been found to persist across more than 2,000 trials (Theeuwes, 1992), indicating that participants cannot learn to ignore them.

Despite many studies showing that certain physical properties (e.g., unique color or an abruptly onsetting item) have inherent power to capture attention, other studies have suggested that we play an active role in directing our attention even in the presence of highly salient stimuli (Leber & Egeth, 2006). For example, when people know in advance where a target will appear, items that appear abruptly elsewhere in a display do not capture attention (Yantis & Jonides, 1990). Meanwhile, results from another task (sometimes known as the "irrelevant precue" task) suggest that stimuli capture attention when they match how people have "tuned" their attention (e.g., Folk et al., 1992). In the typical version of this task, people look for a target in one of several potential locations, and a valid or invalid

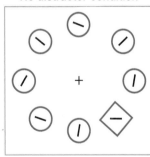
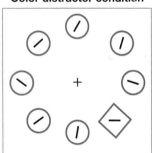

No distractor condition   **Color distractor condition**

FIGURE 4.15 Sample trials from the additional singleton task, used to demonstrate attentional capture Participants are instructed to quickly report the orientation of the line contained within the diamond while ignoring circles. When one of the distractor circles is a salient color (e.g., red, as shown here), people are slower than when there is no distractor present, suggesting that the salient color captures attention. (After J. Theeuwes. 2010. *Acta Psychol* 135: 77–99. Based on J. Theeuwes. 1992. *Percept Psychophys* 51: 699–606.)

cue precedes the target at one of the locations. When participants know the target will be an item with a sudden onset, uniquely colored cues do not affect response time, but cues with sudden onsets do. In contrast, when participants know that the target will have a unique color, the reverse result emerges: cues with sudden onsets no longer affect response time, but cues with unique colors do (Folk et al., 1992). This suggests that when observers tune their attention for a particular feature, they are able to override attentional capture by other, irrelevant information.

History-Based Guidance of Attention

In some cases we direct our attention based on prior experience and learning, even when we're not aware of such learning. One demonstration of this is **contextual cueing**, which is additionally covered in Chapter 7. This refers to an effect that is observed when people search for a target in an array of nontargets over and over again, across many trials. Often unbeknownst to people participating in such experiments, some trials contain spatial arrangements of items that are identical to those seen on previous trials, whereas other trials throughout the experiment present entirely novel spatial arrangements. Results from such experiments show that people are reliably faster at finding a target embedded in repeated configurations than in novel configurations (e.g., Brady & Chun, 2007; Chun, 2000; Chun & Jiang, 1998; Chun & Phelps, 1999; Jiang & Wagner, 2004; also see Brockmole et al., 2006). In short, people learn about patterns in the environment, which then helps them guide their attention even when they are unaware that there have been any patterns to learn about at all!

Emotion-Driven Guidance of Attention

As you are probably aware from your own experience, we often pay attention to things not because of their intrinsic visual properties, but because of their emotional properties (Yiend, 2010). An **attentional bias** refers to our tendency to direct attention to some types of stimuli over others, and when we show a preference to attend to emotional stimuli, this is known as an emotion-driven attentional bias. It is an open question as to how much control we have over our tendency to attend to emotional stimuli (e.g., Grimshaw et al., 2018).

In many respects, modern research on emotion-driven attention was spurred by the research concerns of clinical psychologists, who realized that emotional disorders—such as anxiety—appear to be characterized by heightened tendencies to attend to emotionally negative information (e.g., signs of potential threat; e.g., see Bar-Haim et al., 2007). Such biases are sometimes revealed in the lab. For example, in a **dot probe task**, participants try to respond quickly to a target (e.g., a dot) that can appear in one of two locations. Just prior to the target appearing, the two locations are briefly occupied, with a threatening stimulus at one location and a nonthreatening stimulus at the other (**FIGURE 4.16**). One typical finding is that anxious participants respond more quickly to the target when it appears at the location where the threatening stimulus has just been (e.g., MacLeod et al., 1986), suggesting that their attention had been drawn to that location by the perceived threat.

Provocatively, it has been suggested that it may be possible to train people to overcome such attentional biases and that training might help people disengage from threatening stimuli, thereby imparting a therapeutic effect. Research into the effectiveness of such attentional retraining is known as **attentional bias modification**. Evidence for the effectiveness of this approach is mixed, with some studies revealing therapeutic

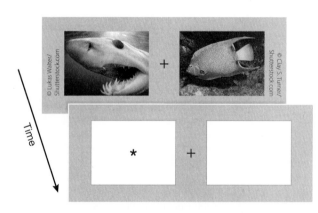

FIGURE 4.16 Example of a dot probe task When the target (here, an asterisk) appears at the location of a threatening picture, people are faster to respond to it than when it appears at the location of the nonthreatening picture. This effect occurs when the delay between the picture and target is a half-second or less. With longer delays, some people are faster at the opposite location. In this task, emotional and non-emotional words are sometimes used instead of pictures.

benefits and others revealing none (e.g., Cristea et al., 2015). Thus, the nature and value of attentional bias modification are currently topics of substantial interest.

What is the nature of these attentional biases? Is it the case that people process the emotional meanings of stimuli preattentively (i.e., before they have attended to them) and *then* orient to them more quickly? Or is it instead the case that people have trouble disengaging from them only once they've been attended? Some evidence seems to suggest that emotional stimuli *are* processed preattentively. For example, when people with a snake phobia searched for a snake among pictures of flowers and mushrooms, they were quick to find it no matter how large the search display, meaning that they registered the emotional stimulus without having to attend serially to each display item. People with a spider phobia were similarly quick to find a spider but did not exhibit the same pattern for snakes (Öhman et al., 2001). Findings such as these have led some psychologists to suggest that evolution has equipped us with a preattentive threat detection module (Öhman & Mineka, 2001; but see Lipp et al., 2004). Such suggestions are consistent with fMRI findings that the amygdala exhibits heightened activity to emotional faces on a computer screen even when people's attention is directed to another location in the display (Vuilleumier et al., 2001).

However, other evidence has suggested otherwise. For example, when perceptual load is high enough, people don't appear to show any particular sensitivity either to emotional words or to that most self-relevant of information, their own name (Harris & Pashler, 2004). Similarly, when people direct attention away from faces on a computer screen under conditions where task demands are high enough, fMRI results indicate no heightened amygdala activity in response to emotional faces (Pessoa et al., 2002). Such findings suggest that emotion-driven attention may reflect more of a difficulty in moving attention away from emotional stimuli rather than a rapid orienting of attention to them (e.g., Fox et al., 2001, 2002). For example, a gory scene may be harder to look away from, even if it may not initially capture our attention more than a non-gory scene does.

EMOTION AND TEMPORAL ATTENTION   The impact of emotional relevance on attention isn't limited to how attention moves in space or to measures of response time. Its influence can be seen in temporal attention tasks that directly probe visual awareness as well. For example, in the attentional blink, emotional stimuli that appear as the first of two targets cause longer and more pronounced impairments for detection of the second target; when they appear as the second target, they appear to "break into" awareness as if not subject to the same processing limitations as non-emotional items (Ihssen & Keil, 2009; Schwabe & Wolf, 2010; Schwabe et al., 2011). Intriguingly, this pattern may involve the amygdala: among patients whose amygdala has been damaged, emotional stimuli do not appear to break through into awareness (Anderson & Phelps, 2001). The fact that emotional stimuli have such impact across multiple tasks reflects the profound degree to which emotions can pervade information processing across the board.

Even when people try to ignore emotional stimuli, such stimuli affect our ability to consciously process other things. For example, when people viewed rapid sequential streams of upright landscapes and tried to find the one landscape that was rotated 90 degrees to the right or left, they could not find the landscape when the target appeared within about a half-second after a task-irrelevant emotional picture, even though they were looking right at it—an effect known as **emotion-induced blindness** (e.g., Most et al., 2005) (**FIGURE 4.17**).

ATTENTION, BIOLOGICAL PREPAREDNESS, AND LEARNED VALUE
Questions about how emotion affects attention also involve questions about

FIGURE 4.17 Schematic of an emotion-induced blindness trial (A) and trial results (B) Participants viewed a rapid stream of landscapes and reported the orientation of the one that was rotated 90 degrees. On most trials, an irrelevant critical distractor appeared prior to the target. When the distractor was emotional and preceded the target by 200-ms items, accuracy suffered relative to when the distractor was non-emotional. This effect was transient, dissipating when the target appeared 800-ms items after the distractor. (After M. Wang et al. 2012. *Front Psychol* 3: Article 438/CC BY 3.0; based on S. B. Most et al. 2005. *Psychon Bull Rev* 12: 654–661. Photos courtesy of Steven Most.)

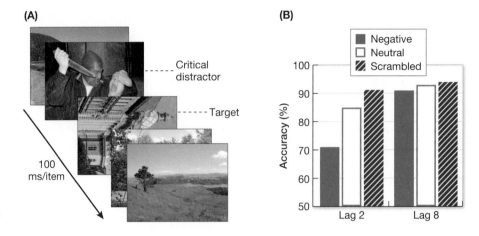

learning. Do we need to learn to attend to emotional information, or are we born with a bias to attend to some potential threats? On the one hand, people appear to have a robust bias to attend to snakes, and some researchers have suggested that such biases have been passed down to us through evolution, as rapid detection of potentially venomous snakes could have had benefits for survival in the distant past (Öhman & Mineka, 2001; Öhman et al., 2001; also see Seligman, 1971). Notions that we are biologically prepared to respond emotionally to some stimuli more than others are consistent with evidence that some stimuli are particularly easy to associate with an emotional response (e.g., fear). For example, in one study rhesus monkeys that had never before encountered snakes watched other monkeys exhibit fearful reactions to either snakes or to artificial flowers, and they themselves were later more likely to exhibit similarly fearful reactions to snakes than to flowers (Cook & Mineka, 1990). In other words, they didn't learn to mimic a fearful reaction to just anything; they were more likely to do so in response to something that may have been dangerous in their evolutionary past.

On the other hand, other evidence suggests that attention can be guided by emotional responses that people learn entirely within a lab context. Neutral stimuli (e.g., a color patch) that have been paired with rewards (e.g., money) or punishments take on power to capture attention (Anderson et al., 2011; Failing & Theeuwes, 2015; Le Pelley et al., 2015, 2019). In some studies, for example, people view displays in which they need to respond to a target quickly in order to earn money. Their responses are particularly slowed when the display contains a non-target distractor indicating that a high amount of money is at stake—in other words, in precisely the condition where it would be strategically important for people *not* to be thrown off by distractors (Le Pelley et al., 2015). Such counterproductive **value-modulated attentional capture** provides compelling evidence that the allocation of attention based on learned value occurs relatively reflexively.

EMOTION AND ATTENTIONAL MODULATION In addition to affecting the selection function of attention, emotional stimuli appear to affect the modulation function. For example, when an emotional face was briefly presented, people's contrast sensitivity for a set of subsequently presented Gabor patches increased (Phelps et al., 2006; also see Bocanegra & Zeelenberg, 2009; Lee et al., 2014). This occurred even though the faces never appeared in the same location as the Gabor patches, suggesting that the effect was independent of spatial selection.

EMOTIONAL STATE How do our moods and emotional states affect fundamental mechanisms of attention? According to the influential **broaden-and-build theory**, positive emotions such as joy, contentment, interest, and love widen the range of information people readily consider and attend to, thereby facilitating individuals' personal growth and connection to others (Fredrickson, 1998, 2001; also see Derryberry & Tucker, 1994). In contrast, this account suggests that negative emotions such as anxiety narrow the range of information people are inclined to consider, which might serve an adaptive function by making it easier for people to take efficient action. Consistent with this, some evidence suggests that negative mood states such as sadness and anxiety cause people to narrow their focus of attention and process details of visual scenes, whereas positive mood states such as joy and contentment cause people to direct attention broadly. In one study, participants viewed film clips designed to elicit positive emotions (amusement or contentment), negative emotions (anger or anxiety), or a neutral emotional state, and the breadth of their attention was then tested using a global-local visual processing task. On each trial, participants saw a target "global" shape composed of smaller "local" shapes that were different shapes (Fredrickson & Branigan, 2005) (**FIGURE 4.18**). Beneath the target shape were two choices, one of which matched the local elements of the target and one of which matched the global form, and participants circled the item that was the best match to the target. The results revealed that participants who had watched positive film clips were the most likely to attend to and match on the basis of the items' global forms (i.e., a "global bias"), consistent with the prediction that positive emotion broadens the scope of attention (also see Curby et al., 2012). In a refinement of the broaden-and-build theory, some evidence suggests that the degree to which positive emotions broaden attention depends on whether the particular positive emotions are strongly associated with approach motivation—a desire to move closer to something. In one study, participants who viewed a positive film designed to elicit approach motivation (i.e., a film showing delicious desserts) were less likely to exhibit a global bias than were participants who viewed clips evoking positive emotion with less intense approach motivation, such as a film showing cats in humorous situations (Gable & Harmon-Jones, 2008).

When taken together, various avenues of research suggest that what we attend to—and thus what we become aware of as we go about our day—is shaped not only by the salience of the features around us, but also potentially by our unique learning histories and by our emotions.

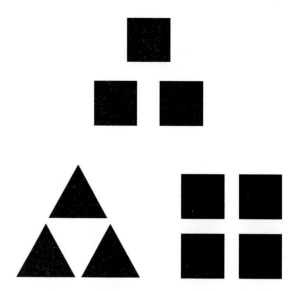

FIGURE 4.18 Example of a trial on a global-local visual processing task Participants circle one of the two bottom figures to indicate which is the best match to the figure at the top. Here, the option on the left matches the target's global form, whereas the option on the right matches its local elements. Positive emotions have been found to be linked with a bias to match on the basis of global form (Fredrickson & Branigan, 2005), but to a lesser degree if the positive emotions elicit approach motivation (Gable & Harmon-Jones, 2008). (After R. Kimchi and S. E. Palmer. 1982. *J Exp Psychol Hum Percept Perform* 8: 521–535.)

➤ **CHECKPOINT 4.6**

1. What are some factors that can guide our attention without our control or intention?

2. Describe different ways that emotion and learning appear to influence attention.

Chapter Summary

4.1 Describe how attention can be directed both outwardly and inwardly.

"Attention" does not refer to one monolithic thing. Instead, it refers to a family of mechanisms that, together, enable us to select subsets of information and modulate our perception of them. We can, for example, direct attention outwardly to the world around us (external attention) or inwardly to select appropriate responses or contents in working memory (internal attention, covered in Chapter 5). When directing attention outwardly, we can do so using just our minds (covert attention) or with the aid of our physical movements (overt attention).

Q: What evidence suggests that visual attention is a function of the mind, not just of the eyes? Describe how internal attention and external attention are related. Are they completely independent of each other? Explain differences between spatial attention, feature-based attention, temporal attention, and object-based attention.

4.2. Describe different ways we can direct attention to select information.

One major function of attention is selection, the prioritization of some information over other information. We can select information on the basis of a range of properties, including (but not limited to) location (spatial attention), features (feature-based attention), and timing (temporal attention). Some tasks, such as the attention network task, have been developed to tap into multiple aspects of attention at once. We can also direct attention voluntarily or reflexively.

Q: It has been claimed that there is no perception without attention. What evidence might support this claim? What do early and late selection accounts of attention suggest about what we might be able to perceive prior to attentional selection? How do inattentional blindness and change blindness differ from each other?

4.3 Distinguish what processing might be like before versus after selection.

Only a small amount of the information available to our senses reaches our awareness. Thus, at some point our minds select what information to process and what to filter out. Where in the flow of information processing does this occur, and what are we able to process (if anything) before this attentional selection (i.e., at a preattentive stage)? According to early selection accounts, we only process rudimentary features prior to selection, but late selection accounts suggest that we are able to glean meaning from the world prior to selection. Load theory suggests that the ultimate locus of attentional selection is flexible and partly determined by the attentional demands of the task we are focusing on. Feature integration theory suggests that we perceive the world as a blur of "primitive" features prior to selection, and only bind these features into meaningful wholes by attending to them.

Q: What is meant by "attentional capture"? What evidence suggests that we are not always in control of what we pay attention to? Describe evidence that experience and emotion can help determine what we pay attention to. How can understanding the relationship between attention and emotion help us understand and potentially treat clinical conditions such as anxiety?

4.4 Explain the role of attention in modulation and vigilance.

Attention increases our perceptual sensitivity, providing benefits to how well, fast, and accurately we can perceive something (modulation). Attention can also enhance our ability to process and respond to something based simply on our expectation that it will appear (vigilance).

Q: Describe examples from this chapter of how attention might modulate what we experience, and of the importance of attentional vigilance for real world safety.

4.5 Explain the link between attention and awareness.

Despite common intuitions that perceiving is something that the eyes or ears do, what we see or hear has just as much to do with how we pay attention. If our attention is occupied by one thing, other things can pass right in front of us without us noticing. In vision, this is known as inattentional blindness. Without attention, we can also miss large changes to a scene or person that occur right in front of our eyes, a phenomenon known as change blindness. Such effects are robust and occur all the time in the real world.

Q: Having read about phenomena such as inattentional blindness and change blindness, name things people do while driving that can impair their ability to notice obstacles.

4.6 Discuss factors that guide our attention that may be beyond our control.

Although we often choose what to pay attention to, sometimes things grab our attention without our meaning to attend to them. This is known as attentional capture. Things that seem to capture attention include items that stand out from their surroundings (e.g., due to their brightness or loudness) or even things that stir emotions within us. Sometimes what we pay attention to can be shaped by our experience. For example, things that we have learned to associate with reward appear to capture attention, and cues that predict where a target will be can guide our attention even when we are not fully aware of such cues (e.g., contextual cuing).

Q: If you and a friend walk through town together, do you think the two of you will notice the exact same things? What might cause you to see things differently from your friend?

Key Terms

ambiguity resolution theory of visual selective attention
attention
attentional bias
attentional bias modification
attentional blink
attentional capture
biased competition model of attention
binding problem
blindsight
bottom-up selection
broaden-and-build theory
capacity-limited
change blindness
cocktail party problem
contextual cueing
continuous performance task
covert attention
dichotic listening
dot probe task
early selection

emotion-induced blindness
endogenous (central) cue
exogenous (peripheral) cue
explicit attention
external attention
eye tracking
feature integration theory
feature-based attention
filter model
Gabor patches
gist
illusory conjuctions
implicit attention
inattentional blindness
inhibition of return
late selection
load theory
masking
modulation
object-based attention
overt attention

parallel processing
perceptual load
Posner cueing task
preattentive processing
receptive field
reflexive attention
saccades
saliency map
selection
serial processing
shadowing
spatial attention
spatial neglect
temporal attention
top-down selection
value-modulated attentional capture
vigilance
visual search task
voluntary attention
working memory
working memory load

Critical Thinking Questions

1. Psychologist and philosopher William James famously said that "everyone knows what attention is." Do you agree? In what ways do most people have an accurate understanding of attention, and in what ways do they not? After reading this chapter, do you believe that cognitive psychologists have a complete understanding of attention? Why or why not?

2. Take a few moments to try to focus on items around you based on different qualities. For example, use spatial attention to pay attention to something on your right; then pay attention to something on your left. Or try tuning your feature-based attention to all the blue things around you, filtering out non-blue things. As you read though this chapter about the different ways people are able to direct attention, try tuning your attention in the ways described. Are you able to do it?

3. Next time you are surfing the Web or using social media on your phone, pause and look around you. What do you see or hear that you weren't aware of while on the phone? What does this tell you about how attention shapes your experience of the world? Based on what you have read in this chapter, do you think you had any experience of these aspects of your environment before paying attention to them? What would that experience have been like?

4. What kinds of things do you have strong emotional reactions to? For example, are you afraid of spiders, or does the rest of the world seem to melt away when you see someone you are attracted to? Think about a time when you had such a strong emotional reaction to something that you couldn't *not* pay attention to it. How does this relate to distinctions between voluntary and reflexive attention?

5. Think about different jobs or occupations you have had, or those held by other people. What aspects of the jobs require you to pay attention? What kinds of consequences could arise when the people in those jobs get distracted?

Discovery Labs

oup.com/he/chun1e

Spatial Cueing

Students explore the spotlight theory of visual attention through the use of spatial cueing experiments. Participants are given cues directing their attention either to the left or right, and then must respond as quickly as possible to the circle that then appears on the screen. Approximate completion time: 30 minutes.

Visual Search

Students learn how more attention must be paid in order to distinguish different features processed in parallel. In this paradigm, participants are asked to look for a specific target among distractor stimuli. The target may differ from distractors in one or more of its features, and there may be a few or a large number of distractors. Approximate completion time: 25 minutes.

Change Blindness

In this experiment, students learn how the brain pieces together snapshots of the world so that it feels like a fluid experience. Using the flicker paradigm, participants are asked to observe ten trials of flickering pictures. Approximate completion time: 5 minutes.

Attentional Blink

In this experiment, students learn how attention cannot be switched to a new stimulus while it is still being used to process a previous stimulus. Using the attentional blink paradigm, stimuli are presented one at a time for 100 ms each. Participants' task is to observe the stream and determine whether specific target stimuli are presented to them. Approximate completion time: 10 minutes.

Suggested Readings

Chabris, C. F., & Simons, D. J. (2010). *The Invisible Gorilla: And Other Ways Our Intuitions Deceive Us*. New York: Crown.

Chun, M. M., Golomb, J. D., & Turk-Browne, N. (2011). A taxonomy of external and internal attention. *Annual Review of Psychology, 62*, 73–101.

Macknik, S. L., & Martinez-Conde, S. (2015). Scientists unveil the secrets of visual attention. *Scientific American,* https://doi.org/10.1038/scientificamericanmind0115-21

Styles, E. (2006). *The Psychology of Attention*. 2nd Edition. London, UK: Routledge.

Cognitive Control and Working Memory

5

Everybody multitasks. But David Strayer and his research team at the University of Utah wanted to know just how well (Strayer & Johnston, 2001; Watson & Strayer, 2010). To investigate this question, they put participants into a driving simulator and tried to distract them to the point of crashing. While participants were driving, the researchers asked them to remember a list of two to five words spoken over a cell phone, and they were quizzed to repeat the words. Making this task even more difficult, simple math problems also appeared amid the word lists. Participants had to answer "True" or "False" to questions such as "Is 6 divided by 2, plus 1, equal to 4?" While trying to juggle these tasks, were the drivers able to stay focused on the road?

Just driving, or just performing the memory and arithmetic tasks, was manageable. However, performance plummeted across the board when the driving and thinking tasks were combined. In these cases, participants made more mistakes in the memory and arithmetic problems, and they were slower to brake, crashing more often.

Multitasking hurts performance. Instead, it is better to perform tasks sequentially, focusing on one job at a time. Even if someone is not multitasking in a given moment, just being a habitual multitasker can make a person less focused (Ophir et al., 2009). And although it sounds tempting to train yourself to be a better multitasker, practice is of limited value. Understanding these limitations can help people perform better and behave more safely.

Courtesy of David Strayer

A high-tech driving simulator can safely test for impairments to driving caused by conversing with someone on a cell phone.

5.1 Cognitive Control

People multitask all the time, listening to music while exercising, talking with friends while walking, or planning dinner while driving. So when can we multitask well enough and when can we not? It's generally difficult to do two things at once, but some tasks are easier to combine than others. While writing a research paper, it would be difficult to carry out a conversation with someone, a little less difficult to watch a TV show at the same time, and easier to listen to music in the background. Multitasking is simpler when at least one of the tasks does not require substantial cognitive effort.

Cognitive control is "the ability to orchestrate thought and action in accordance with internal goals" (Miller & Cohen, 2001, p. 167; also discussed in Diamond, 2013). Most activities involve some control of behavior. Cognitive control, also known as executive control, makes our activities purposeful. It allows us to plan, decide, select behaviors, and coordinate more than one action at a time. Sometimes, we apply cognitive control in anticipation of a challenge, which is known as **proactive control** ("I know there will be candy at the checkout counter, so I have to be strong"). Other times we apply cognitive control only in reaction to a challenge, which is known as **reactive control** ("Ack! Candy! Must. Resist"). These distinct mechanisms of cognitive control recruit different brain regions and each contribute to differences in people's ability to guide their own behavior (Braver, 2012; Braver et al., 2009).

Because the mind has limited capacity, cognitive control requires attention. A mental **resource** refers to limitations in how much information the mind can process at any given time. For example, Chapter 4 showed how we can attend to only a handful of objects in the external environment. On top of this, **internal attention** refers to limitations in how much information can be prioritized within the mind. Try this: Remember the following cities, look away (or close your eyes), and then plot a route through all the cities in alphabetical order: San Francisco, Beijing, London, Paris, Nairobi, Sydney. This task is difficult, consuming much of your limited mental resources, requiring attention to your thoughts rather than to the external world. Cognitive control allows you to prioritize and negotiate all the competing demands from your surrounding environment and from within your mind.

Studying cognitive control can help optimize human performance and understand when that performance breaks down (e.g., Sweller, 1988; Sweller et al., 1998). First we consider when and why performance suffers when people try to do more than one thing at a time.

Task Load, Overlap, and Interference

Two primary factors dictate whether effective multitasking is possible. The first is **cognitive load**, which describes a task's difficulty. If the load is low, the task may be easy to perform simultaneously with another when the combined tasks fit within one's mental capacity. The cognitive demands of walking are relatively low, for example, so you can typically do other low-load tasks while walking, such as listen to a podcast or talk with a friend. But attempting a higher-load task such as texting while walking can be hazardous. Between 2004 and 2010, the number of emergency room visits for pedestrian injuries related to cell phone use tripled (Nasar & Troyer, 2013). More demanding tasks, such as solving a problem set or writing a paper, are best performed one at a time.

The second factor that affects the ability to multitask is **cognitive overlap**, or how much the demands of simultaneous tasks compete for the same mental resources. At one extreme, both texting and driving require you to look. There's a great deal of overlap, so these tasks impede each other, sometimes fatally. In 2015, U.S. highway fatalities increased by the largest annual percentage in 50 years (*New York Times*, 2016), most of them attributable to the increase in phone app usage while driving. By contrast, listening to music and driving overlap

Cognitive control is the ability to orchestrate thought and action, like a conductor leading musicians.

less. One is auditory, while the other is primarily visual and motor. The brain has separate areas devoted to seeing and to listening, and the two activities compete less for common processing. So audio entertainment has long been considered safe enough to be a standard feature in all vehicles (as long as you don't take your eyes off the road while trying to operate it).

Dual-task experiments require participants to do two tasks at the same time. **Cognitive interference** occurs when load is high or when two tasks overlap, and performance suffers as a result. With a lower load or less overlap, less cognitive interference will occur, allowing for better multitasking. By having participants try many different pairings of tasks, as illustrated in the dual-task interference Discovery Lab, researchers can measure which tasks interfere with each other and to what extent.

Distracted driving increases the risk of crashes or near-crashes, especially for novice drivers (Klauer et al., 2014). Compared with listening to music or talking with a passenger in the car, why would talking on a cell phone impede driving? First, the load of talking is higher than passively listening to music. You have to comprehend what the other person is saying while also formulating your own responses. Second, engaging with someone on the phone, who is oblivious to your driving conditions (as opposed to an adult passenger who may adjust their conversation when traffic gets busy), overlaps and interferes more with the demands of driving. Dual-task studies in driving simulators have led researchers to conclude that having cell phone conversations while driving may be as dangerous as driving drunk (Redelmeier & Tibshirani, 1997; Strayer & Johnston, 2001), while texting is even more dangerous (Fitch et al., 2013).

THINK FOR YOURSELF 5.1 explores a common example of multitasking.

It's hard to socialize while everyone is on their own phone.

● DISCOVERY LAB
Dual-Task Interference Encoding Task

▶ **Think for Yourself 5.1**

Does Listening to Music Impair Learning?

Are you listening to music while reading this? Does listening to music help you concentrate? Can listening to certain types of music, such as Mozart, make you smarter?

In 1993, a study claimed that listening to Mozart, compared with sitting in silence, improved spatial abilities. Although the effects were small, brief, and limited to undergraduate populations, the finding had widespread impact, launching an industry of music collections and videos to make infants smarter. Unfortunately, the Mozart effect was not replicated in several subsequent studies. Tragically, all those videos played to infants were not only unhelpful, but they were likely harmful; the passive time seated in front of a TV deprived the infants of live interaction time with caregivers, which is crucial for language development (Brown et al., 2011).

Whatever small benefit occasionally obtained from music listening can be attributed to arousal effects (Chabris et al., 1999). Music can make people feel more alert or pleasant, and such effects of positive arousal can help people perform better on cognitive tasks. But such effects are not unique to music, and again, they tend to be small. Thus, the Mozart effect could also be called the "Schubert effect" or the "Stephen King effect," in which individuals mainly benefit from listening to audio that they enjoy, even if it's not music but a story excerpt from the popular author Stephen King (Nantais & Schellenberg, 1999).

Depending on the person and what's being played, listening to music can either help you focus or it may distract you from what you're studying.

So does listening to music hurt your studying or not? The answer is complicated, but understanding multitasking research can help sort it out. Studying requires lots of thinking and planning—music is more likely to interfere with your study if the type of music overlaps with the type of studying you're trying to do. For example, music listening disrupts **serial recall**, a form of phonological working memory that involves remembering a series of numbers. And serial recall is important for language learning (Perham & Vizard, 2011).

Unlike the ambiguous and possibly distracting effects of music listening (while studying), the effects of music training

(Continued)

Think for Yourself   (continued)

can be beneficial, enhancing verbal intelligence and cognitive control tasks. However, even these findings have been questioned by subsequent studies and analyses (Sala & Gobet, 2020). Regardless, music training should be its own reward.

Follow your experience. If listening to favored music puts you in a good mood and helps you focus in distracting study settings, then it's probably OK. However, if you have trouble studying effectively while listening to music, stick to a quieter atmosphere. If you don't listen to music while studying, there is no reason to pick up the habit.

Automatic and Controlled Processes

Performing a task that requires minimal cognitive effort is called an **automatic process**. In contrast, performing a task that requires more cognitive involvement is called a **controlled process** (Schneider & Shiffrin, 1977; Shiffrin & Schneider, 1977). The cognitive load is much higher for controlled tasks, such as talking on a cell phone, than for automatic tasks, such as listening to a radio. Managing multiple controlled tasks, or one controlled and one automatic, is more difficult than managing multiple automatic tasks. Hence, talking on a cell phone impairs driving more than listening to music.

Controlled activities typically recruit the brain area prefrontal cortex, which implements cognitive control, or what Norman and Shallice (1980) have called supervisory attentional control. The prefrontal cortex serves as a command center to coordinate the brain's activities. Thus, damage to prefrontal cortex, such as from a stroke, impairs cognitive control. Consider the act of brushing your teeth. This simple task is automatic, but a little cognitive control is needed to initiate it—which is why you may skip it when tired, and why you don't do it at inappropriate times. If shown a toothbrush, patients with prefrontal cortex damage may start brushing their teeth even in the middle of a clinical interview, unable to suppress the habitual urge. Such patients lack cognitive control because the "command center" is dysfunctional (Lhermitte, 1983).

Another example of how prefrontal cortex damage can disrupt cognitive control is with delayed-alternation tasks, in which a reward predictably alternates between the two options. For example, a participant would be rewarded for pressing button A, then button B, then button A, and so forth. Typical individuals can pick up on this rule. However, patients with prefrontal damage will keep picking the option that was previously rewarded, no matter the pattern. These **perseveration errors**—persistent responses that fail to adapt to changing rules or circumstances—are typical of individuals with prefrontal damage.

Inhibition

When you drive a vehicle or ride a bike, the ability to stop or slow down is essential. Imagine not having brakes. Mental tasks also need brakes—when speaking up in class, it's best to avoid any profanity, even if what you're saying is f^#%ing cool. An essential function of cognitive control is **inhibition**, the ability to suppress information, thoughts, or actions that may interfere with ongoing behavior—to tap a brake on mental operations (Aron et al., 2004, 2014).

Inhibition reduces distraction and helps people choose how to act. When driving, it's best to ignore texts, for example. While studying for a test, you need to focus on the course material and inhibit distracting worries or thoughts. For police officers, the stakes are high in quickly deciding whether to use force or inhibit the impulse to do so.

Psychologists have developed several tests to measure inhibition in the laboratory, quantifying how individuals vary greatly in their ability to inhibit.

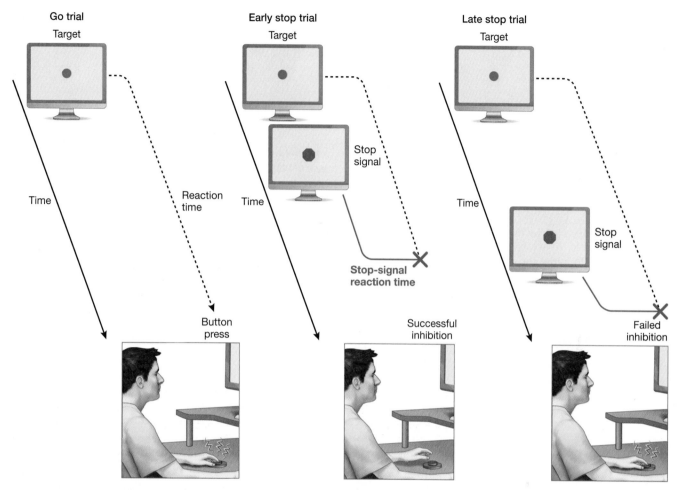

FIGURE 5.1 **The stop-signal task**   Participants respond to the green circle as quickly as possible, except when the stop signal appears. It's hard to stop when the stop signal appears later in the trial, after people have committed to responding to the target. (After S. M. Helfinstein and R. A. Poldrack. 2012. *Nat Neurosci* 15: 803–805.)

The **stop-signal task** (**FIGURE 5.1**) is a classic measure of inhibition (Logan & Cowan, 1984; Logan et al., 1984), in which individuals respond as quickly as possible to a green circle target ("Go trial" in Figure 5.1). Individuals typically respond to this cue within a half-second. On a small proportion of trials, a red circle stop signal appears soon after the target stimulus: participants must stop (withhold) their response to the target on such trials. Most typical individuals are able to inhibit themselves when the stop signal appears early in the trial ("Early-stop trial" in Figure 5.1). However, when the stop signal appears later into the trial, individuals find it more difficult to stop. ("Late-stop trial" in Figure 5.1). The later the stop signal, the harder it is to inhibit the "go" response. People with good inhibition can respond to a late stop signal better than people with poor inhibition.

It is harder to inhibit when rushed, as in the stop-signal task, or when the need to inhibit occurs infrequently. The continuous performance task, introduced in Chapter 4, also requires inhibition—observers must respond differently or withhold their response to an unpredictable and infrequent target (Rosenberg et al., 2013; Rosvold et al., 1956). The continuous performance task reveals decrements in **sustained attention,** or **vigilance** (Barkley, 1997), the ability to maintain focus on a task. Lapses in sustained attention can result in errors on the job or poor grades in school. For truck drivers, air traffic controllers, and soldiers in the field, vigilance can be a matter of life or death.

Classic Tasks

SEE FOR YOURSELF 5.1, and the related Discovery Lab, illustrate how interference and inhibition work in the Stroop task.

▶ See for Yourself 5.1

Stroop Task

Look at **FIGURE A**. For each block of words, say the colors as quickly as possible, while ignoring the words themselves. For example, starting at the top left corner and going across, you would say "red, green, etc." Then try reading the second block of words. The second block is harder because the words conflict with the colors you're trying to name.

According to what's known as **Stroop interference**, it takes longer to name the colors when the word meanings conflict with the ink color (Cohen et al., 1990; MacLeod, 1991; Stroop, 1935). The interference occurs because word reading is highly automatic. Inhibitory processes allow you to suppress the word meanings, so that you focus on naming the color. In the bottom of the figure, the conflicting words cause you to slow down and make more mistakes. The Stroop task shows the importance of cognitive control, which enables

you to inhibit the automatic word meaning to focus on the task of naming the word color.

FIGURE A Stroop interference makes it harder to read the ink colors of the words in the bottom block compared to the top block.

▶ DISCOVERY LAB

Stroop Interference

Real-world examples of Stroop interference can demonstrate bias. Consider a laboratory task in which participants monitored images on a computer screen and were asked to simulate firing at a suspect holding a gun, and to withhold firing at suspects holding a bottle. The task, which requires cognitive control and selective inhibition, tested for unconscious bias by varying the race of the suspects. Participants were more likely to shoot at bottle-holding (i.e., innocent) suspects who were Black than at innocent suspects who were White (Correll et al., 2002). The relation to Stroop interference is that automatic processing may sometimes be linked to unconscious biases that impair cognitive control. Reassuringly, professional police officers did not show this shooting bias in the lab (Correll et al., 2007), although incidents of bias in the real world have fueled activism such as the Black Lives Matter movement.

Another way to test for response conflict is the **Simon task**, also known as the **spatial interference task** (Simon & Rudell, 1967; Simon & Wolf, 1963), in which a spatial incompatibility between the target location and the responding hand slows down response time. **FIGURE 5.2** illustrates an example. Participants fixate their eyes on the middle of the screen, while a target can appear to the right or left of where they're looking. Two conditions are depicted in Figure 5.2. In the compatible condition, the target is blue. When the blue target appears on the left, you press left; when it appears on the right, you press right. In the incompatible condition, the target is green and you make the opposite responses: when the green target appears on the left, you press right, and when the green target appears on the right, you press left. Individuals find it harder to complete the task in the incompatible condition, which requires more cognitive control.

The **flanker task** (**SEE FOR YOURSELF 5.2**) reveals two types of interference: perceptual and response interference

(A) Compatible   **(B) Incompatible**

FIGURE 5.2 The Simon task Participants press the left-hand key for blue targets **(A)** and the right-hand key for green targets **(B)**. However, if the target appears in a location opposite to the finger that is being used, then the incompatibility causes a slowdown and errors, known as the Simon effect. (After W. P. M. van den Wildenberg et al. 2020. *Hum Neurosci* 4: 22.)

(Eriksen & Eriksen, 1974; Hillman et al., 2008). For a demonstration of response interference, in the examples below quickly categorize the middle word as furniture or a metal:

    (A) LAMP DESK LAMP
    (B) GOLD DESK GOLD

This task is much easier in example A, in which the two words on either side belong in the same category, than in example B, in which the two words on either side belong in a different category. Perceptual interference is similar in both cases, but the categorical similarity for "LAMP DESK LAMP" speeds up the judgment, just as the dissimilarity for "GOLD DESK GOLD" slows it down. Similar to what happens in the Stroop task, the flanker words are automatically processed, and need to be inhibited when they are incompatible (Shaffer & LaBerge, 1979).

    To summarize, a wide variety of tasks can test inhibition to resolve interference. The tasks all involve perceptual and response interference, but to different degrees. Some tasks test response inhibition more purely, such as the stop-signal task. Some tasks are more perceptual: the Stroop task involves perceptual conflict between the word meaning and its color, while the Simon task involves interference between the target location and the natural inclination to respond right to things on the right and left to things on the left. Finally, the flanker task allows researchers to separately test both perceptual and response interference.

► **See for Yourself 5.2**

Flanker Task

Start with list 1 (**FIGURE A**) and focus on the middle arrowhead in each row. Try to determine as quickly and accurately as possible whether the middle arrowhead points to the left or right—you can whisper "left" or "right" as you go down the row. Do this again for lists 2 and 3. Compare the difficulty of the three lists.

    The central arrowhead is called the target, and the other distracting stimuli around it are called flankers. Different flankers cause different types of interference. List 2 is harder than list 1 because of **perceptual interference**, caused by distractors that make the target harder to see. It is more difficult to select the middle arrowhead target when the flanker distractors are spaced more closely to the target than when they are spaced farther away. Spatial proximity of distractors causes perceptual interference for target selection.

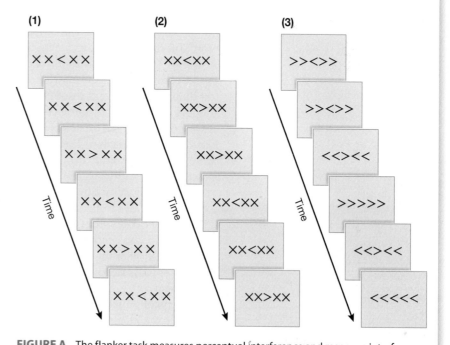

FIGURE A   The flanker task measures perceptual interference and response interference.

    List 3 tends to be harder than list 2 because of **response interference**, a slowing caused by distractors that elicit a conflicting response. In addition to perceptual interference caused by the close spacing, incompatible flankers in the first three and fourth frames of list 3 impose additional response conflict: because the flankers point in the opposite direction as the target arrowhead, the conflicting interference slows you down.

Conflict Monitoring and Resolution

The response to interference is cognitive control, which performs two functions. First, cognitive control processes must detect interference (**conflict monitoring**), such as the word meaning conflict in the Stroop task, a location conflict in the Simon task, or a stop signal in the stop-signal task. Second, once detected, cognitive control mechanisms must reduce that interference (**conflict resolution**), either with inhibition or other behavioral adjustments. This process is what allows people to constantly monitor their own actions, adjust for problems, and compensate for errors. When you make a free throw and miss, you adjust your throw to get the basketball into the hoop on the next try.

Conflict monitoring operates like an alarm system, and a special brain area called the **anterior cingulate cortex** (**ACC**) is the central monitor. Conflict monitoring occurs when multiple perceptual inputs compete for attention or when several response options compete for selection (Botvinick et al., 2001; Carter et al., 1998). Hence, the ACC is active in all the tasks we have discussed that require monitoring for conflicts. The ACC is more active in the Stroop task when the words compete with the colors to be named, or in stop-signal or continuous performance tasks when the signal to withhold a response appears. In the flanker task, the ACC is more active when the distracting stimuli are perceptually close to the target than when they are spaced away from it, and especially when the distractors elicit a response that conflicts with the target response. Trying to respond left to a target appearing on the right-hand side of the screen in the Simon task also activates the ACC.

When the ACC detects these perceptual or cognitive conflicts, it calls out an alarm to other cognitive control mechanisms to inhibit the source of conflict. The **dorsolateral prefrontal cortex** is one of several brain areas important for cognitive control. In the Stroop task, interference activates the ACC and the dorsolateral prefrontal cortex, whose activity correlates with how well participants perform the Stroop task—the more active the dorsolateral prefrontal cortex, the smaller the Stroop interference. The dorsolateral prefrontal cortex inhibits distracting word interference, thus reducing Stroop interference (Carter et al., 1998).

The ACC is important for **error detection** when cognitive control fails. That is, the ACC not only detects interference or problems before people make mistakes, but it also registers and responds to errors. When a mistake happens, the ACC triggers cognitive control mechanisms to adjust performance to reduce further error. Learning from mistakes is important, and the ACC makes that possible, like an internal coach or teacher. If you're playing a car-racing video game and drive too fast around a turn, your car will crash. This is an error that will trigger ACC activity. Accordingly, you—or your dorsolateral prefrontal cortex—will adjust by slowing down the next time you approach a curve.

For all kinds of decisions, the ACC is active whenever a **prediction error** occurs, that is, whenever you do not receive the reward or outcome you predicted. Consider the game rock-paper-scissors. You try to guess what the opponent will throw, and your choice of what you throw depends on that prediction. A prediction error occurs whenever you lose or tie. In decision making, when choosing between two options, one of which provides a reward 80% of the time and the other of which provides a reward 20% of the time, you should choose the one with a higher payoff. However, that option will occasionally not produce a reward (20% of the time), generating a prediction error and activating the ACC (Gehring & Willoughby, 2002).

The ACC initiates an error response (colloquially called the "Oh, sh_t" response), the signal that allows cognitive control mechanisms to respond adaptively to mistakes (Gehring et al., 2000). Natural responses to errors can be easily measured in people using fMRI or EEG. Remember from

Cognitive control helps you race through curves at the right speed to avoid crashing off the track.

Chapter 2 the advantage of EEG over fMRI? EEG is more precise in time, so you can see the response to an error in milliseconds rather than seconds. **FIGURE 5.3** shows a sample EEG response to error called **error-related negativity** (**ERN**) (Gehring et al., 1993). ERN studies have produced many interesting findings. ERN is predictive of various behaviors ranging from substance abuse relapses to severity of obsessive compulsive disorder (OCD) symptoms. A lower ERN is a biomarker (predictor) of relapse from cocaine addiction treatment (Marhe et al., 2013). People with OCD show higher ERNs, suggesting that such individuals are more sensitive to when their standards (e.g., for cleanliness or order) are not met (Gehring et al., 2000).

Speeded Response Selection

People struggle to do more than one thing at a time in rapid succession, constrained by how quickly the brain can control behavior. **Mental chronometry** studies the timing of perceptual and cognitive processing, based on measurements of response time to different stimuli and tasks. From far before the advent of brain imaging, mental chronometry gives important insights into the operations of the mind.

Consider the task, which you can try in the Discovery Lab, of responding to a simple visual signal (which we can call S1) on a computer screen as quickly as possible with a keypress. This response (R1) typically takes less than 600 ms. Now imagine a second, identical signal (S2) appearing on the screen and having to respond (R2) to that as quickly as possible. In theory, the response time R2 to S2 should be similar to that for R1 to S1, because the tasks are the same type. And indeed, when S1 and S2 are spaced apart with enough time, R2 is comparable to R1. However, if S1 appears very soon after S2, R2 is slower than R1. This delay, shown in **FIGURE 5.4**, is called the **psychological refractory period** and reveals a fundamental limitation in information processing (Pashler, 1984, 1994; Welford, 1952).

The psychological refractory period shows a fundamental bottleneck in information processing (Pashler, 1984). Figure 5.4 illustrates how R2 is slowed because the brain is still busy coordinating a response to S1. It's similar to waiting in a line at a fast-food counter: for as long as there is a customer in front of you, you have to wait.

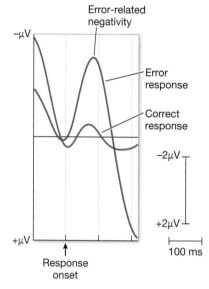

FIGURE 5.3 Error-related negativity (ERN) When people make errors, a large negative signal occurs in the brain potential waveform, shown in red (negative is up), relative to the correct response in blue. (From http://www-personal.umich.edu/~wgehring/research.html, with permission from Bill Gehring.)

 **DISCOVERY LAB**

Dual-Task Interference Psychological Refractory Period Paradigm

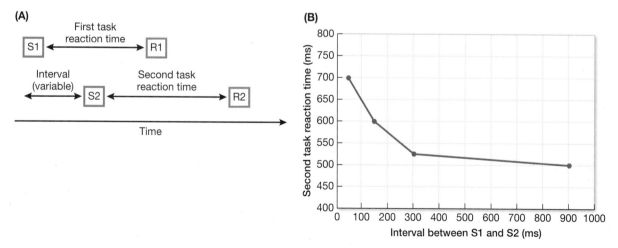

FIGURE 5.4 The dual-task psychological refractory period **(A)** Participants respond to two stimuli (S1 and S2) presented in succession, and the reaction time is measured for each response (R1 and R2). **(B)** The time interval between S1 and S2 varies, and the closer they are in time, the slower the response (R2) is to S2. For short intervals, the slope frequently reaches −1, as if R2 has to wait in a queue until R1 is completed. (From H. Pashler. 1992. *Curr Dir Psychol Sci* 1: 44–48.)

When only one counter is open at a fast-food counter during a busy time, the bottleneck requires customers to wait in line.

The **central bottleneck model** assumes that only one response can be selected at a time, so that the second response is queued. An alternative model for explaining the psychological refractory period is not as a necessary bottleneck but as strategic **resource sharing**. According to this account, responses to both stimuli can be selected at the same time, but priority is strategically given to the first response, slowing the second response (Navon & Miller, 2002; Schumacher et al., 2001; Tombu & Jolicoeur, 2003). To stick with the fast-food analogy, the counter may have multiple cashiers, but perhaps to save money, the restaurant manager may have decided to open only one line. Whether it is explained by the inescapable bottleneck or flexible resource-sharing model, the psychological refractory period reveals limitations in making even the simplest responses in rapid succession (Marois & Ivanoff, 2005; Meyer & Kieras, 1997).

Task Switching and Multitasking

Different forms of study, such as reading, writing a paper, or solving a problem set, all require sustained attention. But while you study, do you check your texts, e-mail, or social media, and if so, how frequently? Does frequent checking affect your focus? Try the demonstration in **SEE FOR YOURSELF 5.3**.

> ▶ **See for Yourself 5.3**
>
> ## Task Switching
>
> For each digit in the first row below, check its color, and if it's red, add 7 to the digit, and if it's black, subtract 7. Do this for each number as quickly as possible. If convenient, use a stopwatch to time how long it takes you to finish the row. Start now:
>
> 48 15 99 67 57 44 81 78 95 41 59 62 34 55 29 35
>
> Now do the same two tasks with the following row. Start timing now:
>
> 97 77 21 64 52 84 13 40 24 31 26 98 92 72 45 81
>
> Which row was harder (slower)?

In lab settings, people find the second row in See for Yourself 5.3 to be more difficult. Participants are slower and less accurate when they have to switch back and forth between tasks, compared with when they can do the same task consecutively without switching (the first row). Note that each row has the same number of addition and subtraction problems. The only difference is that the second row requires you to switch tasks 15 times, while the first row requires you to switch tasks only once. The **task-switch cost** refers to the speed and accuracy penalty that comes with having to switch tasks (Allport et al., 1994; Jersild, 1927; Meiran, 1996; Rogers & Monsell, 1995; Rubinstein et al., 2001). Task-switching away from your study or other work at hand, even momentarily to respond to a text, makes you slower and less accurate.

FIGURE 5.5 shows a common lab task to measure the effects of task switching (Monsell, 2003; Rogers & Monsell, 1995). Each display has a letter or digit target, appearing in one of four positions. The target location shifts around the four locations from trial to trial in a systematic and predictable way, and the task that individuals must perform varies by position. If the target appears in the top row, participants perform the letter task; if the target appears in

(A)

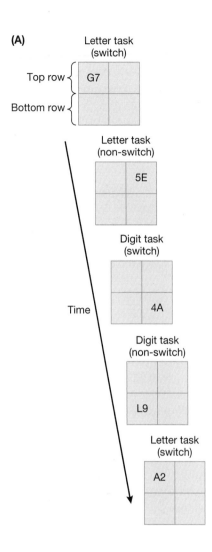

(B)

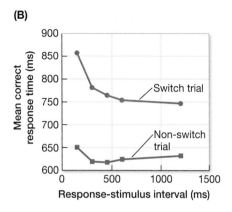

FIGURE 5.5 The task switch cost   (A) Each grid is a trial. When the target appears in the top row, participants respond to the letter (consonant/vowel), and when the target appears in the bottom row, participants respond to the digit (odd/even). From trial to trial, the target changes locations predictably (here, in a counterclockwise direction). **(B)** Despite this predictability, whenever the task switches (from letter to digit or from digit to letter task), people are slower, as indicated by the big difference between the red line for switch trials and the blue line for non-switch trials. The less time people have between targets, the higher the switch cost. (From S. Monsell. 2003. *Trends Cogn Sci* 7: 134–140. Based on R. D. Rogers and S. Monsell. 1995. *J Exp Psychol Gen* 124: 207–231.)

the bottom row, they perform the digit task. Notice that for half the trials, individuals repeat the same task, when the target stays on the top or bottom row. For the other half of the trials, the target switches from top to bottom or bottom to top and individuals must perform the alternate test. The switch is predictable based on location.

The letter/digit task demonstrates the **preparation effect**: increasing the time between targets (trials) gives people more time to prepare and thus reduces the task-switch cost. Back to the example of checking your texts while working on a paper: every time you text, your writing will suffer when you switch back to it, whereas having some transition time between the tasks can lessen the distraction. However, regardless of this preparation, a significant cost persists whenever you switch tasks. In the letter/digit task, even with long delays with ample time to prepare for the next target (again, the task is predictable based on location), the task-switch cost does not completely go away—this is known as the **residual switch cost** (Monsell, 2003; Rogers & Monsell, 1995). Lots of practice will reduce the residual switch cost, but it will not totally eliminate it (Berryhill & Hughes, 2009). That is, no matter how experienced you may be at multitasking while studying, the research suggests that you will always be less efficient and accurate than if you work in a more focused manner that minimizes going back and forth between tasks.

Task switching requires cognitive control. The brain has to work harder to implement the task switch. Cognitive control mechanisms in prefrontal cortex are more active during task switch trials than in trials that do not require a task switch (Braver et al., 2003; Sohn et al., 2000). Thus, when you multitask you're actually making your brain work harder, like hiking with a heavy backpack versus none, or like running in a zigzag rather than a straight line. For most people, the sense of being more efficient while multitasking is an illusion. Evidence shows that it's best to work in a way that minimizes task switching. Silence and put away your phone, and you'll get more work done.

➤ CHECKPOINT 5.1

1. In what ways do task load and overlap help explain dual-task interference?
2. Give examples of automatic tasks versus controlled tasks.
3. Explain the following tasks and what they reveal: stop-signal task, continuous performance task, Stroop task, Simon task, and flanker task.
4. What is the psychological refractory period, and what are the two major theories to explain it?
5. In task switching, what are the preparation effect and the residual switch cost?

5.2 Working Memory

A desktop can be a useful analogy for how the mind works. While writing a paper or studying, you need to pull together the material most essential for your project. On your physical desk you can lay out textbooks, a notebook, and a laptop. Or you can open windows on the virtual desktop of your computer— one for your word processor, and other browser windows for your reference materials. Whether real or virtual, your desktop is physically constrained. There's a limit to how many items you can place on it and easily access. You can display only one or two active windows before you run out of screen space. You can start piling things one on top of one another, but that requires some juggling (task switching!), reducing your efficiency.

Similarly, the mind is limited in how much information it can actively manage at any given moment. Vast amounts of information are stored in long-term memory, retrievable as needed. But at any given time, the mind can actively and efficiently work with only a limited amount of this material on its mental desktop—what researchers call *working memory*.

Working memory is "a brain system that provides temporary storage and manipulation of the information necessary for such complex cognitive tasks as language comprehension, learning, and reasoning," according to Alan Baddeley (1992, p. 556), who developed the most influential model for working memory (Baddeley, 1992; Baddeley & Hitch, 1974). Working memory is essential for almost everything you do with your mind. Not only does it involve how information is manipulated (cognitive control), it also posits temporary storage of information. Working memory is a central concept in cognitive psychology because it is at "the interface between perception, long-term memory, and action" (Baddeley, 2003, p. 829) (**FIGURE 5.6**).

Storage maintains information after it is no longer available in perception— no longer visible, audible, or touchable. Thus, it is a form of internal attention. When you read a textbook or listen to how a professor describes a study, and then look away to your computer to summarize an idea in your own words, you need to temporarily store that information in working memory. Likewise, when you recall information from your past experience in long-term memory, that information gets stored in working memory. The momentary storage of information is short-term memory, and we will consider multiple forms of short-term memory in Chapter 7. But working memory does more than hold information in short-term memory.

Working memory is like a desktop for your mind with easy access to information you need.

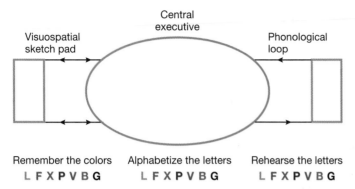

FIGURE 5.6 The basic structure of working memory with examples of its functions
The central executive of working memory manipulates information, as when you need to alphabetize a scrambled list of letters. Different kinds of information are stored in different storage systems of working memory. The visuospatial sketchpad holds visual information such as colors. The phonological loop allows you to remember phonological information, such as a list of letters. (After A. D. Baddeley. 1990. *Human Memory: Theory & Practice*, p. 71. Laurence Erlbaum Associates, East Sussex, UK. © 1990. Reproduced by permission of Taylor and Francis Group, LLC, a division of Informa plc. Based on A. D. Baddeley. 1986. *Working Memory*. Oxford University Press: Oxford; A. Baddeley and G. J. Hitch. 1974. In *The Psychology of Learning and Motivation: Advances in Research and Theory*, G. A. Bower [Ed.], 8: 47–89. Academic Press: New York.)

Working memory is where the mind **manipulates**—performs operations on and transforms—information. In your head, try subtracting 37 from 52. Your ability to do so relies on working memory: the act of sequencing the arithmetic operations in your head requires more than storage of information. You are actively manipulating information, and you can try this in the Discovery Lab on operation span. When people miscalculate simple arithmetic, it is usually not because they have forgotten how to do math or how to solve the problem. Rather, pieces of information slip out from working memory storage, or simple errors occur during manipulation (Hitch, 1978).

Working memory correlates strongly with intelligence, especially mental puzzle-solving abilities (Carpenter et al., 1990; Kyllonen & Christal, 1990). High working memory predicts better reading comprehension and success in school. How people differ in these working memory tasks can also predict how well someone can follow directions (Engle, 2002; Kane & Engle, 2003). For example, beyond the classroom, working memory can predict airplane pilot skills (Carretta et al., 1996; Sohn & Doane, 2004). Active duty U.S. Air Force pilots of F-15 fighter jets were evaluated for their situational awareness, an essential skill for pilots to track their location in space and in time, in addition to other dynamic information required to fly a plane. When also tested for different cognitive skills, scores on working memory, spatial reasoning, and divided attention correlated with situational awareness in these pilots (Carretta et al., 1996).

The Structure of Working Memory

According to Baddeley's model, Working memory involves the *central executive* and three subcomponents (**FIGURE 5.7**). The **central executive** is the primary system for controlling attention and thinking—this is where information is manipulated—and it operates over information temporarily stored in two separate buffers. The **phonological loop** stores and rehearses verbal and acoustic information, while the **visuospatial sketchpad** stores and manipulates visual information. The **episodic buffer** is multimodal, which means it integrates information from multiple internal sources—such as the phonological loop, the visuospatial sketchpad, and long-term memory—into an episodic representation. The term "episodic" refers to the object or event in mind at the moment

DISCOVERY LAB
Operation Span

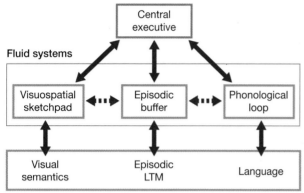

FIGURE 5.7 The structure of working memory with the episodic buffer added as a modern update The central executive integrates information from the visuospatial sketchpad, the phonological loop, and crystallized systems that represent long-term knowledge, memory, and language. The other systems are fluid capacities that involve attention, have limited capacity, and are unchanged by learning. (After A. Baddeley. 2000. *Trends Cogn Neurosci* 4: 417–423.)

or extended across time. A key feature of all of these stores is their limited capacity; each can store only a limited number of items for a brief amount of time.

This proposed architecture of separate components is supported by extensive dual-task studies, neuropsychological evidence, and brain imaging studies. Patterns of dual-task interference support a separation between phonological and visuospatial storage systems. As we discussed in Section 5.1, interference occurs when an individual tries to perform two tasks that use the same storage system. By contrast, when two tasks do not interfere with each other, researchers infer that they are independent. As an example, phonological (verbal) tasks and visuospatial tasks do not strongly interfere with each other, suggesting they use separate storage systems. Consider an experiment with two tasks. One involves visuospatial imagery, such as imagining objects in different locations around the room; the other consists of repeating the names of items either under your breath or in your head. Participants are asked to perform each of these tasks in addition to a visuospatial dual-task, such as tracking a spot of light on a computer screen (Brooks, 1967). The concurrent visuospatial task impairs visuospatial learning more than it impairs phonological repetition learning.

Beyond these patterns of behavioral interference, neuropsychological data distinguish the phonological loop and the visuospatial sketchpad (both of which we discuss in more detail shortly). For example, both are affected separately by different types of brain lesions. Some patients are impaired at short-term memory tasks that use verbal information but not at tasks that rely on spatial information, while other patients have difficulty with spatial tasks but not with verbal tasks. These patterns suggest that the two forms of short-term memory are separate (De Renzi & Nichelli, 1975). Brain imaging studies further reveal that phonological tasks and visuospatial tasks activate different brain regions, with further subdivisions depending on whether storage or active rehearsal is involved (Smith & Jonides, 1999; Wager & Smith, 2003). In addition, as we detail next, tasks that require manipulation of information typically activate prefrontal cortex more strongly than do tasks that require only storage.

The Central Executive

Like the central processing unit (CPU) chip in your computer, the central executive is the command center for working memory, performing all the work of cognitive control reviewed earlier in the chapter: inhibition, response selection, and task switching. It also supports decision making and planning (see Chapters 9 and 10). Finally, the central executive directs attention to important information in the environment (external attention) or in the mind, such as memories and thoughts (internal attention).

The brain recruits prefrontal cortex to perform central executive functions such as dealing with response conflict, divided attention, task switching, working memory load, and problem solving (Duncan & Owen, 2000). The central executive is especially active in situations that require manipulation of information, beyond just storage. Consider the difference between storage and manipulation for a sequence of letters such as *L F X P V B G*. To remember the sequence of letters across a brief delay of a few seconds would require only working memory storage. However, to reorder the sequence of letters into alphabetical order during the delay period would require manipulation. Prefrontal cortex is more strongly activated in the manipulation condition, pointing to the central executive's extra work (D'Esposito et al., 1999). The central executive also manages dual-task demands. Accordingly, the prefrontal cortex is more active when verbal and spatial working memory tasks need to be performed together, as compared with when they are performed in isolation (D'Esposito et al., 1998).

Executive function has separable components, including mental set shifting, information updating, and inhibition (Miyake et al., 2000). Mental set shifting includes task switching. Information updating is closely related to working memory storage and maintenance. Inhibition was reviewed in its own section earlier in this chapter. Evidence for separable components comes from analyzing how people perform in a wide variety of tasks that require executive control. Researchers observe similar performance among tasks associated with the same component, suggesting common mechanisms. Clinical observations reveal that individuals tend to fail at tasks that correlate with each other, but not at executive tasks that do not correlate (Duncan et al., 1997; Godefroy et al., 1999).

The Phonological Loop

The phonological loop is the component of working memory that allows you to briefly remember verbal material. It has two mechanisms: (1) a **phonological store** that holds sound- or speech-based information for 1 to 2 seconds, and (2) an **articulatory rehearsal loop**, which occurs through inner speech (uttering things to yourself without vocalizing out loud) (Baddeley, 1992). Subvocal articulation maintains phonological information either through rehearsal, like when you repeat the spelling of someone's name in your head as you type it in (B-A-D-D-E-L-E-Y), or when you try to learn an important foreign phrase when traveling ("¿Dónde está el baño?"). Articulatory rehearsal happens in real time, and is limited in capacity, such that when the number of items to rehearse increases, the earlier items start to be forgotten.

PHONOLOGICAL STORE   Storage capacity is commonly tested with the **digit-span task**, which you can try in the Discovery Lab. An experimenter reads you a series of numbers, such as "7, 4, 9," and you immediately repeat them back. If you can do this perfectly, the experimenter tests you on longer lists (e.g., "2, 5, 3, 9, 1, 7, 8, 1, 0") until you start to make errors. The point where you start to make errors is the capacity of your articulatory rehearsal loop. The capacity differs across individuals.

DISCOVERY LAB
Memory Span

ARTICULATORY REHEARSAL LOOP   On average, the articulatory rehearsal loop can hold about seven plus or minus two items (Miller, 1956). That is, when a large group of people are tested, their average performance in digit-span tasks is about seven items plus or minus two. These estimates are approximate because individual performance is variable, and because studies demonstrate inconsistency in how to define what an "item" is. Is an item a single digit such as 7, or can a three-digit number, such as 453 count as an item? If you could remember 7 three-digit "items," then your capacity would add up to 21 digits. To address this debate, Miller proposed that working memory capacity was **seven plus or minus two** "**chunks**," where a chunk is flexibly defined to be whatever unit is meaningful to the participant. To illustrate chunking, consider the following list of digits:

1 4 9 1 6 2 5 3 6 4 9 6 4 8 1

This list exceeds the traditional working memory capacity of even the brightest student. However, it becomes easier if you just remember the squares of 1 2 3 4 5 6 7 8 9. Chunking is a useful way to enhance everyday memory, which we will discuss again in Chapter 6.

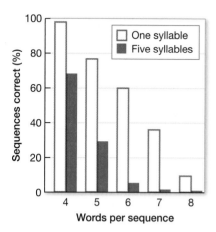

FIGURE 5.8 Effect of word length on memory span People can remember more one-syllable words (e.g., sum, hate, harm, wit, bond, yield, worst, twice) than five-syllable words (association, opportunity, representative, organization, considerable, immediately, university, individual). (From A. D. Baddeley. 1975. *J Verbal Learning Verbal Behav* 14: 575–589.)

VERBAL RECALL IS PHONOLOGICAL What is the capacity of phonological working memory? In what is known as the **word-length effect**, the working memory capacity for words or other phonological stimuli depends on the spoken duration or syllable length of the words (**FIGURE 5.8**). As a rough guide, people can remember about as many items as can be uttered in 2 seconds (Baddeley et al., 1975; Ellis & Hennelly, 1980; Naveh-Benjamin & Ayres, 1986). Interestingly, the word-length effect predicts that people who speak more quickly have higher working memory spans (Baddeley et al., 1975). It also explains the curious finding that English and Chinese speakers have a larger working memory span for digits than do Arabic speakers (Ellis & Hennelly, 1980; Naveh-Benjamin & Ayres, 1986). Digits in English average one syllable in length, excluding 7, as do digits in Chinese: 1 is [ee], 5 is [wu], 9 is [jiu], and so on. In contrast, digits in Arabic average more than two syllables, making them phonologically longer to name: 1 is [wahid], 3 is [thalaatha], and 8 is [thamania]. Thus, rehearsing the same number of digits requires more syllables in Arabic than in English. Since the phonological store is limited by the number of syllables it can maintain, Arabic speakers have been found to fit fewer phonologically long digits into working memory, even while their working memory capacity is otherwise similar to that of English and Chinese speakers.

The acoustic nature of the phonological loop is also shown by the **acoustic similarity effect**, the reduced capacity of working memory for items similar in sound, compared with items that are dissimilar in sound (Baddeley, 1966; Conrad, 1964). Individuals find it harder to recall a series of similar words such as "man, cap, can, map, mad" than one of dissimilar words such as "pit, day, cow, pen, rig." Similar-sounding words are more prone to be confused, suggesting that words are coded in working memory acoustically rather than by meaning.

Since the phonological loop involves rehearsal of spoken material, presenting irrelevant speech disrupts it (Colle & Welsh, 1976; Salamé & Baddeley, 1982), while presenting non-phonological sounds (e.g., bursts of noise) does not. The **irrelevant speech effect** refers to the impairment of working memory by irrelevant spoken material. It occurs even if the irrelevant spoken material involves nonsense words (e.g., "blicket") or words from a foreign language. Thus, it is not the meaning that interferes, but the phonological syllables themselves. On those occasions where a neighboring conversation is so distracting that you "can't hear yourself think," you may be suffering from the irrelevant speech effect.

Patients with working-memory deficits typically have problems with their phonological loop. Because these individuals do not rely on phonological short-term memory, they encode words visually. They thus do not show a acoustic similarity effect or a word-length effect (Vallar & Baddeley, 1984). Furthermore, patients who lack the ability for inner speech show reduced short-term memory span (Baddeley & Wilson, 1985).

These patient effects can be simulated in unaffected individuals with **articulatory suppression**, which is the disruption of working memory that occurs when uttering irrelevant sounds. Individuals who utter an irrelevant sound, which can be repetitive, such as "da da da …," are unable to rehearse material in the phonological loop. Articulatory suppression impairs working memory (Baddeley et al., 1975), but only for verbal, not visual, information (Baddeley et al., 1984). Also, because it directly affects the phonological store, articulatory suppression removes or blocks the word-length effect or the acoustic similarity effect (Baddeley et al., 1984; Murray, 1968).

THE PHONOLOGICAL LOOP AND LANGUAGE LEARNING IN CHILDREN
It's easy to see how the phonological loop is important for language learning, especially in children. Higher phonological loop capacity is predictive of the

ability to learn a second language. Hence, the loop may have evolved to facilitate language acquisition. Children with language disorders typically show specific difficulties in their phonological loops (Gathercole & Baddeley, 1990), revealing deficits in hearing and repeating back unfamiliar nonwords. Furthermore, the ability to repeat words or nonwords in the phonological loop is highly correlated with general vocabulary at the time of testing and even 1 year later.

Better verbal working memory correlates with better reading comprehension skills. Verbal working memory can be measured in a variety of ways. As one example, imagine you are asked to listen to a series of short sentences and remember the last word in each sentence. After hearing "The sailor sold the parrot. The vicar opened the book," you would respond "parrot, book." This task gets harder when more sentences are read. Individual working memory span correlates with reading comprehension abilities (Just & Carpenter, 1992). Reading comprehension can be measured with standardized tests such as the SAT. The correlation between working memory and performance on these tests is strong. The phonological loop facilitates learning a new vocabulary, and children's auditory digit span correlates with their vocabulary levels (Baddeley et al., 1998; Gathercole & Baddeley, 1989; Gathercole et al., 1997; Metsala, 1999).

The phonological loop is important for language, such as when reading.

Several brain regions, especially prefrontal cortex, are active during phonological tasks. Activity levels in several regions in the prefrontal cortex depend on working memory load. As the number of verbal letters to remember increases, so does activity in prefrontal cortex (Braver et al., 1997). Finally, neuroimaging evidence supports the distinction between the phonological store and the subvocal articulatory rehearsal loop, as subvocalization activates Broca's area, an area important for real speech. Studies have found that phonological information is stored differently than non-phonological (e.g., visual) information (Paulesu et al., 1993).

The Visuospatial Sketchpad

In See for Yourself 4.2 you tried several demonstrations in which it was difficult to detect a change between two images. The images are challenging because you can remember only a few details at a time, typically those at fixation. So your eyes need to move around to sample and compare the visual details.

Your ability to detect visual change depends on the visuospatial sketchpad. The visuospatial sketchpad is separate from the phonological loop, and both have limited capacity. The function of the visuospatial sketchpad, also known more generally as **visual short-term memory**, is to retain visual information over time, especially when the perceptual image is no longer available, or has changed, most commonly whenever you move your eyes. Because visual acuity is limited to where you fixate, you move your eyes extensively to explore your surroundings. Visual short-term memory helps stitch together information from one fixation to another.

Defining the limited capacity of visual short-term memory raises unique challenges. For phonological memory, the unit of capacity was phonological length, which seems easy to define: a word is a word, and a syllable is a syllable. Syllables are of similar acoustic length, and more syllables take up more capacity. However, visual objects range in size from the period at the end of this sentence to the size of the room in which you're reading this book. Thus, visual capacity is more ambiguous to define: Is the basic unit a set of pixels in a small area around fixation, and if so, what size? Or is it a visual feature such as color or shape (e.g., red, blue, vertical, horizontal)? Or is the unit of visual short-term memory an object (e.g., a red vertical line)? Are all objects treated equally, regardless of complexity, taking up the same "storage space" in the brain?

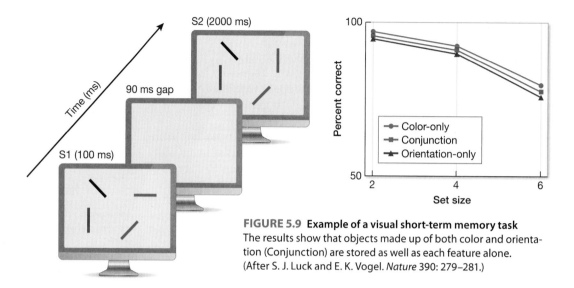

FIGURE 5.9 Example of a visual short-term memory task
The results show that objects made up of both color and orientation (Conjunction) are stored as well as each feature alone. (After S. J. Luck and E. K. Vogel. *Nature* 390: 279–281.)

To examine whether visual short-term memory stores features or objects, researchers have used change-detection tasks. In a typical experiment, illustrated in **FIGURE 5.9**, the number of items can vary from one to six. These items are flashed on a computer screen and then replaced with a blank screen. In the color task, observers are asked to remember the colors of the items, ignoring their orientations. After about 1–2 seconds—an interval that requires the participant to retain the no-longer-visible image in visual short-term memory—a probe item appears in one of the target locations. Participants respond whether the probe matches the color of the target item that previously appeared in the same location or not. Participants in these studies have no problem remembering the colors when only one or two items have to be coded into visual short-term memory. However, they start to make mistakes when the number of items increases beyond four. Based on the mistakes participants make, most individuals have the capacity to remember four color features. Results are similar for remembering four different orientations, when observers are asked to remember the orientations and to ignore the colors. Thus, according to these studies, the capacity of visual short-term memory is about four features (Luck & Vogel, 1997).

However, we usually care about multiple features; when you buy a dress, you care about both the style (shape) and the color. Can features be chunked into objects, so that more features can be attended to and remembered? These questions can be explored using the same type of experiment as that shown in Figure 5.9, but with different task instructions. Instead of focusing on just color or just orientation, participants were asked to remember both the color and the orientation of each item. Then, after a delay, the probe item reappeared with or without a change in color or in orientation. Because these instructions double the number of features that participants have to maintain in visual short-term memory, the task is more demanding. If visual short-term memory capacity is defined by visual features, performance will break down when more than two objects have to be remembered, because that involves more than four features. However, if visual short-term memory capacity is defined by objects, which chunk visual features, then visual short-term memory performance for four objects (eight features) should be comparable to that for four features. The results indicate that individuals chunk features into objects. Participants were able to remember as many multifeatured objects as they could individual features. Visual short-term memory capacity is about four objects, and each object can contain multiple features. **THINK FOR YOURSELF 5.2** explores this topic in more detail.

► **Think for Yourself 5.2**

Object Complexity and Visual Short-Term Memory

Can each object contain an infinite number of features? According to the **slot model** of visual short-term memory, in which a slot corresponds to an object, visual short-term memory can store all of the object's features without reducing the capacity for other objects, up to about four objects. You can think of the slot model as a waiting room with four chairs. Any four people can sit in them, regardless of whether they're small children or large adults. By contrast, the **resource model** of visual short-term memory suggests that capacity is a limited resource that has to be shared by all the objects. So the overall capacity for objects depends on the complexity of each object. In the seating analogy, the resource model is like a bench that seats four people on average, but it can flexibly seat more small children or fewer large adults.

The slot model and the resource model can be pitted against each other by using more complex objects. Objects differ in detail and parts, as illustrated on the left side of **FIGURE A**. If the chunking of features has unlimited capacity, the complexity of objects should not affect visual short-term memory. However, it does—people can hold remember fewer complex objects (e.g., shaded cubes) than simple objects (e.g., colored squares) in visual short-term memory. Capacity correlates with how complex the objects are, as quantified by how quickly participants can scan through them in a separate search task. The more complex the items, the slower people are to search through them (higher search rate), and the fewer they can hold in visual short-term memory (higher threshold on the *x*-axis).

Addressing the debate over whether the slot model or resource model is correct, brain data suggest that the answer is both (Todd & Marois, 2004; Xu & Chun, 2006). One brain imaging study showed that visual short-term memory capacity is constrained by the superior intraparietal sulcus (IPS). As shown in Figure 5.9, visual short-term memory can hold up to about four items and then drops; activity in the superior IPS mirrors this behavioral performance, rising from one to four features and then plateauing. When more complex objects have to be maintained in working memory, performance starts to fail after two objects, and the superior IPS follows that pattern as well, supporting a resource model of visual working memory. However, another brain area, the inferior IPS, shows a different pattern, increasing in activity up to about four objects, regardless of object complexity and performance, which is what a slot model would predict. In sum, the human brain reveals both mechanisms of visual short-term memory: the superior IPS is sensitive to features or resources, like bench seating, and the inferior IPS is sensitive to objects or slots, like individual chairs.

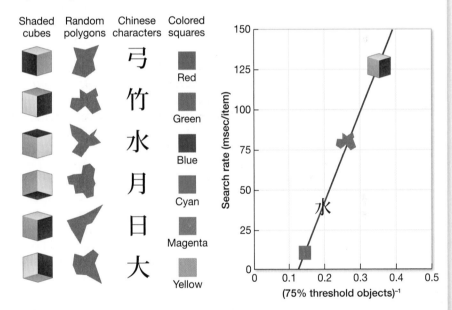

FIGURE A Visual complexity and visual short-term memory   Visual short-term capacity decreases (moving right on the *x*-axis) as visual complexity increases from simple color patches to complex shaded cubes, as measured by slower search rates (moving up on the *y*-axis). (After G. A. Alvarez and P. Cavanagh. 2004. *Psychol Sci* 15: 106–111. © 2004 American Psychological Society. Right panel based on H. Pashler. 1988. *Percept Psycho* 44: 369–378.)

Because visual short-term memory stores objects, one can ask how it represents more complex real-world objects. For example, when you think of a face, such as that of your mother, how does your brain allow you to do this in her absence? Maintaining an image of a face activates the face area of the brain, while maintaining an image of a scene activates the scene area of the brain (Johnson & Johnson, 2009). That is, "thinking" about something involves reactivating the brain regions involved in "perceiving" that object. These working memory representations are so close to those used in perception that fMRI can decode which objects are being held in working memory

FIGURE 5.10 An array of identical dots
How can one track these dots as different, distinct objects when they look the same? Spatial location is an important feature for individuating (distinguishing) objects.

even in the absence of an active perceptual stimulus (Harrison & Tong, 2009; Serences et al., 2009).

Besides object identity, a central feature of visual objects is their location. In fact, location and position should be considered as a special feature, critical because position helps identify and distinguish objects. Consider the display in **FIGURE 5.10**. The objects are all identical, so how do you distinguish them? Position allows you to **individuate** the objects, tracking them as separate entities based on location, as discussed in See for Yourself 4.1.

A separate working memory system holds spatial information. To test this, researchers presented participants with several objects identical in shape, as in Figure 5.10. After a delay, one of the objects may have shifted its location, and participants had to determine if it did or not. This task uses spatial working memory and is associated with activity in dorsolateral brain areas, as opposed to ventrolateral brain areas for objects (Courtney, 1998; D'Esposito et al., 1998; Jonides et al., 1993).

Relation to Long-Term Memory

Working memory is fleeting, compared to the more permanent **long-term memory** (see Figure 6.1). When you make a new friend at a party, you will initially remember his or her name in working memory. However, in order to recognize him or her the next day, you need to store his or her name and face in long-term memory (Atkinson & Shiffrin, 1968).

Researchers debate the relation between working memory and long-term memory. On the one hand, the two systems are independent. By definition, long-term memory has significantly greater capacity and durability than working memory. On the other hand, long-term memory needs to be active or recruited during working memory tasks. For example, chunking effects rely on long-term knowledge. When glancing at a chessboard, chess masters can remember richer configurations of pieces than novices can (Chase & Simon, 1973), not because chess masters have vastly better working memory, but because their knowledge and expertise allow them to group (chunk) more pieces into working memory. If expertise matters, consider what happens if the chess pieces are scrambled on a board in an unusual way that one would not see in a real match. Then the chess master benefit goes away.

Findings like these have led some researchers to propose that working memory is selective activation of long-term memory (Cowan, 1988; Ericsson & Kintsch, 1995). This construes working memory as sustained attention on long-term memory representations. Long-term memory stores knowledge and memories, while attention selects and activates the relevant information according to task.

It is in order to address these points that Baddeley proposed that working memory involves an episodic buffer, a storage space for the executive controller to combine information from the phonological loop and visuospatial sketchpad. Thus, it constructs new representations on the fly rather than reactivating old memories, like freshly mixing olive oil, vinegar, and spices to toss with your salad, rather than pulling out the bottle of premade dressing from the refrigerator. The contents of the episodic buffer are accessible by conscious awareness (Baddeley, 2000; Baddeley & Lieberman, 1980; Dehaene & Naccache, 2001).

A strong link between working memory and attention is evidenced by overlap between brain systems for spatial attention and for spatial working memory. When you are directing attention to a particular location on a screen, working memory is enhanced for that location, and vice versa. The spatial foci of working memory and attention are closely linked, and both tasks activate similar brain regions (Awh & Jonides, 2001).

► CHECKPOINT 5.2

1. What is working memory, and what are its two primary functions?

2. What is the structure of Baddeley's working memory model, and how do the components relate to each other?

3. What is the evidence that the phonological loop is phonological?

4. What is visual short-term memory, and how can its capacity be characterized?

5.3 Influences on Cognitive Control and Working Memory

Cognitive control and working memory are central for intelligent behavior. People vary greatly in their cognitive abilities. These skills take time to fully develop into adulthood, but they are then particularly vulnerable to decline after age 70. Accordingly, it's useful to consider the factors that either impair or enhance cognitive control and working memory.

Cognitive Control and Emotion

The study of internal attention and cognitive control is relevant for clinical disorders such as depression and anxiety. According to estimates published by the National Institute of Mental Health (NIMH, 2021), major depression is one of the most debilitating mental disorders, affecting about 7% of adults in the U.S. each year. Anxiety disorders also create emotional burden for individuals and their families, affecting about 19% of adults each year. Thus, treatment is a high priority, and the two major types are pharmacological and behavioral.

Behavioral intervention has a central role in the treatment of mood disorders, which frequently involve problems with **emotion regulation** (Ochsner & Gross, 2005; Ochsner et al., 2002). The ability to manage one's emotions is a cognitive control function. It is natural to feel depressed or anxious on occasion. However, it becomes debilitating if you can't manage these emotions; instead, they consume your thoughts all the time. Recall that cognitive control inhibits unwanted distraction. It is useful to be able to inhibit maladaptive negative thoughts that do not have a basis in reality, for example, dwelling on how someone dislikes or disrespects you, even though he or she actually may feel neutral about you.

Many people with major depressive disorder show **rumination**, an incessant focus on one's negative thoughts. Rumination occurs when people find it difficult to disengage attention (inhibit) from negative thoughts about oneself, interpersonal relationships, or stressful events (Cisler & Koster, 2010; Koster et al., 2011). Rumination prolongs depression because of negative thinking that interferes with positive problem solving. This focus on negative thoughts and memories is a form of internal attention. Ruminative behaviors are more common in women and start in adolescence (Nolen-Hoeksema, 1991, 2000). Chapters 4 and 12 describe the cognitive control of emotion in more detail.

More generally, emotion regulation manages and even inhibits negative stimuli and thoughts, which otherwise disrupt cognition (and well-being). People get more distracted by emotional stimuli such as a fearful face, spiders, snakes, or a bad grade. In the lab, working memory is impaired more significantly by emotional stimuli than by neutral stimuli (Bishop et al., 2004). The ability to ignore or suppress emotional distraction, as a form of cognitive control,

Cognitive control can help with managing emotions like stress or anger.

© iStock.com/imtmphoto

Fearful faces like this capture attention, and they can cause distraction even when people are instructed to ignore them.

depends on prefrontal cortical mechanisms that are active when a threatening stimulus appears.

People who are more anxious in general show broader difficulties with cognitive control of attention even during nonthreatening situations (Eysenck et al., 2007). Recall that in the flanker task, a participant's response to a target is slowed by a distractor that appears close to the target and that requires a different, conflicting response. Individuals vary in how vulnerable they are to this interference, reflecting differences in cognitive control. Participants who separately report high trait anxiety, not while doing the task but over life in general, perform poorly in the flanker task relative to those who report low trait anxiety. And consistent with the neural substrates of cognitive control described earlier, high-trait-anxiety participants show lower prefrontal activity in high-conflict trials, suggesting that this region of the brain is presumably less effective. In sum, even in a task that does not use emotional stimuli, individuals with high trait anxiety are more susceptible to distraction, suggesting impaired cognitive control (Bishop, 2009).

Stress and Working Memory

Taking an exam can be stressful when you feel pressure to do well or when you do not feel comfortable with the material. Unfortunately, stress itself can make matters worse, causing you to perform more poorly than you would otherwise. The **Yerkes–Dodson curve** describes how performance suffers as a result of anxiety, especially for difficult tasks—those requiring a high degree of cognitive control (**FIGURE 5.11**) (Arnsten, 1998; Diamond, 2013; Liston et al., 2009).

The relation between stress and lower performance is well documented. "Choking" under pressure is evident during exams. Mathematical problem solving is a good domain to study this because it is highly dependent on prefrontal function, and performance can be precisely measured (Beilock & Carr, 2005). Stress and anxiety take up working memory capacity that should be devoted to problem solving (Ashcraft & Kirk, 2001). Participants in one experiment performed simple but demanding math tasks, such as "Subtract 19 from 51. Does this divide evenly by 4 (no remainder)?" In the low-pressure condition, the test was described as practice. In the high-pressure condition that followed, participants were informed that both their speed and accuracy would be monitored, and that they would receive $5 for a 20% improvement over the practice round. To add social pressure, the participants were randomly paired with another individual, and both teammates had to improve for each to receive $5. On top of this, the participants were told that their teammate had already improved by 20%, so participants would feel more pressure and anxiety to do well for both to get the bonus. And if all that were not enough, participants were additionally notified that their performance would be videotaped and reviewed by local math teachers and professors, so a video camera was taping the entire test. Feeling the stress yet?

As you may expect, added pressure hurt performance. Perhaps more surprising, however, was

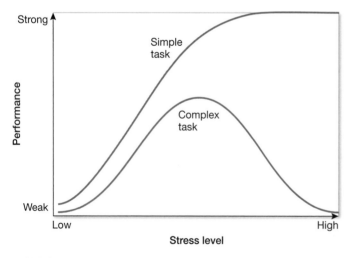

FIGURE 5.11 Arousal (stress) influences performance
Performance is lowest when arousal (stress) levels are either too low or too high, and complex tasks are more severely impaired by arousal than simple tasks are. (From D. M. Diamond et al. 2007. *Neural Plast* 33: 1–33 CC BY 3.0. Based on R. M. Yerkes and J. D. Dodson. 1908. *J Comp Neurol Psychol* 18: 459–482.)

that only the good performers suffered in this study. That is, individuals with high working memory capacity, measured separately, suffered more. Beilock and Carr noted that "individuals most likely to fail under pressure are those who, in the absence of pressure, have the highest capacity for success" (Beilock & Carr, 2005, p. 104).

So you need to find ways to alleviate stress, and here are a few simple tips. Make sure you get enough rest. Physical exercise is good for both mind and body alike. Engage in activities that make you happy, like hanging out with friends or pursuing hobbies. Perform for yourself, and not for others. Even writing about your anxieties can help your grades (Cohen et al., 2006). Mindfulness training can help alleviate the harmful effects of stress (Jha, 2010); common methods include meditation, prayer, yoga, and being out in nature.

Ego Depletion

Just as excessive physical activity makes you physically tired, overuse of mental resources produces mental fatigue. **Ego depletion** occurs when one's energy for mental activity is exhausted, impairing cognitive control and other cognitive activities (Baumeister et al., 1998). Ego refers to the self and self-control, rather than the colloquial sense of someone having a big ego. Even in Sigmund Freud's psychological theory (id-ego-superego), the ego was considered to require energy (as cited in Baumeister et al., 1998). Any of the cognitive control tasks we have discussed earlier in this chapter, such as the Stroop interference task, causes ego depletion. In turn, mental tasks affected by ego depletion are comparably broad. For example, individuals who were asked to suppress their emotions were worse at solving anagram puzzles, compared with individuals who had not been asked to suppress their emotions.

Mental fatigue is a form of physical fatigue, and cognitive control has been described as being like a muscle, which can get tired (Baumeister et al., 1998). Physiologically, ego depletion is associated with lower blood glucose levels. When individuals were asked to perform a task requiring self-control, their blood glucose levels dropped. Furthermore, low levels of blood glucose predicted poorer performance in a subsequent self-control task. Finally, restoring glucose levels with a "glucose drink" promoted better self-control, eliminating these impairments (Gailliot & Baumeister, 2007; Hagger et al., 2010).

All this research suggests that you should not make important decisions on an empty stomach. Your judgment may be impaired, no matter how high the stakes and no matter how fair you are. Consider a study that tested judges on the bench, who—of all people—are trained and respected as rational, deliberative, and fair professionals. We do not expect their judgments to be influenced by anything but the facts of a case and the applicability of law. However, judges are human, and their judgments can be influenced by how hungry (hangry?) they are. In Israel, parole judges get two daily food breaks, dividing their daily work into three sessions. Within each session, the percentage of favorable rulings drops gradually from about 65% to nearly zero before the food break, then returns back up to about 65% after the food break. As judges get hungrier toward their food break, their judgments seem to suffer from ego depletion (Danziger et al., 2011a,b; Weinshall-Margel & Shapard, 2011). **RESEARCH FOCUS 5.1** considers other surprising examples of how scarcity affects cognitive performance.

Ego depletion is an active area of research with over 600 studies on it (Cunningham & Baumeister, 2016). However, several findings have been difficult to replicate, raising a call for caution and more rigorous studies ahead (Carter et al., 2015; Inzlicht & Friese, 2019).

RESEARCH FOCUS 5.1

Scarcity

Global poverty is one of the biggest challenges facing humanity. More than 2 billion people are estimated to be living under the poverty line, where basic needs such as food and shelter are precarious. Even in highly developed nations such as the United States, a large gap separates the rich and the poor. Under financial stress, the poor suffer worse health outcomes, shorter life expectancy, lower performance on intelligence tests, and lower educational achievement. Low-income individuals exhibit behaviors that seem to reflect poor decision making and weak cognitive control, such as borrowing money at high interest rates. When the poor act in ways that seem to make their condition worse, society tends to "blame the victim." People think that the poor are poor because they make bad decisions and have less cognitive control. However, some psychologists and economists believe that the opposite may be true. That is, poverty itself may disrupt cognitive control and decision making.

The **scarcity hypothesis** is that scarcity impairs cognitive control (Mani et al., 2013; Mullainathan & Shafir, 2013). As one example, sugar cane farmers in India suffer from financial uncertainty and poverty before they harvest their crops each year, whereas they are relatively flush right after harvest. When tested before and after harvest on a cognitive control task, sugar cane farmers performed more poorly before harvest—that is, during periods of financial scarcity. This study is fascinating because it was conducted in the real world.

In a more controlled study, adults were randomly recruited at a shopping mall. Everyone participated in a cognitive control task. However, before doing so, they were asked to consider the following question: "Your car is having some trouble and requires $1500 to be fixed. You can pay in full, take a loan, or take a chance and forego the service at the moment. How would you go about making this decision?" After given this question, low-income individuals performed more poorly on the cognitive control task. This question served to induce a mind state of scarcity, making participants worry about money, and thus reduced the mind's bandwidth for the task. When the question was altered so that the amount of the car repair was lowered from $1500 to $150—low enough that it would not induce feelings of scarcity—then the low-income people were not affected by it. They only performed more poorly than wealthier participants when the cost was a more burdensome $1500.

In sum, inducing concerns of financial scarcity made low-income participants perform more poorly in fluid intelligence and cognitive control tasks. It can create tunnel vision, reducing mental bandwidth. Not applicable to you? People can suffer from other kinds of scarcity. Scarcity of money is like scarcity of time (Mullainathan & Shafir, 2013). Consider the table below, which shows how scarcity of time is analogous to scarcity of money.

	Scarcity of money	**Scarcity of time**
Problem	Overspending	Overcommitments
Question	If in debt, why are you spending more?	If behind, why are you taking on more activities?
Result	Giving up basic goods	Giving up activities

Source: A. Mani et al. 2013. *Science* 341: 976–980.

Enhancing Cognitive Control and Working Memory

At the beginning of this chapter we described a dual-task experiment that required participants to drive in a simulator while performing challenging working memory tasks. Almost everyone—about 97%—failed on the dual-task part of the experiment. Interestingly, about 3% of participants demonstrated no multitasking deficits (Watson & Strayer, 2010). The performance of these super-taskers does not deteriorate, and may even improve, when performing more tasks at the same time. But while you would like to think you're a supertasker, chances are you are not. Multitasking is hard for almost everybody.

Still, since attention, working memory, and cognitive control are so important, how can we improve these abilities? Will enhancing these skills make us perform better at school or at work?

The most straightforward way to improve cognitive performance, it would seem, is to train on attentionally demanding tasks (Ball et al., 2002; Holmes et al., 2009; Klingberg et al., 2005). For example, working memory training can benefit intelligence (Jaeggi et al., 2008). Yet training studies overall have produced mixed results. Although some studies demonstrate improvement, others do not (Chooi & Thompson, 2012; Redick et al., 2013; Shipstead et al., 2012; Thompson et al., 2013). So overall, the effects of working memory training require further investigation (Jaeggi et al., 2014).

This does not bode well for the large industry that has sprouted for brain training and enhancement (Simons et al., 2016). By having people do challenging working memory tasks or cognitive control tasks, training software aims to improve intelligence, prevent cognitive declines from aging, and help rehabilitate patients who have suffered from stroke or concussion. Whether these programs produce real-world benefits remains under debate. While researchers can show benefits within tasks being trained, it is not yet clear whether such training generalizes to other tasks or aspects of intelligence (Owen et al., 2010).

However, video games may improve general cognitive capabilities. Certain types of dual-task training produce attentional improvements (Anguera et al., 2013). Action video games improve both external attention and internal attention skills, and even improve low-level visual skills (Green & Bavelier, 2003). It is not clear how these tasks translate to improving IQ or delaying dementia, but no doubt many people find action video games fun to play, so harnessing them toward performance training or educational purposes is an exciting area to pursue further.

What we know for sure is that the way to maximize attentional performance is to first do no harm. Substance abuse, even of legal drugs such as alcohol and marijuana, impairs cognitive skills—not just during the time of consumption, but chronically, even when one is not drunk or high. Some students take off-label prescription drugs, such as Adderall or methamphetamines, thinking that they improve focus. Although these drugs are helpful for students diagnosed with ADHD, it's not clear whether they are helpful for individuals who do not have ADHD (Farah et al., 2004; Greely et al., 2008).

Instead, study after study shows that the best cognitive enhancers are good life habits. Are you getting enough sleep? Not getting enough hours or having irregular sleep patterns, as in waking up at different times every day, not only makes you sleepy during the day, but has direct effects on attention, working memory, and cognitive control (Durmer & Dinges, 2005; Van Dongen et al., 2003). Are you exercising regularly? Physical activity directly benefits cognitive function (Colcombe & Kramer, 2003; Hillman et al., 2008; Kramer et al., 1999). When you do exercise, try to go outside for a walk, ideally within nature. According to **attention restoration theory**, being out in nature can restore cognitive fatigue. Compared with participants who walked in a city, participants who took the same length walk in a forested park performed better on attention and working memory tasks (Berman et al., 2008). So now that you're done reading this chapter, go out for a walk with a friend, or if it's late, go to bed.

Playing action video games can improve your visual skills and attention.

➤ CHECKPOINT 5.3

1. What are some examples of emotion regulation?
2. What does the Yerkes–Dodson curve show? Describe evidence that stress or "choking" impairs working memory.
3. What is the scarcity hypothesis, and how does it relate to ego depletion?
4. List ways to improve cognitive performance (attention, working memory, cognitive control).

Chapter Summary

5.1 Explain cognitive control and its role in multitasking.

Cognitive control is "the ability to orchestrate thought and action in accordance with internal goals" (Miller & Cohen, 2001, p. 167). Also known as executive control, cognitive control makes our activities purposeful and intelligent, allowing us to plan and make good decisions, to select appropriate behaviors, and to coordinate more than one action at a time. Multitasking is dependent on two factors: load—how demanding or difficult each task is—and overlap—how much the demands of simultaneous tasks compete for the same mental resources.

Q: What are different ways that cognitive psychologists study cognitive control in the lab? Can you think of ways that laboratory measures of cognitive control mirror real-world situations from your daily life?

5.2 Discuss the structure of Baddeley's working memory model and the characteristics of each component, especially as they relate to behavior.

Working memory has three subcomponents: the central executive (primary system for controlling attention and thinking—where information is manipulated); the phonological loop (stores and rehearses speech-based information); and the visuospatial sketchpad (stores and manipulates visual information). A key feature of both the phonological loop and the visuospatial sketchpad is their limited storage capacity. Patterns of dual-task interference support a separation between phonological and visuospatial storage systems. Interference occurs when an individual tries to perform two tasks that both use the same storage system. By contrast, when two tasks do not interfere with each other, researchers infer that they are independent.

Q: Describe the evidence that characterizes the phonological loop as phonological, and the visuospatial storage system as visuospatial. What shows that the two storage systems are independent?

5.3 Understand the factors that impair or enhance cognitive control, emotion, and attention.

Emotion regulation—the ability to manage one's emotions, such as our response to stress—is a cognitive control function that affects performance. The Yerkes–Dodson curve describes how performance suffers at both low and high anxiety, stress, and arousal levels, especially for difficult tasks. Ego depletion occurs when one's energy for mental activity is exhausted, impairing cognitive control and other cognitive activities. As for enhancing cognition, study after study shows the beneficial effects of good life habits, such as getting enough sleep and exercising regularly (outdoors when possible). Although working memory training requires further investigation, video game playing may improve general cognitive capabilities.

Q: Consider the kinds of situations you've found to be stressful in your life. How can you reduce the stress levels and their impact on performance? Based on the tips provided to enhance cognition and working memory, what are lifestyle changes that would be feasible for you to try?

Key Terms

7 plus or minus 2
acoustic similarity effect
anterior cingulate cortex (ACC)
articulatory rehearsal loop
articulatory suppression
attention restoration theory
automatic process
central bottleneck model
central executive
chunk
cognitive control
cognitive interference
cognitive load
cognitive overlap
conflict monitoring
conflict resolution
controlled process
digit-span task
dorsolateral prefrontal cortex
dual-task experiments
ego depletion
emotion regulation

episodic buffer
error detection
error-related negativity (ERN)
flanker task
individuate
inhibition
internal attention
irrelevant speech effect
long-term memory
manipulation
mental chronometry
perceptual interference
perseveration errors
phonological loop
phonological store
prediction error
preparation effect
proactive control
psychological refractory period
reactive control
residual switch cost
resource

resource model
resource sharing
response interference
rumination
scarcity hypothesis
serial recall
short-term memory
slot model
spatial interference task (Simon task)
stop-signal task
storage
Stroop interference
sustained attention
task-switch cost
vigilance
visual short-term memory
visuospatial sketchpad
word-length effect
working memory
Yerkes–Dodson curve

Critical Thinking Questions

1. Given cognitive limitations and dual-task interference, should people train to minimize interference or to minimize doing more than one thing at a time?

2. What effect does the constant availability of information (e.g., texting, e-mail, Web browsing, Facebook) have on our minds?

3. How can we leverage our understanding of scarcity effects to improve everyday lives?

4. What are practical and specific things you can do in your life to maximize your attention and performance?

Discovery Labs

oup.com/he/chun1e

Dual-Task Interference Encoding Task

In this experiment, students learn about attention—the capacity-limited cognitive mechanism that we rely on for everything from identifying objects to understanding words to completing all but a very few number of highly learned tasks—by examining dual-task interference. Participants complete a dual-task experiment where the first task is an encoding task and the second task is a timed response to a tone. Approximate completion time: 15 minutes.

Stroop Interference

In this task, students explore the idea of automatic processing. Participants are shown four different lists of words and are asked to read the list aloud for the first two lists, and to name the colors for the second two lists. Approximate completion time: 15 minutes.

Dual-Task Interference Psychological Refractory Period Paradigm

In this experiment, students learn about attention—the capacity-limited cognitive mechanism that we rely on for everything from identifying objects to understanding words to completing all but a very few number of highly learned tasks—by examining dual-task interference. Participants are presented with two stimuli, one a letter and the other a tone. They must respond to each stimulus as quickly and accurately as possible as soon as it is presented. Approximate completion time: 15 minutes.

Operation Span

In this experiment, students generate an estimate of their operation span. Participants are asked to complete arithmetic problems while maintaining a list of words in short-term memory. Approximate completion time: 20 minutes.

Memory Span

In this experiment, students test their own short-term memory using the memory span paradigm, which was devised to explore the argument that short-term memory can hold only a limited amount of information for a short period of time. Participants are presented with a grid of digits, letters, or words, which they must then recall. Approximate completion time: 20 minutes.

Suggested Readings

Carr, N. (2011). *The Shallows: What the Internet Is Doing to Our Brains*. New York: W. W. Norton & Company.

Mullainathan, S., & Shafir, E. (2013). *Scarcity: Why Having Too Little Means So Much*. New York: Times Books.

Everyday Memory

6

In 1984, North Carolina college student Jennifer Thompson lived through a nightmare: a stranger broke into her home and sexually assaulted her at knifepoint. Summoning deep reservoirs of inner strength during the attack, she attempted to memorize her assailant's face and voice. She later identified a man in a police lineup and helped send him to prison. Yet, over 10 years later, DNA testing showed that this man, Ronald Cotton, was not the person who had raped Thompson.

After Cotton's release from prison, he and Thompson met. Trembling, she begged for his forgiveness. "I'm not mad at you," said Cotton. "I've never been mad at you. I just want you to have a good life" (O'Neill, 2001). The two began an unlikely friendship and even coauthored a book, *Picking Cotton*, describing their experience. Their hope is to spread awareness about wrongful convictions and the fallibility of eyewitness identification procedures.

Memory can be a difficult topic on many levels. So much of what we believe about ourselves and others stems from what we remember. How much should we trust our memory, and under what circumstances? As Cotton and Thompson's case shows, questions of memory can have significant implications.

AP photo/Chuck Burton

In 1984, college student Jennifer Thompson (right) was violently assaulted. She later misidentified her assailant as Ronald Cotton (left), who went to prison for someone else's crime. Years later, after Cotton's innocence was proven, the two became unlikely friends—bonded by circumstances caused by the frailty of memory.

LEARNING OBJECTIVES

6.1 Define short-term and long-term memory.

6.2 Describe instances of great memory ability and instances of memory failure.

6.3 Distinguish between encoding and retrieval, and discuss strategies and factors that can improve memory.

6.4 Describe how autobiographical memory is constructive.

6.5 Understand how memory failures can affect the way we perceive past experiences.

6.6 Explain how memory distortions can affect eyewitness testimony.

This chapter focuses on how memory—specifically conscious (or explicit) memory—can work or fail in everyday life. In other words, this chapter focuses on what we might call "everyday memory." Chapter 7 will consider distinctions among the many different types of memory, including memories we might not even be aware we have.

6.1 What Is Memory?

Memory, broadly defined, refers to a family of processes involved in encoding, storing, and retrieving (i.e., recalling or recognizing) information about our experience of the world. Some processes allow us to remember things we learned or experienced seconds ago (*short-term memory*), whereas other processes influence whether we are able to remember things from hours, days, weeks, or years ago (*long-term memory*). **Short-term memory** refers to information stored for a short duration, which fades after several seconds if it is not actively attended to or transferred into long-term memory (Atkinson & Shiffrin, 1968). The term is sometimes used interchangeably with *working memory* (covered in Chapter 5), which holds information briefly so that it can be manipulated in mind (e.g., Cowan, 2008, 2017), although the precise relationship between short-term memory and working memory is a matter of some debate. **Long-term memory** refers to the long-term storage of information, which can stretch back decades. Long-term memory might be likened to a warehouse full of stocked filing cabinets: its capacity is immense, but we are not always accessing its contents and holding them in mind. (Here's an example: What was the name of your kindergarten teacher? If you could recall their name, you had the memory stored in long-term memory but weren't bringing it to mind until asked.)

The sheer variety of memory mechanisms goes beyond the distinction between short-term and long-term memory, and this variety will be covered in more depth in Chapter 7. What all types of memory have in common is that they enable experience to shape thought or behavior down the road.

➤ **CHECKPOINT 6.1**

1. What is memory, broadly defined?
2. How is short-term memory different from long-term memory?

6.2 The Memory Paradox

There is a paradox at the heart of human memory. On the one hand, it is fallible, as demonstrated by cases in which eyewitnesses misidentify a stranger. It is not at all the faithful recording of experience we often assume it to be.

On the other hand, our capacity to store information is immense. Consider the ancient Greek bards who could recite *The Iliad* or *The Odyssey* by heart, or today's **mnemonists** ("memory athletes") (**RESEARCH FOCUS 6.1**), who perform astonishing feats of information retention. How can we make sense of these seemingly incompatible aspects of memory? How can we account for the paradox that memory is both supremely fallible at some times and extraordinary at others?

For clues, we might look to studies of people who demonstrate an ability to remember hundreds of digits or words at a time. We might also look to studies of people who excel at remembering details from their own life. It turns out these functions of memory (i.e., memory for digits or words and memory for personal experiences) might be different from each other (e.g., Roediger & McDermott, 2013). In a classic case, the Russian psychologist Alexander

Painting depicting the Greek bard Homer, by Jean-Baptiste Auguste Leloir.

RESEARCH FOCUS 6.1

The World of Memory Sports

Ben Pridmore of the United Kingdom can, within an hour, memorize the order of cards in 28 consecutive shuffled decks. In that same time, Wang Feng of China can memorize 2,660 written numbers in sequence. And yet they, and many others like them, claim to have average—if not below average—memory in everyday life.

In formal memory competitions, several tests have become standard. Among other things, these aim to see who can remember the longest list of spoken numbers or random words, the order of the most cards, or the most names and faces in a series.

In an address at an annual meeting of the Association for Psychological Science, memory researcher Henry Roediger shared the stage with U.S. memory champion Nelson Dellis. First, Dr. Roediger discussed his team's research on such memory athletes. Dellis then walked the audience through the types of strategies that can turn a memory-challenged individual into a memory champion. He advocated for the power of several techniques to encode information. In what's called a "memory palace," or the **method of loci**, you imagine walking through a highly familiar space or series of rooms (such as your own house) and placing different pieces of information in each room. Each room becomes a cue that later helps you bring to mind the information placed there. Another technique is *visualization* (or mental imagery; see Chapter 3), assigning novel images to represent aspects of the encoded information.

In looking at the difference between memory champions and a control group of university students, Roediger and his colleagues tested memory for words and for nonwords. The researchers presented 100 items at a rate of 1 item every 2

The United Kingdom's Ben Pridmore, a three-time world memory champion.

seconds and then surprised participants with a memory test the next day. The memory champions remembered far more words than the control participants did, but they remembered only slightly more nonwords (both groups had better memory for words than for nonwords). This finding suggests that memory champions may not have elevated memory ability in general, but instead have improved their memory on specific tasks they have practiced. How? It may be telling that the memory champions performed better than the control participants on a task of attentional control and on a task of working memory. Given the role of attention in working memory (see Chapter 5), these findings together seem to indicate that one key to becoming a memory champion is learning to control one's attention.

Luria studied a man (referred to as "S") who earned a living performing memory feats (Luria, 1987). Despite the skill "S" displayed on stage, he claimed to have no special memory of everyday life, and Luria described him as experiencing the world "through a haze" (p. 159). Along similar lines, a study of ten superior memorizers suggested that none of them had above-average memory of details from their lives (Wilding & Valentine, 1997).

The very quirks of memory that allow it to excel in some circumstances might lead it astray in others. The human mind continually seeks meaning, and memories can be distorted when we force it to conform to what we find meaningful. At the same time, some mnemonic (memory) strategies capitalize on this need, making ordinary material memorable by increasing how meaningful it is to us.

Mnemonists' abilities at first seem to contradict research on the limits of memory. In a classic paper, the eminent American psychologist George Miller noted that across a wide range of studies, evidence suggested a "magical number 7." That is, people could retain only seven items at a time, give or take about two, in short-term memory (Miller, 1956). Although estimates have varied somewhat, research has consistently supported the notion of very limited short-term memory capacity (Cowan, 2001).

➤ CHECKPOINT 6.2

1. What evidence suggests that the ability to memorize items (e.g., digits) is different from the ability to recall details from one's life?

2. What evidence suggests that the abilities of memory athletes stem from strategies that they use rather than from some naturally superior memory?

6.3 Making Memory Work

What does it take to retain information? It seems to depend partly on whether you are trying to memorize facts or lists of items, or whether you are trying to remember details from your own life. Here we discuss how memories are initially made (including some strategies you can try while studying) and then how memories are retrieved and strengthened.

Encoding

Mnemonists can remember lists far, far longer than Miller's "magical number 7," and their secret may come down to what they actively do with the information as they receive it.

To remember something, you first need to **encode** it; that is, you need to mentally file that information away where you can later access it. Encoding isn't a one-step process. Instead, it involves the transfer of information at multiple stages. After a stimulus is briefly presented, a detailed representation of it appears to persist in your mind for a fraction of a second. This is known as **sensory memory** (**FIGURE 6.1**), a highly detailed but short-lived impression of sensory information. It's not inevitable that this information will fade away entirely, however: if you direct attention to the impression before it fades, you can hold on to it in short-term memory (Atkinson & Shiffrin, 1968). Evidence suggests that attending to a sensory memory recruits some of the same brain regions as attending to stimuli in the external world (Ruff et al., 2007). It's a race against time: how much you can attend to before the representation deteriorates is one factor that determines how much you can hold in short-term memory.

The American cognitive psychologist George Sperling famously illustrated this principle in a classic series of studies. Sperling presented brief (e.g., 50

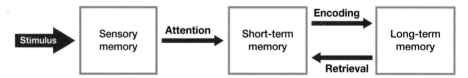

FIGURE 6.1 The relationship between sensory memory, short-term memory, and long-term memory as described in an influential model by Atkinson and Shiffrin (1968)   After a stimulus appears, it persists for a fraction of a second in sensory memory before rapidly fading away. However, paying attention to a subset of its contents before they deteriorate can bring those contents into short-term memory. Although longer-lasting than sensory memory, short-term memory is also short-lived, so information must further be encoded into long-term memory in order to be recalled later. Such encoding can involve rehearsal, as well as other strategies. The contents of long-term memory can exist outside our immediate awareness. When we retrieve them (i.e., bring them into awareness), we temporarily bring them back into short-term memory (or working memory). (After R. C. Atkinson and R. M. Shiffrin. 1968. In *The Psychology of Learning and Motivation: II.* K. W. Spence and J. T. Spence. [Eds.] Academic Press: Oxford, England.)

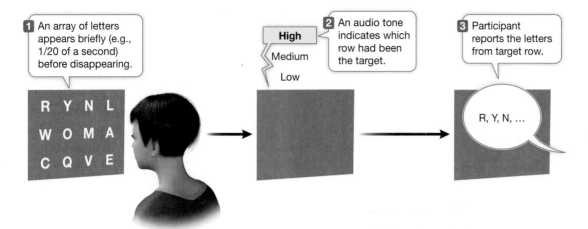

FIGURE 6.2 Sperling's experiment demonstrating the duration of sensory memory   In George Sperling's famous studies of iconic memory (persisting sensory memory), participants saw brief arrays of letters and numbers arranged in rows (e.g., flashed for 50 milliseconds). In some trials, a tone played after the array disappeared, which indicated the row that participants should report. Participants were often accurate even though the arrays were already gone when the tone sounded, suggesting that the visual information continued to persist in sensory memory for a fraction of a second. (After D. H. Hockenbury and S. E. Hockenbury. 1998. *Discovering Psychology.* Worth Publishers, Inc./Macmillan Education: New York; based on G.A. Sperling. 1960. *Psychol Monogr* 74: 1–29.)

millisecond) arrays of letters and numbers (in 3 × 3 or 3 × 4 grids) to experiment participants and asked them to recall as many letters and numbers as they could (**FIGURE 6.2**). Typically, they could report about four items (33–50% of the array). However, in some conditions the array was followed quickly by a tone that indicated which items participants should report, enabling them to select targeted contents of sensory memory. Calculations derived from what people were able to report in this condition revealed that about 75% of the array had persisted for a fraction of a second (Sperling, 1960). In the visual domain, this type of persisting sensory memory is known as **iconic memory**. See the Discovery Lab on this topic to learn more.

Like sensory memory, short-term memory has a limited life span. You can keep it going as long as you don't shift attention away from its contents, but once you move on to other things, it fades. You have probably experienced this for yourself: for example, after being introduced to several new people at a party, you may find you have forgotten their names by the end of your conversation. To keep information that is stored in short-term memory from fading away, you need to find a way to move it into long-term memory. (Next time your professor forgets your name, don't take it personally—consider how many students professors meet each semester.) One approach people often try is **rehearsal**, repeating the information to themselves over and over again. Although this can work, other strategies are more effective. You may have experienced the limitations of rehearsal if you have ever raced to find a pen and paper while repeating someone's address to yourself after it's been told to you. Sometimes you find that pen just a little too late, and crucial elements of the address are gone from your memory.

Before the widespread use of cell phones, people used to be able to cite from memory the phone numbers of family members and close friends. But because most people now use speed-dial functions, you probably don't know many phone numbers by heart. This does not seem to be problematic, but what other facts and knowledge about the world are we giving up? Should we have to remember any information that can be easily looked up on our phone? **THINK FOR YOURSELF 6.1** discusses what's known as the Google effect.

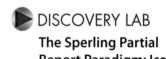
DISCOVERY LAB
The Sperling Partial Report Paradigm: Iconic Memory

► **Think for Yourself 6.1**

Is Google Hurting Your Memory?

The Internet has given us access to an unprecedented amount of information, and the convenience of smart phones, tablets, and laptops puts this wealth of knowledge at our fingertips. When a question comes up during conversation, it is now common for someone to try and answer it by pulling out their phone. The Internet has become our external memory.

But does having access to all this information on the cloud discourage us from storing it in our heads? According to the **Google effect**, when people expect to be able to access relevant information on the Internet or a computer, memory for that information is lowered (Sparrow et al., 2011). In one experiment, participants were asked to type numerous trivia statements into a computer, such as "An ostrich's eye is bigger than its brain." Half the people were told that the information they typed in would be saved on the computer, while the other half were told it would be erased. All participants were later tested on the information they had typed in. When people thought that the computer was saving the information they typed in, their memory was worse than when they thought the computer was erasing the information. Strikingly, this effect persists even when people are explicitly told to remember the information in their heads. On the bright side, people show enhanced memory for where to access the relevant information.

Another aspect of the Google effect is that people are primed to think of search engines such as Google or Yahoo

Google and the Google logo are registered trademarks of Google LLC, used with permission.

when they are prompted with difficult questions, such as "Do all countries have at least two colors in their flags?"

These findings have interesting extensions. People start to mistake access for understanding. Just because you found the Wikipedia article on string theory doesn't mean you understand it. However, simply locating information from a search gives people the illusion of personal understanding (Fisher et al., 2015).

The work extends to pictures. Many people use their smart phones to take photos of their experiences—a form of real memory encoding. However, according to the photo-taking-impairment effect, people remember less about objects they photograph than if they only observe the objects without photographing them (Henkel, 2014). Enjoy the sights before rushing to post them to your Instagram account.

Encoding Strategies

Given the limitations of short-term memory, it can be useful to find ways to reduce the amount of information that must be stored, much like compressing a high-resolution digital photo into a smaller file. You also need to be able to transfer information from short-term memory into long-term memory efficiently. While we will cover more about how encoding works in Chapter 7, here we discuss some encoding strategies, including visualization, chunking, elaboration, hierarchical organization, and spacing. Effective use of such strategies requires having some understanding of how, when, and why memory fails. Understanding of how our own memory works is known as **metamemory** (or more broadly, **metacognition**); it is something that improves over the course of childhood development and is one factor that contributes to better memory performance as children mature (Flavell, 1979; Flavell & Wellman, 1977).

It turns out that highly skilled use of such strategies may be one of the key things that sets memory athletes apart. In one study, cognitive neuroscientists examined the brains of super memorizers and found no structural abnormalities—that is, their brains didn't look physically different from those of other people. There had been reason to hypothesize that their brains *should* look different. For example, the hippocampus is a neural structure that is centrally involved in memory, and Chapter 7 will describe how parts of the hippocampus are larger in people whose daily routines require them to remember a lot of detailed information: taxi drivers who have spent years navigating the labyrinthine streets of London have been found to have enlarged hippocampal regions (Maguire et al., 2000). However, this appears not to be the case for memory athletes. Instead, what does set them apart appears to be which brain regions are particularly active when they try to memorize material. Compared with control participants, memory athletes were found to have greater activity in brain regions that are also involved in spatial navigation and spatial attention, such as the hippocampus, retrosplenial cortex, and parietal cortex (Maguire et al., 2003). This is consistent with the fact that memory athletes frequently use visualization strategies such as the method of loci (see Research Focus 6.1).

CHUNKING   One strategy people can use to reduce the amount of information they need to encode is **chunking**, organizing smaller bits of information into larger, meaningful combinations. If you had to remember the number sequence "1, 4, 9, 2, 1, 7, 7, 6, 1, 8, 1, 2, 1, 9, 8, 4," you might try to memorize it as 16 separate digits, which would be a difficult feat. An easier approach would be to combine the numbers into a smaller number of meaningful wholes, such as 1492 (the year Columbus sailed the ocean blue), 1776 (the year America declared its independence from England), 1812 (as in the War of 1812 or the *1812 Overture*), and 1984 (after George Orwell's famous novel). The ability to chunk information is often one reason that experts in a particular domain seem to have superior memory to novices. One example of this came from a study that compared children's memory with that of adults. Generally, memory improves as children get older, but when participants were asked to remember the positions of multiple chess pieces on a chess board, the children outperformed the adults even though the adults had outperformed the children on memory for digits (Chi, 1978). Why? It was because the children were accomplished chess players, whereas the adults were chess novices. To the children, the configurations of various pieces were meaningful, so they had to remember fewer "chunks" (see Chase & Simon, 1973).

ELABORATION   One powerful encoding strategy is to make links between the material you are trying to learn and knowledge you already hold in long-term memory through a technique known as **elaboration** (Brown & Craik, 2000). This capitalizes on the well-established finding that memory can be influenced by **depth of encoding**, paying attention to meanings and functions versus superficial features (Craik & Lockhart, 1972). In one study, researchers manipulated the depth at which participants encoded words by asking them questions about the typeface (shallow encoding), their rhyming pattern (intermediate encoding), or whether the words fit into a given category (deep encoding) (**FIGURE 6.3**). The results revealed that deep encoding was linked with better memory for the words on a subsequent surprise memory test (Craik & Tulving, 1975). You can try this in **SEE FOR YOURSELF 6.1**.

It can be particularly effective to think of ways that material might be relevant to you or your own interests. This is known as the **self-reference effect** (Rogers et al., 1977; Symons & Johnson, 1997), and it has been found to improve memory performance even among people who have impaired memory due to neurological damage (Grilli & Glisky, 2010). In one study, the memory benefits of a strategy known as **self-imagining**—imagining something from a personal perspective—were compared with the benefits derived from other types of imagery-based and elaboration-based strategies. Participants saw pairs

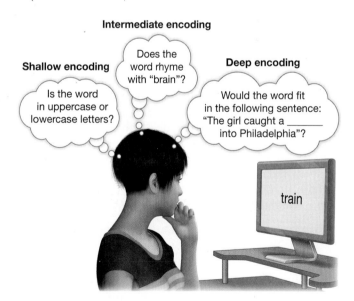

FIGURE 6.3 The deeper people encode the meaning of words, the better they remember them   In a study by Craik and Tulving (1975), shallow encoding was induced by asking people about typeface, intermediate encoding was induced by asking people about rhymes, and deep encoding was induced by asking people to fit words into sentences. Deep encoding led to better memory. (After F. I. M. Craik and E. Tulving. 1975. *J Exp Psych: Gen* 104: 268–294.)

▶ **See for Yourself 6.1**

A. Exercise: Elaboration and Depth of Encoding

Read the words in list 1. As you do so, estimate the number of syllables in each word:

List 1: umbrella, stapler, television, stick, bottle, encyclopedia, cigarette, hose, lightbulb

Now read the words in list 2. This time, decide whether the item would be useful if you were to get lost in the woods for a few days.

List 2: matches, hat, thesaurus, bicycle, computer, wallet, pencil, detergent, aspirin

Now go to See for Yourself 6.1B.

B. Results: Elaboration and Depth of Encoding

Without looking back at the lists in See for Yourself 6.1A, write down as many of the words as you can remember.

Did you remember more words from list 2 than from list 1? Many people do. A major difference is that the instructions for list 1 asked you to engage in shallow encoding—that is, to pay attention to superficial features of the word (e.g., number of syllables). In contrast, the instructions for list 2 asked you to engage in deep encoding, whereby you thought about the meanings and functions of the items. You may also have imagined yourself interacting with the items. In doing so, you also engaged in elaboration: going beyond rote memoriza-tion and linking the words with your existing knowledge of them. This kind of strategy has been found to robustly aid memory. (That's a tip! When studying for a test, don't just highlight or underline terms. Do a little elaboration.)

As an aside, the exercise in See for Yourself 6.1A—although useful for illustrative purposes—has some problems and is not rigorous enough to be an informative experiment (unlike the actual research experiments it is based on, Craik & Tulving, 1975). Can you identify one or two problems with it? If so, how could you fix them to create a more convincing experiment? Think about it and then turn to See for Yourself 6.1C.

C. The Problems with (and Remedies for) See For Yourself 6.1A

In See for Yourself 6.1A, you might have remembered more words from list 2 than from list 1. The purpose of this exer-cise was to demonstrate that elaboration and deep encod-ing can make information easier to remember. In its current form, however, the exercise includes at least two *confound-ing variables*: differences between the two conditions, other than depth of encoding, that could account for the differ-ence in memory. When experimental psychologists wish to make claims about the reasons for what they observe, they need to rule out confounding variables. What are some dif-ferences between the two conditions that could provide al-ternative reasons for different memory performance? Two immediately spring to mind. First, it could be that you re-membered more words from list 2 simply because you read those words more recently than those on list 1 (a *recency effect*, a phenomenon we'll discuss in Chapter 7). Second, it could be that the words on list 2 were inherently more memorable than those on list 1 (e.g., see Madan, 2020). For example, people tend to have better memory for items that have emotional value or that have particular uniqueness on any given list (the latter known as the **von Restorff effect**; von Restorff, 1933; see Hunt, 1995; Wallace, 1965. Also see the Discovery Lab on this topic to learn more). To turn this exercise into a well-controlled experiment, there are a few steps you could take. For example, to control for a possible recency effect, it would be a good idea to have half of the participants engage in deep encoding for list 1 and shallow encoding for list 2. The other half of the participants would complete the tasks in the reverse order. To control for the possibility that words on one list are more memorable than those on the other list, flip which words are assigned to list 1 and list 2 for half the participants.

DISCOVERY LAB
The von Restorff Effect

of words: one naming an object and the other naming a location. In the self-imagining condition, participants were asked to imagine themselves interacting with the object in the paired location. (For example, if the word pair was "typewriter–attic," they might imagine themselves sitting in an attic while typing.) In a follow-up test, participants were presented with an object word and had to recall the location it had been paired with. Memory was bet-ter when people had engaged in self-imagining than when they had engaged in other elaboration strategies (such as constructing a sentence that combined the two words) or other imagery-based strategies (such as simply imagining the object in the location or imagining Arnold Schwarzenegger interacting with the object in the location) (Grilli & Glisky, 2011). It seems that bringing everything back to yourself isn't always narcissistic; where memory is concerned, it can just be good strategy.

HIERARCHICAL ORGANIZATION   Another strategy for encoding material is to rearrange it according to **hierarchical organization**—that is, a meaningful network of associations in which items are linked to increasingly global categories. Here's an example. Try remembering all of these famous names: Robert De Niro, Pablo Picasso, Meryl Streep, Angela Merkel, Georgia O'Keeffe, Chris Hemsworth, Winston Churchill, Elizabeth Warren, Aretha Franklin, Nelson Mandela, Kamala Harris, John Lennon, and Leonardo da Vinci.

That's a lot of names to remember, isn't it? But you can improve your ability to remember them by organizing them hierarchically, as shown in **FIGURE 6.4**.

By organizing the items like this, you create cues that help you reconstruct the information. Rather than needing to retrieve 13 names, you start by retrieving only two items ("artists" and "political figures"). These provide a cue to help remember the subtypes of artists ("actors," "painters," and "singers") and subdivisions of political figures ("USA," "Europe," and "Africa"). These, in turn, provide cues for the names. It is much easier to remember the 3 actors than to remember 13 uncategorized names (Bower et al., 1969; Mandler, 1967). It is, in essence, like laying a trail of bread crumbs to find your way back to the material you learned.

SPACING EFFECT   When you study for an exam, do you typically "cram"— that is, save most of your studying for the days leading up to the test? Or do you start well ahead of time and space out your study sessions? If our experience as teachers is anything to go by, many people opt to cram. After all, life is busy, and sometimes it seems like the best way to study is to get your other obligations out of the way first. However, in what is known as the **spacing effect**, evidence suggests that people remember material better when they space short study sessions apart. The spacing effect was first described by the late-nineteenth-century German psychologist Hermann Ebbinghaus (1885).

Ebbinghaus devoted much of his research career to pioneering the study of memory. He taught himself lists of "nonsense words" and investigated how factors such as encoding strategy and the passage of time influenced his ability to recall them. He found that he retained better memory for the material when his study sessions were distributed over time (**distributed practice**) than when he clustered an equivalent period of study into a single session (**massed practice**).

The benefits of distributed practice are supported by more recent research as well. In one study, people learned Swahili words and their English translations

Hermann Ebbinghaus was a pioneer of rigorous memory research.

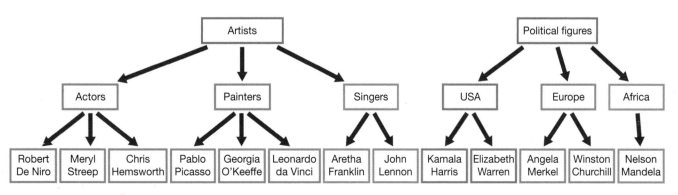

FIGURE 6.4 Hierarchical organization   One strategy for encoding information is to group it according to a hierarchy.

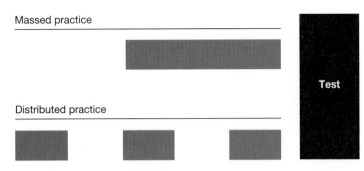

FIGURE 6.5 Massed vs. distributed practice   Even when the total amount of time studying is the same, people tend to remember material better (e.g., such as on an exam) when their study sessions have been spaced out ("distributed practice," bottom) than when crammed together in one session ("massed practice," top).

during two study sessions, which could be separated by as few as 5 minutes or as many as 14 days. When participants were tested on their memory for the material 10 days after the second learning session, their memory improved sharply when the two study sessions had been separated by a day or more (Cepeda et al., 2009). In a follow-up study, the study sessions were separated by as few as 20 minutes or as many as 6 months, and memory was tested 6 months after the second study session (using stimuli other than Swahili–English word pairs). In this case, memory at test was best when the study sessions had been separated by 28 days. Shorter or longer gaps between study sessions yielded worse memory performance (Cepeda et al., 2009). Note that it would probably be incorrect to conclude from this that study sessions should always be separated by 28 days; much depends on the type of material being learned and on how far into the future you expect to be tested. However, the data consistently appear to show that it is best to spread your study sessions out when preparing for an exam rather than cramming your study into one session (**FIGURE 6.5**). (With any luck, you aren't reading this for the first time the night before your exam.)

Retrieval

The act of accessing memories is known as **retrieval** (analogous in some ways to opening a computer file you saved a week earlier). However, although the metaphor of saving and opening a file on a computer is illustrative, it falls short of capturing the way memory actually works. For example, a file that is stored on a computer disk generally takes the form of a faithfully stored array of 1s and 0s that will yield the same output each time it is reaccessed. In contrast, in human memory, quirks of both encoding and retrieval cause memory to be volatile: when we retrieve a memory, there are many aspects of what we remember that will not correspond to what we actually experienced. Even when we do remember things we have encountered before, these memories sometimes take the form of a feeling of familiarity rather than a vivid memory of the circumstances in which we encountered them (e.g., Rajaram, 1993; Tulving, 1985). Failures of memory can often be attributed either to a failure of encoding or a failure of retrieval, but usually—outside the highly controlled artifices of the lab—memory failures in real life are probably due to a combination of encoding and retrieval problems.

TESTING EFFECT & GENERATION EFFECT   Do you ever feel you know the material better after taking an exam than you did going in? If so, you may have experienced something akin to the **testing effect** (**FIGURE 6.6**). Evidence suggests that practice in retrieving information leads to better retention of material than does repeated studying (e.g., Landauer & Bjork, 1978; McDaniel et al., 2007; Roediger & Karpicke, 2006; Thomas et al., 2020). This is also sometimes known as "retrieval practice" (e.g., Agarwal et al., 2017; Karpicke & Blunt, 2011; Smith et al., 2016). In one study, students read a passage and then either restudied it or tested themselves on it. When tested again on it only 5 minutes later, those who had restudied the passage seemed to remember the material better, but when tested on it 2 days or a week later, the students who had read the passage once and then tested themselves did better (Roediger & Karpicke, 2006).

Similarly, in what is known as the **generation effect**, memory is enhanced for a list of items a person has generated versus one that a person was simply asked

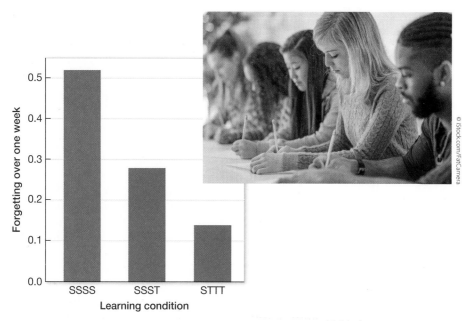

FIGURE 6.6 The testing effect   In one study, people studied material over the course of four study sessions (SSSS), studied over three sessions followed by a single testing session (SSST), or studied for one session followed by three testing sessions (STTT). Consistent with the testing effect, those who studied once and then were tested three times forgot the least amount of material by a week later. (After H. L. Roediger, III and J. D. Karpicke. 2006. *Psychol Sci* 17: 249–255.)

to memorize (e.g., Metcalfe & Kornell, 2007). Although the testing effect and the generation effect are related, there do appear to be differences between them. In one study, participants read a list of target words and then were either shown the words again or were shown word fragments (e.g., "fr_ _nd") and were asked to complete them. Participants exhibited better memory for the words when they had been asked to complete the fragments than when they had simply read them a second time. In a third condition, participants were explicitly instructed to use the word fragments as a retrieval cue. In this condition, participants' memory for the words was even better than when they had completed the word fragment without instructions to recall the word (Karpicke & Zaromb, 2010). Thus, practice retrieving information appears to impart advantages over simply generating information. These kinds of findings have implications for studying: don't just try to answer review questions you have been given—take some time to generate your own and use them to aid your retrieval.

RETRIEVAL CUES   How we use **retrieval cues**—clues in the environment or in our stored representations of experiences—affects our memory. Our memories are suggestible and prone to error in part because we reassemble them each time we access them. Sometimes we simply make mistakes when reconstructing an experience. The nature of these mistakes is often systematic, revealing much about how our memories rely on assumptions, preexisting knowledge, and suggestions.

One example of retrieval cues' importance is **context-dependent memory**, improved memory when the retrieval context is the same as the learning context. In a classic study, researchers asked divers to learn lists of words either underwater or on land. Their memory for the words was then tested in either context. The critical manipulation was that half of the divers were tested in the same environment where they learned the words (i.e., they learned the lists underwater and were tested underwater), whereas half of the divers were tested in the

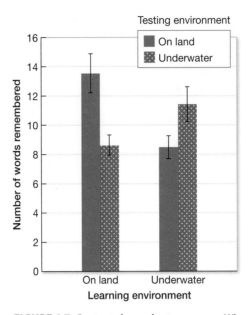

FIGURE 6.7 **Context-dependent memory** When divers learned lists of words underwater, they had better memory for them when tested underwater than when tested on land. When they learned the lists on land, they remembered more when tested on land than when tested underwater. (After D. R. Godden and A. D. Baddeley. 1975. *Br J Psychol* 66: 325–331.)

new environment (i.e., they learned the list on land and were tested underwater) (Godden & Baddeley, 1975). The divers exhibited better memory when their test environment was the same as their study environment (**FIGURE 6.7**).

A related phenomenon is **state-dependent memory**, wherein memory is enhanced when people's internal states at retrieval match their internal states at encoding. This includes **mood-dependent memory** (Eich, 1995). In one study, participants who were placed in a happy or sad mood via hypnosis exhibited better memory for material they had learned when in the same emotional state (Bower, 1981).

Similar effects have been found under the influence of alcohol or marijuana. When people study material while under the influence, they later demonstrate better retrieval of the material when they are again in that state (Eich, 1980; Weissenborn & Duka, 2000). We are not suggesting you smoke or drink before studying or taking an exam, though. It's likely the costs of being under the influence outweigh such state-dependent benefits.

▶ CHECKPOINT 6.3

1. What is the difference between memory encoding and retrieval?
2. How might you use chunking, hierarchical organization, and elaboration to help you encode information into memory?
3. If you were studying for an exam, how might you take advantage of the spacing effect, testing effect, and generation effect?

6.4 Autobiographical Memory

As we noted earlier in this chapter, memory athletes often report having only average memory in everyday life. The strategies they use are effective only after training for specific tasks or situations. Furthermore, remembering lists of items differs from what's called **autobiographical memory**, remembering events in our lives. Typically, most people's autobiographical memories are sparse for events that occurred before the age of 3 or 4 years. This inability to remember the earliest years of our lives is known as **infantile amnesia**, which may be partly attributable to the late development of several brain regions important to memory, such as the hippocampus and prefrontal cortex (Madsen & Kim, 2016). At the other end of development, some evidence suggests that memories of personal experiences among older adults become less specific (Levine et al., 2002), and this may be associated with changing connectivity between the hippocampus and prefrontal cortex (St Jacques et al., 2012).

Autobiographical memory is similar to what is known as "episodic memory," which involves remembering the details of an event, bound to the time and place where it occurred (see Chapter 7). But in addition, autobiographical memory is intimately tied to the self, including personal narratives and beliefs (Conway & Pleydell-Pearce, 2000). Culture appears to play a role too: in one study, Asian Americans were primed to think either of their Asian identity or their American identity before recalling important autobiographical events. Those primed to focus on their American identity reported memories that were more focused on themselves and less on relationships with others than did those who were primed to focus on their Asian identity (Wang, 2008). According to some theorists, it is nearly impossible to avoid having your view of yourself shape your memories.

HIGHLY SUPERIOR AUTOBIOGRAPHICAL MEMORY   Just as some people demonstrate remarkable skill when it comes to memorizing lists, others are unusual in their ability to remember details of their own lives. Researchers have documented rare cases where people have incredibly strong memories of even mundane events. A woman named Jill Price, for example, can remember every day of her life since 1980, when she was 14 years old. "Most have called it a gift, but I call it a burden," she reported when releasing her memoir, *The Woman Who Can't Forget*. "Some memories are good and give me a warm, safe feeling. But I also recall every bad decision, insult, and excruciating embarrassment." Price first came to the attention of memory researchers when she approached Professor James McGaugh at the University of California, Irvine. Her condition is now known as **hyperthymestic syndrome** (*hyper*, "above normal" + *thymesis*, "remembering"), or "highly superior autobiographical memory," and it appears to be very rare. Notably, Price's ability to encode and retrieve material such as strings of digits is no better than normal; it appears that her ability is specifically autobiographical (Parker et al., 2006) (**FIGURE 6.8**).

What might underlie this remarkable autobiographical memory? Unlike memory athletes, whose brains do not appear to be physically different from the average brain, evidence suggests that people with highly superior autobiographical memory may differ in the physical appearance of several brain regions. These include the inferior and middle temporal gyri, temporal pole, anterior insula, and parahippocampal gyrus (LePort et al., 2012). The involvement of these brain regions converges on previous suggestions that these areas are part of a neural network that processes autobiographical memories (Fink et al., 1996; Levine et al., 2004; Maguire, 2001; Svoboda et al., 2006). Individuals with highly superior autobiographical memory also have been found to have significantly more "white matter" (composed of insulated axons that convey signals from one neuron to another), raising the possibility that these individuals are characterized by more efficient transmission of neural signals (LePort et al., 2012).

It is important to note that such evidence of structural differences does not mean that these differences are *why* these individuals have

FIGURE 6.8 The woman who can't forget
Jill Price has astounded memory researchers with her uncanny ability to remember even mundane events from her life in detail. She is one of very few people in the world known to have hyperthymestic syndrome (also called highly superior autobiographical memory). In her memoir *The Woman Who Can't Forget*, she describes the positives and negatives of living with her remarkable memory.

© Karjean Levine/Getty Images

Courtesy of NASA

© PCN Photography/Alamy Stock Photo

FIGURE 6.9 Flashbulb memories   Many people experience "flashbulb memories" of emotional or traumatic moments in their lives. For example, depending on their age, many people feel they have a vivid and clear memory of where they were and what they were doing when they heard about the assassination of John F. Kennedy, the explosion of the space shuttle *Challenger*, or the 9/11 terrorist attack on New York's World Trade Center. What events in your own life have led to the feeling of a flashbulb memory?

highly superior autobiographical memory. Given the brain's well-established plasticity (that is, its tendency to change itself based on experience), it could alternatively be the reverse. In other words, a lifetime of practice recalling autobiographical events might conceivably be what led to these differences in brain structure. Consistent with this possibility, several of the individuals with highly superior autobiographical memory reported compulsively or obsessively practicing recalling their memories. For example, one person would practice recalling events from varying dates when trying to fall asleep or when stuck in traffic (LePort et al., 2012).

Memory and Emotion

Try to remember any specific details about what you did, wore, or ate on April 14 of last year. There's a good chance you can't unless something meaningful happened to you that day. However, if you try to remember something personally meaningful or emotional in itself—perhaps your first kiss or where you were when you received terrible news—you can probably recall vivid details. For example, many Americans who were old enough at the time report high confidence about exactly where they were and what they were doing when the airplanes hit New York's World Trade Center towers in the 9/11 terrorist attacks. (Many can similarly report with confidence what they were doing when the space shuttle *Challenger* broke apart or when President Kennedy was assassinated.)

Vivid memories associated with particularly emotional events are known as **flashbulb memories** (**FIGURE 6.9**). The American psychologists Roger Brown and James Kulik introduced this term into the literature, describing flashbulb memories as a unique type of memory (Brown & Kulik, 1977). Brown and Kulik probed people's memories for salient events, such as the JFK assassination. They concluded that flashbulb memories arise for events that involve a high level of surprise and a high level of emotional arousal.

ENHANCED EMOTIONAL MEMORY: ILLUSION OR REALITY?   Certainly, many of us can think of our own flashbulb memories. But how accurate are they? Some research suggests these are an illusion of confidence rather than a uniquely faithful record of our experience. Evidence for this emerged after the 1986 *Challenger* shuttle disaster. Just over a minute after taking off from Cape Canaveral, Florida, the *Challenger* became engulfed in flames. All aboard were killed, including the first spacebound civilian school teacher, Christa McAuliffe. The disaster was televised live before a shocked nation and horrified schoolchildren across the country. In the aftermath, Ulric Neisser and Nicole Harsch (1992) asked more than 100 students to recall what they were doing and where they were when the tragedy struck. First, they asked within 24 hours of the event. A subset of these students were then asked the same questions two-and-a-half years later and rated how confident they were of their memory. Comparing the answers from those two time points revealed that people remained highly confident in their memory—even though their recollections two-and-a-half years later were not accurate. For example, one respondent who had originally reported being "in my religion class and some people walked in and talked about it" later reported being "in my freshman dorm with my roommate and we were watching TV." Thus, it seems that emotional memories may elicit higher confidence in one's own memory, even though they are as vulnerable to decay and error as any other type of memory.

Similar findings emerged from a later study that improved on the design of Neisser and Harsch's experiment. On September 12, 2001—one day after the 9/11 attacks—more than 50 Duke University students reported how they learned of the attack, as well as their memory for a recent mundane event (Talarico & Rubin, 2003). Instead of only reporting their memories again two-and-a-half years later—which in the Neisser and Harsch study had left open the possibility of slower decay of emotional memories than of mundane memories—students reported their memories again either 1, 6, or 32 weeks later. Consistent with the earlier study, memories of the terrorist attack and of a mundane event decayed similarly over time, even though participants reported a high level of confidence and sense of vividness associated with the emotional memories. Evidence from other studies suggests that despite such vividness and confidence, emotional memories are susceptible to distortion, just as non-emotional memories are (e.g., Strange & Takarangi, 2015).

RETROGRADE MEMORY ENHANCEMENT   Although emotional memories are susceptible to distortion, behavioral and neurobiological research nevertheless suggests that emotional arousal can strengthen memory. Learning material just before emotions are triggered can make it easier to remember (e.g., Anderson et al., 2006; Cahill et al., 2003; Knight & Mather 2009; McGaugh 2006; Nielson et al., 2005), an effect known as a **retrograde memory enhancement**. In one intriguing study, students who watched an emotion-inducing film clip after a classroom lecture performed better on a test 2 weeks later than did students who watched an emotionally neutral clip (Nielson & Arentsen, 2012).

Research from both the human and animal literature suggests that stress hormones help solidify memory of material learned just before an emotional trigger. (In contrast, Chapter 7 will show how excessive stress experienced just before or during learning seems to impair memory; Shields et al., 2017.) For example, when rats were administered stress hormones after a training phase, they subsequently exhibited enhanced memory for their training. However, when the stress hormones were blocked (via injection of what are known as *beta-blockers*), their behavior indicated impaired memory compared with counterparts who received stress hormones without beta-blockers (Liang et al., 1986). This finding raises intriguing possibilities for preventing intrusive memories following trauma, such as those characteristic of post-traumatic stress disorder, or PTSD (**RESEARCH FOCUS 6.2**). Similarly, when human participants were intravenously administered doses of epinephrine (i.e., adrenaline) immediately after viewing a series of pictures, they freely recalled more items a week later than did participants who were injected with saline instead (Cahill & Alkire, 2003). Notably, because the stress hormones were administered after learning, their impact could not be attributed to changes in motivation, emotion, or attention during encoding. Instead, they appeared to affect what's known as memory *consolidation*, which refers to the solidification of memories over time, and which we will cover in more detail in Chapter 7.

RESEARCH FOCUS 6.2

A Pill to Eliminate PTSD?

An intriguing possibility from a clinical psychology perspective is that the mechanisms underlying emotion-driven memory enhancement might play a role in the type of traumatic, intrusive memories at the core of post-traumatic stress disorder (PTSD). If so, then might it be possible to prevent PTSD by administering a beta-blocker soon after a traumatic event?

This is what psychiatrist Roger Pitman and his colleagues set out to test. In one study, trauma-exposed patients from an emergency department were given either a dose of the beta-blocker propranolol (which can block effects of stress hormones) or a placebo (Pitman et al., 2002). They were then assessed 1 and 3 months later in a procedure whereby they first listened to audio recordings of scripts describing the traumatic event and then spent 30 seconds imagining the event. As part of the procedure, researchers collected physiological measures of emotional arousal, such as heart rate, skin conductance, and electromyograms (i.e., the recording of face muscle activity). This procedure has been shown to differentiate between people with and without PTSD (Pitman et al., 1987). Whereas roughly half of the patients who received the placebo showed heightened physiological activity at follow-up, none of those who received the

Knowledge of the mechanisms that cause emotional events to persist in memory might lead to the development of pills to reduce intrusive memories characteristic of PTSD.

beta-blocker did, suggesting the treatment might indeed be effective at preventing PTSD. Research continues on this treatment and on the conditions under which it is most effective (Brunet et al., 2008).

The Constructive Nature of Memory

Think about one of your most personally affecting memories. Maybe it's a perfect moment on a pristine beach on the other side of the world, or maybe it's the first date with the love of your life. It might be a moment of undiluted joy or of profound despair. In many cases, we have the sense that these kinds of memories are what make us who we are today. But what if our memories of such events are not faithful, objective recordings of our experiences and instead are representations that we construct for ourselves during the very act of trying to remember? In many ways, this appears to be the case, and this is what is referred to as the "constructive" nature of memory.

Our minds seek meaning, and this can both increase and decrease the accuracy of memory. As we've already discussed, when it comes to memorizing lists of items or studying for an exam, we can improve memory by attending to the material's deeper meaning, or even by inventing meaning where none naturally exists. However, whereas this can come in handy when done strategically, our minds also have a tendency to spontaneously fill in meanings in ways that can lead our memories astray. It can lead us to have **false memories**: remembrance of things that may never have happened. One way that researchers have shown this in the lab is through what is known as the *Deese/Roediger-McDermott task* (Deese, 1959; Roediger & McDermott, 1995), a task that can induce false memories, and which you can try in **SEE FOR YOURSELF 6.2**.

> ► **See for Yourself 6.2**
>
> ## The Deese/Roediger-McDermott Effect
>
> This is a test. Read the following two lists of words:
>
> **List 1**: nurse, sick, lawyer, medicine, health, hospital, dentist, physician, ill, patient, office, stethoscope, surgeon, clinic, cure
>
> **List 2**: bed, rest, awake, tired, dream, wake, snooze, blanket, doze, slumber, snore, nap, peace, yawn, drowsy
>
> Now, without looking at the lists, write down all the words you remember before reading further.

SPOILER ALERT: Don't read this paragraph until you have tried See for Yourself 6.2! Now let's score your test. Did you write down "nurse"? Good job if you did. How about "blanket"? Great! Okay, how about "doctor" and "sleep"? You did? Lots of people do, but here's the thing: neither of those words appeared on the lists. Yet these are often the first words that people write down. If you take a close look at the two lists, you'll see that although neither "doctor" nor "sleep" appears, the words in list 1 all are closely associated with "doctor" and the words in list 2 are all closely related to "sleep." The **Deese/Roediger-McDermott effect** (that is, the effect elicited by the Deese/Roediger-McDermott task, Roediger & McDermott, 1995) is the tendency to "remember" items that didn't appear but that are meaningfully related to the other items in the list. One reason that this effect is thought to occur is because of how people organize information in their minds, clustering bits and pieces together according to shared meaning and connections with other knowledge. When people read a list of words that are all linked to the word "sleep" (for example), their minds seem to fill in the missing piece, causing them to remember seeing the word "sleep" as well. See the Discovery Lab on false memory to learn more.

DISCOVERY LAB
False Memory

► CHECKPOINT 6.4

1. What is hyperthymestic syndrome? Some people with this syndrome appear to have structural differences in their brains. Why is it not necessarily the case that these structural differences are an underlying cause of a person's superior autobiographical memory?

2. What are flashbulb memories?

3. What is the Deese/Roediger-McDermott effect, and why is it thought to occur?

6.5 Memory Failures

Our memories are constant companions and touchstones in our lives, so it would stand to reason that we are all memory experts to some extent. So how can so many of us be so wrong about how memory works? In one survey, respondents were asked whether they agreed with the following statements:

• "Human memory works like a video camera, accurately recording the events we see and hear so that we can review and inspect them later"—63% agreed.

• "The testimony of one confident eyewitness should be enough evidence to convict a defendant of a crime"—about 37% agreed.

- "Hypnosis is useful in helping witnesses accurately recall details of a crime"—about 55% agreed.
- "Once you have experienced an event and formed a memory of it, that memory does not change"—over 47% agreed.

How many memory researchers and experts agreed with these statements? In each case, none (Simons & Chabris, 2011).

The ramifications of such widespread misunderstanding of memory become clear when you consider that such assumptions heavily influence the workings of the legal system. According to The Innocence Project—an organization dedicated to exonerating wrongfully convicted individuals—in cases where wrongful convictions have been overturned due to DNA evidence, eyewitness testimony had played a heavy hand in over 70% of the convictions.

Much of what we've discussed so far pertains to successful memory and methods for improving its accuracy. However, even under the best of circumstances, memory can be unreliable, suggestible, and subject to distortion. This can be disconcerting: the stories we tell ourselves and others about important events in our lives become woven into our sense of who we are. The idea that we might be constructing it on the spot can throw into question everything we know about ourselves.

And yet, this is what it comes down to: memory works not as a camera that records and faithfully stores our experiences, storing them with high fidelity for us to retrieve later. Instead, each act of remembrance is an act of reconstruction. We may remember isolated bits of information, but the act of bringing to mind a cohesive memory involves binding these isolated bits into a cohesive whole. In many cases, those isolated bits themselves build an incomplete picture and we need to fill in the gaps. Many factors influence how we fill those gaps and whether we bind the bits and pieces together accurately. For example, sitting alongside those bits and pieces in the recesses of our minds are bits and pieces that can come from other experiences we've had, experiences we've only imagined, and assumptions and expectations that we hold about the way things ought to have been. This is a major reason why memory is so suggestible.

The experience of memory failure requires no definition—we all know what it feels like to grope for an answer to a difficult exam question, to later realize we forgot to pick up something at the grocery store, or to be embarrassingly unable to greet an acquaintance by name ("Hey… *you*, …how's it going?").

When a search for something in memory yields nothing, is it because the memory trace is gone forever or is it because the memory couldn't be retrieved at the moment you needed it? It turns out that memory failures can happen during encoding, storage, or retrieval. At the encoding stage, forgetting can be attributed to distraction or inattention. In the storage phase, forgetting can happen when information is poorly consolidated (see Chapter 7 for a discussion of consolidation), often due to distraction, but sometimes due to simple factors such as a poor night's sleep. During retrieval, forgetting can happen when our search for memories fails due to weak memory traces or excessive competition from other memories.

The failings of everyday memory are so common and often so systematic that they could fill a book. In fact, they have: in his excellent (and highly recommended) book *Seven Sins of Memory*, psychology professor Daniel Schacter outlines several ways that memory can fail us, ranging from the routine erosion of memory over time to more provocative aspects of memory distortion such as suggestibility and misattribution. The "seven sins" that Schacter outlines are:

1. *Transience:* The forgetting of information over time
2. *Absent-mindedness:* The failure to encode due to inattention

3. *Blocking:* The inability to access memories that are intact and encoded
4. *Misattribution:* The failure to remember the source of a memory
5. *Suggestibility:* The tendency to reshape one's memory according to misleading external information
6. *Bias:* The tendency to reshape memory according to one's knowledge, beliefs, or feelings
7. *Persistence:* The intrusion of memories that we wish we could forget

Transience

As we all have experienced, sometimes memories simply fade over time. This was documented by Ebbinghaus in his classic studies of memory. As you may recall from Chapter 1 (and from the discussion of the spacing effect earlier in this chapter), Ebbinghaus was a pioneer in the scientific study of memory and ran virtually all his tests on himself. He conducted much of his research by learning nonsense words, which are difficult to link with meanings that might affect how long they linger in memory (e.g., "dax," "yat"), and then testing his memory for them after various intervals of time. By doing so, Ebbinghaus was able to trace what is known as the **forgetting curve**—an estimate of the rate at which information fades from memory (**FIGURE 6.10**).

For his research, Ebbinghaus developed a creative method known as a **"savings measure,"** which refers to how much less you would need to study material in a second study session, compared with a first, in order to learn it perfectly. For example, imagine that you need to cycle through a set of flash cards 100 times in order to remember them perfectly. After some time has passed, your memory will decay and you will need to study them again to remember them all. This time, though, you might find that you need to cycle through them only 80 times in order to remember them all. In this case, you would have saved 20% in terms of study time necessary. If you hadn't waited so long before your second study session, you might have saved even more time. Using this method, Ebbinghaus (1885) found that forgetting occurs most quickly in the first hour

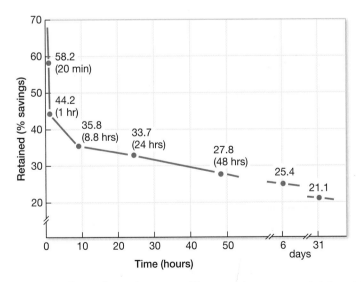

FIGURE 6.10 Ebbinghaus's forgetting curve The curve demonstrates that the relationship between time since studying and how much is retained in memory is curvilinear. Forgetting occurs most rapidly soon after learning and then starts to level off. (After M. H. Erdelyi. 1996. *The Recovery of Unconscious Memories: Hypermnesia and Reminiscence.* University of Chicago Press: Chicago, IL. Based on H. Ebbinghaus. 1913. *Memory: A Contribution to Experimental Psychology.* Trans. by H. A. Ruger and C. E. Bussenius. Teachers College, Columbia University: New York.)

FIGURE 6.11 **Absent-mindedness** Yo-Yo Ma, one of the world's greatest cello players, accidentally forgot his $2.5-million cello in the trunk of a taxi cab after a moment of inattention.

after learning and slows down after that, a finding that has been replicated more recently as well (e.g., Murre & Dros, 2015).

Absent-Mindedness

In many cases, failure to remember something can be traced back to a failure to encode it due to inattention or distraction. This makes sense. After all, as we saw in Chapter 4, inattention can lead to failures to even *see* something (i.e., inattentional blindness), no less remember it. Today it seems that we are more distracted than ever and moving at a faster pace. Consider the story of world-renowned cellist Yo-Yo Ma, who placed his $2.5-million cello into the trunk of a taxi and then forgot to take it when he arrived at his destination. (Fortunately, after a call to the police 10 minutes later, the taxi was tracked down and the cello was recovered.) What could lead to such forgetting? Clearly, the cello was not lost from memory—otherwise, Ma wouldn't have called the police (**FIGURE 6.11**). You can read more about this on Oxford Learning Link.

In Yo-Yo Ma's case, inattention could have come into play either at encoding or when the opportunity for retrieval arose. However, controlled lab experiments have shown that how you pay attention at the time of encoding can indeed affect how much you remember (e.g., Hyman et al., 2018). **SEE FOR YOURSELF 6.3** demonstrates a different memory effect, which we will examine later.

> ▶ **See for Yourself 6.3**
>
> ## Study Phase
>
> This is a demonstration of a memory effect that we will discuss in a few pages. Before we get to that, memorize the following two lists:
>
> **Fruits:** orange, nectarine, pineapple, banana, cantaloupe, lemon
>
> **Drinks:** bourbon, scotch, tequila, brandy, gin, rum
>
> Although it might not be clear yet why we've asked you to do this, we'll come back to it in a few pages in "The Fate of Unselected Memories."
>
> (From M. C. Anderson et al. *J Exp Psychol* 3: 1063–1087.)

Using cues to direct attention to target items and away from nontarget items, researchers have shown that attended items are better remembered than unattended items (Turk-Browne et al., 2013; Uncapher et al., 2011). To simulate distractions common in the real world, researchers can ask participants to do two tasks at the same time in the lab. Such manipulations are known as **divided-attention tasks** (or dual-task experiments, covered in Chapter 5). For example, while viewing a list of words, you may also be required to count backward by three starting with the number 457. Or while viewing a visual list, you may be required to monitor an auditory list for fruit words among general food words. Performing a secondary task reliably impairs memory encoding (Baddeley et al., 1984; Craik et al., 1996). This may be because dual tasks disrupt activity in lateral prefrontal cortex, an area important for encoding and active during subsequent memory (Shallice et al., 1994). This might be something to consider next time you are tempted to study for an exam while watching your favorite show!

Besides actively distracting people with divided-attention tasks, researchers also study how some people are more distractible. Older adults, for example, have more difficulty ignoring distraction than younger adults do (Gazzaley et al., 2005). When viewing scene stimuli, under instructions to ignore face stimuli, older adults were less able to suppress the ignored stimuli. While younger adults showed big differences between neural activity linked with attended stimuli and ignored stimuli in the relevant brain areas (e.g., between a scene area when scenes are attended and a face area when faces are ignored), older adults showed smaller differences. Conversely, think about who would have better memory for the ignored stimuli. It turned out that older adults had better memory for the to-be-ignored faces because they were more easily distracted by them; younger adults were better at ignoring the faces, but consequently had poorer memory for them when given a surprise memory test (Gazzaley & D'Esposito, 2007).

Divided attention helps explain some effects of memory bias (Loftus et al., 1987). For example, when participants viewed a restaurant scene where a customer was pointing a gun at the cashier, they had poorer memory for the customer and other scene details compared with the control condition where the customer was handing the cashier a check. Eye movement recordings suggested that this was because the weapon drew attention to itself and away from other aspects of the scene. This is known as **weapon focus**, the failure to process other things because one's attention is so focused on the threatening weapon, and it works similarly for other types of emotionally salient stimuli, such as a car crash scene (Kensinger et al., 2007; Kern et al., 2005; Steblay, 1992).

It's common for people to try to work or study in front of the TV or with Netflix open on their computer, but evidence suggests that such "divided attention" impairs memory for what you're trying to learn. It's probably better to schedule your studying and entertainment for different times.

Blocking

Failures of memory sometimes stem from problems at the retrieval stage even when material has been well encoded. The feeling of there being some impediment or obstacle standing in the way of successful retrieval is known as **blocking**. A nice demonstration of this is the **tip-of-the-tongue phenomenon**, wherein people experience the feeling of not being able to bring to mind a word despite being able to recall aspects such as the number of syllables, which syllable is stressed, and several letters from the word (Brown & McNeill, 1966). You have probably experienced this feeling yourself. If not, see if you experience it in **SEE FOR YOURSELF 6.4**.

▶ **See for Yourself 6.4**

It's Right on the Tip of My Tongue!

Want to get the feeling that something is right on the tip of your tongue? That you have knowledge buried somewhere in your brain but can't quite access it? Quick: What is the word for underground passageways often used for religious purposes or burials?

In searching your memory for the answer, you may feel like you can almost, but not quite, find the right word. You might know that the word begins with a "c" or even that the first syllable is "cat." You might have the strong sense that the word has three syllables. After fumbling around for a few seconds, you might arrive at the correct answer: "catacombs." This fumbling sensation—the frustrating feeling of "knowing that you know" without being able to put your finger on the answer—is what's meant by the "tip of the tongue phenomenon."

Want to experience it again? What is the capital of Denmark?

Retrieval failure is a common cause of forgetting. The information is intact, but lost in the "stacks" at the moment that you need it. The answer to an exam question may pop into your head after walking out of the room or when reminded by a friend outside the test room. The name of the familiar person that you can't recall will, you hope, come to mind as you engage in banter (but all too embarrassingly, this often happens after you've parted ways). Searching your memory can feel like searching for something in the visual environment. Just as you may scan for the face of a friend at the airport, you must scan your vast stores of memories to retrieve relevant information from your mind.

If we consider how much information is stored in our brain throughout a lifetime of experience and studying, it is remarkable how well we are able to retrieve and bring to mind individual memories. Unfortunately, the brain does not contain an Internet search box. Instead, countless memories occlude and interfere with each other, making successful retrieval difficult—like finding a matching sock when all other sock colors and shapes in a pile or drawer are similar. Thus, memory retrieval can be viewed as an act of internally focused (or reflective) selective attention (Chun & Johnson, 2011), because attention is directed to representations in the mind rather than to objects in the world (as described in Chapter 5; also see Chun et al., 2011).

MEMORY INTERFERENCE   When memories compete with each other and make it harder to recall what you are trying to recall, this is known as interference.

Memory interference is commonly studied with the **A-B, A-C learning paradigm**. Participants are first asked to learn to pair two items, usually unrelated, such as "CAT-CUP." This is called an A-B pair. Following A-B encoding, participants then learn either a new unrelated pair (D-E pair such as "BAT-HAM"), a new related pair (A-C pair such as "CAT-MAP"), or nothing as a control. When memory is tested for the A-B association by asking what the first word associated with CAT was, people do worse when they had to subsequently learn A-C (CAT-MAP) than when they had to learn either the D-E pair (BAT-HAM) or nothing. Interference arises in this case because the word CAT is associated with two items (both CUP and with MAP). This is known as **retroactive interference** because memory (for A-B) was impaired by something that happened later (A-C).

When memory is tested for the A-C pair by asking what the second (or more recent) word associated with CAT was, then people do worse than when retrieving the D-E pair (BAT-HAM). This is **proactive interference** because memory (for A-C) was impaired by something that happened earlier (A-B). In sum, competition or interference between relevant and irrelevant associations directly influences retrieval difficulty, increasing or decreasing the chances of forgetting (Mensink & Raaijmakers, 1988).

Another way to measure retrieval interference is to compare the time it takes to recognize various statements that have overlapping elements (e.g., "the fireman is in the park," "the lawyer is in the park," "the dogwalker is in the park"). The more examples that get associated this way (in this case, more things that are in the park), the slower people are to recognize the statements from memory. This is known as the **fan effect**, and it shows that memory retrieval is dependent on the number of elements associated with the same fact—the more associations there are (i.e., "fan size"), the greater the interference (Anderson, 1974).

QUANTIFYING INTERFERENCE THROUGH NEUROIMAGING   It is possible to quantify the interference during memory retrieval by having competing associations come from different categories that involve distinct neural representations. For example, Kuhl and colleagues employed an A-B, A-C task in which A was a cue word and B and C were faces, scenes, or objects (Kuhl et al., 2011, 2012). Participants first had to learn to pair the word (e.g., ROSE) with an image of a famous place (e.g., the Taj Mahal), and then later had to learn to pair the same word (ROSE) with an image of a famous face (e.g., actor Robert De Niro). When asked to recall the second association (Robert De Niro), memory retrieval should cause reactivation of face activity in the brain,

supporting people's memory of the correct associate. Importantly, the researchers found that fMRI enabled them to quantify the extent to which a face was reactivated versus how much a scene was reactivated. On interference trials, face-related activity (presumably reflecting reactivation of Robert De Niro) co-occurred with scene activity (presumably reflecting reactivation of the Taj Mahal). Strikingly, the more scene-related activity there was, the worse people were at recalling Robert De Niro. This study directly revealed neural evidence for interference effects in memory retrieval.

Amidst all this interference, attentional control plays an important role in successful retrieval, and this relies on intact functioning of the prefrontal cortex. Damage to prefrontal cortex impairs memory retrieval (Janowsky et al., 1989), especially for associative memory tasks that involve interference, as in A-B, A-C tasks (Shimamura et al., 1995). This is not just a general memory deficit, because patients with prefrontal cortex damage do OK with the initial associations (A-B). Instead, prefrontal damage causes bigger problems when there are competing associations (A-C). Neuroimaging studies also reveal strong prefrontal activation during tasks that involve retrieval competition (Badre & Wagner, 2007). Prefrontal activity is higher when fan size (that is, the number of associations) is greater (Sohn et al., 2003), or in A-B, A-C tasks (Kuhl et al., 2007, 2008), or during semantic retrieval tasks with interference (Badre et al., 2005; Thompson-Schill et al., 1999).

THE FATE OF UNSELECTED MEMORIES   When selecting for a memory, what happens to the other competing memories? Retrieval of target memories causes unselected memories to be lost; this phenonmenon is known as **retrieval-induced forgetting**, or retrieval-induced inhibition. This is tested in a three-phase experiment that includes study, retrieval, and test phases. In the study phase, participants learn several items from different categories, as you did for the categories Fruits and Drinks in See for Yourself 6.3 (don't look back yet). During the retrieval phase, participants practice retrieving only half of the items from a category, cued with word-completion tasks. For example, try to recall the following items from the fruit list in See for Yourself 6.3: or_____, nec_____, pine_____. Then, in the test phase, all of the examples from all the categories are probed. Naturally, you should be best at recognizing the words "orange," "nectarine," and "pineapple" because you practiced them in the retrieval phase. However, remembering these items makes it harder to remember the other items from the same category (banana, cantaloupe, and lemon). Memory for these "inhibited" words is even worse than that for any of the words in the category of Drinks, which were also not practiced in the retrieval phase. This shows that the act of retrieving target memories in the Fruits category impaired or caused forgetting of other memories in that category (Anderson et al., 1994; also see Barnier et al., 2004).

Misattribution

How many times has this happened to you: as you are about to leave home for a few days, you remind yourself to check that the windows and doors are locked, but later that day you have a niggling doubt—did you actually lock up or did you only imagine yourself locking up? In this case, you would be having trouble with your **source monitoring**, your ability to keep track of where your memory came from (something you actually did versus something you imagined doing; Johnson et al., 1993).

Confusions about the sources of our memories—**source misattribution**—are a common form of memory failure. Such confusions have sometimes been linked to cases of unintentional plagiarism. If you are a fan of classic rock, you may be able to hum a few bars of George Harrison's "My Sweet Lord." If you are

Courtesy of the Gerald R. Ford Library and Museum/David Hume Kennerly

© Pictorial Press Ltd/Alamy Stock Photo

FIGURE 6.12 Source misattribution In one of the more famous instances of possible source misattribution, former Beatle George Harrison was sued for copyright infringement, as his song "My Sweet Lord" was eerily similar to "He's So Fine" by the Chiffons.

sitting next to other fans of classic rock, they could be excused for thinking that you are humming "He's So Fine" by the Chiffons—they're the same tune! It appears that Harrison had fallen prey to source misattribution, confusing the tune in his head for one of his own creation, resulting in his being sued for copyright infringement (**FIGURE 6.12**).

TYPES OF SOURCE MISATTRIBUTION   Psychologists have distinguished between different types of source misattributions. For example, *external source monitoring* refers to the ability to distinguish between two external sources: Did I have lunch with Melanie at the pizza place or at the Mexican restaurant? *Internal source monitoring* refers to the ability to distinguish between internally generated sources—for example, distinguishing what you might have thought from what you actually said (Johnson et al., 1993). As highlighted in a **reality monitoring** framework by psychologist Marcia Johnson, people often have difficulty distinguishing memories of external events from memories of internally generated information (Johnson & Raye, 1981; also see Garry et al., 1996). This is known as **source confusion**. Earlier, in See for Yourself 6.2, you were asked to recall words from a list of items that were related to the word "doctor." Many people recall seeing the word "doctor" even though it does not appear in the list—in this case, the word "doctor" may have been internally generated, but people often confuse it as having been present. Source confusion errors are common in everyday life and can be easily triggered in the lab. In one study, people were shown or asked to imagine different types of images. For example, they were shown an image of a magnifying glass (external source) and asked to imagine a lollipop (internal source). When their memory was tested later, they had difficulty distinguishing which they had been shown and which they had imagined (Henkel et al., 2000).

MISATTRIBUTION AND JUDGMENT   The importance of knowing the origins of our memories extends beyond the domain of memory itself and influences our attitudes and opinions. For example, if you plan to buy a new camera and have heard a range of positive and negative reviews about a particular model, remembering the sources of the reviews would help you figure out which ones to weigh most heavily. If only you could remember which sources provided which reviews.

In one intriguing demonstration of how easy it is to influence a person's judgment via misattribution, researchers presented participants with lists of names that they had not encountered before. Would you say that "Sebastian Weisdorf" is the name of a famous person? Most people wouldn't, as it was a name invented for the experiment. However, in the experiment, this changed if participants had seen the name previously on a list but couldn't remember that it had been on the list. When participants *could* recollect seeing the name on the list, they were unlikely to say that the name was famous. However, when participants were shown the name after a significant delay, they were more likely to mistake the name as belonging to a famous person. This effect is thought to occur because the name—when seen again—evokes a feeling of familiarity. With the passage of time, participants were less able to attribute this familiarity to its appearance on the previous list and were more likely to misattribute the familiarity to fame (Jacoby et al., 1989).

Source memory appears to improve over the course of child development, reaching relatively mature levels by about 6 years of age, possibly due to the development of children's frontal lobes (Newcombe et al., 2000; Schacter et al., 1995). In one study, young children received information about the contents of a drawer in one of three ways: they either saw the contents for themselves, were told what the contents were, or deduced the contents after being given a clue. The children were then asked, both immediately and after a delay, how they had come to know about the drawer's contents. Whereas 5-years-olds seemed to have no difficulty identifying the source of their knowledge, 3-year-olds had more trouble (Gopnik & Graf, 1988). Intriguingly, intact source memory appears to protect against the power of suggestion. Children who exhibited an ability to keep track of the source of their knowledge were less influenced by leading questions after hearing a story (Giles et al., 2002).

Suggestibility

In a now classic experiment, researchers Elizabeth Loftus and John Palmer showed participants a simulated car accident, which they then had to recollect. Some participants were asked to estimate the speed of the cars when they "hit" each other, and some participants were asked to estimate their speed when they "smashed" into each other. This word change led to a striking effect: those who heard the word "smashed" remembered the cars as going faster than did those who heard the word "hit." In addition, those who heard the word "smashed" were more likely to remember the scene being littered with broken glass even though none had been present (Loftus & Palmer, 1974). If memory is so suggestible that it can be altered through the use of one word, imagine how many other factors might be altering our memories each day! If you are interested in hearing more on this topic from Elizabeth Loftus herself, she discusses her research in a widely watched TED talk.

A fair criticism of such work might be that **memory suggestibility**—the altering of memory through leading questions and cues—is typically demonstrated using controlled, somewhat artificial lab tasks. Could memory be similarly suggestible when someone is trying to recall a truly stressful firsthand experience? The answer appears to be yes. In one study, researchers tested more than 800 military personnel who—as part of training—were imprisoned in a mock POW camp. From the military's perspective, the point of this "imprisonment" was to increase soldiers' resilience in a prison camp environment. As part of training, the military personnel were isolated and subjected to a highly stressful interrogation by a survival school instructor whom they did not know. When they were later presented with misleading information—either in the form of a questionnaire or in the form of photographs—they experienced distorted memory for the event, including misidentifying the aggressive interrogator (Morgan et al., 2013).

Most studies of memory suggestibility seek to change people's memory for an event that they witnessed or experienced, but is it possible to implant a **false memory**—that is, a memory for an event that never occurred at all? Strikingly, the answer again appears to be yes. In one study, participants were given descriptions of four childhood events that they were told had happened when they were with a family member. Three of the events were true, but one of the events—getting lost in a shopping mall—had never actually occurred. Participants were then interviewed twice. At the first interview, they were "reminded" of the four events and were asked to write down everything they could remember about them. One to 2 weeks later, they were asked to remember the four events again and were then

In a classic study on false memory, researchers were able to implant a memory of getting lost in a mall as a child, an event that had not happened.

asked to identify which of the events had never happened. Although most participants were able to identify the false event, several wound up "remembering" getting lost in the mall as if it had actually happened to them (Loftus & Pickrell, 1995). Understanding such memory errors may be especially relevant in today's world of easily manipulated images and "deep fakes," as some evidence suggests that doctored photos may be particularly effective in creating such false memories (Wade, et al., 2002; also see Garry & Gerrie, 2005; Lindsay et al., 2004; Nash, et al. 2009). **RESEARCH FOCUS 6.3** further explores the subject of individual differences in memory suggestibility.

RESEARCH FOCUS 6.3

Individual Differences in Suggestibility

Phenomena such as the Deese/Roediger-McDermott effect (see See for Yourself 6.2) have been used not only to reveal mechanisms of memory, but also to probe individual differences in memory suggestibility. Such work has sometimes stoked controversy precisely because it raises questions about our recollections of powerful experiences that we often assume to have shaped our very being.

Consider, for example, researchers who were concerned about recovered memories among abuse survivors. Recovered memories are ones that don't continuously haunt survivors but instead are memories that people report having forgotten or repressed until they were brought back to awareness through some intervention or event. Although many women who were sexually abused when younger reported having never forgotten the experience, the researchers noted that some reported having had no memory of the experience until entering therapy years later in order to uncover the source of persistent unease. Could it be that the very therapies designed to recover repressed memories accidentally ended up planting false memories of abuse?

To indirectly assess this possibility, the researchers gave a version of the Deese/Roediger-McDermott task to four groups of women:

- Those who reported recovered memories of sexual abuse
- Those who reported no such memories but nevertheless believed that they were sexually abused as children
- Those who were sexually abused and never forgot it
- Those who had never been sexually abused

The data suggested that those who reported having recovered memories of abuse were more prone to false memories in the Deese/Roediger-McDermott task than were the other groups, suggesting that they may indeed have been susceptible to memory distortions during therapy (Clancy et al., 2000).

To be clear, this research does not suggest that most testimonies of traumatic memories are invalid or exaggerated. It does not even indicate that all reports of *recovered* memories are false. Indeed, one study found evidence that some recovered memories of sexual abuse were of real events (Williams, 1995). Taken together, though, research does underscore the fact that memory is not like a video recorder that can be played back accurately each time a memory is accessed. It is precisely because abuse causes devastating pain that it is important to understand circumstances and mechanisms that might differentiate distorted memories from accurate and haunting memories of abuse survivors.

Paralleling the developmental course of source memory (discussed in this section), evidence suggests that the memories of children are particularly suggestible. In one study, children in a school classroom received an uneventful 2-minute visit from a man called Sam Stone. The children were assigned to one of four conditions:

1. In a *control* condition, they received no information about Sam Stone before his visit and were subsequently asked about his visit in a neutral manner, once a week for the next 4 weeks.

2. Children in a *stereotype* condition received information about Sam Stone's "personality" prior to his visit, which depicted him as nice but bumbling. These children were then questioned about his visit in a neutral manner for the next 4 weeks.

3. Children in a *suggestion* condition did not receive any previsit information about Sam Stone but were asked misleading questions about his visit for the next 4 weeks, including suggestions that Sam Stone had ripped a book and had soiled a teddy bear during his visit.

4. Children in a *stereotype-plus-suggestion* condition received both the information about Sam Stone's personality and the misleading questions in the aftermath of his visit.

When interviewed 10 weeks after the visit, children in the control group exhibited relatively accurate memories of the visit, but those in the stereotype, suggestion, and particularly the stereotype-plus-suggestion groups were more likely to report that they had witnessed Sam Stone rip a book and soil a teddy bear, when in fact they had witnessed no such thing. This was truer of children ages 3 to 4 than it was of children ages 5 to 6 (Leichtman & Ceci, 1995).

At the other end of the developmental lifespan, cognitive aging appears to be linked with increased susceptibility to false memories, including those that arise due to misinformation and misattribution (Jacoby, 1999; McDaniel et al., 2008; Wylie et al., 2014). One hypothesis is that this stems from age-related changes in the brain's medial temporal lobe and prefrontal cortex (Devitt & Schacter, 2016).

Bias

When people are said to be looking back with "rose-colored lenses," the implication is that they are not remembering things as they objectively were, but rather that their memories are skewed by the sentimental desire to assume the best of the past. Evidence suggests that such memory bias is more the rule than the exception, and the sources of bias extend well beyond mere sentiment.

All of us color our memories with our preexisting notions of who we are and what should have been. The mind uses **schemas**—that is, knowledge or expectations about an event—to construct memory. When such expectations match the details of what happened, they can help memory. It is when these expectations and assumptions do not match events that such schemas reveal themselves (**SEE FOR YOURSELF 6.5**).

▶ **See for Yourself 6.5**

Remembering "The War of the Ghosts"

A famous example of the influence of schemas on memory comes from a classic study by the British psychologist Frederic Bartlett (1932). Read the following short story:

One night two young men from Egulac went down to the river to hunt seals, and while they were there it became foggy and calm. Then they heard war cries, and they thought: "Maybe this is a war party." They escaped to the shore and hid behind a log. Now canoes came up, and they heard the noise of paddles and saw one canoe coming up to them. There were five men in the canoe, and they said:

"What do you think? We wish to take you along. We are going up the river to make war on the people."

One of the young men said: "I have no arrows."

"Arrows are in the canoe," they said.

"I will not go along. I might be killed. My relatives do not know where I have gone. But you," he said, turning to the other, "may go with them."

So one of the young men went, but the other returned home. And the warriors went on up the river to a town on the other side of Kalama. The people came down to the water, and they began to fight, and many were killed. But presently the young man heard one of the warriors say: "Quick, let us go home; that Indian has been hit." Now he thought: "Oh, they are ghosts." He did not feel sick, but they said he had been shot.

So the canoes went back to Egulac, and the young man went ashore to his house and made a fire. And he told everybody and said: "Behold I accompanied the ghosts,

(Continued)

and we went to fight. Many of our fellows were killed, and many of those who attacked us were killed. They said I was hit, and I did not feel sick."

He told it all, and then he became quiet. When the sun rose, he fell down. Something black came out of his mouth. His face became contorted. The people jumped up and cried. He was dead.

(From F. C. Bartlett. 1932. *Remembering: A Study in Experimental and Social Psychology.* Cambridge University Press: New York.)

Now, try to recall the story in as much detail as possible.

To contemporary Western eyes, the "War of the Ghosts" story can seem unusual—perhaps even more than it did to readers in England during the early twentieth century, when Bartlett used it to arrive at insights about memory that still resonate today. The story actually comes from Canadian Indian folklore, and an interesting thing happened when Bartlett's participants tried to recall the story. They were asked to recall it several times at different time intervals. As you might expect, details faded from memory with time— but what was really striking was the nature of the mistakes they made, which were such that the story began to conform more and more to the norms of Edwardian England. For example, in their memory, the seal hunting party became a "sailing expedition." Bartlett suggested that as people's precise and detailed memory of what they had actually read or heard faded, their recollections grew ever more influenced by their schemas. See the Discovery Lab on memory schemas to learn more.

DISCOVERY LAB
Memory Schemas

Our schemas can come into play in systematic ways. For example, when we try to remember how we felt about an important event from our past—say, a painful breakup of a romantic relationship—we may color our recollections with our feelings from today. In this case, our recollection of the pain we felt may not measure up to our true experience at the time, precisely because our pain over the experience has healed. This tendency to remember the impact of events through the lens of their impact on us today is known as a **consistency bias**.

Persistence

Why should persistence of memory be considered a "sin" of memory? Wouldn't a long-lasting memory be the sign of a particularly adept mind? It turns out that although forgetting seems like a limitation of human memory, many researchers consider it an adaptive feature of the brain. By reducing competition from distracting memories, target memories may be retrieved more easily and reliably. That is, forgetting less important information allows the brain to work less to retrieve the memories important for a task (Kuhl et al., 2007). Without forgetting, the mind would be cluttered with too much useless information.

In some cases, memories persist despite people wishing that they wouldn't. For example, recall the case of Jill Price, discussed earlier in the chapter and who reports being unable to let her most painful experiences fade with time. This is also the reality for many people who have experienced trauma, including those who suffer from PTSD, which is often characterized by the unwanted intrusion of traumatic memories into daily life. These are known as **intrusive memories**, or **flashbacks**, and a large body of clinically related research aims to understand the nature of such unwanted memories and how to decrease them (Ehlers & Clark, 2000; Ehlers & Steil, 1995; Iyadurai et al., 2018; Newby et al., 2014).

➤ CHECKPOINT 6.5

1. What makes autobiographical memory different from memory for learned facts and figures?

2. What evidence suggests that memory is not like a camera that records everything accurately, but is instead something that we construct?

3. Describe the seven sins of memory described by psychologist Daniel Schacter, and give some examples of each.

4. What is the difference between retroactive interference and proactive interference?

6.6 Implications for Eyewitness Testimony

Let's return now to the case that opened this chapter, the story of an unlikely friendship between an accuser and the falsely accused. The high rate at which eyewitness testimony contributes to wrongful convictions suggests that it is important to apply current understanding of memory pitfalls toward improving such testimony. Such understanding may help improve eyewitness testimony generally, and may also help address findings that people can differ in the quality of their eyewitness testimony. For example, older adults are often worse at making eyewitness identifications than younger adults (Erickson, et al., 2016), and particular challenges arise when interrogating children about their memories (e.g., Zajac & Brown, 2018).

Evidence suggests, for example, that several operating procedures and interview techniques are likely to increase the occurrence of false identification and memory. In recognition of the importance of psychology for guiding the collection of eyewitness testimony, the U.S. Department of Justice issued the first set of national guidelines for such procedures (Technical Working Group for Eyewitness Evidence, 1999). Similarly, the U.S. National Research Council issued a set of recommendations for law enforcement agencies and courts in order to improve accuracy of eyewitness identifications (National Research Council, 2014). These included educating law enforcement officers about perception and memory and training them to avoid suggestiveness. Recommendations also included implementation of "double-blind" lineup procedures, whereby the officers overseeing the lineup are not aware of who the true suspect is (in order to avoid the possibility that they might involuntarily influence the witnesses' reports).

Other recommendations pertained to the way lineup procedures are administered. For example, in the stereotypical lineup procedure, eyewitnesses view several people side by side and attempt to identify the suspect from among them (a "simultaneous lineup" procedure). One potential concern with this technique is that it encourages "relative judgments." That is, this viewing procedure engenders a strategy wherein the eyewitness—rather than looking for a person who *matches* their memory—picks out the person who *comes closest* to the person in their memory. This opens the possibility that eyewitnesses will identify a culprit even when the true perpetrator is not present. A suggestion for addressing this issue has been that eyewitnesses should view members of the lineup one at a time, in order to maximize comparison with memory rather than comparison with each other. Some findings suggest that **sequential lineup** procedures—whereby witnesses make a decision about each lineup member before moving on to the next lineup member—are effective in reducing false identifications. This is particularly the case under double-blind conditions, in which the interviewers themselves do not have insight into which individual is the actual suspect (Wells et al., 2015). The double-blind nature of this scenario helps ensure that witnesses make judgments based solely on their own memories rather than being influenced by any suggestive behavior by the interviewer. That said, it is important to note that it is not universally agreed that sequential lineups are always superior to simultaneous lineups; evidence suggests that under some conditions the simultaneous lineup can decrease the number of errors made (Seale-Carlisle et al., 2019). Thus, there is a continuing need to refine our understanding in order to make the best recommendations possible.

Psychologists have contributed to guidelines for interviewing eyewitnesses that capitalize on known memory mechanisms (Fisher et al., 1987). The system they have advocated—known as the **cognitive interview**—stands in contrast

Simultaneous lineups—as in this image—encourage eyewitnesses to compare the suspects to each other. In contrast, sequential lineups, in which suspects are viewed one at a time, are better at encouraging comparisons with memory.

©iStock.com/RichLegg

to some of the procedures often used by police. For example, arguing that recollections of a traumatic event require focused attention, cognitive interviewers are trained to conduct the interview at a slow rate, asking mostly open-ended questions that encourage a witness to recall the event freely. Prior to this, police interviewers often interrupted witnesses with too many questions, thereby disrupting the witnesses' concentration (Wells et al., 2000).

Studies testing the efficacy of the cognitive interview have typically asked participants to watch a videotape or reenactment of a crime and then to describe their memories of it either via the cognitive interview or in the form of a typical police interview. In laboratory studies, the cognitive interview has been found to yield about 35–75% more information than the more standard police interviews, while eliciting fewer incorrect recollections. Field studies have yielded similar results (Fisher et al., 1989; George & Clifford, 1992; Wells et al., 2000). Thus, memory research is an area of cognitive psychology that has had clear and beneficial impacts on important concerns in everyday society.

➤ CHECKPOINT 6.6

1. What are some recommendations for eyewitness testimony that have stemmed directly from cognitive psychology research?

Chapter Summary

6.1 Define short-term and long-term memory.

Short-term memory refers to information held in mind for a short duration, which fades after several seconds if it is not actively attended to or transferred into long-term memory. The term is often used interchangeably with "working memory," although there are also thought to be differences between the two concepts, such as the more complex involvement of attention and other executive processes in working memory. Long-term memory refers to the long-term storage of information, which can stretch back over decades. Long-term memory might be likened to a warehouse full of stocked filing cabinets: its capacity is immense, but we are not always accessing its contents and holding it "in mind."

Q: Describe a time in your own life when you tried to rely on short-term memory. Describe a time in your life when you relied on long-term memory.

6.2 Describe instances of great memory ability and instances of memory failure.

Memory is fallible, as demonstrated by cases in which eyewitnesses misidentify a stranger, but it is also capable of great feats, such as those performed by memory athletes. Factors that contribute to memory for facts and figures may differ from those that underlie autobiographical memory. Many memory athletes report having only average memory for details of their own lives, just as people who have detailed memories of their lives report having only average memory for facts and figures.

Q: The brains of memory athletes do not appear to be structurally unusual. What instead seems to underlie these people's extraordinary memory abilitites?

6.3 Distinguish between encoding and retrieval, and discuss strategies and factors that can improve memory.

When we encounter and store information in memory, this is known as encoding. When we later recall that information, this is known as retrieval. How we remember information depends both on how we encode it and on factors that come into play when we try to retrieve it. Psychologists have identified strategies that can reduce the amount of information we need to encode (e.g., chunking), enhance the effectiveness of encoding (e.g., method of loci, elaboration, distributed practice), and improve the success of efforts to retrieve information (e.g., testing effect, context-dependent memory).

Q: Select a page or two of material from any chapter in this book, and imagine that you will be tested on that material next week. How would you go about learning the material using each of the strategies described in this chapter?

6.4 Describe how autobiographical memory is constructive.

When psychologists say that memory is "constructive," they typically mean that the act of remembering involves reassembling pieces of information into a mental representation that feels true to what we actually experienced—much like assembling the pieces of a puzzle into a coherent image. There may be missing pieces, but we often don't notice because we fill in the gaps—or even overwrite some pieces—with things we believe belonged in that event and with things we misattribute to that event. Sometimes this can lead us to having false memories about things that may never have happened.

Q: Describe the Deese/Roediger-McDermott effect and what it reveals about the suggestibility of memory.

6.5 Understand how memory failures can affect the way we perceive past experiences.

The failings of everyday memory are common and often systematic. Psychologist Daniel Schacter has referred to some of these as transience (forgetting information over time); absent-mindedness (failure to encode due to inattention); blocking (inability to access memories that are intact and encoded); misattribution (failure to remember the source of a memory); suggestibility (tendency to reshape one's memory according to misleading external information); bias (tendency to reshape memory according to one's knowledge, beliefs, or feelings); and persistence (inability to forget information).

Q: Think about one of your earliest memories, from when you were a child. How confident are you that this memory is accurate? Can you think of factors discussed in this chapter that might have helped shape your memory (e.g., confusing memories based on experience with memories based on what others told you about)? Think about a time that you and a friend or relative remembered things differently from each other. Could differences in your biases, expectations, or other factors have contributed to this disagreement?

6.6 Explain how memory distortions can affect eyewitness testimony.

The high rate at which eyewitness testimony contributes to wrongful convictions suggests that it is important to apply current understanding of memory pitfalls toward improving such testimony. Some work has recommended that lineup procedures use sequential presentations of possible suspects rather than simultaneous presentations, although not all researchers are convinced that this marks an improvement. To help remedy memory distortions that might occur during questioning of eyewitnesses, psychologists have developed the cognitive interview (whereby interviewers ask mostly open-ended questions at a slow rate, encouraging the witness to recall events more freely), based on the idea that recollections of a traumatic event require focused attention.

Q: Consider a recent news story where wrongful conviction may have been the result of a misidentified suspect. How would you hope the investigators would have questioned eyewitnesses?

Key Terms

A-B, A-C learning paradigm
autobiographical memory
blocking
chunking
cognitive interview
consistency bias
context-dependent memory
Deese/Roediger-McDermott effect
depth of encoding
distributed practice
divided-attention tasks
elaboration
encode
false memory
fan effect
flashbulb memories
forgetting curve
generation effect
Google effect

hierarchical organization
hyperthymestic syndrome
iconic memory
infantile amnesia
intrusive memories or flashbacks
long-term memory
massed practice
memory
memory suggestibility
metamemory (or, more broadly, metacognition)
method of loci
mnemonists
mood-dependent memory
proactive interference
reality monitoring
rehearsal
retrieval
retrieval cues

retrieval-induced forgetting (or retrieval-induced inhibition)
retroactive interference
retrograde memory enhancement
schemas
self-reference effect
sensory memory
sequential lineup
short-term memory
source confusion
source monitoring
source misattribution
spacing effect
state-dependent memory
testing effect
tip-of-the-tongue phenomenon
weapon focus

Critical Thinking Questions

1. What aspects of your life—for example, the things you like to do, the kind of person you think you are, your dreams for the future—are shaped by memories that you have? If you could voluntarily choose to forget some painful memories, would you do it? Do you think that would change you as a person?

2. What are some strategies for maximizing your own memory performance?

3. Imagine you are serving on jury duty and need to decide whether the defendant is innocent or guilty. You've heard eyewitness testimony. Keeping in mind what you have read in this chapter, what would it take to convince you that the eyewitness testimony should be trusted?

Discovery Labs

oup.com/he/chun1e

The Sperling Partial Report Paradigm: Iconic Memory

In this experiment, students learn about how much memory can be stored in iconic memory, and how long that information is available by completing several trials where they are shown a 9 × 9 grid of numbers and asked to report the top, middle, or bottom of each row based on one of three tones. Approximate completion time: 25 minutes.

The von Restorff Effect

The phenomenon of remembering unique items in a set with better accuracy was first described by Hedwig von Restorff in 1933. It is often referred to as the von Restorff effect, or the isolation effect. Approximate completion time: 25 minutes.

False Memory

In this experiment, students learn about the phenomenon of creating false memories during recall and recognition tasks. Participants are presented with word lists before being asked to perform a recognition task. Approximate completion time: 15 minutes.

Memory Schemas

In this experiment, students explore the possible role of memory schemas in visual long-term memory. Participants complete trials where they are shown an image, complete a series of math problems, and then attempt to recall the image based on a list of items that may or may not have been visible in the image. Approximate completion time: 15 minutes.

Suggested Readings

Schacter, D. L. (2001). *The Seven Sins of Memory: How the Mind Forgets and Remembers*. Boston: Houghton Mifflin.

Schacter, D. L. (1996). *Searching for Memory: The Brain, the Mind, and the Past*. New York: Basic Books.

Memory Systems

7

One of the biggest contributors to the modern understanding of human memory was not a scientist but a patient. Widely known as H.M., the name kept anonymous until he passed away, Henry Molaison (1926–2008) suffered from severe epileptic seizures throughout his early life. These episodes—like lightning storms coursing throughout the brain—are caused by abnormal electrical activity. Treatments at the time were limited to radical measures, such as removing the brain tissue where the seizures were focused.

In 1952, when H.M. was 27, neurosurgeon William Beecher Scoville performed such a surgery, removing H.M.'s medial temporal lobe structures, including the hippocampus. The surgery was successful in its intent, alleviating H.M.'s debilitating epileptic seizures and allowing him to conduct his daily activities. Tragically, however, H.M. lost an essential ability—his ability to remember new information (Scoville & Milner, 1957). Yet, even if he couldn't tell you what he had for dinner yesterday, he could reveal knowledge acquired before his surgery, and he was able to pick up some new skills despite his amnesia.

Observing both what H.M. lost and what he retained after his surgery transformed our understanding of memory. In this chapter we further consider the implications of H.M.'s case as we explore the structure of human memory and underlying brain mechanisms, that is, memory systems. Specifically, we draw a distinction between explicit memory, which is information you can consciously report from the past, and implicit memory, which are skills and habits that depend on learning but are better revealed through performance rather than recollection (such as juggling). We examine the different ways both types of memories can be studied, and we focus in detail on how memories are encoded, stored, and retrieved. Expanding on topics introduced in Chapter 6, this chapter will explain how memory systems in the brain support different types of learning and memory. Finally, we explore a special kind of memory that encodes space for purposes of helping us navigate around the environment.

Photo of Henry Molaison taken by Suzanne Corkin. Copyright © by Suzanne Corkin Estate, used by permission of The Wylie Agency LLC

The famous patient H.M. in 1974, at the age of 48. As a result of radical surgery to control his epileptic seizures, he lost his ability to remember new information, yet he retained many other high-level cognitive functions.

LEARNING OBJECTIVES

7.1 Discuss the roles of different types of memory systems, including explicit and implicit memory, in human memory function.

7.2 Describe how the brain distinguishes long-term versus short-term memory, and how it encodes, stores, and retrieves memories.

7.3 Discuss how spatial memory functions and its role in navigation.

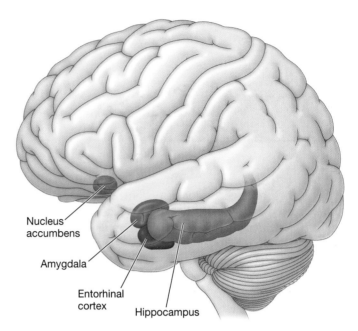

Nucleus accumbens

Amygdala

Entorhinal cortex

Hippocampus

FIGURE 7.1 Schematic of the medial temporal lobe   Key structures include the hippocampus, entorhinal cortex, and the amygdala; not depicted here are the parahippocampal cortex and perirhinal cortex. (After S. M. Breedlove and N. V. Watson. 2019. *Behavioral Neuroscience*, 9th Edition. Oxford University Press/Sinauer: Sunderland, MA.)

7.1 Memory Systems

H.M.'s inability to learn new information revealed the importance of the brain structures that were removed: the **medial temporal lobe**, which includes the **hippocampus** (**FIGURE 7.1**). The surgery left H.M. with **anterograde amnesia**, the inability to learn new information despite retaining old memories. To test his memory abilities, researchers showed him faces of public figures from before and after his surgery. H.M. did poorly in identifying people who became famous only after his surgery, but he could easily recognize those who had already been famous beforehand (Marslen-Wilson & Teuber, 1975). He could also recall information from childhood, and he recognized people he had known before his surgery. In contrast to H.M., patients with **retrograde amnesia** can learn new information but cannot recall information acquired prior to their brain damage.

H.M.'s cognitive abilities that survived the loss of his medial temporal lobe revolutionized the scientific understanding of memory. Researchers originally thought that memory was distributed throughout the brain in a fairly even way (Lashley, 1929; Squire & Wixted, 2011). Extensive studies on amnesic patients such as H.M. have shown, however, that different brain areas play different roles in memory (Hebb, 1949; Squire & Wixted, 2011). That is, the brain contains multiple memory systems—networks that each encode different types of memories (Squire, 1992; Tulving & Schacter, 1990). **THINK FOR YOURSELF 7.1** explores amnesia in more detail.

A central theme of memory is that there are different types of memory, served by different brain mechanisms. The concept of **memory systems** refers to how different systems in the brain support different types of memory. A key distinction is whether we need to consciously access a memory or whether our behavior benefits from a past experience even when we can't articulate the initial learning.

► **Think for Yourself 7.1**

Amnesia in the Movies

Two popular movies illustrate the distinction between anterograde and retrograde amnesia. In the classic thriller *Memento*, the main character suffers from memory loss following the murder of his wife. He searches in vain for his wife's killer, hindered by anterograde amnesia: the inability to remember any new information. In an attempt to keep track of information he uncovers, he tattoos notes all over his body.

In contrast, the character Jason Bourne in *The Bourne Identity* series has retrograde amnesia: in the first installment he wakes up without any idea who he is, but he can remember new information. He soon realizes he is being pursued by assassins. Moreover, he discovers he has fabulous abilities that help him escape: he can speak multiple languages, engage in martial arts, forge a passport, and think and react quickly.

It's important to note that in cases of amnesia, as these movies show, motor and other cognitive skills are preserved. Even with anterograde or retrograde amnesia, patients usually do not forget how to talk, comprehend, read and write, add and subtract, walk, or ride a bike. Real-world cases confirm that memory for facts and events is separate from memory for skills.

Although H.M. could not learn new facts, he was able to learn new skills. The neuropsychologist Brenda Milner tested his ability to learn a mirror tracing task, as shown in **FIGURE 7.2**. This task requires tracing the outline of a star image between double boundary lines without touching the lines. Adding to the challenge, the image is not viewed directly but only as reflected in a mirror, which reverses left and right. At first, this task is very difficult for anyone to do. But after several days of practice, people improve, demonstrating **skill learning**—the cognitive capacity to learn skills such as playing an instrument, surfing, or driving. Tested across multiple days, H.M. couldn't remember the experimenter's name or face, or even that he had seen the apparatus before. But H.M.'s mirror tracing task performance improved each day. His skill learning was so robust that he could still perform the task well when tested a year later. Thus, skill learning occurs independent of whether one can consciously recall practicing (Corkin, 1968). This dissociation hints at different types of memory and memory systems.

Explicit Memory

Analyzing what is remembered and lost in amnesic patients has suggested a distinction between explicit and implicit memory systems (Squire, 1992; Tulving & Schacter, 1990). **Explicit memory**, also known as declarative or conscious memory, is the ability to consciously remember and report facts, events, and associations. It allows you to recall what you had for dinner last night or the name of someone you met. When we say we forget something, this generally means we are unable to retrieve that information from explicit memory.

EPISODIC AND SEMANTIC MEMORY Explicit memory can be further categorized as episodic or semantic memory (Tulving, 1983, 2002). **Episodic memory** allows people to recall past

FIGURE 7.2 H.M.'s performance on a mirror-tracing task Brenda Milner tested H.M.'s ability to learn new skills, which involves the formation of "motor memories," with this star-tracing experiment. (After B. Milner. 1965. In *Cognitive Processes And The Brain: An Enduring Problem in Psychology*, P. M. Milner and S. E. Glickman [Eds.], pp. 97–111. Van Nostrand: Princeton, NJ.)

experiences, single events in specific places at specific times: what, where, and when something happened. For example, you remember you went to the corner store to buy a bagel and a cup of coffee this morning. **Semantic memory** involves facts and knowledge that—as a form of explicit, or declarative, memory—can be stated or recounted, but unlike with episodic memory, the learning of such information accumulates over time across repeated occasions. For example, you know and recall the name of your country's leader based on continual exposure in the news.

Amnesic patients show greater impairments in episodic memory than in semantic memory (Squire et al., 2004; Tulving, 2002). At the age of 30, patient K.C. suffered severe head injury in a motorcycle accident and became amnesic (Tulving et al., 1988). He lost his episodic memory and his conscious experience of memory. K.C. could not remember new events either in his personal experiences or in the world around him. Like H.M., he had anterograde amnesia, and his intelligence and language remained normal. But unlike H.M., who could remember autobiographical memories from before his surgery, K.C. also had a specific form of retrograde amnesia: he could not remember personal events from his life from prior to his accident. K.C.'s episodic memories could not be recovered, whereas the semantic knowledge he had acquired before his accident remained intact. In tests, K.C. was better at learning semantic information than episodic information. He was taught facts in the form of three-word sentences such as "Reporter sent review," and "Student withdrew innuendo." When presented with and tested on these facts repeatedly over several learning sessions, K.C. was able to learn them, albeit slowly, even as he was unable to recall ever participating in the sessions. Sadly, memory loss is not limited to patients who have suffered tragic accidents. **THINK FOR YOURSELF 7.2** discusses the devastating effects of Alzheimer's disease.

► **Think for Yourself 7.2**

Alzheimer's Disease

If you've seen the 2014 film *Still Alice*, based on Lisa Genova's novel of the same name, you may recall this haunting scene, when the protagonist, Dr. Alice Howland, discusses her diagnosis of early-onset Alzheimer's disease:

All my life I've accumulated memories—they've become, in a way, my most precious possessions. The night I met my husband, the first time I held my textbook in my hands. Having children, making friends, traveling the world. Everything I accumulated in life, everything I've worked so hard for—now all that is being ripped away. As you can imagine, or as you know, this is hell. But it gets worse. Who can take us seriously when we are so far from who we once were? Our strange behavior and fumbled sentences change others' perception of us and our perception of ourselves.

"Dementia" refers to the loss of memory and other intellectual abilities, and the most common form of it is Alzheimer's disease. Alzheimer's is not a normal part of aging, although older age is the largest risk factor. Most people with Alzheimer's are over 65, but about 5% of patients have early-onset Alzheimer's, developing it in their thirties, forties, or fifties. According to the Alzheimer's Association, currently almost 6 million Americans are living with Alzheimer's or other dementia, and by 2050 this is projected to rise to 14 million (Alzheimer's Association, 2019).

Symptoms of Alzheimer's Disease. Symptoms usually develop slowly and worsen over time. The most common symptom is memory loss, especially for recently learned information. This may result in asking for the same information over and over. Tasks such as driving to a familiar location or remembering the rules of a favorite game may become increasingly difficult. Other symptoms include difficulties in communicating, focusing, planning and decision making, and even loss of visual and spatial abilities (Alzheimer's Association, 2019; National Institute on Aging, 2019).

Damage in the Brain. Alzheimer's results from microscopic damage to neurons that impairs their function, particularly their ability to communicate (**FIGURE A**). Damage to the brain may begin a decade or more before cognitive problems appear. Two abnormal structures develop and spread through-

Think for Yourself (continued)

out the brain: "plaques" and "tangles." Plaques are fragments of a protein called beta-amyloid that accumulates in the spaces between neurons. Tangles are twisted fibers of a different protein, called tau, that builds up inside cells. The exact role of plaques and tangles is unclear, but they impair neural function and are more prevalent in the brains of Alzheimer's patients than in those of healthy people. The hippocampal system is often the first to be damaged, hence memory loss is one of the earliest and most common symptoms (Alzheimer's Association, 2019; National Institute on Aging, 2019).

Risk Factors. Alzheimer's is irreversible and has no cure yet. The causes are also unclear. For early-onset Alzheimer's, a genetic mutation is usually in play. However, the more common forms of Alzheimer's that develop at a later age usually are the result of a combination of genetic, environmental, and lifestyle factors. For example, vascular conditions such as heart disease, stroke, and high blood pressure can contribute to Alzheimer's disease, as can metabolic conditions such as diabetes and obesity. Accordingly, reducing risk factors for such condi-

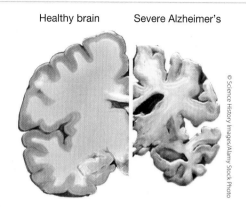

Healthy brain   Severe Alzheimer's

© Science History Images/Alamy Stock Photo

FIGURE A A healthy brain compared with one showing severe damage from Alzheimer's disease.

tions via better nutrition, physical activity, and social engagement may help reduce the risk of Alzheimer's (Alzheimer's Association, 2019; National Institute on Aging, 2019).

THE REMEMBER/KNOW PROCEDURE Have you ever come across a term in an exam question that looked familiar but that you couldn't quite define? For example, "What is the function of the glial cells discussed in Chapter 2?" Similarly, you may struggle to name someone who looks familiar, as in the tip-of-the-tongue phenomenon discussed in Chapter 6.

As these examples show, recognition involves two different kinds of subjective experiences: one is **familiarity**, the sense of having seen something or someone before, which can be either weak or strong. The other is **recollection**, the conscious experience of remembering details (Eichenbaum et al., 2007; Yonelinas, 2002). The distinction between recognition and familiarity can be tested directly using the **remember/know procedure**. In the study phase, participants remember a list of words or pictures. Then later in the test phase, for each item, they have to judge whether they consciously *remember* having viewed the item in the study list. In addition, there may be items for which participants cannot explicitly recollect studying, but that they *know* were on the study list because of a sense of familiarity. Amnesic patients are impaired in both "remember" and "know" responses on a recognition test.

Researchers debate whether recognition (remember) and familiarity (know) responses rely on the same or different neural mechanisms. One proposal is that the hippocampus is important for recollection but not familiarity, while familiarity is supported by neighboring structures in the medial temporal lobe. Supporting this idea, event-related potentials (ERPs; see Chapter 2) in the brain show different signatures for recollection and familiarity during retrieval. Specifically, familiarity is associated with ERP signal changes in midfrontal sites, while recollection is associated with ERP signal changes in parietal sites (Eichenbaum et al., 2007; Duarte et al., 2004.)

Implicit Memory

Explicit memory can be contrasted with **implicit memory**, also known as non-declarative or non-conscious memory, which refers to skills and habits that are learned but that are usually not consciously accessible (Schacter, 1987). Implicit memory is revealed through performance rather than recollection.

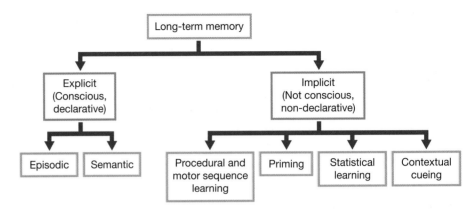

FIGURE 7.3 A taxonomy of long-term memory systems   This is modified to show the types of learning discussed in this chapter. (After L. R. Squire. 2004. *Neurobiol Learn Mem* 82: 171–177.)

Knowing how to ride a bike clearly relies on some kind of learning, but it's not easy to articulate. Likewise, playing the violin or piano well requires years of training and practice, but explaining how we play these instruments is difficult. In contrast, it's easy to tell someone where you had dinner last night—an example of explicit memory.

FIGURE 7.3 diagrams several distinctions between explicit and implicit memory. Explicit memory is more consciously accessible and more flexible in a variety of contexts. It is also more fragile and susceptible to impairment, especially when the hippocampus and medial temporal lobe are damaged, as is common in dementia. Conversely, implicit memory does not depend on conscious recollection and is more resilient to impairment than explicit memory is. It relies on an expansive set of brain areas.

As Figure 7.3 shows, implicit memory is an umbrella category for several memory systems (Gabrieli, 1998; Schacter, 1987; Squire, 1992). Implicit memory includes skills and habits, simple forms of conditioning, emotional learning, priming, and perceptual learning. Implicit memory reveals a form of memory that is dependent on learning, but it does not require asking "Do you remember this?" Implicit memory can be measured even when individuals are unable to report whether they remember an experience or not.

Primary evidence for separate forms of implicit memory is that they survive amnesia, suggesting that they rely on different neural mechanisms. We saw that H.M. improved at the mirror tracing task—a motor skill. Amnesic patients can learn many other types of perceptual and cognitive skills. Try reading the mirror-reversed words in **SEE FOR YOURSELF 7.1**. This is difficult at first, but you will improve with practice. When amnesic patients are tested in this task, they improve at rates similar to those of healthy individuals, even though they are unable to report memory for the task itself and for the specific words they read (Cohen & Squire, 1980). Brain areas involved in reading show changes in

▶ **See for Yourself 7.1**

Mirror-Reversed Words

With practice, you can more quickly read mirror-reversed words like the ones to the right. Both control participants and amnesic patients demonstrate improvement in this perceptually challenging

bedraggled–capricious–grandiose

After N. J. Cohen and L. R. Squire. 1980. *Science* 210: 207–210.

task, showing a form of implicit memory separate from explicit memory.

activation as people become more skilled in mirror reading tasks (Poldrack et al., 1998). That is, these areas are dissociable from brain areas central for explicit memory.

PROCEDURAL LEARNING Practice makes perfect, whether it's playing the piano or learning how to twirl on ice. **Procedural learning** is the acquisition of skills and habits. **Motor sequence learning** is a task for studying procedural learning in the lab, by asking participants to quickly respond to a target that can appear in one of four different locations. Each finger is assigned to a different target position, and participants respond quickly to each target with the correct finger. Targets seemingly appear in random positions on the computer screen, but in reality they form a predictable sequence, like a piano motif. Study findings indicate that participants are faster at responding to repeated sequences even when they are not aware that there is a sequence. **FIGURE 7.4** shows how motor sequence response times improve with repetition.

Given that procedural learning requires some form of memory, you can ask how amnesic patients perform in these tasks. Amnesic patients are capable of normal motor sequence learning (Nissen & Bullemer, 1987), which brain imaging shows to activate motor areas of the brain (Grafton et al., 1995; Jenkins et al., 1994). Along with demonstrations that amnesic patients can improve on mirror tracing tasks (Gabrieli, 1998), procedural learning, which relies on implicit memory, is preserved despite explicit memory impairments. Further evidence that explicit memory and implicit memory are separate comes from patients with the opposite pattern of performance—impaired at skill learning but showing normal explicit memory (Heindel et al., 1989).

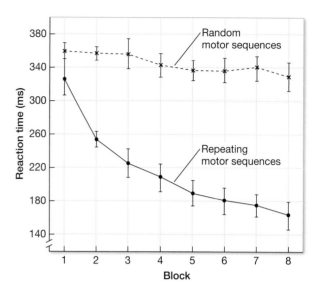

FIGURE 7.4 Response time is faster for repeating motor sequences (solid line) than for random motor sequences (dashed line) Performance improves over time, reflecting motor sequence learning. Bars represent standard errors. (After M. J. Nissen and P. Bullemer. 1987. *Cogn Psychol* 19: 1–32.)

PRIMING **Priming** refers to how a perception, response, or thought is enhanced by prior exposure to an identical or related stimulus, action, or idea. Types of priming include repetition priming, associative priming, perceptual priming, and conceptual priming.

Priming that occurs because of direct repetition is known as **repetition priming**: people are faster at recognizing and responding to repeated items than to new items. This can be studied with a simple **naming task**, in which a participant names a stimulus as quickly and accurately as possible. A basic priming task involves presenting words or pictures to participants during a study phase. During a subsequent test phase, these old stimuli are interleaved with new ones, one at a time, and the naming time is measured for each. Responses are typically faster for repeated (old) items relative to new items (for a review, see Wiggs & Martin, 1998). As a variant of the naming task, priming can be measured by identification of words that are made difficult to see by presenting them very briefly or by degrading them (blurring or adding visual noise). Primed items are recognized at higher rates than novel items.

Priming can also occur from related items, and this is called **associative priming**. For example, when presented with the word "nurse" before being asked to name a word that starts with "d," people are more likely to say "doctor." Associative priming can be studied with a naming task or another method called the **lexical decision task**. In the latter task, people need to quickly judge whether a string of letters forms a word or not: "candy" is a word, while "curfy" is not (yet, at the time of this publication). People can make this lexical decision more quickly if "candy" is preceded by the word "sweet" than "prickly."

We can also distinguish perceptual priming from conceptual priming. Consider the three words "cat," "cot," and "dog." "Cat" and "cot" are perceptually similar in that they share two letters, "c_t", while "cat" and "dog" are perceptually different but are conceptually similar, in that both are common household pets. In **perceptual priming**, perception is improved by repeated exposure to perceptual features. Seeing the word "cat" improves subsequent recognition of the word "cot" because they share perceptual features, but not semantic ones.

While perceptual priming is a matter of having *perceived* stimuli previously, **conceptual priming** reveals how the *meanings* of stimuli were processed. In conceptual priming, as we saw for associative priming, recognition is improved by semantic relations. Seeing the word "cat" improves subsequent recognition of the word "dog" because they share conceptual features, even though they are perceptually dissimilar. Likewise, because of conceptual priming, hearing the word "dog" improves visual recognition of a picture of a dog (reviewed in Gabrieli, 1998; Roediger & McDermott, 1993; Tulving & Schacter, 1990).

Priming is a form of implicit, or non-declarative, memory. Amnesic patients show normal priming, even when they cannot recognize the repeated pictures as familiar, or even remember having done a similar kind of test before (Cave & Squire, 1992; Gabrieli, 1998; Schacter, 1992). Even unaffected participants without amnesia show priming for old stimuli they have forgotten (Roediger & McDermott, 1993) or that are rendered near invisible (Dehaene et al., 2001).

Neuroimaging evidence shows perceptual priming relies on perceptual brain areas. When stimuli are repeated, fMRI responses show lower levels of activity, suggesting that processing requires less effort or work. Known as **repetition suppression**, this signal reduction is specific to the brain areas involved in the processing of a stimulus (Grill-Spector et al., 2006; Schacter & Buckner, 1998). For example, repeating scene images allows participants to respond to them more quickly and is accompanied by reduced activity in the place area, as shown in **FIGURE 7.5** (Turk-Browne et al., 2006).

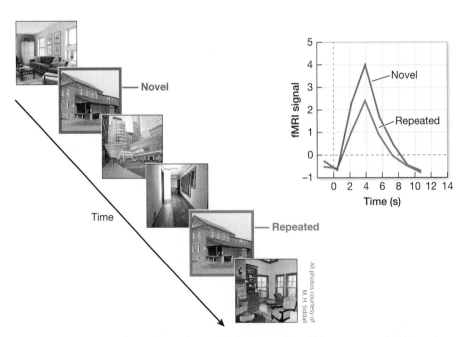

FIGURE 7.5 Perceptual priming and repetition suppression When presented with a series of scenes and asked to make an indoor or outdoor judgment in response to each scene, observers are faster to respond to scenes that appeared before (repeated). The fMRI response in the place area is smaller for repeated scenes than for novel scenes, and this difference is known as repetition suppression.

STATISTICAL LEARNING   We can find meaningful patterns in the sights and sounds we experience daily. These are known as **statistical regularities**, stable and predictable features of an environment, object, or task. The layout of your room does not change from day to day, for example. **Statistical learning** encodes these regularities, which help us function in the world by making it more predictable (Saffran, 2003).

As an example, language is composed of words strung into grammatical sentences. This structure may help us in learning languages. A major challenge for comprehension is that the language input into our ears typically does not contain any pauses or other acoustic boundaries between words. This problem is apparent when you listen to an unfamiliar language. Try to identify the word boundaries in the following and guess how many words are in this Korean sentence: *Shim-ri-hak-eul-yul-shim-hee-gong-boo-hap-shi-da*. The answer is three ("Study psychology hard"). There is a chicken-and-egg problem in that you can segment the sentence if you know the words, but how do you learn the words in the first place? The answer may lie in learning the statistical regularities of the input.

As another example, consider the phrase "pretty baby," and say it out loud: "pri-tee-bay-bee." Throughout the course of experience, the syllables "pri" and "tee" are more likely to go together in succession ("pretty") than "tee" and "bay," which will only go together when the phrase "pretty baby" is heard. In other words, the probability of "pri" and "tee" happening in succession is higher than the probability of "tee" and "bay" happening in succession. These transitional probabilities hint that "pri" and "tee" are part of one word, while "tee" and "bay" are not.

In one study of statistical learning in language, adults and 8-month-old babies were exposed to nonsense utterances such as "golabupabikututibubabupugo-labubabupu" (Saffran et al., 1996). This utterance actually contains novel words that could only be distinguished based on sequential probabilities. Syllables within these fabricated words appeared sequentially with high probability, while syllables across words were much less frequent. The question was whether adults and infants could learn word boundaries from these continuous sequences. After exposure to the long utterance, adults were asked whether they recognized words such as "pabiku," which appeared repeatedly in the sequence, versus non-words such as "bupabi," which spanned word boundaries (**FIGURE 7.6**).

FIGURE 7.6 Statistical learning in language   During training, infants and adults are exposed to continuous speech streams in which artificial words (e.g., "pabiku") are repeated. Then they are tested on these artificial words, or are presented with part-words ("kudaro") that span word boundaries, and hence appeared less frequently (although the individual syllables all appeared the same number of times). Participants show familiarity for the repeated artificial words, showing that based on the statistics of how the syllables string together, they can segment the word boundaries. Bars in the graph represent standard errors. (After J. Sedivy. 2019. *Language in Mind*, 2nd Edition. Oxford University Press/Sinauer: Sunderland, MA; adapted from J. R. Saffran et al. 1996. *Science* 274: 1926–1928.)

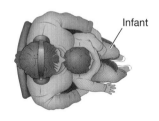

Experimenters create an artificial "language" of three "words":

*pabiku, **golatu**, daropi*

Familiarization phase

Infant hears each "word" repeated 45 times in random order, in an unbroken 2-minute synthesized speech stream:

*pabiku-**golatu**-daropi-pabiku-daropi-pabiku-**golatu**-daropi-pabiku-**golatu**-pabiku* etc.

Test phase

Loudspeakers present infant either a "real" word:

*pabiku, **golatu***

or a sequence of syllables with parts of two words:

kudaro

f Mean listening times

Infants can be tested on the words and non-words using habituation paradigms, which use the fact that infants treat novel and repeated stimuli differently. That is, if you have infants listen to repeated stimuli, they habituate (get bored), which is measurable because they start to look away (fixate on the objects for a shorter duration of time). This habituation reveals that they "recognize" the repeated stimulus. After a series of repeated items, when a novel stimulus is presented, infants will look at it for a longer period of time, indicating that they've noticed the difference.

In the statistical learning paradigm, both adults and infants will habituate to statistically common words like "pabiku" and will treat statistically rare words ("bupabi") as novel. That is, they are sensitive to the statistics of these novel, continuous utterances and learn to distinguish word boundaries in this task (see Figure 7.6). This type of statistical learning has important implications for all types of learning because statistical regularities are a defining feature of the environment.

CONTEXTUAL CUEING   Another way to study how we learn regularities in the environment is by examining context. For example, as discussed in Chapter 3, visual context constrains what we expect and where to look. When shown a picture of a dorm room and asked to look for a pillow, you will first scan the bed and not the desk or bookcase. This reflects the fact that pillows are usually found on beds—a statistical regularity that we've acquired over a lifetime of exposure to bedrooms. "Contextual cueing" refers to learning where to attend and what to expect based on these statistical regularities.

Real-world context is too complex to study in the lab, so the contextual cueing paradigm relies on a computer-based visual search task. Observers were asked to quickly search for a rotated "T" target among rotated "L" distractors (**FIGURE 7.7**). On half of the trials, unbeknownst to the observers, the entire display (configuration of items) repeated throughout the experiment—that is, the spatial layout of the search display formed a consistent context that was predictive of the target location within that display. If your brain learns this predictive regularity, you should be able to find the target faster in repeated displays. This is indeed what observers showed. The faster search time for targets in repeated displays versus targets in novel displays is known as **contextual cueing**. That is, contextual cueing enables faster search of targets whose location or identity is predictable from surrounding context (Chun & Jiang, 1998, 1999). Like statistical learning, contextual cueing shows that people are highly sensitive to useful regularities in the environment.

Furthermore, contextual cueing is implicit. Observers were never told that displays were repeated, and when their memory for the displays was tested

FIGURE 7.7 Computer-based visual search task (A) A sample search array. The task is to search for a rotated T as quickly as possible. (B) Average search times are faster for targets in old, repeated displays than in new displays. The benefit for old configurations is called contextual cueing, as memory for visual context serves to guide search (attention) to the target. The memory traces were implicit (observers were unable to distinguish old contexts from new). (After M. M. Chun. 2000. *Trends Cogn Sci* 4: 170–178; based on M. M. Chun and Y. Jiang. 1998. *Cogn Psychol* 36: 28–71.)

(A)

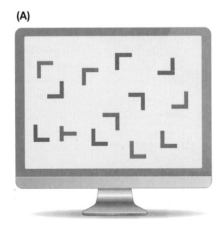

(B)

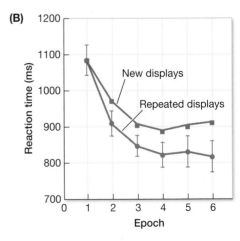

at the end of the session, they were unable to reliably report which search displays were old and which were new. Search was faster for old displays even though observers were not aware that contexts were repeated and predictive of target locations.

Since contextual cueing is an implicit memory task, one should expect amnesic patients to show normal contextual cueing. However, an intriguing feature of contextual cueing is that it relies on contextual learning, which requires the hippocampus and neighboring medial temporal lobe structures. Thus, we have two competing predictions. Will hippocampal damage impair contextual cueing because it relies on contextual learning, or will contextual cueing be intact because it is implicit? As one special counterexample to the finding that amnesic patients have preserved implicit memory, patients with medial temporal lobe damage showed no contextual cueing effects (Chun & Phelps, 1999; Manns & Squire, 2001). Neuroimaging studies also showed hippocampal activation during implicit contextual cueing tasks (Greene et al., 2007; Summerfield et al., 2006).

➤ CHECKPOINT 7.1

1. What is the distinction between explicit memory and implicit memory?
2. Give some examples of episodic memory versus semantic memory.
3. What is procedural learning? Give an example.
4. What is priming? How can you distinguish between associative priming and perceptual priming?
5. Describe an example of statistical learning or contextual cueing.

7.2 Memory Encoding, Storage, and Retrieval

Our experiences are recorded in memory, fleetingly in short-term memory, or more permanently in long-term memory. When you make a new friend at a party, you will initially remember their name in short-term memory, useful throughout the conversation. However, in order to recognize them the next day, you need to store their name and face in long-term memory (Atkinson & Shiffrin, 1968). Compared with long-term memory, short-term memory is more susceptible to distraction, interference, and erasure (for a demonstration, try the Discovery Lab on the Brown–Peterson Paradigm).

Different memory mechanisms are involved in short-term and long-term memory. As we discussed in Chapter 5, working memory actively maintains information for the brief period that it is needed. In this section we discuss ways to study and distinguish long-term memory from short-term memory, introduced in Chapter 6, and then focus on the underlying processes involved in encoding, storing, and retrieving long-term memories. Before you read further, though, try the simple memory test in **SEE FOR YOURSELF 7.2**.

▶ DISCOVERY LAB
The Brown–Peterson Paradigm

▶ **See for Yourself 7.2**

A Simple Memory Test

Study the following list of words, one at a time, two seconds each, reading left-to-right.

stamp	bird	knife	brick	toy	lock	meal
rest	trail	bridge	tank	wood	bike	ring
yak	frog	frame	ocean	bed	crown	skate

Now, without looking at this list, try to write down as many of these words as you can remember. Score them later when prompted in the text.

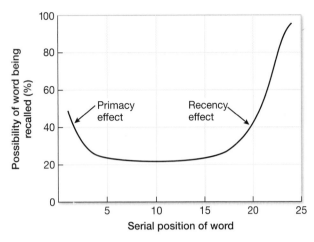

FIGURE 7.8 A serial position curve Better memory for items appearing at the early part of the list is called the primacy effect, and better memory for items appearing toward the end of the list is called the recency effect. (After B. B. Murdock, Jr. 1962. *J Exp Psychol* 64: 482–488. Content in public domain.)

DISCOVERY LAB

Serial Position Effect

Distinguishing Long-Term Memory from Short-Term Memory

The distinction between short-term memory and long-term memory is revealed by trying to recall the items that you just remembered in See For Yourself 7.2 (without looking back!). If you mark which items you remembered according to their position in the list, you may note that you did poorly for the items in the middle. Most people do. Plotting memory performance according to serial position, a U-shaped curve emerges (**FIGURE 7.8**). This is called the **serial position curve**, and it has two features: higher memory performance for the items at the beginning of the list is called the **primacy effect**, and higher memory performance for the items toward the end of the list is called the **recency effect** (Murdock Jr., 1962). The serial position curve, which you can experience again in the relevant Discovery Lab, is quick evidence for the distinction between short-term memory and long-term memory. The primacy effect for items at the beginning of the list may reflect encoding in long-term memory—best for the earlier items because there's more time for rehearsal. The recency effect for items at the end of the list may reflect short-term memory, benefitting from being close to the time of recall with minimal distraction.

A role for short-term memory (or working memory) in the recency effect is easy to demonstrate. As you know, short-term memory is disrupted by interference. When a distraction task (counting backward) was added at the end of the list before participants were asked to recall, they did more poorly on the latter items in the list (**FIGURE 7.9**; also try the Discovery Lab on the serial position effect). (Glanzer & Cunitz, 1966).

Distributed Representation and Reactivation of Memories

Whether they are perceptual encounters or thoughts (reflections), your mind's actions leave neural traces that form the basis for memories (Chun & Johnson, 2011). Amnesic patients with hippocampal and medial temporal lobe damage like that of H.M. have lost their ability to learn new information in long-term memory (anterograde amnesia), while their memories for older information learned prior to their damage remain relatively intact. This means that old memories are not stored in the hippocampus and medial temporal lobe, also known as the **hippocampal system**. Instead, long-term memories must be stored elsewhere in the brain, and evidence indicates that such permanent memories are stored in **neocortex**, the outer layers of neurons forming the bulk of the human brain, that support the initial perception and processing of an experience. That is, memories reside throughout cortex—you can view the entire brain as a large storage device. Unlike a computer, where memory resides in a hard drive or memory stick, compartmentalized and separate from the other processing chips, in the brain, memory is a property of the entire system.

Experiences tend to be multisensory and hence are initially processed in multiple cortical regions. Such cortical processing leaves a **distributed code** (record) in the same multiple regions that were active during the initial

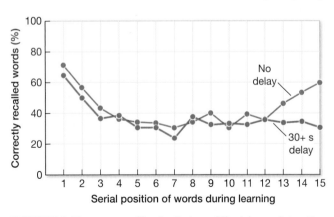

FIGURE 7.9 The recency effect is eliminated if a delay or distracting task is introduced at the end of the list This suggests that the recency effect reflects short-term memory, which is disrupted by delay or distraction. (After M. Glanzer and A. R. Cunitz. 1966. *J Verbal Learning Verbal Behav* 5: 351–360.)

experience (Nyberg et al., 2000; Wheeler et al., 2000). Long-term memories are distributed across the brain, specifically in the same regions that initially performed the processing. Visual memories are processed in visual areas, while auditory memories are processed and stored in auditory areas. The act of remembering is to reactivate these distributed records within the modality-specific or category-specific brain regions that were engaged during initial encoding (Barsalou, 1999; Barsalou et al., 2003; Damasio, 1989; Rissman & Wagner, 2012).

Let's consider the example of when you first met your new college roommate (person) in your new dorm room (place). This episodic event is something you can recall later, ideally with friendly feelings. The face area of your brain would have been active not just when you first saw your new roommate, but also to encode a memory of her face—let's say she looks like Beyoncé. Likewise, the scene area of your brain would have been active not only to perceive the room's layout—more cramped than you would have liked, but with a nice window between the two beds—but also to encode it for future encounters. Furthermore, your brain had to associate these two types of information, the face and the room, forming the episodic details of this initial greeting.

Now, consider what happens as you try to recall this event from memory. From where in the brain will these memory details (the face, the place, and the association of the two) be pulled? Episodic details are not stored in a separate memory vault, but are encoded in the multiple, distributed areas that were active during initial encoding. During retrieval of a memory, these brain mechanisms that were involved during the initial perceptual and cognitive experiences exhibit **reactivation**—they show patterns of activity similar to what occurred during the initial encoding. When remembering or thinking about your college roommate, the face area will be reactivated in a way similar to when you first met the roommate—someone who reminds you of Beyoncé. Also, when remembering your dorm room, the place area will be reactivated in a way similar to when you first perceived the room—the layout of the beds, desks, with the window you liked between the beds. When these two pieces of information are successfully associated, both face and place areas are reactivated together (Ranganath et al., 2004).

The Hippocampal System Associates Information to Form New Memories

To form new memories and to make them accessible for later retrieval, the hippocampal system (hippocampus and medial temporal lobe) initially works together with the specialized regions of cortex. The hippocampal system is active during initial encoding, so damage to its structures results in anterograde amnesia. In healthy participants, the hippocampus and medial temporal lobe are more active for new items (Stern et al., 1996; Tulving et al., 1996) and for items that are successfully encoded compared with items that are later forgotten (Brewer et al., 1998; Wagner et al., 1998).

The hippocampal system associates items and their contexts (time, space, characters, and other details) across different brain areas: visual information from visual cortex, auditory information from auditory cortex, and so on. To link all these disparate parts, the hippocampus binds all the features together so that they are all associated and can activate each other when any of the pieces are activated. Returning to our earlier example, to form an integrated memory of meeting your college roommate, the hippocampal system will associate your roommate's face information from the face area and the dorm room scene information from the scene area. By linking the different parts of a memory together from across the different cortical areas that code the details of the event, the hippocampal system can index a memory's different features (Eichenbaum et al., 2007; Squire et al., 2004).

The hippocampus and medial temporal lobe system are also active during retrieval of memory, reactivating the pieces of information from around cortex. Thinking about the event of first meeting your roommate reactivates the roommate's face representation in the face area and the dorm room scene information from the scene area. If your brain is like a grocery store, the hippocampus serves as the information desk or clerk who can tell you where various items on your shopping list are located throughout the store. For example, if you're shopping for ingredients to serve hot dogs at a cookout, the hippocampus will tell you where to get the hot dogs, buns, and condiments.

The hippocampal system is mainly active during memory retrieval of relatively new memories, and over time the connections in cortical regions are gradually strengthened to a point where the cortical memory can be accessed without hippocampal involvement (McClelland et al., 1995; Squire & Alvarez, 1995). This is why H.M. was able to retrieve older memories that were formed prior to the removal of his hippocampus. That is, after some time, the memories become encoded so strongly in the cortical regions such that the hippocampus is no longer necessary to retrieve the information. To stretch the hot-dog shopping example, you no longer need to ask the information desk where to get your ingredients. Memory retrieval involves direct reactivation of the modality-specific or category-specific cortical areas.

Supporting this view, some patients with damage in non-hippocampal, cortical regions, such as the frontal or temporal lobes, show difficulty recalling episodes from earlier in their life prior to brain damage. This is consistent with the idea that memories are stored outside the hippocampus and medial temporal lobe regions (Squire et al., 2004).

To summarize, when a memory is first formed, its encoding and retrieval depend on the hippocampus and medial temporal lobe, but once memory is fully consolidated, it can be retrieved directly by reactivating cortical regions. Why are there two systems? The hippocampal system (hippocampus + medial temporal lobe) and neocortex form a **complementary memory system** (**FIGURE 7.10**).

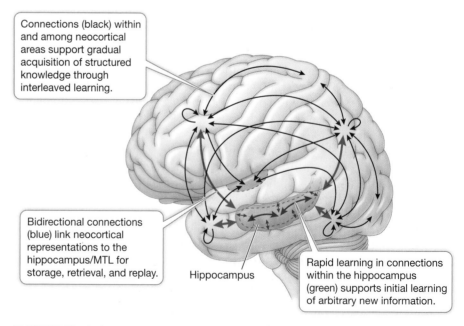

Connections (black) within and among neocortical areas support gradual acquisition of structured knowledge through interleaved learning.

Bidirectional connections (blue) link neocortical representations to the hippocampus/MTL for storage, retrieval, and replay.

Hippocampus

Rapid learning in connections within the hippocampus (green) supports initial learning of arbitrary new information.

FIGURE 7.10 The hippocampus and neocortex form a complementary memory system The hippocampus, which lies deep within the brain, supports rapid learning, while neocortical areas support gradual learning. MTL, medial temporal lobe. (After D. Kumaran et al. 2016. *Trends Cogn Sci* 20: 512–534.)

The hippocampal system allows for quick—even one-shot—learning. Although it may seem desirable for all learning to happen quickly, note that this can be chaotic for existing memories if information can be rewritten so easily. Thus, memory systems require stability, maintaining the integrity of their circuitry and knowledge. Nature's solution is to have two complementary systems. The neocortex learns and changes slowly, while the hippocampal system permits rapid learning of new items (McClelland et al., 1995).

The Neural Mechanisms of Encoding

We can't remember everything we experience. Intuitively, we typically remember experiences and events that were important to us and hence we paid attention to (e.g., an amazing meal); and we don't remember things that were not important and not attended to (e.g., an ad we passed by). The **subsequent memory paradigm** is a common way to study why we successfully encode some things and not others. To reveal the neural mechanisms of whether something is remembered or not, fMRI or EEG data can be collected while participants view a series of items, such as words or pictures. After this encoding session, participants are given a memory test during which they will successfully remember some items and forget others. Researchers can then separate the neural measures collected during encoding, according to whether the stimuli were subsequently remembered versus forgotten during the test phase. Comparing these data reveals how the brain activates differently for items that are later remembered versus those that are forgotten (Brewer et al., 1998; Paller et al., 1987; Wagner et al., 1998).

For items that are subsequently remembered, many brain regions are more active, suggesting that these regions are important for encoding memory (**FIGURE 7.11**). This includes prefrontal cortex, parietal cortex, the hippocampal system, and cortical regions specific to the content of the information being encoded (e.g., face area for encoding faces). Importantly, the regions that show subsequent memory effects are also responsive to attention instructions. When participants are asked to increase their attention to the information to be remembered, the regions that show subsequent memory effects show higher activity, compared with when participants are asked to direct their attention elsewhere (Otten et al., 2006; Paller & Wagner, 2002; Turk-Browne et al., 2006). For example, when viewing stimuli such as those in **FIGURE 7.12**, when attending to scenes instead of faces, activity in the place area of the brain is higher than when attending to faces, and importantly, memory for the scenes is substantially higher. There is barely any memory for the actively ignored stimuli (Johnson & Zatorre, 2005; Yi & Chun, 2005). Thus, a key to better memory is better attention and focus during encoding (Aly & Turk-Browne, 2016b).

Storage and Consolidation in the Brain

Memory is embodied in neural connectivity, but it takes time to solidify the connections that enable memory storage. The act of stabilizing memories is called **consolidation**. Consolidation makes memories durable and resistant to corruption, just as glue hardens bonds.

Synapses, the spaces between neurons across which they signal to each other, can be strong or weak; when they are strong, signals can travel from one neuron to another more effectively. Memory is based on the strengthening of connections between neurons. But what strengthens the connections? Experience does. The more frequently presynaptic neuron A causes firing in postsynaptic neuron B, the stronger the connection will become. This mechanism for strengthening connections is called **Hebb's Rule**, and it is one of the most fundamental

Posterior LIFG

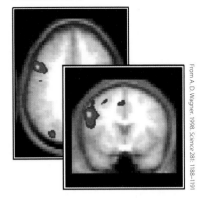

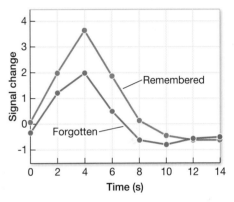

FIGURE 7.11 The subsequent memory effect Brain activity is higher at the time of initial encoding of items that are subsequently remembered versus items that are subsequently forgotten. LIFG, left inferior frontal gyrus. (From A. D. Wagner. 1998. *Science* 281: 1188–1191.)

FIGURE 7.12 You can attend to either the face or the scene when they overlap like this Memory is better for the attended category. (The face is that of the famous neuroscientist Santiago Ramón y Cajal.)

principles in all of neuroscience (Hebb, 1949). It is often paraphrased as "cells that fire together wire together." More specifically, the mechanism behind Hebb's Rule is **long-term potentiation (LTP)**, which refers to how communication across a synapse strengthens future communication between the presynaptic and post-synaptic neurons (Bliss & Collingridge, 1993). LTP is a chemical process that strengthens the synaptic connections between two neurons when both are active, as if clearing a path for information to travel more freely. You would be correct to guess that LTP is more common in the hippocampus than in other brain areas, but LTP also enables plasticity throughout other parts of the brain.

A primary feature of consolidation is that it is a slow process—that is, memory formation does not happen all at once but progresses over time, even in the background when the stimulus is not actively perceived or encoded. It takes time for synapses to be strengthened between individual neurons, and for memories to be incorporated into the extensive brain networks (Dudai, 2004; McGaugh, 2000). To draw an analogy, memory consolidation is more like making fresh popsicles in the freezer than it is like instantaneously creating a file on a computer hard drive. Fragile at first, memories require time to solidify.

The fact that consolidation takes time helps explain many aspects of everyday memory. First, it helps explain interference and distraction effects. If memory consolidation were instantaneous, then distraction after encoding should be minimal. However, studies show that even after an encoding event, distraction will impair memory. The progressive nature of consolidation also explains why trauma to the brain, such as a concussion or drugs, can disrupt memory during the consolidation period. Because recent memories undergoing consolidation are still fragile, they are susceptible to disruption. **THINK FOR YOURSELF 7.3** explores the importance of sleep for consolidating memories.

► **Think for Yourself 7.3**

The Importance of Sleep

During an active day, when can the brain find time to consolidate past experiences? Although consolidation happens in the background amidst other activities, sleep provides an essential time for consolidation to occur. You learn while you sleep. You know the value of sleep based on how lousy you feel after pulling an all-nighter. Almost every aspect of your performance is impaired by such sleep deprivation. But it's not just about fatigue or grumpy moods. Research studies have demonstrated that sleep is central for memory consolidation of not just facts, but also motor and perceptual skills (Stickgold, 2005).

Challenging activities require attention and rapid visuomotor coordination, and these can be tested in the lab in the form of video games. People get better with practice, based on memory consolidation. Now, few parents or teachers will recommend a good night's sleep to improve your Fortnite ranking, but imagine you're an apprentice learning how to pilot a commercial flight

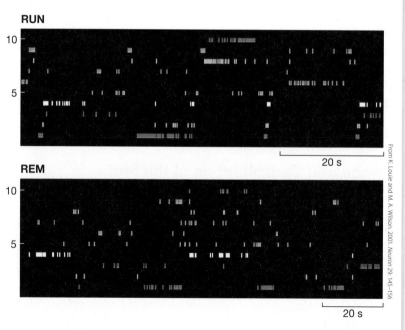

RUN

REM

20 s

From K. Louie and M. A. Wilson 2001. *Neuron* 29: 145–156

Patterns of neural activity across several place cells during maze running (top) correspond well with the activity of the same cells during REM sleep (bottom).

Think for Yourself (continued)

with 400 passengers over the Pacific Ocean, or a medical resident learning how to remove a brain tumor delicately located against a major artery. A night's sleep can improve motor skills by as much as 20% (Walker et al., 2002).

Sleep studies of memory have shown that rapid eye movement (REM) sleep is especially critical (Karni et al., 1994). After an initial training session detecting a brief and camouflaged visible target, participants had their sleep monitored in a sleep lab, and the amount of REM sleep was recorded. A higher proportion of REM sleep corresponded with better performance in this skilled task the next day. However, correlation does not mean that REM sleep played a causal role in perceptual learning. To demonstrate that, the researchers selectively disrupted REM sleep by waking people up whenever they went into REM sleep. As a control, another group was woken up during non-REM sleep. Individuals who had their REM sleep disrupted suffered greater losses of learning during sleep. This suggests that REM sleep is especially important for memory consolidation.

REM sleep is when we dream. So, what's happening when we're dreaming? Anecdotally, dream content can reflect what happens to us during the day, or what we are thinking about. Studies with lab rats can answer the question of what animals dream about rather specifically. Researchers have recorded brain activity in rats while they run around circular mazes. Recordings in hippocampal place cells (discussed further in Section 7.3) can reveal the position of the rat in its environment, like a neural GPS chip (the hippocampus performs many functions in the brain!). Multiple place cells in the hippocampus can be measured simultaneously with such precision that the pattern of activity can be decoded to indicate the position of the rat in its maze with high accuracy. Astonishingly, hippocampal activity during maze-running behavior, when the animal is awake, closely matches that during REM sleep. It appears that rats, at least those living in labs at the Massachusetts Institute of Technology, dream about running around in mazes.

Neural Retrieval and Reactivation

Memory retrieval involves reactivation of the brain regions involved during initial encoding. After being asked to learn a set of picture and sound items, such as a bell or a rooster, participants were given a recall task in which they had to vividly remember the items while their brains were being scanned. Brain imaging revealed that when participants were retrieving memories of the pictures, visual cortex was active, whereas retrieving sound items in memory activated auditory cortex. This shows that retrieval of a memory with sensory information involves reactivation of the same sensory regions that were active during initial perception and encoding of the items (Nyberg et al., 2000; Wheeler et al., 2000). The ability to decode memory reactivation is becoming increasingly specific. Using just visual images and sophisticated analysis methods, fMRI can distinguish whether people are recalling a scene, a face, or an object (**THINK FOR YOURSELF 7.4**) (Polyn et al., 2005). With even richer stimuli such as film clips of everyday actions, researchers are able to decode which film clip participants are reactivating during recall (Chadwick et al., 2010).

In a study that asked people to recognize faces, some of which had been shown to them before and some of which hadn't, fMRI could decode whether people thought they recognized a face from memory and even how familiar or strong their sense of recognition was (Rissman et al., 2010). Unfortunately, such decoding could not distinguish whether the memory was accurate and real. That is, people frequently committed false memories, claiming recognition of a face that was not shown before; or showed the usual memory failures, responding that a face looked new, even if it had been shown before. fMRI could decode what people thought, but it could not distinguish whether an item was old or new. There would be great use for courtroom or applied settings if fMRI could decode whether someone truly saw a face or not, independent of what the participants thought they

From M. J. Chadwick et al., 2010, *Curr Biol* 20: 544–547/CC BY 3.0

fMRI can decode recall of short film clips—in this example, of a woman taking a drink from a cup and disposing of it in a trash can.

► **Think for Yourself 7.4**

Population Coding Increases Brain Capacity

Information is represented as patterns across neurons and not within individual neurons alone. When distinguishing an image of the San Francisco cityscape from that of Miami Beach, it's not as if there's a single neuron A for the city scene and a separate neuron B for the beach scene. Instead, each scene is represented and distinguished by an ensemble (population, or group) of neurons. This is known as **population coding**, and it is more robust and powerful than encoding by single cells.

Consider a toy brain with only four neurons, each of which can be either on or off (**FIGURE A**). In a single-cell coding scheme, each neuron can represent only one object, and hence this toy system can represent only four objects. However, if objects are represented as patterns across this population of four neurons, then the same system can represent many more objects. To be specific, since each neuron can be on or off, a four-neuron ensemble can represent 15 different objects (2^4-1). With billions and billions of neurons, you can see why population coding makes the brain's theoretical capacity practically limitless.

Remarkably, fMRI can discern differences in patterns (Norman et al., 2006). Although fMRI does not have the precision to examine neuron-level activity, different neurons tend to cluster in a way that produces pattern differ-

ences even when probed at (coarse) millimeter resolution. Imagine a satellite image of an area instead of a drone hovering close above the ground. You can still learn a lot from the big-picture image, distinguishing parks from residential areas, for example.

Based on its ability to discern distributed patterns—known as **multivariate pattern analysis**—fMRI can distinguish individual object categories, such as faces, cats, chairs, and so on (Haxby et al., 2001). Even within categories such as scenes, fMRI can tell the difference between whether someone is looking at a city or a beach (Carlson et al., 2003; Walther et al., 2009). Researchers use these capabilities to study how memories are encoded during initial perception and how they are reactivated during retrieval.

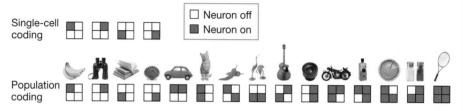

FIGURE A The grid depicts an ensemble of four neurons, each represented by a cell that can be either off (blank) or on (blue) in response to a stimulus. Compared with a single-cell coding scheme (top row), in which each cell codes one type of stimulus (banana, binoculars, book, shell), population coding (bottom row) allows the same ensemble to represent many more stimuli with unique patterns of activity. **Photo credits:** Bananas: © iStock.com/bergamont; Binoculars, shell, cranes, lens, and cooking oil: courtesy of M. H. Siddall; Motorcycle: © iStock.com/goce; Cat: © iStock.com/GlobalP; Little car: © iStock.com/omada; Pumpkin pie: © iStock.com/DebbiSmirnoff; Book: © iStock.com/Fotocam; Guitar: © iStock.com/Puripat1981; Chillies: © iStock.com/Galina Shafran; Salt and pepper: © Tracy Decourcy/Dreamstime.com; Tennis racket: © pukach/Shutterstock.com

could recognize. Alas, more work is needed to develop such capabilities for distinguishing true versus false memories.

Another brain area that is important for memory retrieval is the frontal cortex, located behind the forehead. In brain imaging studies, successful retrieval is accompanied by higher left frontal activity (Tulving et al., 1994). In patient studies, frontal lobe lesions cause learning impairments. Although the damage is not as severe as typically seen with hippocampal damage, frontal patients show problems in recalling past information, and especially recalling the source of information (Janowsky et al., 1989).

Beyond the prefrontal cortex, lateral parietal cortex, above the ears and toward the top back of the head, is also involved in memory retrieval. Activity in parietal cortex is higher when an item is successfully retrieved from memory versus when it is not. That is, the strength of activation reflects the strength of memory evidence. Moreover, the parietal cortex differentiates remember/know responses. When an item is remembered along with its specific details, ventral (lower, closer to the neck) parietal cortex is active. When an item is recognized as familiar but without specific details, dorsal (upper part, closer to the top of the head) parietal cortex is active (Cabeza et al., 2008; Wagner et al., 2005).

Understanding brain mechanisms involved in memory encoding and retrieval helps explain why memory is impaired by brain damage, aging, and environmental factors such as stress. **THINK FOR YOURSELF 7.5** describes how stress impairs neural mechanisms of memory.

► **Think for Yourself 7.5**

Stress and Memory

In studying for an important test, and even while taking one, an essential tip we can offer is to *relax*. Stress impairs memory. When you're stressed, it's harder to encode new information. And under stress, it's also hard to remember information you've already learned.

The body responds to stress by increasing glucocorticoids—hormones that mobilize the body and delay nonurgent functions such as digestion and growth. However, glucocorticoids impair learning in the hippocampus (McEwen, 1999). Glucocorticoids, such as cortisol, not only disrupt thefunctioning of neurons in the hippocampus, but high levels of these hormones cause neurons to wither, and suppress the growth of new neurons (neurogenesis). With long-term exposure to chronic stress, structures such as the hippocampus and prefrontal cortex shrink in size (Arnsten, 2009; Sapolsky, 1996).

Such stress-induced neuronal damage directly affects cognition, especially memory (Kim & Diamond, 2002; McEwen, 1999). In one study, participants were exposed to stress in the lab. A reliable lab method to induce stress is to ask participants to deliver a mock job interview speech and to perform mental arithmetic in front of a panel of judges for 10 minutes, preceded by a 10-minute anticipation period (Kirschbaum et al., 1993). This task reliably induces stress, increasing cortisol levels. Participants who showed high levels of stress, as measured by cortisol levels, showed greater memory impairments. Going beyond this correlation between cortisol and memory impairments, in another experiment participants were given only cortisol or a placebo without a stressful task. Participants who received cortisol were impaired in the memory and spatial tests (Kirschbaum et al., 1996).

Stress impairs retrieval of otherwise well encoded information (de Quervain et al., 1998). Not only does memory retrieval fluctuate along with levels of stress hormones in rats, but blocking the stress hormones with drugs alleviates the stress-induced retrieval impairments.

Hippocampal atrophy is also a feature of many neuropsychiatric disorders such as major depression and post-traumatic stress disorder (Pittenger & Duman, 2008; Sapolsky, 2000). For example, the longer a patient suffers from depres-

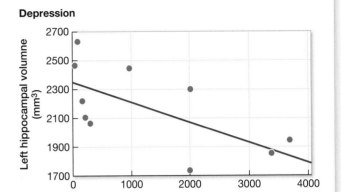

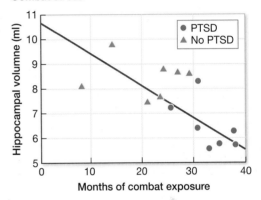

FIGURE A The longer a person has suffered from depression or combat stress, the smaller the volume of their hippocampus is. PTSD, post-traumatic stress disorder. (Top after Y. Sheline et al. 1996. *Proc Natl Acad Sci USA* 93: 3908–3913. © 1996 National Academy of Sciences, U.S.A.; bottom after T. V. Gurvits et al. 1996. *Biol Psychiatry* 40: 1091–1099.)

sion or combat stress, the smaller the size of their hippocampus (**FIGURE A**) (Bremner et al., 1995; Sheline et al., 1996). Although this is correlational evidence, other work in the field suggests that stress plays a causal role in damaging and shrinking the hippocampus and leading to cognitive deficits such as memory impairment.

► CHECKPOINT 7.2

1. How do you test for the serial position curve, and what explains the primacy effect and the recency effect?

2. What is reactivation in memory?

3. Describe the roles of the hippocampal system and the neocortex in forming a complementary memory system.

4. How does the subsequent memory paradigm work, and what does it tell us about how the brain encodes and retrieves memories?

7.3 Spatial Memory

Spatial memory helps us navigate around the environment, functioning like a cell phone's GPS to indicate our location. Because the ability to navigate is fundamental to any mobile organism, spatial memory is heavily studied in animals, from ants to humans.

Cognitive Maps

According to **cognitive map theory**, the hippocampus constructs a map of the environment, providing the basis for spatial memory and navigation. This property is also useful for episodic memory, in which events are typically coded to a spatial and temporal context (Burgess et al., 2002; Eichenbaum & Cohen, 2004; O'Keefe & Nadel, 1978; Squire & Zola-Morgan, 1991).

The hippocampus plays an important role not only in explicit memory but in spatial memory, supporting the abilities to navigate and form mental images of scenes (Maguire, 1998). Recordings from individual neurons in the hippocampus have revealed **place cells**, which fire when an animal is in a particular location within an environment (O'Keefe & Dostrovsky, 1971; O'Keefe & Nadel, 1978). Moreover, the hippocampus interacts with a neighboring brain area called the entorhinal cortex (see Figure 7.1), in which **grid cells** track an individual's position as the individual moves around in space (Hafting et al., 2005; Moser et al., 2008). The properties of grid cells are arranged along a grid that can be visualized across space—different grid cells fire depending on where the individual is located along this two-dimensional grid in space (**FIGURE 7.13**). Thus, place cells

FIGURE 7.13 Recording from grid cells while a rat runs around a box (top panel) activates different grid cells depending on location (middle panel) These firing patterns reveal a grid arrangement (bottom panel), which turns out to be an efficient way to code location in space. (After A. Abbott. 2014. *Nature* 514: 154–157.)

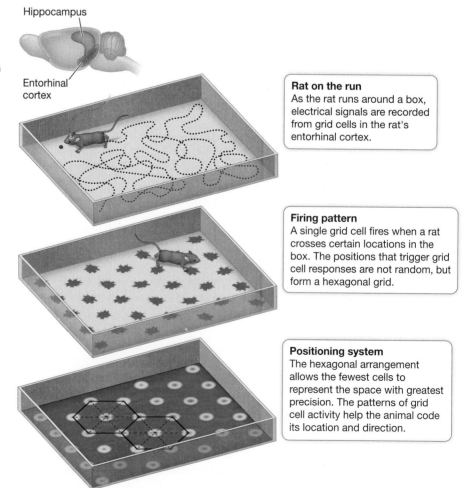

Hippocampus

Entorhinal cortex

Rat on the run
As the rat runs around a box, electrical signals are recorded from grid cells in the rat's entorhinal cortex.

Firing pattern
A single grid cell fires when a rat crosses certain locations in the box. The positions that trigger grid cell responses are not random, but form a hexagonal grid.

Positioning system
The hexagonal arrangement allows the fewest cells to represent the space with greatest precision. The patterns of grid cell activity help the animal code its location and direction.

and grid cells track location within the environment, just like the blue dot that indicates your current location when you navigate using a map app. For their discoveries of place and grid cells, John O'Keefe, May-Britt Moser, and Edvard Moser received the 2014 Nobel Prize in Physiology or Medicine.

Other cortical areas around the hippocampus, such as the parahippocampal place area, also show increased activity when people view scenes, as we saw in Chapter 2 (Epstein, 2008; Epstein & Kanwisher, 1998). In healthy individuals, watching real or virtual film footage through a town layout activates the hippocampus and the parahippocampal place area.

The place area is also active when people recall navigating a route through a city (Maguire et al., 1997). Consider navigating through London, an old city with a very complex road map structure. To be licensed as a taxi driver requires about two years of intensive training—known as being on The Knowledge. Because their spatial knowledge is certified by a stringent set of police examinations, licensed taxi drivers are spatial navigation experts, and they certainly had to be before GPS devices became available. As also described in Chapter 6, their expertise is reflected in the size of their hippocampi. Compared with control participants who lack such navigational expertise, London taxi drivers on The Knowledge have larger hippocampi, the size of which also correlates with years of taxi driving experience (Maguire et al., 2000). This supports the idea that the hippocampus is important for spatial memory and navigation.

Spatial Frameworks

Spatial navigation and memory depend on not only knowing one's location in space (spatial maps), but also on one's relation to the space around oneself. That is, it is not sufficient to know that you're studying in the library right now. Your sense of position depends on which direction you're facing within the library. And explaining your location to another person depends on perspective taking, as we explain here.

Cognitive maps in the brain rely on a **spatial framework** to represent locations in reference to other points. A framework can either be **egocentric**, with the environment's layout defined relative to the viewer, or **allocentric**, with one object's location defined relative to the location of another object or landmark. When you give directions from the perspective of someone following a path, you are using an egocentric framework (e.g., turn left at the first intersection, then turn right at the first stop sign). You could also give directions using an allocentric framework, referencing fixed locations (e.g., head north on College Street, then turn west on Wall Street). Both types of representations are important—you need to know where you are in the environment, and which direction you are facing within it. For example, allocentric coding is more useful for explaining the location of a place to others irrespective of where they are. However, egocentric coding is more useful for the actual navigator (e.g., a map app telling you to turn left as opposed to turning west). **FIGURE 7.14** provides a visual example of the difference between allocentric and egocentric coding systems.

The hippocampus codes space in an allocentric manner, while other brain regions (e.g., the parietal cortex) support egocentric processing. When a lab rat is allowed to roam around a space, place cells in the hippocampus represent the rat's location in a constant way regardless of which direction the rat is facing (Muller et al., 1994; Wilson & McNaughton, 1993), while other parts of the brain—appropriately called "head-direction cells"—encode the direction of the rat's head (Colby & Goldberg, 1999; Snyder et al., 1998; Taube et al., 1990). As you may expect, patients with damage to the hippocampus or the parietal lobe have difficulty remembering and navigating around the environment—something that can be tested with virtual reality setups (Spiers et al., 2001).

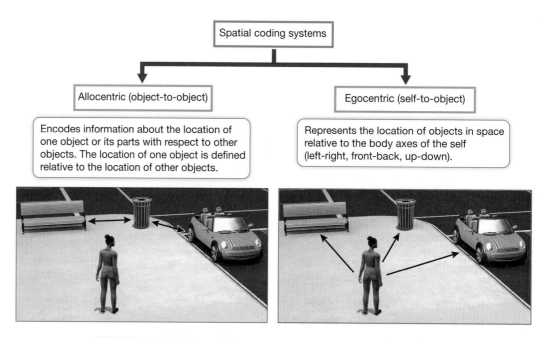

FIGURE 7.14 People can code space in an allocentric way or an egocentric way In an allocentric coding system, the location of the trashcan is referenced with respect to the bench and car. In an egocentric coding system, the location of the trashcan is referenced as located ahead of where the person is facing. (From http://www.nmr.mgh.harvard.edu/mkozhevnlab/?page_id=308, with permission from Maria Kozhevnikov.)

Spatial memory is **viewpoint-dependent**, that is, it is best when the viewer maintains a consistent viewing angle to the spatial array. This can be tested by presenting an array of objects on a circular table for participants to remember. Then a curtain is lowered to block the view of the objects on the table. The curtain is lifted after the table is rotated, and participants have to confirm whether the layout is the same or not. People do more poorly in this task the more the table is rotated (Diwadkar & McNamara, 1997; Simons & Wang, 1998). This shows that spatial memory is viewpoint-dependent and reliant on egocentric representations.

In the real world, people have other ways to update their spatial representations based on how they move around the world. In a different condition of the circular table experiment, instead of rotating the table after the curtain is lowered, viewers are moved around the table. This controls for what the people view with their eyes when the curtain is lifted. However, people do better in this task and show little viewpoint-dependence (that is, little penalty for the change in viewpoint). Patients with hippocampal damage are massively impaired when views are rotated (King et al., 2002).

We use landmarks and the broader geometry of space around us to orient ourselves (Cheng & Newcombe, 2005). When giving directions, we frequently refer people to large landmarks. The importance of geometry can be tested by putting people in rectangular rooms, where one wall is painted a different color as a visual reference. Participants are asked to remember the locations of various hidden objects in the room. Then they are blindfolded and twirled around to disorient them. Adults are able to use the colored surface to reorient themselves to do the task. However, the ability to use color cues appears to be a developing skill, as young children are unable to take advantage of it, relying instead on the geometry of the room alone (Hermer & Spelke, 1994; Shelton & McNamara, 2001).

Spatial skills are important for navigation. However, they are also predictive of achievement in science, technology, engineering, and mathematics (STEM) (Shea et al., 2001; Wai et al., 2009). This relationship raises the possibility that improving spatial skills may improve STEM skills. Of course, in order to fulfill this possibility, one must first ask if spatial skills can be improved in a durable manner and in a way that transfers to tasks other than the one that was practiced. Findings do suggest that training can improve spatial skills in a significant, reliable, and durable manner. In addition, training effects generalize to other tasks. As one example, an interactive physics lecture that involved many spatial demonstrations led to improvement in spatial abilities (Kozhevnikov & Thornton, 2006). Practicing spatial skills such as mental rotation improved math performance in 6- to 8-year-olds (Cheng & Mix, 2014). These findings have implications for education and policy, especially for STEM disciplines. For example, better spatial skills can help students with spatially demanding classes such as engineering and organic chemistry. What kind of training helps? One practical way is to simply add spatially challenging activities to existing classes such as physics, or to use action video games (Uttal et al., 2013).

➤ CHECKPOINT 7.3

1. What is the function of spatial memory?
2. Describe cognitive map theory.
3. Explain what place cells and grid cells are, and what role they play in spatial navigation and memory.
4. Give examples distinguishing an egocentric spatial framework from an allocentric spatial framework.

Chapter Summary

7.1 Discuss the roles of different types of memory systems, including explicit and implicit memory in human memory function.

Explicit memory is the ability to consciously remember and report facts, events, and associations. Episodic memory allows people to recall specific experiences attached to details such as who, what, where, and when. Semantic memory refers to the ability to recall more generic facts and knowledge. In contrast, implicit memory refers to skills and habits that are clearly learned but cannot be articulated consciously or explicitly. Most patients with amnesia, such as H.M., show impaired explicit memory but intact implicit memory. For example, motor skills or priming effects are forms of implicit memory that remain preserved in amnesia. Explicit memory encoding is mostly dependent on brain systems involving the hippocampus, while implicit memory is distributed throughout the brain in a manner that is usually not dependent on an intact hippocampus.

Q: Considering that episodic memory allows you to access some of your earliest memories, what are some of the specific experiences you recall from your past? Take a few minutes to write some of these memories on a piece of paper or on your computer as one-sentence instances. As you do this, do you find that one memory leads to another, and to another, and so on, as one memory primes other associated ones?

7.2 Describe how the brain distinguishes long-term versus short-term memory, and how it encodes, stores, and retrieves memories.

Continuing the discussion of long-term memory and short-term memory in Chapter 6, this chapter focuses on the brain systems supporting memory. The serial position curve demonstrates the difference between long-term memory and short-term memory. The life of a memory can be considered in three stages: encoding, storage, and retrieval. Memories are encoded in a distributed manner, usually within the brain regions that processed them in the first place. Representations in these regions that correspond to memories are strengthened through a process known as consolidation. Retrieval happens when these dormant representations are accessed and reactivated. The hippocampus, prefrontal cortex, and parietal cortex mechanisms help coordinate encoding, storage, and retrieval, especially to associate and bind information across different brain areas. Forming a complementary memory system, the hippocampus and medial temporal lobe enable quick learning, while neocortex provides slower but more stable memory storage.

Q: Using the complementary memory system model, explain why patients with hippocampus and medial temporal lobe damage cannot form new memories but are able to retrieve old ones formed prior to the damage. If one were to scan the brain of an amnesic patient recalling the faces of their parents, which perceptual brain area would you hypothesize to be active?

7.3 Discuss how spatial memory functions and its role in navigation.

Spatial memory allows us to navigate around the environment. Place cells in the hippocampus, grid cells in the entorhinal cortex, and scene representations in the parahippocampal cortex all work together like a GPS device to help us encode and remember where we are located in space. Allocentric representations allow us to encode landmarks around us relative to each other, while egocentric representations help us interact with the environment in a manner that is centered around the observer. People tend to encode spatial information in a viewpoint-dependent manner, egocentric relative to oneself.

Q: Develop a set of directions that you would give to a visiting friend walking to your home on campus from the central library. In addition to an address, and assuming that your friend does not use their map app, how would you explain the route, step by step? Are your directions mostly egocentric or allocentric? Do you instruct your friend to "turn left" or "turn right"? Do you use landmarks? What are the functions of the hippocampus, entorhinal cortex, and parahippocampal cortex as you walk through this route?

Key Terms

allocentric	hippocampal system	reactivation
Alzheimer's disease	hippocampus	recency effect
anterograde amnesia	implicit memory	recollection
associative priming	lexical decision task	remember/know procedure
cognitive map theory	long-term potentiation (LTP)	repetition priming
complementary memory system	medial temporal lobe	repetition suppression
conceptual priming	memory retrieval	retrograde amnesia
consolidation	memory systems	semantic memory
contextual cuing	motor sequence learning	serial position curve
dementia	naming task	skill learning
distributed code	neocortex	spatial framework
egocentric	perceptual priming	spatial memory
episodic memory	place cells	statistical learning
explicit memory	population coding	statistical regularities
familiarity	primacy effect	subsequent memory paradigm
grid cells	priming	viewpoint-dependent
Hebb's Rule	procedural learning	

Critical Thinking Questions

1. In terms of consolidation mechanisms for long-term memory, explain why cramming is bad and why sleep is good.

2. Given what you've learned about how memory works, do you think students should be required to memorize information they can easily look up? Why or why not?

Discovery Labs

oup.com/he/chun1e

The Brown–Peterson Paradigm

In this experiment, students explore how storing even a small amount of information is difficult if they are unable to rehearse it. Participants are shown a series of consonants before solving a series of math problems. Afterward, they are asked to recall the three consonants. Approximate completion time: 30 minutes.

Serial Position Effect

Students explore the notion that individuals use maintenance rehearsal for material they need to keep in short-term memory, and that following sufficient rehearsal, that material becomes part of long-term memory. Participants are shown a series of words and then must try to recall as many of the words as they can in the order they were seen. Approximate completion time: 25 minutes.

Suggested Readings

Genova, L. (2009). *Still Alice*. New York: Pocket Books.

Kandel, E. (2007). *In Search of Memory: The Emergence of a New Science of Mind*. New York: W. W. Norton and Company.

Lemonick, M. (2017). *The Perpetual Now: A Story of Amnesia, Memory, and Love*. New York: Anchor.

Language and Communication

8

Stay in a village in Coahuila, Mexico, and you might hear whistling in the night. The Kickapoo people of this region are known for their "courtship whistling," communicating messages such as "Come on," "Wait a minute," "I'm coming," "No," and "I'm thinking of you." Each couple works together to come up with a unique set of whistling messages. Reportedly, Kickapoo teenagers originally developed this system to communicate with each other in a way their parents could not understand. It gradually replaced an earlier tradition in which young men would call out to their partners with a flute, each flutist having his own tone and melodies (Ritzenthaler & Peterson, 1954). What a beautiful way to communicate! But can this whistling be called a language? Why or why not?

In this chapter we discuss the nature and defining characteristics of language. We delve into how children learn language and whether, or to what extent, the language we learn shapes the way we think.

A young Kickapoo man demonstrating courtship whistling.

8.1 What Is Language?

The answer to the question "What is language?" may seem self-evident: it's how we talk to each other, how we communicate. But probe a little deeper and you find that a clear definition is more elusive. In **psycholinguistics** (the study of the cognitive underpinnings of human language), any satisfying theory of language needs to account for at least the following qualities:

- Language is communicative.
- Language is referential (that is, it refers to things and ideas) and meaningful.
- Language is structured.
- Language is creative (that is, it allows for the creation of meaningful, never-before-spoken sentences).

We expand on each of these qualities in this section.

Language Is Communicative

Language helps us communicate, but we also communicate in other ways, such as through laughter, facial expressions, and posture. These sounds and gestures don't quite satisfy what psychologists call language. In the example that opened this chapter, it may be tempting to think of Kickapoo courtship whistling as a language. What about the flute system it replaced? Both fail to meet some important criteria, and this isn't simply because they don't make use of vocal cords. Indeed, some true expressions of language don't involve vocalizations at all (**THINK FOR YOURSELF 8.1**).

Consider sign language and writing, for example, which are important means of expressing language. You have likely noticed that language doesn't always even need to be transmitted, as it is common to simply think in sentences. But language should not be confused with thought, as we are able to think without words (e.g., through mental imagery). In short, a communicative function may be necessary for something to qualify as a language, but it is not enough. For many psycholinguists, other criteria need to be met as well.

> ► **Think for Yourself 8.1**
>
> ### Animal Communication: Is It Language?
>
> What properties of language are unique to humans? Koko the gorilla, who died in 2018, became famous through reports that she could use language. She demonstrated an understanding of about 2,000 words in spoken English and mastered about 1,000 signs in American Sign Language. But skeptics have argued that Koko's use of words might simply have reflected a learned response to obtain a reward, like a dog learning to sit for a treat (e.g., Terrace, 1980).
>
> A bonobo named Kanzi also gained attention for his communicative abilities. Researchers had been trying to train an older bonobo to point to *lexigrams*—figures or symbols that represented words—when Kanzi began doing so in seemingly meaningful ways. The researchers then shifted their efforts to Kanzi, who soon built up a repertoire allowing him to use more than 400 symbols. According to reports, Kanzi was able to use lexigrams to communicate with his handlers and was also able to comprehend human communication in other instances. In one study, 8-year-old Kanzi's ability to understand novel sentences was found to be comparable with that of a 2-year-old human child in certain tasks (Savage-Rumbaugh et al., 1993).

Think for Yourself   (continued)

Kanzi's communication does not incorporate some hallmarks of human language, however. One is the ability to hierarchically arrange elements of a sentence into what are known as objects and subjects, which allows for linguistic flexibility and creativity. A recent reanalysis of Kanzi's data provides some insight into the nature and degree of Kanzi's comprehension. Kanzi performed just as well as a 2-year-old human child when the meaning could be derived from the simple ordering of the words. Similarly, Kanzi could successfully distinguish between "Put the tomato in the oil" and "Put the oil in the tomato." However, Kanzi's comprehension dropped when the sentences contained hierarchical clustering of words. When instructed to "Give the lighter and the shoe to Rose," he gave Rose only the lighter, failing to assign equal grammatical status to "lighter" and "shoe" (Truswell, 2017).

Such findings highlight the challenge of answering the most basic question one can ask about language: What is it? How is it different from mere communication? There is no doubt that animals across the phylogenetic tree communicate and signal to each other. Meerkats, for example, use different calls to signal the presence of different predators, and these calls can additionally vary depending on their social context (Townsend et al., 2012). Yet arguably, even such complex systems of calls might simply be conditioned responses, learned through chains of associations.

On the left, Koko the gorilla, who famously communicated with humans through sign language with animal psychologist Dr. Francine "Penny" Patterson. On the right, Kanzi the bonobo receives instructions to make a fire from Dr. Sue Savage-Rumbaugh in 2011.

Language Is Referential and Meaningful

Just about every word we utter either has some reference to a real-world object (e.g., "table"), an action (e.g., "eat"), a description (e.g., "blue"), a relationship (e.g., "under"), or a concept (e.g., "justice"), or it helps provide structure to a sentence (e.g., the *a* in the sentence "It is a table"). Thus, language might sometimes be seen as a direct expression of how we represent the world in our minds. Language enables people to communicate about things that are or are not present, about events in the past or future, and about abstract ideas. The "library" of words we use and their links to real-world representations are known collectively as our **mental lexicon**.

ACCESSING THE MENTAL LEXICON   We can access our mental lexicon in several ways. As two examples, we can access them **phonologically** (via their sound) or **orthographically** (via their written form). Understanding these

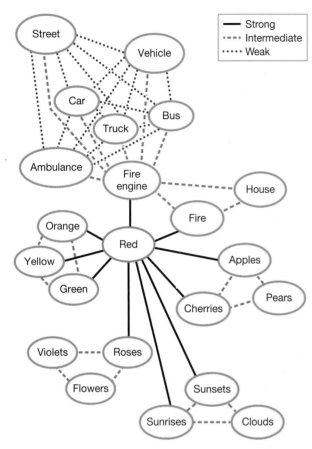

FIGURE 8.1 Schematic example of semantic relatedness between words in the mental lexicon   According to the spreading activation model of semantic priming, exposure to the word "red" might strongly prime the word "apples" and, additionally but more weakly, the word "pears" because of the semantic link between "apples" and "pears." (From A. M. Collins and E. F. Loftus. 1975. *Psychol Rev* 82: 407–428.)

different access routes can provide insight into some impairments of speech production. Likewise, such impairments, which can emerge after stroke or other damage to the brain, reveal how the mental lexicon functions.

In *pure alexia* (a type of *acquired dyslexia*), for example, brain damage in previously literate adults leads to difficulties in orthographic processing but not phonological processing. Evidence suggests that this results specifically from damage to the left occipito-temporal cortex (Binder & Mohr, 1992; Damasio & Damasio, 1983), although there is debate regarding the exact role that this brain region plays during reading (e.g., Price & Devlin, 2011). One intriguing hypothesis is that this region is home to a specialized "visual word form area," which emerges through a repurposing of cortical territory that evolved for object and face recognition (Dehaene & Cohen, 2011). After all, writing systems were developed so recently in evolutionary human history (the Sumerians of ancient Mesopotamia developed cuneiform writing a little over 5,000 years ago) that it seems unlikely that a specialized word form area could have developed through evolutionary pressure alone.

Sometimes a word comes to mind simply because we've encountered a related word. According to an influential **spreading activation model**, word meanings link to each other as if organized like a web within the mental lexicon (e.g., Collins & Loftus, 1975; but for alternative accounts see Dosher & Rosedale, 1989; Ratcliff & McKoon, 1988). According to the spreading activation model, exposure to one word (a "prime" word) activates the corresponding node in this web, and activation spreads along the web, activating other words to different degrees depending on the strength of their connections to the prime word (**FIGURE 8.1**; also see Chapter 11). If you are a fan of the Marvel Cinematic Universe, then you might be able to experience what feels like spreading activation upon seeing the word "Avengers," which likely activates your mental representations of Captain America, Iron Man, and Black Widow. The spread might more weakly activate mental representations of Batman, Superman, and Wonder Woman (who, after all, are members of DC Comics's Justice League, not Marvel's Avengers). Further along the web of connections, devotees might find that the spread activates representations of their favorite comic-book writers and illustrators. In similar fashion, we might often find that some words in our mental lexicon become activated and easily accessed because they are linked with a word or concept currently held in mind.

DISCOVERY LAB
The Word Frequency Effect

THE LEXICAL DECISION TASK AND THE MENTAL ORGANIZATION OF WORD MEANINGS   One way researchers have investigated how word meanings are organized and relate to each other within the mental lexicon is through the **lexical decision task** (**SEE FOR YOURSELF 8.1**). In this task, participants make rapid judgments about strings of letters that are presented to them (e.g., is each string of letters a word or not?). Also see the Discovery Lab on the lexical decision task to learn more. One typical finding, known as the **word frequency effect**, is that people are faster to respond to high-frequency words (words they have encountered a lot) than to low-frequency words (Savin, 1963). See the Discovery Lab on the word frequency effect to learn more.

▶ **See for Yourself 8.1**

The Lexical Decision Task

One of the most robust findings of the lexical decision task is that people are faster at accessing words they encounter with high frequency than they are at accessing words they encounter only infrequently. Try it for yourself.

For list 1 and list 2 below, try to say whether each item is a real word or not, as fast as you can (perhaps by saying yes or no out loud for each item).

List 1		List 2	
Gambastya	Voluble	Mulvow	Gardot
Revery	Boovle	Governor	Norve
Voitle	Chalt	Bless	Busy
Chard	Awry	Tuglety	Effort
Wefe	Signet	Gare	Garvola
Cratily	Trave	Relief	Match
Decoy	Crock	Ruftily	Sard
Puldow	Cryptic	History	Pleasant
Raflot	Ewe	Pindle	Coin
Oriole	Himpola	Develop	Maisle

(Based on K. Hirsh-Pasek et al., 1993. In *Psycholinguistics*, J. B. Gleason and N. B. Ratner [eds.], p. 138. Harcourt Brace Jovanovich: Orlando, FL.)

If you felt yourself responding more slowly to list 1 than to list 2, it may be because the real words in list 1 are less common (e.g., "signet") than those in list 2 (e.g., "effort"). Researchers have adapted this task to investigate how other factors—such as aging or the relationship between words—influence the ease with which we are able to access words in our mental lexicon.

DISCOVERY LAB
Lexical Decision-making

Researchers have used the lexical decision task to explore how words are linked to each other by presenting people with two different words on each trial: (1) a target word about which people need to make the judgment and (2) a preceding word. Researchers measure the degree to which the preceding word affects people's response time to the target word. A typical finding is that participants are faster when the preceding word is related to the target word than when the two words are unrelated. For example, if people need to judge whether "doctor" is a word, an accompanying presentation of "nurse" will quicken reaction time more than an accompanying presentation of "butter." This effect, in which exposure to a word influences a response to a subsequent stimulus, is known as **semantic priming** (**FIGURE 8.2**). In the original report of this type of procedure, participants saw pairs of words alongside each other (rather than a sequential presentation), and the words could be related to each other (e.g., "bread—butter,"

DISCOVERY LAB
Semantic Priming

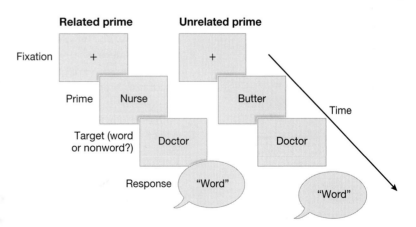

FIGURE 8.2 Schematic illustration of two types of semantic priming trials People are generally faster to answer that the target (e.g., "Doctor") is a word (instead of a nonword) when the preceding prime is a related word (e.g., "Nurse") rather than an unrelated word (e.g., "Butter"). (After D. E. Meyer and R. W. Schvaneveldt. 1971. *J Exp Psychol* 90: 227–234.)

For more than 50 years, *Sesame Street* has helped children learn about language and make connections between words and the objects in their world.

"nurse—doctor") or unrelated to each other (e.g., "bread—doctor," "nurse—butter"). On some additional trials both strings of letters were nonwords, and on other trials one of the pair was a word and the other was not. Participants had to judge whether both members of the pair were words or nonwords. When both were words, participants were faster when the words were related to each other than when they were not (Meyer & Schvaneveldt, 1971). See the Discovery Lab on semantic priming to learn more.

Such patterns are used to draw conclusions about how closely linked the word meanings are in a person's mental lexicon, and they can be useful for understanding the impact of aging and mental health on how we access and link words and concepts. Some evidence suggests that words can be primed not only by preceding items that are semantically related, but also by preceding items that have the same *emotional* quality, an effect known as **affective priming** (e.g., Fazio et al., 1986).

LEARNING THE MEANING OF WORDS   Children who are just learning language face a difficult challenge. Even when they are hearing the people around them speak, the links between the spoken words and the objects they refer to are not always obvious. There are innumerable potential referents in the world. For example, if a parent points to a picture of Big Bird and says "bird," how is the child to know what is being referenced? Is it the color, the size, the long legs? That said, children's rapid pace of language acquisition suggests that they acquire their vocabulary with only minimal exposure to each word. It has been estimated that 1-year-olds can identify a word's meaning after no more than ten exposures (Woodward et al., 1994). Two-year-olds appear to identify meaning after only one exposure, a phenomenon known as **fast mapping** (Carey & Bartlett, 1978; Heibeck & Marman, 1987; Markson & Bloom, 1997; Swingley, 2010).

So how does this fast mapping occur? According to one hypothesis, fast mapping is possible because children don't take the time to consider the full spectrum of a word's referents (Markman, 1989, 1992). The possibility that "bird" could refer to the creature's color rather than to the whole creature itself might not be pondered at all. Instead, it has been suggested that there are constraints on what referents are considered. For example, a proposed **whole-object constraint** suggests that young children will spontaneously assume a word refers to the whole object, not to any specific feature of it (Hollich et al., 2007; Markman, 1991). When generalizing a word to new instances of novel objects, children appear to rely on a **shape bias**, in which they generalize to objects with the same shape rather than to ones with the same color, size, or texture (Baldwin, 1992; Landau et al., 1992; Smith et al., 1992).

Children also appear to factor in what they already know to guide their learning of new words, a phenomenon known as the **mutual-exclusivity constraint**. For example, if children who already know the words "ball" and "flower" are shown both of those items alongside a novel object, and then are asked to identify the "dax," they will typically point to the novel object (Golinkoff et al., 1992).

Language Is Structured

Even when all the words in a sentence have meaning, there is no guarantee that the sentence will be cohesive and coherent. What we say has meaning not only because of the words we use but also because of the way the words are combined. Take this sequence of words:

> *"Furiously sleep ideas green colorless"*

> (From N. Chomsky. 1957. *Syntactic Structures*, p. 15. Mouton & Co., B.V., Publishers, The Hague.)

Obviously, these are all understandable words on their own, but the order seems more like a random jumble (a "word salad") than a meaningful idea. Rearrange them, though, and you get this:

"Colorless green ideas sleep furiously."

(From N. Chomsky. 1957. *Syntactic Structures*, p. 15.
Mouton & Co., B.V., Publishers, The Hague.)

This phrase is one of the most famous in all of psychology because it helped mark the ascension of cognitive science into mainstream psychology during the mid-twentieth century (for reasons we'll return to later). It was coined by Noam Chomsky (1957) and supports one of his many influential insights: sentences have underlying structures that are processed separately from their **semantics**, which refers to the meaning of a word or phrase.

Reading the phrase "Colorless green ideas sleep furiously," your mind might have recognized a meaningful, comprehensible sentence, even though it doesn't make much sense. How can something be colorless and green at the same time? What does it even mean for ideas to sleep? Isn't sleeping the opposite of doing something furiously? Despite these problems, the phrase is grammatically correct. It adheres to the rules and principles that dictate how to combine words (verbs, nouns, adjectives, etc.) into phrases and sentences. Rules about how to structure sentences are known collectively as **syntax** (a subcomponent of what is known as **grammar**, the broader set of rules governing a given language). Violations of proper syntax seem to jar us more profoundly than properly arranged gibberish. A good example of how readily we accept syntactically correct gibberish is Lewis Carroll's famous nonsense poem "Jabberwocky," whose first lines read:

"'Twas brillig, and the slithy toves / Did gyre and gimble in the wabe"

(From L. Carroll. 1872. *Through the Looking Glass and What Alice Found There*.
Henry Altemus Company: Philadelphia.)

You may not know exactly what "brillig," "slithy," "gimble," and "wabe" mean, but the lines' syntactical structure gives most people some sense that these words mean something. You can even figure out which words are verbs, nouns, or adjectives and speculate about what the lines might mean.

Similarly, for those more inclined toward the science-fiction stylings of Douglas Adams, an alternative example comes from the Vogon poetry of *The Hitchhikers Guide to the Galaxy:* "Oh freddled gruntbuggly, thy micturations are to me as plurdled gabbleblotchits on a lurgid bee" (Adams, 1979).

Language Is Creative

One of the most striking and amazing features of language is the flexibility and infinite creativity it allows. Read the following sentence:

"The puzzled sea otter, who had never dreamed of a life beyond
the sea, suddenly found himself floating in orbit and looking
down on Earth after inadvertently nuzzling the launch button."

Considering the millennia over which human language has existed, this statement is remarkable. Specifically, we're reasonably sure that nobody in the history of the universe has ever written or spoken the sentence before. Yet by stringing together words in a highly structured manner, we composed a sentence that is not only original but may also have moved images from our minds to yours.

The ability to produce and understand completely new sentences—that is, the sheer **productivity** of language—is one of the features that any theory of language has to explain. This realm of infinite possibility suggests that language doesn't emerge simply through our having memorized an extensive list of possible sentences. Instead, productivity shows that we have internalized a system of rules for how to combine elements into new meanings. Thus, as Chomsky points out (as did nineteenth-century psychologist Wilhelm Wundt before him), language is a window into the human mind.

An aspect of language that enables us to compose sentences of boundless lyricism, power, and originality is its reliance on rules. Depending on how much of a rebel you are, you may regard rules as things meant to be broken, artificial constraints that limit your potential for self-expression and self-realization. In language, however, rules that guide how parts of a sentence fit together free us. The existence of underlying syntactical rules (i.e., rules related to syntax) allows us to layer shades of meaning in such a way that others can understand us. For example, **recursion** refers to the property of language that enables us to embed structures of language inside other structures, such as sentences within sentences. Take this pithy and undoubtedly true statement:

> "Steve is witty."

The sentence is fully self-contained, but we can expand on it by embedding it within a larger (and, again, undoubtedly true) statement:

> "Marvin thinks that Steve is witty."

There really is no limit to how far we can take this exercise:

> "Lauren knows that Marvin thinks that Steve is witty."

Or

> "The fact that it was Steve who wrote 'Lauren knows that Marvin thinks that Steve is witty' makes the whole exercise a rather shameless bit of self-aggrandizement."

As the psycholinguist Steven Pinker (1994) has noted, such recursion means that there can never be a limit to how long a sentence can be. The instant the *Guinness World Records* book lists the world's longest sentence, it can be immediately topped by one that begins, "The *Guinness World Records* book says that the world's longest sentence is…."

We will delve into some of the syntactical rules that make recursion possible later. For now, suffice it to say that the rules of language free us to build sentences of incomparable creativity and complexity. Such rules are not the "prescriptive rules" of grammar that we learn in elementary school, about how language *should* be expressed. They are "descriptive rules," describing the rules of language as they are naturally and spontaneously instantiated. One might say that a rebel against these rules would be a rebel without a clause.

▶ CHECKPOINT 8.1

1. What are four aspects of language that must be addressed by theory?
2. Describe the lexical decision task, some factors that influence performance on it, and what these suggest about how our mental lexicon is organized.
3. Describe some constraints that help children quickly infer the meanings of words.
4. What is recursion, and how is it important to language?

8.2 An Instinct for Language

If grammar rules are descriptive, where do they come from? This question has puzzled psycholinguists and is central to contemporary attempts to understand what language is. Prior to the mid-twentieth century, linguistics was largely divorced from considerations of cognition or the mind, focusing on the study of language without much regard for the psychological processes that drive it (Bloomfield, 1933; see also Kantor, 1936). At that time, researchers simply described how individual languages worked, with little consideration of the fact that languages, at some deeper level, may have much in common with each other in order to be learnable by all humans.

This is not to say that the mid-twentieth century saw a sudden emergence of interest in the role of the mind from out of nowhere. Decades earlier—before the dawn of Behaviorism—Wundt (1900) argued that an understanding of language was intimately connected with an understanding of the mind. But recall (from Chapter 1) that Behaviorism rejected the need to speculate about the inner workings of the mind, arguing instead that human behavior could be studied by observing how conduct changed as a function of association chains (either between paired stimuli or between actions and their consequences). For many years this approach bore fruit, yielding insights that still ring true today. Then famed behaviorist B. F. Skinner (1957) published *Verbal Behavior*, in which he attempted to explain language development as emerging from such associative learning. Children, for example, were said to learn proper grammar and pronunciation via the feedback they received from adults (e.g., praised when right, corrected when wrong).

Other approaches—such as **Markov models** (named after the early-twentieth-century Russian mathematician Andrey Markov)—sought to explain verbal utterances and language development as probabilistically dependent on preceding words. For example, if a sentence begins with the word "I," it is more probable that the next word is "like" than "orange." If the first two words are "I like," it is more probable that the third word is "oranges" than "run." Such approaches are said to reflect **finite state grammars**, in which sentences are constructed in sequence, with earlier parts of a sentence constraining what subsequent parts of the sentence can be. Finite state grammars are useful for certain situations with a well-defined limit of possible sentences, as in automated announcements or customer-service menus. You may also have seen something similar in action as you type text messages with your phone or enter search terms into Google, which sometimes auto-complete as you type them.

From the start, some scholars expressed doubt about the degree to which these approaches could explain natural language. The neurophysiologist Karl Lashley (1951) pointed out that the meaning of sentences cannot be perfectly derived from the way that words are sequenced. It was at this stage that Noam Chomsky—now one of the towering figures in linguistics and cognitive science—burst onto the scene.

Chomsky, Language Acquisition, and Syntax

Noam Chomsky compellingly argued that neither behaviorist accounts nor finite state grammars could explain the creativity and productivity of human language. His work not only led to a fundamental shift in the field but also helped inspire the Cognitive Revolution.

EVIDENCE OF UNDERLYING RULES GUIDING LANGUAGE ACQUISITION

Chomsky wondered how one could argue for behaviorist principles when the real-world acquisition of language seemed to provide evidence to the contrary. He was particularly struck by the fact that children quickly gain linguistic mastery despite not being exposed to a great amount of information and feedback regarding correct language use. The adults around them often make speech errors, and the limited range of expressions that children typically hear is not enough to be informative about a comprehensive and accurate set of rules. This lack of information in the environment about correct language use is known as the **poverty of the stimulus**. Chomsky's argument

Noam Chomsky's work revolutionized the study of language while also helping lay the foundations for the Cognitive Revolution.

Parents often indicate that they understand what their children are saying even when they make grammatical errors.

suggests that language learning must be supported by some cognitive structures in place that guide how available linguistic information is treated. This claim spelled trouble for Behaviorism's exclusion of the mind from the scientific investigation of behavior.

Consistent with Chomsky's criticism of a behaviorist account of language acquisition, Brown and Hanlon (1970) found that parents tend to respond to ungrammatical and grammatical sentences in the same way. When children make grammatical errors such as "I maked it with water" (Brown, 1973) or "Fill the little sugars up in the bowl" (Pinker, 1989), parents indicate that they understand these utterances—and may even grant praise—just as often as when the sentences are grammatically correct. The researchers also found no evidence that parents reply in such a way as to indicate grammatical approval ("Yes, that's right") or disapproval ("That's wrong") (see Hirsh-Pasek et al., 1984; Marcus, 1993). Parents can be seen to respond affirmatively to an ungrammatical sentence that is factually true (e.g., "Her curling my hair" when a child's hair is being curled) and negatively to grammatically correct sentences that are not true ("There's the animal farmhouse." "No, that's *not* the animal farmhouse.") (Brown & Hanlon, 1970). This kind of parental behavior means that children do not receive **negative evidence** for their ungrammatical sentences (that is, evidence that their utterances have been ungrammatical). Children must be learning language some other way than through parental tutelage.

Further evidence supporting the notion that language learning is guided by a reliance on grammatical rules comes from observations that children engage in **overgeneralization**, the application of grammatical rules in ways unlikely to resemble utterances from adults. That is, children can be seen to apply grammatical rules that are correct in some circumstances to other circumstances in which they are not correct. Few children will have heard their parents say "I runned home," and yet they frequently misapply the past tense in such a way, suggesting that they are somehow extracting and learning underlying, typical grammatical rules of language.

UNIVERSAL GRAMMAR AND THE LANGUAGE ACQUISITION DEVICE

Chomsky believed that every human language involves rules that enable mental representations to be translated into a structured expression of those mental representations, and vice versa. Although these rules may vary from language to language, their presence is a ubiquitous feature of the human mind, and thus they are known as **universal grammar**. One suggestion is that children are born with a **language acquisition device**, an instinct to seek out and master the rules that define their native tongue. Such a notion is consistent with Darwin's (1871) observation that "Man has an instinctive tendency to speak as we see in the babble of our young children while no child has an instinctive tendency to bake, brew, or write."

Because children acquire language at a rate that outstrips the development of other cognitive functions (e.g., working memory), Chomsky proposed that this language acquisition device is **modular**: that it develops and operates independently of other cognitive abilities. Questions about the degree to which language is indeed modular represent an ongoing and intense debate within the literature (as do questions about the degree to which other cognitive functions, such as face perception, are modular). Evidence for the modularity of language is intriguing but not universally agreed on. For example, observations of children with **Williams syndrome**—a genetic condition associated with lower-than-normal IQ and profoundly impaired spatial skills (Hoffman et al., 2003)—suggest that such children are relatively unimpaired in both their grammar and their vocabulary. Preservation of such skills would suggest that language ability may indeed be modular and unconstrained by limitations in other cognitive domains. However, the evidence for preserved linguistic skills in Williams syndrome is not universally regarded as convincing, and calls have been made for further research into the matter (Brock, 2007).

A CRITICAL PERIOD FOR LANGUAGE ACQUISITION   Intriguingly, evidence suggests that there is a **critical period** during which children are optimally equipped to learn the rules of a particular language. Underscoring the notion of children's biological preparedness to learn language, children appear to have more difficulty picking up a language after they reach puberty (Lenneberg, 1967). Obviously, it would be unethical to investigate this by running experiments in which children would be deprived of language exposure until a certain age. Instead, much of what we know about the subject comes from case studies, some of which arose due to unfortunate events. For example, in 1970 authorities rescued a 13-year-old girl, called "Genie," from an intensely abusive situation. Genie had been kept isolated in a room from infancy, often strapped to a bed or toilet, with little exposure to spoken language. Soon after her rescue, she was placed in a foster home, where she was surrounded by spoken English. After years of practice, she developed a large vocabulary, yet her grasp of grammar remained rudimentary, possibly because she was too old by that point to learn grammar fluently (see Curtiss, 1977). Genie's case has been widely cited as evidence for a critical period in language development, but methodological flaws mean that her case can only be interpreted as suggestive or speculative. For example, the kind of isolation she endured would also have included social isolation, which can affect many aspects of cognitive development, and researchers could never satisfactorily rule out the possibility that she had been born with some form of biological or intellectual disability, which could have played a role in her language development (Rolls, 2014).

Although it is difficult to design and run a study on the nature of critical periods in language development, it is not impossible. One of the challenges is that in order to assess how language-learning *ability* changes with age, researchers must somehow control for differences in age of first exposure to a language, years of experience with the language, and the age at which people are tested. In one recent study, researchers tested more than 680,000 participants by recruiting them to take part in an online English grammar quiz that became widely shared by users of social media. In addition to the test of grammatical knowledge, participants answered questions that enabled the researchers to classify them according to their experience learning English. The researchers assessed participants' performance on the grammar test and, via computational modelling, found that grammar-learning ability remained intact until people were more than 17 years old, declining steadily after that. Such findings appear to verify the existence of a critical period for language acquisition but suggest that it lasts longer than previously assumed (Hartshorne et al., 2018).

GRAMMATICAL RULES AND THE CREATIVITY OF LANGUAGE   Compared with behaviorist or probabilistic accounts, the notion that language acquisition stems from learning a set of combinatorial rules is more consistent with the infinite **generativity** of language—that is, with its ability to construct an infinite number of novel sentences (also known as language's *productivity*). According to Chomsky (1957), a finite state grammar could not possibly account for the limitless grammatically correct sentences a person could utter. Consider the sentence "The man who said that [S] is arriving today":

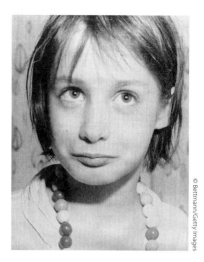

"Genie" was a child rescued from abusive circumstances, where she had been deprived of normal language exposure until her rescue at the age of 13. Although she eventually acquired a large vocabulary, her use of grammar remained impaired, consistent with notions of a critical period for language acquisition that lasts until puberty.

with recursion, the "[S]" can be a placeholder for almost any other sentence you can think of (e.g., "The man who said that [the puzzled sea otter looked down on Earth] is arriving today") (Chomsky, 1957). Only rules that enable such combinations can account for this. Chomsky proposed that a system of rules for translating mental representations into structured verbal output (and vice versa), which he termed **transformational grammar**, lies at the core of human language.

Consider these two sentences:

"The dog bit the man."

"The man was bitten by the dog."

Both have the same meaning and, in the parlance of linguistics, the same **deep structure**: there was a dog, there was a man, the dog did the biting, and the man was bitten. Here, "deep structure" refers to the underlying mental representation of the event. But in changing the sentence from the active voice (the subject performs the action) to the passive voice (the subject experiences the action), we change its **surface structure**, which refers to the way the representation is structured linguistically. The act of comprehending a sentence involves transforming surface structure into deep structure, just as the act of producing a sentence involves translating deep structure into surface structure.

Surface, syntactical structure (or **phrase structure**) is often depicted as a **tree diagram**, which gets its name from the way it branches out. For example, in the first sentence the dog is assigned to the portion of the sentence known as the **noun phrase** (the part that contains the noun and words that modify it), and the man is assigned to the portion known as the **verb phrase** (the part that contains the action, words that modify it, and nouns that clarify the nature of the action). The sentence can be represented as in **FIGURE 8.3**.

The second sentence (**FIGURE 8.4**) reverses the structure, so that the man gets assigned to the noun phrase and the dog gets assigned to the verb phrase.

When the surface structure is hard to determine, it is difficult to understand the underlying deep structure and the sentence is said to be "ambiguous." Read the following headlines, which appeared in actual newspapers:

"Stud Tires Out"

"British Left Waffles on Falkland Islands"

"Gator Attacks Puzzle Experts"

"Squad Helps Dog Bite Victim"

"Juvenile Court to Try Shooting Defendant"

In these cases, the meaning depends on whether words are assigned to a noun phrase or a verb phrase. The first headline can be read as an announcement either about the availability of stud tires (noun phrase: "Stud Tires") or about a breeding horse's exhaustion (verb phrase: "Tires Out"). In the second example (which appeared in British newspaper *The Guardian* in 1982), the meaning changes depending on whether "Left" belongs to the noun phrase ("British Left") and "Waffles" to the verb phrase ("Waffles on

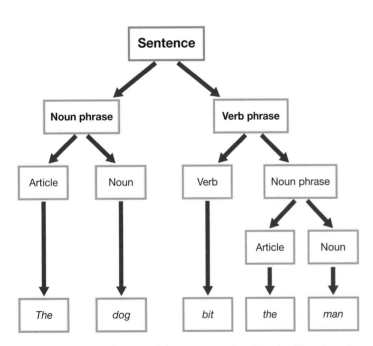

FIGURE 8.3 Tree diagram of the sentence when "the dog" is assigned to the noun phrase (the part that contains the noun and words that modify it), and "the man" is assigned to the overarching verb phrase (the part that contains the action, words that modify it, and nouns that clarify the nature of the action).

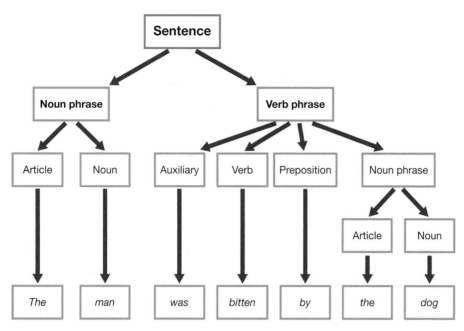

FIGURE 8.4 Tree diagram of the sentence when "the dog" is assigned to the overarching verb phrase, and "the man" is assigned to the noun phrase.

Falkland Islands") or whether "Left" instead belongs to the verb phrase ("Left Waffles on Falkland Islands").

Support for, and Criticism of, a Chomskyan Perspective

Here we consider some of the many arguments for and against Chomsky's theories.

GRAMMAR INSTINCT   Support for an innate grammar instinct comes from many sources, including striking examples from the real world. Historical circumstances have occasionally thrown together people who speak different languages. In such cases, people learn to communicate with each other by stringing together words from their respective languages, forging a shared vocabulary. However, the manner in which such words are combined appears not to adhere to a system of grammatical rules. Such speakers are said to communicate through a **pidgin language**. Strikingly, the children raised in this linguistic environment have been found to impose grammatical rules, with the result that the language evolves into a **creole language**, a synthesis of words from different languages that adheres to rules of grammar (Bickerton, 1984). The emergence of a system of grammatical rules, literally from the mouths of babes, has been taken as evidence for children's innate grammar instinct.

Similar conclusions have been drawn from documentation of a new sign language in Nicaragua. Until the late 1970s, deaf individuals in Nicaragua had little contact with each other. When a new school for the deaf opened, students were taught to speak and lip-read Spanish (Nicaragua's national language) instead of using any form of sign language. Yet students began communicating with each other through gestures, initially through what could be described as a gestural pidgin language. Eventually this spontaneous, organic sign language assumed a complex system of grammatical rules, a shift that was largely driven by the youngest members of the community (Senghas & Coppola, 2001; Senghas et al., 2004).

MODULARITY OF LANGUAGE DEVELOPMENT Some of Chomsky's other ideas, such as the notion of language development as modular, do not enjoy universal agreement. Several findings have suggested that language development is intimately linked with other areas of cognition (e.g., Markson & Bloom, 1997; Mazuka et al., 2009). In some cases, findings have underscored the social pillars of language. For example, caregivers tend to label objects that are the focus of both their and the children's attention, suggesting a role of attention and social skills in language development (Golinkoff et al., 2015; Tomasello & Farrar, 1986). Children seem to infer the meanings of words by taking into account a speaker's intentions. If an adult says a word while appearing to make an accidental action, children don't usually associate the word with the action. If the action is purposeful, though, the children make a link (Tomasello & Barton, 1994). Perhaps the best example of the importance of perceiving others' intentions in learning language comes from a study of children on the autism spectrum. Often found to have difficulty understanding other people's intentions, many children with autism nonetheless do learn language, but in one study, researchers found that the more sensitive children with autism were to the intentions of others, the larger their vocabularies (Parish et al., 2007). These findings suggest that the ability to understand other people's intentions also plays a role in language development.

In line with the notion that language development is interconnected with other cognitive processes such as attention, memory, categorization, and understanding of others' intentions, some theoretical approaches begin by considering the meaning and communicative purpose of language (e.g., Tomasello, 2003). For example, **cognitive-functional linguistics** (also known as **usage-based linguistics**) emphasizes the communicative function of language. Such approaches suggest that the structure of language is not necessarily driven by a modular set of grammar rules, but is instead shaped by the communicative and social context in which language is used (also see Ferreira et al., 2002).

UNIVERSAL GRAMMAR Another criticism of Chomsky's theory concerns the number of languages studied. To make strong claims about universal grammar, one must take an exhaustive inventory of the world's approximately 4,000 languages. The discovery of even one human language that defies the concept's assumptions about how language works could present serious problems.

Linguist Dan Everett (right) with a member of the Pirahã, a group of hunter-gatherers in Brazil. According to Everett, the Pirahã language has many intriguing attributes.

Pirahã could be one such language. In the late 1970s, the American linguist Dan Everett worked as a missionary with the Pirahã, a group of hunter-gatherers in a remote part of the Brazilian Amazon. Bit by bit, he taught himself their unusual language, becoming one of its few speakers in the world. According to Everett, the language has many intriguing attributes, including speakers' ability to whistle entire conversations and a structure that does not appear to incorporate recursion. As you might imagine, such claims have proven controversial and have sparked intense debates among competing theoretical camps.

Although many in the field nibble around the edges of Chomsky's ideas, his main insights and work continue to play a key role in setting the agenda and raising the questions that lie at the core of current psycholinguistics. Such questions include:

1. What makes the unlimited creativity and productivity of language possible?
2. What underlying mental structures enable us to relate words to each other?
3. How do children acquire language?
4. To what degree does language reflect a universal human ability?
5. What does language tell us about the human mind?

➤ CHECKPOINT 8.2

1. How do Chomsky's ideas about language differ from those of Behaviorism and finite state grammar?

2. Discuss arguments for and/or against language being modular or instinctual.

3. What is meant by the difference between "deep structure" and "surface structure" of language?

8.3 From Sound to Meaning

Evolution has given us the ability to make a great variety of sounds, which we rely on to transfer our thoughts to others. Other animals make sounds too, but these various forms of animal communication have not been shown to have the complexity of human language.

Phonemes

The basic units of sound in language (e.g., consonants, vowels) are known as **phonemes**. Some phonemes are present in only some languages; for example, American visitors to Iceland might be struck by sounds Icelandic speakers differentiate between that Americans have never heard before.

DEVELOPING (AND DIMINISHING) SENSITIVITY TO SPEECH SOUNDS

Evidence suggests that infants can distinguish among a wider array of phonemes than adults can (Werker, 1995) (see Research Focus 8.1). It seems that infants enter the world prepared to tune in to the sounds of any language (Eimas et al., 1971; Streeter, 1976). However, by about 6 months of age, children begin to home in on the sounds of their native language and gradually lose sensitivity to sounds that are not present in their native language (Miyawaki et al., 1975; Werker, 1995; Werker et al., 1981).

For example, adult native speakers of Japanese often have difficulty distinguishing between the English sounds /l/ and /r/. In contrast, native English speakers generally maintain their ability to distinguish between these sounds, which are important for telling many English words apart (e.g., "light" vs. "right" or "lead" vs. "read") (Feldman et al., 2013). Children immersed in an English-speaking context learn to place a meaningful boundary between sounds that approximate /l/ and those that approximate /r/—in other words, these two sounds get assigned to different **phonetic categories** (as do other phonemes). Among Japanese speakers, however, the boundaries between phonemes are placed elsewhere. In Japanese, /l/ and /r/ are less likely to reflect meaningful differences between words; the two sounds belong to the same phonetic category, so communicators' sensitivity to the difference between them decreases (Goto, 1971; Miyawaki et al., 1975). Tellingly, Japanese infants have no such trouble—only adults do. The process of learning when phonetic differences are relevant for one's native language is known as the **native language magnet effect** (e.g., Kuhl, 2000) (RESEARCH FOCUS 8.1).

RESEARCH FOCUS 8.1

Effects of Short-Term Exposure and Social Interaction on Phonetic Learning

Before they can even speak, infants fine-tune their sensitivity to phonetic distinctions and begin to lose sensitivity to phonemes outside their native language (e.g., Jusczyk et al., 1993). How is it possible to know this? One method that researchers have used to figure out what babies can do is known as a "head turn" procedure (Polka et al., 1995). In such a procedure, infants are presented with sounds over speakers. The same sound is played over and over again and then is replaced with a slightly different sound for a brief period. Thus, infants might hear the sequence "ba, ba, ba, ba, *bi, bi, bi,* ba, ba." Over many trials, infants learn that, by turning their heads when they recognize the sound as a new one, they can receive a reward such as seeing a toy teddy bear playing the drums. In one experiment using this procedure, American and Japanese infants were exposed to /l/ and /r/ sounds. At 6–8 months of age, the infants performed similarly, but just a few months later—at 10–12 months—the American infants had improved in their ability to distinguish these phonemes, whereas the Japanese infants had grown worse (Kuhl et al., 2006). Such evidence supports the notion that as infants become more proficient in registering the phonemes that are important for their native language, they grow less sensitive to phonetic distinctions that are not.

One particularly interesting aspect of infants learning to distinguish among phonemes is that interacting with a human enhances this process. The infants' learning depends on the nature of their experience with the phonemes. In one study, American babies came to the lab for 12 sessions, during which a native Mandarin speaker read them a storybook and interacted with them. These babies became just as proficient at distinguishing between Mandarin phonemes as did Taiwanese infants in a previous study. However, this did not occur if the American infants were exposed to an equivalent amount of Mandarin speech played over speakers. Thus, it appears that infants are not only prepared to seek out linguistic input but also to prioritize linguistic input that comes from a socially salient source (Kuhl et al., 2003).

Even before they can speak, babies can distinguish phonemes included in their native language.

PHONOLOGY: HOW SOUNDS CAN BE COMBINED   As infants develop, they also become sensitive to their native tongue's **phonology**—the rules that govern how sounds can be combined within that language. Consider the nonsense words "ptak," "plaft," "vlas," "rtut," "thale," "sram," "flutch," "hlad," "mgla," "dnom," and "nyip." You can probably pronounce them, but the tacit rules of English dictate that if any were to be assigned meaning, only "thale," "plaft," and "flutch" would likely become real words (Pinker, 1994).

Phonology differs depending on the language. Take the humble one-syllable word in English, which can often be broken into its *onset* (a consonant or cluster of consonants at the start of the syllable) and its *rime* (the vowel sound plus the consonant sound that trails it). Thus, the onset for "creep" is *cr-* and the rime is *–eep*. Some syllables, such as the word "it," have a rime but no onset. However, Japanese conventions dictate that an onset must contain only a single consonant and a rime only a vowel. Whereas an English speaker may refer to a "girlfriend," the Japanese equivalent is "garufurendo" (Pinker, 1994). These tacit rules establish the sound of a language to such a degree that it is possible to mimic different languages even when one is speaking complete gibberish. Comedian Sid Caesar, who was particularly popular in the mid-20th century, was known for his skill at "double-talk," whereby he could speak at length in what sounded to his audiences like German, French, Italian, or Japanese despite barely saying any true words.

Morphemes and Words

Although phonemes are the smallest units of sound in a language, the smallest units of *meaningful* sound are **morphemes**. According to one study, adult English speakers have, on average, about 80,000 morphemes at their disposal (Miller & Gildea, 1987). The word "bananas" has two: the root word "banana" and the plural specifier *-s*. "Banana" makes sense on its own; *-s* can be appended to a multitude of singular words to make them plural. Although **content morphemes** (those that describe places, people, actions, etc., such as "run," "eat," and "shoe") can be used on their own, **function morphemes** (those that modify content morphemes, such as *-s*, *pre-*, and *-er*) cannot. The rules by which morphemes can be combined into words are known as **morphology**.

Of course, to produce and understand language, one must be able to connect words to their meanings in the mental lexicon. The act of retrieving words and their meanings is called **lexical access** (Forster & Chambers, 1973; Taft, 1979). Insights into the nature of lexical access have come from **speech errors**—the errors made when people are speaking—such as the **tip-of-the-tongue phenomenon**, the feeling one gets when the right word feels just out of reach (see Chapter 6 and See For Yourself 6.4). For example, when people fumble around for the right word, they will often instead recall words that are similar in meaning or in sound, or that start with the same letter, thus giving some insight into what cues people rely on when accessing their mental lexicon (Brown & McNeill, 1966; Rubin, 1975).

Throughout his career, comedian Sid Caesar impressed audiences with his skill at "double-talk," in which he uttered phonemes to sound—at least to an untrained ear— like he was speaking in one of several languages, despite hardly saying any real words at all.

➤ **CHECKPOINT 8.3**

1. What is the difference between phonemes and morphemes?
2. How does infants' sensitivity to phonemes change as they learn their native language?

8.4 Language Production and Comprehension

Language production and comprehension are vital to everyday functioning. When surgery is required to remove a brain tumor, for example, surgeons go to extraordinary lengths—including keeping patients awake as needed—to protect language centers of the brain. Damage to the brain's language centers (either through injury or stroke) can lead to **aphasia**, a condition involving impaired ability to produce or understand language.

Depending on the location and extent of the damage, the impairment can be quite specific, revealing how language ability depends on a coordination of specialized processes. For example, as mentioned in Chapter 2, damage to **Broca's area** (which has functions linked to speech production and is in the inferior frontal gyrus, typically in the brain's left hemisphere) can lead to **Broca's aphasia**. This condition is characterized by difficulty speaking fluently, producing correct sounds, or finding the right words. Although people with Broca's aphasia have difficulty producing speech, they may still be able to comprehend speech, particularly when the grammatical structure is simple. In contrast, as also mentioned in Chapter 2, damage to **Wernicke's area** (which is important for language development and is also in the brain's left hemisphere, near the juncture of the temporal and parietal lobes) leads to **Wernicke's aphasia**. This condition is characterized by difficulty understanding the meaning of words and sentences. People with Wernicke's aphasia not only have difficulty with comprehension but often produce seemingly fluent, grammatically correct sentences that make little sense. Other types of aphasia can range from relatively mild (e.g., **anomic aphasia**, in which people have difficulty finding

[handwritten margin notes:]

aphasia

Broca's aphasia
- difficulty speaking fluently, producing correct speech

wernicke's aphasia
- difficulty understanding the meaning of words and sentences

anomic aphasia
difficulty finding the words they want to say

[handwritten margin note: global aphasia — great difficulty both Producing and comprehending spoken language]

the words they want to say) to severe (e.g., **global aphasia**, in which people have great difficulty both producing and comprehending spoken language).

Production

Speech errors provide interesting insights into how we produce language. For example, the ways people add or swap sounds in a sentence reveal multiple levels of planning that go into producing a simple phrase. As an example of swapping phonemes across words, you might pronounce "snow flurries" as "flow snurries" (not good if you are reporting the weather on TV). You might also exchange morphemes, so that "self-destruct instructions" becomes "self-instruct destructions" (not good if you are a spy). People also sometimes exchange words within a sentence, so that "writing a letter to my mother" becomes "writing a mother to my letter" (e.g., Dell, 1986).

When we assign a part of speech to an incorrect place in the sentence, we most commonly exchange it with a component at the same level (e.g., morphemes with morphemes, phonemes with phonemes, words with words). These exchanges can take place between items at opposite ends of long sentences. A common phenomenon known as an **anticipation error** is when a phoneme early in a sentence is swapped for a phoneme later in the sentence. For example, the nineteenth- and twentieth-century lecturer Reverend Spooner of Oxford University was famously reported to have said to a student "You have hissed all my mystery lectures; you have tasted the whole worm" when he meant to say "You have missed all my history lectures; you have wasted the whole term." (Such errors are now known as "spoonerisms.") Anticipation errors suggest that the planning of speech sounds and the planning of word placement occur at different stages in language production: the correct sounds might be there, but in the wrong places. Based on the evidence from common patterns of errors, one suggestion is that language production involves three primary processes: a prelinguistic process that selects the message one wants to communicate, a process that selects the grammatical structure of the message, and a process that converts the message and structure into a sequence of sounds (Bock, 1996; Levelt, 1989).

Comprehension

Language comprehension is a complex process involving several components.

KNOWING WHICH SYLLABLES COMBINE TO FORM WORDS   The challenge involved in knowing which spoken sounds fit together to form words is not altogether unlike that of programming machine vision (see Chapter 3). Just as it is a puzzle to figure out how to segment the visual world into discrete objects, it is difficult to figure out how to segment the incoming flow of speech sounds. This is a skill that might now seem easy to you, but think of times you might have struggled to be understood by an automated customer-service menu or by your phone's voice assistant, which may not be as adept at factoring in variations of pronunciation, speaking rate, or background noise.

Understanding what someone is saying extends far beyond simply knowing the meanings of the words they say. For one thing, the flow of natural speech does not provide clear **speech segmentation** (boundaries between words). This situation is nicely illustrated by a passage in Beverly Cleary's *Ramona the Pest*:

> *"Beezus, you don't have a very good light for reading," said Mrs Quimby.*
>
> *And she added as she always did, "You have only one pair of eyes, you know."*
>
> *Here was an opportunity for Ramona to show off her new kindergarten knowledge. "Why don't you turn on the dawnzer?" she asked, proud of her new word.*

Beezus looked up from her book. "What are you talking about?" she asked Ramona. "What's a dawnzer?"

Ramona was scornful. "Silly. Everybody knows what a dawnzer is."

"I don't," said Mr Quimby, who had been reading the evening paper. "What is a dawnzer?"

"A lamp," said Ramona. "It gives a lee light. We sing about it every morning in kindergarten."

A puzzled silence fell over the room until Beezus suddenly shouted with laughter. "She—she means—" she gasped, "The Star-Spangled B-banner!" Her laughter dwindled to giggles. "She means the dawn's early light."

(Cleary, 1968, pp. 172–173.)

John Moschitta, Jr., one of the world's fastest speakers, appeared on *Late Night with Jimmy Fallon*. Even when someone is talking incredibly fast, we can usually understand what they're saying.

Yet even when someone is talking incredibly fast, we seem to be able to understand. We have the ability to quickly **parse**, or determine the boundaries between words. For example, we can generally understand speakers such as John Moschitta, Jr., whom the *Guinness Book of World Records* reported as capable of speaking 586 words per minute (a record that has since been broken). (Examples of such fast talkers can be found on YouTube; check out your parsing ability for yourself.) Our parsing ability is only slightly less impressive when it comes to understanding normal speaking rates, which are approximately 250 words per minute for most adult English speakers (Foulke & Sticht, 1969). However, it becomes apparent just how difficult this task can be when you hear someone speaking an unfamiliar language or a language in which you are not fluent.

In contrast with the difficulty of parsing speech in an unfamiliar language, our familiarity with our native language is such that we will often "hear" spoken phonemes that have actually been rendered inaudible due to background noise. This is known as the **phonemic restoration effect** (Warren, 1970). This can be useful when you are trying to have a conversation with a friend in a noisy venue such as a restaurant. For example, imagine that you hear your friend say the following, where the "#" represents noise (e.g., the clanging of dishes) that drowns out your friend's voice: "##y don# w# get s#me de##ert?" Your ability to factor in the interference from the noise should make it feel like you heard their complete question, "Why don't we get some dessert?" In contrast, if those bursts of background noise are replaced by silence, it is harder to understand the sentence: " y don w get s me de ert?"

Phonemic
Restoration effect

LEARNING TO PARSE SPEECH   When trying to understand speech, we must be able to correctly group syllables and phonemes into words and register the underlying grammatical structure very rapidly (Woodard et al., 2016). As discussed in Chapter 7, one line of research suggests that infants and children learn how to parse their native language by noticing the statistical likelihoods of numerous sound combinations (Saffran et al., 1996a,b). Specifically, phonemes that join to form a word (e.g., "bay" and "bee" from the word "baby") will co-occur more often than phonemes taken from different words within a phrase (e.g., "tee" and "bay" from the phrase "pretty baby"). It has been suggested that even very young infants pick up on such statistical probabilities to learn which combinations of sounds form words within their linguistic environment (Saffran et al., 1996a). Because statistical learning plays an important role in language development, this has sometimes been used as evidence against notions of innate cognitive structures dedicated to language learning. However, others have argued that both are important and complement each other (Lidz & Gagliardi, 2015).

NONLINGUISTIC FACTORS IN LANGUAGE COMPREHENSION   Our ability to parse spoken language is also aided by nonlinguistic factors such as our expectations, knowledge, and the context in which we hear language. Although it's sometimes impossible to know the meaning of a sentence until we have heard the whole thing, we begin interpreting it before the sentence ends. Our initial interpretations may be based on our expectations and knowledge, but people are able to revise their interpretation as necessary. In one study, participants sat at a table that displayed a number of objects and were given the instruction "Pick up the candle." Using an eye tracker, the experimenters found that the group typically looked at the candle about 50 milliseconds before the end of the word was spoken. However, if the set of objects also included candy (which shares its first syllable with "candle"), participants did not look at the candle until about 30 milliseconds after the end of the word (Tanenhaus et al., 1995). Thus, our process of interpreting language is influenced by the cues available in the environment.

Evidence also suggests that aspects of executive function (e.g., cognitive flexibility) predict a person's ability to process language in the moment (Novick et al., 2005). This is the case with **garden path sentences**—sentences that begin by suggesting one interpretation only to present another interpretation with their later parts (Pozzan & Trueswell, 2015; Woodard et al., 2016). An example is "After the Martians invaded the town that the city bordered was evacuated" (Ferreira and Henderson, 1991. p. 729). The construction of this sentence at first leads the listener (or reader) to assume that the initial event was Martians invading the town (and that "the town" is part of the verb phrase). However, the subsequent words render the sentence nonsensical unless the initial assumption is corrected (so that "invaded" ends the first verb phrase and "the town" begins the next noun phrase). See the Discovery Lab on garden path sentences to learn more. Evidence indicates that people who have greater cognitive flexibility are better able to adapt "on the fly" to comprehend garden path sentences. Children—who typically are less cognitively flexible than adults (Zelazo & Frye, 1998)—have particular difficulty processing this type of statement, a phenomenon known as the **kindergarten path sentence effect** (Trueswell et al., 1999; see also Choi & Trueswell, 2010; Hurewitz et al., 2001; Weighall, 2008). In one study, children who had more difficulty switching between two cognitive tasks (a measure of cognitive flexibility) showed this effect particularly strongly (Woodard et al., 2016).

Sometimes the words themselves can convey two opposite meanings, again showing that nonlinguistic factors (such as knowing a speaker well) matter for language comprehension. The **prosody**, or the patterns of intonation in a sentence, can make a big difference: a friend's prosody when they tell you they "just love your tie" can inform you whether you should take that as a compliment or as mockery (e.g., Ackerman, 1983; Harris & Pexman, 2003; also see Wagner & Watson, 2010; Watson et al., 2020). The gestures people make while speaking also can play an important role in communication, conveying meanings that may not be captured by spoken language alone (Goldin-Meadow, 1999). In your own experience, you may have found that it is often harder to gauge tone or intention when communicating over e-mail than in person because cues such as prosody and body language are missing.

DISCOVERY LAB
Garden Path Sentences

Pragmatics: Language with the Intention of Communicating

The famous song "Cupid" by Sam Cooke contains the following plea:

> *"Cupid, draw back your bow*
>
> *And let your arrow go*
>
> *Straight to my lover's heart for me, for me"*

Of course, we know the speaker is not actually wishing for their lover's demise. Cupid is the Roman god of erotic desire, whose arrows were said to cause people to fall in love. The songwriter never doubted we would understand his meaning. In short, the song—and our ability to understand its intentions—is an example of how communication often involves a level of shared knowledge between speaker and listener. **Pragmatics** is the study of how the communicative function of language depends on what the speaker knows, what the listener knows, what the speaker knows about what the listener knows, and what the listener knows about what the speaker knows.

Often, we can use context to understand someone's meaning despite the sparseness or ambiguity of their words. For example, on the face of it, the sentence "The boy saw the man with the telescope" is ambiguous (was the boy looking through a telescope or did he see a man who was holding a telescope?), but context—let's say, knowing that the boy was sitting in class, looking out the window at people walking by—can clarify the meaning. Although ambiguity is often seen as impeding clear communication, some theorists have argued that ambiguity can in fact *aid* communication by making it more efficient in some cases. Specifically, in situations where speakers can rely on the context to help specify their meaning, they don't need to find exactly the right words. Instead they can fall back on short, often-used words that might change meaning from one context to the next (Piantadosi et al., 2012). This only works, of course, if speaker and listener share the same understanding or perception of the context or share a degree of knowledge, known as having **common ground** (Clark, 1996).

The degree to which a speaker considers common ground plays an important role in communication (**SEE FOR YOURSELF 8.2**), but such considerations do not always come easy. University students are frequently familiar with the experience of taking classes with professors who are world-renowned experts in their fields but who may also be known among their students for giving seemingly incomprehensible lectures. This may be due to what is known as the **curse of knowledge** (Birch, 2005; Camerer et al., 1989): the difficulty that experts often have in putting themselves into the shoes of a less knowledgeable listener.

▶ **See for Yourself 8.2**

Tappers, Listeners, and the Curse of Knowledge

It's easy to underestimate the degree to which common ground plays a role in communication. But here's a quick game that can help illustrate it: Sit down with a partner and take turns tapping out a famous song on the table. For the purposes of this exercise, pick the most recognizable songs you can think of—ones that almost seem too obvious. You might be surprised at just how few of these songs your partner will be able to guess, even as the songs sound clear as day in your head.

This game was developed in 1990 by a psychology graduate student at Stanford, Elizabeth Newton (see Heath & Heath, 2007). It nicely illustrates the ramifications of the curse of knowledge. Tappers were asked to tap out 120 songs and predicted that their listeners would be able to guess 60 of them (50%). However, the listeners were only able to guess about 3 of the songs (2.5%). If you were a tapper in such a game, this result might surprise you—it's easy for *you* to hear the tune because you already have the song in your head. The same thing often happens in communicating interpersonally or to an audience. When we neglect to consider how much of our experience is unique versus common ground, we may be surprised when our message fails to get across.

Many types of communication failures can occur when speakers and listeners view a situation differently. Imagine you and your friends are at a park when you see a dog leap to catch a Frisbee®. "Amazing!" you say, but your friends won't know what you're talking about if they didn't see it. As it turns out, we often modify what we say based on our assumptions or observations

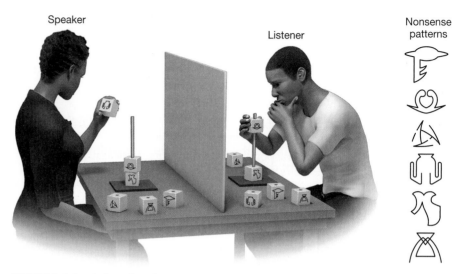

Speaker   Listener   Nonsense patterns

FIGURE 8.5 Depiction of a referential communication task In this case, one participant needs to describe the nonsense patterns on blocks so that their partner can reconstruct the order. (After N. Braisby and A. Gellatly. 2012. *Cognitive Psychology*, 2nd edition. Oxford University Press: Oxford, based on S. Glucksberg et al. 1966. *J Exp Child Psychol* 3: 333–342.)

about the listener's perspective (unless we are under time pressure or in other stressful situations) (Horton & Keysar, 1996). Just as effective speakers need to consider what a listener knows, effective listeners in turn must consider what speakers know (Bergen & Grodner, 2012).

The role of common ground in communication, and adjustments that speakers make to accommodate a lack of common ground, is sometimes studied using the **referential communication task**. In this task, two participants are separated by a partition, and one participant tries to describe layouts of objects that are within their view but not within their partner's view (Glucksberg & Danks, 1975; Krauss & Weinheimer, 1967) (**FIGURE 8.5**). In one such study, a speaker had to communicate the order in which pictures of New York City were arranged, so that a listener on the other side of the partition could duplicate the arrangement (Isaacs & Clark, 1987). In some cases, both participants were from New York, in other cases only one of them was from New York, and in other cases neither of them was from New York. Notably, the way that speakers from New York described their cards differed depending on whether the listeners were also from New York. When speaking to another New Yorker, speakers might simply refer to the name of the depicted places (e.g., "the Citicorp building"), whereas they were more likely to describe features (e.g., "the tall building with the triangular top") to non–New Yorkers. Often a speaker would accommodate their partner's level of knowledge after it became evident that their partner needed more information. This study illustrates how common ground (or lack thereof) gets spontaneously established within the course of conversation, with adjustments made to communicate most effectively.

➤ CHECKPOINT 8.4

1. Describe some common speech errors and provide examples other than those in the text.

2. What evidence suggests that infants use statistical regularity to figure out what phonemes are important in their own language and that they become less sensitive to phonemes in other languages?

3. What is the importance of common ground in communication? How does a lack of common ground change what people say?

8.5 Language and Thought

To what degree does the language we use shape the way we think? Questions about the degree to which perception, memory, and thought are influenced by language are of great interest to many psychologists (e.g., Gleitman & Papafragou, 2005).

Bilingualism

Some evidence suggests that aspects of language such as **bilingualism**—that is, fluency in two languages—affects a range of cognitive processes. On one hand, bilinguals have been found to perform more slowly and make more errors than those who speak only one language ("monolinguals") on tasks that involve picture naming or word production and comprehension (Bialystock et al., 2008; Gollan et al., 2005; Ivanova & Costa, 2008; Ransdell & Fischler, 1987). This may be because it is more difficult for bilinguals than monolinguals to retrieve common words (Bialystock et al., 2012). On the other hand, bilinguals have been found to perform better on tasks that index attentional control, such as response inhibition, task switching, and working memory (e.g., tasks described in Chapter 5). This may be because speaking two languages comes with the constant challenge of juggling and monitoring them both, making sure to inhibit responses in the context-inappropriate language and selecting responses in the language appropriate for the current situation. A lifetime of practice navigating such demands may give rise to the bilingual advantage that has been observed on many attentional control tasks (Bialystock et al., 2012; also see Arredondo et al., 2017). As you may imagine, claims that bilingualism leads to true cognitive advantages have been a source of both great interest and great debate. Counterevidence comes from a recent online study that tested more than 11,000 people on 12 different cognitive tasks, finding no difference between bilinguals and monolinguals (Nichols et al., 2020; also see Lehtonen et al., 2018).

bilingualism
- perform slowly and make more errors than those who speak one language on tasks that involve picture naming or word production and comprehentoin
- perform better on tasks that index attentional control

Language and the Content of Thought

What about the notion that differences in language lead to differences in the contents of people's thoughts and their experience of the world? The notion that language shapes thought seems to have popular appeal. In the world of George Orwell's *1984*, words have been systematically erased from the lexicon in order to limit citizens' ability to engage in rebellious thoughts. In today's world, spin doctors and marketers consult on how to use language to shape people's attitudes and impressions (Luntz, 2007).

Consider this example: In 2006, then-vice president Dick Cheney accidentally shot Texas attorney Harry Whittington while quail hunting. Whittington later suffered a minor heart attack as a result of his injuries but recovered. As psycholinguist Lera Boroditsky (2011) has pointed out, this incident could have been spun to the press in many ways:

> *"Cheney shot Whittington" places the blame squarely on Cheney.*
>
> *"Whittington got shot by Cheney" uses the passive voice to distance Cheney from having direct agency in the shooting.*
>
> *"Whittington got peppered pretty good" removes Cheney from the equation.*

In the end, Cheney said, "Ultimately, I'm the guy who pulled the trigger that fired the round that hit Harry," in effect distancing himself via a long sentence and a series of events from the outcome (Grieve, 2006). Even more strikingly, President Bush said, "He heard a bird flush, and he turned and pulled the trigger and saw his friend get wounded," making Cheney a mere witness (Bumiller & Blumenthal, 2006). Although these descriptions may or may not have influenced public reaction to the incident, they appear to have affected Whittington's assessment, as he subsequently apologized for having put his face in the path of gunshot (Borger, 2006).

The Sapir-Whorf Hypothesis

The **Sapir-Whorf hypothesis** (also known as "linguistic determinism") suggests that differences among languages reflect and contribute to differences in underlying thought processes. That is, language reflects and can even shape how we organize and interpret our perceptual experiences and how we comprehend the meaning of objects and events in our environment (Whorf, 1956; Wolff & Holmes, 2010).

Many investigators draw a distinction between "strong" and "weak" forms of this notion. According to the strong form, language shapes the way we actually perceive and experience the world. According to weak versions, language doesn't affect subjective experience per se, but it does reflect (and can shape) differences in higher cognitive processes such as categorization (e.g., Balaban & Waxman, 1997). Many researchers find weak versions to be more plausible, but both the weak and strong forms have been criticized: in many cases, the strong form has been contradicted by evidence, and some have argued that the weak form is so vague that no evidence could decisively disprove it (Hunt & Agnoli, 1991).

Inconsistent with the notion that cognition is shaped and limited by the language we use, many languages describe experience similarly, suggesting that there may be universal perceptual constraints. Many languages employ similar color vocabularies (Regier et al., 2007) and similar labels for basic tastes (Majid & Levinson, 2008). Meanwhile, the indigenous Amazonian groups the Pirahã and the Mundurukú have languages that are strikingly different from English and other Western languages, but although Mundurukú contains no words for geometrical concepts, its speakers can recognize squares and trapezoids (Dehaene et al., 2006). Although the Pirahã don't have words for numbers, they can perform relatively complex numerical calculations. That said, the Pirahã have been found to have difficulty remembering such calculations, suggesting that language can affect the way we attend to information and encode it into memory (Frank et al., 2008).

The question of whether language shapes or reflects thought remains a vigorous area of research, partly because the question is so compelling and partly because the question is not quite settled. Some evidence does suggest that language can shape perceptual categorization. For example, in one study, speakers of Russian and English—two languages that categorize the color blue differently—performed differently when doing a color-matching task (Winawer et al., 2007). These findings are covered in more detail in **RESEARCH FOCUS 8.2**.

RESEARCH FOCUS 8.2

Does Language Change Color Perception?

The color spectrum is divided differently in Russian and English: Russian differentiates between lighter blues (*goluboy*) and darker blues (*siniy*), whereas English does not. In one study (**FIGURE A**), Russian and English speakers were asked to view stimuli that spanned the divide between light and dark blue and to indicate as fast as they could which of two blue stimuli matched a target blue stimulus (Winawer et al., 2007). The results revealed that the Russian speakers were faster to respond when the two stimuli fell into different categories of blue than when they fell into the same category; this pattern did not emerge among the English speakers. The response-time difference among Russian speakers was eliminated when the participants were asked to do a simultaneous verbal task—the researchers' intention here was to interfere with participants' reliance on language to perform the task. These findings are consistent with the notion that language can influence perceptual categorization.

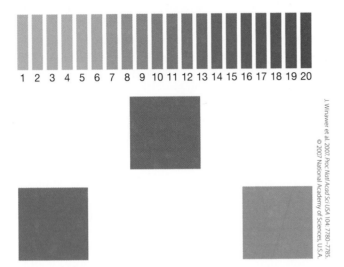

1 2 3 4 5 6 7 8 9 10 11 12 13 14 15 16 17 18 19 20

J. Winawer et al. 2007. Proc Natl Acad Sci USA 104: 7780–7785. © 2007 National Academy of Sciences, U.S.A.

FIGURE A **Color spectrum differentiation study** Participants were asked to choose which of the two squares on the bottom matched the color of the target square above them. Speakers of Russian, who use different color names to refer to the light and dark shades of blue, were quicker at this task than were English speakers, who don't assign the shades to different color names.

Language may also affect how we process spatial information. For example, preschoolers who were exposed to spatial language (e.g., labels of orientation, shape, configurations of objects) while playing were found to outperform children who had not been exposed to such language when later tested on mental rotation tasks (Casasola et al., 2020). Additional evidence comes from Tseltal speakers—Mayans living in Mexico—who do not use egocentric spatial terms such as "left" and "right." Instead they use cardinal directions, as in "The fork is to the north of the plate." In one study, Tseltal speakers were found to remember spatial layouts in terms of absolute coordinates, whereas speakers of Dutch (which does use left–right distinctions) remembered the scenes better in body-centric coordinates (Levinson, 2003). However, it is not clear that the findings from the Tseltal speakers reflected underlying differences in cognitive processing rather than simply different understandings of task instructions or strategies. For example, Tseltal speakers were able to use left–right distinctions when they received hints regarding the solutions to spatial tasks, and in these cases they were sometimes more accurate than when using cardinal directions (Li et al., 2011).

Some evidence suggests that language differences reflect or influence how people think about responsibility and how they regard and remember mistakes made by others. For example, when describing accidents, English speakers are more likely than Spanish speakers to use agentive language (e.g., "She broke the vase") than non-agentive language ("The vase broke"). In one experiment, speakers of both languages watched videos of people breaking eggs, bursting balloons, and spilling drinks, either intentionally or unintentionally. When subsequently asked to remember who did what in the case of accidents, the

English speakers were more likely than the Spanish speakers to remember who had been responsible (Fausey & Boroditsky, 2011).

In the emotional realm, researchers have tested whether language helps shape how we understand emotional experience. Some evidence suggests that access to the meaning of emotion words enhances people's ability to perceive facial expressions of emotions (Gendron et al., 2012; Lindquist et al., 2006, 2014). Relatedly, in a cross-linguistic comparison, speakers of Herero (a dialect of the Himba tribe in Namibia, Africa) and speakers of American English were given images of people making neutral facial expressions and expressions of anger, disgust, fear, happiness, and sadness. When asked to sort them into piles, the English speakers spontaneously separated the images according to these emotion types, whereas the Herero speakers only did so when given emotion labels in advance (Gendron et al., 2014). Such findings are consistent with what is known as a **conceptual act theory of emotion**, whereby processing and experience of emotion are shaped by conceptual knowledge about emotions, which in turn are supported by language (Barrett, 2006; Lindquist et al., 2015). Such conceptualizations depart from classic views of emotions as being universally shared and physiologically distinct from each other (e.g., Ekman & Cordaro, 2011; Izard, 2007).

A vigorous body of research continues to examine the degree to which language reflects and possibly shapes cognition. To date, much evidence suggests that strong forms of the Sapir-Whorf hypothesis may be incorrect: rather than constraining how we think, language might guide our appreciation of which aspects of experience are particularly salient and merit encoding. Some research suggests that children see the world similarly before learning language, but that that language—once learned—heightens or dampens which aspects of the world children notice (Konishi et al., 2019). An additional hypothesis is that language can enhance the sophistication of our thought processes by providing a shared platform. Through language, the outputs of different cognitive computations can be combined, giving rise to the creativity that defines us as a species (Spelke, 2003).

➤ CHECKPOINT 8.5

1. How might bilingualism be linked with better cognitive performance? What evidence suggests that this might be the case, and what evidence suggests that it might not be?

2. What is the difference between "strong" and "weak" forms of the Sapir-Whorf hypothesis?

3. Describe some ways that language has been found to shape or reflect differences in how people experience the world.

Chapter Summary

8.1 Describe four qualities of human language that theories need to explain.

In psycholinguistics, any satisfying theory of language needs to account at least for the following qualities: language is communicative, it is referential and meaningful, it is structured, and it is creative.

Q: Think for Yourself 8.1 described the linguistic capabilities of Koko the gorilla and Kanzi the bonobo, noting that many researchers remain skeptical that non-human primates can learn language. If you were one of these skeptics, what would it take for these animals to convince you that they can use language?

8.2 Discuss evidence that people are biologically prepared to learn language, as well as some core features of Chomsky's contribution to psycholinguistics.

Children rapidly learn the grammar of their native language despite not being exposed to enough linguistic input to support such rapid development on its own (*poverty of the stimulus*). There appears to be a critical time window (*critical period*) during which exposure to the linguistic environment needs to occur. Although some of Chomsky's ideas have been supported by evidence, others—such as the modular nature of language—have been contested.

Q: As described in this chapter, ambiguous sentences can arise when it is unclear how a word fits in with the sentence's surface structure (e.g., "Stud Tires Out"). Try finding more such examples on the Internet, and try writing your own ambiguous sentences.

8.3 Define phonemes and morphemes, their roles in language, and how children become sensitive to the sounds of their native language.

Phonemes are the smallest pronounceable units of language, and different phonemes can be found in different languages. Infants quickly become more sensitive to phonemes in their own language while becoming less sensitive to phonemes in other languages. Morphemes are the smallest units of *meaningful* sound in a language.

Q: Imagine that your friend has a baby and wants to ensure that her baby can remain sensitive to the sounds of many different languages. What advice would you give your friend, and what evidence would you provide to support the soundness of your advice?

8.4 Discuss how people overcome the challenges of producing and comprehending speech, as well as factors that can aid or hinder effective communication.

Language production and comprehension are made possible by a coordination of specialized processes, which have been revealed in part by different patterns of impairment caused by brain damage. Language production has been suggested to involve a prelinguistic process that selects the message one wants to communicate, a process that selects the grammatical structure of the message one intends to utter, and a process that converts the message and structure into a sequence of sounds. Comprehension involves extracting words from an ongoing flow of speech, which is something infants seem to learn to do by tuning in to statistical regularities in their linguistic environments. Language comprehension also appears to be aided by other aspects of cognition such as cognitive flexibility.

Q: What evidence suggests that nonlinguistic aspects of cognition might aid in language comprehension? Think of a time when you adjusted how you explained something upon realizing that you and your conversation partner did not entirely share common ground. Describe a situation in which your expectations caused you to misinterpret what someone was saying.

8.5 Define the Sapir-Whorf hypothesis and critically discuss ways that language may or may not reflect or shape thought.

Also known as linguistic determinism, the Sapir-Whorf hypothesis proposes that differences in language reflect, and even shape, differences in how people think. Weak forms of this hypothesis—whereby language may reflect differences in some aspects of higher-level cognition—are more widely accepted than strong forms of the hypothesis, in which language shapes subjective experience of the world.

Q: In English, we have completely different words for water depending on whether it is in a solid, liquid, or gas state (i.e., "ice," "water," "steam"). Imagine that instead you only knew these forms as "solid water," "liquid water," and "gaseous water." Do you think this would change aspects of how you think about them? If you know a second language, are there words in that language that have no direct English translation (or vice versa)? If so, do you think this affects the way speakers of the two languages experience the world?

Key Terms

affective priming
anomic aphasia
anticipation error
aphasia
bilingualism
Broca's aphasia
Broca's area
cognitive-functional linguistics
common ground
conceptual act theory of emotion
content morphemes
creole language
critical period
curse of knowledge
deep structure
fast mapping
finite state grammar
function morphemes
garden path sentences
generativity
global aphasia
grammar
kindergarten path sentence effect
language acquisition device

lexical access
lexical decision task
Markov models
mental lexicon
modular
morphemes
morphology
mutual-exclusivity constraint
native language magnet effect
negative evidence
noun phrase
orthographically
overgeneralization
parse
phonemes
phonemic restoration effect
phonetic categories
phonologically
phonology
phrase structure
pidgin language
poverty of the stimulus
pragmatics
productivity

prosody
psycholinguistics
recursion
referential communication task
Sapir-Whorf hypothesis
segmentation
semantic priming
semantics
shape bias
speech errors
spreading activation model
surface structure
syntax
tip-of-the-tongue phenomenon
transformational grammar
tree diagram
universal grammar
usage-based linguistics
verb phrase
Wernicke's aphasia
Wernicke's area
whole-object constraint
Williams syndrome
word frequency effect

Critical Thinking Questions

1. The vignette that opened this chapter described the "courtship whistling" of Mexico's Kickapoo people, in which couples whistle coded message to each other, such as "I'm thinking of you" and "Wait a minute." Given what you have read in this chapter, does this courtship whistling qualify as a language? Why or why not? If not, what would courtship whistling need to be like if it were to be a language?

Discovery Labs

oup.com/he/chun1e

Lexical Decision-making

In this experiment, students learn about visual word recognition. Participants are asked to classify visual stimuli as words or non-word as quickly and accurately as possible. Approximate completion time: 25 minutes.

The Word Frequency Effect
Students explore the psychological phenomenon where words that are seen often are recognized more quickly than words that are seen less often. Participants are asked to indicate, as quickly as possible, whether the presented stimulus is a word or not. Approximate completion time: 25 minutes.

Semantic Priming
In this experiment, students learn about the phenomenon of spreading activation. Participants are asked to determine whether a series of characters on a screen do or do not spell a word. Approximate completion time: 25 minutes.

Garden Path Sentences
The study of the psychological factors that underlie language use is known as psycholinguistics. Researchers studying psycholinguistics study a wide variety of topics including speech production and comprehension, reading, and conversational interactions. This lab explores an issue important to psycholinguistics. More details will be provided when you have finished the experiment. Approximate completion time: 5 minutes.

Suggested Readings

Golinkoff, R. M., & Hirsh-Pasek, K. (1999). *How Babies Talk: The Magic and Mystery of Language in the First Three Years of Life*. New York: Dutton.

Jackendoff, R. (2002). *Foundations of Language: Brain, Meaning, Grammar, Evolution*. Oxford, UK: Oxford University Press.

Pinker, S. (1994). *The Language Instinct*. New York: William Morrow and Company, Inc.

Judgment and Decision Making

9

C hris Domine felt so depressed and fatigued that he sought a doctor. But rather than being diagnosed with mental illness, Chris learned that he was suffering from kidney failure and in desperate need of a transplant. After he spent an excruciatingly long two years on the organ waiting list, a kidney donation and transplant gave him life. Reflecting on his story, he says, "The little things? Nothing bothers me. I'm alive!" (U.S. Department of Health and Human Services, 2012).

Chris was lucky; many people in need of a transplant do not fare well. In the United States, due to a shortage of organ donors, about 20 patients die each day while waiting for a kidney (U.S. Department of Health and Human Services, 2015). And the crisis worsens as the gap widens between the number of patients on the waiting list and the number of donors available. Although 95% of Americans support organ donation in principle, only 60% are registered as donors (organdonor.gov, 2021). Why aren't more Americans signing up? What policies or campaigns could increase donation consent rates?

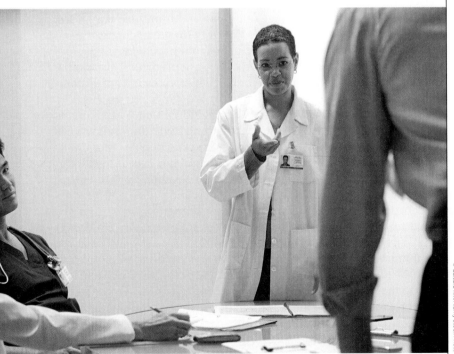

To address a severe shortage of organ donors, medical professionals discuss how to increase organ donation consent rates.

LEARNING OBJECTIVES

9.1 Describe the differences between irrational and rational decision making, and between thinking fast (System 1) and thinking slow (System 2), giving examples.

9.2 Identify examples of intuitive decision making and heuristics.

9.3 Explain how risk, framing, or status quo affects decision making.

9.4 Discuss insights from the field of neuroeconomics based on brain imaging studies and patients with brain damage.

To help answer these questions, we can look to the psychology of judgment and decision making. A classic study by Johnson and Goldstein (2003) showed that in democratic countries, state policy impacts registration rates for organ donation. Countries with high consent rates have an opt-out system: citizens are automatically enrolled as organ donors, a policy of *presumed consent*, and anyone can opt out of being an organ donor. In contrast, countries with low donor rates have an opt-in system: these require *explicit consent* and rely on citizens to sign up as organ donors. The act of opting in involves extra effort—even if it's as minimal as checking a box—and that suppresses participation.

The drastic difference between donation consent rates in opt-in versus opt-out systems shows the power of psychology. People can exercise their preference equally well in either system, so if behavior were rational, there should be no difference in consent rate. But as we will see, human decision making is frequently irrational and surprising.

In this chapter we first distinguish between quick, effortless forms of thinking and more deliberate, effortful forms of thinking. Then we explore how these different modes of thinking come into play when we make judgments under conditions when the outcomes are uncertain (e.g., is this large dog running up to me friendly or not?). We frequently rely on heuristics, which are mental shortcuts. Most of the time, heuristics allow us to make good judgments, but under some conditions they lead to systematic errors. Following our review of heuristics, we consider how we choose an action when presented with one or more options. Decision making aims to maximize utility, the satisfaction and subjective reward that a decision can help us obtain. In the final section of this chapter, we consider how understanding brain mechanisms helps to explain decision-making behavior.

9.1 Fast and Slow Thinking

What does it mean to behave rationally or irrationally? **Rational behavior** can be described as objective and logical. Conversely, **irrational behavior** is more subjective and biased. Some aspects of human behavior are rational. For example, we generally seek to maximize our gains and minimize our losses. We are not consistently rational, however. Not only do we make errors, but we are subject to **psychological bias**, which means that psychological factors affect our decision making in consistent ways. We are **predictably irrational**, according to cognitive psychologist Dan Ariely (2008): our errors are systematic and reliable.

What can we gain by empirically demonstrating how human reasoning is irrational? The applications range from understanding individual behavior to understanding large-scale social problems such as housing bubbles, stock market crashes and vaccine hesitancy. The study of judgment, decision making, and reasoning has implications far beyond cognitive psychology, influencing fields such as behavioral economics, political science, and public policy.

To approach this broad area of research, let's begin by distinguishing between "thinking fast" and "thinking slow," as articulated by Daniel Kahneman (2011), a psychologist who won the 2002 Nobel Prize in Economic Sciences. **Thinking fast** (or **System 1**) refers to decision making that operates quickly, with little effort and less control. **Thinking slow** (or **System 2**) refers to decision making that operates more slowly, with more effort and more deliberate control. For example, after a hard run in hot weather, would you prefer to drink a cold bottle of water or a hot vanilla caramel latte? Using System 1, you would probably choose the water quickly, even if you like lattes. But what if you were trying to determine which local coffee shop offers the best deals over time? Here, you would use System 2, which is for making more complicated calculations.

Both systems are useful—they complement each other depending on the situation. If a new acquaintance asked you out for a cup of coffee, you would probably use System 1 and quickly say yes or no. In the moment, you would not need to go into a long, effortful query and calculation of a person's values, personality, intelligence, attractiveness, sense of humor, interests, emotional stability, political orientation, income potential, and family background. If you were deciding whether to marry someone, however, you would use System 2 to consider many of these factors carefully.

▶ CHECKPOINT 9.1

1. What is rational versus irrational behavior?
2. What are the differences between System 1 and System 2? Suggest examples of when you may use each system.

9.2 Judging Under Uncertainty and Using Heuristics

Decisions are difficult because of uncertainties, such as whether it will rain this afternoon or which of two investments is more likely to yield a high return. Although potentially stressful, uncertainty is what makes life interesting. Would you pay to watch a sports match that was 100% predetermined? Life asks us to gamble all the time, in decisions ranging from whether to carry an umbrella to where to go to college.

To help compare options and make decisions, we have to estimate likelihood, or the chances of events happening, expressing them as *odds*, or *subjective probabilities*, between 0 and 1. For example, the odds that a tossed coin will land as heads are 0.5. The odds that the sun will rise over the east in the morning are 1.0. Most other judgments of probabilities are harder to make and may reflect an individual's subjective experience.

It's easy to say we should always be deliberate and rational when we reason about the world, solve problems, and make decisions. However, decisions are optimal only if we have full knowledge of all relevant alternatives, including their consequences and probabilities, and only if the world is predictable (Simon, 1979). Such perfect knowledge does not exist in the real world; some relevant information is unknown or has to be estimated from small samples. Thus, rational and deliberate modes of reasoning—thinking slow—may not be practical for everyday thinking and decision making. Instead, using **heuristics**—mental shortcuts we take as part of thinking fast (System 1)—can be more practical than using rational models (Gigerenzer & Gaissmaier, 2011; Gigerenzer & Goldstein, 1996).

Although System 1 allows us to make decisions quickly and efficiently through intuitive judgments and heuristics, the disadvantage is that biases and irrelevant information often sway our quick judgments. The following examples show the kinds of predictably irrational decisions that can result from using System 1.

Insensitivity to Prior Probabilities and Representativeness

Many judgments require us to estimate the probability that someone or something belongs to a certain category. Consider the profiles in **SEE FOR YOURSELF 9.1**. (Note: This chapter contains many exercises such as this, which illustrate essential concepts. Please do each one as you come to it.)

► **See for Yourself 9.1**

Profiles and Probabilities

Steve's Profile

"Steve is very shy and withdrawn, invariably helpful, but with little interest in people, or in the world of reality. A meek and tidy soul, he has a need for order and structure, and a passion for detail."

Do you think Steve is more likely to be a librarian or a farmer?

(From A. Tversky and D. Kahneman. 1974. *Science* 185: 1124–1131.)

Jack's Profile

A panel of psychologists has interviewed and administered personality tests to 30 engineers and 70 lawyers, all successful in their respective fields. Thumbnail descriptions have been written on the basis of this information. Below is one description, chosen at random from the 100 available descriptions. After reading it, please indicate how likely you think it is that the person described is an engineer, on a scale from 0% to 100%.

"Jack is a 45-year-old man. He is married and has four children. He is generally conservative, careful, and ambitious. He shows no interest in political and social issues and spends most of his free time on his many hobbies, which include home carpentry, sailing, and mathematical puzzles."

The probability that Jack is one of the 30 engineers in the sample of 100 is _____%.

(From D. Kahneman and A. Tversky. 1973. *Psychol Rev* 80: 237–251.)

Linda's Profile

"Linda is 31 years old, single, outspoken, and very bright. She majored in philosophy. As a student, she was deeply concerned with issues of discrimination and social justice, and also participated in antinuclear demonstrations."

Which of the following is a more probable description of Linda?

  (A) Linda is a bank teller.

  (B) Linda is a bank teller and is active in the feminist movement.

(From A. Tversky and D. Khaneman. 1983. *Psychol Rev* 90: 293–315.)

After reading Steve's profile, most people judge him more likely to be a librarian than a farmer. This is because the description more closely fits our common conceptions and stereotypes of what librarians are like. However, judging probability based on similarity to a preconception can lead to errors, biasing us to ignore other information that may be more objective or accurate.

To demonstrate, now ask yourself this question: Are there more farmers or more librarians in the world? Most people answer that farmers are more numerous, which is correct. Probabilities that reflect the state of the world—how often an event or situation actually occurs—are known as **base rate frequencies**, or **prior probabilities**. Imagine you were told only that Steve is either a librarian or a farmer and then were asked which was more likely. In the absence of any personality description at all, most people would respond "farmer," which is in fact more likely, since farmers outnumber librarians in the population. That is, most people would rely on a base rate probability to answer the question without any context.

The problem is that we often ignore these base rate probabilities when given more descriptive information, such as Steve's profile. This example illustrates the **representativeness heuristic**—the mental shortcut used to estimate the likelihood of an event based on how closely it matches or represents related examples or stereotypes in mind (Kahneman & Tversky, 1973, 1974). Representative information does not change the base rate probabilities, but it causes people to focus on similarity to stereotypes. Representativeness can thus blind us to useful probabilistic information—in this case, base rate frequencies or prior probabilities—and result in misjudgments.

Now review your answer to the question following Jack's profile in See for Yourself 9.1. Other participants estimated an average of about 50% for the probability that Jack was an engineer. What's surprising is that people who received a different version of the profile, in which the base rates were reversed (70 engineers and 30 lawyers), estimated almost the same probability—55%—that Jack was an engineer. That is, people showed minimal sensitivity to the dramatically different base rates across the low-engineer- and high-engineer-proportion samples. Because people were so focused on the description's similarity to stereotypes of engineers, they ignored base rate information, even when it was clearly provided. Rationally, their probability estimates should have been closer to the base rates provided—higher when there were 70 engineers and lower when there were only 30.

Finally, what did you think about Linda's profile? Using the representative heuristic, most people say that Linda is more likely to be a feminist bank teller than just a bank teller, given her description. But now use System 2 to think longer about the question. The probability of a conjunction, let's say of features A and B occurring together, cannot be higher than the probability of either A or B alone. In the world's population, the number of feminist bank tellers (A + B) can never exceed either the total number of bank tellers (A) or the number of feminists (B). To use another example, the number of red cars (A + B) can never exceed either the total number of red things (A) or the number of cars (B). Choosing that Linda is more likely to be both a bank teller and an active feminist is an example of the **conjunction fallacy**, the false assumption that a combination of conditions is more likely than either condition by itself (Kahneman, 2011; Tversky & Kahneman, 1983). The base rate probabilities dictate that Linda is more likely to be just a bank teller. For more examples, see the Discovery Lab on reasoning with probabilities.

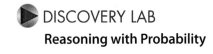

DISCOVERY LAB
Reasoning with Probability

Conjuction Fallacy

Insensitivity to Sample Size and Misconceptions of Chance

Now read **SEE FOR YOURSELF 9.2**. You may find yourself making another type of error in logic.

▶ **See for Yourself 9.2**

Large and Small Hospitals

"A town is served by two hospitals. In the larger hospital about 45 babies are born each day, and in the smaller hospital about 15 babies are born each day. As you know, about 50% of all babies are boys. However, the exact percentage varies from day to day. Sometimes it may be higher than 50%, sometimes lower. For a period of 1 year, each hospital recorded the days on which more than 60% of the babies born were boys."

Which hospital do you think recorded more such days?

(A) The larger hospital

(B) The smaller hospital

(C) About the same (that is, within 5% of each other)

(From D. Kahneman and A. Tversky. 1972. *Cogn Psychol* 3: 430–454.)

In response to the hospital example, most individuals chose (C), judging the probability of obtaining more than 60% boys in a day to be equally likely at both hospitals, regardless of size. Yet mathematically, the answer is (B)—the likelihood for deviation is higher for the smaller hospital because of the **law of sample size**: smaller sample sizes produce more variance. This may seem like a technicality that only statisticians would know. However, intuitively, most people understand that larger sample sizes are more valid, but they fail to apply this knowledge in problems such as this one (Kahneman, 2011).

Consider another example of the law of sample size. Imagine you are trying to choose between two restaurants, each with an average rating of 4 out of 5 stars. Restaurant A received this rating from more than 1,000 customers, whereas restaurant B received this rating from only 3 customers. Independent of the fact that restaurant A is more well known, we intuitively understand that the rating for restaurant A is more reliable. It's useful to know when people understand the law of sample size and when they do not.

In addition, people misunderstand or ignore how chance works in a sequence of events. Read **SEE FOR YOURSELF 9.3**.

▶ **See for Yourself 9.3**

Heads or Tails

When a coin is tossed for heads (H) or tails (T), which of the following sequences is more likely?

(A) H – T – H – T – T – H – H – T

(B) H – H – H – H – T – T – T – T

Likewise, people often expect a short series of events to look random. Upon seeing a streak of reds on a roulette wheel, they believe black is more likely to come up next. But roulette wheels are like coins, so the chances of red or black coming up on the next spin are still 50-50 regardless of what sequence of colors came previously.

In this exercise, most people judge (A) to be more likely because it looks more random (Kahneman, 2011; Tversky & Kahneman, 1973). However, (A) and (B) are equally likely to occur. Such an error in thinking is an example of the **gambler's fallacy**, the faulty reasoning that past events in a sequence affect the likelihood of future events. When flipping a coin multiple times, each toss is independent of the tosses before it. A run of heads or a run of tails does not affect how the next toss will come up.

Related to the gambler's fallacy is the **hot-hand effect**: the perception of being "on a roll." Whereas the gambler's fallacy results from people looking for the appearance of randomness, people also seek patterns even when none exist, inferring causes to explain random events. When a basketball player sinks a few baskets in a row, fans, players, and coaches alike view the player as having a "hot hand" that will lead to more baskets. The notion of hot-hand streaks in sports is irresistible. But it is also testable, and it turns out to be a biased illusion. Of course, some players will have reliably higher averages of baskets, hits, or runs than others, but short-term streaks of peak performance can be explained as random events (Gilovich et al., 1985).

Availability

Most people are averse to risk and danger, but do we fear the right threats? In the summer, we may worry about shark attacks at the beach, especially if an attack has happened recently and has been featured prominently in the media. The threat of a shark attack is statistically quite low, however; we are more likely to die from skin cancer, but beachgoers do not fear sun exposure as much. Essentially, we are wrong about when to be afraid (Ropeik & Holmes, 2003).

There are many reasons for these irrational biases, but one is the **availability heuristic** (or **availability bias**), which shows that people

Most people believe that after a streak of falling on red, the ball is more likely to fall next on black. However, the probability that the ball will fall on red or black is 50% no matter what happened before in the sequence of events.

Photo credits: sun: © Torychemistry/Shutterstock.com; hot dog: © Drozhzhina Elena/Shutterstock.com; thermometer: © Marian Weyo/Shutterstock.com; rollercoaster: © GOLFX/Shutterstock.com; mosquito: © frank60/Shutterstock.com; shark: © Vincent Legrand/Shutterstock.com

← **More risk, less fear**   **More fear, less risk** →

| Event
Odds of injury
requiring
medical
treatment
Odds of dying | Skin cancer
1 in 200
1 in 29,500 | Food poisoning
1 in 800
1 in 55,600 | Heat exposure
1 in 950,000 | Amusement parks
1 in 34,800
1 in 72.3 million | West Nile virus
1 in 68,500
1 in 1 million | Shark attacks
1 in 6 million
1 in 578 million |

FIGURE 9.1 Fearing the wrong things   We fear statistically unlikely events such as shark attacks, even though we should be more concerned and cautious about dangers with higher probabilities, such as skin cancer. (Data from D. Ropeik and N. Holmes. 2003, August 9. *The New York Times*, p. A11.)

estimate the frequency of an event based on how easily examples come to mind (Tversky & Kahneman, 1973). Usually, availability—the ease of thinking of examples—is a useful cue for judging the frequency or probability of an event. Frequently occurring events or cases are easier to recall than uncommon ones. However, there are many cases where availability can be misleading. Media coverage enhances the salience, familiarity, or imaginability of events in the public's mind. That is, anything that increases an event's availability will increase its perceived likelihood, affecting judgment. As **FIGURE 9.1** shows, people are often more afraid of statistically improbable dangers than of more common dangers.

In **SEE FOR YOURSELF 9.4**, try to estimate which words are more common.

▶ **See for Yourself 9.4**

Letter and Word Frequency

Which is more common in the English dictionary, words that start with the letter *r* or words in which *r* is the third letter (counting words that are at least three letters long)?

(After A. Tversky and D. Kahneman. 1973. *Cogn Psychol* 5: 207–232.)

Most people guess that there are more words that begin with *r*, when in fact more words have *r* as the third letter (e.g., "word" and "error"). This estimation problem illustrates the availability heuristic. The ease of thinking of words that start with *r*—as if we are looking them up in a mental dictionary—makes us think they are more common than words with *r* as the third letter. But being able to bring up examples of something more easily does not mean that it is more common in the world.

Consider another example of the availability heuristic. In one study that surveyed 37 heterosexual married couples, when spouses were asked to estimate their responsibility for "cleaning house," the total reported effort added up to more than 100%. That is, each partner overestimated his or her respective contributions. Similar overestimations occurred when participants were asked about "taking out the garbage" or "planning joint leisure activities." This is because it's easier to come up with memories and examples of our own work and contributions, which increases our estimates of their frequency (Ross & Sicoly, 1979).

Anchoring and Adjustment: Everything Is Relative

Another heuristic that reveals biases in judgment and decision making shows that we rely heavily on making relative comparisons. Try **SEE FOR YOURSELF 9.5**.

▶ **See for Yourself 9.5**

Multiplication Estimation

Within 5 seconds, quickly estimate this product:

$$8 \times 7 \times 6 \times 5 \times 4 \times 3 \times 2 \times 1$$

(From A. Tversky and D. Kahneman. 1973. *Cogn Psychol* 5: 207–232.)

This task is from a study in which another group was asked to quickly estimate the product of the exact same numbers presented in the opposite order:

$$1 \times 2 \times 3 \times 4 \times 5 \times 6 \times 7 \times 8$$

The median estimate for the first set of numbers (from higher to lower) was 2,250. The median estimate for the lower-to-higher set was 512—significantly lower than for the descending number group. This is an example of **anchoring**, which refers to how different starting points (initial values) produce different estimates or decisions. The correct answer for both multiplication problems is 40,320. The inaccurate estimates are less surprising than the difference in estimates depending on how the problem is presented (Tversky & Kahneman, 1973).

Let's next examine an application from the real world. Consider the subscription options for *The Economist* used in a study by Ariely (2008) (**SEE FOR YOURSELF 9.6**). The digital subscription at $59 is the cheapest, whereas a print subscription is $125, reflecting the cost of print and delivery. Yet the final option, a combined print and digital subscription, is also $125. Is this a typographical error? Shouldn't the combined subscription be at least slightly more expensive than the print subscription alone? Since it seems certain no one would choose the print-only option, you have to wonder why it's included (Ariely, 2008).

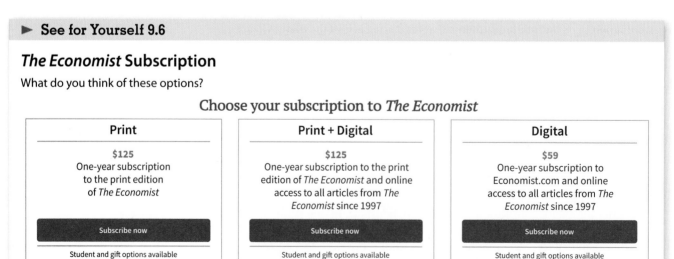

▶ **See for Yourself 9.6**

The Economist Subscription

What do you think of these options?

Choose your subscription to *The Economist*

Print	Print + Digital	Digital
$125	**$125**	**$59**
One-year subscription to the print edition of *The Economist*	One-year subscription to the print edition of *The Economist* and online access to all articles from *The Economist* since 1997	One-year subscription to Economist.com and online access to all articles from *The Economist* since 1997
Subscribe now	Subscribe now	Subscribe now
Student and gift options available	Student and gift options available	Student and gift options available

(From D. Ariely. 2008. *Predictably Irrational*. HarperCollins: New York.)

The "dummy" option (print only) is not useless at all, as it serves to encourage people to buy the combined subscription, which is more expensive than the digital-only subscription. The print-only option makes the combined option look better: people who might have chosen digital only are steered toward the combined subscription because it is a much better deal relative to print only.

In the experiment using this example, 16% of people chose the digital-only subscription and 84% chose the combined subscription. No one chose the print-only subscription—people are irrational, but they're not stupid. But when people had to select between only two options—digital only or combined print and digital subscription—only 32% chose the combined package. So clearly, the print-only option steered people toward choosing the combined subscription when they would otherwise have chosen digital only (Ariely, 2008). Note that these were the options presented in a study for which data were collected—subscription prices are higher now, although they still present the same kinds of options.

Stores offer products across a range of prices, while the cheapest item with the lowest quality can steer consumers to pay more for a better option.

This example highlights an essential factor in decision making: people estimate value *relative to other options.* Accordingly, judgment can be influenced (or manipulated) by changing which options (anchors) are presented. Relative judgments apply to interpersonal relationships as well (Ariely, 2008). If you were to go to a party hoping to meet a romantic prospect, would you rather go with a friend who is more attractive than you or less?

Anchoring is important because people do not have a strong absolute sense of value or pricing. Stores selling TVs or bicycles, for example, typically present a lower-priced option, usually of notably lower quality, than the item they really want consumers to buy. Similarly, restaurants will offer a few cheaper wine options than the one they are steering customers to select (Ariely, 2008). Marketers also anchor products with more expensive options. In another case, the gourmet kitchen store Williams Sonoma struggled to sell a bread-baking machine for $275. But when it began selling a larger and more expensive machine, sales of the original model took off. This tactic is known as the **decoy effect**: the introduction of a more- or less-expensive item provides an anchor to stimulate the sales of the target item (Ariely, 2008).

Intuitive Thinking

Some decisions demand conscious, deliberate thought—thinking slow rather than thinking fast. This is especially true when choosing between complex and expensive products, such as buying a new computer or committing to an apartment lease or home purchase. Yet even in such cases, conscious thought does not always lead to sound choices. Attention is limited, and we can consider only a few factors at a time. Information overload may lead to poorer decisions if the wrong factors are emphasized. Goethe once said "He who deliberates lengthily will not always choose the best" (cited in Wilson et al., 1993, p. 331).

Unconscious thought can be useful for complex decisions that involve multiple factors. Because it is not bound by deliberate focus, it helps people identify and follow their deepest sense of what to do. Imagine you are having trouble deciding between taking a summer session in Paris or at a school in your hometown. Going abroad is appealing, but it is more expensive and requires more preparation. You decide to sleep on it, and after a few days of not dwelling on the options, it suddenly becomes clear to you that you should go abroad. In a process described as the **deliberation-without-attention effect**, you have consciously made a decision, but unconscious processes helped you reach it.

When choosing a car, it can be better to focus on a small number of key attributes such as price and size.

In another example, Wilson and colleagues (1993) presented college students with a set of posters and asked them to select their favorite. Some were instructed to think about why they liked or disliked the posters before making their selection. Compared with those who did not have to articulate their reasoning, these participants were less happy with their choices and even less likely to keep the posters on their dorm room walls. Analyzing and verbalizing reasons for choosing a poster may have caused individuals to ignore their initial, intuitive evaluations. Conscious deliberation therefore does not always lead to more satisfaction with one's decisions.

In many cases, deliberation without attention can help lead to better decisions. Selecting which car to purchase is a classic example that involves many factors and high stakes (given both the expense and the years you will own the car). To study this process, Dijksterhuis and colleagues (2006) asked participants to spend 4 minutes choosing from among four hypothetical cars, some of which were objectively better than others. When the researchers limited the number of attributes to 4 (e.g., gas mileage, legroom), participants were more likely to select the best car than when they had to consider 12 attributes. When researchers distracted participants with difficult anagram puzzles while deciding, participants more easily chose the best car, even when 12 attributes were presented. Moreover, distracted individuals were even happier with their complex decisions than were those who focused on deliberating. The distraction task allowed for deliberation without attention, suggesting that heuristic decision making can be appropriate in certain situations. That said, we do not advocate that you purposefully distract yourself while making important decisions, although it does seem useful to take a break and "sleep on it."

These examples show the value of a less-is-more approach. **Less-is-more effects** refer to situations where too much information, computation, or time devoted to a problem may lead to less accurate, sensible, or satisfying decisions. When faced with more options, people who try to maximize their decisions to achieve the "best" possible outcome, relative to those who choose what's "good enough," tend to be less satisfied and more regretful (Schwartz et al., 2002). Simple heuristics are not only efficient but can also be more adaptive and accurate (Gigerenzer & Gaissmaier, 2011; Gigerenzer & Goldstein, 1996).

Recognition-Based Heuristics

A heuristic is a strategy that uses only a subset of information available, with the goal of "making decisions more quickly, frugally, and/or accurately than more complex methods" (Gigerenzer & Gaissmaier, 2011, p. 454). When choosing hotels, one heuristic may be to choose a brand that you've used in the past and thus know is comfortable and reasonably priced. A more time-consuming alternative is to check customer reviews for all hotels in the area and base your choice on a quality–cost analysis.

According to the **recognition heuristic**, people who are presented with two alternatives place higher value on the one they recognize versus the one that is strange or novel. Name recognition of Swiss cities, such as Basel versus Emmen, is a valid predictor of their populations (Pohl, 2006)—most non-Swiss folks recognize Basel but have never heard of Emmen. Amateur tennis players who recognized professional players made better predictions regarding the 2004 Wimbledon winners (72%) than those who made their predictions by the seedings (69%) and the rankings (66%) (Serwe & Frings, 2006). Election forecasts based on name recognition are shown to be almost as accurate as interviewing voters about their voting intentions (Gaissmaier & Marewski, 2011). And as you may already know, people are more likely to choose brands they recognize. The recognition heuristic is so strong that in a peanut-butter taste test, people favored their familiar brand even when it was labeled as a lower-quality product (Hoyer & Brown, 1990). People prefer things that are familiar to them, and novel options can be made familiar through mere repeated exposure (Zajong, 1968).

When all alternatives are recognizable, the **fluency heuristic** states that people assign higher value to the option that is recognized first, that is, more quickly and easily. Repeated exposure to an item or claim allows you to recognize it faster, which is known as fluency (Jacoby & Dallas, 1981). And, increased fluency can increase the perceived truth of repeated claims or fame of name (Hertwig et al., 1997; Jacoby et al., 1989). For example, stocks that can be pronounced more fluently (Clearman vs. Aegeadux) tend to perform better (Alter & Oppenheimer, 2006).

Peahens use the one-clever-cue heuristic, relying on the number of eyespots on a peacock's train to determine whether to mate with him. Peacocks with fewer eyespots in their plumage have fewer mating opportunities (Petrie & Halliday, 1994).

Cue-Based Heuristics

Many decisions require the consideration of multiple cues or features. For example, choosing a cellphone requires comparing countless features, including price, size, design, camera quality, and battery life. How does a consumer balance all these options? Perhaps the most straightforward heuristic is to base one's decisions on a single cue (the **one-clever-cue heuristic**). In choosing where to get a cup of coffee, you may go to the closest coffee shop. At a party, you might look to meet someone you find attractive. A peahen does not make complex judgments about a peacock but simply chooses the one with the largest number of eyespots on its plumage (Petrie & Halliday, 1994).

If the one-clever-cue heuristic is not apparent, you can adopt the **take-the-best-cue heuristic**. The idea here is that you consider each cue in turn. For example, you may decide that price is the most important feature when choosing a cellphone. This decision will narrow down the number of selections (e.g., all phones under $200), to which you'll then apply another cue, perhaps battery life. You don't consider all possible cues at once but apply them in a sequential way. This process predicts consumer choice better than complex models that calculate all cues simultaneously (Hauser et al., 2009).

Another option is to use **fast-and-frugal search trees**, which involve a limited set of yes–no questions rather than a larger set of probabilistic ones. The benefits of this approach are best seen in emergency medicine, where physicians must quickly decide whether a patient reporting chest pain is having a heart attack. Erring on the safe side, physicians send about 90% of such patients to intensive care, which can result in overcrowding, reduced quality of care, higher cost, and increased risk of infection (Green & Mehr, 1997). Therefore, it's important to have more accurate predictions that can also be performed efficiently. The heart disease predictive instrument (HDPI)—for which doctors fill out a chart with 50 probabilities combined into a complicated statistical formula—may be accurate but is cumbersome. The fast-and-frugal approach is more efficient and seems to be more accurate in predicting actual heart attacks. Doctors favor the heuristic approach because it is more transparent and easier to memorize and understand. Properly used heuristics can improve the efficiency and accuracy of health care (Elwyn et al., 2001).

Tallying is a heuristic that simply involves counting the number of cues that favor one alternative over another. This process does not involve weighting (prioritizing) cues according to their importance. As one example, to help hikers and skiers predict avalanches, among seven cues they can simply tally whether at least three are present (e.g., water is present on the snow surface, an avalanche occurred in the spot during the past 48 hours, or snow appears to be cracking). This tallying strategy has been shown to predict 92% of historical accidents (McCammon & Hägeli, 2007).

Finally, **RESEARCH FOCUS 9.1** looks at a special type of cue called the *zero price effect.*

RESEARCH FOCUS 9.1

The Power of Zero

Assuming that you like chocolate, which of the following would you choose?

A Lindt chocolate truffle for 26 cents

A Hershey's Kiss for 1 cent

In this trial, 40% of participants chose the truffle and 40% the Kiss. What do you think happened when the options were changed to the following?

A Lindt chocolate truffle for 25 cents

A Hershey's Kiss for free

In this trial, 90% chose the Hershey's Kiss (Ariely, 2008). Although the price difference between the two options is the same and rational economic theory does not predict such a change in demand, the participants were drawn to getting a free chocolate. Ariely (2008, p. 49) calls this the **zero price effect**: "Zero is an emotional hot button—a source of irrational excitement."

Marketers are well aware of the zero price effect. To sell more books, Amazon once offered free shipping to customers who bought two books instead of one. Suppose the book you want costs $16.95 and the shipping is $3.95 (a total of $20.90). If you choose a second book at the same price to take advantage of the promotion, you would spend $33.90. You spend more money and buy a book that you perhaps wouldn't have otherwise, but the powerful allure of free shipping is irresistible. Interestingly, this strategy did not initially work in France because the French division of the company charged 1 franc (approximately 20 cents) for shipping. This

Which chocolate would you choose? What criteria would you consider in your decision?

was still an incredible discount, but as we saw in the chocolate example, even the tiniest charge affects the power to entice customers. "Zero is not just another discount. Zero is a different place" (Ariely, 2008, p. 54).

Campaigns that entice you to buy more are boundless—free sodas if you order a larger pizza, a free cup of coffee after a dozen purchases, free add-ons for your car. But the power of zero can be used for social good. The town of New Haven, CT, encouraged the use of environmentally friendly hybrid vehicles by allowing such cars to park for free at city meters. At least for one author of this book, this plan encouraged him to purchase a hybrid vehicle even though the price premium over a conventional car will not outweigh the total cost of parking. On a broader public health note, Ariely (2008) suggests that if health insurance companies want to ensure regular checkups, which can prevent more costly procedures by detecting serious illnesses early, they should provide them for free.

▶ **CHECKPOINT 9.2**

1. How are heuristics useful in decision making?
2. What are the different types of heuristics? Identify examples for each.
3. Why should we care about base rate frequencies?
4. What is the law of sample size, and what kind of samples give better estimates?
5. What is anchoring? Give an example.

9.3 Decision Making

Whereas Section 9.2 focused on how people make judgments about the likelihood of uncertain events, here we focus on decision making, which involves selecting a course of action from one or more options. Many of the options involve uncertain outcomes, so this section builds on our understanding of how people judge probabilities. You can try a few examples in the Discovery Lab on risky decisions.

DISCOVERY LAB

Risky Decision

Risky Choice

Let's start with a no-brainer decision. If someone offers you a choice of accepting a gift of $1,000 or an alternative gift of $100, no strings attached, you should take the larger amount. We make choices that maximize **utility,** the satisfaction that we obtain from choosing an option. Utility can be positive or negative. We try to maximize **positive utility** (gains) and minimize **negative utility** (losses or costs). If you are required to pay either $2,000 or $1,000 for the exact same laptop, you will choose to pay $1,000, minimizing the negative utility (cost).

However, everyday choices are complicated by uncertainty and **risk**, which is the probability of a negative outcome, such as losing something of value. Very few things in life are certain, and rarely will you be asked to choose between a sure gift of $1,000 or one of $100. To study our decision-making processes, social scientists frequently rely on gambling tasks that attach specific probabilities to wins or losses. Try **SEE FOR YOURSELF 9.7**.

▶ **See for Yourself 9.7**

The Better Bet

Which of the following bets would you choose?
  (A) A 5% chance of earning $1,000
  (B) A 95% chance of earning $100

Although you're free to follow your gut instinct, rationally speaking you should choose option B, because the probability of getting a reward is so much higher for option B than for option A. Intuitively, this sounds right, and mathematically one can precisely calculate which option is more lucrative by simply multiplying the probability by the value. The product is known as the **expected value**:

$$\text{Expected value} = \text{value} \times \text{probability}$$

For example, the expected values for the two options in See for Yourself 9.7 are as follows:

  (A) Expected value of 5% (5/100) chance of earning
       $1,000 = 0.05 \times \$1,000 = \$50$
  (B) Expected value of 95% (95/100) chance of earning
       $100 = 0.95 \times \$100 = \$95$

According to **rational choice theory**, we make decisions by comparing the expected value of our options. In See For Yourself 9.7, when expected value can be calculated based on the given values and probabilities, rational choice theory predicts that we should choose the option with higher utility: option B. The rational models that help us calculate these choices are called "normative." **Normative theories** are based on rational, logical, and mathematical calculations to compare decision options, explaining how decisions *should* be made in order to maximize utility and rewards.

Of course, life is more complicated, and human decision making frequently deviates from what normative analysis recommends. **Descriptive theories** are concerned with how we *actually* decide, describing beliefs and preferences as they are, not as they should be. Cognitive psychology and behavioral economics use these theories to help us understand how people make decisions and behave in the real world. The concept of being predictably irrational, mentioned at the beginning of the chapter, involves understanding when descriptive theory predictions don't match up with normative analysis. Now try **SEE FOR YOURSELF 9.8**.

▶ **See for Yourself 9.8**

Risk versus a Sure Bet: Reward

Choose one of the following:
  (A) A sure gain of $240
  (B) A 25% chance of gaining $1,000 and a 25% chance of gaining nothing

(After A. Tversky and D. Kahneman. 1981. *Science* 211: 453–458.)

Given these options, most people choose A. Does this seem obvious? It does from a descriptive standpoint because people prefer the sure bet. But from a normative standpoint, it is not ideal. Rational analysis shows that the expected payout is larger for option B ([0.25 × $1,000] + [0.75 × $0] = $250) than for option A (1.00 × $240 = $240). That is, your chances of making more money are higher with option B. Or if a group of people were asked to make this choice individually, the group as a whole would make more money by choosing option B (Bernoulli, 1738, 1954; Kahneman, 2011).

Decision making in everyday life deviates from normative analysis for two main reasons. First, options are **ambiguous**, or open to more than one interpretation—life does not always give us clear probabilities on which we can base our decisions (Hsu et al., 2005). When you flip a coin, the outcome is uncertain, but you can specify an unambiguous probability of 50%. However, could you put a precise number on the probability that you would be happier at College Y than at College H? What is the specific likelihood that the stock market will go down or that housing prices will go up within the next year? Not only are these outcomes uncertain, it's difficult to even put a number on them.

Second, even if likelihoods were well defined, value (utility) is subjective. Bernoulli introduced the concept of **subjective value**, the notion that utility is not objective but dependent on the decision maker and context. People make judgments not on exact monetary amounts, but on the subjective values of these monetary amounts, an insight that grounds much of Kahneman and Tversky's work (Kahneman, 2011). When choosing an apartment or dorm, how do you compare the value of its location relative to the value of the room's size? When choosing where to go for dinner, how much more are you willing to pay for better food or for nicer ambiance? Even the value of money is not straightforward. Sure, $1,000 is better than $100, but the difference in value matters more for an average college student than for a billionaire. A college student may choose a $100 coat because it's cheaper than a $1,000 coat, but a billionaire will choose the latter if it looks better.

Normative approaches and descriptive approaches frequently conflict, and cognitive psychology has played a central role in identifying where and why. For example, as we saw at the beginning of the chapter, the huge difference in outcomes for organ donation registration conflicts with what a rational model would predict. Decision making is so fundamental that it is studied in many other disciplines as well, including mathematics, statistics, economics, political science, and neuroscience. Taking a cross-disciplinary approach helps us compare how decisions are made with how they should be made.

Prospect Theory

The concept of utility helps explain many decision-making behaviors, but try **SEE FOR YOURSELF 9.9**.

▶ **See for Yourself 9.9**

Risk versus a Sure Bet: Loss

Consider the following two options, a slight variation from the choices in See for Yourself 9.8. Which would you choose?

(C) A sure loss of $750

(D) A 75% chance of losing $1,000 and a 25% chance of losing nothing

(After A. Tversky and D. Kahneman. 1981. *Science* 211: 453–458.)

Here, most people choose option D rather than option C. That is, people avoid choosing the sure loss, even though normative analysis shows that C is financially preferable: the expected value of the loss is smaller. Just as we saw earlier, human psychology deviates from normative theory. This example demonstrates the principle of **loss aversion**: people hate losses more than they enjoy equivalent gains, and they tend to prefer a sure gain over risky gains (Kahneman & Tversky, 1984; Tversky & Kahneman, 1981, 1992). Recall that given a choice between a sure gain of $240 versus a 25% chance of gaining $1,000 (A vs. B in See for Yourself 9.8), people opted for the sure gain of $240. In sum, when an amount is presented as a gain, people go for the riskless gain, but when an amount is presented as a loss, people avoid risk and go for the risky option over the sure loss.

An influential model called **prospect theory**, developed by Daniel Kahneman and Amos Tversky, explains loss aversion (Kahneman & Tversky, 1979). Prospect theory works as follows. Which seems like a greater difference: losing $200 versus losing $100, or losing $10,200 versus losing $10,100? The larger the dollar amount, the less the same absolute difference of $100 matters. **FIGURE 9.2** shows this concept in a graph. The value function has two essential features. First, it is S-shaped rather than a straight line—this describes how subjective value gets smaller with increasing monetary value, for both gains and losses. Again, a gain or loss of $100 looms larger if relative to $200 than to $10,000. Second, the curve is not symmetrical around the center of the graph—it is steeper for losses than it is for gains (Kahneman & Tversky, 1979). This means that people treat the same dollar loss as psychologically larger than the same dollar gain. Losing $100 gives you more pain (larger drop in psychological value along the y-axis) than gaining $100 gives you joy (smaller gain in psychological value). That is, loss aversion and the choices that result from it can be described and predicted mathematically, based on the value functions.

Here's another example to quantify loss aversion. Would you accept a bet that will pay you $10 if a coin shows up heads, but requires you to pay $10 if it shows up tails? The expected value of this bet is 0 ([0.5 × $10] + [0.5 × –$10] = 0), so most people would not accept this bet. How about if heads pays better than even money, say $20, while tails still requires you to pay only $10? The expected value of this bet is $5 ([0.5 × $20] + [0.5 × –$10] = $5), so you stand to gain. However, most people still refuse to take this bet. The payout would need to exceed $30 for people to start accepting the bet. The reason is that the attraction to the potential dollar gain is much less than the aversion to the possible loss.

In summary, we've seen that when evaluating gains, people are **risk averse**: they would rather take a sure gain than a risky option for slightly more money. Yet the situation flips for losses. When faced with a sure loss, people become **risk seeking**. Rather than accept a sure loss, they are willing to lose more if the bet allows them a small chance of avoiding any loss. These ways of thinking are incredibly powerful—even monkeys show loss aversion (**RESEARCH FOCUS 9.2**).

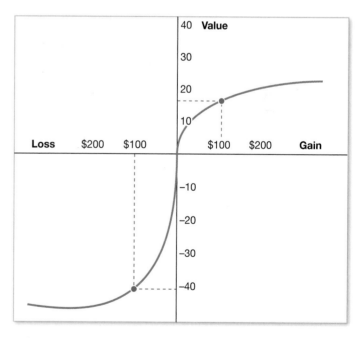

FIGURE 9.2 Prospect theory On the x-axis, a gain of $100 in the positive direction and a loss of $200 in the negative direction are equivalent in size. However, their impact on psychological value differs greatly along the y-axis. As a hypothetical example, a $100 gain may give about 15 units of positive psychological value in this plot, while a comparable $100 loss gives around 40 units of negative psychological value. (After Laurenrosenberger/CC BY-SA 4.0, based on D. Kahneman. 2011. *Thinking, Fast and Slow*. Farrar, Straus and Giroux: New York.)

RESEARCH FOCUS 9.2

Decision Making in Monkeys and Humans

Studying other animal species is fascinating because it shows that many decision-making processes, and even biases, are not unique to humans.

In one experiment, cognitive psychologist Laurie Santos of Yale University trained monkeys to trade tokens for treats. The monkeys were introduced to two human salespersons, each of whom showed the monkeys a grape. One salesperson represented the safe option: when monkeys gave him a token, they always received two grapes (the one in the salesman's hand plus one more). The other salesperson represented the risky option. When monkeys chose to give him a token, half the time they received three grapes (the one shown plus two more)—a large gain. However, the other half of the time, the risky salesperson gave nothing to the monkeys. Choosing like a human would, monkeys preferred the safe option.

To test whether monkeys demonstrate loss aversion or risk aversion, they were given a different version of the task, now involving losses. Both salespersons started with three grapes in their hand. When monkeys chose the first salesperson, who represented the safe loss option, they always received two out of the three grapes presented. When they chose the second salesperson, who represented the risky option, half the time the monkeys would lose two grapes (and only receive one), but the other half of the time they received all three grapes. In this case, more monkeys chose the risky option in an attempt to avoid the sure loss, again like humans tend to do.

Courtesy of Laurie Santos

Cognitive psychologist Laurie Santos studies comparative cognition, examining what is common and what is different between humans and other species.

For gains, both people and monkeys are risk averse, while for losses, both people and monkeys are risk seeking. Accordingly, one can conclude that these patterns of decision-making biases are not unique to humans (Chen et al., 2006). This means there is something fundamental about decision making that does not depend on human intelligence, language, or education.

Framing

Now we illustrate another prominent factor that makes decision making predictably irrational. Try **SEE FOR YOURSELF 9.10**.

> ### ▶ See for Yourself 9.10
>
> ### Outbreak Options: Gains
>
> Imagine the United States is preparing for the outbreak of a rare disease that is expected to kill 600 people. Two alternative programs to combat the disease have been proposed. Assume that the exact scientific estimates of the consequences of the programs are as follows:
>
> If Program A is adopted, 200 people will be saved.
>
> If Program B is adopted, there is a one-third probability that 600 people will be saved and a two-thirds probability that no one will be saved.
>
> Which of the two programs would you favor?
>
> (From A. Tversky and D. Kahneman. 1981. *Science* 211: 453–458.)

The vast majority (72%) of 152 participants chose Program A. Saving 200 people is a sure gain, and people are risk averse when it comes to sure gains (Kahneman, 2011; Tversky & Kahneman, 1981).

Another group of participants was presented with the options in **SEE FOR YOURSELF 9.11** for the same scenario.

▶ **See for Yourself 9.11**

Outbreak Options: Losses

The options here are a variation of those in See for Yourself 9.10. Which would you choose?

If Program C is adopted, 400 people will die.

If Program D is adopted, there is a one-third probability that no one will die and a two-thirds probability that 600 people will die.

(From A. Tversky and D. Kahneman. 1981. *Science* 211: 453–458.)

Given these options, only 22% of 155 participants chose Program C: The result can be explained in terms of loss aversion. People hate losses, and so they become risk seeking to avoid sure losses.

Yet there's an illogical discrepancy here. "Safe" Program A is equivalent to "safe" Program C: The way the problem is set up, saving 200 lives in Program A is the same as losing 400 lives in Program C. Likewise, the risky options presented to each group were equivalent: "risky" Program B is exactly the same as "risky" Program D.

The only difference between the two groups was in how the problems were framed, or presented, but they produced radically different decisions. **Framing** effects occur for naive participants and scholarly experts alike. The inconsistency can even arise within the same people given both sets of options (Kahneman, 2011; Tversky & Kahneman, 1981).

Framing is like a perceptual illusion. In the ambiguous **FIGURE 9.3** you can view the same image as a lady in front of a vanity mirror or as a skull. Likewise, framing problems are like ambiguous perceptual illusions: ground beef sold in the supermarket can be framed as 80% meat or 20% fat. People are less likely to buy a package framed as fat.

Our choices are governed by the subjective value of options coupled with the probability that we will realize them. We saw how subjective value, or utility, changes with larger amounts. We assumed the probability is even across 0% to 100%. However, even probabilities are subjective.

Imagine a small-scale lottery, where the probability of winning varies from 0% to 100%. The difference between a 5% chance of winning and a 0% chance of winning seems large compared with the difference between a 35% chance of winning and a 30% chance of winning. Likewise, the difference between a 95% probability and a 100% certainty is significant. That is, our perception of probabilities is different near the boundaries of impossibility (0%) and certainty (100%) compared with equivalent changes in the middle of the scale.

People tend to put too much weight on low-probability events. That is, the prospect of a rare event plays a larger role in our decision making than it should. We amplify the value of long-shot gains (e.g., lotteries) or exaggerate the impact of the rare chance of a severe loss (e.g., life insurance for flight travel) (Kahneman, 2003).

Framing effects can help encourage healthier behaviors (McNiel et al., 1982; Rothman & Salovey, 1997). For example, people understand that wearing sunscreen is important to prevent skin damage and to reduce cancer risk from sun exposure. But putting on

"All is Vanity" – Charles Allan Gilbert (1873–1929)

FIGURE 9.3 Framing is like a perceptual illusion that you can see two ways Here, you can see either a skull or a woman looking into a vanity mirror.

sunscreen is a greasy nuisance, so how do you encourage people to use it? On a study conducted on a beach, researchers tested different types of brochure messages that were framed as either gains or losses. A brochure with gain-framed messaging included statements such as "Using sunscreen decreases your risk for skin cancer and prematurely aged skin." A loss-framed message expressed the same thing as "Not using sunscreen increases your risk for skin cancer and prematurely aged skin." People who received the gain-framed messages were more likely to request and to repeatedly apply sunscreen while at the beach (Detweiler et al., 1999).

Status Quo

One of the most powerful biases on decisions is a passive one: people prefer to maintain the status quo. The **status quo bias** is a preference for the current state of affairs. Any change from how things are, or even the act of considering a change, requires time, effort, and frequently money. These negatives are known as **transaction costs**. People try to avoid even minimal transaction costs, from getting up off the sofa to grab a piece of candy, to going online to transfer money into savings. The desire to avoid any transaction cost contributes to the status quo bias.

Status quo effects can be described in terms of loss aversion. Many decisions in life do not introduce two or more new options, but involve one new option relative to the status quo. In such cases, choosing a new option requires weighing its gain relative to giving up the status quo (a loss). Loss aversion dictates that the aversion of potential losses is more intense than the perceived benefits of equivalent gains. This is why people seek higher incomes or higher status when switching jobs. If pay or working conditions are roughly equivalent between job A and job B, then workers are hesitant to switch.

OPTIMAL DEFAULTS　The status quo bias affects decision making and behavior in many ways, and it can be used for a good purpose. We already considered the example of organ donation: the opt-in/opt-out effect can be explained in terms of status quo. People tend to accept the option given to them by default, such that opting in or opting out of a default state entails a transaction cost that people avoid. Hence, the goal of policy makers should be to set **optimal defaults**—that is, automatically place people into options that have the greatest benefit.

Optimal defaults can help people help themselves. Consider the essential need to save for retirement. No one wants to be poor in retirement, but putting money aside from one's paycheck requires discipline and effort. According to one study, when new employees have to actively sign up to contribute a portion of their income to retirement savings (a 401[k] plan), the average proportion of employees who participate starts at less than 40% (**FIGURE 9.4**). However, if the company automatically signs up people to make contributions as an optimal default, while preserving their ability to opt out (decline participation), a much greater proportion—about 85%—save (Choi et al., 2004; Madrian & Shea, 2001).

Another example of an optimal default is to promote healthy eating and sustainability. Making healthy choices more convenient can reduce caloric intake (Wisdom et al., 2010). In cafeteria settings, simply eliminating trays reduces food waste by about 30% (Levin, 2012). When people have trays, they tend to take more food than they need. With trayless dining, people take what they can fit on a plate. Even when they have the option to go back through the line to get more food, the transaction cost of that effort discourages them from doing so. The result is that trayless diners take less, eat less, and waste less.

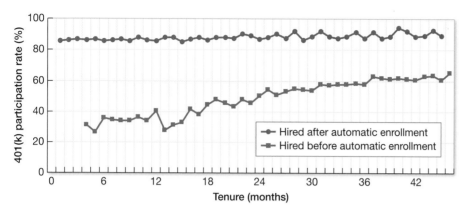

FIGURE 9.4 Optimal defaults can help people save for retirement Regardless of time at the company (tenure on the *x*-axis), participation rates for saving for retirement are much higher for employees who are automatically enrolled (optimal default) compared with those who have to actively sign up. (From J. J. Choi et al. 2004. *Natl Tax J* 57: 275–298, with permission from the National Tax Association.)

THE ENDOWMENT EFFECT This tendency to overvalue what one has in hand is called the **endowment effect**, and one of its major researchers, Richard Thaler, won the Nobel Prize in Economic Sciences (Thaler, 1980). The endowment effect can be tested as follows. Imagine that for purchasing this book, the publisher sent you a souvenir mug. Now, suppose that someone offered you money for it. How much would you be willing to sell it for? The average asking price reflects the value that owners place on the mug. Others are asked how much they would pay for the mug, and their average price represents the value that buyers place on the mug. Since potential sellers and buyers are pricing the same mug, the prices should be similar. Indeed, free market principles state that buying and asking prices should be similar, or no transactions would occur. However, the average asking price is significantly higher than the average price people are willing to pay for the mug. The endowment effect shows that people attach a premium to what they own. It is a type of status quo bias, and it is commonly seen in real estate markets (Kahneman, 2011; Kahneman et al., 1986; 1990; Knetsch & Sinden, 1984).

THE SUNK COST EFFECT A downside of loss aversion and status quo effects is that they may cause you to stick with a losing position or harmful course of action when it's better to get out or quit. The **sunk cost effect** is a maladaptive behavior, the "greater tendency to continue an endeavor once an investment in money, effort, or time has been made" (Arkes & Ayton, 1999, p. 591). Resistance to change or attachment to money or time invested makes people lose more. It is also known as the Concorde fallacy (Dawkins & Carlisle, 1976), named after the commercial supersonic airliner that lost a huge amount of money despite early and accurate predictions that it would be a failure. In a sports example, professional basketball coaches give more playing time to players who were higher draft picks, and hence more expensive, whether their current performance merits playing time or not (Staw & Hoang, 1995). Other everyday examples include holding onto a stock that is clearly declining in value, or staying in a relationship that is abusive and hurtful.

On the bright side, loss aversion and the endowment effect provide stability amid options for change. If everyone focused on the grass being greener on the other side, then few people would stay satisfied and committed to their relationships or jobs.

Imagine you received this mug as a bonus gift for purchasing this textbook. If you were to sell the mug to someone else, how much would you charge? Because the endowment effect makes you overvalue your possessions, your proposed selling price is likely to be significantly higher than what buyers are willing to pay.

➤ **CHECKPOINT 9.3**

1. How do you calculate expected value?
2. According to prospect theory, how does psychological value change as the monetary value of gains and losses increases? How does psychological value differ for gains and losses?
3. Under what conditions do people or monkeys act in a risk-seeking manner (vs. a risk-averse manner)?
4. What is framing? Give an example.
5. What is the status quo effect? Give an example.

9.4 Neuroeconomics

Rational decision making can be easily implemented by computers, given their ability to crunch numbers instantaneously. However, human decision making is powered by brains, which operate differently from computers—slower in some ways, but smarter in others. Thus, it is important to study how the brain represents reward and makes decisions to maximize gain. Furthermore, the objective to maximize gains and rewards is hardly unique to humans. From bees to lions, animals must forage effectively to survive. That is, just as people make financial decisions that maximize their profits while minimizing the risk of loss, animals must act in ways that maximize survival and minimize energy spent.

To understand how the brain makes decisions, **neuroeconomics** is a field that combines insights from economics, neuroscience, and psychology. Economics provides models and tasks to understand decision-making behavior, while psychology also provides methods and theory to collect and understand the behavioral data. Neuroscience links these behaviors to the brain and neural activity (Balleine et al., 2007; Camerer et al., 2005; Rangel et al., 2008).

Why should decision scientists and economists care about the brain? First, psychology and neuroscience help define value and reward. Understanding the brain can inform why and when people experience positive or negative utility. Unlike a computer, the brain and its decisions are influenced by motivation and emotion: people don't just think about their choices, they *feel* differently about different options (Phelps et al., 2014). Unlike a machine, emotions, motivation, and physiological states come into play for biological decision making. A hungry person will respond differently to a food offer than a satiated person will.

Second, we saw earlier that much of human decision making relies on automatic processes, such as heuristics. Studying the brain helps reveal the differences between automatic decision making (System 1) and more effortful decision making (System 2). Understanding the characteristics of each system can explain why judgment and decision making can go awry, such as in addictions or with some types of brain damage.

Third, while economic models are not suited to explain why individuals differ, psychology and neuroscience are keenly interested in individual differences. Neuroeconomics can inform why people differ in being impulsive or deliberate, decisive or indecisive, depressed or optimistic (Camerer et al., 2005). A can of soda will appeal to some people and disgust others. Neuroeconomics reveals why different people respond differently to the same offer, that is, why the subjective value of an option differs.

Value and Willingness to Pay

Neuroeconomics can provide biological explanations of how people value things and whether they will buy them or not. The prefrontal cortex processes reward (Wallis, 2007) and encodes

What would you choose? Cola, orange soda, or sparkling water?

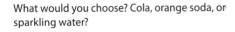

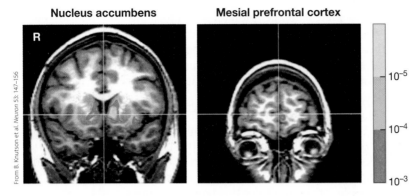

Nucleus accumbens   **Mesial prefrontal cortex**

R

10^{-5}

10^{-4}

10^{-3}

From B. Knutson et al. *Neuron* 53: 147–156

FIGURE 9.5 A signal in the brain reveals whether someone is willing to buy something or not   Higher activity in the nucleus accumbens (a part of the ventral striatum) and mesial prefrontal cortex revealed a person's willingness to pay even before choices were physically made. The color scale up to yellow indicates more statistically significant activations.

willingness to pay, which is the decision of whether someone will purchase an option or item (Knutson et al., 2007; Plassmann et al., 2007). Willingness to pay is an essential part of any economic transaction, and the more you want something, the more you're likely to pay for it. For example, for a cup of frozen yogurt, you may be willing to pay $5 but not $10. To test purchasing behavior in the lab, researchers showed enticing photos of various sweet and salty junk foods such as chips and candy bars on a computer screen one at a time. Participants were asked how much they would be willing pay for each of them. To enhance their desire (appetite), participants were asked to fast for 4 hours before the experiment and to plan on staying for an additional 30 minutes, during which time they could consume some of the food that they purchased during the experiment. To make the choices real, participants were given money at the beginning of the experiment, and they were told they could keep the money that they did not spend on the snacks. Activity in prefrontal regions and ventral striatum was positively correlated with willingness to pay (Knutson et al., 2007), that is, a signal in the brain reveals whether someone is willing to buy something or not (**FIGURE 9.5**). In theory, a consumer's preference about a product can be decoded from brain signals alone.

As another exploration of how the brain represents value, people in an auction setting could declare how much they would pay for a certain kind of food. For example, you may be willing to pay $1 for a chocolate bar but only 20 cents for a stick of gum. In one such study, activity in the orbitofrontal cortex and other prefrontal cortex regions corresponded to the values that participants assigned to different options (Knutson et al., 2007; Plassmann et al., 2007). Value is not restricted to material items or money. Orbitofrontal cortex activity also reveals social preferences by showing higher activity in response to attractive faces versus unattractive faces (O'Doherty et al., 2003).

In turn, the price of items can influence the value that people assign to them. Wine bottles vary dramatically in price: some bottles cost just a few dollars, while special wines can fetch several hundred or even several thousand dollars. Naturally, people believe that expensive wines taste better (Rao & Monroe, 1989). Hence, more selectively produced, fine wines command higher prices. Conversely, price itself can affect how much you will enjoy a wine, due to expectations and framing. Because rare or special items and services tend to be more expensive (a steak vs. a hamburger; a smartphone vs. a clamshell phone; a five-star hotel vs. a hostel), in the absence of other information, price itself influences how people perceive the quality of items. When presented with a new taste of an unlabeled wine, people will gain more pleasure and assign a higher-quality rating to a wine that is described as coming from a $90 bottle than from a $10 bottle—even if it's the same wine. Moreover, when this task is performed inside an fMRI scanner, neural systems that respond to pleasure are more highly activated when people think they are drinking an expensive wine versus when they are drinking an inexpensive wine (Plassmann et al., 2008). Thus, the price of a product directly influences how people enjoy it, not just in behavioral ratings, but also as revealed by neural activity.

Findings like these raise the prospect of using brain scanning to predict product preferences, a field known as **neuromarketing**. Note that fMRI would be impractical and too expensive for everyday purposes—arguably, marketers can just ask people, "Do you prefer this handbag from Gucci or this other one from Prada?" However, more affordable brain scanning methods such as EEG offer the opportunity to refine products in ways that people may not be able to articulate well. EEG signals can reveal levels of attention, and when recorded while viewers are watching a show or an advertisement, they can provide an ongoing measure of when people tune in or tune out. This feedback can help producers edit their content to better engage viewers. Companies such as Nielsen, which gathers statistics on television viewership, provide neuromarketing services. According to Nielsen's website, "It's important to pinpoint which aspects of your marketing materials are the most provocative…By studying people at their most fundamental level—by measuring brainwaves—we provide a real-time view of their subconscious reactions" (Nielsen, n.d.).

Brain Damage and Decision Making

The neuroeconomics approach gains even more traction when you consider how brain damage impairs the ability to make good decisions. If you're offered a "double-or-nothing" option (risking everything for the chance to win double), the safe choice would be to pass, ensuring that you keep your winnings. When people choose to gamble like this, a brain region called the insula in prefrontal cortex becomes more active (Paulus et al., 2003). However, patients with prefrontal damage act differently. They make riskier choices (Bechara et al., 1994; Rahman, 1999), respond less adversely to ambiguity (Hsu et al., 2005; Levy et al., 2010), and act more impulsively (Bechara, 2005; Davidson, 2000).

In an experiment that measured risk-seeking or risk-averse decision making in both prefrontal patients and unaffected control groups, researchers presented participants with four decks of cards, in which each card presented a gain or loss of variable amounts. Participants were asked to choose cards from any deck at will, and the goal was to maximize one's gains. Two of the decks were advantageous with positive expected value—that is, participants who chose to continue drawing from one of them would end the session with a gain. The other two decks were disadvantageous with negative expected value, so that drawing from them would result in an overall loss. As a clever manipulation, the decks also differed in whether they presented extreme wins and losses. Large gains are rewarding, while large losses cause anxiety and fear. The advantageous decks with positive expected value were safer, offering smaller gains, but also smaller losses. The disadvantageous decks with negative expected value offered more thrills: larger gains, but also larger losses. Most people without brain damage opted to choose the risk-averse, safer decks of cards. However, patients with prefrontal damage acted in a more risk-seeking manner, choosing the disadvantageous decks that offered larger gains, even though they also presented larger losses and negative expected value. That is, patients with prefrontal damage showed impaired decision making, choosing decks that were worse for them and making them more likely to go bankrupt in this game (Bechara, 1997).

Even without brain damage, people differ in whether they are risk seeking or risk averse. One way to distinguish people is to see how they react emotionally to negative events. People who are more emotionally reactive will choose safer options in another version of the card task, even if the safe decks are set up to offer smaller payoffs with lower expected value (Peters & Slovic, 2000)—that is, on average, they pay out less money. In the real world, a classic example is whether to save money in savings accounts that are safe but pay less interest, as opposed to in the stock market, which poses greater risk of losing money but historically offers larger gains. In the lab, researchers can design tasks that reward risk taking. Consider a gamble where you can participate in a series of take-it-or-leave-it choices with a 50% chance of losing $1 or gaining $1.50. You should play this gamble because the expected value is positive ($1.25 to be exact), and most people will choose to play at least one round. However, some people will decline any bet, and among those who do play a round, if they experience a loss, they tend to quit. Patients with prefrontal damage are not dissuaded by an initial loss and will keep playing, which in this case is the smarter thing to do (Shiv et al., 2005).

➤ CHECKPOINT 9.4

1. What is neuroeconomics, and why should we care about how the brain makes decisions? Why do we study patients with brain damage?

2. What is neuromarketing, and how does it relate to the study of willingness to pay?

Chapter Summary

9.1 Describe the differences between irrational and rational decision making, and between thinking fast (System 1) and thinking slow (System 2), giving examples.

In everyday life, we need to judge uncertain (probabilistic) information and make decisions with uncertain outcomes. Judgments and decisions can either be made in a rational manner (objective and logical), or they can be predictably irrational (subjective and biased). While System 2 allows us to make carefully calculated decisions, we also need System 1, which provides a way to make rapid decisions given noisy, imperfect information.

Q: From your life, come up with two situations in which you typically rely on thinking fast (System 1) and two other examples in which you rely on thinking slow (System 2).

9.2 Identify examples of intuitive decision making and heuristics.

Decisions typically involve situations in which the outcomes are uncertain, and so you need to estimate their likelihood of occurrence. But for many everyday decisions, we don't have the time or motivation to deliberate using System 2. Instead, we rely on heuristics, that is, mental shortcuts: availability, anchoring, representativeness, intuition, recognition, fluency, and other cues.

Q: During course selection period, when you're trying to choose which classes to take, what kind of cues do you rely on? Cues may include instructor quality, requirements for graduation or your major, intellectual stimulation, novelty, scheduling convenience, course workload, class size, and so on. How good is the information you collect from others? Do you consider base rates, availability, anchoring, or sample size? What kind of heuristics do you employ, or do you use System 2? Is System 2 always best for optimizing your decisions?

9.3 Explain how risk, framing, or status quo affects decision making.

Decisions require choosing between different options to maximize utility, maximizing gains or minimizing losses. Because decision outcomes are usually uncertain, it is necessary to take some risks. People are usually averse to risk when it comes to seeking gains, but they typically seek risky options if it helps avoid losses. One reason for this is because people dislike a loss more than they favor a comparably priced gain. Accordingly, people will make different decisions if an outcome is framed as a loss than when it is presented as a gain. It is also useful to know that people favor the status quo and items that they possess. Understanding when decisions fail can help inform how to present options in a way that leads people to make better decisions.

Q: People generally do not like change, favoring current arrangements over novel options. Imagine that your university launches an environmental sustainability campaign to encourage students to walk or use bikes instead of shuttle services. Explain potential student resistance in terms of transaction costs, loss aversion, status quo, and endowment effects.

9.4 Discuss insights from the field of neuroeconomics based on brain imaging studies and patients with brain damage.

Neuroeconomics combines insights from economics, neuroscience, and psychology to explain how people make economic decisions. For example, imaging studies have demonstrated mechanisms underlying willingness to pay. Studies of patients with brain damage provide insight into risk-seeking versus risk-averse decision making.

Q: How can neuroscience be used for neuromarketing, measuring brain responses to assess how much people value different products, services, or even political candidates? What are the ethical issues to consider?

Key Terms

ambiguous

anchoring

availability heuristic (availability bias)

base rate frequencies (prior probabilities)

conjunction fallacy

decoy effect

deliberation-without-attention effect

descriptive theories

endowment effect

expected value

fast-and-frugal search trees

fluency heuristic

framing

gambler's fallacy

heuristics

hot-hand effect

irrational behavior

law of sample size

less-is-more effect

loss aversion

negative utility

neuroeconomics

neuromarketing

normative theories

one-clever-cue heuristic

optimal defaults

positive utility

predictably irrational

prospect theory

psychological bias

rational behavior

rational choice theory

recognition heuristic

representativeness heuristic

risk

risk averse

risk seeking

status quo bias

subjective value

sunk cost effect

take-the-best-cue heuristic

tallying

thinking fast (System 1)

thinking slow (System 2)

transaction cost

utility

willingness to pay

zero price effect

Critical Thinking Questions

1. Can we develop machine-based systems that perform decision making (e.g., medical decision making) better than humans? Why or why not?

2. Considering the research presented in this chapter, what additional research could be conducted at a policy level to help people save for retirement?

Discovery Labs

oup.com/he/chun1e

Reasoning with Probability

This experiment is a popular paradigm used to show how human decision making can sometimes defy the laws of probability. Participants are asked to choose between two scenarios based on which scenario they think is more likely. Approximate completion time: 20 minutes.

Risky Decision

In this experiment, students discover the fairly consistent pattern psychologists have discovered for how people deal with risk. Participants are asked to choose between two possible outcomes for a variety of scenarios. Approximate completion time: 15 minutes.

Suggested Readings

Akerlof, G. A. & Shiller, R. J. (2009). *Animal Spirits: How Human Psychology Drives the Economy and Why It Matters for Global Capitalism*. Princeton, NJ: Princeton University Press.

Ariely, D. (2008). *Predictably Irrational: The Hidden Forces That Shape Our Decisions*. New York: HarperCollins.

Kahneman, D. (2011). *Thinking, Fast and Slow*. New York: Farrar, Straus and Giroux.

Reasoning and Problem Solving

10

In December 2015, government ministers of 195 nations reached an unprecedented agreement to lower greenhouse gas emissions, a major factor in the global-warming crisis. Such climate-change diplomacy, the first of its kind in scope, is all the more impressive when you consider the numerous factors that have worked against such an accord. Most of these hurdles are not technical but psychological, and many of the phenomena described in this chapter can help explain why solutions have proven so elusive (Newell & Pitman, 2010).

First, the threats related to global warming—including extreme weather, rising sea levels, and diminished food supply—seem far away, so many people do not feel an urgency to address them. People do not like to think ahead. Instead, they are more focused on pressing needs, frequently sacrificing a greater good in the future in favor of a smaller convenience in the present. For example, a commitment to reducing greenhouse gas emissions requires adjustments that may slow down ongoing economic development (Zhang et al., 2017).

Second, despite considerable scientific evidence that global warming is a serious threat that requires immediate action, some citizens remain skeptical. Drawing rational conclusions involves deductive reasoning, inductive reasoning, and causal reasoning, all described in this chapter. Other factors, discussed in Chapter 9, are also relevant for understanding why people disagree about whether climate change is a real threat (Newell & Pitman, 2010). As a function of the availability heuristic (see Section 9.2),

Climate change is an existential threat.

LEARNING OBJECTIVES

10.1 Describe delay discounting, considering examples from everyday life.

10.2 Discuss the different forms of deductive reasoning, inductive reasoning, and confirmation bias.

10.3 Examine how we determine causality.

10.4 Describe Bayesian reasoning.

10.5 Compare different problem-solving techniques, including factors that contribute to creativity.

10.6 Discuss the role of theory of mind and trust in social reasoning.

people may see an unusually cold stretch of winter days as evidence that the climate is not getting warmer. Meanwhile, framing effects (see Section 9.3) can make the science less obscure. Hearing that odds are 1 out of 5 is more compelling than hearing the equivalent probability value of 0.2 (Gigerenzer & Hoffrage, 1995). Images matter, as does wording. People show more concern for the problem described as "global warming" than as "climate change" (Whitmarsh, 2008).

Finally, even if everyone agrees that immediate global solutions are needed to address climate change, psychological factors (e.g., selfishness) can prevent cooperation. In this chapter we look at how people reason with each other and, in particular, when people cooperate or compete with each other. The social decision-making tasks described later in this chapter show that every partner needs to sacrifice a little to maximize overall gain.

10.1 Delay Discounting and Self-Control

Let's begin by looking at **SEE FOR YOURSELF 10.1**.

> ▶ **See for Yourself 10.1**
>
> ## Now or Later
>
> If given the choice, would you take $1,000 now or $1,500 one year later?

In this situation, most people would take the immediate payout of $1,000, even though it's better to take the later payout of $1,500. You may claim that life is too uncertain, but chances are probably good that one year from now, you will be alive and well, so it's still better to take the later payout. In fact, should you choose to defer, you could take out a $1,000 loan in the meantime. Even if you had a high annual interest rate of 20%, when you received the $1,500 one year later, you could pay off the loan plus interest ($1,200). You would still be $300 ahead—that's a lot of pizza money.

Delay Discounting

Because of a psychological tendency known as **delay discounting**, or **temporal discounting**, people diminish the value of future gains the longer they have to wait for them. Delay discounting explains many problems in personal finance. People do not save enough money because they prefer to consume now rather than defer spending, even though saving ultimately benefits them more. Let's suppose you invest $1,000 into a brokerage account at age 20 and do not add to it. By age 65, that money will have grown to a little under $180,000, assuming an average annual growth rate of 8%. You put in only $1,000, but compounding interest will have added nearly $178,000. Contrast this outcome with what happens if you wait until age 40 to put $1,000 into a savings account. By age 65, and assuming the same return rate, you will have a much smaller total—less than $40,000 (**FIGURE 10.1**). Despite the obvious advantages of saving, people still do not put enough money aside, because they want to consume immediately.

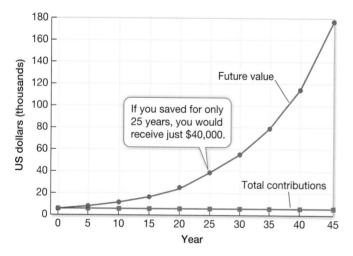

FIGURE 10.1 Delay discounting A one-time investment of $5,000 (depicted in blue squares) will grow to about $180,000 in 45 years (shown in red dots) just by the power of compounding interest (8% per year assumed here). If you only saved for 25 years, you would receive only $40,000. (Derived from https://www.investor.gov/financial-tools-calculators/calculators/compound-interest-calculator)

Self-Control

For individuals, delay discounting also relates to a lack of **self-control**, which is a crucial function of the self that involves initiating, sustaining, and inhibiting behavior—that is, executive function. As we described in Chapter 5, people have limited cognitive resources, such that they may suffer from ego depletion, using up their ability to perform executive functions well (Baumeister et al., 1998). Ego depletion leads to more delay discounting (Joireman et al., 2008).

Viewing patience as a form of self-control links to other problems such as addiction. Although addiction is usually caused by physiological dysfunctions, the pathology is associated with increased delay discounting. Harmful behaviors such as smoking or drug abuse are, in part, a form of these phenomena, in that immediate pleasure is chosen over future health and well-being. For example, drug addicts show higher discount rates for money options (more impatience or greater delay discounting) than others do, especially when they are craving drugs (Giordano et al., 2002).

Delay discounting starts in childhood, as shown in Walter Mischel's Stanford marshmallow experiment (Mischel, 2014). Preschoolers were presented with a choice: enjoy one marshmallow immediately or wait a bit longer and receive two. Many children were unable to wait, especially with the marshmallow placed right in front of them. This measure of self-control had long-term, real-world implications. When the same children were tested as teenagers, those who could not wait for two marshmallows in their preschool years showed lower standardized test scores and higher rates of behavioral problems (Mischel et al., 1989).

Self-control and delay discounting vary with age. Most individuals enjoy strong physical health and increasing intelligence during adolescence, yet mortality rates increase by 200% relative to childhood (Dahl, 2001). Could this alarming surge result from diminished self-control, leading to bad choices that put adolescents in harm's way? Adolescents tend to perform worse than adults on behavioral measures of self-control. The ability to inhibit inappropriate desires, emotions, and actions can be measured in the lab using tests such as the Simon task, continuous performance task, and task switching (described in Chapters 4 and 5). According to these measures, adolescents act more impulsively than adults and make riskier choices, especially when reward incentives are higher (Casey, 2014; Cohen & Casey, 2014). However, differences in adolescent decision making do not have to be viewed as a deficit but rather as an aspect of normal brain development, just as an infant's inability to speak is normal (Steinberg, 2008).

At the other end of the developmental trajectory, individuals over age 65 also show brain and behavioral differences. Working memory, attention, and executive control start to decline steadily with age, which affects decision-making abilities, especially when multiple pieces of information need to be considered, such as trying to choose a hotel for a trip. However, it would be wrong to say that older people are impaired at decision making across the board, as they are similar to younger adults in many ways and even show more optimal choices in tasks that involve delayed rewards (Samanez-Larkin & Knutson, 2015). Older adults are more patient than younger adults, which earns them more money in such tasks.

A child tries to resist eating one marshmallow now so that she can instead have two later. This test of self-control is related to delayed discounting.

© Josie Garner/Shutterstock.com

► CHECKPOINT 10.1

1. Explain delay discounting and its connection to self-control.
2. How does age affect self-control and decision-making?

Just because some apple types are red does not mean that all apples are red.

10.2 Types of Reasoning

Thinking, or **reasoning**, allows us to gain new knowledge and understanding from existing information. **Deductive reasoning** involves moving from general knowledge and principles to more specific knowledge and examples. Its opposite, **inductive reasoning**, moves from specific to general. That is, when we think inductively, we use specific observations and real examples to infer general theories about the world. **SEE FOR YOURSELF 10.2** provides an example of reasoning that asks us to think beyond what is known.

> ▶ **See for Yourself 10.2**
>
> ## Apple Logic
>
> 1. All apples are fruits. Fuji is a type of apple. Is Fuji a fruit?
>
> 2. Fuji apples are red. Gala apples are red. Is an Empire apple red?
>
> According to logic, the answer to the first question is yes. Using *deductive reasoning*, we can take the two general statements ("All apples are fruits" and "Fuji is a type of apple") to logically form a specific conclusion (Fuji is a type of fruit). The answer to the next question, using *inductive reasoning*, is "maybe." From the specific examples, we can infer that other types of apples would be red, but we cannot be certain. General conclusions from specific examples are probabilistic (i.e., they are based on probability), not logically defined. How do the two types of reasoning differ? The apple examples show that as long as the premises are true, deductive reasoning can allow for true conclusions based on logic. Inductive reasoning, by contrast, involves educated guesswork and relies more on existing knowledge about categorization or causation (Hayes & Heit, 2013). Here's a tip to help you remember the two types of reasoning: *deduction* is *definite*, while *induction* is *indefinite* (Jarrard, 2001).

Deductive Reasoning

SEE FOR YOURSELF 10.3 features two deductive reasoning tasks.

> ▶ **See for Yourself 10.3**
>
> ## Deductive Reasoning Tasks
>
> **Problem 1**
> Is the conclusion below logically valid or invalid?
>
> - No A are B.
> - Some C are B.
> - Therefore, some A are not C.
>
> | A | 3 | D | 7 |
>
> **Problem 2**
> To validate the rule "If a card has an A on one side, it has a 3 on the other," which of the following cards do you need to check: A, D, 3, and/or 7?
>
> (After J. S. B. T. Evans. 2013. In *The Oxford Handbook of Cognitive Psychology*, D. Reisberg [Ed.], https://doi.org/10.1093/oxfordhb/9780195376746.013.0040.)

Problem 1 involves a **syllogism**, a logical system devised by Aristotle in which a conclusion is drawn from two given propositions (called "premises"). In this example, 63% of participants thought the argument was logically valid, which is incorrect (Evans et al., 2001). The conclusion here is not valid, because the first two statements provide no information about the relationship between A and C. For example, it is possible that A could be completely subsumed by C while still not being B. Drawing a picture is often helpful in thinking through this type of problem.

For Problem 2, known as the Wason selection task (or four-card problem), the correct answer is A and 7. More than 80% of participants get this wrong; most incorrectly choose A and 3 or just A alone. Choosing A makes sense because the rule is disproved if the other side does not have a 3. Choosing D is irrelevant. Choosing 3 does not provide a valid test because the rule allows for any letter to be on the other side. That is, the rule would still hold if the letter B were on the other side. However, 7 must be checked. An A on the other side of the 7 would directly violate the rule being tested. Logically, you must seek evidence to disconfirm the rule. You can practice with more examples in the Discovery Lab.

DISCOVERY LAB
The Wason Task

The Wason selection task relies on a form of logical reasoning that contains two principles—modus ponens and modus tollens described below—essential for science and for legal reasoning. For example, the LSAT exam, used to assess readiness for law school in the United States, uses these forms of logic.

To understand these principles, let's consider a few examples and variants. Consider the statement "If p is true, then q is true." Here, p is called the **antecedent**, and q is the **consequent**; **modus ponens** states that under conditions when the statement is accepted and the antecedent (p) holds as true, the consequent (q) can be treated as true. Let's consider this statement, "If a student is funny [the antecedent, p], the student is popular [the consequent, q]." If you accept this statement, and you know that Tina is funny (p is true), then you may logically conclude that Tina is popular (q is true).

"If p is true, then q is true," then **modus tollens** allows for the following: "If q is false, then p is false." If you know that Jack is not popular (q is false), then you may conclude that Jack is not funny either (p is false). If Jack is funny, then the statement dictates that he should be popular.

However, given the statement "If p is true, then q is true," you may not conclude that "If p is false, then q is false." This fallacy (error) is known as **denial of the antecedent (p)**. If Joe is not funny (the antecedent p is false), you may not conclude that Joe is not popular (the consequent q is false). The statement leaves open for Joe to be popular for other reasons (e.g., he is tall and athletic).

Furthermore, given the statement "If p is true, then q is true," you may not conclude that "If q is true, then p is true." This fallacy is known as **affirmation of the consequent (q)**. If Jennifer is popular (the consequent q is true), you may not conclude that she is funny (the antecedent p is true). Again, the statement leaves open the possibility for Jennifer to be popular for other reasons even if she is not funny.

Let's look now at **SEE FOR YOURSELF 10.4**.

> ► **See for Yourself 10.4**
>
> ## Deductive Reasoning Tasks, Continued
>
> Evaluate whether the conclusion in the next problems is valid.
>
> **Problem 3**
> - No police dogs are vicious.
> - Some highly trained dogs are vicious.
> - Therefore, some police dogs are not highly trained.

Here, about 90% of participants correctly indicated that Problem 3 (about the police dogs) is logically invalid. This example takes the same logical form as Problem 1 in See for Yourself 10.3, but you may have noticed that it is intuitively easier to judge. We often have difficulty evaluating syllogistic arguments when they are presented abstractly (e.g., using *p*'s and *q*'s), but we tend to reason more logically when the same arguments have semantically rich content (Evans et al., 1983). People are better at solving logical problems with semantic content because our thinking styles are designed to handle real-world problems, not logical abstractions, especially when they involve social context, as will be described in more detail in Chapter 12.

Inductive Reasoning

Inductive reasoning involves "using past observations and knowledge to make predictions about novel cases" (Hayes & Heit, 2013). When told that robins, eagles, and ducks all have sesamoid bones, you can guess—but cannot be completely sure—that other birds also have them. Choosing political candidates in an election is a form of induction. When you choose to vote for someone based on his or her past record and values, you are predicting that the person will advocate for your needs and priorities (Hayes & Heit, 2013).

Reasoning in everyday life is mostly inductive. We frequently make guesses based on our past experience: "I am hopeful that my favorite football team will win the Super Bowl this year because it won last year." "I think I will like this course because I enjoyed the professor's other classes." These examples illustrate **property induction**, which is how people generalize properties or features from one exemplar of a category to another (Hayes & Heit, 2013; Osherson et al., 1990; Rips, 1975). Essential for learning about the world, inductions are made by children throughout development (Gelman & Markman, 1986). By trying to answer the fictional questions in **SEE FOR YOURSELF 10.5**, you will learn some examples of induction logic.

▶ See for Yourself 10.5

Property Induction

Given the first sentence in each fictional example below, how would you answer each question? How confident are you in your answers?

1. Orangutans are susceptible to an illness called woseness. Are gorillas susceptible to woseness?

2. Crows have an anatomical part called slabido. Do all birds have slabido?

3. The French and the Chinese observe the cultural tradition of Thanksgiving in some form. Do all people around the world observe Thanksgiving in some form?

(Based on B. K. Hayes and E. Heit. 2013. In *The Oxford Handbook of Cognitive Psychology*, D. Reisberg [Ed.], https://doi.org/10.1093/oxfordhb/9780195376746.013.0039. Nonsense words from B. A. Wilson. 2010. *Fundations, nonsense word lists: Level 3, unit 1*. Wilson Language Training: Oxford, MA.)

The **premise–conclusion similarity** states that the more similar the premise and conclusion categories, the stronger the inductive argument will be (Osherson et al., 1990; Sloman, 1993). For example, people are more likely to conclude that gorillas have property X when told that orangutans do than if they are told that lizards do. This is because gorillas are more similar to orangutans than to lizards. Thus, for Example 1 in See for Yourself 10.5, people will be more likely to say that gorillas have woseness than if they were asked if lizards have woseness. If the premises are more typical or representative of a category, they will lead to stronger inductions—this is known as **premise typicality** (Osherson et al., 1990). People will conclude that birds have property X because crows are typical of birds. However, induction will be weaker when participants are given a different premise using an atypical bird, such as a penguin. Again, in Example 2 in See for

Yourself 10.5, more people will be comfortable saying that birds have slabido given that crows have it than if told that penguins have it. These typicality effects are observed even in children (López et al., 1992).

Properties shared by diverse or dissimilar categories linked by a superordinate category (e.g., the mammal category is superordinate to its subordinate categories lions and goats) are more likely to be generalized than properties shared by similar categories (e.g., lions and leopards). This process is known as **premise diversity** (Feeney & Heit, 2011; Kim & Keil, 2003). In Example 3 in See for Yourself 10.5, people are likely to conclude that all people observe Thanksgiving because the French and the Chinese are diverse cultures. However, people would be less likely to think that all people observe Thanksgiving when given less diverse examples, such as "The French and the Belgians observe Thanksgiving." Likewise, the larger the number of premises that share a property, the stronger the induction, an effect described as **premise monotonicity** (Osherson et al., 1990). Therefore, people would be even more likely to say that all people observe Thanksgiving if told "The French, the Chinese, the Nigerians, the Brazilians, and the Australian Aboriginal people observe the cultural tradition of Thanksgiving in some form."

Consider the following fictional statement about Captain America (right) and try answering the accompanying question about Captain Marvel (left). "Captain America has a blicket compound in his blood that grants him superpowers. Does Captain Marvel, who also has superpowers, have this blicket compound?

Confirmation Bias

In testing one's hypotheses about the world, people exhibit a common pattern of thinking known as **confirmation bias**. Confirmation bias refers to the favoring of evidence that supports one's beliefs, expectations, or hypotheses (Nickerson, 1998). We already saw one example of the confirmation bias in the Wason selection task in Problem 2 in See for Yourself 10.3 (Wason, 1968). We saw that people commonly chose the card with 3, which allows them to confirm the rule, expecting to see an A on the other side, but that is the logical problem. This card cannot "test" (disconfirm) the rule because if it had a different letter besides A, the rule would still hold (i.e., the rule allows for other letters to be on the other side of 3. People tend to choose the card that is consistent with their hypothesis—the confirmation bias. Instead, one must also check the card that would disconfirm the rule, which would be the card with a 7. Only these two cases would contradict the rule, providing a test of the rule's validity. For further consideration of the confirmation bias concept, let's look at the studies in **SEE FOR YOURSELF 10.6** and the Discovery Lab.

 DISCOVERY LAB
The 2-4-6 Task

▶ **See for Yourself 10.6**

Confirmation Bias

Use your evaluative powers to think about what the author of the study did, what the critics had to say, and whether the research provided support for one side or the other.

Kroner and Phillips (1977) compared murder rates for the year before and the year after adoption of capital punishment in 14 states. In 11 of the 14 states, murder rates were lower after adoption of the death penalty. This research supports the deterrent effect of the death penalty.

Palmer and Crandall (1977) compared murder rates in 10 pairs of neighboring states with different capital punishment laws. In 8 of the 10 pairs, murder rates were higher in the state with capital punishment. This research opposes the deterrent effect of the death penalty.

(From C. G. Lord et al. 1979.
J Pers Soc Psychol 37: 2098–2109.)

How do you process relevant data, especially when you disagree with them? One might hope that such data would moderate the views of those contradicted. However, the confirmation bias suggests the opposite. To test this, undergraduate students were identified as either supporting or opposing capital punishment. Then the students were exposed to two purported studies: one that apparently confirmed the idea that the death penalty deters crime, while the other presented evidence against such deterrent effects (i.e., the studies cited in See for Yourself 10.6 are not real and were presented in counterbalanced order across participants). Students were asked to rate the results and procedures of these studies as their details were revealed to them. Demonstrating the confirmation bias, students favored the study that supported their original views. Furthermore, their beliefs became even stronger over time, and exposing everyone to the contrasting studies produced polarization: people's views became even more extreme than they were before (Lord et al., 1979).

> ## CHECKPOINT 10.2

1. What is the difference between deductive and inductive reasoning?
2. What is the common error in the Wason selection task? What role do pragmatic reasoning schemas play in everyday reasoning?
3. Given the statement "If p is true, then q is true," according to modus tollens, what else can you conclude? What can you not conclude?
4. What is property induction, and what are the effects of premise typicality, premise diversity, premise monoticity, and premise–conclusion similarity?
5. What is confirmation bias? Suggest an example.

10.3 Causal Reasoning

If you get sunburned, one can reasonably guess that you were out in the sun without sunscreen. But understanding why Israel and Palestine are in perpetual conflict is more complex. **Causal reasoning** is the ability to understand why something happens, to determine the causes of specific effects (Holyoak & Cheng, 2011; Sloman & Lagnado, 2015; Waldmann & Hagmayer, 2013). Such reasoning is fundamental in everyday life as it helps us predict the future and diagnose when something goes wrong. When someone is sick, doctors need to understand the causes of illness in order to prescribe the proper treatment. Likewise, when your car or computer malfunctions, a mechanic or technician looks for causes in order to fix it. Causal reasoning is also important in the sciences, the law, and history. Assigning blame and moral responsibility depends on determining the causes for a behavior, and the resulting punishment varies accordingly. For example, was the murder premeditated or accidental (Cushman & Young, 2011)?

Consider how shaking a bell (event A) causes a sound (event B). This can be illustrated as "A causes B," where event A is the cause and event B is the effect. Causal relationships have **directionality**: causes precede effects. People represent this directionality in their minds. For example, they are faster to verify the causal relation for two items presented in a cause–effect order (e.g., *spark* prior to *fire*) than for items presented in the opposite order (*fire* prior to *spark*). This asymmetry is absent when people have to verify that the two concepts are only related to each other (Fenker et al., 2005).

From simple perceptual animations, people can perceive what we call **causal launching**, or causation associated with a direction. When presented with a sequence such as the one in **FIGURE 10.2**, study participants understand that the red ball seems to have caused the green ball to move, like in the game of pool (Michotte, 1963; Scholl & Tremoulet, 2000). Notably, even infants correctly

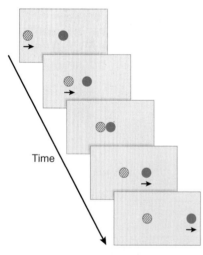

FIGURE 10.2 Causal launching   Adults and children, even infants, perceive this sequence of events as causal launching—the red striped ball appears to bump into the solid green ball, causing it to move—showing their understanding of physics and physical causality. (After B. J. Scholl and P. D. Tremoulet. 2000. *Trends Cog Sci* 8: 299–309.)

Time

perceive causal launching. Given this same series of illustrations, they stare longer or act surprised if the red ball hits the green ball but the latter does not launch (Leslie & Keeble, 1987). This reaction reveals an understanding of physics and physical causality.

Causes are usually *probabilistic*—the presence of a cause does not guarantee an effect—which can make them difficult to determine. Suppose you get sick with a stomach flu. Any number of things you ate or touched could have caused your illness. Causal reasoning is also difficult since causes are frequently unobservable and thus need to be inferred. For example, hand washing is an obvious sanitary procedure now, but in the mid-nineteenth century Ignaz Semmelweis had difficulty convincing his fellow physicians to wash their hands, especially after examining cadavers before delivering babies. He believed there was a relationship between handling cadavers and birth mortality rates (for the mother and child), but at the time, no one could imagine it (cited in Spellman & Mandel, 2006).

Cause–effect relations can be depicted in arrow format, with the cause appearing at the origin. For example, "A causes B" would be depicted as A → B. Turning on a light can be represented as flip switch → light on. The strength of the relation can be listed as a probabilistic weight, where weights closer to 1 mean that the presence of A is more likely to cause B, and weights closer to 0 represent weaker causal links. Cause–effect relations can be organized into **causal models** (**FIGURE 10.3**), which are networks of interconnected relationships (Holyoak & Cheng, 2011; Pearl, 2011).

How do people acquire the causal structure of events around them? **Causal learning** (or **causal induction**) involves learning cause–effect relationships from observations. The challenge is that causal power is not directly observable, so it must be inferred. People use a variety of cues to determine causal relations. Statistical relations, or **covariation** (the likelihood of two events occurring together), are essential. Consider events A (being happy), B (sleeping more than 7 hours a night), and C (sleeping less than 7 hours a night). If you observe that A occurs more frequently with B (more people are happy and sleep well) than with C (fewer people are happy and do not sleep well), then A and B have higher covariation, leading you to view A and B as being in a causal relationship. However, additional information is required to determine the direction.

Covariation is basic, but it is not sufficient to determine causal direction. Another important cue is **temporal order**, the arrangement of events over time. As mentioned earlier, directionality matters, since causes precede effects. So if event A occurs before event B, A is more likely to be a cause of B. People treat causal features as more important than other features. Consider an artificial animal category described as having three features—eats fruit (X), has sticky feet (Y), and builds nests in trees (Z)—that are causally linked in a chain (X → Y → Z) such that eating fruit causes the animal to have sticky feet, which allows it to build its nests. When asked to categorize examples that varied in whether they were missing a causal feature X versus an effect feature Z, people viewed feature X (eating fruit) as more central than Z (builds nests in trees) (Ahn et al., 2000).

Intervention, which involves observing the consequences of one's own actions, is also important. For example, a baby may learn that shaking a rattle causes a noise. Active intervention can help distinguish causal relations from noncausal associations (Sloman & Lagnado, 2005; Steyvers et al., 2003). But keep in mind that correlations do not equal causation. When ice-cream sales increase or decrease, the murder rate in the area does the same. However, ice-cream sales are unlikely to influence murder rates. Instead, heat seems to be the causal factor for changes in both. As another example, people once had difficulty comprehending that bacteria could cause ulcers. A correlation between bacteria and ulcers cannot show a causal relation (or a third common cause),

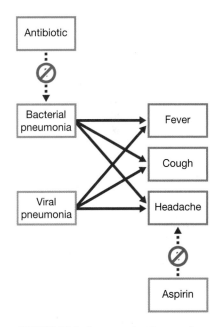

FIGURE 10.3 An example of a causal model The solid lines indicate generative causal links, while the dashed lines indicate preventative (inhibitory) causal links. To spell out this causal model, bacterial pneumonia and viral pneumonia both cause fever, cough, and headache symptoms, while antibiotics can prevent bacterial pneumonia, and aspirin can alleviate headaches. (After K. J. Holyoak and P. W. Cheng. 2011. *Annu Rev Psychol* 62: 135–163.)

but causal directionality can be established by an intervention that removes bacteria and reduces ulcers (Waldmann & Hagmayer, 2013). In science, experiments are basically interventions to determine causal relationships between correlated events, while everyday learners benefit from interventions (Gopnik et al., 2004; Steyvers et al., 2003).

Finally, **prior knowledge** (or **causal mechanism**) influences causal reasoning. Roosters crow before the sun rises, providing both covariation and temporal order cues for causality. However, people do not infer that the rooster causes the sunrise because they know that animals cannot influence the movement of astronomical bodies (Lien & Cheng, 2000). When given the opportunity to indicate the questions they would like answered about an event (e.g., an accident), people seek out and prefer hypotheses about causal mechanisms ("Was John drunk?") over information about covariation ("Was there a mechanical problem with the car?") (Ahn et al., 1995). Having a potential causal mechanism is so powerful that it will increase estimates of covariation, even when none exists—known as illusory correlations.

Illusory Correlations and Superstition

Because covariation information is useful for finding relationships and causes, people are sensitive to it. However, observing relationships between events can also lead to errors, known as **illusory correlations**, which refers to when people make connections between variables that have no relation to each other. As a medical example, arthritis pain is commonly thought to be influenced by the weather, but there is no scientific support for this association. To test this further, a group of patients was studied for over a year, but no association was found between their arthritis pain and the weather conditions (Redelmeier & Tversky, 1996). In sum, the relationship between arthritis pain and weather is an illusory correlation.

Illusory correlations tend to occur for statistically infrequent events, that is, distinctive events (Chapman, 1967). Salient or unusual events draw attention, and hence are remembered better, making them more likely to be associated in an illusory manner. Illusory correlations can lead to superstitious behavior. For example, you may care more about what you wore on the day your favorite team won a championship, causing you to wear the same clothing, even if ragged, at future games. Athletes themselves are also prone to such superstitions. Tennis legend Björn Borg grew a beard and wore the same Fila shirt to the annual Wimbledon tournament, which he won five straight times (Murphy, n.d.).

Counterfactual Reasoning

When trying to understand why something happened, people frequently ask about alternative scenarios: "What if …?" If you fail to answer an exam question that was covered in a class you had missed, you might wonder if you could have gotten it correct if you had attended the relevant lecture. Counterfactual thinking is important to many disciplines that do not include the luxury of doing experiments, such as political science, economics, history, and the law. For example, if Archduke Franz Ferdinand had not been assassinated, would World War I have started (Spellman & Mandel, 2006)?

These examples demonstrate **counterfactual reasoning**, in which people consider alternative outcomes, contrary to what has already occurred in reality—your mind plays out an alternative history that can be either beneficial or aversive ("counterfactual" as in counter or contrary to the facts). This type of thinking is important for causal reasoning because people use mental replay to understand the causes of events, especially negative outcomes. Imagine that you forgot your significant other's birthday and he or she broke up with you a few days later. You may ask yourself whether you would still be together if you had given him or her a nice gift. There is no knowing for sure because there

Legendary golfer Tiger Woods wears a red shirt in the final round of competition. Is this his brand or is it a superstition?

may have been other causes. Thus, counterfactual reasoning helps us understand past events and plan for future behaviors. It's useful for developing new ideas to test and adjusting our behaviors for better outcomes (Roese, 1997).

➤ CHECKPOINT 10.3

---

1. Describe three types of causal relationships.
2. What factors help determine causal direction? Explain how each operates.
3. What is the relation between covariation and causation? Can you treat a correlation as causation?
4. Give an example of an illusory correlation.
5. What is counterfactual reasoning? Try to come up with your own example.

10.4 Bayesian Reasoning and Ambiguity

As discussed in the section on inductive reasoning, people (and increasingly machines) need to learn general knowledge from specific examples. This ability to learn from sparse input is central to perception, categorization, and reasoning (Chater et al., 2006). In all these domains, the brain needs to infer new information from other material delivered through the senses or stored in memory. By nature, this information is typically uncertain and incomplete; thus, much thinking is probabilistic. **Bayesian inference** allows you to estimate the probability of a hypothesis being true based on the evidence at hand and your knowledge of the world.

Bayes' Rule

In many ways, Bayesian approaches help capture the essence of how we reason and make predictions in everyday life. Imagine that you have a flight booked to the Bahamas. How much time do you give yourself to get to the airport? Your decision might depend on your previous experience. Perhaps you know that traffic often comes to a standstill near the airport during rush hour or that security lines tend to be particularly long and slow at the terminal. This prior knowledge might lead you to leave earlier than someone who is new to the area. In similar fashion, Bayesian inference takes into account the way we adjust our predictions from one experience to the next.

Researchers describe this process as

$$P(H \mid E) = \frac{P(E \mid H) \times P(H)}{P(E)}$$

With this important equation, called **Bayes' Rule**, you are trying to estimate the **posterior probability**—$P(H \mid E)$—which is the probability of the hypothesis being true given the evidence. As an example, if you got a B+ on the midterm (evidence), how likely is it that you may get a final grade of A (hypothesis)? Bayes' Rule is a powerful formula that allows you to make this estimate. It is based on the prior probability, $P(H)$, and the likelihood, $P(E \mid H)$. The **prior probability**, $P(H)$, is the probability of the hypothesis being true even before any evidence is obtained (e.g., the probability that you get an A independent of your midterm grade), while the **likelihood**, $P(E \mid H)$, is the probability that the evidence would be observed when the hypothesis is true (e.g., the probability that you could have a B+ on the midterm and get a final grade of A). $P(E)$ is the probability of the evidence you have in hand (e.g., the probability that you get a B+ on the midterm). Although this may seem complicated, it's neat that one can plug these numbers in to get an estimate of what you care about: the probability of getting a final grade of A, given a midterm grade of B+. This example is hopefully intuitive, but the power of Bayesian inference is that it explains counterintuitive examples, as shown in **SEE FOR YOURSELF 10.7**.

▶ **See for Yourself 10.7**

A Real-World Medical Application of Bayesian Inference

A woman has a 0.8% chance of having breast cancer and if she does, she is 90% likely to show a positive result on a mammogram. If she does not have breast cancer, the likelihood of her mammogram showing a positive result is 7%. What is the closest likelihood that this woman has breast cancer?

1. 1%   4. 70%
2. 10%   5. 90%
3. 50%

(After G. Gigerenzer and A. Edwards. 2003. *BMJ* 327: 741–744.)

When doctors were asked the question in See for Yourself 10.7 about a patient having breast cancer, their estimates varied radically: approximately one-third responded about 10%, another one-third between 50% and 80%, and the remaining one-third approximately 90% (Gigerenzer, 2002, cited in Gigerenzer & Edwards, 2003). Think how confusing and upsetting this would be if you were a patient seeking multiple opinions, especially since the correct answer is 9%! The reason it is so low is that the priori probability of having breast cancer is low. However, people don't use conditional probabilities well. Fortunately, there's a way to make the problem easier by reframing the problem in terms of frequencies instead of probabilities, as shown in **SEE FOR YOURSELF 10.8**.

▶ **See for Yourself 10.8**

A Real-World Medical Application of Bayesian Inference, Continued

Out of every 1,000 women, eight have breast cancer. Mammographies of these eight women with breast cancer will reveal a positive result in seven of these women. Mammographies of the 992 women who do not have breast cancer will still reveal a positive result in some 70 of these women. Now consider a sample of women with positive mammogram results—how many of these women have breast cancer?

(After G. Gigerenzer and A. Edwards. 2003. *BMJ* 327: 741–744.)

In this example, you can see that 77 women have positive mammograms, but only 7 have breast cancer. The math is simple: 7 divided by 77 is 0.9, or 9%. When presented the information as frequencies, doctors were much better, with about 8 out of 10 doctors providing the correct estimate (Gigerenzer, 2002, cited in Gigerenzer & Edwards, 2003). This example makes two points. First, people are better at working with frequencies than with probabilities. Second, conditional probabilities are important in everyday life, and one must consider a priori probabilities when computing them.

More broadly, Bayesian estimation happens for all kinds of problems. Every act of perception involves taking perceptual evidence and making an inference (hypothesis) about what it corresponds to in the real world (Yuille & Kersten, 2006). In causal reasoning, we must estimate the likelihood of causes given evidence. In categorization, we learn labels for objects and must infer what other objects can be named with the same label (Tenenbaum et al., 2006). Bayesian estimation is also useful for prediction, from presidential election outcomes to World Series baseball championships (Silver, 2012).

➤ CHECKPOINT 10.4

1. What is Bayesian inference? How does it help us make choices in our everyday lives?

2. Explain the following terms: posterior probability, prior probability, and likelihood. How do they work together to determine whether a hypothesis is true?

3. For estimating likelihoods, is there an advantage to using one of the following types of information: probabilities versus frequencies?

10.5 Problem Solving and Creativity

A problem is a situation where someone has a goal but does not know how to achieve it (Mayer, 2013). Hence, problem solving is the effort directed toward finding ways to obtain one's goals, whether the agent is a person, animal, or machine. Problems start with the given state, the current situation. The goal state, or the desired state, is where the problem solver wants to be. Finally, there are the **actions**, or **operators**, that he or she needs to determine and enact in order to move from the given state to the goal state. If you are a college junior (the given state) looking for a job next summer (the goal state), problem solving involves your figuring out and executing the actions (operators) needed to help you get the job. Creativity contributes to problem solving, not just in finding novel solutions to problems, but also in helping identify novel problems. For example, the military needed to solve the problem of controlling computers from a distance, and the solution was the Internet. Over time, people came up with new problems or uses for the Internet, such as e-mail and e-commerce.

Problem Solving

Let's start with a few examples of problem solving. Try the problems in **SEE FOR YOURSELF 10.9**—please feel free to put some thought into them. Then we will discuss the answers to illustrate how problem solving works.

➤ **See for Yourself 10.9**

Thinking Outside the Box

A. Try to connect all the dots in the 3 × 3 grid below by drawing four straight lines without lifting your pencil from the paper (Maier, 1930).

```
•  •  •

•  •  •

•  •  •
```

B. Suppose you are a doctor faced with a patient who has a malignant tumor in his stomach. It is impossible to operate on the patient, but unless the tumor is destroyed, the patient will die. There is a kind of ray that can be used to destroy the tumor. If the rays are directed at the tumor at a sufficiently high intensity, the tumor will be destroyed. Unfortunately, at this intensity the healthy tissue that the rays pass through on the way to the tumor will also be destroyed. At lower intensities the rays are harmless to the healthy tissue but they will not affect the tumor either. What type of procedure might be used to destroy the tumor with the rays, and at the same time avoid destroying the healthy tissue?

(Excerpt from M. L. Gick and K. J. Holyoak. 1980. *Cogn Psychol* 12: 306–355. Based on K. Duncker. 1945. *On Problem-Solving*. [Psychological Monographs, No. 270]. American Psychological Association.)

Problems can be distinguished as routine or nonroutine (Mayer, 2013). **Routine problems** are familiar, such that the solutions are known. For example, if you need to figure out how many $20 bills make $80, you know that you divide

80 by 20 to get the correct answer of 4. **Nonroutine problems** are more difficult because they are not familiar and the solution is not apparent. The given state and goal state are clear, but the way to achieve the goal is not. For example, how can we get more people to stop drinking sugary soda, which contributes to obesity and other health problems? We could tax soft drinks, like we do cigarettes, but this idea has met with public opposition. Most problems in life, whether personal or social, are nonroutine.

A related distinction exists between well-defined and ill-defined problems. In **well-defined problems**, the given state, goal state, and operators are well specified. Arithmetic problems fall within this domain. These parts are poorly delineated in **ill-defined problems**. The problems we encounter in everyday life are more characteristic of the ill-defined type: How can you become happier? What does it mean to be happier?

Problem-solving research has focused on three classic issues: insight, transfer, and heuristics (Mayer, 2013). **Insight** describes the process of suddenly gaining a solution to a problem, typically with an "aha!" sensation (Bassok & Novick, 2012). Insight is common for creative solutions (Metcalfe & Wiebe, 1987). The problem "What is the superordinate for newspaper?" can be solved by thinking of a similar category, such as magazine, which then helps form the superordinate "publications" (Selz, cited in Fridja & de Groot, 1982). The nine-dot problem in See for Yourself 10.9 is also typically solved via insight. As shown in **FIGURE 10.4A**, once you realize that your lines can go outside the implicit boundary defined by the square grid, the solution becomes apparent. Another form of insight involves visualization. The second problem in See for Yourself 10.9 asked how you can destroy a tumor without destroying the patient's surrounding healthy tissue. **FIGURE 10.4B** shows that the solution is to concentrate many weak rays on the tumor from different angles (Duncker, 1945). It is also useful to come up with novel (new, unique, unexpected) uses for an object (Wertheimer, 1959). How do you find the area of a parallelogram? The insight shown in **FIGURE 10.4C** is that you can cut off the triangle on one side, place it on the other to form a rectangle, and then multiply the height by the width.

Another way to solve problems is to **transfer** solutions, so that learning how to solve one problem generalizes to solving others. This is fundamental in education, because when you teach a student how to do one thing, you want the student to be able to extend that learning. For example, a student's writing class might benefit other classes that require writing. Participating in sports teaches teamwork, persistence, and resilience—all useful skills for schoolwork and for life. Performing in theater teaches communication and may improve social intelligence (Schellenberg, 2004).

Unfortunately, people are not always good at shifting their learning to new contexts (Singley & Anderson, 1989). Ideally, one wants to be able to teach a general strategy that can be transferred to new problems (Mayer, 2013). **Analogical reasoning** helps people find solutions by transferring their knowledge from other problems. This requires that people recognize analogies (similarities) between the new problem and older problems that they know how to solve. People who first read a story about a military problem and its solution (**FIGURE 10.4D**) were better at solving the radiation problem in See For Yourself 10.9 (Gick & Holyoak, 1980).

Finally, people also use **heuristics**, shortcuts or simple strategies, to solve problems (Newell & Simon, 1972). One problem-solving heuristic is simply **random trial and error**, which involves randomly selecting and applying different potential solutions until the problem is solved. For complex problems, this process tends to be unsuccessful—and frustrating. Try solving the Rubik's Cube puzzle without any guidance, and it may take you weeks or months.

(A)

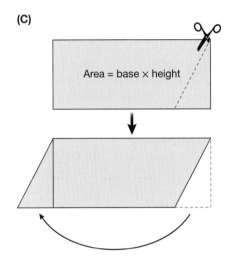

(B)

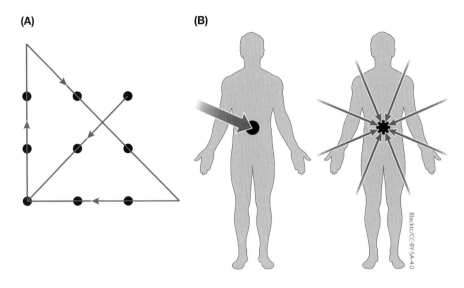

Blacktc/CC-BY-SA-4.0

FIGURE 10.4 **Problem solving using insight, transfer, and heuristics** **(A)** The solution to the nine-dot problem requires thinking out of the box (the boundaries of the grid, that is). **(B)** A patient needs radiation treatment on a tumor inside the body, but a single high-intensity beam of radiation will harm the healthy tissue on the way in. The solution is to target the tumor with low-level rays coming from different directions, and have them converge on the tumor. **(C)** Computing the area of a parallelogram becomes trivial once you realize that you can cut off a triangle and just move it to the other side, forming a rectangle. **(D)** Reading this fortress passage helped people solve the radiation problem via analogical transfer. (A,C from M. Bassok and L. R. Novick. 2012. In *The Oxford Handbook of Thinking and Reasoning*, K. J. Holyoak and Robert G. Morrison [Eds.], Oxford University Press: Oxford; D from M. L. Gick and K. J. Holyoak. 1980. *Cog Psych* 12: 306–355.)

(C)

Area = base × height

(D)

A small country fell under the iron rule of a dictator. The dictator ruled the country from a strong fortress. The fortress was situated in the middle of the country, surrounded by farms and villages. Many roads radiated outward from the fortress like spokes on a wheel. A great general arose who raised a large army at the border and vowed to capture the fortress and free the country of the dictator. The general knew that if his entire army could attack the fortress at once it could be captured. His troops were poised at the head of one of the roads leading to the fortress, ready to attack. However, a spy brought the general a disturbing report. The ruthless dictator had planted mines on each of the roads. The mines were set so that small bodies of men could pass over them safely, since the dictator needed to be able to move troops and workers to and from the fortress. However, any large force would detonate the mines. Not only would this blow up the road and render it impassable, but the dictator would then destroy many villages in retaliation. A full-scale direct attack on the fortress therefore appeared impossible.

The general, however, was undaunted. He divided his army into small groups and dispatched each group to the head of a different road. When all was ready he gave the signal, and each group charged down a different road. All of the small groups passed safely over the mines, and the army then attacked the fortress in full strength. In this way, the general was able to capture the fortress and overthrow the dictator.

Hill climbing includes selecting options that move the problem solver a little closer to the end state. A shortcoming is that some problems require people to move away from a goal state temporarily to solve the problem. Improving one's tennis serve may require breaking it down into different components, fixing one at a time. This commonly results in one's tennis serve performance getting worse before it gets better. **Means-ends analysis** requires being specific about creating goals and, importantly, subgoals to find moves that solve the problem (Gigerenzer et al., 1999; Kahneman & Tversky, 1984). How do you complete a long research paper? Ideally, you don't just sit down and try to write it out in one sitting. Instead, you break it down into smaller steps, completing one at a time. First, you list several topics to consider. Second, you do some preliminary research into each topic. Third, you choose a topic and outline the paper. Then you write each section of the paper.

© gd_project/Shutterstock.com

The Rubik's Cube is a three-dimensional puzzle; each face can be rotated independently, and the goal is to make every face have the same color.

Finally, you do multiple rounds of editing before submitting it. For each stage, you get feedback and comments from a teacher or tutor.

Expert Problem Solving

In almost every domain, ranging from medicine to finance to sport, specialists solve problems in their domain of expertise better than novices do; therefore, studying experts helps us better understand problem solving. Overall, experts notice meaningful patterns not obvious to novices, experts organize and remember information in a way that reflects their deeper understanding of the material, and expert knowledge appears to be more specific and contextualized than novice knowledge (Bransford et al., 2000). An experienced editor can make writing more clear and tight, an expert programmer can detect errors better and make code run faster, and a proficient coach can detect problems in an individual athlete's form or in a team's play.

Experience matters, arguably more than innate ability (Ericsson & Charness, 1994). Experts are not required to be generally smarter than novices, but rather, expertise is specific. As a classic example, chess masters are better at remembering the layout of pieces on the board. However, this is only the case if the pieces are arranged in a legal way, not randomly placed. That is, experts do not have better general memory than chess novices, but their expertise allows them to create configurations—to group, or "chunk," the layout of pieces—that increase the amount of information they can remember (Chase & Simon, 1973; de Groot, 1965). Thus, their memory is better only when the pieces are arranged in meaningful ways. This ability to recognize lawful chess configurations helps chess masters better understand their strategic implications and potential moves (de Groot, 1965).

Across the domains of physics, biology, chemistry, and math, novice problem solvers are more focused on superficial features of problems, while experts are more attuned to deeper features and principles related to the solutions for the problems (Bassok & Novick, 2012). When given a set of physics problems and asked to group them, novices focus on superficial aspects of the problems such as whether they involve pulleys or ramps, while the experts group them according to what principles and equations are needed to solve each problem (Chi et al., 1981). Thus, expert knowledge contributes to how people organize, represent, and interpret information.

Ultimately, we want to understand how people solve problems in the real world. For example, a study of children who are street vendors showed that they were good at solving arithmetic problems involved in their transactions (adding the cost of different items and figuring out correct change) but did poorly when the same problems were presented in school. Thus, assessing problem-solving skills in school is not sufficient (Nunes et al., 1993). Important findings such as this one highlight the need to understand **situated cognition**, the idea that thinking is shaped by its physical and social context (Robbins & Aydede, 2008).

Master's game
Experts recall the entire position almost perfectly, but novices perform poorly.

Random position
There is no difference in recall of random positions between experts and novices.

Expert chess players are more successful than novices because, if the pieces are arranged in a way that makes sense in a chess game (e.g., pawns cannot appear in the top or bottom rows; bishops need to be on differently colored squares), experts can remember more information and thus solve the problem of winning the game. This is not simply because chess masters have better memory—when pieces are placed in random positions (forming illegal placements given the rules of chess), experts are not better than novices.

Creative Thinking

When it comes to problem solving and creating solutions, the basic reasoning mechanisms we have described thus far will only get you so far (Guildford, 1950). Many of today's revolutionary advancements arose because people thought "outside the box." In the words of Apple's famous ad campaign, such advances come from people who "think different." Best-selling author Daniel Pink (2006) has argued that, partly due to increasing automation of knowledge-based jobs, the future belongs to those who can think creatively.

Creativity is a broad construct that has somewhat different meanings depending on whom you ask, but it often refers to the generation of a novel product or idea that is useful for some purpose (Diedrich et al., 2015; Runco & Jaeger, 2012). It has been suggested that although creativity is often associated with original behavior, such conduct alone does not meet the definition of creativity (Runco, 2004).

A central challenge for the field of creativity research is how to study it, a decision that depends on what one views as most important for creativity. For example, should researchers operationalize creativity as the number of creative outputs one produces, the degree to which one's outputs affect others' ideas and outputs, the cognitive processes engaged when one is being creative, or individual differences that determine a person's potential for creativity? A widely used approach to structuring the field is to distinguish between factors involving the person, press, product, and process (otherwise known as the four P's of creativity) (Rhodes, 1961, 1987).

"Person" refers to within-individual characteristics such as personality, interests, and motivation. A substantial body of work shows that motivation plays an important role in creativity: people's work tends to be more creative when they are driven by their own passion, interest, and satisfaction (i.e., **intrinsic motivation**) than by external rewards such as money or status (**extrinsic motivation**) (Amabile, 1987, 1998). In some cases, the offer of extrinsic motivators seems to impede creativity (Amabile, 1982).

"Press" refers to environmental factors (or perceived pressures in the environment) that shape the creative process (Murray, 1938). Environments that foster creativity give people freedom, autonomy, sufficient resources, and encouragement to take chances (without penalties for failure) (Amabile & Gryskiewicz, 1989; Witt & Beorkrem, 1989).

"Product" focuses on creativity's outputs. This approach often starts by identifying a creative person (e.g., Einstein, Curie, Shakespeare, Hopper) and exploring factors that may have caused him or her to be so creative (e.g., Gardner, 1993). A pitfall here is the potential to conflate productivity and creativity. The most creative individuals are not always the most productive (see Runco, 2004).

"Process" is perhaps most relevant from a cognitive perspective, as investigations following this approach include those that examine mental processes contributing to creativity.

The cognitive processes that support creativity are sometimes referred to as **creative cognition** (Beaty et al., 2016). Understanding these processes may help come up with novel solutions and ideas, that is, make them more creative. For example, smartphones put a portable computing device and access to the Internet into your pocket. Some of these creative cognitive processes are geared toward finding new ways to frame questions and perceiving unrecognized needs and problems. This latter ability is known as **problem finding** (Getzels, 1975; Getzels & Csikszentmihalyi, 1972, 1976; Runco, 2004). Before social media was established, people did not have the ability to stay constantly connected with access to a worldwide audience. Some argue that problem finding can best be understood by distinguishing between **problem identification** (whereby people notice a problem in need of a solution) and **problem definition and**

U.S. Navy admiral Grace Hopper, an innovating pioneer in computer science and technology, invented one of the first high-level programming languages and introduced the word "bug" to describe programming errors, after discovering an actual bug had disrupted her computer system.

redefinition (whereby people develop an approach that renders a problem tractable, or manageable) (Runco, 2004).

Remote Associations and Creativity

Noted psychologist Sarnoff Mednick (1962) suggested that creative ideas tend to be removed, or remote, from the original formulation of a problem and that it takes time to find one's path to such **remote associates**. To measure the ease with which people could think of remote associates, the **remote associates test** requires participants to think of what links three specific words. In many cases, the association is far from obvious (Mednick, 1968). Before moving on, try a few remote association task questions in **SEE FOR YOURSELF 10.10**.

▶ **See for Yourself 10.10**

Remote Associations

How would you link the three words in each line?

surprise line birthday

rat blue cottage

(From S. Mednick. 1962. *Psychol Rev* 69: 220–232.)

For the first example in See for Yourself 10.10, one associate might be "party," as in *surprise party, party line*, and *birthday party*. An associate for the second list of words may be "cheese," as in *rat* and *cheese, blue cheese*, and *cottage cheese*. According to one perspective on creativity, our thinking about the world is characterized by hierarchies of associations: it is easy to associate "table" with "chair" but harder to associate "table" with "resolution" ("we will table this resolution"). Particularly creative individuals, however, may have relatively **flat associative hierarchies**, wherein the less obvious associations are nearly as accessible as the obvious ones (Kaufman, 2014; Mednick, 1962).

A related approach to testing creative potential asks people to generate remote associations. Imagine that your study group meets at a table in the library. The first thing you might look for would be available chairs; after all, chairs are closely associated with sitting. If there are more people than chairs, someone might offer to sit on the floor. Someone else, however, might make a remote association and stack a bunch of thick books to provide additional seats. This person has overcome **functional fixedness**, the tendency for our thinking to be boxed in by predefined uses and associations. Going back to See for Yourself 10.9, solving the nine-dot problem involved overcoming functional fixedness that lines needed to stay within the implicit square shape defined by the dots.

Divergent thinking—the ability to generate a wide range of associations from a given starting point—is often associated with creative cognition (Berlyne, 1965). A widely used measure to tap into this type of thinking is the **Torrance Test of Creative Thinking** (Torrance, 1966). In the verbal version of this test, participants view a picture and need to respond to it in writing for different activities, which include providing ideas for product improvement and unusual uses. In the figural version of the test, participants are asked to construct pictures incorporating a given shape and to use incomplete figures to piece together a cohesive object or picture. Participants' performance is scored in terms of the number of ideas and images produced (referred to as "fluency"), the number of unusual responses provided ("originality"), the degree of elaboration reflected in their responses, the abstractness of the titles they provide, and evidence of psychological "openness" (e.g., see Kim, 2006).

A hypothesis regarding creative cognition claims that it proceeds according to a two-stage process: **idea generation** and **idea evaluation** (Finke et al., 1992). Idea generation is proposed to occur, at least in part, during states of diffuse attention, that is, when one is unfocused, like during daydreaming, taking a shower, or on a leisurely walk. In contrast, idea evaluation involves the application of cognitive control and focused attention (Jung et al., 2013).

➤ CHECKPOINT 10.5

1. What are the three main parts of a problem? Explain each one and provide examples.
2. What roles do insight and transfer play in problem solving?
3. What differentiates chess masters from novice chess players?
4. What is the remote associates test, and how does it differentiate creative individuals?
5. What is functional fixedness?
6. What is divergent thinking?

10.6 Social Reasoning

Everyday economic decisions—such as purchasing a used bicycle from someone on campus, or bidding on a house—are not made in isolation but typically involve social interactions (see Chapter 12). Whatever the situation, someone decides how much to charge and someone decides whether the amount is acceptable. Each party wants to maximize his or her gain, but each must also consider what's reasonable to the other party or the transaction will fail and no one will gain. That is, the seller wants to get the highest price possible but knows that, if it is too high, no one will buy the item. Likewise, if the buyer will pay only a low price, he or she will not find a seller. The ability to consider what the other party is thinking is called the **theory of mind**.

There are many ways to study these social interactions, but the **ultimatum game** is especially interesting because it reveals how social decision making can get emotional or "personal." The game has two players who will split a sum of money. Each player has a different role: the proposer suggests how the money should be divided, and the responder can either accept or reject the offer. If the responder accepts, the money is shared as proposed. However, it's a one-trial game—if the responder rejects the offer, neither player receives any money. Pretend you're the proposer. How would you suggest splitting $10? A fair offer would be to split the money evenly ($5 each), and you can feel assured that the responder would accept the proposal. But say you want more money, so you consider proposing $8 for yourself and $2 for the responder. What makes this game social is that you have to figure out whether the responder would accept this uneven offer. Rationally speaking, he or she should accept it because it's the only way either of you will get any of the money. Yet people are both emotional and social, such that a low offer may be poorly received. Indeed, data from numerous ultimatum game studies show that low offers are rejected at higher rates than fair offers. Remarkably, even chimpanzees behave similarly in these games, suggesting that the sense of fairness is not uniquely human (Proctor et al., 2013).

When you take the perspective of the responder, you can understand why low offers are rejected (**FIGURE 10.5**). People care about fairness—if the offer is too low, the responder may feel a need to signal that the offer is unfair, even at a cost to oneself. When these tasks are conducted on responders in an fMRI scanner, a brain area that

You need to make a fair offer to close a deal.

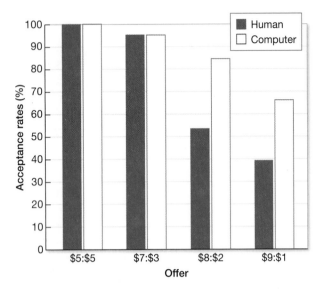

FIGURE 10.5 In an ultimatum game where $5 is an even split, responders would rather receive nothing than receive a low-ball offer of just $1 or $2 In the graph featured here, it's clear that responders are, however, more likely to accept unsatisfactory offers from a computer (rates shown in solid bars) than from a human (rates shown in striped bars). (From A. G. Sanfey et al. 2003. *Science* 300: 1755–1758.)

is typically activated by negative emotions (e.g., pain, disgust) is more active when the responders receive an unfair offer for consideration. Although one cannot conclude from such activations that people were upset, their rejections of the offer are consistent with a negative emotional response. In sum, social and emotional factors influence decision making (Sanfey et al., 2003).

If theory of mind is important, people with less capacity to consider other people's thoughts should behave differently in the ultimatum game. Autism is a developmental disorder that results in impairments of theory of mind (Baron-Cohen et al., 1985; Gallagher & Frith, 2003). Compared with unaffected children who demonstrate theory of mind in a separate task, children diagnosed with autism make more low-ball offers (Sally & Hill, 2006; Takagishi et al., 2010).

A unique feature of human societies is their ability to cooperate. Cooperation depends on social norms—rules are enforced by law but require people to agree to follow the law. **Social norms** are standards of behavior based on widely shared beliefs about how individual group members should behave (Fehr & Fischbacher, 2004). In families, parents are expected to care for their children, and children are expected to follow their parent's direction. On sports teams, each player has a role in relation to the other players and the coach. At the level of nations, world peace relies on countries respecting boundaries and resources.

Cooperation enables individuals to achieve a public good, an outcome that benefits a group as a whole. This requires that people or groups act in unselfish ways or make small personal sacrifices. To study cooperation, a classic scenario is known as the **prisoner's dilemma**, which reveals why individuals may act selfishly instead of cooperatively. Imagine that two criminals (A and B) working together are arrested and imprisoned. The prosecutor wants to convict both, but only has evidence to convict them of a lesser crime; a confession from at least one of them is needed to charge them with a more serious crime that carries a longer term of imprisonment. Thus, the prosecutor offers a bargain to each prisoner in which either prisoner can betray the other by confessing to the larger crime, and each prisoner is isolated so that they cannot communicate with each other. The following bargain is offered to each prisoner. If both A and B remain silent (cooperate), they will both serve only one year in prison. If A confesses to the crime (defecting from cooperation and betraying the other), while B does not (tries to cooperate), A goes free, while B will serve five years in prison (and vice versa). If both confess (defecting from cooperation), both will serve three years. The ideal choice is to cooperate, but because you can't trust what the other person is going to do, many will choose to defect.

One way to simulate this behavior in a lab setting is the **prisoner's dilemma game** (Axelrod & Hamilton, 1981). In this game, two players choose whether to cooperate. Each player is told that his or her reward depends not only on what he or she decides but also on what the other player chooses. If both independently decide to cooperate, both receive $3. However, the players are told that if one player decides to cooperate, while the other player defects (does not cooperate), the defector receives $5, while the cooperator gets nothing. If both players choose to defect, they each receive $1. Each player is given the options independently, and must decide without discussing the decision with the other player. **FIGURE 10.6** shows the different payoffs for each player depending on how they act. Because the players don't know what the other is going to decide, the game involves trust, cooperation, and reciprocity.

At least in the first round, it seems that the safe thing to do is to defect; otherwise you risk getting nothing. But if played for multiple rounds, each player learns what the other player decided after each round, commonly leading to mutual cooperation that maximizes profit for both individuals. However, one player starting to defect causes the other to do the same, reducing cumulative benefits.

Returning to the example at the beginning of this chapter, a global treaty to reduce carbon emissions requires everyone's cooperation and buy-in, and if a large industrial power defects, the deal would lose its effectiveness and fall apart. At the individual level, mutual cooperation seems rewarding, activating brain areas related to reward processing. That is, the brain may be wired to cooperate (Rilling et al., 2002).

The prisoner's dilemma game reveals the importance of **trust**, a social and emotional behavior that is indispensable in social interactions ranging from friendships to economic exchanges and politics. When trust among trading partners is lacking, market transactions cease. When a country's institutions and leaders lose trust in each other, political legitimacy breaks down (Kosfeld et al., 2005). The **trust game** studies these factors even more directly. Two players interact anonymously as either an investor or a trustee. The investor must decide on an amount of money to give or not to give the trustee. Any amount "invested" will be increased according to the game's rules. For example, the experimenter may announce that any invested amount will be tripled: if the investor sends $2 to the trustee, that amount will be tripled to $6. The trustee initially receives the entire increase and must decide how much to share with the investor.

This game poses a quandary similar to that in the prisoner's dilemma. The investor wants to entrust the maximum amount of money to the trustee in order to increase his or her payoff, but doing so comes with the risk that the trustee will run off with the investment. However, the real world requires that people trust others; in the game, trustees tend to reciprocate by transferring money back to investors. They do not necessarily split the profits evenly, but they return a little more than the initial investment so that both parties gain.

People playing these games act differently when they think they are interacting with a person than when they think they are interacting with a computer (even if the interface is a computer in both cases). Figure 10.5 showed that people playing the ultimatum game were more likely to accept low bids from computer opponents than from other humans. Overall, however, people are more likely to cooperate with human opponents (McCabe et al., 2001). Given these social-emotional influences, neuroeconomics also considers the role of social hormones. Can you imagine a serum that increases trust? An investor's trust in the trust game can be increased by administering the hormone **oxytocin** (Kosfeld et al., 2005), a neuropeptide that is important for pair bonding, maternal care, and sexual behavior (Insel & Young, 2001). Oxytocin also increased generosity in the ultimatum game (Zak et al., 2007).

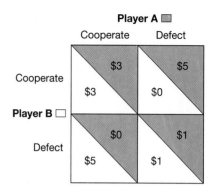

FIGURE 10.6 The prisoner's dilemma This payoff matrix illustrates the four possible outcomes of the prisoner's dilemma game. Player A's decisions and payoffs are shown in dark, purple regions, and player B's decisions and payoffs are shown in white regions. Each cell represents the four possible decision combinations and resulting payoffs. (After R. Axelrod and W. D. Hamilton. 1981. *Science* 211: 1390–1396.)

➤ **CHECKPOINT 10.6**

1. What is the theory of mind? What role does it play in the ultimatum game?
2. How does the prisoner's dilemma game work, and how does it reveal trust and cooperation?

Chapter Summary

10.1 Describe delay discounting, considering examples from everyday life.

When thinking ahead, delay discounting frequently comes into play, such that people prefer immediate gains over larger long-term ones (spending or consuming now vs. saving for the future). Overcoming this bias requires self-control.

Q: Along with the examples of combating climate change and saving for retirement, please offer an example from your life in which you should favor a larger long-term gain over immediate gratification.

10.2 Discuss the different forms of deductive reasoning, inductive reasoning, and confirmation bias.

Via deductive reasoning, people can take general knowledge and principles to definitely deduce specific knowledge. Inductive reasoning requires a bit more indefinite guessing of general knowledge based on specific observations and examples. People are not always logical about the conclusions they draw, revealing denial of the antecedent, affirmation of the consequent, or confirmation bias.

Q: Can you think of an example when you or someone around you was stuck in confirmation bias? If you had the opportunity, how would you have reversed the bias?

10.3 Examine how we determine causality.

Causal reasoning helps us understand why things happen. It starts with noting that two events tend to co-occur. To distinguish causal relationships from simple associations, it is useful to consider temporal order, intervention, and prior knowledge. Our desire to understand causes and note relationships between variables can also lead to illusory correlations and counterfactual reasoning.

Q: You did poorly on an exam. Think about how hard it is to determine the causes behind it. Did you study enough? Did you miss some classes? Did you avoid multitasking? Did you feel stressed before or during the exam? Was the exam hard? Did you get a good night's sleep?

10.4 Describe Bayesian reasoning.

Bayes' Rule helps us reason with the probabilistic world, allowing us to make predictions or test hypotheses based on the evidence at hand and our knowledge of the world.

Q: Not to obsess about grades, but imagine that you are trying to get a final grade of at least A– in the class, but you received a disappointing grade of C+ on the midterm. The professor assures the class that around 45% will receive a final grade of A–. From a Bayesian reasoning perspective for estimating your final grade, why would it matter whether 45% or 25% of the class receive at least an A– for the course?

10.5 Compare different problem-solving techniques, including factors that contribute to creativity.

Problem solving tries to figure out the actions required to go from the present state to a desired goal state. People solve problems using insight or by drawing analogies with other solved problems. Creative cognition allows people to identify and solve problems in novel ways, and the ability to think divergently appears to contribute to creativity.

Q: Think about the most creative activity that you engage in. Is it for a hobby or for work? What helps you be creative?

10.6 Discuss the role of theory of mind and trust in social reasoning.

We are social beings, interacting with others, and social reasoning helps us maximize individual or group benefits. We use theory of mind to think about how others approach a situation, influencing the kinds of actions that we would take. Cooperation and trust are important to maximize social benefits.

Q: To reduce the spread of COVID-19, what are the ways in which individuals needed to constrain their behaviors for the greater public health good? Try to frame this in terms of the prisoner's dilemma game.

Key Terms

actions (operators)
affirmation of the consequent (q)
analogical reasoning
antecedent
Bayes' Rule
Bayesian inference
causal launching
causal learning (causal induction)
causal models
causal reasoning
cause–effect relationships
confirmation bias
consequent
counterfactual reasoning
covariation
creative cognition
deductive reasoning
delay discounting (temporal discounting)
denial of the antecedent (p)
directionality
divergent thinking
extrinsic motivation
flat associative hierarchies

functional fixedness
heuristics
hill climbing
idea evaluation
idea generation
ill-defined problem
illusory correlation
inductive reasoning
insight
intervention
intrinsic motivation
likelihood
means-ends analysis
modus ponens
modus tollens
nonroutine problem
oxytocin
posterior probability
premise diversity
premise monotonicity
premise typicality
premise–conclusion similarity
prior knowledge (causal mechanism)
prior probability

prisoner's dilemma
prisoner's dilemma game
problem definition and redefinition
problem finding
problem identification
property induction
random trial and error
reasoning (thinking)
remote associates
remote associates test
routine problem
self-control
situated cognition
social norms
syllogism
temporal order
theory of mind
Torrance Test of Creative Thinking
transfer
trust
trust game
ultimatum game
well-defined problem

Critical Thinking Questions

1. How can we encourage people to favor long-term benefits over short-term ones?
2. How can education promote logical thinking?
3. How can we best measure creativity and enhance it?

Discovery Labs

oup.com/he/chun1e

The Wason Task
Students explore one of the first experimental studies of human conditional reasoning. First they try the selection task themselves, structured around conditional statements, and then they consider the general results from conditional reasoning experiments and their implications for our understanding of human cognition. Approximate completion time: 15 minutes.

The 2-4-6 Task

In this experiment you will be asked to uncover the pattern governing a sequence of numbers. You will learn more about how this relates to problem solving when you have completed the experiment. Approximate completion time: 5 minutes.

Suggested Readings

Gigerenzer, G. (2003). *Calculated Risks: How to Know When Numbers Deceive You*. New York: Simon & Schuster.

Markman, A. (2012). *Smart Thinking: Three Essential Keys to Solve Problems, Innovate, and Get Things Done*. New York: Penguin Group.

Pearl, J. (2009). *The Book of Why: The New Science of Cause and Effect*. New York: Basic Books.

Knowledge, Intelligence, and Cognitive Development

11

Does artificial intelligence need to be as good as—or better than—human intelligence? In 2016, an artificial intelligence system called AlphaGo made international news by defeating nine-time world champion Lee Se-dol in Go, an abstract strategy game. The accomplishment seemed unimaginable to the public, and even more so, to the experts. In 1997, IBM's Deep Blue computer had defeated world chess champion Garry Kasparov using trial-and-error analysis, but Go is far more complex than chess. The number of potential moves is so vast in Go that Deep Blue would have taken a year and half to consider a single stone placement.

In this chapter we focus on knowledge and intelligence, and on how they develop. Humans have enormous capacity to acquire and apply knowledge, and we have the intelligence to adapt to new situations. Furthermore, our knowledge and intelligence improve across most of our lifespan. These topics draw heavily on the other basic cognitive skills we have discussed throughout the book, especially perception, memory, decision making, and reasoning.

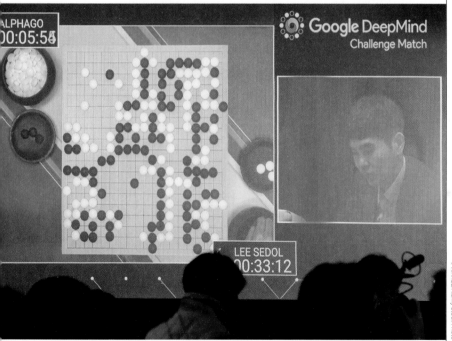

© Xinhua/Alamy Stock Photo

The artificial intelligence system AlphaGo made international news by defeating nine-time world champion Lee Se-dol in Go, an abstract strategy game. The accomplishment seemed unimaginable to the public, and even more so, to the experts.

11.1 Knowledge

Knowledge is what we've learned about the world around us. Much of this information is obtained through perception, refined through reasoning, and stored in memory. We learn through our sensory abilities—from viewing, hearing, tasting, smelling, and touching. Beyond our immediate surroundings, we acquire more information from other people and through media. Reasoning allows us to expand our knowledge, while experience and memory ground our expertise.

Knowledge is tightly linked to perception. As Chapter 3 explained, imagery relies on perceptual mechanisms in the brain. And in Chapter 7 we saw that recalling a memory activates the brain areas involved in perceiving the original event. Accordingly, a theory known as **embodied cognition**, or **grounded cognition**, argues that shared representations are used for perception, action, and knowledge (Barsalou, 1999, 2008). The acts of seeing a pen, using a pen, and thinking about a pen are supported by shared representations.

Categorization is the process of grouping items or ideas together and distinguishing them from other items or ideas. Object recognition is essentially an act of categorization. Recognizing a chicken as a chicken, or a goat as a goat, is an act of categorization, not just perceptual analysis. Categorization allows us to group similar things together, distinguishing them from other things. Categories can also be understood as **concepts**, the mental representations in the brain that correspond to objects or ideas in the world (Markman & Rein, 2013). Some concepts and categories are concrete—for example, books and roses—while others are more abstract—for example, fairness and happiness. Should a fetus be categorized as an infant or as just another cluster of cells in the body? The contentious abortion debate hinges on this categorization.

Categorization is useful for at least three primary reasons. First, categorization facilitates communication, allowing us to convey ideas to others in an effective manner (Brown, 1958). Categories allow us to summarize multiple properties of an object using a single label. Instead of telling your friend that at the zoo you saw a cute, bamboo-eating, black-and-white animal that weighs several hundred pounds, you can simply say that you saw a panda bear.

Second, categories permit inference, which allows you to generalize from prior experience to understand a new object or event. That is, you can use categorization to infer or assume properties of the object even when they are not present, which then enables you to predict features of a new instance based on what you know about its category (Anderson, 1990; Osherson et al., 1990). If you learn that a robin has sesamoid bones (bones that are tiny like a sesame seed), then you may infer that other birds have sesamoid bones.

Third, categories enable us to make better decisions and predictions. Based on inference from past experience, you already know that to do well in a new class, you should do your readings on time, attend class, and see your professor during his or her office hours when you have questions.

Categorization

So how do we form and distinguish categories? One idea is to agree on *definitions* for different categories. For example, a rectangle is an object that has four sides. If a new object appears, such as a square, you may ask if it's a rectangle. Since a square has four sides, it satisfies the definition, whereas a triangle or circle would not. Unfortunately, the definition approach breaks down quickly when you consider that it's frequently impossible to develop a comprehensive definition that works in the real world. Consider a chair, which can be defined as an object on which you sit. Given this definition, it seems easy enough to categorize a chair, but there are some challenges: Is a boulder a chair? Is the

Languag → Creativity
The ability to arrive to completely Novel Solutions and creations

floor a chair? Is the spiky object in **FIGURE 11.1** still a chair if you can't sit on it comfortably? Another example would be the word "game." Merriam-Webster defines game as "activity engaged in for diversion or amusement." This applies well to games such as hide-and-go-seek or Halo. What about recreational running or sex? Few people would describe the latter two as games.

Another common approach is **feature-based categorization**; categories are defined according to a set of characteristic features (Smith & Medin, 1981). For example, the category of bird consists of robins, sparrows, and hawks, which all have wings and lay eggs. Wings and laying eggs are therefore features of this category. A key feature of categorical knowledge is that once you possess a category, you can place novel examples or prototypes into it based on their **similarity**, or **resemblance**, to other members of the category. According to this similarity-based categorization, if it looks like a dog, it's a dog, and if it sounds like jazz, it's jazz. **Family resemblance** refers to the fact that items in a category tend to share features (Wittgenstein, 1953). Some variation is tolerable. Defining features are probabilistic, usually not absolute. "Can fly" may be a common feature of birds, but it is not a necessary feature; ostriches are birds, but they cannot fly.

There are two ways to determine how similar an item is to its category: prototypes and exemplars. According to one approach, categories are exemplified by a **prototype**—that is, a typical or ideal member (Rosch, 1973; Rosch & Mervis, 1975). For example, a robin is a prototypical example of a bird, whereas a penguin is not. A prototype or typical member of a category is usually an average of the examples that a person has encountered. For example, we often encounter birds—most of us see them on a daily basis flittering about the yard, or in parking lots, or at the seashore—but we rarely encounter penguins, unless we're at the zoo or in the Antarctic, South Africa, Australia, or New Zealand. People categorize things according to how closely they match a category's prototype.

A classic experiment studied prototypes by exposing people to numerous dot patterns. Half of these patterns are variations of one prototype, forming one category (**FIGURE 11.2**); the other half are variations of another prototype, forming another category. People learn to distinguish these novel, artificial categories, as well as the underlying average pattern, even if it was not shown during the course of their training. People not only learn prototypes well, they

FIGURE 11.1 A medieval torture chair If it is not suitable for sitting, is this still considered a chair?

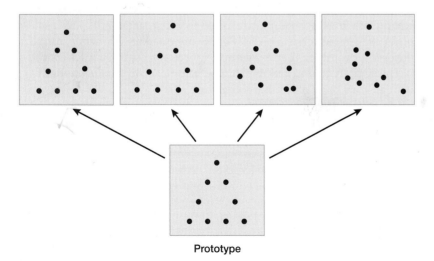

Prototype

FIGURE 11.2 Distinguishing prototypes People can categorize the patterns in the top row across different levels of distortion. The underlying triangle pattern in the second row is called the prototype, but it doesn't need to be shown for people to categorize the variants. (After M. I. Posner et al. 1967. *J Exp Psychol* 73: 28–38.)

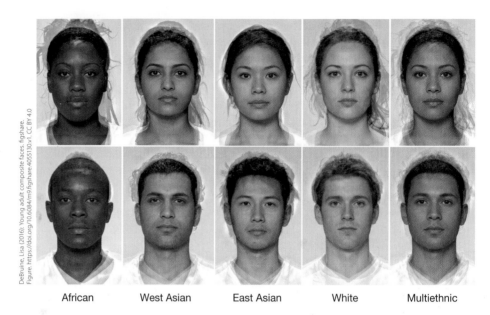

African West Asian East Asian White Multiethnic

FIGURE 11.3 These faces were constructed by a computer imaging program that averages several individual faces Averaged faces are usually rated as more attractive than the individual faces from which they were composed, possibly because the former are closer to a facial prototype.

also tend to prefer them over individual exemplars of a category (Posner & Keele, 1968) (**FIGURE 11.3**).

The **typicality effect** refers to how some members of a category are more representative than others. Another way to study prototypes is to ask what is typical in a category. If you ask people to name examples from a category, prototypes come up first. For example, suppose you ask people to name as many dogs as they can (Rosch et al., 1976). The Labrador retriever is frequently named, as it is the most popular breed of dog in America. Or suppose you ask people to rate how typical, or "good," examples of a particular category are (Rosch & Mervis, 1975). For the category fruit, apples, peaches, and pears show high typicality ratings, while avocados, pumpkins, and olives show low typicality ratings (Malt & Smith, 1984). As a final example, consider the **sentence verification task**, in which people are asked to verify statements such as "A crow is a bird" or "An ostrich is a bird." People are quicker to affirm examples that are closer to a prototype than they are to affirm atypical examples (Smith et al., 1974). This reveals **graded membership**, which means that some items are closer to their category prototypes than others are.

Exemplar-based categorization is related to the prototype idea in that it is a family resemblance theory that depends on similarity among items within a category. However, instead of relying on average instances or ideal prototypes, the exemplar approach appeals to actual examples or specimens of a category (Medin & Schaffer, 1978; Nosofsky, 1987). Whereas prototype models propose that we store an average instance in our mind, exemplar models suggest that we store all the specific examples shown in our mind. When a new instance is observed, our mind matches it against all the stored exemplars.

Exemplar models predict many of the findings used in support of prototype models, such as typicality effects that allow us to quickly categorize common category examples such as Labrador retrievers. Exemplar models can predict typicality effects because they imply that there will be more exemplars of common objects in mind. Why bother storing all experienced exemplars? Exemplars work better for outliers that deviate from typical category members, such as an ostrich, which is very different from the prototype of a bird, but can be categorized as one because we store it as an exemplar. Importantly, exemplar models and prototype models do not exclude each other. Most researchers believe that both exemplars and prototypes exist in the mind to form our concepts and categories.

The classic, feature-based models of categorization do not work for many categories in the real world. Some categories cannot be defined with features. As noted earlier, one problem is that it's hard to find a great way to describe defining features in a way that encompasses outliers (Markman & Rein, 2013). If the category of bachelor is defined as "an unmarried man," the pope would fit in this category. However, some people would feel uncomfortable describing the pope as a bachelor. Thus, an additional approach is to define some categories in terms of goals or themes, or what psychologist Lawrence Barsalou (1983) calls **ad-hoc categories**. One example is exercise equipment: a treadmill, balancing ball, and weight machine look very different from each other, but people readily group them together as equipment used for exercise. The unifying feature here is the goal to work out and be healthy, not some shared set of perceptible characteristics, such as size, shape, accessory features, and whether or not the equipment needs to be plugged in to operate. People can make such goal-based categories rather quickly. Barsalou asked people what they would save from their house if it was on fire. Although most people do not have real-life experience with this task (thankfully), no one required much time to come up with a coherent list, such as children, pets, family photos, house documents, jewelry, and money. However, these ad-hoc category items are unlikely to be perceptually similar to each other in a way that they could be categorized based on appearance.

Knowledge Representation

Given that categories are used to carve up the world, **knowledge representation** studies how these categories are organized in the mind. Regardless of how you define them, categories are in a **hierarchical relationship** with each other, such that general categories subsume more specific categories (the category "animal" contains "elephants" and "squirrels"). Categories can, however, have other categories within them (making them **superordinate**) or may be part of larger categories (making them **subordinate**). This hierarchical structure of superordinate and subordinate categories raises the question: What is the most useful level of categorization in everyday life? The most common categorization is considered to be the **basic-level category**, which is more typical and comes to mind more naturally (**FIGURE 11.4**). As noted, people use basic-level categories in naming tasks, and learning these concepts is an important part of learning language.

HIERARCHICAL NETWORKS   Work on categorization has led many researchers to believe that knowledge is organized in **hierarchical networks** containing nodes and links. Nodes are pieces of information, while links are associations between them (Collins & Quillian, 1969). Consider the network in **FIGURE 11.5**. Properties of categories are stored at higher levels so that they can be generalized to categories underneath them, which helps avoid duplication. Specific properties that are unique to certain categories are stored at lower levels. This hierarchical structure minimizes redundancy in the organization of knowledge. One does not need to separately

FIGURE 11.4 Name this object quickly, as if you're telling a child, "Look at that _____"   Most people will say that it's a car (basic-level category); however, it's also a vehicle (superordinate category) and, more specifically, a 2020 Tesla Model S (subordinate category).

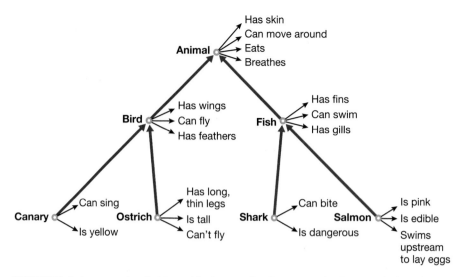

FIGURE 11.5 An example of a hierarchical network Concept nodes (e.g., "Bird") have features (e.g., "Has wings") and are organized hierarchically via links (the lines between concepts). Activations spread across links more quickly for closer links ("Canary" to "Bird" vs. "Canary" to "Salmon"). (After A. M. Collins and M. R. Quillian. 1969. *J Verbal Learning Verbal Behav* 8: 240–247.)

specify that each of the specific examples of pine, oak, rose, and daisy all have roots. Instead, since all of these are plants, you can specify the feature of having roots at the superordinate plant node.

Activation or processing at a node will travel across links—this is called spreading activation (see Chapter 8). The longer the distance, the longer it will take for information to travel. Like an airplane flying routes between airports, information travels across the connections between nodes. The longer the connections, or the more nodes that need to be traversed, the more time it will take to answer questions about the two nodes. Thus, the structure of knowledge networks can be probed by measuring the speed of spreading activation. Such investigations are possible with sentence verification tasks for which simple statements are presented and participants just need to quickly respond true or false. As one example, people will be faster to verify "A canary is yellow" than "A canary is an animal." As suggested in Figure 11.5, the latter requires longer connections; thus, it takes longer for activations to travel across them. These measurements can be used to sketch the structure of semantic networks; facts that are quick to verify can be placed closer together than facts that are slow to verify.

DISTRIBUTED NETWORKS In semantic networks, the nodes explicitly represent pieces of knowledge or information. A different approach is to represent knowledge in a distributed manner across connections between multiple nodes—this is known as **connectionism**, **parallel distributed processing**, or **neural nets**. Again, like the semantic network approach, connectionist models have nodes and links. However, unlike in semantic networks, facts in connectionist models are not stored in single nodes, but are more widely distributed across nodes influencing each other in parallel. Active nodes can spread their activity to other connected nodes with links that have different strengths, also known as connection weights (Rumelhart et al., 1988).

Connectionism mimics principles of brain processing. People are better than machines at perceiving the world around them, not because the brain operates faster than computers, but because of its design. More so than silicon chips, neurons are massively connected and process information in parallel, helping the brain handle imperfect information better and allowing the "simultaneous consideration of many pieces of information or constraints" (Rumelhart et al., 1988, p. 3). Such parallel processing is important in a variety of tasks—everything from reaching out for a pen (while avoiding obstacles like the sharp corner of your desk, or a cup of hot coffee) to recognizing words in natural language. Let's explore reading in more detail.

In **FIGURE 11.6**, ink blotches—a form of visual noise—make letters ambiguous. Yet the meaning of the words and the presence of unambiguous letters help people read these words with no problem. Parallel processing can resolve ambiguous or noisy information because it simultaneously considers context and other information.

Let's take a closer look at the process of reading, which starts with units that detect the visual features distinguishing alphabet letters in different positions in a word. **FIGURE 11.7** is seemingly complex but conceptually simple. At the bottom of this model is a "layer" of different visual features, which in different combinations will activate different letters in the next layer. Finally, different combinations of letters will activate different concepts in the word layer at the top. In this example, the feature and letter units are for only one letter-position in a word, replicated for different letter positions.

Now imagine that this model is viewing the letter *T* as input. The horizontal and vertical lines in *T* will activate the first two units in the feature layer, which in turn will activate the *T* in the letter layer—these connections are **excitatory**, represented with arrows, meaning that feature units make it more likely that the receiving letter unit will be activated. At the letter layer, when *T* is active, it

FIGURE 11.6 What are the four words? The inkblots make some letters ambiguous (R/P, E/F, B/D), but context allows you to read the words as "RED," "SPOT," "FISH," and "DEBT." (After J. L. McClelland et al. 1986. In *Parallel Distributed Processing: Explorations in the Microstructure of Cognition*, Vol. 1, D. E. Rumelhart et al. [Eds.], pp. 3–40. MIT Press: Cambridge, MA. Based in part on P. H. Lindsay and D. A. Norman. 1972. *Human Information Processing: An Introduction to Psychology*, p. 142. Academic Press: New York.)

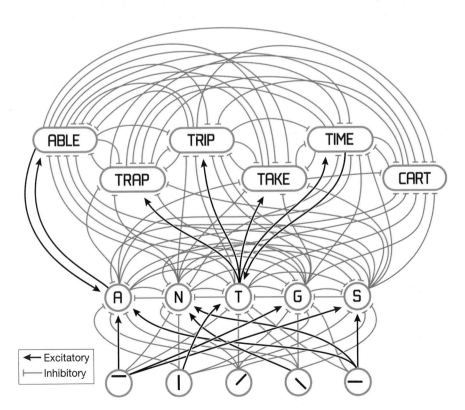

FIGURE 11.7 A parallel distributed processing model Features in the bottom row can be combined to activate letters in the middle row, which can be combined to activate words in the top row (not all features or letters shown here). (After D. Purves et al. 2012. *Principles of Cognitive Neuroscience*, 2nd ed., Oxford University Press/Sinauer: Sunderland, MA. Based on J. L. McClelland and D. E. Rumelhart. 1981. *Psychol Rev* 88: 375–407.)

should try to reduce the chances that other letters will be active, so it has **inhibitory** connections with the other letters (represented with flat arrowheads). And when the *T* is activated in the first letter position, it will increase the chances that the words TRAP, TRIP, TAKE, and TIME will be active, while reducing the activation of ABLE and CART since those words do not start with the letter *T*. This model demonstrates how different types of information are considered together in a parallel manner.

Neural Representation of Concepts

How do you organize files on your computer or in the cloud? Do you sort them in different folders based on categories such as "Personal" and "Schoolwork"? Do you organize based on file type, such as "Photos," "Music," and "Documents?" Or do you use a combination? The answer determines how easy it will be to search for files, and it will explain what kinds of losses you will suffer if a folder is accidentally deleted or is damaged. Likewise, cognitive psychologists are interested in how the brain stores and organizes information.

The organization of the brain's data folders can be inferred from patient data and from neuroimaging data. We saw in Chapter 2 that people with prosopagnosia (face blindness) have selective deficits for face processing, while their object processing remains intact. Further sharpening this dissociation, some people show normal face processing but are selectively impaired at object recognition, ruling out the possibility that face processing is just a more difficult form of object recognition (Moscovitch et al., 1997). Brain imaging has revealed separate cortical areas for face recognition and object recognition.

Similarly, to study how concepts are organized in the brain, one can search for categories that show selective impairments and brain activation. For example, representations of living things and human-made artifacts appear to be segregated in the brain. Some patients are unable to label living things and foods, while being able to identify inanimate objects (Warrington & Shallice, 1984). Another patient showed the opposite problem, with difficulties comprehending inanimate objects but being able to label foods and living things (Warrington & Mccarthy, 1987). Another patient was not able to name animals but had no trouble naming non-animals. She was also unable to name animals based on their typical sounds, suggesting that the deficit was not a visual agnosia but a deeper semantic problem (Caramazza & Mahon, 2003; Caramazza & Shelton, 1998) (**FIGURE 11.8**). Accordingly, researchers infer that animals, foods, and artifacts are stored separately in the brain.

Returning to the computer file analogy, these deficits suggest that the brain stores information categorically, as if you had separate file folders for animals versus nonanimals or for living things versus tools. Accidentally deleting or misplacing one of the folders will make an entire category inaccessible. Several theories try to explain this pattern of semantic organization. The examples above support the **domain-specific hypothesis**—the idea that, throughout the course of evolution, certain categories of objects gained privileged processing in the brain, leading to specialized circuitry and brain areas, such as for face processing and body movements and for living versus nonliving things (Caramazza & Shelton, 1998). It is easy to understand why living things and foods, and inanimate objects such as tools, may have gained privileged status in the brain.

"Kangaroo"   "Chicken"

"Squirrel"   "Some kind of bug"

FIGURE 11.8 Examples of errors that a patient with agnosia made in naming animals   (After A. Caramazza and B. Z. Mahon. 2003. *Trends Cogn Neurosci* 7: 354–361.)

Another way to understand the distinction between animate and inanimate categories is that sensory and functional properties may be processed separately in the brain. According to the **sensory-functional account** (Warrington & Shallice, 1984), which is related to the embodied cognition theory put forth at the beginning of this chapter, object concepts are grounded in perception and action (Barsalou, 1999, 2008). Rather than being symbolic or abstract, semantic knowledge is stored according to whether it is primarily sensory or primarily functional. That is, the meaning of objects and words and object properties—such as how they look, or how they are used—is stored in the sensory and motor systems activated by that object (Martin, 2007). The ability to name living things, such as a people-eating tiger, is based on sensory information on how tigers look and sound. However, the ability to name tools and artifacts, such as a hammer and nail, depends more on motor actions involved with grasping and performing actions with such objects.

Supporting the sensory-functional account, neuroimaging studies have revealed separate cortical activations for the naming of people, tools, and animals, similar to those areas damaged in patients. Naming pictures of animals activates regions important for processing perceptual features, while naming tools activates brain regions involved in action (Martin et al., 1996). Even answering questions about animals and tools activated corresponding brain areas (Chao et al., 1999). In one study, individuals were presented with achromatic (uncolored) object pictures or word names, such as "wagon," and then were asked to generate words related to an action associated with the object ("pull") or a color ("red"). The word task activated areas related to action and motion, while the color task activated regions associated with sensory and color processing (Martin et al., 1995). In a different study of word processing, the verb "eat" produced activity in a brain area involved in gustatory responses, while the verb "run" activated a brain area involved in the perception of biological motion (Mitchell et al., 2008).

Not all categories are special. Most categories, such as shoes and purses, do not have devoted brain areas that can be isolated by brain imaging or that lead to specific deficits in patients; rather than being localized and independent, their representations are more distributed and intermingled with other categories, such as balls and tools. Because most categories do not have special, localized brain areas, you will rarely see a patient with a selective deficit for bicycles but not for vehicles in general. Instead, most of our knowledge is represented in distributed and interconnected networks spanning different areas of the brain (Haxby et al., 2001; Ishai et al., 2000).

➤ CHECKPOINT 11.1

1. Define embodied cognition.
2. What are the three benefits of categorization?
3. What are the different ways to define categories? What are typicality effects?
4. What is a basic-level category, and what does it tell us about knowledge representation?
5. What are the key differences in how knowledge is represented between semantic networks (e.g., Collins & Quillian, 1969) and connectionist models?
6. Cite brain imaging evidence for sensory-functional accounts of knowledge representation in the brain.

11.2 Intelligence

If knowledge represents what we know about the world, intelligence may be the ability to apply that knowledge to real-world situations and problems. Two

Intelligence involves the ability to reason and solve problems. Katherine Johnson performed mathematical calculations of orbital mechanics that enabled NASA's first manned missions to space. Her work inspired the book and movie *Hidden Figures*, which chronicles the contributions of Johnson and other Black female mathematicians to the development of the American space program.

pioneers of intelligence measurement, Alfred Binet and Theophile Simon (Binet & Simon, 1916/1905), defined **intelligence** as

> *a fundamental faculty the alteration or lack of which is of the utmost importance for practical life. This faculty is judgment, otherwise called good sense, practical sense, initiative, the faculty of adapting oneself to circumstances. To judge well, to comprehend well, to reason well, these are the essential activities of intelligence* (pp. 42–43).

Generally speaking, intelligence refers to the ability to reason, solve problems, and gain new knowledge. This definition is broad enough to elicit agreement from most intelligence researchers and experts, but attempts to create a more concrete definition have been less successful. For example, when two dozen theorists were asked to define the term, they gave two dozen answers (see Neisser et al., 1996; Sternberg & Detterman, 1986).

Understanding what we mean by intelligence has become more important than ever, as society comes to terms with a world in which computer-driven, automated systems are increasingly charged with decision-making responsibilities. Computers are now able to defeat the world's best chess players and Go players, but are there aspects of intelligence that people uniquely bring to the table and that computers cannot match? To what degree should we define human intelligence in the same way that we define **artificial intelligence (AI)**— the technology that increasingly enables computers to engage in or mimic complex cognitive functions?

We all know people who seem to be better at some things than others. Perhaps one of your friends always gets good grades while another comes in at the bottom of the class every time. You might know someone whose judgment and problem-solving ability have led him or her to be promoted several times and another person who can't seem to hold down a job. Why are some people more successful than others at meeting society's cognitive challenges? This question is obviously complex, with many contributing factors—including motivation, values, personality, interpersonal skills, socioeconomic advantages, and upbringing. Intelligence research attempts to understand the degree to which **individual differences** in cognitive ability—that is, variations among people— contribute to such outcomes.

Another question to ask is whether intelligence is fixed or malleable. Is intelligence more innate, like height, or learnable, like the ability to play basketball? Both height and ability are useful, but only the latter can be improved with effort. Likewise, intelligence—which has been conceived by some as "mental energy" (Spearman, 1904)—might contribute to a person's raw information-processing power, but expertise, practice, and determination (as well as other characteristics) shape how such power translates into real-world outcomes. Even differences in how we define intelligence can cloud attempts to answer questions about what shapes it and whether it can be improved through training and education.

Perhaps more than any other subject in cognitive psychology, intelligence is often defined in terms of its utility within society. Today's intelligence tests evolved largely from efforts to predict academic success.

Modern intelligence research has been motivated by different communities of interested parties and has followed several approaches. The measurement of intelligence is seen as important for society (whether for identifying learning difficulties or for recruiting military personnel). The approach that seeks to understand the most valid way to measure intelligence is the **psychometric approach**, which gave us IQ tests. The psychometric approach has provided grist for clashes between theoretical perspectives, with some criticizing the very notion of intelligence measurement. Because different cultures value different traits and skills, and because the challenges they face can vary, cultural biases can shape ideas about what outcomes and skills are most central to the concept of intelligence. Whereas some cultures may value vocational training and technical skills, others may put more emphasis on literature and the arts. Issues of circular reasoning in how we define intelligence can also emerge. Assumptions about the correct predictive outcomes guide the development of the measures employed; therefore, it is only natural for people who score high in intelligence tests to go on to enjoy success, leading some to quip sardonically that "intelligence is what intelligence tests measure."

The **information-processing approach** provides a complementary, but not exclusive, perspective on intelligence. Researchers from this tradition try to understand the neurocognitive processes that are involved in intelligent behavior. This approach can explain how much of intelligence is heritable, and how it can be predicted from brain activity and other biological differences. In addition, it considers how intelligence is correlated with other cognitive skills such as speed of processing, working memory, and executive control.

The Psychometric Approach

In many ways, modern intelligence research began as an attempt to develop measures of cognitive ability that predicted real-world outcomes. Such efforts can be traced back to the pioneering works of Alfred Binet, who was hired by the French educational system in the early twentieth century to develop a test that would aid in placing schoolchildren in the appropriate classes. Binet and his collaborator, Theophile Simon, created a system for identifying normally and subnormally intelligent children. Items on their test—for example, questions that asked children to repeat three numbers, state facts, think of rhymes for a given word, and critique absurd statements—were designed to tap into mental abilities that contribute to academic aptitude and success. One of the test's strengths was its ability to compare children based on **mental age** (the average score of children at a certain age). If a 6-year-old's score equaled that of the average 7-year-old, he or she would have a mental age of 7.

American psychologist and Stanford University professor Lewis Terman adapted Binet and Simon's test into the **Stanford–Binet intelligence scales**. This test gave us the term **intelligence quotient** (**IQ**), which is calculated by dividing a person's mental age by his or her chronological age and multiplying by 100. Thus, a person of "normal" intelligence (e.g., a 7-year-old with the mental age of 7) has an IQ of 100. Note that this method is meaningful only for children and teenagers. After a certain age, it doesn't make sense to compare. A 5-year-old who performs at the level of an average 8-year-old would have a high IQ: $(8/5) \times 100 = 160$. But there shouldn't be such a robust difference between the average 35-year-old and 38-year-old.

Terman found a positive correlation between children's IQs and the degree to which teachers rated their intelligence. This discovery helped the Stanford–Binet test become widely adopted. The U.S. military became interested in the tests because, with its involvement in World War I, it had a pressing need to make efficient recruit assignments (i.e., ascertain which soldiers were officer material). With this goal in mind, intelligence tests were modified so that—unlike the original Stanford–Binet test—they could be administered to many people at once.

Perhaps the most widely used intelligence tests today are the **Wechsler scales**, named after their developer, David Wechsler, who aimed to measure "the global capacity of a person to act purposefully, to think rationally, and to deal effectively with his/her environment" (Wechsler, 1939, p. 3). These tests provided a significant advance for the psychometric approach by attempting to minimize the degree to which intelligence scores were shaped by linguistic

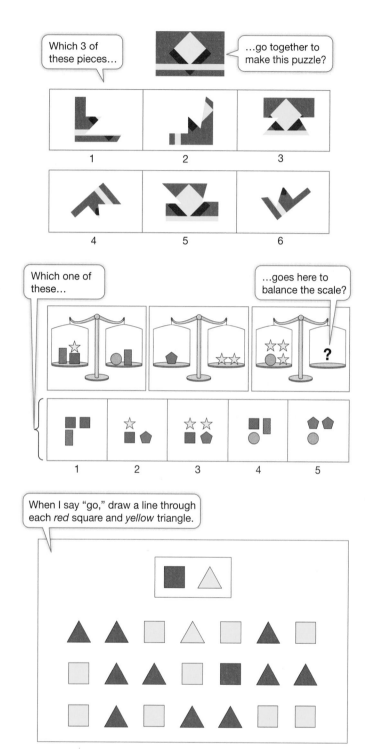

FIGURE 11.9 Sample items from the Wechsler Adult Intelligence Scale (WAIS-IV) Try each problem according to the prompts in the bubbles. The answer to the top problem is 1, 3, and 6. The second problem's answer is 3. The bottom problem is scored based on how quickly and accurately people can cross out the red squares and yellow triangles. (From Weschler Adult Intelligence Scale 4th Edition. Copyright © 2008 NCS Pearson, Inc. Reproduced with permission. All rights reserved. Weschler Adult Intelligence Scale 4th Edition is a trademark, in the US and/or other countries, of Pearson Education, Inc. or its affiliates(s).)

and cultural differences. The tests have been developed for both adults and children. Individuals over the age of 16 are given the **Wechsler Adult Intelligence Scale** (WAIS-IV) (Wechsler, 2008), whereas children are given the **Wechsler Intelligence Scale for Children** (WISC-V) (Wechsler, 2014).

The Wechsler scales assess performance on several subscales; some rely on a verbal response from the test-takers, and some require them to perform visuospatial tasks (**FIGURE 11.9**). Verbal items assess general knowledge, vocabulary, comprehension, and math performance. Nonverbal (or visuospatial) tasks include arranging a series of pictures into an appropriate sequence, completing unfinished pictures correctly, and piecing together segments of an object into a whole (much like doing a jigsaw puzzle).

For example, the Wechsler scales comprise the following subscales or indices, which focus on specific types of assessments:

- The Verbal Comprehension Index includes tests of vocabulary, factual knowledge, abstract verbal reasoning, and ability to comprehend abstract rules and expressions. Tests that contribute to this index assess vocabulary and general knowledge and ask test-takers to recognize similarities.
- The Perceptual Reasoning Index features block design and matrix reasoning tests (which are used to assess spatial perception and visual problem solving), nonverbal abstract problem solving, visual puzzles, and picture completion.
- The Processing Speed Index includes speeded visual search tests and tests of visual-motor coordination.
- The Working Memory Index tests digit span (the number of digits a person can accurately remember for a short period of time), mental manipulation of math problems, and combined tests of attention and working memory.

The concept of IQ also changed with the Wechsler tests. Rather than calculating an individual's mental age, IQ is derived by placing an individual's score on a frequency distribution relative to other same-age test-takers. A greater number of scores cluster around the middle, with low scores and high scores becoming ever less frequent as they become extreme. When this distribution is more or less symmetrical, it is referred to as a normal distribution (**FIGURE 11.10**). The resulting graphical depiction is known as a **bell curve** because the shape resembles a bell.

WHAT DO INTELLIGENCE SCORES PREDICT?
Intelligence tests are generally good predictors of

academic performance (Cronbach & Snow, 1977). This connection makes sense, as school performance is exactly what Binet's original tests were designed to predict. Nonetheless, IQ scores account for only a portion of the variance among students; other factors include motivation to study and persistence. An unmotivated or lazy tennis player who uses a high-tech racquet will not outperform a player who has a less-advanced racquet but trains hard and plays with passion. Similarly, an unengaged student with a high IQ won't perform better in school than someone who is passionate, persistent, and dedicated. In one study, measures of self-discipline in the first semester of an eighth-grade academic year predicted grades in the second semester better than IQ scores did (Duckworth & Seligman, 2005).

The relationship between intelligence scores and academic outcome is affected by factors such as teaching practices and cultural values. This is apparent in the finding that Chinese and Japanese children score better in math than do American children, despite being matched on intelligence scores (Neisser et al., 1996; Stevenson & Stigler, 1992). Scores taken as early as the elementary school years also appear to predict how many years a child will stay in school, although this might reflect the influence of social factors: children who achieve higher test scores are likely to receive greater amounts of encouragement from their teachers.

Beyond academic success, scores on intelligence tests have been found to predict several life outcomes, such as job performance (Barrett & Depinet, 1991). They have even been shown to predict how long a person is likely to live. In one study, women who had scored at least 1 standard deviation below average when they were 11 years old were only 75% as likely to live to age 76 as were women who scored higher (Whalley & Deary, 2001). One possibility is that longevity depends partly on learning, reasoning, and problem-solving skills that are useful in avoiding accidents and adhering to complicated treatment regimens—skills that are related to intelligence (Gottfredson & Deary, 2004). In an interesting twist on this story, one study found that efficiency of information processing—as measured by reaction time—accounted for the finding that people with high IQs live longer on average (Deary & Der, 2005).

THE CONCEPT OF GENERAL INTELLIGENCE   In the early twentieth century, British psychologist Charles Spearman found that people who tend to perform highly on one subscale of intelligence perform highly on others as well. This isn't to say that they correlate perfectly, but why should they? Someone who is gifted at math is not necessarily as prodigious in his or her vocabulary. Still, it is interesting that people who are good at one cognitive skill tend to be good at other cognitive tasks, so it's worth studying what's shared and what's specialized. This discovery became a major finding in the field of intelligence research and helped turn Spearman into one of its towering figures.

That said, Spearman noted that there seemed to be some source of individual variation that caused some people's scores to be higher than those of others across the board. He labeled this invisible source **general intelligence (g)** and the variation in the individual subtests **specific intelligences (s)**. Together, these types form Spearman's **two-factor theory of intelligence**. The distinctions between general and specific ability are similar to those that can be found in many domains. For example, a pro basketball player might excel at playing defense and be an overall high scorer but might not be particularly strong at making 3-point shots. Nevertheless, his or her general ability will likely be higher than that of the average recreational player.

The concept of general intelligence suggests that although there may be variation across many measures, a single *g* factor accounts for a large degree of

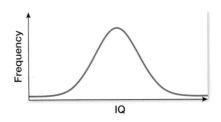

FIGURE 11.10 A normal distribution, or bell curve For any given population, the greatest concentration of IQ scores likely falls in the middle, with fewer test-takers represented as the scores become extremely high or extremely low.

variation among people. The finding that intelligence subtests correlate across individuals is so robust that at least one theorist has proposed that a "law of general intelligence" should be regarded as a fundamental principle of cognitive science (Jensen, 1998). However, others claim that variation among people can best be accounted for by assuming the existence of seven or more different dimensions of intelligence. How do researchers and theorists decide which number of intelligences makes the most sense? Often, they rely on a statistical procedure known as **factor analysis**, which takes several independently measured variables and determines the number of underlying factors (or **latent variables**) that best explains the data variance. In many cases, this process results in fewer factors than measures. **SEE FOR YOURSELF 11.1** provides a hypothetical example outside the realm of intelligence.

▶ **See for Yourself 11.1**

Factor Analysis

Stepping away from the intelligence domain for a moment, imagine that you plan to try online dating and want to determine which advertised traits attract the most interest on dating sites. You obtain access to thousands of dating profiles and information about the amount of interest each received. What variables do you measure? You might choose love of movies, enthusiasm for hiking, general disdain for people, love of books, enthusiasm for kayaking, enthusiasm for art museums, enthusiasm for camping, enthusiasm for bullying, and enthusiasm for vandalism (we didn't say it was a *good* dating website).

Your data might reveal that the variables of loving movies, books, and art museums correlate with each other. You might also notice that enthusiasms for hiking, camping, and kayaking correlate, as do enthusiasms for vandalism, bullying, and disdain for people. If you were to conduct a factor analysis of these nine variables, they might "load" onto—be consolidated

and summarized as—three underlying factors that could be categorized as love of arts, active lifestyle, and antisocial tendencies. You could then analyze the contributions of these factors to profile success, rather than the contributions of each variable on its own.

Key to this example is that the factor analysis identified three factors that accounted for variance among the profiles, even though they were not directly indexed by the individual measures. The ability to identify these latent variables is important for several reasons. For example, because love of camping, hiking, and kayaking correlated so highly with each other, they each emerge as accounting for less unique variance than if they were grouped into a more informative and representative construct. In intelligence research, this technique has played a central role in theorists' understanding of how many kinds of intelligence might exist.

A Factor Analysis of Online Dating Traits

	Movies	Books	Art	Hiking	Kayaking	Camping	Bullying	Disdain	Vandal
Movies	1.00								
Books	0.78[1]	1.00							
Art	0.56[1]	0.60[1]	1.00						
Hiking	0.05	0.13	0.21	1.00					
Kayaking	0.12	0.20	0.17	0.66[2]	1.00				
Camping	0.16	0.11	0.09	0.82[2]	0.56[2]	1.00			
Bullying	-0.03	-0.08	-0.10	0.09	0.05	-0.04	1.00		
Disdain	-0.19	-0.11	-0.20	-0.01	0.03	0.02	0.85[3]	1.00	
Vandal	-0.22	-0.04	0.12	-0.40	-0.12	-0.32	0.61[3]	0.81[3]	1.00

[1]Factor 1; [2]Factor 2; [3]Factor 3.

CRYSTALLIZED INTELLIGENCE AND FLUID INTELLIGENCE Raymond Cattell (1943, 1971), a student of Spearman, made an important and influential distinction within the intelligence literature by dividing g into **crystallized intelligence (Gc)** and **fluid intelligence (Gf)**. Crystallized intelligence pertains to people's knowledge, as reflected in tests of vocabulary and facts about the world. Fluid intelligence involves content-independent analytical processes, which come into play when discerning patterns in the environment, understanding analogies, and drawing inferences. Measures of fluid intelligence attempt to index this ability independently of experiences and knowledge and are sometimes regarded as central to—if not the very definition of—general intelligence (Lubinski, 2004).

The distinction between crystallized and fluid intelligence makes intuitive sense. Indeed, you might have noticed in your own experience that the ability to learn and use new knowledge (one of the core working definitions of intelligence) appears to be shaped by two very different components: the content of what we already know and the ease with which we can recognize patterns and regularities in the world and information around us. Imagine that you are trying to learn how to program in a new computer language. If you already know the basics of programming in one computer language, you will likely have an easier time than someone who has never programmed before. However, someone else might demonstrate a knack for understanding and applying general principles, allowing them to learn programming rapidly without prior experience.

But how can we measure fluid intelligence? How can tests tap into abilities without regard for one's knowledge? An influential approach has been to test people's abilities to perceive and learn patterns involving unfamiliar stimuli, as is done in the **Raven's Progressive Matrices** (Carpenter et al., 1990; Raven, 2000). In this test, people see configurations of an undisclosed pattern and must pick the next one in the sequence (**FIGURE 11.11**).

As our discussion shows, most intelligence research focuses on the individual or on what makes some people particularly intelligent. But people often find themselves working together and making decisions in groups. What makes some groups "smarter" than others? Is there anything akin to g at the group

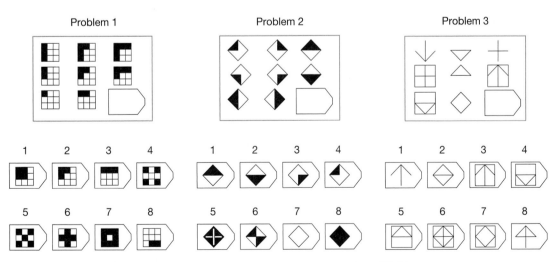

FIGURE 11.11 Examples of problems from the Raven's Progressive Matrices of fluid intelligence From the eight options below each problem box, choose the one that best completes the pattern. Try Problems 1–3 before seeing the answers: 3, 8, and 5. (From P. A. Carpenter et al. 1990. *Psychol Rev* 97: 404–431.)

level? In a study reported in the prestigious journal *Science*, a team of researchers investigated the possible existence of **collective intelligence**, or **c** (Woolley et al., 2010). **RESEARCH FOCUS 11.1** explores these experiments.

RESEARCH FOCUS 11.1

The Intelligence of Groups

In one experiment, Woolley and her colleagues (2010) assigned people to groups of three, wherein they collaborated on tasks involving visual puzzles, brainstorming, making moral judgments, negotiating about limited resources, and playing checkers against a computer. The results were intriguing: as with general intelligence, groups that perfromed well on some tasks also tended to perform well on the other tasks. This was driven neither by the average intelligence of the group members nor by the highest individual intelligence score within each group.

In a second experiment, the researchers assigned people to work in 152 groups consisting of two to five members each; the groups worked together on an even greater range of tasks. The results were largely the same as in the first experiment (replication being one of the most important indicators that a researcher might be onto something). Once again, the apparent existence of collective intelligence appeared unrelated to the average or highest individual intelligence score within a given group or to intuitive factors such as group cohesion, motivation, or satisfaction. However, three factors seemed to account for the collective intelligence of groups:

- The average social sensitivity of group members was positively correlated with collective intelligence. This feature was measured via the Reading the Mind in the Eyes test, in which people attempt to identify facial expressions of emotion when seeing only the models' eye.
- Groups in which members contributed relatively equally to the conversations tended to score high on

Across a variety of tasks, collective intelligence predicts performance better than individual intelligence.

collective intelligence; groups in which conversations were dominated by a few people exhibited lower collective intelligence.

- Groups with a higher proportion of female members scored higher in collective intelligence. The authors suggested that this result might have been driven by the female participants' higher scores in social sensitivity.

Of these factors, social sensitivity emerged as the strongest predictor. Although the jury is still out on the applicability of such findings to real-world teams, the next time you work on a group project, you may also want to ensure equal contributions from your group members and do what you can to foster social sensitivity.

ONE INTELLIGENCE OR MANY?   Although much research focuses on the notion of general intelligence, a complementary (or sometimes competing) view is that intelligence is better viewed as a collection of different competencies. Examples of this perspective can be traced back thousands of years. Aristotle suggested that people could exhibit theoretical intelligence, defined as the ability to learn the nuances of math, science, and complex reasoning, which he distinguished from practical intelligence, or the ability to govern one's actions wisely. He also suggested that people could be characterized in terms of their productive intelligence, defined as their ability to create and make things (Tigner & Tigner, 2000). This way of characterizing aspects of intelligence has been echoed in more modern times by theorists such as Robert Sternberg, whose **triarchic theory of intelligence** differentiates between analytical, practical, and creative intelligences (Sternberg, 1984).

According to Sternberg's theory, **analytical intelligence** maps roughly onto IQ measures and is the intelligence most linked with traditional notions of general intelligence. **Creative intelligence** involves people's abilities to reason in novel, or "non-entrenched," ways. **Practical intelligence** pertains to people's abilities to meet the challenges they encounter in everyday life. Each type relies on metacomponents, the kinds of executive processes that are crucial for planning, monitoring, and decision making (Sternberg, 1984), and on performance components, processes involved in putting plans and strategies into action. Despite its widespread influence, the triarchic theory of intelligence has been criticized in the face of evidence that the different forms of intelligence correlate with each other, questioning the assertion that they are separable (e.g., Brody, 2003).

Some theorists—such as L. L. Thurstone (1938)—argued against the notion of *g*, suggesting instead that evidence favors the existence of seven separate intelligences:

1. Verbal fluency
2. Comprehension
3. Numerical computation
4. Spatial ability
5. Associative memory
6. Reasoning
7. Perceptual speed

Like Spearman, Thurstone used factor analysis to derive his factors. In another multifactor theory of intelligence, arrived at via an analysis of more than 400 data sets, Carroll (1993) suggested three levels of factors: an overarching general intelligence, a middle level of factors similar to those identified by Thurstone, and a lower level made up of basic processes such as visual processing speed.

One of the most widely known accounts of independent intelligences is the **multiple intelligences theory** of Howard Gardner (1983, 1999). According to this theory, which argues against the notion of general intelligence, intelligence is best viewed as a collection of abilities that people use to solve problems or produce useful creations. These abilities or intelligences include (Gardner, 1999):

- Musical
- Bodily/kinesthetic
- Spatial
- Verbal
- Logical/mathematical
- Intrapersonal (managing oneself) and interpersonal (interacting with others) domains
- An ability to understand patterns in the environment

A key observation that proponents of multiple intelligences often highlight is that people can be profoundly impaired in some mental skills while retaining impressive skills in another domain. Such **savant syndrome** is characterized by generally low intelligence (as traditionally measured) but incredible skill in a particular domain. Kim Peek, the original inspiration for the savant character in the film *Rain Man* (1988), had exceptional memory. Despite his seemingly low IQ, he knew all the area and zip codes in the United States and could name all the television stations that transmitted to those regions. He could also identify most classical music compositions, along with their composer's birth place and birth date, and remember the approximately 7,600 books he had read in great detail.

The theory of multiple intelligences has been profoundly influential in school settings, where it speaks to teachers' experiences working with hundreds of children every day. There is even a school, the Howard Gardner School in Alexandria, Virginia, dedicated to providing a curriculum that

Kim Peek demonstrated incredible feats of memory despite having a seemingly low IQ. Individuals with such savant syndrome have been argued to support notions of multiple intelligences.

accommodates children who learn best through nontraditional means. But this theory is not without its critics; some argue that it is not well supported by objective data (e.g., Chen, 2004).

The Information-Processing Approach

Several researchers have sought to understand how cognitive and neural processes contribute to intelligence, a perspective referred to as the information-processing approach. For example, research has examined the degree to which factors such as processing speed, prior knowledge, and use of cognitive strategies account for intelligence scores and intelligent behavior. This approach has seen some success: measures of executive function, cognitive control, and working memory seem to correlate more with *g* than do measures of implicit learning and face recognition.

The roots of the information-processing approach can be traced back to the British polymath Sir Francis Galton (1822–1911) who regarded intelligence as a relatively fixed, biologically driven capacity. Inspired by Darwin's work on evolution (as well he should have been—Darwin was his half-cousin!), Galton published *Hereditary Genius* (1869), in which he suggested that intellectual ability was biologically inherited and transmitted from generation to generation. (One can't help but wonder if Galton's interest in intelligence was a case of research as "me-search," the idea that people do research to better understand themselves. A brilliant individual, gifted and productive in many areas, he developed the statistical notions of correlation and factor analysis, which remain staples of the field. He also developed the first weather maps and furthered the field of forensics by creating a system for classifying fingerprints, to name just a few of his accomplishments.)

Galton hypothesized that the properties of neural transmission contributing to intelligence also contribute to enhanced perceptual, sensory, and motor abilities. This hypothesis guided his attempts to measure intelligence: setting up a lab at London's 1884 International Exhibition, he tested thousands of visitors on reaction time and sensory acuity. Contrary to his predictions, he found no relationship between these measures and the criteria that he regarded as being influenced by intelligence (e.g., social status).

MENTAL SPEED   Although Galton found little support for his hypothesis, more recent studies suggest that he wasn't completely wrong: some evidence indicates that IQ scores are correlated with speed of processing (Ryan et al., 2000; Vernon & Weese, 1993). For example, in studies measuring **inspection time** (the shortest exposure at which people can render accurate judgments), people have viewed brief displays of two parallel lines and tried to determine which was longer (with the typical ratio being 1:1.4). Such studies have found that inspection time correlates with measures of both fluid and crystallized intelligence (Sheppard & Vernon, 2008; Vernon & Kantor, 1986).

Similar approaches have asked people to determine whether pairs of letters (e.g., *EE* and *Ee*) are physically identical or have the same name (**FIGURE 11.12**). Judging that the letters have the same name requires access to and scanning of long-term memory, but judging that they are physically identical does not; it has been argued that the difference in response time reflects the efficiency and speed of pulling information from memory (e.g., Posner et al.,

Match each uppercase letter to its lowercase letter.

FIGURE 11.12 IQ is correlated with how you quickly you can perform tasks such as matching letters   This is an informal paper-based version with pictures added to make it friendly for kids, but letter-matching performance is better measured in carefully controlled tasks run on computers.

1969). Intriguingly, evidence suggests that students who exhibit high scholastic aptitude tend to perform such tasks more quickly than their peers do (Lindley & Smith, 1992). However, a pitfall in the study of mental speed is that its many measures—including computerized response-time tasks, paper-and-pencil tests, and tests on low-level sensory acuity—may be confounded with other skills not related to intelligence. For example, great vision may allow you to perform some tasks more quickly, but it doesn't directly show that you're smarter—otherwise, intelligence tests would be replaced with eye exams.

WORKING MEMORY AND EXECUTIVE FUNCTION   It has been suggested that links between processing speed and IQ are driven by processing speed's role in the efficiency and capacity of working memory (see Chapter 5). Given that working memory is central to holding and manipulating information, it makes intuitive sense that the factors that enhance it enhance IQ. Indeed, measures of working memory correlate moderately highly with measures of fluid intelligence (Miller & Vernon, 1992). For example, a task known as the three-back test has a high correlation. In this test, people must indicate when a presented item is the same as the item they saw or heard three items previously, which requires that participants not only keep a number of items in mind but also constantly update their store so that they add each new item and discard the fourth previous one (Conway et al., 2003; Engle, 2002; Gray et al., 2003).

Another type of working memory task, known as the active-span task, involves alternating between different types of questions. For example, people might be asked to judge whether a mathematical equation is true and then to read a word aloud, with these two tasks switching across multiple trials. Such working memory tasks have been shown to correlate with reasoning ability, reading comprehension, and IQ (e.g., Carpenter et al., 1990; Engle et al., 1992; Just & Carpenter, 1992; Kyllonen & Christal, 1990).

Limitations of Intelligence

Although evidence suggests that individual differences in intelligence are predictive of real-life outcomes, intelligence—at least as traditionally defined and measured—is not the only determining factor. For example, traditional approaches fail to consider people's ability to recognize and manage emotions (both theirs and others'), something that has been labeled **emotional intelligence** (Mayer & Salovey, 1997). Emotional intelligence has been found to predict both more positive social relationships and less deviant behavior (see Salovey & Grewal, 2005).

Underscoring the possibility that real-world outcomes can depend on more than just raw processing power, a person's beliefs about whether his or her abilities are hardwired or malleable can be a greater predictor of achievement than scores on intelligence tests. Such beliefs have been referred to as a **mindset** (Dweck, 2015). Some people maintain a **fixed mindset**, in which they regard qualities such as intelligence as unchanging. Others hold what Dweck (2006) calls a **growth mindset**, which regards intelligence as something that can improve with practice and hard work. Some suggest that those with a growth mindset may perform better than those with a fixed mindset (e.g., Blackwell et al., 2007; but see Bahnik & Vranka, 2017).

Many perspectives also ignore people's **creativity**, the ability to arrive at completely novel solutions and creations (see Chapter 10). Let's suppose that humankind is forever doomed to lose to computers at strategic games like chess and Go. If you were the CEO of a company, or the principal investigator of a lab, should you ditch human employees in favor of supercomputers? Perhaps not: People have the advantage of being able to do lots of different tasks. They can solve different types of problems, and they have the creativity to come up with novel solutions when traditional ones don't work.

Finally, there are long-running controversies about whether there are group differences between males and females or between different races (Deary, 2012; Nisbett et al., 2012). These debates focus on whether any reports of group differences are valid, and if they are, whether they can be attributed to innate, biological differences or sociological factors such as bias and injustice against women or marginalized racial groups (Steele, 1997). A review of the literature reveals stronger evidence for socioeconomic influences on IQ over genetic explanations (Nisbett et al., 2012). It is also useful to remember that individual differences in IQ are much greater than any purported group differences. Namely, don't judge people by their gender or race.

➤ CHECKPOINT 11.2

1. What is intelligence?
2. What are some differences between research on intelligence and other areas of cognitive psychology?
3. How does factor analysis distinguish general intelligence and specific intelligence?
4. What is the difference between crystallized and fluid intelligence? What are some other examples of different types of intelligence?
5. Describe evidence for the role of mental speed, working memory, and executive function in intelligence.
6. What are some limitations of the concept or application of intelligence?

11.3 The Development of Knowledge and Intelligence

How do we come to learn about the world? How does intelligence develop over time and across schooling? How do we go from being passive and helpless babies to active and thinking grownups, unique from each other? Coming into the world, babies seem similar in that they don't appear to be capable of doing much except to sleep a lot, but then they quickly diverge and develop into unique children and adults. How much knowledge do infants possess when they are born, and what role does the environment play throughout their growth? This classic question is known as the nature–nurture debate.

Nature and Nurture

Nature refers to skills that develop regardless of experience—suggesting that specialized learning systems are present or native at birth (nativism). Philosophers such as Plato and René Descartes argued that knowledge is more than acquired associations, explaining how people naturally differ in talent and temperament, born equipped to learn specific types of information such as language, physics, numbers, and psychology—domains known as **core knowledge** (Spelke & Kinzler, 2007). Children come into the world with these core cognitive systems that equip them to acquire a language, understand physical and numerical properties of the world, and socialize with their caregivers. Infants universally around the world share these core domains, while experiences serve to elaborate and refine these skills over the course of development.

In contrast to nativism is the empiricist view, which according to John Locke asserts that infants are like a blank canvas, a tabula rasa. Human knowledge is built up by forming associations through experience. Empiricists such as George Berkeley and David Hume described development in terms of general learning, viewing infants as having very little innate bias toward particular kinds of information.

Rather than treating nature and nurture as mutually exclusive, both factors shape development. Much is learned from experience, but infants come into the world with innate capabilities and assumptions that help them learn more effectively. Studying the development of knowledge informs us not only of innate and learned capabilities, it also gives us insight into mature cognition. Furthermore, the study of cognitive development has direct implications for social policy, education, and welfare (Keil, 2013). For example, how important is early schooling? What are the effects of poverty? How can we best help students with special needs? Is it ever acceptable to separate children from their parents?

Studying identical twins helps tease apart the effects of nature versus nurture on intelligence.

BIOLOGICAL CONTRIBUTIONS TO INTELLIGENCE   Illustrating a role for nature, intelligence is highly heritable. **Heritability** refers to the extent that genetics can explain variation (differences) among people. It is quantified by the following formula, where h^2 represents the **heritability coefficient**:

$$h^2 = \text{variance due to genes} / \text{total variance}$$

The more that variations in intelligence can be attributed to genes, the closer the IQs of close relatives should be. One challenge to conducting such analyses is that siblings often grow up in a shared environment, making it hard to determine what the relative contributions of genes and environment are. To isolate the role of genes, researchers compare IQs among both identical and fraternal twins. Another approach compares the IQs of identical twins who were raised apart (e.g., through adoption into separate homes at an early age). In some studies, investigators estimate heritability by comparing the degree to which the IQs of identical twins are correlated with how much those of fraternal twins are correlated. Because both types of twins have comparable environmental influences, the degree to which the IQs of identical twins correlate more strongly helps estimate genetic (heritable) influences (e.g., Plomin, 1990). Such methods suggest that the contribution of genetics plays a larger role among adults than among children and adolescents. This conclusion makes sense: some characteristics (such as height) develop more fully as people mature, and as adults set out on their own, they and their siblings experience less of a shared environment.

With recent advances in **genotyping**, whereby the presence or absence of particular genes is investigated using biological samples provided by participants, investigators have been able to look more directly at the role of genes in shaping IQ. However, the evidence is mixed. In one attempt to replicate published links between general intelligence and 12 different genes (with a combined data set of almost 10,000 data points), only 1 out of 32 tests was nominally significant, a much lower success rate than predicted. Thus, many reports of genetic associations with general intelligence might be "false positives" (Chabris et al., 2012).

Consistent with notions of a close link between fluid intelligence and working memory, one neuroimaging study found that people who scored high in fluid intelligence exhibited greater activation in lateral prefrontal and parietal cortex when engaging in difficult verbal and nonverbal working memory tasks than did people with low scores (Gray et al., 2003) (**FIGURE 11.13**). A study using positron emission technology (PET) revealed that activation of frontal lobes might contribute to individual differences in g. The researchers found that the frontal areas associated with working memory (e.g., DLPFC) were highly responsive regardless of whether or not the general intelligence tasks the participants completed were visual or verbal (Duncan, 2000).

Beyond prefrontal and parietal cortex, intelligence may reflect the coordinated activity across multiple areas of the brain. One way to assess this is by

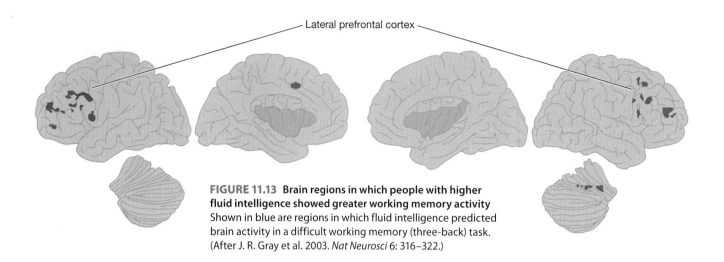

Lateral prefrontal cortex

FIGURE 11.13 Brain regions in which people with higher fluid intelligence showed greater working memory activity Shown in blue are regions in which fluid intelligence predicted brain activity in a difficult working memory (three-back) task. (After J. R. Gray et al. 2003. *Nat Neurosci* 6: 316–322.)

measuring how different brain regions are in synchrony or out of synchrony with each other. From such brain scans, researchers can estimate a person's IQ (Finn et al., 2015).

CAN INTELLIGENCE BE INCREASED?   From the empiricist, nurture approach, an important question behind much of intelligence research is whether training can increase people's overall intelligence. Fundamentally, education is based on the idea that a person's knowledge and skills can be enhanced. However, beyond school settings, expert opinions vary on whether other forms of training, such as computer-based brain training programs, can improve everyday cognition.

Within the span of 2 months during 2014, one group of more than 70 psychologists and neuroscientists published an open letter decrying claims that brain training regimens can improve real-world cognitive performance (Max Planck Institute for Human Development and Stanford Center on Longevity, 2014), and another group of 133 therapists and scientists published a different open letter arguing that such cognitive benefits are real! Notions that brain training can improve cognition tap into a vein of optimism that can be exploited. In 2016, Lumosity—a company specializing in brain training programs—agreed to pay the Federal Trade Commission (FTC) $2 million to settle charges of deceptive advertising. The FTC argued that the company did not have the science to support the claim that its product—an app with cognitively challenging games and exercises—could enhance users' performance at work and in school and slow the progression of age-related cognitive impairments (Federal Trade Commission, 2016). In the wake of such controversies, an extensive survey of the literature suggested that although training can improve performance on the trained cognitive tasks, there is little evidence that such benefits generalize beyond those tasks (Simons et al., 2016). As an example of one of the shortcomings identified in the relevant literature, the authors noted that many studies failed to account for what's known as a **placebo effect**. In this case, a placebo effect comes into play when people who undergo extensive training guess the hypothesis of the study in which they are taking part. This intuiting then results in their subsequent cognitive performance being tainted by their expectations of how they should perform rather than reflecting an objective improvement in cognitive ability. Other potential problems stem from the use of less than ideal (or absent) control groups for comparison.

When it comes to questions about whether training regimens can improve memory, attention, and intelligence, the principle of **neuroplasticity**—wherein neural connections change with experience—gives us reason to think the answer is yes. Nevertheless, the evidence is mixed. Some positive evidence comes from a study in which people who trained on difficult working memory tasks performed better on tests of fluid intelligence than did people who had no such training (Jaeggi et al., 2008; also see Au et al., 2015). In a follow-up study on children, only those who improved on the working memory task exhibited increases in fluid intelligence (Jaeggi et al., 2011). Other studies have found that such improvements did not translate into higher fluid intelligence (Colom et al., 2013; Harrison et al., 2013).

Some evidence suggests music education provides at least one example of training that can improve cognitive ability.

Some evidence suggests that, rather than transferring to real-world cognitive performance (the "holy grail" of brain training), the benefits of brain training are task-specific. In one massive study, more than 11,000 participants trained several times per week for 6 weeks on tasks designed to improve memory, attention, reasoning, planning, and visuospatial skills. The results revealed that people improved in each of these tasks, yet the benefits did not carry over to even closely related but untrained tasks (Owen et al., 2010).

Some kinds of cognitive exercise can broadly improve cognitive performance. Take musical education: several studies—but not all (Sala & Gobet, 2020)— have found that music training and education produce benefits for measures of intelligence and academic performance (Ho et al., 2003; Hyde, 2009; Moreno et al., 2011; Schellenberg, 2004).

Piaget's Theory of Cognitive Development, with Modern Updates

Education and training aside, much of cognitive development occurs naturally. We take for granted our understanding of the physical world, but how do infants come to learn about basic physical properties like gravity, momentum, and solidity? Are newborns born with this knowledge or is it learned? Jean Piaget (1896–1980) was one of the most influential and impressive psychologists to have tried to answer these questions. Although many of his ideas no longer hold today, they have influenced modern research in such a fundamental way that we can organize our study of cognitive development around how modern studies have updated his thinking.

Piaget believed that development progresses in discrete periods and stages, with qualitative leaps in abilities occurring between them, as follows:

- The sensorimotor period, from birth to 2 years
- The preoperational period, from 2 to 7 years
- The concrete operational period, from 7 to 12 years
- The formal operational period, from 12 years and beyond

The actual age brackets are less important than the sequence of hypothesized periods. Piaget proposed that within each period, children acquire new ways of understanding the world, which trigger a transformation that leads to the progression to the next period. Each period is necessary for the next. Most important, Piaget emphasized the importance of active exploration and engagement. Children are not passive, nor are they blank tablets. They are like little investigators, proactively learning about the world around them. Read more about how infants learn in **THINK FOR YOURSELF 11.1**.

► **Think for Yourself 11.1**

Studying Infant Abilities

Infants cannot talk, and they can perform only a small number of limited behaviors, requiring psychologists to create ingenious methods to study their abilities. Measurable in infants are their looking preferences and looking time. Whenever an infant shows a preference for one stimulus over another, either by fixating it or by staring at it longer, one can infer that the infant perceives the difference. The **preferential looking method** is based on the fact that infants prefer to look at patterns rather than at blank displays. For example, when infants are presented with dim, subtle patterns that push the limits of their visual acuity, any preference for such a pattern reveals that the infants can "see" it over a blank display. Another method, **habituation** (discussed in Chapter 7), is based on how infants (and older individuals) get bored by looking at the same thing over and over again. When you show a stimulus repeatedly, the first time the infant will look for a certain amount of time; the infant will then look at each repetition for a measurably shorter amount of time until a new stimulus is shown. When the infant looks longer at the novel stimulus, this is known as **dishabituation**, revealing that the infant noticed the difference.

By measuring preferential looking and habituation, researchers demonstrated that visual acuity, color perception, and depth perception improve over time. More complex forms of understanding can be measured as well. Face perception is important for social interactions, and from the moment of birth, newborns prefer intact faces over nonsense faces that have the same features (e.g., eyes, nose, mouth)

FIGURE A   Newborns prefer intact faces (left) over nonsense faces (right) that contain the same features but scrambled into a meaningless configuration. (After P. R. Koopman and E. W. Ames. 1968. *Child Dev* 39: 481–487.)

but scrambled into a meaningless configuration (**FIGURE A**) (Goren et al., 1975). Infants as young as newborns even prefer attractive faces over unattractive faces (Langlois et al., 1987; Slater et al., 1998). Newborns have no race preference, but by 3 months they show an own-race preference (Kelly et al., 2005). This is called **perceptual narrowing** (Kelly et al., 2007), which also occurs for sounds in one's native language (see Chapter 8).

SENSORIMOTOR PERIOD   Across the first 2 years of life, the **sensorimotor period** is essential for developing knowledge about the physicality of objects. Infants interacts with objects, including parts of their own body, as shown in **FIGURE 11.14**. A basic property to know about the physical world is **object permanence**, which is the understanding that objects persist and are stable even when they are out of sight. Piaget thought that infants lacked object permanence, such that they failed to understand that objects continued to exist once they went out of sight. To test this hypothesis, Piaget observed that infants would not look for objects placed out of view behind an occluder, such as a toy hidden under a blanket. From that observation, he concluded that for infants, out of sight meant out of mind. Piaget believed that across the sensorimotor period, infants had to learn about object permanence.

Subsequent research has shown that infants' knowledge about the physical world is more sophisticated and advanced than Piaget had assumed. Indeed, modern research has convincingly demonstrated that babies are a lot smarter than originally thought! In contrast to Piaget's claim that infants lacked object permanence, which was based on how infants did not reach out for objects that were hidden under a blanket (in plain view), it turns out that

FIGURE 11.14 Sensorimotor period   A baby in the sensorimotor period, actively exploring her own feet.

infants know that the object persisted, and they just had difficulty or a lack of motivation to retrieve it (why bother?).

In a classic study by Renée Baillargeon (1987), demonstrating that infants have object permanence and physical knowledge that objects are solid (that they do not disappear into thin air), infants watched a screen swing back and forth, reaching the table on either side of the swinging motion (**FIGURE 11.15**). When this is shown repeatedly to infants aged 3.5 months, they habituate to the event. Then the experimenter introduces a box on the far side of the screen away from the infant. Physics determines that as the screen swings, it must stop where it hits the box, even though the box would be out of the infant's view. This is called the possible event condition. In the impossible event, like magic, the screen continues to swing through its full arc, reaching the table. (This magic is made possible by having the box drop through a hidden opening in the table's surface.) The question is whether infants look longer at the possible event or the impossible event. Even though the latter is more consistent with the original swinging motion to which infants have habituated, infants look at the impossible event than the possible event. It is as if they understand that the screen should not have been able to swing all the way down to the table because of the box. These looking-time differences reveal an infant's understanding of object solidity. Through clever experiments like this, researchers have demonstrated that infants possess knowledge of several additional physical principles such as gravity, inertia, and physical causation (Graner et al., 2013; Kim & Spelke, 1992; Oakes & Cohen, 1990; Spelke et al., 1994).

One of the most impressive demonstrations of infant cognition is an understanding of number concepts and basic arithmetic (Fei & Carey, 1996; Feigenson et al., 2004; Wynn, 1992). Infants can certainly distinguish a display of three objects versus two objects, but that may be simply because the objects are perceptually different. Infants are not only sensitive to numerosity; they can also add and subtract (Wynn, 1992). Five-month-old infants were habituated to a single toy placed on a stage (**FIGURE 11.16**). Then a screen came up, hiding the toy on the stage. At this point, the infant watched the experimenter take another identical toy and place it behind the screen. Then the screen was removed and two alternative scenarios were presented. In some trials, there were two toy mice on the stage (possible outcome). In other trials, there was only one toy on the stage (impossible outcome). If infants have a basic understanding of arithmetic and object solidity (the notion that objects are solid and have mass), and if their memory is good enough to remember the first object, they should expect two toy mouse figures on the stage (expected condition), and they should be surprised if only one toy mouse is left on the stage (unexpected condition). Infants looked longer at the unexpected condition in which only one mouse was left on the stage, which can be interpreted as a violation of their expectation, and as suggestive evidence that infants can add. Subtraction can be demonstrated by starting with two displays on the screen, putting the screen up, taking one of the toys away, and then leaving one (possible) or two (impossible) for infants to view.

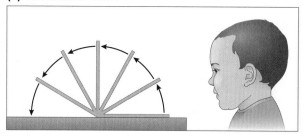

(A) Habituation event

(B)

Possible event

Impossible event

The infant stares longer at the screen when it rotates a full 180°.

FIGURE 11.15 Screen-and-box study of object permanence **(A)** An infant is habituated to a screen rotating back and forth on a table, making a 180° arc. **(B)** A box is placed in the path of the screen. The infant gazes at the screen longer when it proceeds to rotate the full 180 degrees (i.e., as if it went right through the box) compared to the situation shown in the top panel of (B), in which the screen stops where the box should have been. This finding suggests that infants expect the block to obstruct the screen, and that they visually represent the block despite the fact they can no longer see it. (After D. Purves et al. 2008. *Principles of Cognitive Neuroscience*. Oxford University Press/ Sinauer: Sunderland, MA. Based on R. Baillargeon. 1987. *Dev Psychol* 23: 655–664.)

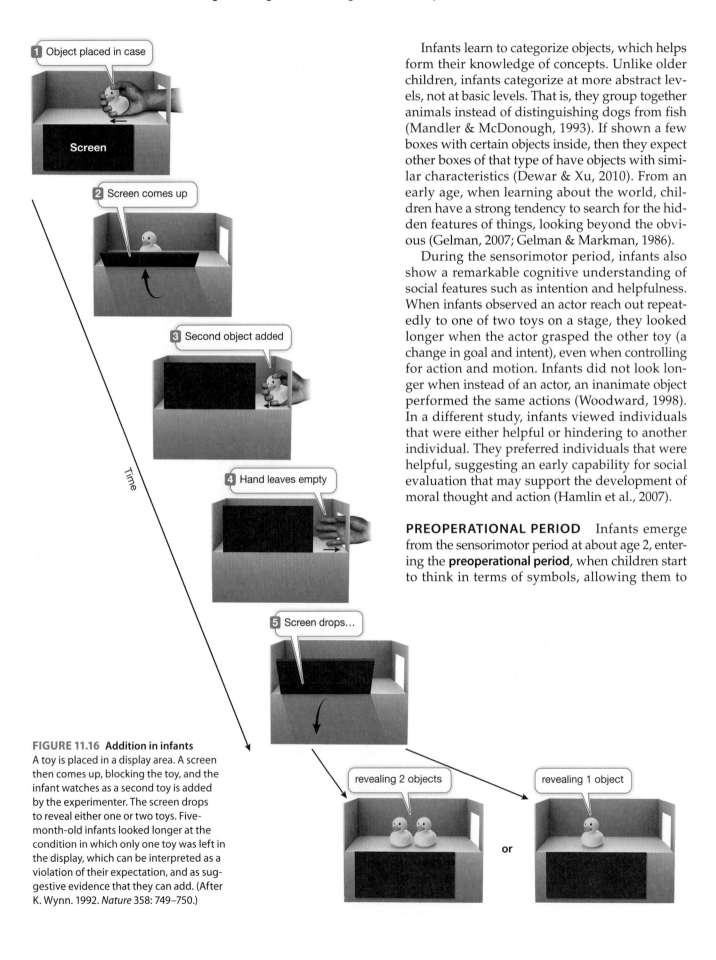

FIGURE 11.16 Addition in infants A toy is placed in a display area. A screen then comes up, blocking the toy, and the infant watches as a second toy is added by the experimenter. The screen drops to reveal either one or two toys. Five-month-old infants looked longer at the condition in which only one toy was left in the display, which can be interpreted as a violation of their expectation, and as suggestive evidence that they can add. (After K. Wynn. 1992. *Nature* 358: 749–750.)

Infants learn to categorize objects, which helps form their knowledge of concepts. Unlike older children, infants categorize at more abstract levels, not at basic levels. That is, they group together animals instead of distinguishing dogs from fish (Mandler & McDonough, 1993). If shown a few boxes with certain objects inside, then they expect other boxes of that type of have objects with similar characteristics (Dewar & Xu, 2010). From an early age, when learning about the world, children have a strong tendency to search for the hidden features of things, looking beyond the obvious (Gelman, 2007; Gelman & Markman, 1986).

During the sensorimotor period, infants also show a remarkable cognitive understanding of social features such as intention and helpfulness. When infants observed an actor reach out repeatedly to one of two toys on a stage, they looked longer when the actor grasped the other toy (a change in goal and intent), even when controlling for action and motion. Infants did not look longer when instead of an actor, an inanimate object performed the same actions (Woodward, 1998). In a different study, infants viewed individuals that were either helpful or hindering to another individual. They preferred individuals that were helpful, suggesting an early capability for social evaluation that may support the development of moral thought and action (Hamlin et al., 2007).

PREOPERATIONAL PERIOD Infants emerge from the sensorimotor period at about age 2, entering the **preoperational period**, when children start to think in terms of symbols, allowing them to represent ideas. Language is a major hallmark of this period, which runs from age 2 to 7, as discussed in Chapter 8.

Piaget believed that young children lacked the ability to think abstractly. For example, a preoperational child will note that a ball of dough gets wider when flattened with a rolling pin (Keil, 2013)—but the same child would fail at a **conservation task**, which tests how physical properties remain conserved (do not change) even when their appearance is changed. As an example of a conservation task, children are asked to compare the number of coins in each of two equal lines. Then the experimenter spreads them apart, and the child says that the one with a longer line has more coins (**FIGURE 11.17**). This failure suggests that young children do not understand conservation.

However, it is also possible that the child did not understand what the researcher was asking. The question can be confusing for kids—why would an adult ask me the same question when they themselves changed the length? In a different version of the task, a naughty teddy bear messes up the display—in this case, preschoolers do better, saying that the number of objects did not change. So contrary to Piaget's initial proposal, young children are now known to have good conservation skills (McGarrigle & Donaldson, 1974).

An understanding of space also develops over childhood. We discussed the difference between egocentric and allocentric spatial frames of reference in Chapter 7. Young children are egocentric, perceiving spatial relations from their

(A) Conservation of liquid volume

(B) Conservation of numbers

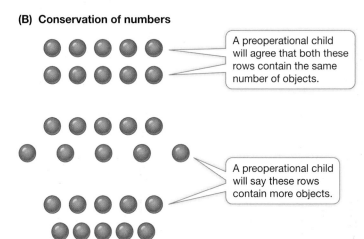

A preoperational child will agree that both these rows contain the same number of objects.

A preoperational child will say these rows contain more objects.

FIGURE 11.17 Examples of conservation tasks   (A) Preoperational children tend to make mistakes on conservation of liquid tests, thinking that the taller glass contains more water. (B) A preoperational child agrees that both top rows have the same number of objects. A preoperational child will say the longer rows toward the bottom of the figure contain more objects. (After S. M. Breedlove. 2015. *Principles of Psychology*. Oxford University Press/Sinauer: Sunderland, MA.)

FIGURE 11.18 Piaget's three mountain task   To test egocentrism in young children, the child is asked questions about what the scene looks like from the doll's point of view. (After J. Piaget and B. Inhelder. 1956. *The Child's Conception of Space.* Routledge & Kegan Paul: London.)

own point of view, and are less adept at allocentric frames of reference (based on the external environment and not focused on one's own location in it). In **FIGURE 11.18**, the child is seated at one end of the table, and a doll is at the other. With a selection of pictures, the child can be asked what the mountain scene looks like to the doll. Or you can show a picture of one of the four views of the mountain scene, and ask the child to place the doll in the position that would yield that view. Children younger than 7 are egocentric, not able to demonstrate how the scene would look from a point of view different from their own. That said, consider a "hide-and-seek" example, such as asking the child to place a doll where it could hide from a police officer. This requires understanding the police officer's viewpoint, and children are more successful with this task (Hughes & Donaldson, 1979).

Children between the ages of 2 and 3 begin to be able to use symbolic representations or models. Adults use map apps to get around, and we take it for granted that the maps represent the world we are trying to navigate. Map representations are like models that correspond to the real world. To test whether young children understand that a model can represent the world, an experimenter shows a child a small model of a room, such as a dollhouse, and hides a small object in it while the child watches (**FIGURE 11.19**). Then the child is introduced to a real full-size room that corresponds to the model, and is asked to find a larger version of the object in the bigger room. Three-year-old children can do this task, but 2.5-year-old children struggle, likely because they can't make the connection between the dollhouse and the real room—that is, mapping the representation to reality. As a clever instruction, the experimenter introduced a magic "shrinking machine" to illustrate

(A)

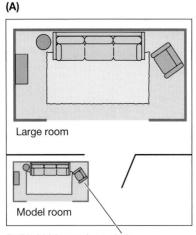

Doll is hidden under a chair
in the model room

(B)

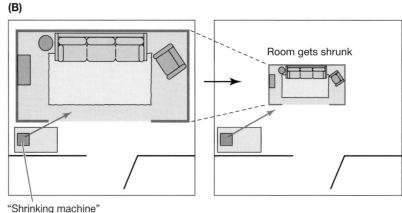

FIGURE 11.19 Children aged 2.5 years have difficulty understanding that a model can represent the world   **(A)** Using the model, the child is told that a doll is hidden under the chair (purple chair in this figure). Then the child is taken into an actual room that is a real-size version of the model that they just saw. However, the child is not able to use the model's hint to find the doll in the real room because they don't understand the model as a representation of the room. **(B)** To help the child match the model to the room, they are shown a "shrinking machine" that makes the doll small enough to fit into the model room. When told that the shrinking machine can also make the room as small as the model, they are able to use the model to find where the doll is hidden in the larger room. (After C. Tamis-LeMonda. 2021. *Child Development: Contexts and Cascades.* Oxford University Press: New York. Based on J. S. DeLoache et al. 1997. *Psychol Sci* 8: 308–313.)

that the dollhouse room was just a miniature of the larger room next to it. When given this information to better link the model to the world, the younger children performed much better (DeLoache, 1987; DeLoache et al., 1997).

CONCRETE OPERATIONAL PERIOD AND FORMAL OPERATIONAL PERIOD   The **concrete operational period**, defined as the time when children acquire mental **operators** (thinking and reasoning abilities) that allow for conservation of properties even as objects change, begins around age 7, although as noted earlier, children may have these operators before age 7. The **formal operational period**, when scientific thinking skills begin to emerge, begins around age 12 (Inhelder & Piaget, 1958). Formal operational skills in scientific tasks allow a child to isolate variables and see how they change when systematically manipulated one at a time (Kuhn, 1989; Kuhn & Brannock, 1977). Children without formal operational skills will vary things randomly. For example, if you want to understand what determines the length of time for a pendulum to swing back and forth, you can vary the length of the pendulum's string, the pendulum bob's weight, or the height from which the bob is let go, setting the pendulum into motion (**FIGURE 11.20**). All three variables can be changed, and children in the concrete operational period do not vary these systematically one at a time, while formal operational children do. Ultimately, string length is critical and the bob weight and drop height do not matter. Not all children achieve full competence in formal operations.

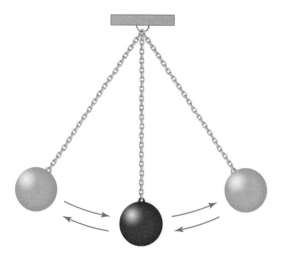

FIGURE 11.20 Formal operational skills are needed to determine what affects the length of time for a pendulum to swing back and forth   To answer this, you should separately vary the length of the string, the bob weight, or the height from which the bob is set into motion.

Schools play an important role in cognitive development and social development. Schooling increases intelligence. The number of years of schooling influences academic performance (Ceci, 1991), and as interesting evidence of the positive impact of schooling, intelligence scores drop over summer vacation (Cooper et al., 1996).

➤ CHECKPOINT 11.3

1. What is the nature–nurture debate?
2. What are some ways that researchers can investigate the role of biology in shaping intelligence?
3. What are reasons to think that intelligence can be increased through training, and what are some of the shortcomings of the studies purporting to demonstrate this?
4. Describe the preferential looking and habituation methods of studying infant abilities.
5. What is the evidence that infants have object permanence?
6. What is a conservation task? When do children in the preoperational period succeed or fail at conservation tasks?
7. What do formal operational skills allow children to do in scientific reasoning tasks?

Chapter Summary

1.1 Explain how categories are defined and represented in the mind and brain.

Through our perceptual experiences, actions, and thoughts, we acquire knowledge about the world. According to embodied cognition, the brain stores knowledge using common mechanisms for perception, action, and knowledge. To organize this information, categorization groups items or ideas together to make it easier to communicate concepts, and to infer other properties and features of concepts (e.g., when you say "dog," you communicate a pet with four legs that is friendly, barks, and likes to take walks). Finally, categories permit better decisions and predictions. There are many ways to define categories. One way is to define categories according to typical features (e.g., birds have wings). Exemplars within a category tend to be similar to one another, which is known as family resemblance. Categories can also be determined by definitions (e.g., an even number is divisible by 2). Brain data suggest that at least some forms of knowledge are stored categorically with a distinction between living things and human-made artifacts. Another distinction found in the brain is between knowledge that is primarily sensory (e.g., flower) and primarily functional (e.g., pen).

Q: Consider the way we might categorize types of college students. For example, when observing your own peer groups, are you aware of different personality types or any form of hierarchy? Are any stereotypical character types taking your attention, along the lines of those depicted in movies, novels, and TV shows? If so, how would you label these "types" as categories of students?

11.2 Discuss subtleties in the meaning of "intelligence."

Intelligence is the ability to reason, solve problems, and gain new knowledge. Research on intelligence focuses on individual differences and the utility of intelligence measures within society, such as predicting academic success. The psychometric approach seeks to measure intelligence, such as the intelligence quotient, and to characterize the behaviors that IQ predicts. Factor analysis helps identify why some people are better or worse at an array of tasks, known as general intelligence, as well as specific skills that vary independent of general intelligence. Another distinction is between crystallized intelligence, which reflects knowledge, and fluid intelligence, which supports analytical skills independent of knowledge. Overall, rather than a single type of intelligence, multiple forms seem to exist. The information-processing approach aims to identify the neurocognitive processes involved in intelligent behavior, using tasks that incorporate mental speed, working memory, or executive function. Although intelligence is rich and practically useful, it is limited by not incorporating the role of emotions and creativity in predicting everyday behavior and success.

Q: There are many ways to be successful in school and in life. Do intelligence tests cover the range of abilities important for doing well in school? How does doing well in school predict how one will do in life? Consider the many ways and examples a person can make an impact in life without high grades in school.

11.3 Outline how cognitive capacities develop across childhood.

Both knowledge and intelligence increase enormously over the course of development, as the forces of nature (genetics) and nurture (environment) interact. Nativists believe that specialized learning systems are present at birth, while empiricists believe that human knowledge and skills must be acquired through experience. As an example of both influences, intelligence is highly heritable, but it is also modified by learning and education. To study the skills that infants bring into the world, two major methods include preferential looking and habituation. Piaget, a prominent psychologist, proposed that infants and children interact with the world in qualitatively different ways from one period to the next. Piaget posited that infants lacked object permanence and that young children were challenged to conserve object properties such as number and size. However, modern research has shown that infants and children are more sophisticated than originally thought, demonstrating evidence for both object permanence and conservation when presented with the right kinds of tasks to reveal these capabilities. In the final period of development, adolescent children learn thinking skills important for scientific and abstract reasoning.

Q: What are your own views on nature versus nurture? Can you cite a specific example (whether from your personal life or from your observations) to support one or the other of these views as the prominent driving force in human development? If you have siblings, how do you differ from them and why?

Key Terms

ad-hoc categories
analytical intelligence
artificial intelligence (AI)
basic-level category
bell curve
categorization
collective intelligence (c)
concepts
concrete operational period
connectionism/parallel distributed processing/neural nets
conservation task
core knowledge
creative intelligence
creativity
crystallized intelligence (Gc)
dishabituation
domain-specific hypothesis
embodied cognition/grounded cognition
emotional intelligence
excitatory
exemplar-based categorization
factor analysis
family resemblance
feature-based categorization

fixed mindset
fluid intelligence (Gf)
formal operational period
general intelligence (g)
genotyping
graded membership
growth mindset
habituation
heritability
heritability coefficient
hierarchical relationship
hierarchical networks
individual differences
information-processing approach
inhibitory
inspection time
intelligence
intelligence quotient (IQ)
knowledge
knowledge representation
latent variables
mental age
mindset
multiple intelligences theory
neuroplasticity
object permanence

operators
perceptual narrowing
placebo effect
practical intelligence
preferential looking method
preoperational period
prototype
psychometric approach
Raven's Progressive Matrices
savant syndrome
sensorimotor period
sensory-functional account
sentence verification task
similarity, or resemblance
two-factor theory
specific intelligences (s)
Stanford–Binet intelligence scales
subordinate
superordinate
triarchic theory of intelligence
typicality effect
Wechsler Adult Intelligence Scale
Wechsler Intelligence Scale for Children
Wechsler scales

Critical Thinking Questions

1. Artificial intelligence can beat human masters at complex games such as chess and Go. Consider new domains in which artificial intelligence may surpass human intelligence.

2. How can intelligence be improved in broad ways that generalize beyond the specific task used for training? For example, training people with a video game will improve their gaming performance, but can it also enhance other cognitive and perceptual skills?

3. How can we incorporate an understanding of cognitive development to enhance educational effectiveness?

Suggested Readings

Doidge, N. (2007). *The Brain That Changes Itself.* New York: Penguin Books.

Dweck, C. (2006). *Mindset: The New Psychology of Success.* New York: Random House.

Ritchie, S. (2015). Intelligence: *All That Matters.* London: John Murray Learning.

Social Cognition

12

umans are a social species. Many of us crave, need, and thrive on social connection. The drive for social connection is one reason why so many people—perhaps including you—had such difficulty in 2020, when the rapid worldwide spread of the dangerous illness COVID-19 led health officials to mandate long periods of social isolation. And it was this very same need for social connection that led to moving displays of solidarity, as if in defiance of the virus, with neighbors gathering on their balconies to sing and dance together, even from a distance.

Given people's strong drive for community, it would make sense for the way that we process social information to be different from the way we process nonsocial information. There are costs of going without social connection: for example, loneliness and perceived social isolation appear to contribute to impaired cognitive function, sleep, and mental and physical health (Cacioppo & Cacioppo, 2014), and social disconnection has been found to trigger responses in some of the same brain areas as does physical pain (Eisenberger, 2012; Eisenberger et al., 2003). So profound is our need for social connection that in 2011 the United Nations Special Rapporteur on Torture and Other Cruel, Inhuman or Degrading Treatment or Punishment decried prolonged solitary confinement as a form of cruel and inhumane punishment.

During the 2020 COVID-19 pandemic, people in many parts of the world were quarantined in their homes to slow the spread of the illness. The need for social connection was evident in the way these neighbors in Italy gathered on their balconies to sing and dance together, even at a distance.

LEARNING OBJECTIVES

12.1 Understand how social cognition connects with other areas of cognitive psychology, and how and why social cognition may differ from nonsocial cognition.

12.2 Describe evidence that people are particularly sensitive to social information and that we may be "wired" to process social information.

12.3 Discuss shortcuts that our minds use in order to reduce the complexity of the social world, as well as some consequences of such shortcuts.

12.4 Understand "motivated reasoning" and how it can impede fruitful discussions over disagreements.

Yet for social creatures, we have some strangely antisocial tendencies. People can be resistant to welcoming others with open arms. Our drive to bond with others sits side by side with a tendency to carve the social world into "us" and "them," to sometimes treat those in the "them" group as if they are less than fully human, sometimes with devastating consequences. This was experienced firsthand by many terrified Asian Americans who were spit on, yelled at, and attacked as COVID-19 made its way through the United States and other countries, finding themselves to be easy scapegoats because the virus had begun its deadly march in China (Tavernise & Oppel, 2020). Such attacks were facilitated by people's tendency to draw divisions between those with whom they seek solidarity and those they vilify.

In 2020, massive protests shook cities across the United States following the death of 46-year old George Floyd, a Black man who died after a police officer knelt on his neck for nine and a half minutes. Coming after years of police shootings of often unarmed Black men and women, the widely viewed footage mobilized people in one of the largest protest movements the nation had seen. The rallying cry "Black Lives Matter" was, in turn, interpreted by some as suggesting that White lives did not. Depending on who you spoke or listened to, the protesters were described either as fed-up citizens seeking change or as riotous thugs. What is it about humans that so often prevents us from seeing one another as flesh-and-blood individuals, even as we seek social connection? Why do we often fall into the trap of caricaturing and harming those we perceive to be "other"?

There are no simple answers here, and those that cognitive psychology can offer are just a small part of a much larger picture. Yet we live in a time when we can't ignore these underlying questions. We must make an effort to understand what science has to tell us about how we perceive ourselves, other people, and other groups. This area of research is known as social cognition.

In this chapter we briefly survey a few topics in the field that are relevant to how we think about and interact with others. We also discuss how we regulate our behavior in the face of thoughts and feelings that might impede our ability to get along with others.

12.1 The Unique Place of Social Cognition within Cognitive Psychology

The study of cognition (how we encode, store, and use information) has long had a home among social psychology researchers. During the mid-twentieth century, when considerations of cognition were largely ignored within the behaviorist movement, social psychologists continued to probe the relationship between human behavior and human thinking about the social world.

Kurt Lewin—now recognized as one of the founders of social psychology—pointed out that we respond not merely to the actions of people and the groups they comprise but also to our interpretations of and beliefs about them. These interpretations, beliefs, and attributions contribute to what he called the **psychological field** surrounding each person (Lewin, 1939): the concept that the social world and our responses to it are determined not only by the way things objectively are but also by our cognitions about ourselves and the people around us. Thus, understanding social behavior necessitates understanding cognition.

In a way, the field of social cognition fulfills some of the ideals of cognitive psychology's founders, such as Ulric Neisser and Jerome Bruner. Not long after the Cognitive Revolution, Neisser and Bruner began to worry that the field they had created was becoming increasingly isolated from how cognition operates in the real world (see Chapter 1 to refresh your memory of the Cognitive Revolution). Neisser's ideal of keeping cognitive psychology grounded in the real world was reflected in the title of his classic book *Cognition and Reality* (1976). In the book, he addressed what he viewed as an unfortunate dissociation between lab-based cognitive psychology experiments and any sense of their implications for everyday life. Since that time, cognitive psychologists have narrowed this gap, and social cognition has helped; using the methods and techniques of cognitive science, the field of social cognition looks for the mental mechanisms that explain how people interact with and view each other. Issues in social cognition, for example, often build on and extend topics found elsewhere in cognitive psychology, such as categorization, reasoning, and attention.

Although social cognition research builds on these topics, it is also important to note that when we move from isolated testing booths (often used in cognitive psychology research) to the full richness of social reality, our cognition may change in ways far more complex than can be explained by a simple switch of stimuli (Fiske & Taylor, 2017). Social cognition involves more than simply redirecting the focus of cognitive processes toward social stimuli (e.g., swapping patches of color for people). Perhaps most saliently, the foci of social cognitions (people) are active agents who are trying to influence the environment, including you. Social cognition is inherently mutual: the perceived perceive you in return, and your cognitive processing of others can change their behavior because people are both hyperaware of being judged and motivated to be seen in a certain way (e.g., to be loved, feared, or respected).

The writer and scholar Garnette Cadogan eloquently captured the sense of regulating one's own behavior in response to social judgments. In his essay "Walking While Black," he reminisced about his experience in New Orleans soon after moving there from Jamaica to attend college:

> On one occasion, less than a month after my arrival, I tried to help a man whose wheelchair was stuck in the middle of a crosswalk; he threatened to shoot me in the face, then asked a white pedestrian for help.
>
> I wasn't prepared for any of this. I had come from a majority-black country in which no one was wary of me because of my skin color. Now I wasn't sure who was afraid of me. I was especially unprepared for the cops. They regularly stopped and bullied me, asking questions that took my guilt for granted. I'd never received what many of my African-American friends call "The Talk": No parents had told me how to behave when I was stopped by the police, how to be as polite and cooperative as possible, no matter what they said or did to me. So I had to cobble together my own rules of engagement. Thicken my Jamaican accent. Quickly mention my college. "Accidentally" pull out my college identification card when asked for my driver's license.

(From G. Cadogan. 2015. In Freeman's: *Arrival: The Best New Writing on Arrival*, J. Freeman [Ed.]. Grove Atlantic: New York. Permission by Chris Calhoun Agency, © Garnette Cadogan.)

Other people's views of you can change the way you behave even when you may not be aware of it. In a classic study, researchers gave elementary school students an intelligence test and then told their teachers which children were likely to show great progress over the next several months. When the children were given a follow-up test 8 months later, those whose names had been given to the teachers showed greater improvement than their classmates did, even though the researchers had chosen the names at random. In other words, although there was no actual reason to label them as likely achievers, the students performed according to their teachers' expectations. This **Pygmalion effect** (or **self-fulfilling prophecy**) provides an interesting demonstration of the power of people's expectations of us, even when we aren't explicitly aware of them (Rosenthal, 1974; Rosenthal & Jacobsen, 1968; also see Jussim & Harber, 2005).

The essay "Walking While Black" describes how the writer Garnette Cadogan tried to adjust his behavior to counter social judgments people made simply because of his skin color. It is a situation commonly encountered by members of groups facing discrimination.

> CHECKPOINT 12.1

1. How was cognition an integral consideration within social psychology even before the Cognitive Revolution?
2. How might cognition become even more complex when focused on other people rather than objects?

12.2 Are We Specially Wired to Process Social Information?

Just as we inevitably see meaningful shapes in the clouds, we seem wired to perceive social information even when there objectively is none. In one famous study, Fritz Heider and Marianne Simmel (1944) created an animation in which abstract shapes moved around a display, appearing to mimic social interactions (**FIGURE 12.1**). Even when participants were simply asked to view the movie and describe what happened—without the investigators instructing them to make social inferences—nearly all of them attributed social motives and relationships to the figures. Researchers have argued that the inference of social behavior in this case occurred at an early, perceptual stage of processing, as such impressions were fast and irresistible (Scholl & Tremoulet, 2000). This suggestion appears consistent with recent claims that the brain's wiring includes a visual pathway for social information (Pitcher & Ungerleider, 2021). It is as if we can't help but see motives and intentions around us, even when there are none. When we perceive these invisible motives and intentions accurately, our exquisite sensitivity toward them can enable us to navigate complex social dynamics. However, there is vast potential to get things wrong when we perceive motives and intentions that aren't there, and for hostilities to arise based on incorrect assumptions. **RESEARCH FOCUS 12.1** discusses some factors that appear to influence whether people see—or don't see— humanizing qualities in others.

FIGURE 12.1 Still frame from an animation by Heider and Simmel (1944)   In the animation, the triangles and circle moved around the display, appearing to interact in meaningful ways (such as hiding from, chasing, bullying, and outsmarting each other). Participants who were asked to describe what they saw almost always described the video in terms of social motives and relationships. (Derived from video associated with F. Heider and M. Simmel. 1944. *Am J Psychol* 57: 243–259.)

RESEARCH FOCUS 12.1

Individual Differences in Humanization and Dehumanization

People's sensitivities to social connections and motivations are so strong that they often see them where they don't actually exist. But it may be that people differ in how *much* they see them. Evidence suggests that there are individual differences in how likely people are to attribute human mental states to inanimate objects and animals. According to some research, people who are lonely are more likely than non-lonely people to attribute human emotions, motivations, and intentions to objects and pets (Epley et al., 2008; Epley et al., 2008).

For example, in one study 20 participants filled out an online survey that also described four gadgets:

- A wheeled alarm clock that made users chase it to turn it off
- A pillow that could be programmed to give a hug
- A battery charger designed to prevent overcharging
- An air purifier

Participants rated the degree to which they viewed the gadgets as having minds of their own, intentions, free will, consciousness, and emotions. Strikingly, the participants' ratings of

their own loneliness correlated with how much they attributed these humanlike qualities to the gadgets (Epley et al., 2008).

Conversely, and perhaps counterintuitively, people with abundant social connections appeared to be less likely to attribute thoughts and feelings to other people when those other people were outside their circle of social connections; in other words, they were more likely to dehumanize people outside their social circle. In one experiment, some participants were made to feel connected to others by writing about how they met, knew, or felt supported by a close friend or associate (Waytz & Epley, 2012). Participants in the control group wrote about a person in their life with whom they hardly ever interacted. All participants were then asked to indicate whether the average middle-class American, disabled person, rich person, or drug addict was able to act intentionally, think deeply, experience pain, and experience pleasure. Perhaps surprisingly, participants who had been made to feel socially connected were not as generous in endorsing these humanizing traits in others! The investigators replicated this effect in several follow-up experiments, and some tweaks of experimental design revealed that participants who wrote about a person close to them were particularly likely to engage in dehumanization when they were asked to evaluate people far removed from their social group.

Why should feeling close to some people make it more likely that you might dehumanize others with whom you do not have a personal connection? One speculation is that considering other people's perspectives is effortful and that people need to be motivated to do so. The more that people feel socially connected, the less motivated they may be to step outside their own perspective (Waytz & Epley, 2012). Thus, the dark side of having a tight-knit circle of friends may be a tendency—although not an inevitable one—to disregard the needs or mental states of people outside it.

Social Wiring of the Brain

Evidence that we are wired to spontaneously treat social information differently than nonsocial information also comes from neuroimaging studies. In one study, people watched animated movies of geometric shapes moving around a display in a variety of ways. They also were told that the movements either reflected the shapes' mental states (e.g., involving feelings, thoughts, and social motives), reflected simple goals (e.g., chasing or dancing), or were simply random physical movements (e.g., floating or bouncing). Even though all participants saw the same stimuli, the act of attributing mental states to the shapes elicited heightened activity in brain regions that have been suggested to be part of what is known as the **social cognition neural network**, a network of brain regions that play a role in social interaction (Frith & Frith, 2001; Harris & Fiske, 2006, 2007; Harris et al., 2007) (**FIGURE 12.2**). These brain regions include the medial prefrontal cortex, superior temporal sulcus (or temporoparietal junction), and fusiform gyrus,

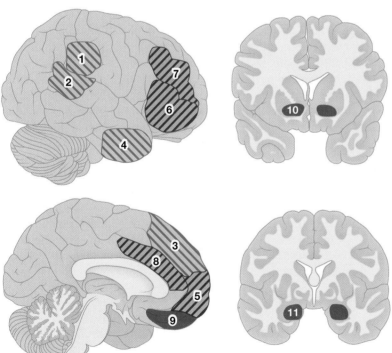

Social cognition
1. Temporal parietal junction
2. Posterior superior temporal sulcus
3. Dorsomedial prefrontal cortex
4. Temporal poles
5. Medial prefrontal cortex

Cognitive control
5. Medial prefrontal cortex
6. Ventrolateral prefrontal cortex
7. Dorsoolateral prefrontal cortex
8. Anterior cingulate cortex

Affective
9. Orbitofrontal cortex/ventromedial prefrontal cortex
10. Ventral striatum
11. Amygdala

FIGURE 12.2 **Some of the brain regions implicated in social cognition, cognitive control, and emotion (affective) processing (not mutually exclusive)** Areas in green, in addition to the medial prefrontal cortex and the fusiform gyrus, have been linked to what is called the social cognition neural network, which has key functions for social interaction. (After E. H. Telzer et al. 2018. In *Advances in Child Development and Behavior* [Vol. 54], J. B. Benson [Ed.], pp. 215–258. Academic Press: New York.)

(A)

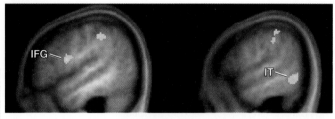

(B)

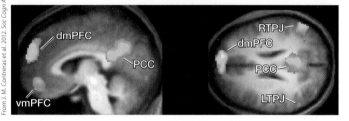

From J. M. Contreras et al. 2012. Soc Cogn Affect Neurosci 7: 764–770

FIGURE 12.3 Thinking about nonsocial versus social categories
Judgments about social and nonsocial categories were found to increase activity in different brain regions. **(A)** Increased activity in brain regions linked with thinking about nonsocial categories (inferior frontal gyrus [IFG], inferotemporal cortex [IT]) versus **(B)** increased activity in brain regions linked with thinking about social categories (dorsomedial prefrontal cortex [dmPFC], ventromedial prefrontal cortex [vmPFC], posterior cingulate cortex [PCC], right and left temporoparietal junction [RTPJ and LTPJ]).

which has been widely implicated in the processing of faces (Castelli et al., 2000; Kanwisher et al., 1997; also see Mitchell et al., 2002).

In another neuroimaging study, investigators tested whether knowledge about social categories is represented differently in the brain than knowledge about nonsocial categories. When people were asked to make semantic judgments about nonsocial categories (e.g., musical instruments), researchers observed increased activity in the left inferior frontal gyrus and inferotemporal cortex. In contrast, judgments about social categories were accompanied by increased activity in brain areas that have previously been linked with social cognition, such as the medial frontal cortex, posterior cingulate cortex, bilateral temporoparietal junction, and anterior temporal cortex (Contreras et al., 2012) (**FIGURE 12.3**).

Perceiving Mental States in Others

One reason perceiving people is different from perceiving objects is that we tend to understand that people differ in their thoughts, knowledge, motivations, and intentions. Such understanding is known as **theory of mind** (Premack & Woodruff, 1978), and the inference of such internal states in others has been linked to neural regions such as the temporoparietal junction (e.g., Saxe & Kanwisher, 2003; Saxe et al., 2004). The attainment of theory of mind is regarded as one of the major milestones in child development. Disorders characterized by social difficulties, such as autism, have been associated with failures of theory of mind to develop normally (Baron-Cohen et al., 1985). See Section 10.6 for more about theory of mind.

When it comes to how we treat others, perceiving them as having minds of their own appears to help us view them as beings worthy of moral treatment (Gray et al., 2007, 2012). Conversely, failure to perceive mental states in others—known as **dehumanized perception** (Harris & Fiske, 2011)—may contribute to prejudiced and cruel treatment (Hackel et al., 2014). Intriguingly, some neuroimaging studies have found reduced activity in brain areas associated with the social cognition neural network under conditions where dehumanized perception has occurred (Harris & Fiske, 2006, 2007).

Reasoning about Social and Nonsocial Information

Consistent with the suggestion that we may be wired to think in social terms, reasoning about social information appears to be easier than reasoning about nonsocial information. For example, consider the **Wason selection task** (Cosmides, 1989; Cosmides & Tooby, 1992; Wason, 1968), a logic puzzle demonstrated in **SEE FOR YOURSELF 12.1**.

Understanding that other people's emotions, thoughts, and goals may be different from yours is a developmental milestone known as theory of mind.

▶ **See for Yourself 12.1**

The Role of Social Information in the Wason Selection Task

In Chapter 10, we introduced the Wason selection task, in which four cards are supposed to follow a rule: each card that has a vowel on one side must have an even number on the other side. Which two cards do you need to turn over to confirm the rule?

See for Yourself (continued)

Although See For Yourself 10.4 showed how performance improves when such problems are stated more concretely, additional benefits come from framing them in social terms. For example, imagine that you are a bouncer at a bar and your job is to make sure that nobody under 21 drinks alcohol. Each patron holds a card with his or her age on one side and drink on the other. So, if their card has an alcoholic drink on one side, it must have a number on the other side that is 21 or higher. Of the following cards, which two do you need to turn over?

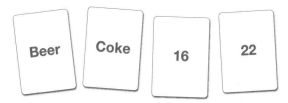

In the first case, the answers are the "E" and "3" cards. In the second case, and the "Beer" and "16" cards are correct. Did you choose correctly? The logic behind these two versions is identical, so why did the version with the drinks and ages seem so much easier?

(After L. Cosmides. 1989. *Cognition* 31: 187–276; P. C. Wason. 1968. *J Exp Psychol* 20: 273–281.)

The interesting thing about these tasks is that, although many people often get the first puzzle wrong and the second puzzle correct, the logic for both is the same. In the first puzzle in the box, it doesn't matter what's on the other sides of the "K" or "4" cards because the former isn't a vowel and the latter won't break the rule if it has a consonant on the other side. The rule is broken only if the "E" card has an odd number on the other side or if the "3" has a vowel. Similarly, it doesn't matter what's on the other side of the "Coke" or "22" card: the Coke drinker won't be violating the rule no matter his or her age, and the 22-year-old can drink whatever he or she wants.

As discussed in Chapter 10, people find problems like this more difficult when they are phrased abstractly instead of in concrete terms, but difficulties arise even when they are framed concretely. For example, if the problem is framed in a concrete but non-social context—"Every time I eat haddock then I drink gin"—it doesn't make people more likely to arrive at the right answer (Manktelow & Evans, 1979).

According to evolutionary psychologists Leda Cosmides and John Tooby (1992), situating this kind of problem in a social context may help because people are endowed with an evolutionarily derived system for detecting cheaters. According to this notion, it's not simply any social context that will kick problem-solving into high gear. Evidence suggests that people are less adept at problem-solving when the goal is to detect altruists rather than cheaters (Cosmides, 1989).

➤ **CHECKPOINT 12.2**

1. How might the perception of mental states in others (or the failure to perceive mental states in others) influence the way we treat other people?

2. What evidence suggests that people process social information differently than nonsocial information?

We encounter so many people from day to day that it would be impossible to encode and remember what makes each person unique. Instead, our minds seek shortcuts to keep the amount of information we process manageable. Although such shortcuts enhance cognitive efficiency, they can often lead us to make incorrect assumptions.

12.3 Reducing the Cognitive Burden of a Complex Social World

Despite the fact that people appear particularly adept at processing social information, there are limits to how large a social network our brains can handle. (Think about your Facebook friends or your Instagram followers: although social media may connect you to hundreds or thousands of people, how many of them would you count as close friends?) According to what is known as the **social brain hypothesis**, the size of social networks among primates is related to the size of brain regions such as the frontal lobe (Dunbar, 1993, 1998). Compared with most other animals, people have relatively large social networks, with one well-known estimate placing the average at about 150 meaningful relationships (known as **Dunbar's number**). Beyond this number, other people take on the quality of mere acquaintants (see Dunbar, 2014 ; but see Lindenfors et al., 2021). Neuroimaging studies appear to show that the size of people's social networks is correlated with the size of brain regions linked with emotional coding of social signals (e.g., the amygdala; Bickart et al., 2011; Kanai et al., 2012) **(FIGURE 12.4)** and regions linked with theory of mind (e.g., left middle temporal gyrus, right superior temporal sulcus, right entorhinal cortex; Kanai et al., 2012). In a similar vein, people's cognitive abilities related to theory of mind and memory have also been correlated with the size of their friend networks (Stiller & Dunbar, 2007).

Of course, the world has far more than 150 people. You probably regularly encounter and interact with more than 150 people in your own immediate surroundings—across your neighborhood, school, and workplace. With so many social relationships to navigate, it can be adaptive—purely from the perspective of reducing computational demands—for our minds to cut corners and seek shortcuts to minimize the need to process each person's intrinsic complexities. Such shortcuts include carving the social world into smaller in-groups and out-groups, relying on stereotypes, and making rapid judgments based on superficial appearances (e.g., tattoos, a hijab, or darker skin color). Unfortunately, these shortcuts frequently guide us in the wrong direction and can contribute to intergroup tension.

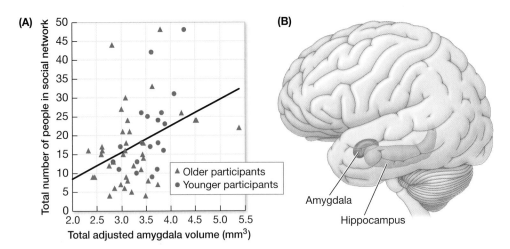

FIGURE 12.4 Social network size is correlated with amygdala size   (A) As the size of people's social networks increases (*y*-axis), so does the size of the amygdala (*x*-axis), a brain region heavily involved in emotional coding of social signals. This has been found for both young participants (circles) and older participants (triangles). **(B)** Location of the amygdala, deep inside the brain near the hippocampus. (A after K. C. Bickart et al. 2011. *Nat Neurosci* 14: 163–164; B after S. M. Breedlove and N. V. Watson. 2019. *Behavioral Neuroscience*, 9th Edition. Oxford University Press/Sinauer: Sunderland, MA.)

First Impressions

One way that our minds attempt to lessen the amount of cognitive effort involved in navigating the social world is by relying heavily on rapid first impressions. There are many situations in which first impressions leave a lasting impact, such as when you are starting at a new school or job and begin to meet new people. This may not seem fair: people are fascinatingly complex, full of contradictions. As the poet Walt Whitman so eloquently stated, "I am large, I contain multitudes." Yet although in truth it might take months or years before you develop a deep and lasting friendship with someone, it is not uncommon to get an immediate sense of how you feel about them—perhaps wary, intrigued, or attracted.

FIGURE 12.5 Example of a baby-faced person (left) and a mature-faced person (right) Baby-faced adults are often assumed to be honest, if somewhat naive and bumbling.

PHYSICAL APPEARANCE Rightly or wrongly, people's physical appearances can have a big impact on how we form first impressions. Facial features, for example, play a role in how trustworthy or guilty we judge a person to be. One well-known example is the **baby-face bias** (**FIGURE 12.5**). Some of the people around us might have particularly round, youthful, soft-looking faces, reminiscent of a child's face; these features can have a robust effect on how we judge them. In one study that used simulated civil court cases, male baby-faced defendants were more likely to lose when accused of negligent actions (e.g., underreporting income to the IRS because of poor record keeping) but more likely to win when accused of intentional actions (e.g., underreporting income intentionally) (Berry & Zebrowitz-McArthur, 1988). Such findings were consistent with the notion that baby-faced adults are often assumed to be honest, if somewhat naive and bumbling (Berry & McArthur, 1985). Even when defendants admitted wrongdoing, the baby-faced defendants were penalized less. Similar findings were found in a survey of 506 real small-claims outcomes (Zebrowitz & McDonald, 1991). Attractiveness also appeared to play an independent role, with defendants more likely to lose when contesting attractive plaintiffs, consistent with the literature on **attractiveness bias** (e.g., Dion et al., 1972). Of course, attractiveness is in the eye of the beholder—features that are attractive to one person may not be attractive to another. That said, some features, such as facial symmetry, have been linked with higher ratings of attractiveness (Perrett et al., 1999).

Facial structure (e.g., whether one has a broad or narrow jawline, high or low forehead) appears to affect how people judge someone's specific traits as well. Participants in one study were asked to rate—based only on photographs of faces—the competence of several congressional candidates. These ratings correctly predicted the election outcomes (Todorov et al., 2005). Why should this be? Surely most people know that a person's facial structure doesn't tell us anything about his or her competence, trustworthiness, extraversion, or likeability. One suggestion is that inferences based on physical appearance occur rapidly and effortlessly, though they can be superseded by slower, effortful deliberation (Todorov et al., 2005). A study by Willis and Todorov (2006) attests to the rapidity of such inferences: when people were asked to rate others' attractiveness, likeability, trustworthiness, competence, and aggressiveness based on 100-millisecond exposures to photographs, their judgments did not differ much from judgments they made without time constraints.

NONVERBAL BEHAVIOR Likewise, we appear to infer a great deal even from very brief exposures to people's **nonverbal behavior**, which refers to the ways that people behave, gesture, or express themselves without words. This ability has been demonstrated through studies that evaluate people based on extremely brief videos, often with the sound turned off. These are known as **thin-slice judgments**. In one example, participants viewed 30-second silent video clips of college instructors teaching. On the basis of these videos, participants rated the teachers' effectiveness. Strikingly, the ratings correlated with the teachers' end-of-semester ratings. Similar accuracy occurred when the clips were as short as 6 seconds (Ambady & Rosenthal, 1993). In other studies, participants proved capable of making reliable judgments about a person—about everything from their emotional state to their sexual orientation—just by looking at his or her gait. The gaits in such cases were conveyed with only **point light walkers**, wherein participants did not see the actual person but instead saw only dots where the person's joints would be (Ambady et al., 1999). **SEE FOR YOURSELF 12.2** discusses this further.

▶ **See for Yourself 12.2**

Nonverbal Communication in Point Light Walkers

When you want someone to know how you feel, you might choose to tell them using words. But people can also be sensitive to nonverbal behavior, picking up on a wealth of information just from the way that someone gestures or walks. In fact, people are so good at this that they can glean this information from simple, moving arrays of dots arranged so that each dot is placed where a person's joints would be. This is known as a point light walker. You can see this for yourself on Oxford Learning Link.

Imagine how much more knowledge people can pick up from nonverbal information that is not reduced to arrays of dots!

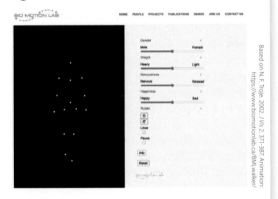

Based on N. F. Troje. 2002. *J Vis* 2, 371–387. Animation: https://www.biomotionlab.ca/BMLwalker/

Image of the animated interface at York University's BioMotion Lab, in Toronto, Ontario, with a point light walker on the left.

In-Groups and Out-Groups

In the face of the vast number of people we might encounter in our lives, how do our minds cope with the daunting cognitive burden such numerous encounters might impose? It turns out that people are strongly inclined to divide the world's sea of humanity into smaller, easier-to-think-about **in-groups** ("those like me") and **out-groups** ("those unlike me"), which guide how and to whom we allocate our limited cognitive and emotional resources.

The sorting of people into in-groups and out-groups can have benefits for how we perceive in-group members and costs for how we perceive out-group members. **In-group identification** refers to a feeling of solidarity that we tend to have with other members of what we perceive to be "our" group, leading to preferential, benevolent treatment of our fellow group members, who we are more likely to treat as distinct individuals. In contrast, it is not uncommon for out-groups to be perceived as being uniform, with little differentiation among the group members.

ENTITATIVITY AND EMPATHY When regarding one's own in-group it is easy to appreciate the full spectrum of opinions, personalities, and values held by the people in it; but when regarding members of an out-group, people often default to the assumption that they are uniform in these characteristics. Examples might include a White person who perceives all Asian people as having similar personalities or a Democrat who assumes that all Republicans have similar attitudes toward immigrants. This perceived uniformity of out-group members is known as **entitativity** (Campbell, 1958). Related effects have been observed even in perceptual tasks: for example, the **other race face effect** refers to the difficulty that people have individuating and recognizing people from a race different from their own (Malpass & Kravitz, 1969; Meissner & Brigham, 2001).

One consequence of entitativity is that it becomes difficult to empathize with people as individuals. This was painfully apparent in the aftermath of Hurricane Katrina, which devastated swaths of New Orleans in 2005. It took several days before food, water, and medical supplies reached those in dire need, and the Federal Emergency Management Agency's handling of the disaster was widely seen as insensitive. Psychologists investigated the degree to which people felt empathy for the victims, who were largely Black or Latino. Participants were asked to infer the emotional states of individual Black, Latino, and White victims, as well as indicate their willingness to help them (Cuddy et al., 2007). The participants were less likely to ascribe "uniquely human" emotions such as anguish, mourning, and remorse (sometimes called "secondary" emotions) to individuals perceived as belonging to an out-group. That is, participants who self-identified as White were less likely to ascribe such emotions to Black and Latino victims than to White victims, and those who self-identified as Black or Latino were less likely to ascribe such emotions to White victims (**FIGURE 12.6**). Those who did ascribe such emotions to victims expressed greater motivation to help. A similar failure to identify with those perceived as different may explain the tepid emergency response to the devastation of Puerto Rico by Hurricane Maria in 2017.

Consistent with such decreased identification with out-group members, in another study Black and White participants watched a video of a hand being pricked by a pin, and the hand itself appeared to belong to a Black or a White individual. In these cases, fMRI revealed that neural activity in brain regions linked with sensitivity to other people's pain—and other physiological indices of sensitivity to another person's pain—was greater when observing the

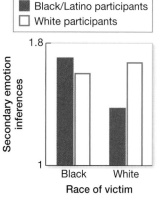

FIGURE 12.6 **It is easier to identify and empathize with people who belong to your in-group than to an out-group** This tendency may have contributed to delayed emergency responses in the aftermath of Hurricane Katrina, which devasted large areas of New Orleans in 2005. Many of the victims were Black or Latino, whereas many of the decision makers in power were White. After the hurricane, one study found that White participants were less likely to attribute humanizing emotions such as anguish and mourning to Black and Latino victims than to White victims, whereas Black and Latino participants were less likely to ascribe such emotions to White victims. (From A. J. C. Cuddy et al. 2007. *Group Process Intergr Relat* 10: 107–118.)

hand of one's own race getting pricked than when observing the hand of an out-group member getting pricked (Avenanti et al., 2010; Azevedo et al., 2013; also see Xu et al., 2009).

Such findings highlight how social divisions can get in the way of what has been proposed to be a fundamental human capacity for empathy. Although **empathy** has been defined in several different ways, its definition usually involves a sensitivity to what and how other people are thinking and feeling (Batson & Ahmad, 2009; Preston & de Waal, 2002). Empathy can be "cognitive," in that it involves knowing or imagining what other people are thinking or feeling, or it can be more vicarious, in that it involves "feeling" what other people are feeling (Batson, 2009). Research suggests that empathizing with people is effortful and takes energy (Cameron et al., 2019). It may be that people have a tendency to conserve their energy, expending it more readily when they feel they have something in common with the person with whom they are empathizing.

The degree to which we distance ourselves from out-groups is also observable in how we process people's physical actions. When watching someone perform a motor action (such as reaching for a cookie), regions of our motor cortex sometimes respond as if we were performing the action ourselves. Such neural activity is said to reflect a **mirror-neuron system** (Rizzolatti & Craighero, 2004)—that is, a set of neurons that appear to mirror the actions of other people. In one study, two groups of children imitated and observed others making emotional facial expressions. The children were either high-functioning children with autism (who are often documented to experience deficits in social functioning) or matched controls. When the children were observing the facial expressions, fMRI revealed greater activation of a brain region linked with the mirror-neuron system (the pars opercularis) in the matched controls than in the children with autism. What's more, among the children with autism, activity in the pars opercularis was weakest in those with the most severe deficits in social functioning (Dapretto et al., 2006). One theoretical account of empathy, known as the **perception-action-coupling** model, suggests that our brains' mirroring of other people's actions reflects processes that enable us to vicariously experience other people's outwardly exhibited states (Decety & Jackson, 2004; Dimberg et al., 2000).

It is notable, then, that such neural activity seems to be influenced by social factors. In a study by Gutsell and Inzlicht (2010), participants watched other people perform motor actions such as picking up a glass and taking a sip of water. By recording electrical activity above the participant's motor cortices, the researchers found that perception-action-coupling was reduced when people watched the actions of out-group members, and that such reductions were especially profound when the participants held prejudiced attitudes toward the out-groups. Along similar lines, neural activity associated with the actual experience of pain was observed more when people witnessed the pain of in-group members being penetrated by a needle than of out-group members (Xu et al., 2009). Such results echo other findings in which pictures representing extreme out-groups failed to elicit activity in brain areas involved in a range of social cognitions (Harris & Fiske, 2006; Van Bavel et al., 2008) (**FIGURE 12.7**).

EASE OF FORMING IN-GROUPS AND OUT-GROUPS   People appear to leap to use the smallest, most insignificant differences to sort people into in-groups and out-groups. The ease with which we form such divisions has been demonstrated in study after study. One compelling demonstration was not a controlled laboratory study but an exercise conducted in a third-grade classroom on April 5, 1968, the day after Martin Luther King, Jr. was assassinated. Guided by a belief that children should understand the flimsy bases on which group hatreds can arise, teacher Jane Elliott divided her class into two groups:

(A)   (B)   (C)

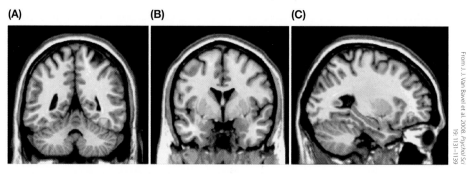

From J. J. Van Bavel et al. 2008 *Psychol Sci* 19: 1131–1139

FIGURE 12.7 Responses to in-group and out-group faces   In one study, brain areas that were more active when viewing images of in-group than out-group faces included **(A)** the fusiform gyri, **(B)** the amygdala, and **(C)** the orbitofrontal cortex.

those with brown eyes and those with blue eyes. She told the groups that the brown-eyed children were better than the blue-eyed children and that they were not to play together. The purpose of this exercise was for the children to experience firsthand how societal divisions and conflict can arise from the most superficial differences. In Elliott's class exercise, intergroup conflict between the blue- and brown-eyed children arose almost immediately (Peters, 1985).

To understand just how arbitrary these superficial differences can be, researchers often use the **minimal group paradigm** (e.g., Tajifel, 1970; Tajifel et al., 1971), a procedure in which people spontaneously form in-groups and out-groups on the basis of the most trivial features.

In this procedure, people are placed into separate groups, either at random or on the basis of a superficial feature. Sometimes they are then tasked with divvying up resources among members of the different groups. For example, in an early experiment, 14- and 15-year-old boys were recruited into a lab and were asked simply to estimate the numbers of dots in a display. The boys were then (misleadingly) told that some of them were "overestimators" and some of them were "underestimators." Subsequently, they were asked to allocate money to the other recruits in the study. Those who had been told they were overestimators gave more money to other overestimators than to underestimators, and vice versa (see Tajifel, 1970). That is, as soon as the most arbitrary distinctions between "their group" and "the other group" were made, a bias to favor one's in-group emerged. In contrast, when no such group differentiation was made, the participants tended to adopt a strategy that maximized fairness for the whole group of recruits.

The consequences of dividing the world into in-groups and out-groups are observable at an early age. This is so even though many people—including children—mistakenly perceive themselves to be less biased than other people, something that is known as the **bias blind spot** (Hagá et al., 2018; Pronin et al., 2002). In one study, researchers randomly assigned children (ages 6–12) to a "red team" and a "blue team" and assessed both their social anxiety and the degree to which they felt their group membership was important to them. Several weeks later, the researchers introduced a stressful situation: the children were told that they had not been selected for a special team and were asked to describe their feelings about it. When asked about how much empathy they felt for other children who had been left out, socially anxious children for whom group membership had been important—and who were distressed by the rejection—reported feeling more empathy for other members of their color team than for members of the other color team (Masten et al., 2010).

In the classic *Star Trek* series of the 1960s, the starship *Enterprise* encountered a society doomed by internal strife. Hatred arose because one group was white on their right side and black on the other, whereas another group had their colors reversed. The bases of our divisions in the real world are often similarly superficial.

RELISHING THE MISFORTUNE OF OUT-GROUPS   Beyond simply feeling more empathy for fellow in-group members, it is not uncommon for people to experience **schadenfreude**, the feeling of reward or pleasure at out-group members' (or sometimes even in-group members') failures or suffering (Leach & Spears, 2009; Smith et al., 2009). For example, Red Sox and Yankees fans have reported feeling pleasure at seeing their rival team lose, and when they were placed in an fMRI scanner while watching their rival team lose, such feelings were reflected in higher activity in the nucleus acumbens, an area of the brain sensitive to reward (Cikara et al., 2011). Such reward-related activity extended beyond the confines of the game. Fans of rival soccer teams exhibited reward-related neural activity when watching the other team's fans receive painful electric shocks, and this neural activity predicted a later unwillingness to alleviate their rival team's pain by stepping into their place (Hein et al., 2010). Similarly, reward-related neural activity was observed among participants when learning that someone they were envious of suffered from the spread of rumors about them (Takahashi et al., 2009).

The allure of schadenfreude can be so strong that people sometimes appear to relish feelings of schadenfreude more than they relish their own self-interests. In one study, people who strongly identified as Democrats appeared to feel some degree of schadenfreude when reading an article about an economic downturn that occurred during a Republican administration, even though the downturn would have been bad for their own financial interests as well (Combs et al. 2009).

STEREOTYPE CONTENT MODEL   What makes the difference between whether we empathize with out-group members or relish their misfortune? According to an influential framework known as the **stereotype content model**, not all out-group members are equally regarded. This model suggests that much of how we regard "others" can be attributed to a combination of how "warm" and how "competent" we perceive them to be (Fiske et al., 2002). In this case, "warmth" refers to how trustworthy or friendly we perceive a group to be, which has implications for what we believe their intentions toward us are. "Competence" refers to how capable or assertive we perceive the group to be, which would have implications for their ability to follow through on their intentions. According to the stereotype content model, where we place a group on a combination of these dimensions affects how we relate to them and our feelings toward them (**TABLE 12.1**). For example, groups that are perceived to be warm but incompetent might elicit feelings of pity or sympathy, whereas groups that are perceived as cold but competent might elicit feelings of envy or resentment (see Fiske, 2018). It is the latter group that might inspire feelings of schadenfreude. For example, in one experiment participants envisioned different misfortunes befalling different individuals who varied in how warm and competent the participants perceived

TABLE 12.1 Attributing warmth and competence to others[a]

	Low competence	High competence
High warmth	Common stereotypes: elderly, disabled, children Emotions evoked: pity, sympathy	Common stereotypes: citizens, middle class, defaults Emotions evoked: pride, admiration
Low warmth	Common stereotypes: poor, homeless, immigrants Emotions evoked: disgust, contempt	Common stereotypes: rich, professional, technical experts Emotions evoked: envy, jealousy

[a] Different groups of people are stereotypically associated with different levels of "warmth" and "competence." According to the stereotype content model, the emotions that these groups evoke depend at least partly on whether the groups are perceived to be high or low on a combination of the warmth and competence dimensions. (Based on S. Fiske. 2018. *Curr Dir Psychol Sci* 27: 67–73.)

them to be. When participants envisioned an investment banker (low perceived warmth, high perceived competence) sitting on some gum on a park bench, electrodes recording the activity of the participants' face muscles revealed hints of a smile—schadenfreude (Cikara & Fiske, 2012). Notably, in a follow-up experiment in which participants began by reading a newspaper article that highlighted investment bankers' cooperativeness (e.g., working with small businesses to help the economy) or that diminished their status or enviability (e.g., many bankers are unemployed), signs of schadenfreude decreased substantially.

FLEXIBILITY OF GROUP MEMBERSHIP AND CONSIDERATIONS OF "SELF"

In many lab-based experiments, groups are differentiated on the basis of one characteristic prechosen by the researchers (e.g., overestimators vs. underestimators, as in the aforementioned work of Tajifel, 1970). However, in the real world we hold many representations of ourselves and we belong to many groups. How does this complexity affect whom we consider to be in-group members and out-group members? For example, imagine someone who identifies as White, Christian, American, and Democratic. Will they view their in-group as being other Americans? Other Christians (regardless of nationality)? Other White people (regardless of nationality or religion)? Other Democrats? It turns out that whom we see as an in-group versus out-group member depends on which aspects of our identity we focus on at a given time (Gaertner & Dovidio, 2000). In one study, university students viewed faces spatially arranged by race (Black vs. White) or by university (Black and White students hypothetically at the participant's own university or a different university). When the faces were organized on the basis of race, people were better at subsequently recognizing faces from their own racial group. But when the faces were organized on the basis of university affiliation, people were better at recognizing those purportedly from their own university, with race having no effect (Hehman et al., 2010).

Merely being exposed to everyday events brings us into contact with innumerable cues that can spontaneously lead us to assign people to particular social groups—a process known as **social categorization**. For example, we might find ourselves categorizing people based on their dark skin, Asian appearance, or if they are adorned with tattoos, military garb, a doctor's coat, or a hijab (Allport, 1954; Brewer & Lui, 1989; Dovidio et al., 1986; Fiske & Neuberg, 1990; Fiske et al., 1999; Ito et al., 2007; Olsson et al., 2005). Intriguingly, the degree to which we regard others as part of our in-group or of an out-group may not be driven purely by these social categorization cues. Instead, it also may be linked with moment-to-moment fluctuations in how we regard ourselves. For example, you can view yourself as a student, as a member of your university, and as a citizen of your country. None of these are exclusive of the others, but they may differ in how important they are to you depending on the situation (see Van Bavel & Cunningham, 2010). If a person enters a situation in which their gender is rendered salient, this act of self-categorization might influence how the person categorizes other people. That is, the gender identities of his or her neighbors might become particularly relevant. But if a person's race is particularly salient in the moment, it might lead them to register their neighbors' races. People who typically view themselves through the lens of their occupation might find that their racial identity becomes more salient following news reports of a racially charged shooting, and this might make them especially attuned to races of the people around them. Such a possibility is consistent with **self-categorization theory**, which posits that people can view themselves according to several hierarchically nested identities, which can vary in their relative salience at any given time (Turner et al., 1987; see also Van Bavel & Cunningham, 2010).

People can view themselves according to several nested identities, any one of which can be rendered particularly salient at any given time. What aspect of her identity might the woman in this photo feel is salient in this moment?

OVERCOMING DIVISIONS BETWEEN GROUPS Is there anything that can be done to increase people's ability to empathize with out-group members, or with those with whom they have conflicts? This question may be among the most important that can be asked today, when some of history's worst ethnopolitical conflicts continue to unfold—whether one thinks of the Rwandan genocide of the 1990s or the ongoing violence between Israelis and Palestinians. To stem the hatred, some governments have run programs in which young people from communities in conflict attend workshops where they live together for days or weeks, engage in role playing and group projects, and discuss ways to resolve conflict and the value of diversity (see Malhotra & Liyanage, 2005). Intergroup contact is often seen as a way of increasing empathy and understanding between groups (e.g., Allport, 1954), but not much is known about whether such workshops lead to lasting changes once participants return to their communities.

Fortunately, some evidence suggests that the benefits of such intergroup contact can be lasting. For example, in Sri Lanka, where protracted ethnic conflict exists between Tamils and Sinhalese, a 4-day peace workshop led to greater empathy between groups that still persisted 1 year later. Beyond simply reflecting reports of whether they felt empathy, people who had participated in the workshop were also more likely to donate money to help poor children belonging to the "other" ethnicity than were people who had not participated (Malhotra & Liyanage, 2005). Field experiments from other sites of ethnic conflict additionally offer evidence that intergroup contact can raise between-group empathy even when such "contact" is not in person, but is instead provided through the media. For example, in Rwanda, where tensions between Hutus and Tutsi persist following the Rwandan Civil War and genocide in the 1990s, 600 citizens, prisoners, and genocide survivors listened to a radio soap opera about Rwandan communities dealing with prejudice and violence and which contained positive interactions. Over the course of the study, listeners' perceptions and behaviors regarding social norms changed and they reported increased empathy toward the other group (Paluck, 2009). It seems that exercises that encourage perspective taking or exposure to positive interactions may be an effective way to counter the worst consequences of people's strong tendencies to divide the world into "us" and "them" (also see Cikara et al., 2017).

Stereotyping, Prejudice, and Behavior

When it comes to the cognitive processes that shape how we ultimately treat others, it is important to distinguish between social categorization (sorting people into group memberships, discussed in the preceding section), stereotyping, and prejudice (Fiske & Neuberg, 1990; Kunda & Sinclair, 1999). Although these processes often occur together, their co-occurrence isn't guaranteed. These different processes may differ in the degree of control we have over them.

Some social cognitive processes appear to proceed efficiently, without effort, without intention, and to such a degree that they are difficult to inhibit (qualities that have been referred to as the "four horsemen of automaticity"; Bargh, 1994). These are often referred to as **automatic processes** and are contrasted with **controlled processes** of social cognition, which appear to require effort, to unfold more slowly, and to be easier for us to inhibit or overcome (Bargh & Williams, 2006). That said, it is important to note that the distinction between automatic and controlled processes is neither clean nor all-or-nothing. Many social cognitive processes involve

Contact between groups can increase empathy and understanding. That may be one positive outcome of projects such as this set of seesaws at the Mexico–U.S. border—developed by Ronald Rael and Virginia San Fratello—that allows children on opposite sides of the border wall to play together.

both automatic and controlled processes, to varying degrees and in different combinations (Bargh, 1994). Thus, although cognitive mechanisms of stereotyping and prejudice are often discussed in terms of whether they are automatic or controlled, this distinction is better regarded as a sometimes useful shorthand than as a rigid division.

The ways we judge and relate to others often have no necessary connection to what a person is actually like. We frequently make assumptions about others on the basis of their social group membership—such as their race, religion, or sexuality—as well as on the mental associations we link with that group. This is known as **stereotyping**.

As we noted earlier, from a cognitive efficiency perspective, our tendency to rely on stereotypes makes adaptive sense. As the noted psychologist Gordon Allport stated:

> We like to solve problems easily. We can do so best if we can fit them rapidly into a satisfactory category and use this category as a means of prejudging the solution. . . . So long as we can get away with coarse overgeneralizations we tend to do so. Why? Well, it takes less effort, and effort, except in the area of our most intense interests, is disagreeable.

(From G. W. Allport. 1954. *The Nature of Prejudice*. Addison-Wesley.)

But the story is a bit more complex than Allport describes in this passage (see Amodio & Cikara, 2021). Although stereotyping might happen in a blink of an eye, there are different cognitive processes involved, which may be differentially open to our attempts to inhibit them. One account, known as a **dual-process theory of stereotyping**, suggests that the act of stereotyping involves two stages (Devine, 1989). The first stage, known as **stereotype activation**, refers to the bringing to mind of traits and characteristics that are commonly associated with a particular social group. Our cultures are so saturated with these types of associations that it can be difficult to avoid stereotype activation even when we don't personally believe the stereotypes.

The second stage, known as **stereotype application**, involves evaluations of, judgments of, and behaviors toward people based on our activated stereotypes. This process lies closer to what we commonly refer to as **prejudice**, which is the typically negative evaluation or prejudgment of others in accordance with stereotypes. Often, prejudice leads to real-world harm. One doesn't need to look hard to find examples. Consider the events of June 17, 2015, when a young man in South Carolina opened fire in a historically Black church, killing nine innocent members of a Bible study group. "You rape our women and you're taking over our country," Dylann Roof said, claiming that his motivation was to start a race war. Similar prejudices, against Hispanics, appear to have been at the root of the August 2019 mass shooting at a Walmart store in El Paso, Texas, which killed 22 people. Even more recently, in 2020 a wave of anti-Asian prejudice swept the globe in the wake of the illness COVID-19, sparked by the virus's initial emergence in China—never mind that China's population initially bore the brunt of the virus's toll.

Stereotype application is thought to be more under our control than stereotype activation, with people able to mentally correct the initial associations that come to mind (also see Fazio, 1990; Fazio et al., 1995; Krieglmeyer & Sherman, 2012; Kunda & Sinclair, 1999). In a seminal series of experiments, people who scored high and low in prejudice demonstrated equivalent knowledge of cultural stereotypes. When placed under cognitive load—which impeded people's ability to apply corrections once stereotypes were activated—both high- and low-prejudiced people tended to make evaluations in line with common stereotypes. However, in the absence of cognitive load, only those who scored high in prejudice rendered evaluations consistent with common stereotypes (Devine, 1989). This suggests that people are able to overcome stereotype application when motivated to do so, assuming that their cognitive resources are not overly taxed or distracted. Such findings give reason for hope, as they suggest that prejudice is not an inevitable consequence of stereotype knowledge—at least not for everyone (see Allport, 1954; Billig, 1985; Ehrlich, 1973; Hamilton, 1981; Tajfel, 1981).

The mechanisms that underlie stereotyping and prejudice can be subtle. In one set of experiments, people who were distracted by a cognitive task were less likely to activate stereotype knowledge but were more likely to apply it once it was activated (Gilbert & Hixon, 1991).

Some stereotypes may gain their power by virtue of being internalized from an early age. For example, research suggests that children differentiate between male and female gender roles from as early as age 3 (Kuhn et al., 1978) and that they begin to categorize and evaluate others on the basis of race at a similar age (Aboud, 1988). Children play with sex-typed toys (e.g., Bradbard et al., 1986; O'Brien & Huston, 1985), segregate themselves with same-sex peers (Maccoby & Jacklin, 1987), and make sex-based inferences about appropriate behavior (Biernat, 1991; Kuhn et al., 1978). Eventually, gender-based associations become effortless, fast, implicit, and difficult to inhibit (e.g., Banaji & Hardin, 1996; Most et al., 2007). That said, evidence suggests that children's gender-based stereotypes have evolved over time, in line with changes in societal expectations. When nearly 5,000 children in the United States and Canada, in the 1960s and 70s, were asked to draw a scientist, only 28 drew a picture of a woman (and all 28 children were girls themselves; Chambers, 1983). However, over the course of five decades of collecting data with this "draw a scientist" task, this proportion has increased (Miller et al., 2018). Even with such progress, though, children draw female scientists less than they draw male scientists.

IMPLICIT ATTITUDES   Closely related to the concept of prejudice is the concept of **attitude**, which refers to the generally positive or negative evaluations people hold of others. (And, of course, people can hold attitudes toward abstract concepts and inanimate objects as well.) One challenge of studying people's attitudes is that research participants are not always forthcoming about them. To get around this, researchers have developed methods that aim to measure people's **implicit attitudes**—that is, attitudes or associations that people exhibit unintentionally and without necessarily being aware of or able to verbalize them. Attempts to measure implicit attitudes are important because sometimes such attitudes have real-world consequences. For example, consider a study in which more than 120 faculty members from research-intensive universities were asked to rate applications from students who were applying for a laboratory manager position. The applications were equivalent, except that some were attributed to a male applicant and some to a female applicant. Overall, regardless of the whether the rater was a man or woman, they rated the male applicant as more competent and hireable, recommended a higher starting salary for him, and offered to provide him with more career mentoring (Moss-Racusin et al., 2012).

Among the best known and widely studied lab-based measures of implicit bias is the **implicit association test (IAT)** (Greenwald et al., 1998), which has been claimed to reveal people's unconscious attitudes about different social groups. In a classic example, people rapidly categorized stereotypically White and stereotypically

Women in science often need to combat systematic implicit biases that their male colleagues do not. In one study, female applicants to a laboratory manager position were perceived to be less competent than male applicants despite equivalent qualifications, and even when the evaluators were women themselves.

© iStock.com/sanjeri

Black names as each name appeared on a computer screen. In a separate phase, the participants viewed positive and negative words one at a time and had to rapidly categorize each as good or bad. These tasks were combined in a critical phase: people were instructed to press one key if the word was a stereotypically White name (e.g., Betsy, Katie) or a good word (e.g., lucky, happy), and another key if the word was a stereotypically Black name (e.g., Latonya, Shanise) or a bad word (e.g., grief, disaster). Most people found this task became harder (reflected in slower response times) when when the mapping was reversed, with the instructions to press one key for a White name or a bad word and another key for a Black name or a good word. That is, it was easier for people to link Black with bad than with good. You may have already noticed that the principle underlying the IAT is that interference or response conflict slows people down, as in the Stroop effect described in Chapter 5. Versions of the IAT have been developed to assess implicit attitudes pertaining to age, sexuality, religion, gender, and many other social dimensions. An interesting question is: What happens when the participants themselves are members of the stigmatized group? Evidence suggests that they show the same bias, albeit to a sometimes lesser degree. **SEE FOR YOURSELF 12.3** provides more information on the IAT.

> ▶ **See for Yourself 12.3**

The Implicit Association Test

The IAT reveals biases that people have when they associate social groups (e.g., old people, Black people, women) with positive or negative evaluations. Implicit biases often emerge even among people who believe they hold no preconceived notions about different groups. For this reason, seeing your own results on an IAT can be uncomfortable. You can try one on Oxford Learning Link.

Although the IAT was introduced to the literature over 20 years ago, controversy still exists over what it truly measures and what it predicts about real-world behavior. Does it really reveal unconscious prejudice, as some of its proponents initially suggested, or does it simply reflect participants' knowledge of the biased messages that pervade society? According to one large review of the literature, the IAT was a poor predictor of several measures of discrimination (Oswald et al., 2013; also see Blanton et al., 2009). And yet, taken on their own, some studies show tantalizing evidence that measures such as the IAT can predict real-world behaviors, including:

- Voting behavior (Arcuri et al., 2008; Galdi et al., 2008)
- Suicidal ideation and self-injuring behavior (Nock & Banaji, 2007a, 2007b)
- Severity of panic symptoms (Teachman et al., 2007)
- Racial bias among emergency room physicians (Green et al., 2007)
- Drug and alcohol use (Thush & Wiers, 2007)
- Biases in hiring decisions (Agerström & Rooth, 2011)

Clearly, the jury is still out on the value of such implicit measures and what they can reveal about implicit biases in the real world. Proponents of the IAT have pointed out that even if effects are statistically small in the lab, they can have a societal impact either because they affect many people at once or because they can affect a limited number of people repeatedly (Greenwald et al., 2015).

CAN CHANGES TO IMPLICIT ATTITUDES AFFECT REAL-WORLD BEHAVIOR?

If you tried to get coffee from a U.S. Starbucks on May 29, 2018, or a Canadian Starbucks 2 weeks later, chances are that you had to go without your caffeine fix. A large number of Starbucks shops were closed so that staff could be trained about implicit biases. Why? A month-and-a-half earlier, an employee had called police to report two Black men who were sitting in the store without ordering. The men explained that they were waiting for a friend before ordering, but they were handcuffed and detained by the police nevertheless. The incident caused nationwide outrage, and indeed it is hard to imagine similar treatment of White men in the same situation. The initiative to train the Starbucks employees about implicit bias seemed driven, in part, by a hope that changing implicit attitudes —or at least raising awareness of them—might lead to changes in real-world treatment of customers.

Efforts to change implicit biases take on additional urgency because in addition to their reported impact on voting, hiring, and health behavior, implicit biases have been linked to the kinds of split-second life or death decisions that we often hear about on the news. Imagine: You are about to participate in an experiment that has been appealingly described as being similar to playing a video game. In this game, you are a police officer. On the screen in front of you, a number of potentially dangerous people appear one at a time. Some are Black, some are White. Some have a gun, and you need to shoot them before they shoot you. Other people on the screen, however, are innocent bystanders holding only a cell phone. You are sworn to protect these people, and you need to withhold your fire each time they appear. In real life, this would be a nerve-racking situation.

This experiment is real; the task is known as the **police officer's dilemma** (Corell et al., 2002). The results from this task are as striking as they are alarming. Consistently, participants are more likely to shoot innocent Black bystanders than to shoot innocent White bystanders, and they are slower to shoot the White bad guys than to shoot the Black ones. In Australia, this effect has been replicated substituting people wearing Muslim headgear for bystanders and criminals for Black people (Unkelbach et al., 2008).

Can anything counter such automatic biases? As it turns out, even these relatively unconscious biases appear to be modulated by one's motivations and how people construe their current social environment (Blair, 2002; Forscher et al., 2019). For example, in lab experiments, reductions in automatic, racially driven biases have been observed among White participants in the following instances (among others):

- When they are assigned a role that is subordinate to that of a Black partner (Richeson & Ambady, 2003)
- When they are confronted with examples of Black individuals they admire (Dasgupta & Greenwald, 2001)
- When the experimenter they interact with is Black (Lowery et al., 2001)

Other research demonstrates that the nature of activated implicit biases depends on which social dimensions people attend to. For example, in one study participants were presented with Black athletes and White politicians. When asked to categorize these people according to race, they exhibited an implicit preference for the White individuals. However, when asked to categorize the people on the basis of their occupation, participants exhibited an implicit preference for the Black athletes (Mitchell et al., 2003). Evidence suggests that some interventions—such as manipulations of goals, associations, motivations, or concurrent cognitive load—can change how people perform on measures of implicit bias; but the evidence is not yet clear that changes to implicit bias translate into changes in behavior or in the attitudes that people consciously express (Forscher et al., 2019). As is often the case, more research is needed.

ASSERTING CONTROL OVER OUR THOUGHTS AND BEHAVIOR   In line with the notion that stereotypes can reduce the demands on our cognitive resources, it can be effortful to assert control over them and mold our behavior to our ideals rather than being led by the first associations that come to mind.

Ironically, attempts to suppress stereotypical thoughts may sometimes actually heighten their activation in one's mind. This possibility was illustrated by a classic series of studies in which people were asked to inhibit thoughts that researchers had activated through the instructions they gave: participants were explicitly instructed *not* to think of a "white bear" and were asked to indicate each time their attempts to suppress the thought of a white bear failed. Subsequently, participants were asked to dictate their stream of thought while again trying not to think of a white bear. The key result was that the group that had initially been instructed to suppress thoughts of a white bear subsequently reported thinking of the bear with greater frequency than did a control group that had not been instructed to suppress thoughts of a white bear. To the researchers, this result suggested that attempts to suppress a thought caused it to become more salient in participants' minds later on (Wegner et al., 1987). (The choice of a white bear was inspired by the Russian novelist Fyodor Dostoevsky, who in 1863 wrote "Try… not to think of a polar bear, and you will see that the cursed thing will come to mind every minute.")

It has been proposed that this **white bear effect** reflects the operation of dual processes in which people (a) monitor their thoughts for instances of what they are trying to suppress and then (b) attempt to suppress each instance they detect. The monitoring process proceeds relatively automatically, whereas attempts to suppress each instance are effortful and easily exhausted. Because attempts at thought suppression are effortful, they become less effective over time, even as the monitoring process continues unabated, leading the "forbidden" thought to enter awareness more often. Such findings and mechanisms have implications for what might happen when we try to avoid activating stereotype knowledge. As with the white bear example, it is possible that dual processes involved in monitoring one's thoughts for—and then trying to suppress—instances of stereotype knowledge might lead to greater activation of stereotype knowledge in the end.

STRATEGIES FOR SUPPRESSING UNWANTED THOUGHTS   Given the dilemma of "forbidden" thoughts taking center stage in the mind, there appear to be some strategies that people can use to suppress these unwanted notions. For example, in a follow-up study, researchers found that asking people to think of a red Volkswagen in place of a white bear reduced the effect. That is, substituting an acceptable thought for the unwanted one can be more effective than simply trying to suppress the unwanted thought (Wegner et al., 1987).

Just as suppressing unwanted stereotyped thoughts can be effortful, the same can be said for inhibiting inappropriate behaviors that may stem from them. In one study, participants took an IAT that revealed them to have high- or low-implicit biases against Black people, and then spent a period of time interacting with a Black individual. At the end of the interaction, the participants engaged in a Stroop task, a classic measure of executive function. Researchers found that participants who scored high in implicit bias against Black people, and who then interacted with a Black person, performed worse on the subsequent Stroop task than did participants who scored low on implicit bias and than those who interacted with a White person (Richeson & Shelton, 2003; also see Richeson et al., 2003). The researchers interpreted these findings as evidence that interracial interactions are cognitively taxing for people who score high in implicit bias and who therefore need to engage in self-regulation to prevent implicit attitudes from affecting their behavior. As discussed in Chapter 5, cognitive control is effortful.

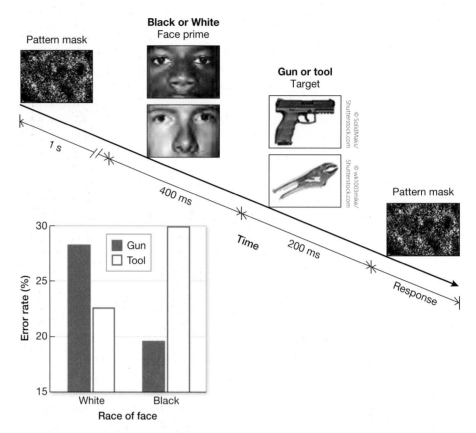

FIGURE 12.8 Weapons Identification Task Participants were asked to report whether each briefly presented picture of an object was a weapon or a tool. When the object was preceded by a briefly presented Black face, people often mistook the tool for a weapon. When the object was preceded by a White face, people often perceived the weapon as a tool. Although this occurred without intention, some evidence suggests that people may be able to exert control over such biases. (After D. M. Amodoio et al. 2004. *Psychol Sci* 15: 88–93.)

Some research suggests that people are able to control the degree to which their minds engage in implicit stereotyping and prejudice, as long as they prepare to apply such control in advance (see Chapter 5 for a consideration of proactive control). In one series of studies, researchers used Black and White faces to prime positive versus negative evaluations or stereotyped thinking. For example, in a Weapons Identification Task, people saw briefly presented pictures of handheld objects, one at a time, and had to indicate whether each item was a weapon or a tool. Critically, each item was preceded by a picture of a Black face or a White face (i.e., a Black or White "prime") (**FIGURE 12.8**). Consistent with the activation of implicit biases, people were more likely to mistakenly categorize tools as weapons when they were preceded by a Black face prime (Amodio et al., 2004; Payne, 2001). In follow-up experiments, participants were more likely to correctly categorize positive words (e.g., "pleasure") as positive and mental tasks (e.g., "math") as mental after the presentation of White face primes than Black face primes. However, when Black faces served as the primes on a high proportion of trials, all of these effects disappeared (Amodio & Swencionis, 2018). The researchers suggested that the frequent presentation of stereotypically "incongruent" pairings (e.g., Black faces followed by positive words) led participants to proactively increase the degree to which they recruited cognitive control. If this interpretation is correct, then it suggests that implicit stereotyping and prejudice in real life may be reduced by designing situations and strategies that encourage people to proactively apply cognitive control rather than try to gain control over their implicit cognitions once they have been activated.

EMOTION REGULATION   Sometimes, controlling your behavior toward others is really an exercise in controlling your emotions—otherwise known as **emotion regulation**. In some cases emotion regulation also appears to be cognitively taxing. In one experiment, people watched an emotional movie while trying to suppress their reactions to it. When subsequently asked to perform a Stroop task, they exhibited more Stroop interference than did participants who watched the movie without engaging in emotion regulation. What's more, when making errors on the subsequent Stroop task, those who had tried to regulate their emotions exhibited weaker *error-related negativity*, an event-related potential (ERP; see Chapter 2) component linked with registering one's own mistakes, which is a crucial component of cognitive control (Inzlicht & Gutsell, 2007) (**FIGURE 12.9**; see Chapter 5 for more on the error related negativity).

Of course, we can regulate our emotions in various ways, and not all of these ways appear to be equally demanding—at least not to the degree that they interfere with other cognitive functions. One of the most researched distinctions among emotion regulation strategies is that between **expressive suppression**, which involves attempting to hide one's emotional reactions, and **cognitive reappraisal**, which involves strategically reinterpreting whatever is eliciting your emotional reaction (Gross, 2001; Gross & John, 2003; John & Gross, 2004; Ochsner & Gross, 2005). An example of the latter is reinterpreting an anxiety-provoking job interview as an opportunity to learn more about the company instead of a situation in which you are being judged (Gross, 2002).

It has been suggested that these two strategies—expressive suppression and cognitive reappraisal—affect emotional processing at different points of an emotional episode (**FIGURE 12.10**). Cognitive reappraisal has been proposed to be "antecedent-focused," meaning that it targets the meaning of what elicited the emotion prior to the completion of an emotional episode. In contrast, expressive suppression has been proposed to be "response-focused": it targets the expression of emotion after a person has begun to generate an emotional response (e.g.,

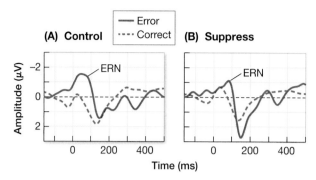

FIGURE 12.9 Emotion regulation can be cognitively taxing When people were instructed to suppress their emotional reactions to an emotional movie, errors on a subsequent Stroop task elicited a neural response of greater amplitude (solid line) than did correct answers (dashed line) **(A)**. This error-related negativity (ERN) was reduced after people had suppressed their emotional reactions to the emotional movie **(B)**. The findings suggested that the act of regulating emotion requires and depletes cognitive control. Note that in ERP research, it is customary to depict negative waveforms upward. (From M. Inzlicht and J. N. Gutsell. 2007. *Psychol Sci* 18: 933–937.)

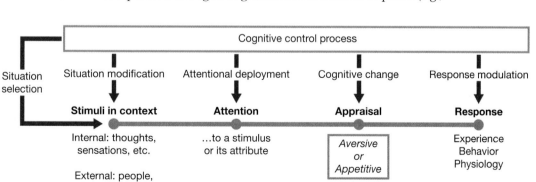

FIGURE 12.10 Steps involved in emotion generation and how they can be regulated by cognitive control From left to right (mirroring the unfolding of an emotional episode over time): people can alter their emotional experience by selecting or modifying the situation they find themselves in (where possible), by choosing which aspects of an event or stimulus to attend to, by changing their interpretation (or appraisal) of a situation or stimulus, or by altering how they express their emotion (response modulation). The last two strategies map onto cognitive reappraisal and expressive suppression, as described in the text. (From K. N. Ochsner et al. 2012. *Ann NY Acad Sci* 1251: E1–E24.)

facial expression). Several studies have found that expressive suppression strategies of emotion regulation are draining and impair subsequent cognitive processing (e.g., Inzlicht & Gutsell, 2007; Schmeichel, 2007; Shamosh & Gray, 2007). The cognitive consequences of cognitive reappraisal are less clear (Deveney & Pizzagalli, 2008; Moser et al., 2010). Importantly, the notion that some emotion regulation strategies are uniformly more beneficial than others has been suggested to be overly simplified. Instead, what may be more important is people's **regulatory flexibility**, or the degree to which they use different emotion regulation strategies depending on context and feedback (Bonanno & Burton, 2013).

➤ CHECKPOINT 12.3

1. Describe evidence that people make judgments about others quickly and without detailed information.
2. What do studies using the minimal group paradigm suggest about our tendency to divide people into in-groups and out-groups?
3. What evidence suggests that the way we categorize people influences our empathy toward them? Describe a real-world example that might illustrate this.
4. What does the distinction between automatic and controlled processes suggest about people's ability to overcome stereotyping and prejudice?
5. In what ways might the processes underlying social judgments translate into real-world consequences?
6. What are different ways that people can regulate their emotions?

12.4 Motivated Reasoning: A Roadblock to Seeing Eye to Eye

We live in difficult, divided times. It seems that whereas once upon a time people may have disagreed with each other, it appears difficult today even to have a civil discussion about disagreements due to demonization of "the other side." In the United States, in 2018 Republican Senator Jeff Flake told a New Hampshire crowd that "tribalism is ruining us. It is tearing our country apart. It is no way for sane adults to act." In a similar vein, *New York Times* columnist Thomas Friedman wrote:

> We can't find common ground on which to respectfully disagree; the other side is "the enemy." We shout at each other on television, unfollow each other on Facebook and fire verbal mortars at each other on Twitter—and now everyone is on the digital battlefield, not just politicians.

(Thomas Friedman in *The New York Times* October 2, 2018)

This dilemma is exacerbated by people's tendency to seek out information that supports and validates their own beliefs and attitudes, a tendency known as **confirmation bias** (which we covered in Chapter 10) and which only serves to make people more certain in the correctness of their beliefs. It's not merely that consumers of *Fox News* and the *Huffington Post* receive differently slanted news coverage and opinions (with *Fox* leaning right and the *Huffington Post* leaning left); it's also that audiences often actively seek out information that conforms to their world views (**FIGURE 12.11**). Not too long ago, there were limited opportunities to indulge this tribal aspect of human behavior, but an explosion of media and internet outlets in recent years has unleashed myriad such opportunities. What's more, when people limit their contact and conversations only to people who already agree with them, there's a tendency for them to emerge with even more extreme views than they initially had, a well-known effect called **group polarization**.

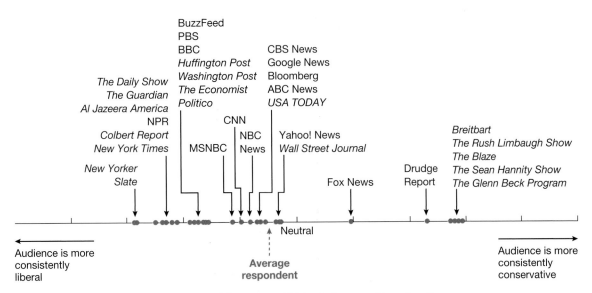

FIGURE 12.11 Graphical representation of the average ideological composition of audiences for several American media outlets as of 2014 Survey data suggest that people of different political stripes prefer to rely on different sources of news and analysis. (After A. Mitchell et al. 2014. *Political Polarization and Media Habits.* Pew Research Center. Washington, D.C. https://www.journalism.org/2014/10/21/political-polarization-media-habits/)

As a hypothetical solution, one could imagine implementing some policy that might encourage a broader representation of views across all media platforms. But in addition to confirmation bias, there are other cognitive biases that make people resistant to changing their views. The biases that keep us from changing our views are so entrenched that they even operate in the absence of contact with other people. For example, people frequently overestimate the degree to which their own opinions and attitudes are shared by others, a phenomenon known as the **false consensus effect** (Ross et al., 1977).

Motivated Reasoning

People have a tendency to fit their interpretation of information to their own preexisting beliefs or emotions, a phenomenon known as **motivated reasoning** (Kunda, 1990; Lord et al., 1979; Westen et al., 2006). According to one study, which was conducted at the time of the 2004 U.S. presidential election, signatures of motivated reasoning processes can be observed at the neural level: when people were confronted with information counter to their own strongly held viewpoint, heightened activity was observed in brain regions distinct from those often linked with dispassionate deliberation (Westen et al., 2006). In this study, passionate Democratic and Republican partisans were shown a series of statements about the Democratic and Republican presidential candidates, which progressed in such a way that an initial statement was then followed by a statement suggesting hypocrisy on the part of the candidate.

It turned out that participants were more likely to view the statements as hypocritical or contradictory when they came from the candidate belonging to the opposite party as themselves. It was when people were confronted with the evidence of hypocrisy from their preferred candidate that they exhibited heightened activation in brain regions previously linked with emotion, emotional conflict, and pain, such as the orbital prefrontal cortex, ventromedial prefrontal cortex, ventral anterior cingulate cortex, and insula (Westen et al., 2006). Consistent with the role of emotion in resistance to changing one's mind, participants in another study who did change their opinion when presented with evidence against their strongly held political beliefs were characterized by weaker activity in the emotion-linked areas such as the insula and amygdala (Kaplan et al., 2016).

An upshot is that it is difficult for people to change their strongly held opinions even when confronted with evidence that contradicts them, perhaps because of their emotional investment. Although many of us would like to believe our opinions are based on our understanding of the facts, it frequently is the case that we simply use and pay attention to the facts that support a view we already have. People have a singular, exceptional ability to convince themselves that their beliefs and attitudes are based in reason. As psychologists Richard Nisbett and Timothy Wilson (1977) highlighted in a classic survey of the literature, this idea is often false. Instead, we have a tendency to create seemingly rational justifications after making a decision. The notion that our beliefs—say, about right and wrong—stem from quick intuition, only then to be followed by slow deliberation, is known as the **social intuitionist model** (Haidt, 2001). Note that this does not mean that our beliefs and values are wrong per se—only that we appear to have limited conscious access to the processes that form them. **THINK FOR YOURSELF 12.1** provides an example.

▶ **Think for Yourself 12.1**

Judging Right and Wrong without Knowing Why

Consider your reaction to the following scenario, described by psychologist Jonathan Haidt (2001):

> *Julie and Mark are brother and sister. One night during their summer vacation in France, they stay alone in a cabin near the beach. They decide that it would be interesting and fun to make love; at the very least, it would be a new experience for each of them. Julie is already taking birth control pills, but Mark uses a condom just to be safe. They both enjoy the sex, but they decide not to do it again. They keep the night as a special secret, which makes them feel even closer to each other than they did before.*
>
> (From J. Haidt. 2001. *Psychol Rev* 108: 814–834.)

Was it OK for Julie and Mark to have sex? Many people can't help but feel that they did the wrong thing. When people are pressed to explain why they object to the siblings' actions, they often scramble to find a logical reason.

"Because they're related! If Julie had gotten pregnant, the child would have had an increased chance of having a genetic defect!" (But the story emphasizes how careful they were to use birth control.)

"Because if anyone ever found out, they would think they were perverts!" (But the story explicitly says that they never told anyone.)

"Because it could emotionally damage them!" (But the story tells us that they enjoyed it and felt closer to one another afterward.)

Don't get us wrong: we're not endorsing incest. What we are pointing out, however, is that our judgments and evaluations don't always come from a place that we can articulate. Our guess is that even though you might recognize logical

flaws in every reasoned objection you come up with, you won't be able to shake the feeling that there is something wrong with Julie's and Mark's actions. Recall the "trolley problem" described in See For Yourself 1.3, where people tend to find it less palatable to save five people's lives by pushing a man in front of a trolley to stop it than to switch the trolley onto a parallel track, where it will run over and kill the man. Although the outcomes are the same in both cases (i.e., number of lives saved), behavioral and neuroimaging data suggest that it is harder to contemplate such personal transgressions because they additionally engage a conflicting emotional response (Greene et al., 2001). Multiple factors contribute to such moral decision-making (e.g., Crockett, 2013; Cushman, 2013), and it is hard for people to always verbalize their reasons.

Is it wrong for siblings to have sex? Many people strongly believe that it is, even in hypothetical scenarios with no negative consequences. Our sense of right and wrong does not always rely on a rational consideration of pros and cons.

© Yuril/stock.adobe.com

THE DIFFICULTY OF CORRECTING MISINFORMATION   Even after it has been rescinded or corrected, the influence of misinformation has been found to persist (Ecker et al., 2011; Johnson & Seifert, 1994; Wilkes & Leatherbarrow, 1988). In one study that might be particularly deflating for believers in the power of facts and logic, researchers discovered that people sometimes "dig in their heels" and recommit to their worldviews when their understanding of the facts is corrected. For example, in one set of experiments, participants read mock news articles containing a misleading claim by a politician, which either was or was not followed by a correction. In some cases, the correction appeared to lead people to agree even more with the initial misleading claim, particularly when the misleading claim aligned with their worldview (Nyhan & Reifler, 2010). This has been called the **backfire effect**, and it may be important to keep in mind for those seeking to develop strategies to counter the influence of misinformation. In one study, conservatives who followed a liberal bot on Twitter were likely to become more conservative in their views, whereas liberals who followed a conservative bot on Twitter became slightly more liberal (Bail et al., 2018).

Fortunately, evidence suggests that the backfire effect may not be as inevitable as initial findings suggested: studies that have failed to replicate it suggest that people's understanding of the facts can indeed be changed by counterevidence (Redlawsk et al., 2010; Wood & Porter, 2018). This is good news for those who fear we may be living in a "post-truth" world. Nevertheless, there is a difference between changing someone's understanding of the facts and changing someone's opinion. As the eminent philosopher John Stuart Mill once wrote, "So long as opinion is strongly rooted in the feelings, it gains rather than loses instability by having a preponderating weight of argument against it" (Mill, 1869; also see Lewandowsky et al., 2012).

Despite the power of motivated reasoning, evidence suggests that we are not inevitably bound by our pre-existing biases and ideological leanings. People who tend to engage in analytical reasoning have been found to successfully distinguish accurate information from misinformation regardless of whether the information aligned with their ideology (Pennycook & Rand, 2019). Consistent with this, such individuals also appear less likely to share information from unreliable sources on social media (Mosleh et al., 2021). Findings such as these may hold clues for slowing the rampant spread of misinformation. Indeed, one study found that subtly priming participants to focus on the accuracy of information subsequently improved the quality of information they shared online (Pennycook et al., 2021).

➤ CHECKPOINT 12.4

1. How can aspects of motivated reasoning such as confirmation bias and the false consensus effect prevent people from appreciating each other's perspectives?

2. What evidence suggests that differentiating right from wrong is not always based on rational deliberation?

3. What evidence suggests that motivated reasoning may facilitate the spread of misinformation? What evidence suggests that critical thinking may counter this?

Chapter Summary

12.1 Understand how social cognition connects with other areas of cognitive psychology, and how and why social cognition may differ from nonsocial cognition.

Social cognition comprises a rich area of research and theory at the intersection of cognitive psychology and social psychology. It encompasses what science has to tell us about how we perceive, attend to, remember, and think about ourselves, other people, and social groups. The field of social cognition has helped fulfil the ideals of the architects of the Cognitive Revolution by addressing how cognition operates in the real world. Social cognition often builds on and extends research found elsewhere in cognitive psychology.

Q: Consider again this statement from the chapter: "Social cognition is inherently mutual: the perceived perceive you in return.… Other people's views of you can change the way you behave even when you may not be aware of it." Can you think of times in your life when this has rung true for you and would provide a good example of this concept?

12.2 Describe evidence that people are particularly sensitive to social information and that we may be "wired" to process social information.

People have a strong need to connect with each other. Loneliness and perceived social isolation have been linked with impairments in physical and mental health. People appear to be so sensitive to social information that they have been found to perceive social motives and interactions even in the movements of nonsentient objects. The ability to understand the mental states of others is known as theory of mind, the emergence of which constitutes an important developmental milestone. Researchers have identified brain areas that are particularly involved in social interactions, and which have been proposed to form the social cognition neural network.

Q: Although social cognition research incorporates topics such as attention, categorization, and reasoning, one can argue that the field amounts to more than simply applying cognitive principles to people instead of objects. Why? What is different about the social world?

12.3 Discuss shortcuts that our minds use in order to reduce the complexity of the social world, as well as some consequences of such shortcuts.

With many social relationships to navigate, our minds look for ways to cut corners and seek shortcuts to minimize the need to process each person's intrinsic complexities. Such shortcuts include carving the social world into smaller in-groups and out-groups, relying on stereotypes, and making rapid judgments based on superficial appearances. Unfortunately, these shortcuts frequently guide us in the wrong direction. Some of these processes occur very quickly, and they appear to vary in how much control we have over them. For example, we may have less control over stereotype activation than over the degree to which we apply stereotypes. Regulating our own behavior, whether by attempting to suppress stereotype-related thoughts or by regulating our emotional reactions, can be more or less cognitively effortful depending on which strategy we choose.

Q: Intergroup hostility, prejudice-driven violence, and problems that people can't seem to agree on appear frequently in the news. What aspects of social cognition might be important for trying to understand some of this, and what solutions might the study of social cognition have to offer?

12.4 Understand "motivated reasoning" and how it can impede fruitful discussions over disagreements.

People have a tendency to fit their interpretation of information to their own preexisting beliefs or emotions, a phenomenon known as motivated reasoning. Thus, even when people receive the same information as each other, they may come away with different understandings. Phenomena such as confirmation bias can lead people to attend to only the bits of information that conform to what they already believe. Phenomena such as the false consensus effect can make it harder for people to change their own views because they have a false impression of how widely held their own beliefs are. Frameworks such as the social intuitionist model of moral reasoning suggest that people's judgments of morality are often rooted in their intuitive and emotional reactions, and that people often use reasoning to support their conclusions after the fact.

Q: Think of a friend or relative with whom you strongly disagree about political issues. To what degree are your differing opinions a function of getting your information from different sources or of cognitive biases or motivated reasoning? Now consider your feelings on that subject in general and ask yourself whether you would be open to seeing the other person's point of view, and even being willing to adapt it to your way of thinking.

Key Terms

attitude
attractiveness bias
automatic process
baby-face bias
backfire effect
bias blind spot
cognitive reappraisal
confirmation bias
controlled processes
dehumanized perception
dual-process theory of stereotyping
Dunbar's number
emotion regulation
empathy
entitativity
expressive suppression
false consensus effect

group polarization
implicit association test (IAT)
implicit attitudes
in-group identification
in-groups
minimal group paradigm
mirror-neuron system
motivated reasoning
nonverbal behavior
other race face effect
out-groups
perception-action-coupling
point light walkers
police officer's dilemma
prejudice
psychological field
Pygmalion effect

regulatory flexibility
schadenfreude
self-categorization theory
self-fulfilling prophecy
social brain hypothesis
social categorization
social cognition neural network
social intuitionist model
stereotype activation
stereotype application
stereotype content model
stereotyping
theory of mind
thin-slice judgments
Wason selection task
white bear effect

Critical Thinking Questions

1. The field of social cognition has yielded insights into cognitive processes that are involved in stereotyping, prejudice, persuasion, and between-group hostility. What real-world problems can be addressed through such understanding, and what real-world problems can only be addressed through a different lens (e.g., economic, political, etc.)? When is it useful to combine such other perspectives with an understanding of social cognition?

2. Society bombards us with messages constantly, whether through television, movies, radio, advertisements, etc. Can you think of examples from mass media that might be helping to break down barriers or increase empathy between social groups? Can you think of examples that might be helping drive people apart?

Suggested Readings

Amodio, D. M., & Cikara, M. (2021). The social neuroscience of prejudice. *Annual Review of Psychology, 72*, 439–469.

Fiske, S. T., & Taylor, S. E. (2017). *Social Cognition: From Brains to Culture*, 3rd Edition. London: Sage Publications.

Lewandowsky, S., Ecker, U. K., Seifert, C. M., Schwarz, N., & Cook, J. (2012). Misinformation and its correction: Continued influence and successful debiasing. *Psychological Science in the Public Interest, 13*, 106–131.

Lieberman, M. D. (2013). *Social: Why Our Brains Are Wired to Connect.* New York: Crown Publishers/Random House.

Zaki, J. (2019). *The War for Kindness: Building Empathy in a Fractured World.* New York: Crown Publishing Company.

Glossary

7 plus or minus 2   Miller's proposal for the number of items that can be stored in working memory.

A

A-B, A-C learning paradigm   A task used to study memory interference; for example, memory for a pairing (A & B) is worse when participants also learn an overlapping pairing (A & C) than a non-overlapping pairing (D & E).

acoustic similarity effect   The reduced capacity of working memory for items similar in sound, compared with items that are dissimilar in sound.

action pathway   A visual pathway in the brain that uses perceptual information to guide ongoing actions.

action potential   An electrical signal in a neuron, which travels down the axon once an activation threshold is crossed.

actions (operators)   In problem solving, the steps needed to move from a given state to a goal state.

ad-hoc categories   Categories defined in terms of goals or themes.

affective primacy hypothesis   The hypothesis that an emotional response typically precedes cognitive interpretation.

affective priming   Response enhancement that results from prior exposure to items that have the same emotional quality.

affirmation of the consequent (q)   In reasoning, a formal fallacy of declaring an antecedent true if the consequent is true.

agnosia   A visual condition involving difficulty recognizing objects.

algorithmic level of analysis   An analytical framework centered on understanding the rules, mechanisms, and representations the mind uses.

allocentric   Referring to a spatial framework in which an object's location is defined relative to the location of another object.

Alzheimer's disease   A degenerative brain disease characterized by memory loss and dementia.

ambiguity resolution theory of visual selective attention   The theory that, because activations within the visual system can support multiple perceptual interpretations, attention helps resolve such ambiguities.

amodal completion   A visual process that supports an illusory sense of seeing past blocked views due to the mind's filling in of missing visual information.

analogical reasoning   Reasoning that helps an individual find solutions by transferring their knowledge from other problems.

analytical intelligence   A type of intelligence that maps roughly onto IQ measures, and is most linked with traditional notions of general intelligence.

anchoring   The concept that different starting points (initial values) produce different estimates or decisions.

anomic aphasia   A condition characterized by difficulty finding the words one wants to say.

antecedent   In reasoning, the first part of a hypothetical proposition ("if" in "if/then").

anterior cingulate cortex (ACC)   A brain area implicated in the detection of errors and cognitive interference.

anterograde amnesia   An inability to form new conscious memories.

anticipation error   An error in which a speech segment (e.g., a phoneme) early in a sentence is swapped for a speech segment later in the sentence.

aphantasia   An inability to engage in mental imagery.

aphasia   A condition characterized by impaired ability to produce or understand language.

apperceptive agnosia   The inability to perform simple visual feature tasks, implying impaired object recognition stems from deficits in early vision.

articulatory rehearsal loop   A component of the phonological loop in working memory that allows a person to briefly remember verbal material by repeating it in their mind.

articulatory suppression   The disruption of rehearsal in working memory, induced by uttering irrelevant sounds.

artificial intelligence (AI)   The technology that enables computers to engage in or mimic complex cognitive functions.

associative agnosia   The inability to recognize or name objects, despite functioning early vision.

associative priming   Response enhancement that results from prior exposure to related items.

attention   A family of cognitive mechanisms that combine to help us select, modulate, and sustain focus on information that might be most relevant for behavior.

attention restoration theory   The theory that being out in nature can restore cognitive fatigue.

attentional bias   An often involuntary tendency to attend to a particular type of (often emotional) stimulus.

attentional bias modification   A therapeutic approach aiming to help people reduce maladaptive biases to attend to clinically relevant stimuli.

attentional blink   The failure to see the second of two targets in a rapid succession of items when it appears soon after the first target.

attentional capture   Involuntary (reflexive) grabbing of attention by certain kinds of stimuli.

attitude   The generally positive or negative evaluations that people hold of other people or things.

attractiveness bias   The tendency to attribute other good qualities to people we find attractive.

autobiographical memory   Memory of events from one's own life.

automatic processes   Cognitive, or social cognitive, processes that can proceed efficiently, without effort or intention, and are more difficult to inhibit than controlled processes.

availability heuristic (availability bias)   A bias whereby people estimate the frequency of an event based on how easily examples come to mind.

axon   The part of a neuron that carries nerve impulses away from the cell body, toward the receiving dendrites of other neurons.

B

baby-face bias   A tendency to attribute honesty and naivety to baby-faced adults.

backfire effect   An effect in which an attempt to correct a person's misinformed belief leads the person to adhere more strongly to their belief.

base rate frequency (prior probability)   Probabilities that reflect how often an event or situation actually occurs.

basic-level category   The level of category that typically comes easily to most people's minds (e.g., car); in contrast with a superordinate category (e.g., vehicle) and subordinate category (e.g., Toyota Camry).

Bayes' Rule   An equation estimating the probability of a hypothesis being true given the evidence.

Bayesian inference   Estimation of the probability of a hypothesis being true given the evidence at hand and one's knowledge of the world.

behavioral genetics   The field that attempts to link behavior (phenotypes) and genes (genotypes).

behavioral neuroscience   The branch of neuroscience that uses animal models to understand neural mechanisms underpinning behavior.

Behaviorism   A psychological movement characterized by its focus only on outwardly observable behavior.

bell curve   A graphical depiction of a normal distribution, which is more or less symmetrical and shaped like a bell.

bias blind spot   The mistaken perception of oneself as less biased than other people.

biased competition model of attention   A model of attention in which visual stimuli falling within the same receptive field compete with each other, and in which attention biases the competition in favor of one over the other.

bilingualism   Fluency in two languages.

binding problem   The challenge of figuring out which visual features in the environment combine together to form cohesive perceptions of objects.

binocular depth cues   Visual cues that support depth perception but which require the use of both eyes.

binocular disparity   A phenomenon in which the closer something is to you, the greater the difference between what your two eyes see.

blind spot   An area toward the outside of the visual field corresponding to where the optic nerve passes through the retina, and where there is no visual stimulation due to an absence of photoreceptors.

blindsight   The condition in which a patient who has suffered damage to the visual cortex (e.g., through stroke) is able to respond to and localize visual stimuli that they report not being able to see.

blocking   Difficulty retrieving memories that are intact and encoded due to other memories getting in the way.

blood-oxygen-level-dependent (BOLD) signal   The signal used to generate images in functional magnetic resonance imaging (fMRI), indicating blood oxygen levels throughout the brain.

bottom-up information   The sensory input in perception.

bottom-up selection   Attentional selection driven by the salience of the physical features in the external environment.

brain stimulation   The stimulation or disruption of brain activity to study causal effects on perceptual and cognitive function.

broaden-and-build theory   The theory that positive emotions widen the range of information people readily consider and attend to.

Broca's aphasia   A condition characterized by difficulty speaking fluently, producing correct sounds, or finding the right words.

Broca's area   An area in the brain's left frontal lobe, with functions linked to speech production.

C

capacity-limited   Referring to the mind's ability to handle only limited amounts of information at a time.

categorization   The process of grouping items or ideas together and distinguishing them from other items or ideas.

causal launching   In an animated display, the perception that one moving stimulus causes a stationary one to move (or "launch") when it collides with it.

causal learning (causal induction)   Learning about cause–effect relationships from observations.

causal models   Modeled networks of interconnected relationships that organize understanding of cause-effect relationships.

causal reasoning   The ability to understand why something happens, to determine the causes of specific effects.

cause–effect relationships   Relationships in which one factor or set of factors causes an outcome (or effect); often depicted with an arrow leading from the cause to the effect.

cell body (soma)   The neuron's core, which receives input and provides the metabolic machinery for the neuron.

central bottleneck model   A model of attention that assumes that only one response can be selected at a time, so that a subsequent response is queued.

central executive   The primary system for controlling attention and thinking, responsible for manipulating information held in working memory.

cerebellum   A major structure of the brain, located near the brainstem; responsible for control of fine motor movements and possibly the coordination of complex thought.

cerebral cortex   A thin, folded sheet of neurons constituting the outer layer of the brain.

change blindness   The failure to notice often large changes from one view to the next.

chromosome   A long strand of DNA; in humans, each cell normally contains 23 pairs.

chunk   A unit of information in working memory, flexibly defined in terms of what is meaningful to the person; historically, Miller claimed that working memory capacity was 7-plus-or-minus-2 chunks.

chunking   The memory-encoding strategy of organizing smaller bits of information into larger, meaningful combinations.

classical conditioning   A form of learning in which observable changes in behavior result from learned associations between stimuli.

cocktail party problem   An analogy referring to people's ability to attend to one channel of information while ignoring others that impinge on the senses.

cognitive control   The ability to orchestrate thought and action in accordance with internal goals.

cognitive interference   A condition that occurs when task load is high or when two tasks overlap significantly, and performance suffers as a result.

cognitive interview   A psychologist-developed system for interviewing eyewitnesses, in which the interview is conducted at a slow rate and asks mostly open-ended questions that encourage a witness to recall events freely.

cognitive load   The cognitive burden caused by holding information in working memory; related to the difficulty of a task.

cognitive map   A mental representation of locations within an individual's environment.

cognitive map theory   A theory according to which the hippocampus constructs a map of the environment, providing the basis for spatial memory and navigation.

cognitive neuroscience   The interdisciplinary study of the neural mechanisms of cognition and behavior.

cognitive overlap   The degree to which the demands of simultaneous tasks compete for the same mental resources.

cognitive primacy hypothesis   The hypothesis that cognitive interpretation typically precedes an emotional response.

cognitive psychology   The scientific study of how the mind encodes, stores, and uses information.

cognitive reappraisal   An emotion regulation strategy involving reinterpretation of what is eliciting an emotional reaction.

Cognitive Revolution   A period during the 1950s and 1960s marked by rapid and radical shifts in approaches to the study of cognition.

cognitive science   A formal effort to synthesize insights across diverse disciplines attempting to understand the mind.

cognitive-functional linguistics   A branch of linguistics that emphasizes the communicative function of language; also known as usage-based linguistics.

cognitively impenetrable   Referring to a property of perceptual processing that is not influenced by high-level cognition (e.g., by beliefs, knowledge, or motivation).

collective intelligence (c)   The intelligence exhibited when individuals work together and make sound decisions in groups.

color constancy   In color perception, the ability to factor in differences in illumination.

common ground   A shared understanding or perception of context, or a shared degree of knowledge.

complementary memory system   A system in which the hippocampus and medial temporal lobe support rapid learning, and the neocortex supports gradual learning.

computational level of analysis   An analytical framework centered on understanding what the mind is trying to compute and why.

computational modeling   The use of mathematical functions to constrain and predict aspects of human cognition.

concepts   Mental representations that correspond to objects or ideas in the world.

conceptual act theory of emotion   A theory according to which the processing and experience of emotion are shaped by conceptual knowledge about emotions.

conceptual priming   Response enhancement that results from having previously processed the meaning of a related stimulus.

concrete operational period   According to Piaget, the time (around age 7) when children acquire thinking and reasoning abilities that allow them to understand conservation of properties even as objects change.

cones   The light-sensitive photoreceptors in the eye that enable color vision.

confirmation bias   The favoring of evidence that supports one's beliefs, expectations, or hypotheses.

conflict monitoring   A core component of cognitive control, involving the detection of interference.

conflict resolution   In cognitive control, the ability to reduce interference, either through inhibition or other behavioral adjustments.

conjunction   In attention and perception, a combination of features, such as color and shape, that distinguish a target stimulus.

conjunction fallacy   The false assumption that a combination of conditions is more likely to occur than any one of the conditions by itself.

connectionism (parallel distributed processing, neural nets)   The representation of knowledge in a distributed manner across connections between multiple nodes.

consequent   The second part of a hypothetical proposition ("then" in "if/then").

conservation task   A test, typically of children's cognitive abilities, to see whether participants understand that physical properties do not change even when an appearance is changed.

consistency bias   The tendency to remember the impact of events in the past through the lens of their impact on us today.

consolidation   The solidification of connections that enable memory storage.

content morphemes   The smallest units of meaningful sound that describe places, people, actions, or things.

context-dependent memory   The enhancement of memory when the retrieval context is the same as the learning context.

contextual cueing   Learning where to attend and what to expect based on statistical regularities in past experience.

continuous performance task   An experimental task in which participants are required to stay focused for a prolonged period.

controlled processes   Cognitive, or social cognitive, processes that require more effort, unfold more slowly, and are easier to inhibit than automatic processes.

core knowledge   Knowledge of specific types of information, such as language, physics, numbers, and psychology.

corpus callosum   A large bundle of neural fibers (axons) forming a massive interconnection between the two hemispheres of the brain.

correlation and causation problem   The mistaken assumption that correlation implies causation.

counterfactual reasoning   Thinking in which an individual considers alternative outcomes, contrary to what has already occurred in reality.

covariation   The likelihood of events occurring together.

covert attention   Attention directed in a manner that is not outwardly observable.

creative cognition   The cognitive processes that support creativity.

creative intelligence   Intelligence that involves the ability to reason in novel ways.

creativity   The ability to arrive at novel solutions and creations.

creole language   A synthesis of words from different languages that adheres to rules of grammar.

critical period   A developmental period during which children appear to be optimally equipped to learn the rules of language.

crystallized intelligence (Gc)   Knowledge as reflected in tests of vocabulary and facts about the world.

curse of knowledge   The difficulty experts often have in putting themselves into the shoes of someone less knowledgeable.

D

decoy effect   The phenomenon whereby the introduction of a more- or less-expensive item provides an anchor to stimulate the sales of a target item.

deductive reasoning   Thinking that involves moving from general knowledge and principles to more specific knowledge and examples.

deep learning   A form of artificial intelligence that uses deep neural nets (brainlike algorithms) to attempt to interpret natural images.

deep structure   In language, the underlying mental representation, which is translated into surface structure in order to be communicated through language.

Deese/Roediger-McDermott effect   The tendency to falsely remember an item that did not appear on a list of related items.

dehumanized perception   Failure to perceive humanizing mental states in others.

delay discounting (temporal discounting)   The psychological tendency to diminish the value of future gains the longer one has to wait for them.

deliberation-without-attention effect   The effect that occurs when unconscious processes help an individual consciously make a decision.

dementia   A chronic disorder characterized by the loss of memory and other intellectual abilities.

dendrite   A branchlike component of a neuron, receiving input from sensory receptors or other neurons.

denial of the antecedent (p)   In reasoning, a formal fallacy of declaring a consequent false if the antecedent is false.

depictive   In mental imagery, referring to the view that the brain creates representations of mental images the same way it creates real images perceived through the eyes.

depth of encoding   The degree to which a person encodes information. Deep encoding is associated with better memory than shallow or intermediate encoding.

descriptive theories   Theories concerned with how individuals *actually* make decisions, describing beliefs and preferences as they are, not as they should be.

dichotic listening   An experimental task in which participants listen to two different messages played simultaneously over headphones.

digit-span task   An experimental task in which the participant listens to and then repeats a series of numbers; used to test the storage capacity of working memory.

directionality   The principle that in causal relationships, causes precede effects.

dishabituation   The reemergence of a behavioral response that had previously diminished (e.g., over time or with repetition).

distributed code   A cortical record of information processing across multiple brain regions, which can be reactivated when remembering the initial experience.

distributed practice   The strategy of distributing study sessions over time to help improve memory.

divergent thinking   The ability to generate a wide range of associations from a given starting point.

divided-attention tasks   Research tasks in which participants are asked to complete two tasks at the same time.

DNA (deoxyribonucleic acid)   A molecule shaped like a twisted ladder, known as a double-helix configuration, and containing genes.

domain-specific hypothesis   The hypothesis that, throughout the course of evolution, certain categories of objects gained privileged processing in the brain, leading to specialized circuitry and brain areas.

dorsolateral prefrontal cortex   One of several brain areas important for cognitive control.

dot probe task   An experimental task in which participants respond quickly to a target (e.g., a dot) that could appear in one of two locations, and where an emotional or personally relevant stimulus may precede the target at the target or non-target location.

dual-process theory of stereotyping   The theory that stereotyping involves two stages, activation and application.

dual-task experiment   An experiment that requires participants to do two tasks at the same time.

dualism   The idea, credited to the seventeenth-century philosopher René Descartes, that there is a distinction between the physical world, where the brain resides, and a nonphysical world, where the mind and soul reside.

Dunbar's number   An estimation of the average number of meaningful relationships an individual has in their social network, about 150.

E

early selection   In attention, the theory that we attentionally select stimuli on the basis of physical features such as color, pitch, or location, and that we register their meaning only after we have selected them.

ego depletion   An effect in which exhausting one's self-regulatory energy leads to subsequently impaired self-regulation and cognitive control.

egocentric   Referring to a spatial framework in which spatial layout and locations are defined relative to the observer.

elaboration   A memory-encoding strategy of making links between new material and existing knowledge held in long-term memory.

electrocorticography (ECoG) (intracranial recording)   A method of recording electrical signals from electrodes placed on surgically exposed cerebral cortex.

electroencephalography (EEG)   A method of using electrodes on the scalp to measure electrical activity in the brain.

electrophysiology   The direct measurement of electrical activity from neurons, either from single cells or from an aggregate of cells.

embodied cognition (grounded cognition)   The theory that shared representations are used for perception, action, and knowledge, and that the body and physical experience help shape cognition.

emotion regulation   The ability to manage, modulate, and alter one's emotions.

emotion-induced blindness   The failure to see rapidly presented targets that appear right after a rapidly presented emotional non-target.

emotional intelligence   The ability to recognize and manage emotions.

empathy   A feeling of sharing in what and how other people are thinking and feeling.

encode   To mentally process information in a way that enables you to later have conscious access to it.

endogenous (central) cue   A cue that engages voluntary attention and symbolically directs attention to a potential target location.

endowment effect   The tendency to overvalue what one has in hand.

entitativity   A perceived uniformity of out-group members.

epigenetics   The study of external factors that affect how genes operate.

epiphenomenon   A phenomenon that occurs together with a process of interest but is not central for its function.

episodic buffer   The component of working memory that integrates information from multiple internal sources into an episodic representation.

episodic memory   Memory that enables recall of past events in specific places at specific times: what, where, and when something happened.

error detection   The detection of cognitive interference or response errors, an important component of cognitive control.

error-related negativity (ERN)   An electrical brain signal (event related potential) that occurs when a person makes an error.

event-related potential (ERP)   The time-locked EEG waveform that occurs in response to a stimulus, event, or task.

excitatory   Refers to connections between features or neurons in which activating one raises the likelihood of activating the other.

exemplar-based categorization   A theory of categorization proposing that we store numerous, previously encountered exemplars from a category in mind and then match new instances to the stored representations when deciding whether or not they belong.

exogenous (peripheral) cue   A cue that engages reflexive attention and can appear at one of multiple target locations, it attracts attention to its location instead of directing attention symbolically.

expected value   In decision making, the assessment of the lucrativeness of an option, derived by multiplying its value by the likelihood of obtaining it.

explicit attention   Attention resulting in conscious awareness; measures of it usually rely on conscious report.

explicit memory   The ability to consciously remember facts, events, and associations; also known as declarative or conscious memory.

expressive suppression   An emotion regulation strategy involving hiding or suppressing one's emotional reactions.

external attention   Attention directed outwardly to the world.

extrinsic motivation   Motivation based on external rewards such as money or status.

eye tracking   A research tool whereby cameras track and record where participants are looking.

F

factor analysis   A statistical procedure that takes several independently measured variables and determines the number of underlying factors that best explains the data variance.

false consensus effect   The phenomenon whereby an individual overestimates the degree to which their own opinions and attitudes are shared by others.

false memories   Recollections of events that never happened.

familiarity   The sense of having seen something or someone before.

family resemblance   The similarity of exemplars within a category.

fan effect   The phenomenon of having greater difficulty retrieving memories that have a greater number of associations or overlapping elements with other memories.

fast mapping   A young child's ability to identify a word's meaning after only one exposure to it.

fast-and-frugal search tree   An approach to decision making that relies on a limited set of yes–no questions rather than a larger set of probabilistic questions.

feature integration theory   The theory that focusing attention on an object causes its features to become bound (integrated) together and perceived as a cohesive subject.

feature-based attention   Tuning attention to prioritize features such as color, shape, or motion.

feature-based categorization   Categorization in which categories are defined according to a set of characteristic features.

Fechner's Law   The principle that the intensity of subjective experience of a stimulus increases in proportion to the stimulus's measurable intensity.

feedforward   Referring to a hierarchical account of the flow of visual information processing, from rudimentary visual features to increasingly complex visual processing.

figure-ground organization   The perceptual segmentation of a visual scene into objects ("figure") and backgrounds ("ground").

filter model of attention   The notion that attention acts as a filter determining which information gains entry to more complex processing and which information gets excluded; in Broadbent's version, information is filtered based on "early" stimulus characteristics (e.g., pitch or loudness) prior to the processing of semantic meaning.

finite state grammar   Grammar in which sentences are constructed in sequence, with earlier parts of a sentence constraining what subsequent parts of the sentence can be.

fixed mindset   The belief that qualities such as intelligence are unchanging.

flanker task   A cognitive interference task in which participants respond to a target that is flanked by non-targets that activate a conflicting or non-conflicting response.

flashbulb memories   Vivid memories associated with particularly emotional events.

flat associative hierarchies   Networks of mental associations in which the less obvious ones are nearly as accessible as the obvious ones; may be linked with creativity.

fluency heuristic   An approach to decision making that assigns higher value to the option that is recognized more quickly and easily.

fluid intelligence (Gf)   Content-independent analytical processes that come into play when discerning patterns in the environment, understanding analogies, and drawing inferences.

fMRI subtraction method   An fMRI analysis technique that compares patterns of brain activity elicited by different stimuli or tasks.

forgetting curve   An estimate of the rate at which information fades from memory.

formal operational period   According to Piaget, the developmental period (beginning around age 12) when scientific thinking skills begin to emerge.

fovea   The center of the eye's retina, where photoreceptors known as cones are concentrated, involved in high resolution visual processing.

framing   The way in which a problem or situation is presented, which can affect decision making.

frontal lobe   A region in the front of each brain hemisphere, involved in thinking, planning, decision making, and cognitive control.

function morphemes   Units of meaningful sound that modify content morphemes.

functional brain imaging   Imaging that uses medical technology to noninvasively study brain activity.

functional brain mapping   The task of linking cognitive and perceptual functions to specific brain regions.

functional fixedness   The tendency for thinking to be boxed in by predefined uses and associations.

functional magnetic resonance imaging (fMRI)   A technique that measures and localizes blood oxygen levels throughout the brain to infer brain activity.

functional specialization   The principle that different brain areas serve different perceptual and cognitive skills.

Functionalism   A historical movement that aligned itself with William James's focus on psychological functions.

G

Gabor patches   Versatile stimuli used in vision research, characterized by undulating dark and light stripes that can vary along dimensions such as orientation, contrast, and width.

gambler's fallacy   The faulty reasoning that past events in a sequence affect the likelihood of future events.

garden path sentence   A sentence that begins by suggesting one interpretation, only to then present another interpretation.

general intelligence (g)   The idea of intelligence as a source of individual variation that causes some people to score higher than others on a broad range of cognitive measures.

generation effect   The enhancement of memory for a list of items a person has generated versus one that the person was asked to memorize.

generativity   The ability to construct an infinite number of novel sentences.

genes   Heritable codes in almost every cell that dictate how an organism develops and functions.

genotype   The entire set of genes that an organism carries.

genotyping   The investigation of the presence or absence of particular genes using biological samples.

geons   Basic shapes or component parts, in two or three dimensions, that the brain may use to recognize objects.

Gestalt movement   An early-twentieth-century movement promoting the idea that conscious experience as a whole cannot be sufficiently explained by examining individual components.

gist   The overall idea or meaning of a visual scene.

glial cells   Non-neuronal cells in the brain and spinal cord that provide both structural and functional support to the neurons.

global aphasia   A condition characterized by difficulty both producing and comprehending spoken language.

Google effect   A phenomenon that occurs when people expect to be able to access information on the Internet, lowering their own memory for that information.

graded membership   The idea that some items are closer to their category prototypes than others are.

grammar   The broad set of rules that govern a given language.

grid cells   Neurons in the entorhinal cortex that track position as an individual moves.

group polarization   A phenomenon in which people tend to develop more extreme views when they limit their contact and conversations to people with whom they already agree.

growth mindset   The idea that intelligence can improve with practice and hard work.

H

habituation   Familiarity or boredom that results from repetition.

Hebb's Rule   A rule describing a mechanism for strengthening neural connections, often paraphrased as "cells that fire together wire together."

hemisphere   The left or right half of the brain.

heritability   The extent to which genetics can explain variation (differences) among people.

heritability coefficient   A formula for quantifying heritability: variance due to genes divided by total variance.

heuristics   Shortcuts or simple strategies to solve problems and make decisions quickly.

hierarchical network   The organization of knowledge into nodes (pieces of information) and links (the connections between nodes) using a hierarchical structure; higher-level properties can be generalized to subcategories.

hierarchical organization   Arrangement into a meaningful network of associations in which items are linked to increasingly global categories; can be used strategically to aid memory.

hierarchical relationship   A categorical relationship in which general categories subsume more specific categories.

hill climbing   In problem solving, the phenomenon of selecting options that move the problem solver a little closer to the end state.

hippocampal system   The hippocampus and neighboring structures in the medial temporal lobe.

hippocampus   A structure in the medial temporal lobe of each brain hemisphere, important to emotion, memory, and the autonomic nervous system.

holistic perception   The processing of a whole object at once, including the relations of the individual parts to each other.

hot-hand effect   The perception of being "on a roll," for example in a gambling situation.

hyperthymestic syndrome   A condition in which an individual has a highly superior autobiographical memory.

I

iconic memory   Very short-term visual memory; highly detailed but largely fades within a fraction of a second.

idea evaluation   The process of judging the merit of an idea developed during idea generation; a component of creative cognition that involves focused attention and cognitive control.

idea generation   A component of creative cognition that involves coming up with ideas; sometimes linked with being in an unfocused, daydream-like state.

ill-defined problem   A problem in which the given state, goal state, and operators are not well defined.

illusory conjunction   The incorrect combining of features that are not actually combined in the real world.

illusory correlation   An incorrect perception of connections between variables that have no relation to each other.

implementational level of analysis   An analytical framework centered on understanding how the brain physically enables the processes of human cognition.

implicit association test (IAT)   A lab-based measure of implicit bias that has been used to study unconscious attitudes about different social groups.

implicit attention   Attention that does not necessarily lead to conscious awareness; measured via response time, eye-movements, and other measures that do not rely on conscious report.

implicit attitudes   Attitudes or associations that people exhibit unintentionally and are not necessarily aware of or able to verbalize.

implicit memory   Memory for learned skills, associations, and habits, which can manifest without conscious recollection; also known as non-declarative or non-conscious memory.

in-group identification   The feeling of solidarity that people tend to have with other members of what they perceive to be their own group.

in-groups   People we see as being like ourselves or part of our "tribes."

inattentional blindness   The failure to notice an unexpected item right in plain view when our attention is preoccupied.

individual differences   Variations among people.

individuate   In attention and perception, the ability to tell items apart from each other.

inductive reasoning   Thinking that involves moving from specific knowledge and examples to more general knowledge and principles.

infantile amnesia   The inability to remember the earliest years of our lives.

information theory   A cross-disciplinary field that focuses on the processes by which information can be coded, stored, transmitted, and reconstructed.

information-processing approach   In the study of intelligence, an approach that seeks to understand how cognitive and neural processes underlie and contribute to intelligence.

inhibition   In reference to cognitive control, the ability to suppress information, thoughts, or actions that may interfere with ongoing behavior.

inhibition of return   Short-lived suppression of information processing at a just-attended location.

inhibitory   Referring to connections between features or neurons in which activating one decreases the likelihood of activating the other.

insight   The experience of suddenly gaining a solution to a problem.

inspection time   The shortest exposure at which people can render accurate judgments.

intelligence   Generally speaking, the ability to reason, solve problems, and gain new knowledge.

intelligence quotient (IQ)   A performance-based metric of a person's intelligence, the derivation of which has changed over time.

internal attention   Attention that is directed to one's thoughts and response selections rather than to the external world.

intervention   In causal reasoning, implementing an action and observing its consequences to infer a causal relationship.

intrinsic motivation   Motivation based on an individual's own passion, interest, and satisfaction.

introspection   A method whereby some early psychologists attempted to objectively observe their own mental experiences.

intrusive memories (flashbacks)   Unwanted memories that persist and intrude into our thoughts unbidden.

invasiveness   Among cognitive neuroscience techniques, the degree to which a research method impacts the individual whose brain is being studied.

inverse projection problem   The challenge our visual system faces in enabling us to perceive a three-dimensional world despite the input to our eyes being a two-dimensional projection.

irrational behavior   Behavior that is subjective and emotional rather than objective and logical.

irrelevant speech effect   The impairment of working memory by irrelevant speech.

J

just-noticeable difference   The minimum perceptual difference between two stimuli (e.g., in length, brightness, or pitch) needed for the difference to be detected.

K

kindergarten path sentence effect   The phenomenon, seen particularly among children, of having difficulty processing garden path sentences.

knock-out   A research technique that involves rendering a gene absent or unexpressed.

knowledge   What we have learned about the world around us.

knowledge representation   The study of how categories are organized in the mind.

L

language acquisition device   An instinct to seek out and master the rules of one's native language.

late selection   The attention theory that we process the meaning of everything around us before we select what will gain entry to heightened awareness.

latent variables   Underlying factors.

law of sample size   The principle that smaller sample sizes produce more variance.

less-is-more effect   The phenomenon whereby too much information, computation, or time devoted to a problem may lead to a less accurate, sensible, or satisfying decision.

lexical access   The act of retrieving words and their meanings.

lexical decision task   An experimental task in which participants make rapid judgments about strings of letters that are presented to them (e.g., do they spell out words or not?).

lightness constancy   In brightness perception, the ability to factor in illumination conditions.

likelihood   The probability that the evidence will be observed when a hypothesis is true.

linear perspective   The phenomenon by which parallel lines appear to move closer together and converge on a single point (a *vanishing point*) as they recede into the distance.

load theory   The theory that the availability of mental resources to process information depends partly on the demands of an attended task.

lobe   One of four major zones in each brain hemisphere: frontal, parietal, temporal, and occipital.

long-term memory   Memory responsible for storing information for a relatively long time.

long-term potentiation (LTP)   A principle by which communication across a synapse strengthens future communication between the presynaptic and postsynaptic neurons.

loss aversion   The principle of disfavoring losses more than favoring equivalent gains.

M

magnetic resonance imaging (MRI)   A widely used technique for studying brain structure and cognition, involving the use of a powerful magnetic field and brief radio pulses.

manipulation   The ability to use or manipulate information in working memory.

Markov models   Approaches that sought to explain verbal utterances and language development as probabilistically dependent on preceding words.

masking   A method of making a stimulus imperceptible.

massed practice   Practicing a task in a single session rather than taking breaks.

materialism   The modern view that the mind is entirely a product of the brain.

means-ends analysis   A problem-solving strategy that involves creating specific goals and subgoals in steps.

medial temporal lobe   A region in the cortex that includes the hippocampus and plays a central role in memory processing.

memory   A family of processes involved in encoding, storing, and retrieving (i.e., recalling or recognizing) information about our experience of the world.

memory retrieval   A memory process that typically involves reactivation of the brain regions involved during initial encoding.

memory suggestibility   The altering of memory through leading questions and cues.

memory systems   Brain networks that encode different types of memories.

mental age   In intelligence testing, the measure of an individual's performance compared against that of the average score of children that age.

mental chronometry The study of perceptual and cognitive processing speed or timing, based on measurements of response time to different stimuli and tasks.

mental imagery The ability of the mind to construct images without immediate input from the environment.

mental lexicon The words one uses and their links to real-world representations.

mental rotation The ability of the mind to compare and match rotated images.

mental scanning The process of moving from one point in a mental image to another.

metamemory (metacognition) The understanding of how our own memory works.

method of loci A memory technique in which a person imagines walking through a familiar space, such as their house, and placing different pieces of information at each location.

mindset Beliefs about whether abilities are hardwired or malleable.

minimal group paradigm A research procedure used to study how people spontaneously form in-groups and out-groups on the basis of the simplest criteria, such as random assignment.

mirror-neuron system A set of neurons that appear to mirror the actions of other people.

mnemonist A person who has trained to become a memory athlete.

modular Referring to an ability that develops and operates independently of other cognitive abilities.

modulation The process by which attention affects perception of a stimulus.

module A specialized region in the brain that performs a specific function.

modus ponens In logical reasoning, the principle stating that when the antecedent holds true, the consequent can be treated as true.

modus tollens In logical reasoning, the principle stating that when the consequent is false, the antecedent is false.

monocular depth cues Visual cues that the mind uses to construct a three-dimensional understanding when the eyes have the same view.

mood-dependent memory The phenomenon of exhibiting better memory retrieval for material learned when in the same mood.

morphemes The smallest units of *meaningful* sound in a language.

morphology The rules by which morphemes can be combined into words.

motivated reasoning The tendency for people fit their interpretation of information to their own preexisting beliefs or emotions.

motor sequence learning An experimental task for studying procedural learning, in which participants must quickly respond to a target that can appear in one of four locations.

multiple intelligences theory The theory that intelligence is not a general ability but a collection of abilities that people use to solve problems or produce useful creations.

multiple-trace memory model The idea that we store multiple mental representations corresponding to multiple views (or templates) of the same object, allowing us to quickly match an incoming object to the corresponding representation.

mutual-exclusivity constraint A phenomenon whereby children factor in what they already know to guide their learning of new words.

N

naming task An experimental task in which participants must name a stimulus as quickly and accurately as possible.

native language magnet effect The process of learning when phonetic differences are relevant for one's native language.

negative evidence Feedback indicating that an utterance is ungrammatical.

negative utility The losses or costs incurred by a decision.

neocortex The layers of the cortex that support higher-order brain functions such as the initial perception and processing of experiences.

neural nets Brainlike algorithms that analyze information in multiple, parallel steps.

neuroeconomics A field of study that combines insights from economics, neuroscience, and psychology.

neuromarketing A field of study that uses brain scanning to understand and predict product preferences.

neurons Specialized cells that receive and transmit signals in the nervous system.

neuroplasticity The ability of neural connections to change with experience.

neuropsychology The study of the behavioral consequences of brain damage.

neurotransmitter A chemical through which neurons communicate with other networked neurons.

nonroutine problem A problem that is unfamiliar and does not have an immediately known or apparent solution.

nonverbal behavior The ways in which individuals behave, gesture, or express themselves without words.

normative theories Theories based on rational, logical, and mathematical calculations to compare decision options, explaining how decisions *should* be made in order to maximize utility and rewards.

noun phrase The part of a sentence that contains the noun and the words that modify it.

O

object-based attention   Attention directed to an object rather than to a point in space.

object constancy   The ability to recognize objects despite different orientations, lighting, and other variation.

object permanence   The understanding that objects persist and are stable even when they are out of sight.

object segmentation   The visual assignment of the elements of a scene to separate objects and backgrounds.

occipital lobe   A region in the back of each brain hemisphere, devoted to visual perception.

occlusion   The blockage of one's view of an object by other objects.

one-clever-cue heuristic   An approach to decision making that relies on a single cue (e.g., price).

operant conditioning   Learning in which observable changes in behavior result from associations between an organism's actions and desired or undesired outcomes.

operators   Thinking and reasoning abilities.

optimal defaults   Automatic placement into options that have the greatest benefits.

orthographically   Through written form, as opposed to sound.

other race face effect   The difficulty people have individuating and recognizing people from a race different from their own.

out-groups   People we see as being different from ourselves or as belonging to a different social group.

overgeneralization   The broad application by children of grammatical rules in ways unlikely to resemble utterances by adults.

overt attention   Attention directed in an outwardly observable way, such as by moving the eyes to the attended location.

oxytocin   A hormone important for pair bonding, maternal care, and sexual behavior.

P

parallel processing   Processing that occurs by taking in stimuli all at once.

parietal lobe   A region in the upper back side of each brain hemisphere, important for controlling action.

parse   A process of determining the boundaries between spoken words.

perception   The ability to recognize and interpret information from the senses.

perception-action-coupling   A theoretical account of empathy suggesting that our brain's mirroring of other people's actions reflects processes that enable us to vicariously experience others' exhibited states.

perception pathway   A mental pathway that allows us to determine what is located where.

perceptual interference   A condition in which perception is affected by distractors that make a target harder to see.

perceptual load   The perceptual demands of a task.

perceptual narrowing   A developmental process in which environmental experiences shape perception to lose the ability to distinguish similar input.

perceptual priming   Response enhancement that results from having previously perceived a stimulus.

perseveration error   A persistent response that fails to adapt to changing rules or circumstances.

phenotype   All of an organism's observable traits resulting from the interactions of its genotype and its environment.

phonemes   The smallest units of sound in a language.

phonemic restoration effect   The phenomenon whereby individuals seem to hear spoken phonemes that have been rendered inaudible by background noise or omission.

phonetic categories   Categories that humans use to distinguish meaningful sounds.

phonological loop   The component of working memory that stores and rehearses speech-based information.

phonological store   The part of the phonological loop that holds sound- or speech-based information.

phonologically   Through sound, as opposed to written form.

phonology   The rules that govern how sounds can be combined within a language.

photoreceptors   Specialized cells on the retina at the back of each eye, sensitive to light.

phrase structure   See *surface structure*.

pidgin language   A simplified form of communication, typically used between people that do not share a language, that does not adhere to a system of grammatical rules.

place cells   Neurons that fire when an animal is in a particular location within an environment.

placebo effect   An effect that cannot be due to a treatment but must result from a patient's belief in the treatment.

plastic   Referring to the ability for the strength of neuronal connections to change with learning and experience.

point light walkers   Simple, moving arrays of dots arranged so that each dot is placed where a person's joints would be; these sparse animations can be perceived as humans moving.

police officer's dilemma   An experimental task designed to assess the role of bias or stereotyping in choosing to shoot or not shoot at individuals who may be holding weapons or non-weapons.

population coding   Representation or coding by an ensemble (population, or group) of neurons.

positive utility   The gains incurred by a decision.

Posner cueing task   An experimental task used to reveal the movement of attention in space; participants respond to targets on a screen as quickly as they can, and attention can be directed toward or away from the target location by exogenous or endogenous cues.

posterior probability The probability of a hypothesis being true given the evidence.

postsynaptic Referring to the receiving neuron in the transmission of a neural signal.

poverty of the stimulus A lack of information in the environment about correct language use.

practical intelligence The ability to meet the challenges one encounters in everyday life.

pragmatics The study of how the communicative function of language depends on what the speaker knows, what the listener knows, what the speaker knows about what the listener knows, and what the listener knows about what the speaker knows.

preattentive processing The processing of information before it is attentionally selected.

predictably irrational Systematic errors or biases in decision making.

prediction error The failure to receive the reward or outcome that a person predicted.

predictive coding The ability of the visual brain to predict what input the eyes are about to receive.

preferential looking method An experimental method based on the fact that infants prefer to look at patterns rather than at blank displays.

prejudice The typically negative evaluation or prejudgment of others in accordance with stereotypes.

premise diversity The principle that properties shared by diverse or dissimilar categories linked by a superordinate category are more likely to be generalized than properties shared by similar categories.

premise monotonicity The principle that the larger the number of premises that share a property, the more likely people will conclude that the property generalizes broadly.

premise typicality The principle that if premises are more typical or representative of a category, they will lead to stronger inductions.

premise–conclusion similarity The principle that the more similar the premise and conclusion categories of a logical statement, the stronger the inductive argument will be.

preoperational period According to Piaget, a developmental period extending from about ages 2 to 7, when children start to think in terms of symbols, allowing them to represent ideas; language is a major hallmark of this period.

preparation effect The effect seen when increasing the time between trials gives people more time to prepare and thus reduces the task-switch cost.

presynaptic Referring to the sending neuron in the transmission of an electrical impulse.

primacy effect The phenomenon of having improved memory for items at the beginning of a list.

primary visual cortex An area at the back of each brain hemisphere, specialized for basic visual feature processing.

priming An effect in which a perception, response, or thought is enhanced by prior exposure to an identical or related stimulus, action, or idea.

prior knowledge (causal mechanism) Background knowledge that influences the determination of causes for events.

prior probability The probability of a hypothesis being true even before any evidence is obtained.

prisoner's dilemma A decision making scenario in which participants (the "prisoners") must decide whether to betray or cooperate with the other(s) without knowing what the other(s) will do; the rewards or consequences depend on the prisoners' combined decisions.

proactive control The process of applying cognitive control in anticipation of a challenge.

proactive interference The phenomenon whereby previously learned material can interfere with subsequent learning.

problem definition and redefinition A problem-solving step whereby an individual develops an approach that renders a problem manageable.

problem finding Creative cognitive processes that are geared toward finding new ways to frame questions and perceiving unrecognized needs and problems.

problem identification A problem-solving step whereby an individual notices a problem in need of a solution.

procedural learning The acquisition of skills and habits.

processes Ways of encoding, transforming, storing, interpreting, and acting on information.

productivity The ability to produce and understand completely new sentences.

property induction The generalization of properties or features from one exemplar of a category to another.

propositional Referring to the view that mental images are held in a post-perceptual, abstract way, more like a linguistic description than a picture.

prosody The patterns of intonation in a sentence.

prosopagnosia A neurological condition characterized by difficulty recognizing faces; also known as face blindness.

prospect theory A mathematical model to explain loss aversion; people treat a monetary loss as psychologically larger than the same monetary gain, and the larger the dollar amount, the less the same absolute difference matters.

prototype A typical or ideal member of a category.

psycholinguistics The study of the cognitive underpinnings of human language.

psychological bias The effect of psychological factors on decision making.

psychological field   The concept that the social world and an individual's responses to it are determined not only by the way things objectively are but also by the individual's cognitions about themselves and the people around them.

psychological refractory period   A cognitive delay that reveals a fundamental limitation in information processing; the response to a second stimulus is significantly slowed because a first stimulus is still being processed.

psychometric approach   In the study of intelligence, an approach that seeks to measure intelligence quantitatively.

psychophysics   The study of the relationship between physical stimuli and mental experience.

punishments   Negative outcomes that decrease the likelihood that an action will be repeated.

Pygmalion effect (self-fulfilling prophecy)   A phenomenon in which your expectations of someone can lead them to behave or perform in a way that matches your expectations, even when they aren't consciously aware of your expectations.

R

random trial and error   The process of randomly selecting and applying different potential solutions until a problem is solved.

rational behavior   Behavior that is objective and logical.

rational choice theory   The theory that people make decisions by comparing the expected value of their options.

Raven's Progressive Matrices   A measure of fluid intelligence in which people see configurations of an undisclosed pattern and must pick the next one in the sequence.

reactivation   The phenomenon of exhibiting patterns of brain activity similar to those that occurred during the initial encoding of a memory.

reactive control   The process of applying cognitive control only after a challenge is known.

reality monitoring   Distinguishing real (external) from imagined (internally-generated) events.

reasoning (thinking)   The process of gaining new knowledge and understanding from existing information.

recency effect   The phenomenon of having improved memory for items at the end of a list.

receptive field   The area of the environment or body to which a neuron responds.

recognition by components   A model proposed by Biederman to explain object recognition according to basic shapes or component parts, called geons.

recognition heuristic   An approach to decision making that places higher value on a recognized option versus one that is strange or novel.

recollection   The conscious experience of remembering details.

recursion   The property of language that enables us to embed structures of language inside other structures, such as sentences within sentences.

referential communication task   A task in which two participants are separated by an opaque partition, and one participant tries to describe the layout of objects that are within their view but not within their partner's view.

reflexive attention   Attention to a stimulus without actively choosing to attend to it.

region of interest (ROI)   A brain area designated by an investigator to be the focus of study.

regulatory flexibility   The degree to which people use different emotion regulation strategies depending on context and feedback.

rehearsal   The memory-encoding strategy, often of limited success, of repeating information to oneself over and over again.

reinforcers   Positive outcomes that increase the likelihood that an action will be repeated.

remember/know procedure   An experimental task used to test the distinction between recognition and familiarity.

remote associates   Creative ideas that are remote from the original formulation of a problem.

remote associates test   A cognitive test in which participants must think of what links three specific words.

repetition priming   Response enhancement that results from repetition.

repetition suppression   A brain signal reduction that occurs when a stimulus is repeated, suggesting that processing requires less effort or work.

representations   The mind's way of storing and processing information about the world.

representativeness heuristic   A mental shortcut used to estimate the likelihood of an event based on how closely it matches or represents related examples or stereotypes.

residual switch cost   The speed and accuracy penalty that comes with long delays between tasks.

resource   The limitation in how much information the mind can process at any given time.

resource model   A visual short-term memory model suggesting that capacity is a limited resource that has to be shared by all objects.

resource sharing   A model suggesting that attention can be split across two or more stimuli at the same time, for example, allowing for multi-tasking.

response interference   A slowing in response, caused by distractors that elicit a conflicting response.

retina   The light-sensitive part of the eye.

retrieval   The act of accessing memories.

retrieval cues   Memory clues in our environment or in our stored representations that help us reconstruct our experiences.

retrieval-induced forgetting (retrieval-induced inhibition) The phenomenon whereby retrieval of target memories causes unselected memories to be lost.

retroactive interference The phenomenon of forgetting something when new information is learned.

retrograde amnesia The inability to remember information from before brain damage occurred.

retrograde memory enhancement The phenomenon whereby learning material just before emotions are triggered can make it easier to remember.

reverse inference The illogical inference of a mental process (cognitive or emotional) from the activation of a particular brain region.

risk The probability of a negative outcome, such as losing something of value.

risk averse Preferring to make a sure gain rather than take a risky option for slightly more money.

risk seeking Rather than accepting a sure loss, preferring to lose more if a bet allows a small chance of avoiding any loss.

rods The light-sensitive photoreceptors in the eye that are responsive even in dim light but that do not distinguish among colors.

routine problem A problem that is familiar and has a known solution.

rumination Incessant focus on one's negative thoughts.

S

saccades Rapid eye movements.

saliency map Across a field of view, areas with sharp visual contrast (e.g., a yellow dandelion flower in a green lawn) are salient and draw attention.

Sapir-Whorf hypothesis A hypothesis suggesting that differences among languages reflect and contribute to differences in underlying thought processes; also known as linguistic determinism.

savant syndrome A condition characterized by having impressive skill in a particular domain despite having what appears to be generally low intelligence as traditionally measured.

savings measure A measure of how much less one would need to study material in a second study session, compared with a first, in order to remember information.

scarcity hypothesis The hypothesis that scarcity impairs cognitive control.

schadenfreude The feeling of reward or pleasure one feels at another person's failures or suffering.

schemas Knowledge or expectations about an event.

segmentation The boundaries between words.

selection The singling out of certain pieces of information among many.

self-categorization theory The theory that people can view themselves according to several hierarchically nested identities, which can vary in their relative salience at any given time.

self-control A crucial function of the self that involves initiating, sustaining, and inhibiting behavior.

self-imagining A memory-encoding strategy whereby a person imagines something from a personal perspective.

self-reference effect A memory-encoding strategy whereby a person thinks of ways material might be relevant to them or their interests.

semantic memory Memory for facts and common knowledge that can be stated or recounted and that accumulate over time across repeated occasions.

semantic priming An effect in which exposure to a word influences a response to a subsequent stimulus.

semantics The meaning of a word or phrase.

sensation Stimulation of the sensory receptors for perception.

sensorimotor period A developmental period from birth to about 2 years, during which infants and toddlers learn about the physicality of objects.

sensory memory Following presentation of a stimulus, the phenomenon whereby a detailed representation of the stimulus appears to persist in one's mind for a fraction of a second.

sensory-functional account The idea that object concepts are grounded in perception and action.

sentence verification task An experimental task in which people are asked to verify statements such as "A crow is a bird" or "An ostrich is a bird"; they are quicker to affirm examples that are more typical.

sequential lineup A police procedure in which witnesses make a decision about each member in a lineup before moving on to the next one.

serial position curve A U-shaped curve that emerges when plotting memory performance according to serial position.

serial processing Processing that occurs by taking in items one at a time.

serial recall A form of phonological working memory that involves remembering a series of items.

shadowing An experimental task in which participants repeat a message out loud as it is played to them.

shape bias A bias in which children, when generalizing a word to new instances of novel objects, appear to generalize to objects with the same shape rather than to objects with the same color, size, or texture.

short-term memory Memory responsible for storing information only momentarily.

similarity (resemblance) How well examples or prototypes fit into a category.

situated cognition The idea that thinking is shaped by its physical and social context.

size constancy   The ability to perceive the sizes of objects as stable despite radical differences in their image size, which vary with distance, on the retina.

skill learning   The cognitive capacity to learn skills, such as playing an instrument, surfing, or driving.

slot model   A model of visual short-term memory in which a slot corresponds to an object, and all of the object's features can be stored without reducing the capacity for other objects (up to about four).

social brain hypothesis   The hypothesis that the size of an individual's social network is related to the size of brain regions such as the frontal lobe.

social categorization   A process in which exposure to everyday events brings us into contact with innumerable cues that can spontaneously lead us to assign people to particular social groups.

social cognition neural network   A network of brain regions that play a role in social interaction.

social intuitionist model   The notion that our beliefs stem first from quick intuition, and only then by slow deliberation.

social norms   Standards of behavior based on widely shared beliefs about how individual group members should behave.

somatic marker hypothesis   The hypothesis that people learn to link their physiological responses to outcomes associated with their actions.

source confusion   Difficulty in correctly remembering the source of information.

source misattribution   Incorrect attribution of the source of a memory.

source monitoring   The ability to keep track of where a memory came from (e.g., something you did versus something you only imagined doing).

spacing effect   The phenomenon whereby people remember new material or tasks better when they take short breaks or space study sessions apart.

spatial attention   Selection of a stimulus on the basis of location.

spatial framework   A way of representing locations in reference to other points.

spatial interference task (Simon task)   A task in which a spatial incompatibility between the target location and the responding hand slows down response time.

spatial memory   Memory that helps an individual navigate around their environment.

spatial neglect   Following a brain injury, the failure to process stimuli on one side of the visual field.

spatial resolution   The ability of a research method to pinpoint where neural activity occurs (e.g., ranging from neurons to brain areas of varying size).

specific intelligences (s)   Intellectual abilities that are specific (e.g., math) rather than general (e.g., all subjects in school).

speech error   An error made in speaking.

split-brain patient   A patient whose corpus collosum, which helps the two brain hemispheres communicate with each other, has been severed.

spreading activation model   A model according to which word meanings link to each other as if organized like a web within the mental lexicon. Activation of words within this web spread and activate related words.

Stanford–Binet intelligence scales   A widely used test of intelligence, and the source of the term "intelligence quotient."

state-dependent memory   The enhancement of memory when a person's internal state at retrieval matches their internal state at encoding.

statistical learning   A type of learning that encodes patterns or regularities in the sights and sounds one experiences.

statistical regularities   Stable and predictable features of an environment, object, or task, based on experience.

status quo bias   A preference for the current state of affairs.

stereotype activation   The act of bringing to mind traits and characteristics that are commonly associated with a particular social group.

stereotype application   The act of evaluating, judging, and behaving toward people based on one's activated stereotypes.

stereotype content model   A framework according to which much of how we regard "others" can be attributed to a combination of how "warm" and how "competent" we perceive them to be.

stereotyping   The act of making assumptions about others on the basis of their social group membership—such as their race, religion, or sexuality—as well as on the basis of mental associations one has with that group.

stop-signal task   An experimental task in which participants need to abort a response when a stop signal appears; a classic measure of inhibition.

storage   A capacity that helps sustain access to information after it is no longer available in perception—no longer visible, audible, or touchable.

Stroop interference   People are slower to name the ink color of a color word when the two conflict (e.g., the word "green" printed in red ink).

structural descriptions   Models that represent objects as sets of three-dimensional parts organized in spatial relationships to each other.

Structuralism   A movement, founded by Wilhelm Wundt, that focuses on the structural components of mental life.

subjective value   The notion that utility is not objective but is dependent on the decision maker and context.

subordinate   Part of a larger category.

subsequent memory paradigm   A way to study what supports successful memory encoding by separately analyzing items that are subsequently remembered from items that are subsequently forgotten—why people successfully encode some things and not others.

sunk cost effect   The maladaptive tendency to continue an endeavor once an investment in money, effort, or time has been made.

superordinate   Containing other categories.

surface structure   The way a mental representation is structured linguistically; also known as phrase structure.

sustained attention   The ability to maintain focus on a task, including vigilance.

syllogism   A logical system, devised by Aristotle, in which a conclusion is drawn from two given propositions (called "premises").

synapse   A gap between neurons, across which chemical or electrical signals are transmitted.

syntax   The rules that govern how sentences are structured.

T

take-the-best-cue heuristic   An approach to decision making that considers the best options in turn.

tallying   A heuristic that involves counting the number of cues that favor one alternative over another.

task-switch cost   The speed and accuracy penalty that comes with having to switch tasks.

template   A mental representation that fully describes the shape of an object.

temporal attention   The ability to pay attention to points in time.

temporal lobe   A region in the lower side of each brain hemisphere, important for complex perception, memory, and language.

temporal order   The arrangement of events over time.

temporal resolution   The ability of a research method to pinpoint when neural activity occurs over milliseconds, seconds, minutes, or longer.

testing effect   The phenomenon whereby practice retrieving information (e.g., while taking a test) improves memory of that material.

texture gradient   The phenomenon by which textural elements that are presumably of similar size appear to get smaller and more densely packed together as they recede into the distance.

theory of constructed emotion   The theory that the experience of emotion is one we construct based on external cues, bodily cues, and our existing concepts and categories.

theory of mind   The ability to consider what someone else is thinking.

thin-slice judgments   Inferences or judgments that individuals make even from very brief exposures to people's nonverbal behavior.

thinking fast (System 1)   Decision making that operates quickly, with little effort and less control.

thinking slow (System 2)   Decision making that operates slowly, with effort and deliberate control.

tip-of-the-tongue phenomenon   The feeling that the right word is just out of reach.

top-down information   The knowledge and expectations that influence and enhance the interpretation of sensory input.

top-down selection   Stimulus selection driven by relevance to a goal.

topographic   Referring to a feature of the occipital cortex, whereby items adjacent in visual space are represented by neurons that are close to each other in the cortex.

Torrance Test of Creative Thinking   A cognitive test that scores participants' performance in terms of fluency, originality, elaboration, abstractness, and openness of responses.

transaction cost   The time, effort, or money required to consider or make a change.

transcranial direct current stimulation (tDCS)   A brain stimulation technique that involves applying a weak electrical current across the skull to modify brain activity, thereby increasing or decreasing the likelihood that underlying neurons will fire.

transcranial magnetic stimulation (TMS)   A method to temporarily disrupt brain activity using focal magnetic pulses targeted over different areas of the scalp.

transduction   The process by which physical signals from the environment are translated to neural signals the brain can use.

transfer   To generalize a solution from one problem to another.

transformational grammar   A system of rules for translating mental representations into structured verbal output, and vice versa.

tree diagram   A branched diagram showing the surface structure of a sentence or fragment.

triarchic theory of intelligence   A theory that differentiates among analytical, practical, and creative intelligences.

trust   A social and emotional behavior that is indispensable in social interactions ranging from friendships to economic exchanges and politics.

trust game   A game that studies what happens when players interact anonymously, one as an investor and one as a trustee; the investor must decide on an amount of money to give or not to give the trustee, who must then decide how much to share with the investor.

Turing machine   A hypothetical machine, proposed by Alan Turing, that could implement any conceivable calculation.

two-factor theory   The theory that intelligence is a combination of a general ability combined with specific abilities.

typicality effect   A principle by which some members of a category are more representative than others.

U

ultimatum game   A game in which two players have one opportunity to split a sum of money; the proposer suggests how the money should be divided, and the responder can either accept or reject the offer.

unconscious inference   The perceptual process of making educated guesses based on visual clues, without being aware of this process.

universal grammar   A theoretical system of rules shared by all languages.

usage-based linguistics   See *cognitive-functional linguistics*.

utility   The satisfaction and subjective reward obtained by making a decision.

V

value-modulated attentional capture   The reflexive allocation of attention based on learned value.

verb phrase   The part of a sentence that contains the action, words that modify it, and nouns that clarify the nature of the action.

view-based approach   In the study of object recognition, the idea that we match real-world images to mental representations that are like two-dimensional pictures, or templates.

viewpoint-dependent   Referring to a property of spatial memory, meaning it is best when the viewer maintains a consistent viewing angle to a spatial array.

vigilance   Related to sustained attention, a state of heightened attentional anticipation that enables people to better respond to stimuli before they appear.

visual cognition   The field of psychology that studies how cognitive processes contribute to perception.

visual search task   An experimental task in which participants look for a target embedded in an array of nontargets.

visual short-term memory   The temporary storage of visual information, especially when the perceptual image is no longer available or has changed.

visuospatial sketchpad   The component of working memory that stores and manipulates visual information.

voluntary attention   The intentional effort to select goal-relevant information.

W

Wason selection task   A logic puzzle to test deductive reasoning.

weapon focus   The failure to process other aspects in the environment when attention is focused on a threatening weapon or similarly stress-inducing stimulus.

Weber's Law   The first precise formula specifying the relationship between a physical aspect of the environment and the mind's ability to perceive it.

Wechsler Adult Intelligence Scale   A test aimed at measuring the global capacity of an adult to act purposefully, to think rationally, and to deal effectively with environments.

Wechsler Intelligence Scale for Children   A test aimed at measuring the global capacity of a child to act purposefully, to think rationally, and to deal effectively with environments.

Wechsler scales   Widely used contemporary tests of several subscales of intelligence in adults and children.

well-defined problem   A problem in which the given state, goal state, and operators are well specified.

Wernicke's aphasia   A condition characterized by difficulty understanding the meaning of words and sentences.

Wernicke's area   A region in the brain's left temporal lobe, important for comprehension of language.

white bear effect   An ironic process in which monitoring and trying to suppress one's thoughts of something (e.g., a white bear) ultimately lead to more instances of that thought intruding into awareness.

whole-object constraint   The idea that young children spontaneously assume that a new word refers to a whole object, not to any specific feature of it.

Williams syndrome   A genetic condition associated with a lower than normal IQ and profoundly impaired spatial skills.

willingness to pay   The decision of whether to purchase an option or item.

word frequency effect   The phenomenon whereby people are faster to respond to high-frequency words (i.e., words they have encountered often) than to low-frequency words.

word-length effect   An effect in which the working memory capacity for words or other phonological stimuli depends on the spoken duration or syllable length of the words.

working memory   A brain system for temporary storage and manipulation of the information necessary for cognitive tasks such as language, learning, and reasoning.

working memory load   The working memory demands of a task.

Y

Yerkes–Dodson curve   A model that describes how performance, especially on difficult tasks, suffers as a result of increased arousal, anxiety, or stress.

Z

zero price effect   The enticement of a free option or item.

References

Chapter 1

Baillargeon, R. (1987). Object permanence in 3½- and 4½-month-old infants. *Developmental Psychology, 23*(5), 655–664.

Barrett, L. F. (2006). Are emotions natural kinds? *Perspectives on Psychological Science, 1*(1), 28–58.

Bechara, A. (2004). The role of emotion in decision-making: evidence from neurological patients with orbitofrontal damage. *Brain and Cognition, 55*(1), 30–40.

Bradley, D. R., Dumais, S. T., & Betry, H. M. (1976). Ambiguous cognitive contours: A reply. *Nature, 261*(5555), 78.

Broadbent, D. E. (1958). *Perception and Communication.* London: Pergamon Press.

Bruner, J. S., Goodnow, J. J., & Austin, G. A. (1956). *A Study of Thinking.* Hoboken, NJ: John Wiley and Sons.

Bruner, J. (1990). *Acts of Meaning.* Cambridge, MA: Harvard University Press.

Bruner, J. S., & Goodman, C. C. (1947). Value and need as organizing factors in perception. *The Journal of Abnormal and Social Psychology, 42*(1), 33–44.

Castles, A., Rastle, K., & Nation, K. (2018). Ending the reading wars: Reading acquisition from novice to expert. *Psychological Science in the Public Interest, 19*(1), 5–51.

Chomsky, N. (1959). A review of B. F. Skinner's *Verbal Behavior. Language, 35,* 26–58.

Dehaene-Lambertz, G., Monzalvo, K., & Dehaene, S. (2018). The emergence of the visual word form: Longitudinal evolution of category-specific ventral visual areas during reading acquisition. *PLOS Biology, 16*(3), e2004103.

Damasio, A. R. (1994). *Descartes' Error: Emotion, reason, and the human brain.* New York: G. P. Putnam.

Duncan, S., & Barrett, L. F. (2007). Affect is a form of cognition: A neurobiological analysis. *Cognition & Emotion, 21*(6), 1184–1211.

Dunn, B. D., Dalgleish, T., & Lawrence, A. D. (2006). The somatic marker hypothesis: A critical evaluation. *Neuroscience and Biobehavioral Reviews, 30,* 239–271.

Ebbinghaus, H. (1885). *Über das Gedächtnis. Untersuchungen zur experimentellen Psychologie.* Leipzig: Duncker & Humblot.

Firestone, C., & Scholl, B. J. (2016). Cognition does not affect perception: Evaluating the evidence for "top-down" effects. *The Behavioral and Brain Sciences, 39,* e229.

Foot, P. (1967). The problem of abortion and the doctrine of the double effect. *The Oxford Review, 5,* 5–15.

Gardner, H. (1985). *The Mind's New Science: A history of the cognitive revolution.* New York: Basic Books.

Howard, I. P. (1996). Alhazen's neglected discoveries of visual phenomena. *Perception, 25*(10), 1203–1217.

Stolarova, M., Keil, A., & Moratti, S. (2006). Modulation of the C1 visual event-related component by conditioned stimuli: Evidence for sensory plasticity in early affective perception. *Cerebral Cortex, 16*(6), 876–887.

Lazarus, R. S. (1984). On the primacy of cognition. *American Psychologist, 39*(2), 124–129.

Leary, D. E. (1980). One hundred years of experimental psychology: An American perspective. *Psychological Research, 42,* 175–189.

Marr, D. (1982). *Vision: A computational investigation into the human representation and processing of visual information.* San Francisco: W. H. Freeman.

Miller, G. A. (1956). The magical number seven, plus or minus two: Some limits on our capacity for processing information. *Psychological Review, 63*(2), 81–97.

Miller, G. A. (2003). The cognitive revolution: A historical perspective. *Trends in Cognitive Sciences, 7*(3), 141–144.

Moore, T. V. (1939). *Cognitive Psychology.* Philadelphia: J. B. Lippincott.

Neisser, U. (1967). *Cognitive Psychology.* New York: Appleton-Century-Crofts.

Neisser, U. (1976). *Cognition and Reality: Principles and implications of cognitive psychology.* New York: W. H. Freeman/Times Books/Henry Holt & Co.

Pessoa, L. (2015). *The Cognitive-Emotional Brain: From interactions to integration.* Cambridge, MA: The MIT Press.

Pylyshyn Z. (1999). Is vision continuous with cognition? The case for cognitive impenetrability of visual perception. *Behavioral and Brain Sciences, 22*(3), 341–423.

Rayner, K., & Raney, G. E. (1996). Eye movement control in reading and visual search: Effects of word frequency. *Psychonomic Bulletin & Review, 3*(2), 245–248.

Reingold, E. M., Reichle, E. D., Glaholt, M. G., & Sheridan, H. (2012). Direct lexical control of eye movements in reading: Evidence from a survival analysis of fixation durations. *Cognitive Psychology, 65*(2), 177–206.

Rozin, P. & Jonides, J. (1977). Mass reaction time: Measurement of the speed of the nerve impulse and the duration of mental processes in class. *Teaching of Psychology, 4*(2), 91–94.

Russell, J. A. (2003). Core affect and the psychological construction of emotion. *Psychological Review, 110*(1), 145–172.

Shannon, C. E. (1948). A mathematical theory of communication. *The Bell System Technical Journal, 27*(3), 379–423.

Skinner, B. F. (1948). *Walden Two.* New York: Macmillan.

Skinner, B. F. (1957). *Verbal Behavior.* New York: Appleton-Century-Crofts.

Sloan Foundation. 1978. Cognitive Science, 1978. Report of the State of the Art Committee to the Advisors of The Alfred P. Sloan Foundation. New York.

Spelke, E. S., Breinlinger, K., Macomber, J., & Jacobson, K. (1992). Origins of knowledge. *Psychological Review, 99*(4), 605–632.

Sternberg, S. (1969). The discovery of processing stages: Extensions of Donders' method. *Acta Psychologica, 30,* 276–315.

Surprenant, A. M., & Neath, I. (1997). T. V. Moore's (1939) Cognitive Psychology. *Psychonomic Bulletin & Review, 4*(3), 342–349.

Thomson, J. J. (1976). Killing, letting die, and the trolley problem. *The Monist, 59*(2), 204–217.

Tolman, E. C., & Honzik, C. H. (1930). Introduction and removal of reward, and maze performance in rats. *University of California Publications in Psychology, 4,* 257–275.

Tolman, E. C. (1948). Cognitive maps in rats and men. *Psychological Review, 55*(4), 189–208.

Treisman, A. M. (1960). Contextual cues in selective listening. *The Quarterly Journal of Experimental Psychology, 12,* 242–248.

Watson, J. B. (1913). Psychology as the behaviorist views it. *Psychological Review, 20*(2), 158–177.

Watson, J. B. (2009). *Behaviorism.* Seventh printing. New Brunswick, NJ: Transaction Publishers.

Wynn, K. (1992). Addition and subtraction by human infants. *Nature, 358*(6389), 749–750.

Zajonc, R. B. (1980). Feeling and thinking: Preferences need no inferences. *American Psychologist, 35*(2), 151–175.

Chapter 2

Aguirre, G. K., Detre, J. A., Alsop, D. C., & D'Esposito, M. (1996). The parahippocampus subserves topographical learning in man. *Cerebral Cortex, 6*(6), 823–829.

Allison, T., Puce, A., Spencer, D. D., & McCarthy, G. (1999). Electrophysiological studies of human face perception. I: Potentials generated in occipitotemporal cortex by face and non-face stimuli. *Cerebral Cortex, 9*(5), 415–430.

Aron, A., Badre, D., Brett, M., et al. (2007). Politics and the brain. *New York Times,* November 14, 2007. https://www.nytimes.com/2007/11/14/opinion/lweb14brain.html.

Associated Press. (2013). NFL, ex-players agree to $765M settlement in concussions suit. *Associated Press,* August 29,

2013. https://apnews.com/article/8b60113432d94194819a99a461c539bd.

Barton, J. J. S., Press, D. Z., Keenan, J. P., & O'Connor, M. (2002). Lesions of the fusiform face area impair perception of facial configuration in prosopagnosia. *Neurology, 58*(1), 71–78.

Bentin, S., Allison, T., Puce, A., et al. (1996). Electrophysiological studies of face perception in humans. *Journal of Cognitive Neuroscience, 8*(6), 551–565.

Breedlove, S. M., & Watson, N. V. (2019). *Behavioral Neuroscience,* 9th Edition. Sunderland, MA: Oxford University Press/Sinauer.

Bruce, C., Desimone, R., & Gross, C. G. (1981). Visual properties of neurons in a polysensory area in superior temporal sulcus of the macaque. *Journal of Neurophysiology, 46*(2), 369–384.

Bryant, P., Trinder, J., & Curtis, N. (2004). Sick and tired: Does sleep have a vital role in the immune system? *Nature Reviews Immunology, 4,* 457–467.

Canli, T., Sivers, H., Whitfield, S. L., et al. (2002). Amygdala response to happy faces as a function of extraversion. *Science, 296*(5576), 2191.

Cowen, A. S., Chun, M. M., & Kuhl, B. A. (2014). Neural portraits of perception: reconstructing face images from evoked brain activity. *NeuroImage, 94,* 12–22.

"Definition of mind". Oxford University Press. Lexico.com. 24 March 2021. https://www.lexico.com/en/definition/mind

Demertzi, A., Liew, C., Ledoux, D., et al. (2009). Dualism persists in the science of mind. *Annals of the New York Academy of Sciences, 1157,* 1–9.

Desimone, R., Albright, T. D., Gross, C. G., & Bruce, C. (1984). Stimulus-selective properties of inferior temporal neurons in the macaque. *The Journal of Neuroscience, 4*(8), 2051–2062.

Downing, P. E. (2007). Face perception: Broken into parts. *Current Biology, 17*(20), R888–R889.

Duchaine, B. (2015). Individual differences in face recognition ability: Impacts on law enforcement, criminal justice and national security. *Psychological Science Agenda.* https://www.apa.org/science/about/psa/2015/06/face-recognition.

Eagleman, D. (2011). The brain on trial. *The Atlantic.* https://www.theatlantic.com/magazine/archive/2011/07/the-brain-on-trial/308520.

Eagleman, D., & Downar, J. (2015). *Brain and Behavior: A Cognitive Neuroscience Perspective.* New York: Oxford University Press.

Epstein, R., & Kanwisher, N. (1998). A cortical representation of the local visual environment. *Nature, 392*(6676), 598–601.

Fregni, F., Boggio, P. S., Nitsche, M., et al. (2005). Anodal transcranial direct current stimulation of prefrontal cortex enhances working memory. *Experimental Brain Research, 166*(1), 23–30.

Friedman, N. P., Miyake, A., Young, S. E., et al. (2008). Individual differences in executive functions are almost entirely genetic in origin. *Journal of Experimental Psychology. General*, 137(2), 201–225.

Gazzaniga, M. S. (2000). Cerebral specialization and interhemispheric communication. Does the corpus callosum enable the human condition? *Brain*, 123(7), 1293–1326.

Gazzaniga, M. S. (2005a). Forty-five years of split-brain research and still going strong. *Nature Reviews Neuroscience, 6*, 653–659.

Gazzaniga, M. S., Ivry, R. B., & Mangun, G. R. (2018). *Cognitive Neuroscience: The Biology of the Mind*, 5th Edition. New York: W.W. Norton & Company.

Gazzaniga, M. S. (2005b). *The Ethical Brain*. New York/ Washington, DC: Dana Press.

Gilbertson, M. W., Shenton, M. E., Ciszewski, A., et al. (2002). Smaller hippocampal volume predicts pathologic vulnerability to psychological trauma. *Nature Neuroscience*, 5(11), 1242–1247.

Golan, O., & Baron-Cohen, S. (2006). Systemizing empathy: Teaching adults with Asperger syndrome or high-functioning autism to recognize complex emotions using interactive multimedia. *Development and Psychopathology*, 18(2), 591–617.

Greene, J., & Cohen, J. (2004). For the law, neuroscience changes nothing and everything. *Philosophical Transactions of the Royal Society B: Biological Sciences*, 359(1451), 1775–1785.

Hebb, D. O. (1949). *The Organization of Behavior*. New York: Wiley.

Hubel, D. H., & Wiesel, T. N. (1962). Receptive fields, binocular interaction and functional architecture in the cat's visual cortex. *The Journal of Physiology*, 160(1), 106–154.

Hubel, D. H., & Wiesel, T. N. (1968). Receptive fields and functional architecture of monkey striate cortex. *Journal of Physiology*, 195(1), 215–243.

Huettel, S. A., Song, A. W., & McCarthy, G. (2014). *Functional Magnetic Resonance Imaging*, Third Edition. Sunderland, MA: Oxford University Press/Sinauer.

Iacoboni, M., Freedman, J., Kaplan, J., et al. (2007). This is your brain on politics. *New York Times*, November 11, 2007. https://www.nytimes.com/2007/11/11/opinion/11freedman.html.

Kanwisher, N., McDermott, J., & Chun, M. M. (1997). The fusiform face area: A module in human extrastriate cortex specialized for face perception. *Journal of Neuroscience*, 17(11), 4302–4311.

Kennerknecht, I., Grueter, T., Welling, B., et al. (2006). First report of prevalence of non-syndromic hereditary prosopagnosia (HPA). *American Journal of Medical Genetics Part A*, 140A(15), 1617–1622.

Murphy, B., & Garcia-Roberts, G. (2018). NFL players with brain trauma receive notice of settlements stripped to nothing. *USA TODAY*, October 23, 2018. https://www.usatoday.com/story/sports/nfl/2018/10/23/nfl-players-family-members-settlement/1736602002.

NFL Concussion Settlement. Last modified May 10, 2021. https://www.nflconcussionsettlement.com/.

Nishimoto, S., Vu, A. T., Naselaris, T., et al. (2011). Reconstructing visual experiences from brain activity evoked by natural movies. *Current Biology*, 21(19), 1641–1646.

Nitsche, M. A., Cohen, L. G., Wassermann, E. M., et al. (2008). Transcranial direct current stimulation: State of the art 2008. *Brain Stimulation*, 1(3), 206–223.

Nitsche, M. A., Schauenburg, A., Lang, N., et al. (2003). Facilitation of implicit motor learning by weak transcranial direct current stimulation of the primary motor cortex in the human. *Journal of Cognitive Neuroscience*, 15(4), 619–626.

Nobre, A. C., Allison, T., & McCarthy, G. (1994). Word recognition in the human inferior temporal lobe. *Nature*, 372(6503), 260–263.

Norman, K. A., Polyn, S. M., Detre, G. J., & Haxby, J. V. (2006). Beyond mind-reading: Multi-voxel pattern analysis of fMRI data. *Trends in Cognitive Sciences*, 10(9), 424–430.

Ogawa, S., Lee, T. M., Kay, A. R., & Tank, D. W. (1990). Brain magnetic resonance imaging with contrast dependent on blood oxygenation. *Proceedings of the National Academy of Sciences of the United States of America*, 87(24), 9868–9872.

Pascual-Leone, A. (1999). Transcranial magnetic stimulation: Studying the brain-behavior relationship by induction of "virtual lesions." *Philisophical Transactions of the Royal Society of London, B*, 354, 1229–1238.

Pascual-Leone, A., Rubio, B., Pallardó, F., & Catalá, M. D. (1996). Rapid-rate transcranial magnetic stimulation of left dorsolateral prefrontal cortex in drug-resistant depression. *Lancet*, 348(9022), 233–237.

Pascual-Leone, A., Walsh, V., & Rothwell, J. (2000). Transcranial magnetic stimulation in cognitive neuroscience—Virtual lesion, chronometry, and functional connectivity. *Current Opinion in Neurobiology*, 10(2), 232–237.

Perrett, D. I., Rolls, E. T., & Caan, W. (1982). Visual neurones responsive to faces in the monkey temporal cortex. *Experimental Brain Research*, 47(3), 329–342.

Pitcher, D., Charles, L., Devlin, J. T., et al. (2009). Triple dissociation of faces, bodies, and objects in extrastriate cortex. *Current Biology*, 19(4), 319–324.

Plomin, R., Owen, M. J., & McGuffin, P. (1994). The genetic basis of complex human behaviors. *Science*, 264, 1733–1739.

Poldrack, R. A. (2006). Can cognitive processes be inferred from neuroimaging data? *Trends in Cognitive Sciences*, 10(2), 59–63.

Puce, A., Allison, T., Gore, J. C., & McCarthy, G. (1995). Face-sensitive regions in human extrastriate cortex studied by functional MRI. *Journal of Neurophysiology*, 74(3), 1192–1199.

Quiroga, R. Q., Reddy, L., Kreiman, G., Koch, C., & Fried, I. (2005). Invariant visual representation by single neurons in the human brain. *Nature*, 435(7045), 1102–1107.

Ramirez, S., Liu, X., Lin, P.-A., et al. (2013). Creating a false memory in the hippocampus. *Science*, 341(6144), 387–391.

Ro, T., Cheifet, S., Ingle, H., et al. (1998). Localization of the human frontal eye fields and motor hand area with transcranial magnetic stimulation and magnetic resonance imaging. *Neuropsychologia, 37*(2), 225–231.

Robson, S. (2013). Epilepsy sufferer who refused to stop driving after being diagnosed with condition killed passenger in crash when he had fit at the wheel. *Daily Mail*, June 20, 2013. https://www.dailymail.co.uk/news/article-2345125/Epilepsy-sufferer-refused-stop-driving-diagnosed-condition-killed-passenger-crash-fit-wheel.html.

Rossi, S., Hallett, M., Rossini, P. M., & Pascual-Leone, A. (2009). Safety, ethical considerations, and application guidelines for the use of transcranial magnetic stimulation in clinical practice and research. *Clinical Neurophysiology, 120*(12), 2008–2039.

Sacks, O. (2010). Face-blind. *New Yorker*, August 30, 2010. https://www.newyorker.com/magazine/2010/08/30/face-blind.

Schmahmann, J. D., Guell, X., Stoodley, C. J., & Halko, M. A. (2019). The theory and neuroscience of cerebellar cognition. *Annual Review of Neuroscience, 42*(1), 337–364.

Schultz, R. T., Gauthier, I., Klin, A., et al. (2000). Abnormal ventral temporal cortical activity during face discrimination among individuals with autism and Asperger syndrome. *Archives of General Psychiatry, 57*(4), 331–340.

Sejnowski, T. J., Churchland, P. S., & Movshon, J. A. (2014). Putting big data to good use in neuroscience. *Nature Neuroscience, 17*(11), 1440–1441.

Singh, R., Meier, T. B., Kuplicki, R., et al. (2014). Relationship of collegiate football experience and concussion with hippocampal volume and cognitive outcomes. *JAMA, 311*(18), 1883–1888.

Smith, S. (2014). Former NFLer: "Your mind just goes crazy." *CNN*, February 1, 2014. https://www.cnn.com/2014/02/01/health/jenkins-nfl/index.html.

Tanaka, J. W., Wolf, J. M., Klaiman, C., et al. (2010). Using computerized games to teach face recognition skills to children with autism spectrum disorder: The Let's Face It! program. *Journal of Child Psychology and Psychiatry, and Allied Disciplines, 51*(8), 944–952.

Toga, A. W., & Thompson, P. M. (2005). Genetics of brain structure and intelligence. *Annual Review of Neuroscience, 28*, 1–23.

Weaver, I. C. G., Cervoni, N., Champagne, F. A., et al. (2004). Epigenetic programming by maternal behavior. *Nature Neuroscience, 7*(8), 847–854.

Chapter 3

Adelson, E. H. (2005). MIT. Checkers Shadow Illusion. http://web.mit.edu/persci/people/adelson/CheckersShadow_description.html.

Anderson, B. A., & Winawer, J. (2005). Image segmentation and lightness perception. *Nature, 434*, 79–83.

Anderson, J. A., Healey, M. K., Hasher, L., & Peterson, M. A. (2016). Age-related deficits in inhibition in figure-ground assignment. *Journal of Vision, 16*, 6.

Balcetis, E., & Dunning, D. (2010). Wishful seeing: More desired objects are seen as closer. *Psychological Science, 21*(1), 147–152.

Bar, M. (2004). Visual objects in context. *Nature Reviews Neuroscience, 5*, 617–629.

Bartolomeo, P., Hajhajate, D., Liu, J., & Spagna, A. (2020). Assessing the causal role of early visual areas in visual mental imagery. *Nature Reviews Neuroscience, 21*, 517.

Beck, D. M., & Clevenger, J. (2016). The folly of boxology. *Behavioral & Brain Sciences, 39*, e231.

Behrmann, M. (2000). The mind's eye mapped onto the brain's matter. *Current Directions in Psychological Science, 9*(2), 50–54.

Benson, D. F., & Greenberg, J. P. (1969). Visual form agnosia: A specific defect in visual discrimination. *Archives of Neurology, 20*(1), 82–89.

Berkeley, G. (1710). Treatise Concerning the Principles of Human Knowledge. Dublin.

Bhalla, M., & Proffitt, D. R. (1999). Visual–motor recalibration in geographical slant perception. *Journal of Experimental Psychology: Human Perception and Performance, 25*(4), 1076–1096.

Biederman, I. (1981) On the semantics of a glance at a scene perceptual organization. In Kubovy, M., Pomerantz, J. R., (Eds.) *Perceptual Organization*. Hillsdale, NJ: Laurence Earlbaum Associates. pp. 213–253.

Biederman, I. (1987a). Matching image edges to object memory. In *Proceedings of the First International Conference on Computer Vision, IEEE Computer Society*, 384–392.

Biederman, I. (1987b). Recognition-by-components: A theory of human image understanding. *Psychological Review, 94*(2), 115–147.

Biederman, I., & Bar, M. (1999). One-shot viewpoint invariance in matching novel objects. *Vision Research, 39*, 2885–2899.

Biederman, I., & Bar, M. (2000). Differing views on views: Response to Hayward and Tarr (2000). *Vision Research, 40*, 3901–3905.

Biederman, I., Mezzanotte, R. J., & Rabinowitz, J. C. (1982). Scene perception: Detecting and judging objects undergoing relational violations. *Cognitive Psychology, 14*(2), 143–177.

Bisiach, E., & Luzzatti, C. (1978). Unilateral neglect of representational space. *Cortex, 14*(1), 129–133.

Bonnet, G. (2013). "Amodal nudity," *Skeptophilia* (blog). January 18, 2013, http://skeptophilia.blogspot.com/2013/01/amodal-nudity.html.

Breedlove, S. M., & Watson, N. V. (2010). *Biological Psychology: An Introduction to Behavioral, Cognitive, and Clinical Neuroscience*, 6th Edition, Sunderland, MA: Oxford University Press/Sinauer.

Bregman, A. S. (1981). Asking the "what for" question in auditory perception. In Kubovy M., Pomerantz J. (Eds.) *Perceptual Organization*, Hillsdale, NJ: Routledge, pp. 99–118.

Bruner, J. S., & Goodman, C. C. (1947). Value and need as organizing factors in perception. *The Journal of Abnormal and Social Psychology, 42*(1), 33–44.

Bruner, J. S., & Minturn, A. L. (1955). Perceptual identification and perceptual organization. *The Journal of General Psychology, 53*, 21–28.

Bullier, J. (2001). Integrated model of visual processing. *Brain Research Reviews, 36*, 96–107.

Burton, A. M., White, D., & McNeill, A. (2010). The Glasgow Face Matching Test. *Behavior Research Methods, 42*, 286–291.

Butter, C. M., Kosslyn, S., Mijovic-Prelec, D, & Riffle, A. (1997). Field-specific deficits in visual imagery following hemianopia due to unilateral occipital infarcts. *Brain, 120*, 217–228.

Chetverikov, A., & Ivanchei, I. (2016). Seeing "the dress" in the right light: Perceived colors and inferred light sources. *Perception, 45*, 910–930.

Chua, K. W., Richler, J. J., & Gauthier, I. (2015). Holistic processing from learned attention to parts. *Journal of Experimental Psychology: General, 144*(4), 723–729.

Clark, A. (2013). Whatever next? Predictive brains, situated agents, and the future of cognitive science. *Behavioral and Brain Sciences, 36*(3), 181–204.

Crane, C., Shah, D., Barnhofer, T., & Holmes, E. A. (2012). Suicidal imagery in a previously depressed community sample. *Clinical Psychology & Psychotherapy, 19*(1), 57–69.

Curby, K. M., Entenman, R. (2016). Framing faces: Frame alignment impacts holistic face perception. *Attention, Perception, & Psychophysics, 78*, 2569–2578.

Dayan, P., Hinton, G., Neal, R., et al. (1995). The Helmholtz Machine. *Neural Computation, 7*, 889–904.

De Renzi, E., & Spinnler, H. (1967). Impaired performance on color tasks in patients with hemispheric damage. *Cortex: A Journal Devoted to the Study of the Nervous System and Behavior, 3*(2), 194–217.

De Valois, R. L., & De Valois, K. K. (1988). *Oxford Psychology Series, No. 14. Spatial Vision*. New York: Oxford University Press.

de Vreese, L. P. (1991). Two systems for colour-naming defects: Verbal disconnection vs colour imagery disorder. *Neuropsychologia, 29*(1), 1–18.

Diamond, R., & Carey, S. (1986). Why faces are and are not special: An effect of expertise. *Journal of Experimental Psychology: General, 115*(2), 107–117.

Dijkstra, N., Bosch, S. E., & van Gerven, M. A. J. (2019). Shared neural mechanisms of visual perception and imagery. *Trends in Cognitive Sciences, 23*, 423–434.

Di Lollo, V., Enns, J. T., & Rensink, R. A. (2000). Competition for consciousness among visual events: the psychophysics of reentrant visual processes. *Journal of Experimental Psychology: General, 129*, 481–507.

Edelman, S., & Bulthoff, H. H. (1992). Orientation dependence in the recognition of familiar and novel views of 3D objects. *Vision Research, 32*, 2385–2400.

Erdelyi, M. H. (1974). A new look at the new look: Perceptual defense and vigilance. *Psychological Review, 81*(1), 1–25.

Farah, M. J. (1988). Is visual imagery really visual? Overlooked evidence from neuropsychology. *Psychological Review, 95*(3), 307–317.

Farah, M. J. (1989). The neural basis of mental imagery. *Trends in Neurosciences, 12*(10), 395–399.

Farah, M. J. (1990). *Issues in the Biology of Language and Cognition. Visual Agnosia: Disorders of Object Recognition and What They Tell Us about Normal Vision*. Cambridge, MA: The MIT Press.

Farah, M. J., Hammond, K. M., Levine, D. N. et al. (1988). Visual and spatial mental imagery: dissociable systems of representation. *Cognitive Psychology, 20*, 439–462.

Farah, M. J., Soso, M. J., & Dasheiff, R. M. (1992). Visual angle of the mind's eye before and after unilateral occipital lobectomy. *Journal of Experimental Psychology: Human Perception & Performance, 18*, 241–246.

Felleman, D. J., & Van Essen, D. C. (1991) Distributed hierarchical processing in the primate cerebral cortex. *Cerebral Cortex, 1*, 1–47.

Finks, R. A., et al. (1989). Reinterpreting visual Patterns in mental imagery. *Cognitive Science, 13*, 51–78.

Firestone, C., & Scholl, B. J. (2016). Cognition does affect perception: Evaluating the evidence for "top-down" effects. *Behavioral and Brain Sciences, 39*, e229.

Gauthier, I., Curran, T., Curby, K. M., & Collins, D. (2003). Perceptual interference support a non-modular account of face processing. *Nature Neuroscience, 6*, 428–432.

Gauthier, I., Klaiman, C., & Schultz, R. T. (2009). Face composite effects reveal abnormal face processing in Autism spectrum disorders. *Vision Research, 49*(4), 470–478.

Gauthier, I., Skudlarski, P., Gore, J. C., & Anderson, A. W. (2000). Expertise for cars and birds recruits brain areas involved in face recognition. *Nature Neuroscience, 3*, 191–197.

Gibson, J. J. (1979). *The Ecological Approach to Visual Perception*. Boston, MA: Houghton Mifflin and Company.

Goebel, R., Khorram-Sefat, D., Muckli, L. et al. (1998). The constructive nature of vision: direct evidence from functional magnetic resonance imaging studies of apparent motion and motion imagery. *European Journal of Neuroscience, 10*, 1563–1573.

Goodale, M. A., & Milner, A. D. (1992). Separate visual pathways for perception and action. *Trends in Neurosciences, 15*, 20–25.

Goodale, M. A. & Milner, A. D. (2013). *Sight Unseen: An Exploration of Conscious and Unconscious Vision*, 2nd Edition. Oxford, UK: Oxford University Press.

Goodale, M. A., Milner, A. D., Jakobson, L. S., & Carey, D. P. (1991). A neurological dissociation between perceiving objects and grasping them. *Nature, 349*, 154–156.

Gregory, R. L. (1966). *Eye and Brain: The Psychology of Seeing*. New York: McGraw-Hill.

Grossberg, S. (1994). 3-D vision and figure-ground separation by visual cortex. *Perception & Psychophysics, 55,* 48–121.

Hackel, L. M., Larson, G. M., Bowen, J. D., et al. (1986). "Schema abstraction" in a multiple-trace memory model. *Psychological Review, 93*(4), 411–428.

Hintzman, D. L. (1986). "Schema abstraction" in a multiple-trace memory model. *Psychological Review, 93*(4), 411–428.

Hintzman, D. L., Curran, T., & Oppy, B. (1992). Effects of similarity and repetition on memory: Registration without learning? *Journal of Experimental Psychology: Learning, Memory, and Cognition, 18*(4), 667–680.

Hill, K. (2013). "The lurking pornographer: Why your brain turns bubbles into nude bodies" (blog), January 17, 2013, http://archive.randi.org/site/index.php/swift-blog/1985-the-lurking-pornographer-why-your-brain-turns-bubbles-into-nude-bodies.html?widthstyle=w-wide

Hollingworth, A., & Henderson, J. M. (1998). Does consistent scene context facilitate object perception? *Journal of Experimental Psychology: General, 127,* 398–415.

Holmes, E. A., James, E. L., Kilford, E. J., & Deeprose, C. (2010). Key steps in developing a cognitive vaccine against traumatic flashbacks: Visuospatial Tetris versus verbal Pub Quiz. *PLOS ONE, 5*(11). e13706.

Holmes, E. A., & Mathews, A. (2005). Mental imagery and emotion: A special relationship? *Emotion, 5*(4), 489–497.

Hubel, D. H., & Wiesel, T. N. (1959). Receptive fields of single neurones in the cat's striate cortex. *The Journal of Physiology, 148*(3), 574–591.

Hummel, J. E. (2013). Object recognition. In D. Reisberg (Ed.), *Oxford Library of Psychology. The Oxford Handbook of Cognitive Psychology* (pp. 32–45). New York: Oxford University Press.

Intraub, H., & Dickinson, C. A. (2008). False memory 1/20th of a second later: What the early onset of boundary extension reveals about perception. *Psychological Science, 19,* 1007–1014.

Intraub, H., & Richardson, M. (1989). Wide-angle memories of close-up scenes. *Journal of Experimental Psychology: Learning, Memory and Cognition, 15,* 179–187.

Ishai, A., & Sagi, D. (1995). Common mechanisms of visual imagery and perception. *Science, 268*(5218), 1772–1774.

James, T. W., Culham, J., Humphrey, G. K., et al. (2003). Ventral occipital lesions impair object recognition but not object-directed grasping: An fMRI study, *Brain, 126,* 2463–2475.

Kanizsa, G., & Gerbino, W. (1976). Convexity and symmetry in figure–ground organization. In M. Henle (Ed.), *Vision and Artifact.* New York: Springer.

Kanwisher, N., & Yovel, G. (2006). The fusiform face area: a cortical region specialized for the perception of faces. *Philosophical Transactions of the Royal Society of London. Series B, Biological Sciences, 361*(1476), 2109–2128.

Keogh, R., & Pearson, J. (2018). The blind mind: no sensory visual imagery in aphantasia. *Cortex, 105,* 53–60.

Kornmeier, J., & Bach, M. (2004). Early neural activity in Necker-cube reversal: evidence for low-level processing of a gestalt phenomenon. *Psychophysiology, 41,* 1–8.

Kosslyn, S. M. (1973). Scanning visual images: Some structural implications. *Perception & Psychophysics, 14*(1), 90–94.

Kosslyn, S. M. (1976). Can imagery be distinguished from other forms of internal representation? Evidence from studies of information retrieval times. *Memory & Cognition, 4,* 291–297.

Kosslyn, S. M. (1994). *Image and Brain: The Resolution of the Imagery Debate.* Cambridge, MA: The MIT Press.

Kosslyn, S. M., Alpert, N. M., Thompson, W. L., et al. (1993). Visual mental imagery activates topographically organized visual cortex: PET investigations. *Journal of Cognitive Neuroscience, 5*(3), 263–287.

Kosslyn, S. M., Ball, T. M., & Reiser, B. J. (1978). Visual images preserve metric spatial information: Evidence from studies of image scanning. *Journal of Experimental Psychology: Human Perception and Performance, 4*(1), 47–60.

Kosslyn, S. M., Pascual-Leone, A., Felician, O., et al. (1999). The role of area 17 in visual imagery: Convergent evidence from PET and rTMS. *Science, 284,* 167–170.

Kosslyn, S. M., Thompson, W. L., Kim, I. J., & Alpert, N. M. (1995). Topographical representations of mental images in primary visual cortex. *Nature, 378*(6556), 496–498.

Kreiman, G., Kock, C., & Fried, I. (2000). Category-specific visual responses of single neurons in the human medial temporal lobe. *Nature Neuroscience, 3,* 946–953.

Lafer-Sousa, R., Hermann, K. L., & Conway, B. R. (2015). Striking individual differences in color perception uncovered by 'the dress' photograph. *Current Biology, 25*(13), R545–R546.

LeCun, Y., Bengio, Y., & Hinton, G. (2015). Deep learning. *Nature, 521,* 436–444.

Levine, D. N., Warach, J., & Farah, M. J. (1985). Two visual systems in mental imagery: Dissociation of "what" and "where" in imagery disorders due to bilateral posterior cerebral lesions. *Neurology, 35,* 1010–1018.

Liu, Z., Knill, D. C., & Kersten, D. (1995). Object classification for human and ideal observers. *Vision Research, 35*(4), 549–568.

Lotto, R. B., & Purves, D. (2002). The empirical basis of color perception. *Consciousness and Cognition, 11*(4), 609–629.

Lund, N. (2016). A World Record Big Year for Birds. *Slate.* https://slate.com/technology/2016/01/noah-strycker-broke-birdings-worldwide-big-year-record.html

Marks, D. F. (1973). Visual imagery differences in the recall of pictures. *British Journal of Psychology, 64,* 17–24.

Marr, D., & Nishihara, H. K. (1978). Representation and recognition of the spatial organization of three-dimensional shapes. *Proceedings of the Royal Society of London. Series B, Biological Sciences, 200,* 269–294.

Mathews, A., Ridgeway, V., & Holmes, E. A. (2013). Feels like the real thing: imagery is both more realistic and emotional than verbal thought. *Cognition & Emotion, 27*(2), 217–229.

McKone, E., Kanwisher, N., & Duchaine, B. (2007). Can generic expertise explain special processing for faces? *Trends in Cognitive Sciences, 11,* 8–15.

Milner, A. D., & Goodale, M. A. (1995). *Visual Brain in Action.* Oxford, UK: Oxford University Press.

Miskovic, V., Kuntzelman, K., Chikazoe, J., & Anderson, A. K. (2016). Representation of affect in sensory cortex. *Behavioral & Brain Sciences, 39,* e252.

Mishkin, M., Ungerleider, L. G., & Macko, K. A. (1983). Object vision and spatial vision: two cortical pathways. *Trends in Neurosciences, 6,* 414–417.

Molyneux, W., (1688). Letter to John Locke, 7 July, in *The Correspondence of John Locke* (9 vols.), E.S. de Beer (Ed.), Oxford: Clarendon Press, 1978, vol. 3, no. 1064.

New York University. (2017). "Why did we see 'the dress' differently? The answer lies in the shadows, new research finds." ScienceDaily. https://www.sciencedaily.com/releases/2017/04/170407132747.htm.

Nundy, S., Lotto, R. B., Coppola, D., et al. (2000). Why are angles misperceived? *Proceedings of the National Academy of Sciences U.S.A., 97*(10), 5592–5597.

O'Callaghan, C., Kveraga, K., Shine, J. M., et al. (2016). Convergent evidence for top-down effects from the "predictive brain." *Behavioral & Brain Sciences, 39,* e254.

O'Callaghan, C., Kveraga, K., Shine, J. M., et al. (2017). Predictions penetrate perception: Converging insights from brain, behaviour and disorder. *Consciousness and Cognition, 47,* 63–74.

O'Craven, K. M., & Kanwisher, N. (2000). Mental imagery of faces and places activates corresponding stimulus-specific brain regions. *Journal of Cognitive Neuroscience, 12,* 1013–1023.

O'Malley, E. E., Mesquita, B., & Barrett, L. F. (2016). On the neural implausibility of the modular mind: evidence for distributed construction dissolves boundaries between perception, cognition, and emotion. *Behavioral & Brain Sciences, 39,* e246.

O'Toole, A. J., Jiang, F., Abdi, H., & Haxby, J. V. (2005). Partially distributed representations of objects and faces n ventral temporal cortex. *Journal of Cognitive Neuroscicence, 17,* 580–590.

Ostrovsky, Y., Meyers, E., Ganesh, S., et al. (2009). Visual parsing after recovery from blindness. *Psychological Science, 20,* 1484–1491.

Palmer, E. M., Kellman, P. J., & Shipley, T. F. (2006). A theory of dynamic occluded and illusory object perception. *Journal of Experimental Psychology: General, 135,* 513–541.

Palmer, S. E. (1975). The effects of contextual scenes on the identification of objects. *Memory & Cognition, 3,* 519–526.

Pearson, J. (2019). The human imagination: the cognitive neuroscience of visual mental imagery. *Nature Reviews Neuroscience, 20*(10), 624–634.

Pearson, J., Naselaris, T., Holmes, E. A., & Kosslyn, S. M. (2015). Mental imagery: functional mechanisms and clinical applications. *Trends in Cognitive Sciences, 19,* 590–602.

Peterson, M. A., Gerhardstein, P. C., Mennemeier, M., & Rapcsak, S. Z. (1998). Object-centered attentional biases and object recognition contributions to scene segmentation in left- and right-hemisphere-damaged patients. *Psychobiology, 26*(4), 357–370.

Peterson, M. A., & Gibson, B. S. (1991). The initial identification of figure-ground relationships: Contributions from shape recognition processes. *Bulletin of the Psychonomic Society, 29,* 199–202.

Peterson, M. A., & Gibson, B. S. (1994). Object recognition contributions to figure-ground organization: Operations on outlines and subjective contours. *Perception & Psychophysics, 56,* 551–564.

Peterson, M. A., Harvey, E. M., & Weidenbacher, H. J. (1991). Shape recognition contributions to figure-ground reversal: Which route counts? *Journal of Experimental Psychology: Human Perception and Performance, 17*(4), 1075–1089.

Peterson, M. A., & Kimchi, R. (2013). Perceptual organization in vision. In D. Reisberg (Ed.), *Oxford Library of Psychology. The Oxford Handbook of Cognitive Psychology* (pp. 9–31). New York: Oxford University Press.

Poggio, T., & Edelman, S. (1990). A network that learns to recognize 3D objects. *Nature, 343,* 263–266.

Press, C., Kok, P., & Yon, D. (2020). The perceptual prediction paradox. *Trends in Cognitive Sciences, 24,* 13–24.

Proffitt, D. R., Stefanucci, J., Banton, T., & Epstein, W. (2003). The role of effort in perceiving distance. *Psychological Science, 14*(2), 106–112.

Purves, D. & Lotto, R. B. (2011). *Why We See What We Do Redux: A Wholly Empirical Theory of Vision.* Sunderland, MA: Oxford University Press/Sinauer.

Pylyshyn, Z. W. (1973). What the mind's eye tells the mind's brain: A critique of mental imagery. *Psychological Bulletin, 80*(1), 1–24.

Pylyshyn, Z. W. (1999). Is vision continuous with cognition? The case for cognitive impenetrability of visual perception. *Behavioral and Brain Sciences, 22,* 341–365.

Raune, D., MacLeod, A., & Holmes, E. A. (2005). The simulation heuristic and visual imagery in pessimism for future negative events in anxiety. *Clinical Psychology & Psychotherapy, 12*(4), 313–325.

Richler, J. J., & Gauthier, I. (2014). A meta-analysis and review of holistic face processing. *Psychological Bulletin, 140*(5), 1281–1302.

Rubin, E. (1921). *Visuell Wahrgenommene Figuren.* Copenhagen, Denmark: Gyldendalske Boghandel.

Shepard, R. N. (1990). *Mind Sights: Original Visual Illusions, Ambiguities, and Other Anomalies, with a Commentary on the Play of Mind in Perception and Art.* New York: W. H. Freeman & Co.

Shepard, R. N., & Metzler, J. (1971). Mental rotation of three-dimensional objects. *Science, 171,* 701–703.

Shine, J. M., Muller, A. J., O'Callaghan, C., et al. (2015). Abnormal connectivity between the default mode and the visual system underlies the manifestation of visual hallucinations in Parkinson's disease: a task-based fMRI study. *NPJ Parkinson's Disease, 1*, 15003.

Spehar, B., & Halim, V. A. (2016). Created unequal: Temporal dynamics of modal and amodal boundary. *Vision Research, 126*, 97–108.

Szpunar, K. K., & Schacter, D. L. (2013). Get real: effects of repeated simulation and emotion on the perceived plausibility of future experiences. *Journal of Experimental Psychology: General, 142*(2), 323–327.

Tanaka, J. W., & Farah, M. J. (1993). Parts and wholes in face recognition. *The Quarterly Journal of Experimental Psychology A: Human Experimental Psychology, 46A*(2), 225–245.

Tanaka, J. W., Wolf, J. M., Klaiman, C., et al. (2010). Using computerized games to teach face recognition skills to children with autism spectrum disorder: The Let's Face It! program. *Journal of Child Psychology and Psychiatry, and Allied Disciplines, 51*, 944–952.

Tarr, M. J., & Bülthoff, H.H. (1998). Image-based object recognition in man, monkey, and machine. *Cognition, 67*, 1–20.

Tarr, M. J., & Pinker, S. (1990). When does human object recognition use a viewer-centered reference frame? *Psychological Science, 1*, 253–256.

Trapp, S., & Bar, M. (2015). Prediction, context, and competition in visual recognition. *Annals of the New York Academy of Sciences, 1339*, 190–198.

Tsao, D. Y., Freiwald, W. A., Tootell, R. B., & Livingstone, M. S. (2006). A cortical region consisting entirely of face-selective cells. *Science, 311*(5761), 670–674.

Ullman, S., & Basri, R. (1991). Recognition by linear combinations of models. *IEEE Transactions on Pattern Analysis and Machine Intelligence, 13*, 992–1006.

Vinson, D. W., Abney, D. H., Amso, D., et al. (2016). Perception, as you make it. *Behavioral & Brain Sciences, 39*, e260.

Vinyals, O., Toshev, A., Bengio, S., & Erhan, D. (2014). Show and tell: A neural image caption generator. *2015 IEEE Conference on Computer Vision and Pattern Recognition (CVPR)*, 3156–3164.

Vogelsang, M. D., Palmeri, T. J., & Busey, T. A. (2017). Holistic processing of fingerprints by expert forensic examiners. *Cognitive Research: Principles and Implications, 2*(1), 15.

Wallisch, P. (2017). Illumination assumptions account for individual differences in the perceptual interpretation of a profoundly ambiguous stimulus in the color domain: "the dress." *Journal of Vision, 17*, 5.

Wallisch, P., as quoted in Wong, S. (2017). The science behind the world's most divisive dress. Published in NewsHub, 10/04/2017. © 2017 Discovery New Zealand - All Rights Reserved.

Watson, T. L. (2013). Implications of holistic face processing in autism and schizophrenia. *Frontiers in Psychology, 4*, Article 414.

White, D., Kemp, R. I., Jenkins, R., et al. (2014). Passport officers' errors in face matching. *PLOS ONE, 9*(8), e103510.

Winerman, L. (2012). "Neuroscientist brings light to the blind—and to vision research" *American Psychological Association, 43*, 26. https://www.apa.org/monitor/2012/12/neuroscientist-sinha

Wolfe, J., et al. (2018). *Sensation and Perception*, 5th Edition, Sunderland, MA: Oxford University Press/Sinauer.

Wolfe, J., et al. (2020). *Sensation and Perception*, 6th Edition, Sunderland, MA: Oxford University Press/Sinauer.

Wong, A. C.-N., Bukach, C. M., Hsiao, J., et al. (2012). Holistic processing as a hallmark of perceptual expertise for nonface categories including Chinese characters. *Journal of Vision, 12*(13). Article 7.

Wong, Y. K., & Gauthier, I. (2012). Music-reading expertise alters visual spatial resolution for musical notation. *Psychonomic Bulletin & Review, 19*(4), 594–600.

Zeman, A. Z., Della Sala, S., Torrens, L. A., et al. (2010). Loss of imagery phenomenology with intact visuo-spatial task performance: A case of 'blind imagination.' *Neuropsychologia, 48*, 145–155.

Chapter 4

Anderson, A. K., & Phelps, E. A. (2001). Lesions of the human amygdala impair enhanced perception of emotionally salient events. *Nature, 411*, 305–309.

Anderson, B. A., Laurent, P. A., & Yantis, S. (2011). Value-driven attentional capture. *Proceedings of the National Academy of Sciences of the United States of America, 108*(25), 10367–10371.

Anton-Erxleben, K., & Carrasco, M. (2013). Attentional enhancement of spatial resolution: linking behavioural and neurophysiological evidence. *Nature Reviews Neuroscience, 14*(3), 188–200.

Anton-Erxleben, K., Herrmann, K., & Carrasco, M. (2013). Independent effects of adaptation and attention on perceived speed. *Psychological Science, 24*(2), 150–159.

Arguin, M., & Bub, D. (1993). Evidence for an independent stimulus-centered spatial reference frame from a case of visual hemineglect. *Cortex, 29*, 349–357.

Awh, E., Belopolsky, A. V., & Theeuwes, J. (2012). Top-down versus bottom-up attentional control: a failed theoretical dichotomy. *Trends in Cognitive Sciences, 16*(8), 437–443.

Awh, E., & Vogel, E. K. (2008). The bouncer in the brain. *Nature Neuroscience, 11*(1), 5–6.

Barbot, A., Landy, M., & Carrasco, M. (2011). Exogenous attention enhances 2nd-order contrast sensitivity, *Vision Research, 51*, 1086–1098.

Bar-Haim, Y., Lamy, D., Pergamin, L., et al. (2007). Threat-related attentional bias in anxious and nonanxious individuals: A meta-analytic study. *Psychological Bulletin, 133*(1), 1–24.

Beanland, V., & Pammer, K. (2010). Looking without seeing or seeing without looking? Eye movements in sustained inattentional blindness. *Vision Research, 50*, 977–988.

Beck, D. M., & Kastner, S. (2007). Stimulus similarity modulates competitive interactions in human visual cortex. *Journal of Vision, 7*(2), 1–12.

Beck, D. M., & Kastner, S. (2009). Top-down and bottom-up mechanisms in biasing competition in the human brain. *Vision Research, 49*(10), 1154–1165.

Becklen, R., & Cervone, D. (1983). Selective looking and the noticing of unexpected events. *Memory & Cognition, 11,* 601–608.

Bocanegra, B. R., & Zeelenberg, R. (2009). Emotion improves and impairs early vision. *Psychological Science, 20,* 707–713.

Boynton, G. M. (2005). Attention and visual perception. *Current Opinion in Neurobiology, 15,* 465–469.

Brady, T. F., & Chun, M. M. (2007). Spatial constraints on learning in visual search: Modeling contextual cuing. *Journal of Experimental Psychology: Human Perception and Performance, 33*(4), 798–815.

Breedlove, S. M., & Watson, N. V. (2019). *Behavioral Neuroscience,* 9th Edition. Sunderland, MA: Oxford University Press/Sinauer.

Broadbent, D. E. (1958). *Perception and Communication.* London: Pergamon Press.

Broadbent, D. E. (1971). *Decision and Stress.* London: Academic Press.

Broadbent, D. E., & Broadbent, M. H. (1987). From detection to identification: Response to multiple targets in rapid serial visual presentation. *Perception and Psychophysics, 42*(2), 105–113.

Brockmole, J. R., Castelhano, M. S., & Henderson, J. M. (2006). Contextual cueing in naturalistic scenes: Global and local contexts. *Journal of Experimental Psychology: Learning, Memory, and Cognition, 32*(4), 699–706.

Buetti, S., Cronin, D. A., Madison, A. M., et al. (2016). Towards a better understanding of parallel visual processing in human vision: Evidence for exhaustive analysis of visual information. *Journal of Experimental Psychology: General, 145*(6), 672–707.

Bundesen, C. (1990). A theory of visual attention. *Psychological Review, 97,* 523–547.

Carrasco, M., Ling, S., & Read, S. (2004). Attention alters appearance. *Nature Neuroscience, 7,* 308–313.

Chelazzi, L., Miller, E. K., Duncan, J., & Desimone, R. (2001). Responses of neurons in macaque area V4 during memory-guided visual search. *Cerebral Cortex, 11,* 761–772.

Cherry, E. C. (1953). Some experiments on the recognition of speech with one and with two ears. *Journal of the Acoustical Society of America, 25,* 975–979.

Chun, M. M., (2000). Contextual cueing of visual attention. *Trends in Cognitive Sciences,* 4(5), 170–178.

Chun, M. M., Golomb, J. D., & Turk-Browne, N. (2011). A taxonomy of external and internal attention. *Annual Review of Psychology, 62,* 73–101.

Chun, M. M., & Jiang, Y. (1998). Contextual cueing: Implicit learning and memory of visual context guides spatial attention. Cognitive Psychology, 36, 28–71.

Chun, M. M., & Phelps, E. A. (1999). Memory deficits for implicit contextual information in amnesic subjects with hippocampal damage. *Nature Neuroscience, 2,* 844–847.

Chun, M. M., & Potter, M. C. (1995). A two-stage model for multiple target detection in rapid serial visual presentation. *Journal of Experimental Psychology: Human Perception & Performance, 21,* 109–127.

Cook, M., & Mineka, S. (1990). Selective associations in the observational conditioning of fear in rhesus monkeys. *Journal of Experimental Psychology: Animal Behavior Processes, 16*(4), 372–389.

Corbetta, M., Akbudak, E., Conturo, T. E., et al. (1998). A common network of functional areas for attention and eye movements. *Neuron, 21*(4), 761–773.

Corbetta, M., Miezin, F. M., Dobmeyer, S., et al. (1991). Selective and divided attention during visual discriminations of shape, color, and speed: Functional anatomy by positron emission tomography. *Journal of Neuroscience, 11,* 2383–2402.

Corbetta, M. & Shulman, G. L. (2002). Control of goal directed and stimulus driven attention in the brain. *Nature Reviews Neuroscience, 3,* 201–215.

Cosman, J. D., Lowe, K. A., Zinke, W., et al. (2018). Prefrontal control of visual distraction. *Current Biology, 28*(3), 414–420.

Cristea, I. A., Mogoaşe, C., David, D., & Cuijpers, P. (2015), Practitioner Review: Cognitive bias modification for mental health problems in children and adolescents: A meta-analysis. *Journal of Child Psychology and Psychiatry, 56,* 723–734.

Curby, K. M., Johnson, K. J., & Tyson, A. (2012). Face to face with emotion: Holistic face processing is modulated by emotional state. *Cognition & Emotion, 26,* 93–102.

Cutzu, F., & Tsotsos, J. K. (2003). The selective tuning model of attention: Psychophysical evidence for a suppressive annulus around an attended item. *Vision Research, 43,* 205–219.

de Fockert, J. W., Rees, G., Frith, C. D., & Lavie, N. (2001). The role of working memory in visual selective attention. *Science, 291,* 1803–1806.

Derryberry, D., & Tucker, D. M. (1994). Motivating the focus of attention. In P. M. Neidenthal & S. Kitayama (Eds.), The Heart's Eye: Emotional influences in perception and attention (pp. 167–196). San Diego, CA: Academic Press.

Desimone, R. (1998). Visual attention mediated by biased competition in extrastriate visual cortex. *Philosophical Transactions of the Royal Society B: Biological Sciences, 353*(1373), 1245–1255.

Desimone, R., & Duncan, J. (1995). Neural mechanisms of selective visual attention. *Annual Review of Neuroscience, 18,* 193–222.

Detling, D. (2014). Driver blames mannequin for car crash. *KOCO News 5,* June 28, 2014. https://www.koco.com/article/driver-blames-mannequins-for-car-crash/4298981

Deutsch, J. A., & Deutsch, D. (1963). Attention: Some theoretical considerations. *Psychological Review, 70,* 80–90.

Di Lollo, V., Enns, J. T., & Rensink, R. A. (2000). Competition for consciousness among visual events: The psychophysics of reentrant visual processes. *Journal of Experimental Psychology: General, 129,* 481–507.

Drew, T., Võ, M. L., & Wolfe, J. M. (2013). The invisible gorilla strikes again: Sustained inattentional blindness in expert observers. *Psychological Science, 24*(9), 1848–1853.

Driver, J., Davis, G., Ricciardelli, P., et al. (1999). Gaze perception triggers reflexive visuospatial orienting. *Visual Cognition, 6*, 509–540.

Driver, J., & Halligan, P. W. (1991). Can visual neglect operate in object-centered coordinates: An affirmative study. *Cognitive Neuropsychology, 8*, 475–496.

Duncan, J. (1984). Selective attention and the organization of visual information. *Journal of Experimental Psychology: General, 113*, 501–517.

Duncan, J., & Humphreys. G. W. (1989). Visual search and stimulus similarity. *Psychological Review, 96*, 433–458.

Dux, P. E., & Marois, R. (2009). The attentional blink: A review of data and theory. *Attention, Perception & Psychophysics, 71*(8), 1683–1700.

Egeth, H. E. (1966). Parallel versus serial processes in multidimensional stimulus discrimination. *Perception & Psychophysics, 1*(8), 245–252.

Egly, R., Driver, J., & Rafal, R. D. (1994). Shifting visual attention between objects and locations: Evidence from normal and parietal lesion subjects. *Journal of Experimental Psychology: General, 123*, 161–177.

Eriksen, C., & St. James, J. (1986). Visual attention within and around the field of focal attention: A zoom lens model. *Perception & Psychophysics, 40*, 225–240.

Failing, M. F., & Theeuwes, J. (2015). Nonspatial attentional capture by previously rewarded scene semantics. *Visual Cognition, 23*(1–2), 82–104.

Fan, J., McCandliss, B. D., Sommer, T., et al. (2002). Testing the efficiency and independence of attentional networks. *Journal of Cognitive Neuroscience, 14*, 340–347.

Folk, C. L., & Gibson, B. S. (Eds.). (2001). *Attraction, Distraction, and Action: Multiple perspectives on attentional capture* (Vol. 133). Amsterdam: Elsevier.

Folk, C. L., Remington, R. W., & Johnston, J. C. (1992). Involuntary covert orienting is contingent on attentional control settings. *Journal of Experimental Psychology: Human Perception and Performance, 18*, 1030–1044.

Fougnie, D., Cockhren, J., & Marois, R. (2018). A common source of attention for auditory and visual tracking. *Attention, Perception, & Psychophysics, 80*(6), 1571–1583.

Fox, E., Russo, R., Bowles, R., & Dutton, K. (2001). Do threatening stimuli draw or hold visual attention in subclinical anxiety? *Journal of Experimental Psychology: General, 130*, 681–700.

Fox, E., Russo, R., & Dutton, K. (2002). Attentional bias for threat: Evidence for delayed disengagement from emotional faces. *Cognition & Emotion, 16*(3), 355–379.

Franconeri, S. L., Alvarez, G. A., & Cavanagh, P. (2013). Flexible cognitive resources: Competitive content maps for attention and memory. *Trends in Cognitive Sciences, 17*(3), 134–141.

Franconeri, S. L., & Simons, D. J. (2003). Moving and looming stimuli capture attention. *Perception & Psychophysics, 65*, 999–1010.

Fredrickson, B. L. (1998). What good are positive emotions? *Review of General Psychology, 2*, 300–319.

Fredrickson, B. L. (2001). The role of positive emotions in positive psychology: The broaden-and-build theory of positive emotions. *American Psychologist, 56*, 218–226.

Fredrickson, B. L., & Branigan, C. (2005). Positive emotions broaden the scope of attention and thought-action repertoires. *Cognition & Emotion, 19*(3), 313–332.

Friesen, C. K., & Kingstone, A. (1998). The eyes have it! Reflexive orienting is triggered by nonpredictive gaze. *Psychonomic Bulletin & Review, 5*, 490–495.

Gable, P. A., & Harmon-Jones, E. (2008). Approach-motivated positive affect reduces breadth of attention. *Psychological Science, 19*, 476–482.

Goodhew, S. C., Lawrence, R. K., & Edwards, M. (2017). Testing the generality of the zoom-lens model: Evidence for visual-pathway specific effects of attended-region size on perception. *Attention, Perception & Psychophysics, 79*(4), 1147–1164.

Grabowecky, M., Robertson, L. C., & Treisman, A. (1993). Preattentive processes guide visual search: evidence from patients with unilateral visual neglect. *Journal of Cognitive Neuroscience, 5*(3), 288–302.

Greene, M. R., & Oliva, A. (2009). The briefest of glances: The time course of natural scene understanding. *Psychological Science, 20*(4), 464–472.

Grimshaw, G. M., Kranz, L. S., Carmel, D., et al. (2018). Contrasting reactive and proactive control of emotional distraction. *Emotion, 18*(1), 26–38.

Harris, A. M., Dux, P. E., Jones, C. N., & Mattingley, J. B. (2017). Distinct roles of theta and alpha oscillations in the involuntary capture of goal-directed attention. *NeuroImage, 152*, 171–183.

Harris, C. R., & Pashler, H. (2004). Attention and the processing of emotional words and names: Not so special after all. *Psychological Science, 15*, 171–178.

Hoffman, J. E., & Subramaniam, B. (1995). The role of visual attention in saccadic eye movements. *Perception & Psychophysics, 57*, 787–795.

Holcombe, A. O. (2009). Seeing slow and seeing fast: two limits on perception. *Trends in Cognitive Sciences, 13*(5), 216–221.

Horowitz, T. S., & Wolfe, J. M. (1998). Visual search has no memory. *Nature, 394*, 575–577.

Hsieh, P. J., Colas, J. T., & Kanwisher, N. (2011). Pop-out without awareness: Unseen feature singletons capture attention only when top-down attention is available. *Psychological Science, 22*(9), 1220–1226.

Ihssen, N., & Keil, A. (2009). The costs and benefits of processing emotional stimuli during rapid serial visual presentation. *Cognition and Emotion, 23*(2), 296–326.

Itti, L., & Koch, C. (2001). Computational modelling of visual attention. *Nature Reviews Neuroscience, 2*(3), 194–203.

James, W. (1890). *The Principles of Psychology*, in two volumes. New York: Henry Holt and Company.

Jiang, Y., Costello, P., Fang, F., et al. (2006). A gender- and sexual orientation-dependent spatial attentional effect of invisible images. *Proceedings of the National Academy of Sciences of the United States of America, 103*(45), 17048–17052.

Jiang, Y., & Wagner, L. C. (2004). What is learned in spatial contextual cuing—Configuration or individual locations? *Perception & Psychophysics, 66*(3), 454–463.

Jones, W., & Klin, A. (2013). Attention to eyes is present but in decline in 2–6-month-old infants later diagnosed with autism. *Nature, 504*(7480), 427–431.

Kastner, S., & Ungerleider, L. G. (2000). Mechanisms of visual attention in the human cortex. *Annual Review of Neuroscience, 23*, 315–341.

Kastner, S., & Ungerleider, L. G. (2001). The neural basis of biased competition in human visual cortex. *Neuropsychologia, 39*, 1263–1276.

Kearney, L. (2013). Absorbed smartphone users oblivious to gunman before fatal California train shooting. *Chicago Tribune*, October 9, 2013. https://www.chicagotribune.com/news/ct-xpm-2013-10-09-sns-rt-usa-crimecommuters-20131009-story.html

Kentridge, R. W., Heywood, C. A., & Weiskrantz, L. (1999). Attention without awareness in blindsight. *Proceedings of the Royal Society of London, Series B, 266*, 1805–1811.

Kentridge, R. W., Heywood, C. A., & Weiskrantz, L. (2004). Spatial attention speeds discrimination without awareness in blindsight. *Neuropsychologia, 42*, 831–835.

Kimchi, R., & Palmer, S. E. (1982). Form and texture in hierarchically constructed patterns. *Journal of Experimental Psychology: Human Perception and Performance, 8*(4), 521–535.

Klein, R. M. (1988). Inhibitory tagging system facilitates visual search. *Nature, 334*, 430–431.

Klein, R. M. (2000). Inhibition of return. *Trends in Cognitive Sciences, 4*, 138–146.

Klein, R. M. & MacInnes, J. (1999). Inhibition of return is a foraging facilitator in visual search. *Psychological Science 10*(4): 346–352.

Klin, A., Jones, W., Schultz, R., et al. (2002). Visual fixation patterns during viewing of naturalistic social situations as predictors of social competence in individuals with autism. *Archives of General Psychiatry, 59*, 809–816.

Koch, C., & Tsuchiya, N. (2007). Attention and consciousness: Two distinct brain processes. *Trends in Cognitive Sciences, 11*(1), 16–22.

Koch, C., & Ullman, S. (1985). Shifts in selective visual attention: Towards the underlying neural circuitry. *Human Neurobiology, 4*, 219–227.

Koivisto, M., Hyönä, J., & Revonsuo, A. (2004). The effects of eye movements, spatial attention, and stimulus features on inattentional blindness. *Vision Research, 44*, 3211–3221.

Kowler, E., Anderson, E., Dosher, B., & Blaser, E. (1995). The role of attention in the programming of saccades. *Vision Research, 35*, 1897–1916.

Kristjánsson, Á. (2015). Reconsidering visual search. *i-Perception, 6*(6), Article 2041669515614670.

Lamy, D., & Egeth, H. (2002). Object-based selection: The role of attentional shifts. *Perception & Psychophysics, 64*, 52–66.

Lavie, N. (1995). Perceptual load as a necessary condition for selective attention. *Journal of Experimental Psychology: Human Perception and Performance, 21*, 451–468.

Lavie, N. (2005). Distracted and confused? Selective attention under load. *Trends in Cognitive Sciences, 9*, 75–82.

Lavie, N., & Cox, S. (1997). On the efficiency of visual selective attention: Efficient visual search leads to inefficient distractor rejection. *Psychological Science, 8*(5), 395–398.

Leber, A. B., & Egeth, H. E. (2006). It's under control: Top-down search strategies can override attentional capture. *Psychonomic Bulletin & Review, 13*(1), 132–138.

Lee, T. H., Baek, J., Lu, Z. L., & Mather, M. (2014). How arousal modulates the visual contrast sensitivity function. *Emotion, 14*(5), 978–984.

Lee, J., & Maunsell, J. H. (2009). A normalization model of attentional modulation of single unit responses. *PLOS ONE, 4*(2), e4651.

Le Pelley, M. E., Pearson, D., Griffiths, O., & Beesley, T. (2015). When goals conflict with values: Counterproductive attentional and occulomotor capture by reward-related stimuli. *Journal of Experimental Psychology: General, 144*, 158–171.

Le Pelley, M. E., Watson, P., Pearson, D., et al. (2019). Winners and losers: Reward and punishment produce biases in temporal selection. *Journal of Experimental Psychology: Learning, Memory, & Cognition, 45*, 822–833.

Lim, J., & Dinges, D. F. (2008). Sleep deprivation and vigilant attention. *Annals of the New York Academy of Sciences, 1129*, 305–322.

Lincoln's Gettysburg address, November 19, 1863.

Lipp, O. V., Derakshan, N., Waters, A. M., & Logies, S. (2004). Snakes and cats in the flower bed: Fast detection is not specific to pictures of fear-relevant animals. *Emotion, 4*(3), 233–250.

Liu, T., Slotnick, S. D., Serences, J. T., & Yantis, S. (2003). Cortical mechanisms of feature-based attentional control. *Cerebral Cortex, 13*, 1334–1343.

Luck, S. J., Girelli, M., McDermott, M. T., & Ford, M. A. (1997). Bridging the gap between monkey neurophysiology and human perception: An ambiguity resolution theory of visual selective attention. *Cognitive Psychology, 33*, 64–87.

Luck, S. J., & Hillyard, S. A. (1994). Electrophysiological correlates of feature analysis during visual search. *Psychophysiology, 31*, 291–308.

Mack, A., & Rock, I. (1998). *Inattentional Blindness*. Cambridge, MA: The MIT Press.

MacLeod, C., Mathews, A., & Tata, P. (1986). Attentional bias in emotional distractors. *Journal of Abnormal Psychology, 95*, 15–20.

Marois, R., Yi, D. J., & Chun, M. M. (2004). The neural fate of consciously perceived and missed events in the attentional blink. *Neuron, 41*(3), 465–472.

Martens, S., & Wyble, B. (2010). The attentional blink: Past, present, and future of a blind spot in perceptual awareness. *Neuroscience and Biobehavioral Reviews, 34*(6), 947–957.

Martinez-Trujillo, J. C., & Treue, S. (2004). Feature-based attention increases the selectivity of population responses in primate visual cortex. *Current Biology, 14,* 744–751.

Mather, M., & Sutherland, M. R. (2011). Arousal-biased competition in perception and memory. *Perspectives on Psychological Science, 6*(2), 114–133.

Mathews, A., & MacLeod, C. (2002). Induced processing biases have causal effects on anxiety. *Cognition & Emotion, 16,* 331–354.

Mathewson, K. E., Prudhomme, C., Fabiani, M., et al. (2012). Making waves in the stream of consciousness: Entraining oscillations in EEG alpha and fluctuations in visual awareness with rhythmic visual stimulation. *Journal of Cognitive Neuroscience, 24*(12), 2321–2333.

McCarley, J. S., & Mounts, J. R. W. (2007). Localized attentional interference affects object individuation, not feature detection. *Perception, 36,* 17–32.

Memmert, D. (2006). The effects of eye movements, age, and expertise on inattentional blindness. *Consciousness & Cognition, 15,* 620–627.

Mitroff, S. R., & Biggs, A. T. (2014). The ultra-rare-item effect: Visual search for exceedingly rare items is highly susceptible to error. *Psychological Science, 25*(1), 284–289.

Mitroff, S. R., Simons, D. J., & Levin, D. T. (2004). Nothing compares 2 views: Change blindness can occur despite preserved access to the changed information. *Perception & Psychophysics, 66,* 1268–1281.

Montagna, B., & Carrasco, M. (2006). Transient covert attention and the perceived rate of flicker. *Journal of Vision, 6*(9), 955–965.

Moore, C. M., Yantis S., & Vaughan, B. (1998). Object-based visual selection: Evidence from perceptual completion. *Psychological Science, 9,* 104–110.

Moray, N. P. (1959). Attention in dichotic listening: Affective cues and the influence of instructions. *Quarterly Journal of Experimental Psychology, 11,* 56–60.

Most, S. B., & Astur, R. S. (2007). Feature-based attentional set as a cause of traffic accidents. *Visual Cognition, 15*(2), 125–132.

Most, S. B., Chun, M. M., Widders, D. M., & Zald, D. H. (2005). Attentional rubbernecking: Cognitive control and personality in emotion-induced blindness. *Psychonomic Bulletin & Review, 12,* 654–661.

Most, S. B., Simons, D. J., Scholl, B. J., et al. (2001). How not to be seen: The contribution of similarity and selective ignoring to sustained inattentional blindness. *Psychological Science, 12,* 9–17.

Mounts, J. R. W. (2000). Evidence for suppressive mechanisms in attentional selection: Feature singletons produce inhibitory surrounds. *Perception & Psychophysics, 62,* 969–983.

Müller, H. J., & Rabbitt, P. M. (1989). Reflexive and voluntary orienting of visual attention: time course of activation and resistance to interruption. *Journal of Experimental Psychology: Human Perception & Performance, 15,* 315–330.

Müller, N. G., Bartelt, O. A., Donner, T. H., et al. (2003). A physiological correlate of the "Zoom Lens" of visual attention. *The Journal of Neuroscience, 23*(9), 3561–3565.

Nakayama, K., & Mackeben, M. (1989). Sustained and transient components of focal visual attention. *Vision Research, 29,* 1631–1647.

Neisser, U. (1979). The control of information pickup in selective looking. In A. D. Pick (Ed.), *Perception and Its Development: A tribute to Eleanor J. Gibson* (pp. 201–219). Hillsdale, NJ: Erlbaum.

Nobre, A. C., Gitelman, D. R., Dias, E. C., & Mesulam, M. M. (2000). Covert visual spatial orienting and saccades: overlapping neural systems. *Neuroimage, 11,* 210–216.

O'Craven, K. M., Downing, P. E., & Kanwisher, N. (1999). fMRI evidence for objects as the units of attentional selection. *Nature, 401*(6753), 584–587.

Öhman, A., Flykt, A., & Esteves, F. (2001). Emotion drives attention: Detecting the snake in the grass. *Journal of Experimental Psychology: General, 130,* 466–478.

Öhman, A. & Mineka, S. (2001). Fears, phobias, and preparedness: Towards an evolved module of fear and fear learning. *Psychological Review, 108,* 483–522.

Olivers, C. N., & Meeter, M. (2008). A boost and bounce theory of temporal attention. *Psychological Review, 115*(4), 836–863.

O'Regan, J. K., Rensink, R. A., & Clark, J. J. (1999). Change-blindness as a result of "mudsplashes." *Nature, 398,* 34.

Panichello, M. F., & Buschman, T. J. (2021). Shared mechanisms underlie the control of working memory and attention. *Nature, 592*(7855), 601–605.

Pashler, H. E. (1998). *The Psychology of Attention*. Cambridge, MA: The MIT Press.

Pessoa, L., McKenna, M., Gutierrez, E., & Ungerleider, L. G. (2002). Neural processing of emotional faces requires attention. *Proceedings of the National Academy of Sciences, 99,* 11458–11463.

Phelps, E. A., Ling, S., & Carrasco, M. (2006). Emotion facilitates perception and potentiates the perceptual benefits of attention. *Psychological Science, 17*(4), 292–299.

Pilz, K. S., Roggeveen, A. B., Creighton, S. E., et al. (2012). How prevalent is object-based attention?. *PLOS ONE, 7*(2), e30693.

Posner, M. I. (1980). Orienting of Attention. *The Quarterly Journal of Experimental Psychology, 32,* 3–25.

Posner, M. I., & Cohen, Y. P. C. (1984). Components of visual orienting. In H. Bouma & D. Bouwhuis (Eds.), *Attention and Performance X: Control of language processes* (pp. 531–556). London: Laurence Erlbaum.

Posner, M. I., & Petersen, S. E. (1990). The attention system of the human brain. *Annual Review of Neuroscience, 13,* 25–42.

Posner, M. I., Snyder, C. R. R., & Davidson, B. J. (1980). Attention and the detection of signals. *Journal of Experimental Psychology: General, 109,* 160–174.

Potter, M. C. (1976). Short-term conceptual memory for pictures. *Journal of Experimental Psychology: Human Learning and Memory, 2*(5), 509–522.

Potter, M. C. (1984). Rapid serial visual presentation (RSVP): A method for studying language processing. In D. Kieras & M. Just (Eds.), *New Methods in Reading Comprehension Research* (pp. 91–118). Hillsdale, NJ: Erlbaum.

Potter, M. C., Wyble, B., Hagmann, C. E., & McCourt, E. S. (2014). Detecting meaning in RSVP at 13 ms per picture. *Attention, Perception & Psychophysics, 76*(2), 270–279.

Pylyshyn, Z. W., & Storm, R. W. (1988). Tracking multiple independent targets: Evidence for a parallel tracking mechanism. *Spatial Vision, 3,* 179–197.

Raymond, J. E., Shapiro, K. L., & Arnell, K. M. (1992). Temporary suppression of visual processing in an RSVP task: An attentional blink? *Journal of Experimental Psychology: Human Perception and Performance, 18,* 879–860.

Reynolds, J. H., & Heeger, D. J. (2009). The normalization model of attention. *Neuron, 61*(2), 168–185.

Robertson, L. C. (2003). Binding, spatial attention and perceptual awareness. *Nature Reviews Neuroscience, 4*(2), 93–102.

Rolfs, M., & Carrasco, M. (2012). Rapid simultaneous enhancement of visual sensitivity and perceived contrast during saccade preparation. *Journal of Neuroscience, 34,* 13744–13752.

Rosvold, H. E., Mirsky, A. F., Sarason, I., et al. (1956). A continuous performance test of brain damage. *Journal of Consulting Psychology, 20,* 343–350.

Ruff, C. C., Kristjánsson, A., & Driver, J. (2007). Readout from iconic memory and selective spatial attention involve similar neural processes. *Psychological Science, 18*(10), 901–909.

Scholl, B. J. (2001). Objects and attention: The state of the art. *Cognition, 80*(1–2), 1–46.

Scholl, B. J., & Pylyshyn, Z. W. (1999). Tracking multiple items through occlusion: Clues to visual objecthood. *Cognitive Psychology, 38,* 259–290.

Schwabe, L., Merz, C. J., Walter, B., et al. (2011). Emotional modulation of the attentional blink: The neural structures involved in capturing and holding attention. *Neuropsychologia, 49,* 416–425.

Schwabe, L., & Wolf, O. (2010). Emotional modulation of the attentional blink: Is there an effect of stress? *Emotion, 10,* 283–288.

Seligman, M. E. P. (1971). Phobias and preparedness. *Behavior Therapy, 2,* 307–320.

Serences, J. T., & Boynton, G. M. (2007). Feature-based attentional modulations in the absence of direct visual stimulation. *Neuron, 55,* 301–312.

Shapiro, K. L., & Raymond, J. E. (1994). Temporal allocation of visual attention: Inhibition or interference? In D. Dagenbach & T. H. Carr (Eds.), *Inhibitory Processes in Attention, Memory, and Language* (pp. 151–188). New York: Academic Press.

Sheliga, B. M., Riggio, L., & Rizzolatti, G. (1994). Orienting of attention and eye movements. *Experimental Brain Research, 98,* 507–522.

Shomstein, S., & Behrmann, M. (2008). Object-based attention: Strength of object representation and attentional guidance. *Perception & Psychophysics, 70*(1), 132–144.

Simons, D. J. (2000). Attentional capture and inattentional blindness. *Trends in Cognitive Sciences, 4,* 147–155.

Simons, D. J. (2010). Monkeying around with the gorillas in our midst: Familiarity with an inattentional-blindness task does not improve the detection of unexpected events. *i-Perception, 1*(1), 3–6.

Simons, D. J., & Chabris, C. F. (1999). Gorillas in our midst: Sustained inattentional blindness for dynamic events. *Perception, 28,* 1059–1074.

Simons, D. J., & Levin, D. T. (1998). Failure to detect changes to people during a real-world interaction. *Psychonomic Bulletin & Review, 5,* 644–649.

Spering, M., & Carrasco, M. (2012). Similar effects of feature-based attention on motion perception and pursuit eye movements at different levels of awareness. *Journal of Neuroscience, 32,* 7594–7601.

Theeuwes, J. (1992). Perceptual selectivity for color and form. *Perception & Psychophysics, 51,* 599–606.

Theeuwes, J. (1994). Stimulus-driven capture and attentional set: Selective search for color and visual abrupt onsets. *Journal of Experimental Psychology: Human Perception and Performance, 20,* 799–806.

Theeuwes, J. (2010). Top-down and bottom-up control of visual selection. *Acta Psychologica, 135,* 77–99.

Tipper, S., Jordan, H., & Weaver, B. (1999). Scene-based and object-centered inhibition of return: evidence for dual orienting mechanisms. *Perception & Psychophysics, 61,* 50–60.

Townsend, J. T., & Wenger, M. J. (2004). The serial-parallel dilemma: A case study in a linkage of theory and method. *Psychonomic Bulletin & Review, 11*(3), 391–418.

Tran, A., & Hoffman, J. E. (2016). Visual attention is required for multiple object tracking. *Journal of Experimental Psychology: Human Perception and Performance, 42*(12), 2103–2114.

Treisman, A. (1960). Contextual cues in selective listening. *Quarterly Journal of Experimental Psychology, 12,* 242–248.

Treisman, A., & Gelade, G. (1980). A feature-integration theory of attention. *Cognitive Psychology, 12,* 97–136.

Treisman, A., & Schmidt, H. (1982). Illusory conjunctions in the perception of objects. *Cognitive Psychology, 14,* 107–141.

Treue, S., & Martinez Trujillo, J. C. (1999). Feature-based attention influences motion processing gain in macaque visual cortex. *Nature, 399,* 575–579.

Treue, S., & Maunsell, J. H. (1996). Attentional modulation of visual motion processing in cortical areas MT and MST. *Nature, 382,* 539–541.

Vogel, E. K., Luck, S. J., & Shapiro, K. L. (1998). Electrophysiological evidence for a postperceptual locus of suppression during the attentional blink. *Journal of Experimental Psychology: Human Perception & Performance, 24,* 1656–1674.

Vogel, E. K., & Machizawa, M. G. (2004). Neural activity predicts individual differences in visual working memory capacity. *Nature, 428,* 748–751.

Vogel, E. K., McCollough, A. W., & Machizawa, M. G. (2005). Neural measures reveal individual differences in controlling access to working memory. *Nature, 423,* 500–503.

Vuilleumier, P., Armony, J. L., Driver, J., & Dolan, R. J. (2001). Effects of attention and emotion on face processing in the human brain: An event-related fMRI study. *Neuron, 30,* 829–841.

Wang, L., Kennedy, B. L., & Most, S. B. (2012). When emotion blinds: A spatiotemporal competition account of emotion-induced blindness. *Frontiers in Psychology: Special Topic on Emotion and Cognition, 3,* 438.

Weichselgartner, E., & Sperling, G. (1987). Dynamics of automatic and controlled visual attention. *Science, 238,* 778–780.

Weiskrantz, L. (1986). *A Case Study and Implications.* Oxford: Oxford University Press.

Wolfe, J. M. (1994). Guided Search 2.0: A revised model of visual search. *Psychonomic Bulletin & Review, 1,* 202–238.

Wolfe, J. M. (1998). Visual search. In H. Pashler (Ed.), *Attention* (pp. 13–73). London: Psychology Press.

Wolfe, J. M. (2007). Guided Search 4.0: Current progress with a model of visual search. In W. D. Gray (Ed.), *Integrated Models of Cognitive Systems* (pp. 99–119). New York: Oxford University Press.

Wolfe, J. M., et al. (2017). *Sensation & Perception,* 5th Edition. Sunderland, MA: Oxford University Press/Sinauer.

Wolfe, J. M., Võ, M. L., Evans, K. K., & Greene, M. R. (2011). Visual search in scenes involves selective and nonselective pathways. *Trends in Cognitive Sciences, 15*(2), 77–84.

Wood, N. L., & Cowan, N. (1995). The cocktail party phenomenon re-visited: Attention and memory in the classic selective listening procedure of Cherry (1953). *Journal of Experimental Psychology: Learning, Memory, & Cognition, 21,* 255–260.

Woodman, G. F., & Luck, S. J. (2003). Dissociations among attention, perception, and awareness during object-substitution masking. *Psychological Science, 14,* 605–611.

Yantis, S., & Jonides, J. (1984). Abrupt visual onsets and selective attention: Evidence from visual search. *Journal of Experimental Psychology: Human Perception and Performance, 10,* 601–621.

Yantis, S., & Jonides, J. (1990). Abrupt visual onsets and selective attention: Voluntary versus automatic allocation. *Journal of Experimental Psychology: Human Perception and Performance, 16,* 121–134.

Yarbus, A. L. (1967). *Eye Movements and Vision.* New York: Plenum Press.

Yi, D. J., Woodman, G. F., Widders, D., et al. (2004). Neural fate of ignored stimuli: Dissociable effects of perceptual and working memory load. *Nature Neuroscience, 7*(9), 992–996.

Yiend, J. (2010). The effects of emotion on attention: A review of attentional processing of emotional information. *Cognition and Emotion, 24*(1), 3–47.

Chapter 5

Allport, D. A., Styles, E. A., & Hsieh, S. (1994). Shifting intentional set: Exploring the dynamic control of tasks. In C. Umiltà & M. Moscovitch (Eds.), *Attention and Performance Series. Attention and Performance XV: Conscious and Nonconscious Information Processing* (pp. 421–452). Cambridge, MA: The MIT Press.

Alvarez, G. A., & Cavanaugh, P. (2004). The capacity of visual short-term memory is set both by visual information load and by number of objects. *Psychological Science, 15,* 106–111.

Anguera, J. A., Boccanfuso, J., Rintoul, J. L., et al. (2013). Video game training enhances cognitive control in older adults. *Nature, 501*(7465), 97–101.

Arnsten, A. F. (1998). Catecholamine modulation of prefrontal cortical cognitive function. *Trends in Cognitive Sciences, 2*(11), 436–447.

Aron, A. R., Robbins, T. W., & Poldrack, R. A. (2014). Inhibition and the right inferior frontal cortex: One decade on. *Trends in Cognitive Sciences, 18*(4), 177–185.

Aron, A. R., Robbins, T. W., & Poldrack, R. A. (2004). Inhibition and the right inferior frontal cortex. *Trends in Cognitive Sciences, 8*(4), 170–177.

Ashcraft, M. H., & Kirk, E. P. (2001). The relationships among working memory, math anxiety, and performance. *Journal of Experimental Psychology: General, 130*(2), 224–237.

Atkinson, R. C., & Shiffrin, R. M. (1968). Human memory: A proposed system and its control processes. In K. W. Spence and J. T. Spence (Eds.), *Psychology of Learning and Motivation* (Vol. 2, pp. 85–195). New York: Academic Press.

Awh, E., & Jonides, J. (2001). Overlapping mechanisms of attention and spatial working memory. *Trends in Cognitive Sciences, 5*(3), 119–126.

Baddeley, A. (1990). *Human Memory: Theory & Practice.* East Sussex, UK, Laurence Erlbaum Associates, 71.

Baddeley, A. (2000). The episodic buffer: A new component of working memory? *Trends in Cognitive Neuroscience, 4,* 829–839.

Baddeley, A. (1986). *Working Memory.* Oxford, UK, Oxford University Press.

Baddeley, A. (1992). Working memory. *Science, 255*(5044), 556–559.

Baddeley, A., Gathercole, S., & Papagno, C. (1998). The phonological loop as a language learning device. *Psychological Review, 105*(1), 158–173.

Baddeley, A., & Hitch, G. J. (1974). In *The Psychology of Learning and Motivation: Advances in Research and Theory,* G. A. Bower (Ed.), 8, New York, Academic Press, 47–89.

Baddeley, A., & Lieberman, K. (1980). Spatial working memory. In R. S. Nickerson (Ed.), *Attention and Performance VIII*. Hillsdale, NJ: Laurence Erlbaum Associates, 521–539.

Baddeley, A., Lewis, V., & Vallar, G. (1984). Exploring the articulatory loop. *The Quarterly Journal of Experimental Psychology Section A, 36*(2), 233–252.

Baddeley, A., & Wilson, B. (1985). Phonological coding and short-term memory in patients without speech. *Journal of Memory and Language, 24*(4), 490–502.

Baddeley, A. D. (1966). Short-term memory for word sequences as a function of acoustic, semantic and formal similarity. *The Quarterly Journal of Experimental Psychology, 18*(4), 362–365.

Baddeley, A. D., Thomson, N., & Buchanan, M. (1975). Word length and the structure of short-term memory. *Journal of Verbal Learning and Verbal Behavior, 14*(6), 575–589.

Baddeley, A. D. (2003). Working memory: Looking back and looking forward. *Nature Reviews Neuroscience, 4*(10), 829–839.

Baddeley, A. D., & Hitch, G. (1974). Working Memory. *Psychology of Learning and Motivation—Advances in Research and Theory, 8*, 47–89.

Ball, K., Berch, D. B., Helmers, K. F., et al. (2002). Effects of cognitive training interventions with older adults. *JAMA, 288*(18), 2271.

Barkley, R. A. (1997). Behavioral inhibition, sustained attention, and executive functions: Constructing a unifying theory of ADHD. *Psychological Bulletin, 121*(1), 65–94.

Baumeister, R. F., Bratslavsky, E., Muraven, M., & Tice, D. M. (1998). Ego depletion: Is the active self a limited resource? *Journal of Personality and Social Psychology, 74*(5), 1252–1265.

Beilock, S. L., & Carr, T. H. (2005). When high-powered people fail: Working memory and "choking under pressure" in math. *Psychological Science, 16*(2), 101–105.

Berman, M. G., Jonides, J., & Kaplan, S. (2008). The cognitive benefits of interacting with nature. *Psychological Science, 19*(12), 1207–1212.

Berryhill, M. E., & Hughes, H. C. (2009). On the minimization of task switch costs following long-term training. *Attention, Perception & Psychophysics, 71*(3), 503–514.

Bishop, S., Duncan, J., Brett, M., & Lawrence, A. D. (2004). Prefrontal cortical function and anxiety: controlling attention to threat-related stimuli. *Nature Neuroscience, 7*(2), 184–188.

Bishop, S. J. (2009). Trait anxiety and impoverished prefrontal control of attention. *Nature Neuroscience, 12*(1), 92–98.

Botvinick, M. M., Braver, T. S., Barch, D. M., et al. (2001). Conflict monitoring and cognitive control. *Psychological Review, 108*(3), 624–652.

Braver, T. S. (2012). The variable nature of cognitive control: A dual mechanisms framework. Trends in Cognitive Sciences, 16(2), 106–113.

Braver, T. S., Cohen, J. D., Nystrom, L. E., et al. (1997). A parametric study of prefrontal cortex involvement in human working memory. *NeuroImage, 5*(1), 49–62.

Braver, T. S., Paxton, J. L., Locke, H. S., & Barch, D. M. (2009). Flexible neural mechanisms of cognitive control within human prefrontal cortex. *Proceedings of the National Academy of Science of the United States of America, 106*(18), 7351–7356.

Braver, T. S., Reynolds, J. R., & Donaldson, D. I. (2003). Neural mechanisms of transient and sustained cognitive control during task switching. *Neuron, 39*(4), 713–726.

Brooks, L. R. (1967). The suppression of visualization by reading. *The Quarterly Journal of Experimental Psychology, 19*(4), 290–299.

Brown, A., Mulligan, D. A., Altmann, T. R., et al. (2011). Media use by children younger than 2 years. *Pediatrics, 128*(5), 1040–1045.

Carpenter, P. A., Just, M. A., & Shell, P. (1990). What one intelligence test measures: A theoretical account of the processing in the Raven progressive matrices test. *Psychological Review, 97*(3), 404–431.

Carretta, T. R., Perry Jr., D. C., & Ree, M. J. (1996). Prediction of situational awareness in F-15 pilots. *International Journal of Aviation Psychology, 6*(1), 21–41.

Carter, C. S., Braver, T. S., Barch, D. M., et al. (1998). Anterior cingulate cortex, error detection, and the online monitoring of performance. *Science, 280*(5364), 747–749.

Carter, E. C., Kofler, L. M., Forster, D. E., & McCullough, M. E. (2015). A series of meta-analytic tests of the depletion effect: Self-control does not seem to rely on a limited resource. *Journal of Experimental Psychology: General, 144*(4), 796–815.

Chabris, C. F., Steele, K. M., Dalla Bella, S., et al. (1999). Prelude or requiem for the "Mozart effect"? *Nature, 400*(6747), 827.

Chase, W. G., & Simon, H. A. (1973). Perception in chess. *Cognitive Psychology, 4*(1), 55–81.

Chooi, W.-T., & Thompson, L. A. (2012). Working memory training does not improve intelligence in healthy young adults. *Intelligence, 40*(6), 531–542.

Cisler, J. M., & Koster, E. H. W. (2010). Mechanisms of attentional biases towards threat in anxiety disorders: An integrative review. *Clinical Psychology Review, 30*(2), 203–216.

Cohen, G. L., Garcia, J., Apfel, N., & Master, A. (2006). Reducing the racial achievement gap: A social-psychological intervention. *Science 313*(5791), 1307–1310.

Cohen, J. D., Dunbar, K., & McClelland, J. L. (1990). On the control of automatic processes: A parallel distributed processing account of the stroop effect. *Psychological Review, 97*(3), 332–361.

Colcombe, S., & Kramer, A. F. (2003). Fitness effects on the cognitive function of older adults: A meta-analytic study. *Psychological Science, 14*(2), 125–130.

Colle, H. A., & Welsh, A. (1976). Acoustic masking in primary memory. *Journal of Verbal Learning and Verbal Behavior, 15*(1), 17–31.

Conrad, R. (1964). Acoustic confusions in immediate memory. *British Journal of Psychology, 55*(1), 75–84.

Correll, J., Park, B., Judd, C. M., & Wittenbrink, B. (2002). The police officer's dilemma: Using ethnicity to disambiguate potentially threatening individuals. *Journal of Personality and Social Psychology, 83*(6), 1314–1329.

Correll, J., Park, B., Judd, C. M., et al. (2007). Across the thin blue line: Police officers and racial bias in the decision to shoot. *Journal of Personality and Social Psychology, 92*(6), 1006–1023.

Courtney, S. M. (1998). An area specialized for spatial working memory in human frontal cortex. *Science, 279*(5355), 1347–1351.

Cowan, N. (1988). Evolving conceptions of memory storage, selective attention, and their mutual constraints within the human information-processing system. *Psychological Bulletin, 104*(2), 163–191.

Cunningham, M. R., & Baumeister, R. F. (2016). How to make nothing out of something: Analyses of the impact of study sampling and statistical interpretation in misleading meta-analytic conclusions. *Frontiers in Psychology, 7*, Article 1639.

Danziger, S., Levav, J., & Avnaim-Pesso, L. (2011). Reply to Weinshall-Margel and Shapard: Extraneous factors in judicial decisions persist. *Proceedings of the National Academy of Sciences, 108*(42), E834–E834.

Danziger, Shai, Levav, J., & Avnaim-Pesso, L. (2011). Extraneous factors in judicial decisions. *Proceedings of the National Academy of Sciences of the United States of America, 108*(17), 6889–6892.

Dehaene, S., & Naccache, L. (2001). Towards a cognitive neuroscience of consciousness: Basic evidence and a workspace framework. *Cognition, 79*(1–2), 1–37.

D'Esposito, M., Aguirre, G. K., Zarahn, E., et al. (1998). Functional MRI studies of spatial and nonspatial working memory. *Cognitive Brain Research, 7*(1), 1–13.

D'Esposito, M., Postle, B. R., Ballard, D., & Lease, J. (1999). Maintenance versus manipulation of information held in working memory: An event-related fMRI study. *Brain and Cognition, 41*(1), 66–86.

De Renzi, E., & Nichelli, P. (1975). Verbal and non verbal short term memory impairment following hemispheric damage. *Cortex, 11*(4), 341–354.

Diamond, A. (2013). Executive functions. *Annual Review of Psychology, 64*, 135–168.

Diamond, D. M., Campbell, A., Park, M., et al. The temporal dynamics model of emotionl memory processing: A synthesis on the neurobiological basis of stress-induced amnesia, flashbulb memories, and the Yerkes-Dodson law. *Neural Plasticity, 33*.

Duncan, J., Johnson, R., Swales, M., & Freer, C. (1997). Frontal lobe deficits after head injury: Unity and diversity of function. *Cognitive Neuropsychology, 14*(5), 713–741.

Duncan, J., & Owen, A. M. (2000). Common regions of the human frontal lobe recruited by diverse cognitive demands. *Trends in Neurosciences, 23*(10), 475–483.

Durmer, J. S., & Dinges, D. F. (2005). Neurocognitive consequences of sleep deprivation. *Seminars in Neurology, 25*, 117–129.

Ellis, N. C., & Hennelly, R. A. (1980). A bilingual word-length effect: Implications for intelligence testing and the relative ease of mental calculation in Welsh and English. *British Journal of Psychology, 71*(1), 43–51.

Engle, R. W. (2002). Working memory capacity as executive attention. *Current Directions in Psychological Science, 11*(1), 19–23.

Ericsson, K. A., & Kintsch, W. (1995). Long-term working memory. *Psychological Review, 102*(2), 211–245.

Eriksen, B. A., & Eriksen, C. W. (1974). Effects of noise letters upon the identification of a target letter in a nonsearch task. *Perception & Psychophysics, 16*(1), 143–149.

Eysenck, M. W., Derakshan, N., Santos, R., & Valco, M. G. (2007). Anxiety and cognitive performance: Attentional control theory. *Emotion, 7*(2), 336–353.

Farah, M. J., Illes, J., Cook-Deegan, R., et al. (2004). Neurocognitive enhancement: What can we do and what should we do? *Nature Reviews Neuroscience, 5*, 421–425.

Fitch, G. A., Soccolich, S. A., Guo, F., et al. (2013). The impact of hand-held and hands-free cell phone use on driving performance and safety-critical event risk. Washington, DC: National Highway Traffic Safety Administration.

Gailliot, M. T., & Baumeister, R. F. (2007). The physiology of willpower: Linking blood glucose to self-control. *Personality and Social Psychology Review, 11*(4), 303–327.

Gathercole, S. E., & Baddeley, A. D. (1989). Evaluation of the role of phonological STM in the development of vocabulary in children: A longitudinal study. *Journal of Memory and Language, 28*(2), 200–213.

Gathercole, S. E., & Baddeley, A. D. (1990). Phonological memory deficits in language disordered children: Is there a causal connection? *Journal of Memory and Language, 29*(3), 336–360.

Gathercole, S. E., Hitch, G. J., Service, E., & Martin, A. J. (1997). Phonological short-term memory and new word learning in children. *Developmental Psychology, 33*(6), 966–979.

Gehring, W. J., Goss, B., Coles, M. G. H., et al. (1993). A Neural System for Error Detection and Compensation. *Psychological Science, 4*(6), 385–390.

Gehring, W. J., Himle, J., & Nisenson, L. G. (2000). Action-monitoring dysfunction in obsessive-compulsive disorder. *Psychological Science, 11*(1), 1–6.

Gehring, W. J., & Willoughby, A. R. (2002). The medial frontal cortex and the rapid processing of monetary gains and losses. *Science, 295*(5563), 2279–2282.

Godefroy, O., Cabaret, M., Petit-Chenal, V., et al. (1999). Control functions of the frontal lobes. Modularity of the central-supervisory system? *Cortex, 35*(1), 1–20.

Greely, H., Sahakian, B., Harris, J., et al. (2008). Towards responsible use of cognitive-enhancing drugs by the healthy. *Nature, 456*(7223), 702–705.

Green, C. S., & Bavelier, D. (2003). Action video game modifies visual selective attention. *Nature, 423*(6939), 534–537.

Hagger, M. S., Wood, C., Stiff, C., & Chatzisarantis, N. L. D. (2010). Ego depletion and the strength model of self-control: a meta-analysis. *Psychological Bulletin*, *136*(4), 495–525.

Harrison, S. A., & Tong, F. (2009). Decoding reveals the contents of visual working memory in early visual areas. *Nature*, *458*(7238).

Helfinstein, S. M., & Poldrack, R. A. (2012). The young and the reckless. *Nature Neuroscience*, *15*, 803–805.

Hillman, C. H., Erickson, K. I., & Kramer, A. F. (2008). Be smart, exercise your heart: Exercise effects on brain and cognition. *Nature Reviews Neuroscience*, *9*(1), 58–65.

Hitch, G. J. (1978). The role of short-term working memory in mental arithmetic. *Cognitive Psychology*, *10*(3), 302–323.

Holmes, J., Gathercole, S. E., & Dunning, D. L. (2009). Adaptive training leads to sustained enhancement of poor working memory in children. *Developmental Science*, *12*(4), F9–15.

Inzlicht, M., & Friese, M. (2019). The past, present, and future of ego depletion. *Social Psychology, 50*, 370–378.

Jaeggi, S. M., Buschkuehl, M., Jonides, J., & Perrig, W. J. (2008). Improving fluid intelligence with training on working memory. *Proceedings of the National Academy of Sciences of the United States of America*, *105*(19), 6829–6833.

Jaeggi, S. M., Buschkuehl, M., Shah, P., & Jonides, J. (2014). The role of individual differences in cognitive training and transfer. *Memory & Cognition*, *42*(3), 464–480.

Jersild, A. T. (1927). Mental set and shift. *Archives of Psychology, 89*, 1–81.

Jha, A. P., Stanley, E. A., Kiyonaga, W., et al. (2010). Examining the protective effects of mindfulness training on working memory capacity and affective experience. *Emotion, 10*, 54–64.

Johnson, M. R., & Johnson, M. K. (2009). Top-down enhancement and suppression of activity in category-selective extrastriate cortex from an act of reflective attention. *Journal of Cognitive Neuroscience*, *21*(12), 2320–2327.

Jonides, J., Smith, E. E., Koeppe, R. A., et al. (1993). Spatial working memory in humans as revealed by PET. *Nature*, *363*(6430), 623–625.

Just, M. A., & Carpenter, P. A. (1992). A capacity theory of comprehension: Individual differences in working memory. *Psychological Review*, *99*(1), 122–149.

Kane, M. J., & Engle, R. W. (2003). Working-memory capacity and the control of attention: The contributions of goal neglect, response competition, and task set to Stroop interference. *Journal of Experimental Psychology: General*, *132*(1), 47–70.

Klauer, S. G., Guo, F., Simons-Morton, B. G., et al. (2014). Distracted driving and risk of road crashes among novice and experienced drivers. *The New England Journal of Medicine*, *370*(1), 54–59.

Klingberg, T., Fernell, E., Olesen, P. J., et al. (2005). Computerized training of working memory in children with ADHD--a randomized, controlled trial. *Journal of the American Academy of Child and Adolescent Psychiatry*, *44*(2), 177–186.

Koster, E. H. W., De Lissnyder, E., Derakshan, N., & De Raedt, R. (2011). Understanding depressive rumination from a cognitive science perspective: The impaired disengagement hypothesis. *Clinical Psychology Review*, *31*(1), 138–145.

Kramer, A. F., Hahn, S., Cohen, N. J., et al. (1999). Ageing, fitness and neurocognitive function. *Nature*, *400*(6743), 418–419.

Kyllonen, P. C., & Christal, R. E. (1990). Reasoning ability is (little more than) working-memory capacity?! *Intelligence*, *14*(4), 389–443.

Lhermitte, F. (1983). "Utilization behaviour" and its relation to lesions of the frontal lobes. *Brain*, *106*(2), 237–255.

Liston, C., McEwen, B. S., & Casey, B. J. (2009). Psychosocial stress reversibly disrupts prefrontal processing and attentional control. *Proceedings of the National Academy of Sciences of the United States of America*, *106*(3), 912–917.

Logan, G. D., & Cowan, W. B. (1984). On the ability to inhibit thought and action: A theory of an act of control. *Psychological Review*, *91*(3), 295–327.

Logan, G. D., Cowan, W. B., & Davis, K. A. (1984). On the ability to inhibit simple and choice reaction time responses: A model and a method. *Journal of Experimental Psychology: Human Perception and Performance*, *10*(2), 276–291.

Luck, S. J., & Vogel, E. K. (1997). The capacity of visual working memory for features and conjunctions. *Nature*, *390*(6657), 279–281.

MacLeod, C. M. (1991). Half a century of reseach on the stroop effect: An integrative review. *Psychological Bulletin*, *109*(2), 163–203.

Mani, A., Mullainathan, S., Shafir, E., & Zhao, J. (2013). Poverty impedes cognitive function. *Science*, *341*(6149), 976–980.

Marhe, R., Waters, A. J., van de Wetering, B. J. M., & Franken, I. H. A. (2013). Implicit and explicit drug-related cognitions during detoxification treatment are associated with drug relapse: An ecological momentary assessment study. *Journal of Consulting and Clinical Psychology*, *81*(1), 1–12.

Marois, R., & Ivanoff, J. (2005). Capacity limits of information processing in the brain. *Trends in Cognitive Sciences*, *9*(6), 296–305.

Meiran, N. (1996). Reconfiguration of processing mode prior to task performance. *Journal of Experimental Psychology: Learning Memory and Cognition*, *22*(6), 1423–1442.

Metsala, J. L. (1999). Young children's phonological awareness and nonword repetition as a function of vocabulary development. *Journal of Educational Psychology*, *91*(1), 3–19.

Meyer, D. E., & Kieras, D. E. (1997). A computational theory of executive cognitive processes and multiple-task performance: Part 1. Basic mechanisms. *Psychological Review, 104*(1), 3–65.

Miller, E. K., & Cohen, J. D. (2001). An integrative theory of prefrontal cortex function. *Annual Review of Neuroscience*, *24*, 167–202.

Miller, G. A. (1994). The magical number seven, plus or minus two: Some limits on our capacity for processing information. *Psychological Review, 101*(2), 343–352.

Miyake, A., Friedman, N. P., Emerson, M. J., et al. (2000). The unity and diversity of executive functions and their contributions to complex "frontal lobe" tasks: A latent variable analysis. *Cognitive Psychology, 41*(1), 49–100.

Monsell, S. (2003). Task switching. *Trends in Cognitive Sciences, 7*(3), 134–140.

Moreno, S., Marques, C., Santos, A., et al. (2009). Musical training influences linguistic abilities in 8-year-old children: More evidence for brain plasticity. *Cerebral Cortex, 19*(3), 712–723.

Moreno, S., Bialystok, E., Barac, R., et al. (2011). Short-term music training enhances verbal intelligence and executive function. *Psychological Science, 22*(11), 1425–1433.

Mullainathan, S., & Shafir, E. (2013). *Scarcity: Why Having Too Little Means So Much*. New York: Times Books.

Murray, D. J. (1968). Articulation and acoustic confusability in short-term memory. *Journal of Experimental Psychology, 78*, 679–684.

Nantais, K. M., & Schellenberg, E. G. (1999). The Mozart effect: An artifact of preference. *Psychological Science, 10*(4), 370–373.

Nasar, J. L., & Troyer, D. (2013). Pedestrian injuries due to mobile phone use in public places. *Accident, Analysis and Prevention, 57*, 91–95.

National Institute of Mental Health. (2021). *Statistics*. Mental Health Information. https://www.nimh.nih.gov/health/statistics/index.shtml.

Naveh-Benjamin, M., & Ayres, T. J. (1986). Digit span, reading rate, and linguistic relativity. *The Quarterly Journal of Experimental Psychology A: Human Experimental Psychology, 38*(4-A), 739–751.

Navon, D., & Miller, J. (2002). Queuing or sharing? A critical evaluation of the single-bottleneck notion. *Cognitive Psychology, 44*(3), 193–251.

Nolen-Hoeksema, S. (1991). Responses to depression and their effects on the duration of depressive episodes. *Journal of Abnormal Psychology, 100*(4), 569–582.

Nolen-Hoeksema, S. (2000). The role of rumination in depressive disorders and mixed anxiety/depressive symptoms. *Journal of Abnormal Psychology, 109*(3), 504–511.

Norman, D. A., & Shallice, T. (1981). Attention to action: Willed and automatic control of behavior. *Consciousness and Self-Regulation, 4*, 1–18.

Ochsner, K. N., Bunge, S. A., Gross, J. J., & Gabrieli, J. D. E. (2002). Rethinking feelings: an FMRI study of the cognitive regulation of emotion. *Journal of Cognitive Neuroscience, 14*(8), 1215–1229.

Ochsner, K. N., & Gross, J. J. (2005). The cognitive control of emotion. *Trends in Cognitive Sciences, 9*(5), 242–249.

Ophir, E., Nass, C., & Wagner, A. D. (2009). Cognitive control in media multitaskers. *Proceedings of the National Academy of Sciences of the United States of America, 106*(37), 15583–15587.

Owen, A. M., Hampshire, A., Grahn, J. A., et al. (2010). Putting brain training to the test. *Nature, 465*(7299), 775–778.

Pashler, H. (1992). Attentional limitations in doing two tasks at the same time. *Current Directions in Psychological Science, 1*(2), 44–48.

Pashler, H. (1984). Processing stages in overlapping tasks: Evidence for a central bottleneck. *Journal of Experimental Psychology: Human Perception and Performance, 10*(3), 358–377.

Pashler, H. (1988). Familiarity and visual change detection. *Perception & Psychophysics, 44*, 369–378.

Pashler, H. (1994). Dual-task interference in simple tasks: Data and theory. *Psychological Bulletin, 116*(2), 220–244.

Pashler, H. (2003). Task switching. *Trends in Cognitive Sciences, 7*(3), 134–140.

Patel, A. D. (2011). Why would musical training benefit the neural encoding of speech? The OPERA hypothesis. *Frontiers in Psychology, 2*, 142.

Paulesu, E., Frith, C. D., & Frackowiak, R. S. J. (1993). The neural correlates of the verbal component of working memory. *Nature, 362*(6418), 342–345.

Perham, N., & Vizard, J. (2011). Can preference for background music mediate the irrelevant sound effect? *Applied Cognitive Psychology, 25*(4), 625–631.

Redelmeier, D. A., & Tibshirani, R. J. (1997). Association between cellular-telephone calls and motor vehicle collisions. *The New England Journal of Medicine, 336*(7), 453–458.

Redick, T. S., Shipstead, Z., Harrison, T. L., et al. (2013). No evidence of intelligence improvement after working memory training: A randomized, placebo-controlled study. *Journal of Experimental Psychology. General, 142*(2), 359–379.

Rogers, R. D., & Monsell, S. (1995). Costs of a predictable switch between simple cognitive tasks. *Journal of Experimental Psychology: General, 124*(2), 207–231.

Rosenberg, M., Noonan, S., DeGutis, J., & Esterman, M. (2013). Sustaining visual attention in the face of distraction: a novel gradual-onset continuous performance task. *Attention, Perception & Psychophysics, 75*(3), 426–439.

Rosvold, H. E., Mirsky, A. F., Sarason, I., et al. (1956). A continuous performance test of brain damage. *Journal of Consulting Psychology, 20*(5), 343–350.

Rubinstein, J. S., Meyer, D. E., & Evans, J. E. (2001). Executive control of cognitive processes in task switching. *Journal of Experimental Psychology: Human Perception and Performance, 27*(4), 763–797.

Sala, G., & Gobet, F. (2020). Cognitive and academic benefits of music training with children: A multilevel meta-analysis. *Memory & Cognition, 48*, 1429–1441.

Salamé, P., & Baddeley, A. (1982). Disruption of short-term memory by unattended speech: Implications for the structure of working memory. *Journal of Verbal Learning and Verbal Behavior, 21*(2), 150–164.

Schellenberg, E. G. (2004). Music lessons enhance IQ. *Psychological Science, 15*(8), 511–514.

Schneider, W., & Shiffrin, R. M. (1977). Controlled and automatic human information processing: I. Detection, search, and attention. *Psychological Review, 84*(1), 1–66.

Schumacher, E. H., Seymour, T. L., Glass, J. M., et al. (2001). Virtually perfect time sharing in dual-task performance: Uncorking the central cognitive bottleneck. *Psychological Science, 12*(2), 101–108.

Serences, J. T., Ester, E. F., Vogel, E. K., & Awh, E. (2009). Stimulus-specific delay activity in human primary visual cortex. *Psychological Science, 20*(2), 207–214.

Shaffer, W. O., & LaBerge, D. (1979). Automatic semantic processing of unattended words. *Journal of Verbal Learning and Verbal Behavior, 18*(4), 54–67.

Shiffrin, R. M., & Schneider, W. (1977). Controlled and automatic human information processing: II. Perceptual learning, automatic attending and a general theory. *Psychological Review, 84*(2), 127–190.

Shipstead, Z., Redick, T. S., & Engle, R. W. (2012). Is working memory training effective? *Psychological Bulletin, 138*(4), 628–654.

Simon, J. R., & Rudell, A. P. (1967). Auditory S-R compatibility: The effect of an irrelevant cue on information processing. *Journal of Applied Psychology, 51*(3), 300–304.

Simon, J., & Wolf, J. D. (1963). Choice reaction time as a function of angular stimulus-response correspondence and age. *Ergonomics, 6*(1), 99–105.

Simons, D. J., Boot, W. R., Charness, N., et al. (2016). Do "brain-training" programs work? *Psychological Science in the Public Interest: A Journal of the American Psychological Society, 17*(3), 103–186.

Smith, E. E., & Jonides, J. (1999). Storage and executive processes in the frontal lobes. *Science, 283*(5408), 1657–1661.

Sohn, M.-H., Ursu, S., Anderson, J. R., et al. (2000). The role of prefrontal cortex and posterior parietal cortex in task switching. *Proceedings of the National Academy of Sciences, 97*(24), 13448–13453.

Sohn, Y. W., & Doane, S. M. (2004). Memory processes of flight situation awareness: Interactive roles of working memory capacity, long-term working memory, and expertise. *Human Factors, 46*(3), 461–475.

Strayer, D. L., & Johnston, W. A. (2001). Driven to distraction: Dual-task studies of simulated driving and conversing on a cellular telephone. *Psychological Science, 12*(6), 462–466.

Stroop, J. R. (1935). Studies of interference in serial verbal reactions. *Journal of Experimental Psychology, 18*(6), 643–662.

Sweller, J. (1988). Cognitive load during problem solving: Effects on learning. *Cognitive Science, 12*(2), 257–285.

Sweller, J., van Merrienboer, J. J. G., & Paas, F. G. W. C. (1998). Cognitive architecture and instructional design. *Educational Psychology Review, 10*, 251–296.

Thompson, T. W., Waskom, M. L., Garel, K.-L. A., et al. (2013). Failure of working memory training to enhance cognition or intelligence. *PLOS ONE, 8*(5), e63614.

Todd, J. J., & Marois, R. (2004). Capacity limit of visual short-term memory in human posterior parietal cortex. *Nature, 428*(6984), 751–754.

Tombu, M., & Jolicoeur, P. (2003). A central capacity sharing model of dual-task performance. *Journal of Experimental Psychology: Human Perception & Performance, 29*(1), 3–18.

Vallar, G., & Baddeley, A. D. (1984). Fractionation of working memory: Neuropsychological evidence for a phonological short-term store. *Journal of Verbal Learning and Verbal Behavior, 23*(2).

van den Wildenberg, W. P., Wylie, M., Forstmann, S. A., et al. (2010). To head or to heed? Beyond the surface of selective action inhibition: a review. *Human Neuroscience, 4*, 22.

Van Dongen, H. P. A., Maislin, G., Mullington, J. M., & Dinges, D. F. (2003). The cumulative cost of additional wakefulness: Dose-response effects on neurobehavioral functions and sleep physiology from chronic sleep restriction and total sleep deprivation. *Sleep, 26*(2), 117–126.

Wager, T. D., & Smith, E. E. (2003). Neuroimaging studies of working memory: A meta-analysis. *Cognitive, Affective and Behavioral Neuroscience*, Vol. 3, pp. 255–274.

Watson, J. M., & Strayer, D. L. (2010). Supertaskers: Profiles in extraordinary multitasking ability. *Psychonomic Bulletin & Review, 17*(4), 479–485.

Weinshall-Margel, K., & Shapard, J. (2011). Overlooked factors in the analysis of parole decisions. *Proceedings of the National Academy of Sciences of the United States of America, 108*(42), E833; author reply E834.

Welford, A. T. (1952). The "psychological refractory period" and the timing of high speed performance—A review and a theory. *British Journal of Psychology, 43*, 2–19.

Yerkes, R. M., & Dodson, J. D. (1908). The relation of strength stimulus to rapidity of habit-formation. *Journal of Comparative Neurology and Psychology, 18*(5), 459–482.

Xu, Y., & Chun, M. M. (2006). Dissociable neural mechanisms supporting visual short-term memory for objects. *Nature, 440*(7080), 91–95.

Chapter 6

Agarwal, P. K., Finley, J. R., Rose, N. S., & Roediger, H. L. (2017). Benefits from retrieval practice are greater for students with lower working memory capacity. *Memory, 25*(6), 764–771.

Anderson, A. K., Wais, P. E., & Gabrieli, J. D. (2006). Emotion enhances remembrance of neutral events past. *Proceedings of the National Academy of Sciences of the United States of America, 103*(5), 1599–1604.

Anderson, J. R. (1974). Retrieval of propositional information from long-term memory. *Cognitive Psychology, 6*(4), 451–474.

Anderson, M. C., Bjork, R., & Bjork, E. L. (1994). Remembering can cause forgetting: retrieval dynamics in long-term memory. *Journal of Experimental Psychology: Learning, Memory, and Cognition, 20*, 1063–87.

Atkinson, R. C., & Shiffrin, R. M. (1968). Human memory: A proposed system and its control processes. In K. W. Spence & J. T. Spence (Eds.). *The Psychology of Learning and Motivation: II.* Oxford, UK: Academic Press.

Baddeley, A., Lewis, V., Eldridge, M., & Thomson, N. (1984). Attention and retrieval from long-term memory. *Journal of Experimental Psychology: General, 113*(4), 518–540.

Badre, D., Poldrack, R. A., Paré-Blagoev, E. J., et al. (2005). Dissociable controlled retrieval and generalized selection mechanisms in ventrolateral prefrontal cortex. *Neuron, 47,* 907–918.

Badre, D., & Wagner, A. D. (2007). Left ventrolateral prefrontal cortex and the cognitive control of memory. *Neuropsychologia, 45,* 2883–2901.

Bower, G. H. (1981). Mood and memory. *American Psychologist, 36*(2), 129–148.

Barnier, A. J., Hung, L., & Conway, M. A. (2004). Retrieval-induced forgetting of emotional and unemotional autobiographical memories. *Cognition and Emotion, 18*(4), 457–477.

Bartlett, F. C. (1932). *Remembering: A study in experimental and social psychology.* New York: Cambridge University Press.

Bower, G. H. (1981). Mood and memory. *American Psychologist, 36*(2), 129–148.

Bower, G. H., Clark, M. C., Lesgold, A. M., & Winzenz, D. (1969). Hierarchical retrieval schemes in recall of categorized word lists. *Journal of Verbal Learning and Verbal Behavior, 8,* 323–343.

Brown, S. C., & Craik, F. I. M. (2000). Encoding and retrieval of information. In E. Tulving & F. I. M. Craik (Eds.), *The Oxford Handbook of Memory.* New York: Oxford University Press, 93–107.

Brown, R., & Kulik, J. (1977). Flashbulb memories. *Cognition, 5*(1), 73–99.

Brown, R., & McNeill, D. (1966). The "tip of the tongue" phenomenon. *Journal of Verbal Learning & Verbal Behavior, 5*(4), 325–337.

Brunet, A., Orr, S. P., Tremblay, J., et al. (2008). Effect of post-retrieval propranolol on psychophysiologic responding during subsequent script-driven traumatic imagery in post-traumatic stress disorder. *Journal of Psychiatric Research, 42,* 503–506.

Cahill, L. & Alkire, M. T. (2003). Epinephrine enhancement of human memory consolidation: interaction with arousal at encoding. *Neurobiology of Learning & Memory, 79,* 194–198.

Cahill, L., Gorski, L., & Le, K. (2003). Enhanced human memory consolidation with post-learning stress: interaction with the degree of arousal at encoding. *Learning & Memory (Cold Spring Harbor, N.Y.), 10*(4), 270–274.

Cepeda, N. J., Coburn, N., Rohrer, D., et al. (2009). Optimizing distributed practice: Theoretical analysis and practical implications. *Experimental Psychology, 56*(4), 236–246.

Chase, W. G., & Simon, H. A. (1973). Perception in chess. *Cognitive Psychology, 4*(1), 55–81.

Chi, M. T. H. (1978). Knowledge structures and memory development. In R. S. Siegler (Ed.), *Children's Thinking: What Develops?* Hillsdale, NJ: Lawrence Erlbaum Associates, Inc. 73–96.

Chun, M. M., Golomb, J. D., & Turk-Browne, N. B. (2011). A taxonomy of external and internal attention. *Annual Review of Psychology, 62,* 73–101.

Chun, M. M., & Johnson, M. K. (2011). Memory: enduring traces of perceptual and reflective attention. *Neuron, 72*(4), 520–535.

Clancy, S. A., Schacter, D. L., McNally, R. J., & Pitman, R. K. (2000). False recognition in women reporting recovered memories of sexual abuse. *Psychological Science, 11*(1), 26–31.

Conway, M. A., & Pleydell-Pearce, C. W. (2000). The construction of autobiographical memories in the self-memory system. *Psychological Review, 107*(2), 261–288.

Cowan, N. (2001) The magical number 4 in short-term memory: A reconsideration of mental storage capacity. *Behavioral & Brain Sciences, 24,* 87–114; discussion 114–185.

Cowan, N. (2008). What are the differences between long-term, short-term, and working memory? *Progress in Brain Research, 169,* 323–338.

Cowan, N. (2017). The many faces of working memory and short-term storage. *Psychonomic Bulletin & Review, 24,* 1158–1170.

Craik, F. I. M., Govoni, R., Naveh-Benjamin, M., & Anderson, N. D. (1996). The effects of divided attention on encoding and retrieval processes in human memory. *Journal of Experimental Psychology: General, 125*(2), 159–180.

Craik, F. I., & Lockhart, R. S. (1972). Levels of processing: A framework for memory research. *Journal of Verbal Learning & Verbal Behavior, 11*(6), 671–684.

Craik, F. I. M., & Tulving, E. (1975). Depth of processing and the retention of words in episodic memory. *Journal of Experimental Psychology: General, 104*(3), 268–294.

Deese, J. (1959). On the prediction of occurrence of particular verbal intrusions in immediate recall. *Journal of Experimental Psychology, 58*(1), 17–22.

Devitt, A. L., & Schacter, D. L. (2016). False memories with age: Neural and cognitive underpinnings. *Neuropsychologia, 91,* 346–359.

Ebbinghaus, H. (1913). *Uber das Gedachtnis: Untersuchungen zur Experimentellen Psychologie.* Leipzig: Dunke and Humboldt. Trans. by H. A. Ruger and C. E. Bussenius as *Memory: A Contribution to Experimental Psychology.* New York: Columbia University Teacher's Collge.

Ehlers A., & Clark, D. M. (2000). A cognitive model of posttraumatic stress disorder. *Behaviour Research and Therapy, 38,* 319–345.

Ehlers, A., & Steil, R. (1995). Maintenance of intrusive memories in posttraumatic stress disorder: A cognitive approach. *Behavioural and Cognitive Psychotherapy, 23*(3), 217–249.

Eich, J. E. (1980). The cue-dependent nature of state-dependent retrieval. *Memory & Cognition, 8*(2), 157–173.

Eich, E. (1995). Searching for mood dependent memory. *Psychological Science, 6*(2), 67–75.

Erdelyi, M. H. (1996). *The Recovery of Unconscious Memories: Hypermnesia and Reminiscence.* Chicago, IL: University of Chicago Press.

Erickson, W. B., Lampinen, J. M., & Moore, K. N. (2016). Eyewitness identifications by older and younger adults: A meta-analysis and discussion. *Journal of Police and Criminal Psychology, 31*(2), 108–121.

Fink, G. R., Markowitsch, H. J., Reinkemeier, M., et al. (1996). Cerebral representation of one's own past: Neural networks involved in autobiographical memory. *The Journal of Neuroscience, 16*(13), 4275–4282.

Fisher, R. P., Geiselman, R. E., & Amador, M. (1989). Field test of the cognitive interview: Enhancing the recollection of actual victims and witnesses of crime. *Journal of Applied Psychology, 74*(5), 722–727.

Fisher, R. P., Geiselman, R. E., Raymond, D. S., et al. (1987). Enhancing enhanced eyewitness memory: Refining the cognitive interview. *Journal of Police Science & Administration, 15*(4), 291–297.

Fisher, M., Goddu, M. K., & Keil, F. C. (2015). Searching for explanations: How the Internet inflates estimates of internal knowledge. *Journal of Experimental Psychology: General, 144*(3), 674–687.

Flavell, J. H. (1979). Metacognition and cognitive monitoring: A new area of cognitive–developmental inquiry. *American Psychologist, 34*(10), 906–911.

Flavell, J., & Wellman, H. (1977). Metamemory. In R. V. Kail, Jr. & J. Hagen (Eds.), *Perspectives on the Development of Memory and Cognition.* Hillsdale, NJ: Lawrence Erlbaum Associates, Inc. 3–33.

Garry, M., & Gerrie, M. P. (2005). When photographs create false memories. *Current Directions in Psychological Science, 14*(6), 321–324.

Garry, M., Manning, C. G., Loftus, E. F., & Sherman, S. J. (1996). Imagination inflation: Imagining a childhood event inflates confidence that it occurred. *Psychonomic bulletin & review, 3*(2), 208–214.

Gazzaley, A., Cooney, J. W., Rissman, J., & D'Esposito, M. (2005). Top-down suppression deficit underlies working memory impairment in normal aging. *Nature Neuroscience, 8,* 1298–1300.

Gazzaley, A., & D'Esposito, M. (2007). Top-down modulation and normal aging. *Annals of the New York Academy of Sciences, 1097,* 67–83.

George, R. C., & Clifford, B. R. (1992). Making the most of witnesses. *Policing, 8,* 185–98.

Giles, J. W., Gopnik, A., & Heyman, G. D. (2002). Source monitoring reduces the suggestibility of preschool children. *Psychological Science, 13*(3), 288–291.

Godden, D. R., & Baddeley, A. D. (1975). Context-dependent memory in two natural environments: On land and underwater. *British Journal of Psychology, 66*(3), 325–331.

Gopnik, A., & Graf, P. (1988). Knowing how you know: Young children's ability to identify and remember the sources of their beliefs. *Child Development, 59*(5), 1366–1371.

Grilli, M. D., & Glisky, E. L. (2010). Self-imagining enhances recognition memory in memory-impaired individuals with neurological damage. *Neuropsychology, 24*(6), 698–710.

Grilli, M. D., & Glisky, E. L. (2011). Imagine that: Self-imagination improves prospective memory in memory-impaired individuals with neurological damage. *Neuropsychological Rehabilitation, 21*(6), 847–859.

Henkel L. A., (2014). Point-and-shoot memories: the influence of taking photos on memory for a museum tour. *Psychological Science, 25*(2), 396–402.

Henkel, L. A., Franklin, N., & Johnson, M. K. (2000). Cross-modal source monitoring confusions between perceived and imagined events. *Journal of Experimental Psychology: Learning, Memory, and Cognition, 26*(2), 321–335.

Hockenbury, D. H., & Hockenbury S. E. (1998). *Discovering Psychology.* New York: Worth Publishers, Inc./Macmillan Education.

Hunt, R. R. (1995). The subtlety of distinctiveness: What von Restorff really did. *Psychonomic Bulletin & Review, 2*(1), 105–112.

Hyman, I. E., Wulff, A. N., & Thomas, A. K. (2018). Crime blindness: How selective attention and inattentional blindness can disrupt eyewitness awareness and memory. *Policy Insights from the Behavioral and Brain Sciences, 5*(2), 202–208.

Iyadurai, L., Blackwell, S. E., Meiser-Stedman, R., et al. (2018). Preventing intrusive memories after trauma via a brief intervention involving Tetris computer game play in the emergency department: A proof-of-concept randomized controlled trial. *Molecular Psychiatry, 23*(3), 674–682.

Jacoby, L. L. (1999). Ironic effects of repetition: measuring age-related differences in memory. *Journal of experimental psychology: Learning, Memory, and Cognition, 25*(1), 3–22.

Jacoby, L. L., Kelley, C., Brown, J., & Jasechko, J. (1989). Becoming famous overnight: Limits on the ability to avoid unconscious influences of the past. *Journal of Personality and Social Psychology, 56*(3), 326–338.

Janowsky, J. S., Shimamura, A. P., & Squire, L. R. (1989). Source memory impairment in patients with frontal lobe lesions. *Neuropsychologia, 27,* 1043–1056.

Johnson, M. K., Hashtroudi, S., & Lindsay, D. S. (1993). Source monitoring. *Psychological Bulletin, 114*(1), 3–28.

Johnson, M. K., & Raye, C. L. (1981). Reality monitoring. *Psychological Review, 88*(1), 67–85.

Karpicke, J. D., & Blunt, J. R. (2011). Retrieval practice produces more learning than elaborative studying with concept mapping. *Science, 331,* 772–775.

Karpicke, J. D., & Zaromb, F. M. (2010). Retrieval mode distinguishes the testing effect from the generation effect. *Journal of Memory and Language, 62*(3), 227–239.

Kensinger, E. A., Garoff-Eaton, R. J., & Schacter, D. L. (2007). Effects of emotion on memory specificity: Memory trade-offs elicited by negative visually arousing stimuli. *Journal of Memory and Language, 56*(4), 575–591.

Kern, R. P., Libkuman, T. M., Otani, H., & Holmes, K. (2005). Emotional Stimuli, Divided Attention, and Memory. *Emotion, 5*(4), 408–417.

Knight, M., & Mather, M. (2009). Reconciling findings of emotion-induced memory enhancement and impairment of preceding items. *Emotion, 9*(6), 763–781.

Kuhl, B. A., Bainbridge, W. A., & Chun, M. M. (2012). Neural reactivation reveals mechanisms for updating memory. *The Journal of Neuroscience, 32*(10), 3453–3461.

Kuhl, B. A., Dudukovic, N. M., Kahn, I., & Wagner, A. D. (2007). Decreased demands on cognitive control reveal the neural processing benefits of forgetting. *Nature Neuroscience, 10,* 908–914.

Kuhl, B. A., Kahn, I., Dudukovic, N. M., & Wagner, A. D. (2008). Overcoming suppression in order to remember: Contributions from anterior cingulate and ventrolateral prefrontal cortex. *Cognitive, Affective & Behavioral Neuroscience, 8*(2), 211–221.

Kuhl, B. A., Rissman, J., Chun, M. M., & Wagner, A. D. (2011). Fidelity of neural reactivation reveals competition between memories. *Proceedings of the National Academy of Sciences of the United States of America, 108*(14), 5903–5908.

Landauer, T. K., & Bjork, R. A. (1978). Optimum rehearsal patterns and name learning. In M. M. Gruneberg, P. E. Morris, & R. N. Sykes (Eds.), *Practical Aspects of Memory.* London: Academic Press. 625–632.

Leichtman, M. D., & Ceci, S. J. (1995). The effects of stereotypes and suggestions on preschoolers' reports. *Developmental Psychology, 31*(4), 568–578.

LePort, A. K. R., Mattfeld, A. T., Dickinson-Anson, H., et al. (2012). Behavioral and neuroanatomical investigation of highly superior autobiographical memory (HSAM). *Neurobiology of Learning and Memory, 98,* 78–92.

Levine, B., Svoboda, E., Hay, J. F., et al. (2002). Aging and autobiographical memory: Dissociating episodic from semantic retrieval. *Psychology and Aging, 17*(4), 677–689.

Levine, B., Turner, G. R., Tisserand, D., et al. (2004). The functional neuroanatomy of episodic and semantic autobiographical remembering: A prospective functional MRI study. *Journal of Cognitive Neuroscience, 16,* 1633–1646.

Liang, K. C., Juler, R. G., & McGaugh, J. L. (1986). Modulating effects of posttraining epinephrine on memory: Involvement of the amygdala noradrenergic system. *Brain Research, 368*(1), 125–133.

Lindsay, D. S., Hagen, L., Read, J. D., et al. (2004). True Photographs and False Memories. *Psychological Science, 15*(3), 149–154.

Loftus, E. F., Loftus, G. R., & Messo, J. (1987). Some facts about "weapon focus." *Law and Human Behavior, 11*(1), 55–62.

Loftus, E. F., & Palmer, J. C. (1974). Reconstruction of automobile destruction: An example of the interaction between language and memory. *Journal of Verbal Learning & Verbal Behavior, 13*(5), 585–589.

Loftus, E. F., & Pickrell, J. E. (1995). The formation of false memories. *Psychiatric Annals, 25*(12), 720–725.

Luria, A. R. (1987). *The Mind of a Mnemonist: A Little Book About a Vast Memory* (L. Solotaroff, Trans.). Cambridge, MA: Harvard University Press.

Madan, C. R. (2020). Exploring word memorability: How well do different word properties explain item free-recall probability?. *Psychonomic Bulletin & Review, 28,* 583–595.

Madsen, H. B., & Kim, J. H. (2016). Ontogeny of memory: An update on 40 years of work on infantile amnesia. *Behavioural Brain Research, 298,* 4–14.

Maguire, E. A. (2001). Neuroimaging studies of autobiographical event memory. *Philosophical Transactions of the Royal Society of London B Biological Sciences, 356,* 1441–1451.

Maguire, E. A., Gadian, D. G., Johnsrude, I. S., et al. (2000). Navigation-related structural change in the hippocampi of taxi drivers. *Proceedings of the National Academy of Sciences of the United States of America, 97*(8), 4398–4403.

Maguire, E. A., Valentine, E. R., Wilding, J. M., & Kapur, N. (2003). Routes to remembering: The brains behind superior memory. *Nature Neuroscience, 6*(1), 90–95.

Mandler, G. (1967). Organization and memory. In K. W. Spence and J. T. Spence (Eds.), *Psychology of Learning and Motivation.* Vol. I. New York: Academic Press.

McDaniel, M. A., Anderson, J. L., Derbish, M. H., & Morrisette, N. (2007). Testing the testing effect in the classroom. *European Journal of Cognitive Psychology, 19*(4-5), 494–513.

McGaugh, J. L. (2006). Make mild moments memorable: add a little arousal. *Trends in Cognitive Sciences, 10,* 345–347.

Mensink, G.-J., & Raaijmakers, J. G. (1988). A model for interference and forgetting. *Psychological Review, 95*(4), 434–455.

Metcalfe, J. & Kornell, N. (2007). Principles of cognitive science in education: The effects of generation, errors, and feedback *Psychonomic Bulletin & Review, 14,* 225–229.

Miller, G. A. (1956). The magical number seven, plus or minus two: some limits on our capacity for processing information. *Psychological Review, 63*(2), 81–97.

Morgan, III, C. A., Southwick, S., Steffian, G., et al. (2013). Misinformation can influence memory for recently experienced, highly stressful events. *International Journal of Law and Psychiatry, 36,* 11–17.

Murre, J. M. J., & Dros, J. (2015). Replication and analysis of Ebbinghaus' forgetting curve. *PLOS ONE, 10,* e0120644.

Nash, R. A., Wade, K. A., & Lindsay, D. S. (2009). Digitally manipulating memory: effects of doctored videos and imagination in distorting beliefs and memories. *Memory & Cognition, 37*(4), 414–424.

National Research Council. (2014). *Identifying the Culprit: Assessing Eyewitness Identification.* Washington, DC: The National Academies Press.

Newby, J. M., Lang, T., Werner-Seidler, A., et al. (2014). Alleviating distressing intrusive memories in depression: a comparison between computerised cognitive bias modification and cognitive behavioural education. *Behaviour Research and Therapy, 56*(100), 60–67.

Newcombe, N. S., Drummey, A. B., Fox, N. A., et al. (2000). Remembering early childhood: How much, how, and why (or why not). *Current Directions in Psychological Science, 9,* 55–59

Nielson, K. A., & Arensten, T. J. (2012). Memory modulation in the classroom: Selective enhancement of college examination performance by arousal induced after lecture. *Neurobiology of Learning & Memory, 98,* 12–16.

Nielson, K. A., Yee, D., & Erickson, K. I. (2005). Memory enhancement by a semantically unrelated emotional arousal source induced after learning. *Neurobiology of Learning & Memory, 84,* 49–56.

Neisser, U., & Harsch, N. (1992). Phantom flashbulbs: False recollections of hearing the news about Challenger. In E. Winograd & U. Neisser (Eds.), *Emory Symposia in Cognition, 4. Affect and Accuracy in recall: Studies of "Flashbulb" Memories.* New York: Cambridge University Press. 9–31.

O'Neill, H. (2001, March 4). The Perfect Witness. *The Washington Post.* Retrieved from http://www.washingtonpost.com. Washington, DC.

Parker, E. S., Cahill, L., & McGaugh, J. L. (2006). A case of unusual autobiographical remembering. *Neurocase, 12,* 35–49.

Pitman, R. K., Orr, S. P., Forgue, D. F., de Jong, J., & Claiborn, J. M. (1987). Psychophysiologic assessment of posttraumatic stress disorder imagery in Vietnam combat veterans. *Archives of General Psychiatry, 44*(11), 970–975.

Pitman, R. K., Sanders, K. M., Zusman R. M., et al. (2002). *Biological Psychiatry, 51,* 189–192.

Price, J. (2008). *The Woman Who Can't Forget.* New York: Free Press.

Rajaram, S. (1993). Remembering and knowing: Two means of access to the personal past. *Memory & Cognition, 21,* 89–102.

Roediger, H. L., III, & Karpicke, J. D. (2006). Test-enhanced learning: Taking memory tests improves long-term retention. *Psychological Science, 17,* 249–255.

Roediger, H. L., & McDermott, K. B. (1995). Creating false memories: Remembering words not presented in lists. *Journal of Experimental Psychology: Learning, Memory, and Cognition, 21*(4), 803–814.

Roediger, H. L., III, & McDermott, K.B. (2013). Two types of event memory. *Proceedings of the National Academy of Sciences, 110,* 20856–20857.

Rogers, T. B., Kuiper, N. A., & Kirker, W. S. (1977). Self-reference and the encoding of personal information. *Journal of Personality and Social Psychology, 35*(9), 677–688.

Ruff, C. C., Kristjánsson, Á., & Driver, J. (2007). Readout from iconic memory and selective spatial attention involve similar neural processes. *Psychological Science, 18*(10), 901–909.

Schacter, D. L. (1996). *Searching for Memory: The Brain, the Mind, and the Past.* New York: Basic Books.

Schacter, D. L. (2001). *The Seven Sins of Memory: How the Mind Forgets and Remembers.* Boston: Houghton Mifflin.

Schacter, D. L., Kagan, J., & Leichtman, M. D. (1995). True and false memories in children and adults: A cognitive neuroscience perspective. *Psychology, Public Policy, and Law, 1,* 411–428.

Seale-Carlisle, T. M., Wetmore, S. A., Flowe, H. D., & Mickes, L. (2019). Designing police lineups to maximize memory performance. *Journal of Experimental Psychology: Applied, 25*(3), 410–430.

Shallice, T., Fletcher, P., Frith, C. D., et al. (1994). Brain regions associated with acquisition and retrieval of verbal episodic memory. *Nature, 368*(6472), 633–635.

Shields, G. S., Sazma, M. A., McCullough, A. M., & Yonelinas, A. P. (2017). The effects of acute stress on episodic memory: A meta-analysis and integrative review. *Psychological bulletin, 143*(6), 636–675.

Shimamura, A. P., Jurica, P. J., Mangels, J. A., et al. (1995). Susceptibility to memory interference effects following frontal lobe damage: Findings from tests of paired-associate learning. *Journal of Cognitive Neuroscience, 7*(2), 144–152.

Simons, D. J., & Chabris, C. F. (2011). What people believe about how memory works: a representative survey of the U.S. population. *PLOS ONE, 6*(8), e22757.

Smith, A. M., Floerke V. A., Thomas A. K. (2016). Retrieval practice protects memory against acute stress. *Science, 354*(6315), 1046–1048.

Sohn, M. H., Goode, A., Stenger, V. A., et al. (2003). Competition and representation during memory retrieval: roles of the prefrontal cortex and the posterior parietal cortex. *Proceedings of the National Academy of Sciences of the United States of America, 100*(12), 7412–7417.

Sparrow, B., Liu, J., & Wegner, D. M. (2011). Google effects on memory: cognitive consequences of having information at our fingertips. *Science, 333*(6043), 776–778.

Sperling, G. (1960). The information available in brief visual presentations. *Psychological Monographs: General and Applied, 74*(11), 1–29.

St Jacques, P. L., Rubin, D. C., & Cabeza, R. (2012). Age-related effects on the neural correlates of autobiographical memory retrieval. *Neurobiology of Aging, 33*(7), 1298–1310.

Steblay, N. M. (1992). A meta-analytic review of the weapon focus effect. *Law and Human Behavior, 16*(4), 413–424.

Strange, D., & Takarangi, M. K. (2015). Memory distortion for traumatic events: the role of mental imagery. *Frontiers in Psychiatry, 6,* 27.

Svoboda, E., McKinnon, M. C., & Levine, B. (2006). The functional neuroanatomy of autobiographical memory: a meta-analysis. *Neuropsychologia, 44*(12), 2189–2208.

Symons, C. S., & Johnson, B. T. (1997). The self-reference effect in memory: A meta-analysis. *Psychological Bulletin, 121*(3), 371–394.

Talarico, J. M., & Rubin, D. C. (2003). Confidence, not consistency, characterizes flashbulb memories. Psychological Science, 14(5), 455–461.

Technical Working Group for Eyewitness Evidence. (1999). *Eyewitness Evidence: A Trainer's Manual for Law Enforcement.* Research Report. Washington, DC: U.S. Department of Justice.

Thomas, A. K., Smith, A. M., Kamal, K., & Gordon, L. T. (2020). Should you use frequent quizzing in your college course? Giving up 20 minutes of lecture time may pay off. *Journal of Applied Research in Memory and Cognition, 9,* 83–95.

Thompson-Schill, S. L., D'Esposito, M., & Kan, I. P. (1999). Effects of repetition and competition on prefrontal activity during word generation. *Neuron, 23,* 513–522.

Tulving, E. (1985). Memory and consciousness. *Canadian Psychology/Psychologie Canadienne, 26*(1), 1–12.

Turk-Browne, N. B., Golomb, J. D., & Chun, M. M. (2013). Complementary attentional components of successful memory encoding. *NeuroImage, 66*, 553–562.

Uncapher, M. R., Hutchinson, J. B., & Wagner, A. D. (2011). Dissociable effects of top-down and bottom-up attention during episodic encoding. *The Journal of Neuroscience, 31*(35), 12613–12628.

von Restorff, H. (1933). Über die wirkung von bereichsbildungen im spurenfeld. *Psychologische Forschung, 18*, 299–342.

Wade, K. A., Garry, M., Don Read, J., & Lindsay, D. S. (2002). A picture is worth a thousand lies: Using false photographs to create false childhood memories. *Psychonomic Bulletin & Review, 9*, 597–603.

Wallace, W. P. (1965). Review of the historical, empirical, and theoretical status of the von Restorff phenomenon. *Psychological Bulletin, 63*(6), 410–424.

Wang, Q. (2008). Being American, being Asian: the bicultural self and autobiographical memory in Asian Americans. *Cognition, 107*(2), 743–751.

Weissenborn, R., & Duka, T. (2000). State-dependent effects of alcohol on explicit memory: the role of semantic associations. *Psychopharmacology, 149*, 98–106.

Wells, G. L., Malpass, R. S., Lindsay, R. C. L., et al. (2000). From the lab to the police station: A successful application of eyewitness research. *American Psychologist, 55*(6), 581–598.

Wells, G. L., Steblay, N. K., & Dysart, J. E. (2015). Double-blind photo lineups using actual eyewitnesses: An experimental test of a sequential versus simultaneous lineup procedure. *Law and Human Behavior, 39*(1), 1–14.

Wilding, J., & Valentine, E. (1997). *Essays in Cognitive Psychology. Superior Memory.* Hove, England: Psychology Press/Laurence Erlbaum Associates, Inc. (UK) Taylor & Francis.

Williams, L. M. (1995). Recovered memories of abuse in women with documented child sexual victimization histories. *Journal of Traumatic Stress, 8*(4), 649–673.

Wylie, L. E., Patihis, L., McCuller, L. L., et al. (2014). Misinformation effect in older versus younger adults: A meta-analysis and review. In M. P. Toglia, D. F. Ross, J. Pozzulo, & E. Pica (Eds.), *The Elderly Eyewitness in Court* (pp. 38–66). London, UK: Psychology Press.

Zajac, R., & Brown, D. A. (2018). Conducting successful memory interviews with children. *Child & Adolescent Social Work Journal, 35*(3), 297–308.

Chapter 7

Abbott, A. (2014). Neuroscience: Brains of Norway. *Nature, 514*, 154–147.

Aly, M., & Turk-Browne, N. B. (2016b). Attention promotes episodic encoding by stabilizing hippocampal representations. *Proceedings of the National Academy of Sciences of the United States of America, 113*(4), E420–429.

Alzheimer's Association. (2019). 2019 Alzheimer's disease facts and figures. Retrieved January 2, 2020, from https://www.alz.org/media/Documents/alzheimers-facts-and-figures-infographic-2019.pdf.

Arnsten, A. F. T. (2009). Stress signalling pathways that impair prefrontal cortex structure and function. *Nature Reviews. Neuroscience, 10*(6), 410–422.

Atkinson, R. C., & Shiffrin, R. M. (1968). Human memory: A proposed system and its control processes. In K. W. Spence & J.T. Spence (Eds.), *Psychology of Learning and Motivation* (Vol. 2, pp. 89–195).

Barsalou, L. W. (1999). Perceptual symbol systems. *Behavioral and Brain Sciences, 22*(4), 577–609.

Barsalou, L. W., Simmons, W. K., Barbey, A. K., & Wilson, C. D. (2003). Grounding conceptual knowledge in modality-specific systems. *Trends in Cognitive Sciences, 7*(2), 84–91.

Bliss, T. V., & Collingridge, G. L. (1993). A synaptic model of memory: Long-term potentiation in the hippocampus. *Nature, 361*(6407), 31–39.

Breedlove, S. M., & Watson, N. V. (2019). *Behavioral Neuroscience,* 9th Edition. Sunderland, MA: Oxford University Press/Sinauer.

Bremner, J. D., Randall, P., Scott, T. M., et al. (1995). MRI-based measurement of hippocampal volume in patients with combat- related posttraumatic stress disorder. *American Journal of Psychiatry, 152*(7), 973–981.

Brewer, J. B., Zhao, Z., Desmond, J. E., et al. (1998). Making memories: Brain activity that predicts how well visual experience will be remembered. *Science, 281*(5380), 1185–1187.

Burgess, N., Maguire, E. A., & O'Keefe, J. (2002). The human hippocampus and spatial and episodic memory. *Neuron, 35*(4), 625–641.

Cabeza, R., Ciaramelli, E., Olson, I. R., & Moscovitch, M. (2008). The parietal cortex and episodic memory: an attentional account. *Nature Reviews Neuroscience, 9*(8), 613–625.

Carlson, T. A., Schrater, P., & He, S. (2003). Patterns of activity in the categorical representations of objects. *Journal of Cognitive Neuroscience, 15*(5), 704–717.

Cave, C. B., & Squire, L. R. (1992). Intact and long-lasting repetition priming in amnesia. *Journal of Experimental Psychology: Learning, Memory, and Cognition, 18*(3), 509–520.

Chadwick, M. J., Hassabis, D., Weiskopf, N., & Maguire, E. A. (2010). Decoding individual episodic memory traces in the human hippocampus. *Current Biology, 20*(6), 544–547.

Cheng, K., & Newcombe, N. S. (2005). Is there a geometric module for spatial orientation? Squaring theory and evidence. *Psychonomic Bulletin and Review, 12*, 1–23.

Cheng, Y.-L., & Mix, K. S. (2014). Spatial training improves children's mathematics ability. *Journal of Cognition and Development, 15*(1), 2–11.

Chun, M. M., & Phelps, E. A. (1999). Memory deficits for implicit contextual information in amnesic subjects with hippocampal damage. *Nature Neuroscience, 2*(9), 844–847.

Chun, M. M. (2000). Contextual cueing of visual attention. *Trends in Cognitive Sciences, 4*(5), 170–178.

Chun, M. M., & Jiang, Y. (1998). Contextual cueing: Implicit learning and memory of visual context guides spatial attention. *Cognitive Psychology, 36*(1), 28–71.

Chun, M. M., & Jiang, Y. (1999). Top-down attentional guidance based on implicit learning of visual covariation. *Psychological Science, 10*(4), 360–365.

Chun, M. M, & Johnson, M. K. (2011). Memory: Enduring traces of perceptual and reflective attention. *Neuron, 72*(4), 520–535.

Cohen, N. J., & Squire, L. R. (1980). Preserved learning and retention of pattern-analyzing skill in amnesia: Dissociation of knowing how and knowing that. *Science, 210*(4466), 207–210.

Colby, C. L., & Goldberg, M. E. (1999). Space and attention in parietal cortex. *Annual Review of Neuroscience, 22*(1), 319–349.

Corkin, S. (1968). Acquisition of motor skill after bilateral medial temporal-lobe excision. *Neuropsychologia, 6*(3), 255–265.

Damasio, A. R. (1989). Time-locked multiregional retroactivation: A systems-level proposal for the neural substrates of recall and recognition. *Cognition, 33*(1–2), 25–62.

de Quervain, D. J., Roozendaal, B., & McGaugh, J. L. (1998). Stress and glucocorticoids impair retrieval of long-term spatial memory. *Nature, 394*(6695), 787–790.

Dehaene, S., Naccache, L., Cohen, L., et al. (2001). Cerebral mechanisms of word masking and unconscious repetition priming. *Nature Neuroscience, 4*(7), 752–758.

Diwadkar, V. A., & McNamara, T. P. (1997). Viewpoint dependence in scene recognition. *Psychological Science, 8*(4), 302–307.

Duarte, A., Ranganath, C., Winward, L., et al. (2004). Dissociable neural correlates for familiarity and recollection during the encoding and retrieval of pictures. *Cognitive Brain Research, 18*(3), 255–272.

Dudai, Y. (2004). The neurobiology of consolidations, or, how stable is the engram? *Annual Review of Psychology, 55*, 51–86.

Eichenbaum, H., & Cohen, N. J. (2004). *From Conditioning to Conscious Recollection: Memory systems of the brain*. New York: Oxford University Press.

Eichenbaum, H., Yonelinas, A. P., & Ranganath, C. (2007). The medial temporal lobe and recognition memory. *Annual Review of Neuroscience, 30*, 123–152.

Epstein, R. A. (2008). Parahippocampal and retrosplenial contributions to human spatial navigation. *Trends in Cognitive Sciences, 12*(10), 388–396.

Epstein, R., & Kanwisher, N. (1998). A cortical representation of the local visual environment. *Nature, 392*(6676), 598–601.

Fisher, M., Goddu, M. K., & Keil, F. C. (2015). Searching for explanations: How the internet inflates estimates of internal knowledge. *Journal of Experimental Psychology: General, 144*(3), 674–687.

Gabrieli, J. D. E. (1998). Cognitive neuroscience of human memory. *Annual Review of Psychology, 49*, 87–115.

Genova, L. (2009). *Still Alice*. New York: Gallery Books.

Glanzer, M., & Cunitz, A. R. (1966). Two storage mechanisms in free recall. *Journal of Verbal Learning and Verbal Behavior, 5*(4), 351–360.

Glatzer, R., & Westmoreland, W. (2014). *Still Alice*. Sony Pictures Classics.

Grafton, S. T., Hazeltine, E., & Ivry, R. (1995). Functional mapping of sequence learning in normal humans. *Journal of Cognitive Neuroscience, 7*(4), 497–510.

Greene, A. J., Gross, W. L., Elsinger, C. L., & Rao, S. M. (2007). Hippocampal differentiation without recognition: an fMRI analysis of the contextual cueing task. *Learning & Memory, 14*(8), 548–553.

Grill-Spector, K., Henson, R., & Martin, A. (2006). Repetition and the brain: Neural models of stimulus-specific effects. *Trends in Cognitive Sciences, 10*(1), 14–23.

Gurvits, T. V., Shenton, M. E., Hokama, H., et al. (1996). Magnetic resonance imaging study of hippocampal volume in chronic, combat-related posttraumatic stress disorder. *Society of Biological Psychiatry, 40*(11), 1091–1099.

Hafting, T., Fyhn, M., Molden, S., et al. (2005). Microstructure of a spatial map in the entorhinal cortex. *Nature, 436*(7052), 801–806.

Haxby, J. V, Gobbini, M. I., Furey, M. L., et al. (2001). Distributed and overlapping representations of faces and objects in ventral temporal cortex. *Science, 293*(5539), 2425–2430.

Hebb, D. O. (1949). *The Organization of Behavior*. New York: Wiley.

Heindel, W. C., Salmon, D. P., Shults, C. W., et al. (1989). Neuropsychological evidence for multiple implicit memory systems: A comparison of Alzheimer's, Huntington's, and Parkinson's disease patients. *Journal of Neuroscience, 9*(2), 582–587.

Henkel, L. A. (2013). Point-and-shoot memories: The influence of taking photos on memory for a museum tour. *Psychological Science, 25*(2), 396–402.

Hermer, L., & Spelke, E. S. (1994). A geometric process for spatial reorientation in young children. *Nature, 370*(6484), 57–59.

Janowsky, J. S., Shimamura, A. P., Kritchevsky, M., & Squire, L. R. (1989). Cognitive impairment following frontal lobe damage and its relevance to human amnesia. *Behavioral Neuroscience, 103*(3), 548–560.

Jenkins, I. H., Brooks, D. J., Nixon, P. D., et al. (1994). Motor sequence learning: A study with positron emission tomography. *Journal of Neuroscience, 14*(6), 3775–3790.

Johnson, J. A., & Zatorre, R. J. (2005). Attention to simultaneous unrelated auditory and visual events: Behavioral and neural correlates. *Cerebral Cortex, 15*(10), 1609–1620.

Karni, A., Tanne, D., Rubenstein, B. S., et al. (1994). Dependence on REM sleep of overnight improvement of a perceptual skill. *Science, 265*(5172), 679–682.

Kim, J. J., & Diamond, D. M. (2002). The stressed hippocampus, synaptic plasticity and lost memories. *Nature Reviews Neuroscience, 3*, 453–462.

King, J. A., Burgess, N., Hartley, T., et al. (2002). Human hippocampus and viewpoint dependence in spatial memory. *Hippocampus, 12*(6), 811–820.

Kirschbaum, C., Pirke, K. M., & Hellhammer, D. H. (1993). The "Trier social stress test"—A tool for investigating psychobiological stress responses in a laboratory setting. *Neuropsychobiology, 28*(1–2), 76–81.

Kirschbaum, C., Wolf, O., May, M., et al. (1996). Stress- and treatment-induced elevations of cortisol levels associated with impaired declarative memory in healthy adults. *Life Sciences, 58*(17), 1475–1483.

Kumaran, D., Hassabis, D., & McClelland, J. L. (2016). What learning systems do intelligent agents need? Complementary learning systems theory updated. *Trends in Cognitive Sciences, 20*, 512–534.

Lashley, K. S. (1929). *Brain Mechanisms and Intelligence: A quantitative study of injuries to the brain.* Chicago: Chicago University Press.

Louie, K., & Wilson, M. A. (2001). Temporally structured replay of awake hippocampal ensemble activity during rapid eye movement sleep. *Neuron, 29*(1), 145–156.

Maguire, E. A. (1998). Knowing where and getting there: A human navigation network. *Science, 280*(5365), 921–924.

Maguire, E. A., Gadian, D. G., Johnsrude, I. S., et al. (2000). Navigation-related structural change in the hippocampi of taxi drivers. *Proceedings of the National Academy of Sciences of the United States of America, 97*(8), 4398–4403.

Maguire, Eleanor A., Frackowiak, R. S. J., & Frith, C. D. (1997). Recalling routes around London: Activation of the right hippocampus in taxi drivers. *Journal of Neuroscience, 17*(18), 7103–7110.

Manns, J. R., & Squire, L. R. (2001). Perceptual learning, awareness, and the hippocampus. *Hippocampus, 11*(6), 776–782.

Marslen-Wilson, W. D., & Teuber, H.-L. (1975). Memory for remote events in anterograde amnesia: Recognition of public figures from newsphotographs. *Neuropsychologia, 13*(3), 353–364.

McClelland, J. L., McNaughton, B. L., & O'Reilly, R. C. (1995). Why there are complementary learning systems in the hippocampus and neocortex: Insights from the successes and failures of connectionist models of learning and memory. *Psychological Review, 102*(3), 419–457.

McEwen, B. S. (1999). Stress and hippocampal plasticity. *Annual Review of Neuroscience, 22*, 105–122.

McGaugh, J. L. (2000). Memory—A century of consolidation. *Science, 287*, 248–251.

Milner, B. (1965). Memory disturbance after bilateral hippocampal lesions. In *Cognitive Processes and the Brain: An Enduring Problem in Psychology*, P. M. Milner & S. E. Glickman (Eds.), Princeton, NJ: Van Nostrand, 97–111.

Moser, E. I., Kropff, E., & Moser, M.-B. (2008). Place cells, grid cells, and the brain's spatial representation system. *Annual Review of Neuroscience, 31*, 69–89.

Muller, R. U., Bostock, E., Taube, J. S., & Kubie, J. L. (1994). On the directional firing properties of hippocampal place cells. *Journal of Neuroscience, 14*(12), 7235–7251.

Murdock Jr., B. B. (1962). The serial position effect of free recall. *Journal of Experimental Psychology, 64*(5), 482–488.

National Institute on Aging. (2019). Alzheimer's disease and related dementias. Retrieved January 2, 2020, from https://www.nia.nih.gov/health/alzheimers.

Nissen, M. J., & Bullemer, P. (1987). Attentional requirements of learning: Evidence from performance measures. *Cognitive Psychology, 19*(1), 1–32.

Norman, K. A., Polyn, S. M., Detre, G. J., & Haxby, J. V. (2006). Beyond mind-reading: Multi-voxel pattern analysis of fMRI data. *Trends in Cognitive Sciences, 10*(9), 424–430.

Nyberg, L., Habib, R., McIntosh, A. R., & Tulving, E. (2000). Reactivation of encoding-related brain activity during memory retrieval. *Proceedings of the National Academy of Sciences of the United States of America, 97*(20), 11120–11124.

O'Keefe, J., & Dostrovsky, J. (1971). The hippocampus as a spatial map. Preliminary evidence from unit activity in the freely-moving rat. *Brain Research, 34*(1), 171–175.

O'Keefe, J., & Nadel, L. (1978). *The Hippocampus as a Cognitive Map.* New York: Oxford University Press.

Otten, L. J., Quayle, A. H., Akram, S., et al. (2006). Brain activity before an event predicts later recollection. *Nature Neuroscience, 9*(4), 489–491.

Paller, K.A., Kutas, M., & Mayes, A. R. (1987). Neural correlates of encoding in an incidental learning paradigm. *Electroencephalography and Clinical Neurophysiology, 67*(4), 360–371.

Paller, Ken A., & Wagner, A. D. (2002). Observing the transformation of experience into memory. *Trends in Cognitive Sciences, 6*(2), 93–102.

Pittenger, C., & Duman, R. S. (2008). Stress, depression, and neuroplasticity: A convergence of mechanisms. *Neuropsychopharmacology, 33*(1), 88–109.

Poldrack, R. A., Desmond, J. E., Glover, G. H., & Gabrieli, J. D. E. (1998). The neural basis of visual skill learning: An fMRI study of mirror reading. *Cerebral Cortex, 8*(1), 1–10.

Polyn, S. M., Natu, V. S., Cohen, J. D., & Norman, K. A. (2005). Category-specific cortical activity precedes retrieval during memory search. *Science, 310*(5756), 1963–1966.

Ranganath, C., Cohen, M. X., Dam, C., et al. (2004). Inferior temporal, prefrontal, and hippocampal contributions to visual working memory maintenance and associative memory retrieval. *The Journal of Neuroscience, 24*(16), 3917–3925.

Rissman, J., & Wagner, A. D. (2012). Distributed representations in memory: Insights from functional brain imaging. In *Annual Review of Psychology, 63*, 101–128.

Rissman, Jesse, Greely, H. T., & Wagner, A. D. (2010). Detecting individual memories through the neural decoding of memory states and past experience. *Proceedings of the National Academy of Sciences of the United States of America, 107*(21), 9849–9854.

Roediger, H. L., & McDermott, K. B. (1993). Implicit memory in normal human subjects. *Handbook of Neuropsychology, 8,* 63–131.

Saffran, J. R., Aslin, R. N., & Newport, E. L. (1996). Statistical learning by 8-month-old infants. *Science, 274*(5294), 1926–1928.

Saffran, Jenny R. (2003). Statistical language learning: Mechanisms and constraints. *Current Directions in Psychological Science, 12*(4), 110–114.

Sapolsky, R. M. (1996). Why stress is bad for your brain. *Science, 273,* 749–750.

Sapolsky, R. M. (2000). Glucocorticoids and hippocampal atrophy in neuropsychiatric disorders. *Archives of General Psychiatry, 57,* 925–935.

Schacter, D. L. (1987). Implicit memory: History and current status. *Journal of Experimental Psychology: Learning, Memory, and Cognition, 13,* 501–518.

Schacter, D. L. (1992). Priming and multiple memory systems: Perceptual mechanisms of implicit memory. *Journal of Cognitive Neuroscience, 4*(3), 244–256.

Schacter, D. L., & Buckner, R. L. (1998). Priming and the brain. *Neuron, 20*(2), 185–195.

Scoville, W. B., & Milner, B. (1957). Loss of recent memory after bilateral hippocampal lesions. *Journal of Neurology, Neurosurgery, and Psychiatry, 20*(1), 11–21.

Sedivy, J. (2019). *Language in Mind,* 2nd Edition. Sunderland, MA: Oxford University Press/Sinauer.

Shea, D. L., Lubinski, D., & Benbow, C. P. (2001). Importance of assessing spatial ability in intellectually talented young adolescents: A 20-year longitudinal study. *Journal of Educational Psychology, 93*(3), 604–614.

Sheline, Y. I., Wang, P. W., Gado, M. H., et al. (1996). Hippocampal atrophy in recurrent major depression. *Proceedings of the National Academy of Sciences, 93*(9), 3908–3913.

Shelton, A. L., & McNamara, T. P. (2001). Systems of spatial reference in human memory. *Cognitive Psychology, 43*(4), 274–310.

Simons, D. J., & Wang, R. F. (1998). Perceiving real-world viewpoint changes. *Psychological Science, 9*(4), 315–320.

Snyder, L. H., Grieve, K. L., Brotchie, P., & Andersen, R. A. (1998). Separate body- and world-referenced representations of visual space in parietal cortex. *Nature, 394*(6696), 887–891.

Sparrow, B., Liu, J., & Wegner, D. M. (2011). Google effects on memory: Cognitive consequences of having information at our fingertips. *Science, 333*(6043), 776–778.

Spiers, H. J., Burgess, N., Maguire, E. A., et al. (2001). Unilateral temporal lobectomy patients show lateralized topographical and episodic memory deficits in a virtual town. *Brain, 124*(12), 2476–2489.

Squire, L. R., & Zola-Morgan, S. (1991). The medial temporal lobe memory system. *Science, 253*(5026), 1380–1386.

Squire, L.R., & Wixted, J. T. (2011). The cognitive neuroscience of human memory since H.M. *Annual Review of Neuroscience, 34,* 259–288.

Squire, L. R. (1992). Memory and the hippocampus: A synthesis from findings with rats, monkeys, and humans. *Psychological Review, 99*(2), 195–231.

Squire, L. R. (2004). Memory systems of the brain: A brief history and current perspective. *Neurobiology of Learning and Memory, 82*(3), 171–177.

Squire, L. R., & Alvarez, P. (1995). Retrograde amnesia and memory consolidation: a neurobiological perspective. *Current Opinion in Neurobiology, 5*(2), 169–177.

Squire, L. R., Stark, C. E. L., & Clark, R. E. (2004). The medial temporal lobe. *Annual Review of Neuroscience, 27,* 279–306.

Stern, C. E., Corkin, S., González, R. G., et al. (1996). The hippocampal formation participates in novel picture encoding: Evidence from functional magnetic resonance imaging. *Proceedings of the National Academy of Sciences of the United States of America, 93*(16), 8660–8665.

Stickgold, R. (2005). Sleep-dependent memory consolidation. *Nature, 437*(7063), 1272–1278.

Summerfield, J. J., Lepsien, J., Gitelman, D. R., et al. (2006). Orienting attention based on long-term memory experience. *Neuron, 49*(6), 905–916.

Taube, J. S., Muller, R. U., & Ranck, J. B. (1990). Head-direction cells recorded from the postsubiculum in freely moving rats. I. Description and quantitative analysis. *Journal of Neuroscience, 10*(2), 420–435.

Tulving, E. (1983). *Elements of Episodic Memory.* Oxford: Clarendon.

Tulving, E. (2002). Episodic memory: From mind to brain. *Annual Review of Psychology, 53,* 1–25.

Tulving, E., Kapur, S., Craik, F. I. M., et al. (1994). Hemispheric encoding/retrieval asymmetry in episodic memory: Positron emission tomography findings. *Proceedings of the National Academy of Sciences of the United States of America, 91*(6), 2016–2020.

Tulving, E., Markowitsch, H. J., Craik, F. I. M., et al. (1996). Novelty and familiarity activations in pet studies of memory encoding and retrieval. *Cerebral Cortex, 6*(1), 71–79.

Tulving, E., & Schacter, D. L. (1990). Priming and human memory systems. *Science, 247*(4940), 304–306.

Tulving, E., Schacter, D. L., McLachlan, D. R., & Moscovitch, M. (1988). Priming of semantic autobiographical knowledge: A case study of retrograde amnesia. *Brain and Cognition, 8*(1), 3–20.

Turk-Browne, N. B., Yi, D.-J., & Chun, M. M. (2006). Linking implicit and explicit memory: common encoding factors and shared representations. *Neuron, 49*(6), 917–927.

Uttal, D. H., Meadow, N. G., Tipton, E., et al. (2013). The malleability of spatial skills: A meta-analysis of training studies. *Psychological Bulletin, 139*(2), 352–402.

Wagner, A. D., Schacter, D. L., Rotte, M., et al. (1998). Building memories: Remembering and forgetting of verbal experiences as predicted by brain activity. *Science, 281*(5380), 1188–1191.

Wagner, A. D., Shannon, B. J., Kahn, I., & Buckner, R. L. (2005). Parietal lobe contributions to episodic memory retrieval. *Trends in Cognitive Sciences, 9*(9), 445–453.

Wai, J., Lubinski, D., & Benbow, C. P. (2009). Spatial ability for STEM domains: Aligning over 50 years of cumulative psychological knowledge solidifies its importance. *Journal of Educational Psychology, 101*(4), 817–835.

Walker, M. P., Brakefield, T., Morgan, A., et al. (2002). Practice with sleep makes perfect. *Neuron, 35*(1), 205–211.

Walther, D. B., Caddigan, E., Fei-Fei, L., & Beck, D. M. (2009). Natural scene categories revealed in distributed patterns of activity in the human brain. *The Journal of Neuroscience, 29*(34), 10573–10581.

Wheeler, M. E., Petersen, S. E., & Buckner, R. L. (2000). Memory's echo: Vivid remembering reactivates sensory-specific cortex. *Proceedings of the National Academy of Sciences of the United States of America, 97*(20), 11125–11129.

Wiggs, C. L., & Martin, A. (1998). Properties and mechanisms of perceptual priming. *Current Opinion in Neurobiology, 8*(2), 227–233.

Wilson, M. A., & McNaughton, B. L. (1993). Dynamics of the hippocampal ensemble code for space. *Science, 261*(5124), 1055–1058.

Wilson, M. A., & McNaughton, B. L. (1994). Reactivation of hippocampal ensemble memories during sleep. *Science, 265*(5172), 676–679.

Yi, D.-J., & Chun, M. M. (2005). Attentional modulation of learning-related repetition attenuation effects in human parahippocampal cortex. *Journal of Neuroscience, 25*(14).

Yonelinas, A. P. (2002). The nature of recollection and familiarity: A review of 30 years of research. *Journal of Memory and Language, 46*(3), 441–517.

Chapter 8

1911 December, *The Strand* Magazine, Volume 42, Spooneriana by A. T. Corke, Start Page 770, Quote Page 771, Column 2, Published by George Newnes, Strand, London.

Ackerman, B. P. (1983). Form and function in children's understanding of ironic utterances. *Journal of Experimental Child Psychology, 35*, 487–508.

Adams, D. (1979). *The Hitchhiker's Guide to the Galaxy.* London: Pan Books, Ltd.

Arredondo, M. M., Hu, X. S., Satterfield, T., & Kovelman, I. (2017). Bilingualism alters children's frontal lobe functioning for attentional control. *Developmental Science, 20*(3), 10.1111/desc.12377.

Balaban, M. T., & Waxman, S. R. (1997). Do words facilitate object categorization in 9-month-old infants?. *Journal of Experimental Child Psychology, 64*(1), 3–26.

Baldwin, D. A. (1992). Clarifying the role of shape in children's taxonomic assumption. *Journal of Experimental Child Psychology, 54*(3), 392–416.

Barrett, L. F. (2006). Solving the emotion paradox: Categorization and the experience of emotion. *Personality and Social Psychology Review, 10*, 20-46.

Bergen, L. & Grodner, D. J. (2012). Speaker knowledge influences the comprehension of pragmatic inferences. *Journal of Experimental Psychology: Learning, Memory, & Cognition, 38*, 1450-1460.

Bialystok, E., Craik, F. I., & Luk, G. (2008). Cognitive control and lexical access in younger and older bilinguals. Journal of experimental psychology. *Learning, Memory, and Cognition, 34*, 859–873.

Bialystok, E., Craik, F. I., & Luk, G. (2012). Bilingualism: Consequences for mind and brain. *Trends in Cognitive Sciences, 16*(4), 240–250.

Bickerton, D. (1984). The language bioprogram hypothesis. *Behavioral and Brain Sciences, 7*(2), 173–221.

Binder, J. R., & Mohr, J. P. (1992). The topography of callosal reading pathways: A case-control analysis. *Brain, 115*, 1807–1826.

Birch, S. A. (2005). When knowledge is a curse: Children's and adults' reasoning about mental states. *Current Directions in Psychological Science, 14*, 25–29.

Bloomfield, L. (1933). *Language.* New York: Henry Holt.

Bock, K. (1996). Language production: Methods and methodologies. *Psychonomic Bulletin & Review, 3*, 395–421.

Bögels, S., & Torreira, F. (2015). Listeners use intonational phrase boundaries to project turn ends in spoken interaction. *Journal of Phonetics, 52*, 46–57.

Borger, J. (2006, February 18). Cheney shooting victim says sorry—to Cheney. *The Guardian.* February 18, 2006. https://www.theguardian.com/world/2006/feb/18/usa.dickcheney.

Boroditsky, L. (2001). Does language shape thought? Mandarin and English speakers' conceptions of time. *Cognitive Psychology, 43*(1), 1–22.

Boroditsky, L. (2011). How language shapes thought. *Scientific American, 304*, 62–65.

Boroditsky, L., & Gaby, A. (2010). Remembrances of times east: Absolute spatial representations of time in an Australian Aboriginal community. *Psychological Science, 21*(11), 1635–1639.

Braisby, N. & Gellatly, A. (2012). *Cognitive Psychology,* 2nd Edition. New York: Oxford University Press.

Brock, J. (2007). Language abilities in Williams syndrome: A critical review. *Development and Psychopathology, 19*, 97–127.

Brown, R. (1973). *A First Language.* Cambridge, MA: Harvard University Press.

Brown, R., & Hanlon, C. (1970). *Derivational complexity and order of acquisition in child speech.* In J. R. Hayes. (Ed.), Cognition and the Development of Language. New York: Wiley.

Brown, R., & McNeill, D. (1966). The "tip of the tongue" phenomenon. *Journal of Verbal Learning & Verbal Behavior, 5*(4), 325–337.

Bumiller, E., & Blumenthal, R. (2006). Bush 'satisfied' with Cheney response. *New York Times.* February 17, 2006. https://www.nytimes.com/2006/02/17/politics/bush-satisfied-with-cheney-response.html.

Camerer, C., Loewenstein, G., & Weber, M. (1989). The curse of knowledge in economic settings: An experimental approach. *Journal of Political Economy, 97*, 1232–1254.

Carey, S., & Bartlett, E. (1978). Acquiring a single new word. *Proceedings of the Stanford Child Language Conference, 15*, 17–29.

Carroll, D. W. (2008). *Psychology of Language,* 5th Edition. Belmont, CA: Thomson Wadsworth.

Carroll, L. (1872). *Through the Looking Glass and What Alice Found There.* Philadelphia: Henry Altemus Company.

Casasola, M., Wei, W. S., Suh, D. D., et al. (2020). Children's exposure to spatial language promotes their spatial thinking. *Journal of Experimental Psychology: General, 149*(6), 1116–1136.

Choi, Y., & Trueswell, J. C. (2010). Children's (in)ability to recover from garden paths in a verb-final language: Evidence for developing control in sentence processing. *Journal of Experimental Child Psychology, 106*(1), 41–61.

Chomsky, N. (1957). *Syntactic Structures.* Mouton & Co., B.V., Publishers, The Hague.

Clark, H. H. (1996). *Using Language.* Cambridge: Cambridge University Press.

Clark, H. H., & Chase, W. G. (1972). On the process of comparing sentences against pictures. *Cognitive Psychology, 3*, 472–517.

Cleary, B. (1968). *Ramona the Pest.* New York: William Morrow and Company, 173–173.

Collins, A. M., & Loftus, E. F. (1975). A spreading-activation theory of semantic processing. *Psychological Review, 82*(6), 407–428.

Curtiss, S. (1977). *Genie: A Psycholinguistic Study of a Modern-Day "Wild Child".* New York: Academic Press.

Damasio, A. R., & Damasio, H. (1983). The anatomic basis of pure alexia. *Neurology, 33*(12), 1573–1583.

Darwin, C. (1871). *The Descent of Man, and Selection in Relation to Sex.* London: John Murray.

Dehaene, S., & Cohen, L. (2011). *The unique role of the visual word form area in reading. Trends in Cognitive Sciences, 15*, 254–262.

Dehaene, S., Izard, V., Pica, P., & Spelke, E. S. (2006). Core knowledge of geometry in an Amazonian indigene group. *Science, 311*, 381–384.

Dell, G. S. (1986). A spreading-activation theory of retrieval in sentence production. *Psychological Review, 93*(3), 283–321.

Dosher, B. A., & Rosedale, G. (1989). Integrated retrieval cues as a mechanism for priming in retrieval from memory. *Journal of Experimental Psychology: General, 118*(2), 191–211.

Eimas, P. D., Siqueland, E. R., Jusczyk, P., & Vigorito, J. (1971). Speech perception in infants. *Science, 171*(3968), 303–306.

Ekman, P., and Cordaro, D. (2011). What is meant by calling emotions basic. *Emotion Review, 3*, 364–370.

Fausey, C. M., & Boroditsky, L. (2011). Who dunnit? Cross-linguistic differences in eye-witness memory. *Psychonomic Bulletin & Review, 18*(1), 150–157.

Fazio, R. H., Sanbonmatsu, D. M., Powell, M. C., & Kardes, F. R. (1986). On the automatic activation of attitudes. *Journal of Personality and Social Psychology, 50*(2), 229–238.

Feldman, N. H., Griffiths, T. L., Goldwater, S., & Morgan, J. L. (2013). A role for the developing lexicon in phonetic category acquisition. *Psychological review, 120*(4), 751–778.

Ferreira, F., & Henderson, J. M. (1991). Recovery from misanalyses of garden-path sentences. *Journal of Memory and Language 30*(6): 725–745.

Ferreira, F., Bailey, K. G. D., & Ferraro, V. (2002). Good-enough representations in language comprehension. *Current Directions in Psychological Science, 11*, 11–15.

Forster, K. I., & Chambers, S. M. (1973). Lexical access and naming time. *Journal of Verbal Learning & Verbal Behavior, 12*(6), 627–635.

Foulke, E., & Sticht, T. G. (1969). Review of research on the intelligibility and comprehension of accelerated speech. *Psychological Bulletin, 72*, 50–62.

Frank, M. C., Everett, D. L., Fedorenko, E., & Gibson, E. (2008). Number as a cognitive technology: Evidence from Pirahã language and cognition. *Cognition, 108*, 819–824.

Fuhrman, O., & Boroditsky, L. (2010). Cross-cultural differences in mental representations of time: Evidence from an implicit nonlinguistic task. *Cognitive Science, 34*, 1430–1451.

Gendron, M., Lindquist, K. A., Barsalou, L. W., and Barrett, L. F. (2012). Emotion words shape emotion percepts. *Emotion, 12*, 314–325.

Gendron, M., Roberson, D., van der Vyver, J. M., & Barrett, L. F. (2014). Perceptions of emotion from facial expressions are not culturally universal: Evidence from a remote culture. *Emotion, 14*, 251–262.

Gleitman, L., & Papafragou, A. (2005). Language and thought. In K. J. Holyoak & R. G. Morrison (Eds.), *The Cambridge Handbook of Thinking and Reasoning* (pp. 633–661). Cambridge: Cambridge University Press.

Glucksberg, S., & Danks, J. H. (1975). *Experimental Psycholinguistics: An introduction.* Hillsdale, NJ: Lawrence Erlbaum.

Glucksberg, S., Krauss, R. M., & Weisberg, R. (1966). Referential communication in nursery school children: Method and some preliminary findings. *Journal of Experimental Child Psychology, 3*, 333–342.

Goldin-Meadow, S. (1999). The role of gesture in communication and thinking. *Trends in Cognitive Sciences, 3*(11), 419–429.

Golinkoff, R. M., Deniz Can, D., Soderstrom, M., & Hirsh-Pasek, K. (2015). (Baby)talk to me: The social context of infant-directed speech and its effects on early language acquisition. *Current Directions in Psychological Science, 24*, 349–344.

Golinkoff, R. M., Hirsh-Pasek, K., Bailey, L. M., & Wenger, N. R. (1992). Young children and adults use lexical principles to learn new nouns. *Developmental Psychology, 28*(1), 99–108.

Gollan, T. H., Montoya, R. I., Fennema-Notestine, C., et al. (2005). Bilingualism affects picture naming but not picture classification. *Memory & Cognition, 33*, 1220–1234.

Goto, H. (1971). Auditory perception by normal Japanese adults of the sounds "l" and "r." *Neuropsychologia, 9*(3), 317–323.

Grieve, T. (2006). Cheney: "I'm the guy who pulled the trigger that shot my friend". *Salon*, February 16, 2006. https://www.salon.com/2006/02/15/cheneyfox/

Harris, M., & Pexman, P. M. (2003). Children's perceptions of the social functions of verbal irony. *Discourse Processes, 36*(3), 147–165.

Hartshorne, J., Tenenbaum, J., B., & Pinker, S. (2018). A critical period for second language acquisition: Evidence from 2/3 million English speakers. *Cognition, 177, 263–277.*

Heath, C., & Heath, D. (2007). *Made to Stick: Why Some Ideas Survive and Others Die.* New York: Random House.

Heibeck, T. H., & Markman, E. M. (1987). Word learning in children: An examination of fast mapping. *Child Development, 58*(4), 1021–1034.

Hirsh-Pasek, K., Reeves, L. M., & Golinkoff, R. (1993). In *Psycholinguistics*, J. B. Gleason and N. B. Ratner (Eds.), Orlando, FL: Harcourt Brace Jovanovich, 138.

Hirsh-Pasek, K., Treiman, R., & Schneiderman, M. (1984). Brown & Hanlon revisited: Mothers' sensitivity to ungrammatical forms. *Journal of Child Language, 11*(1), 81–88.

Hoffman, J. E., Landau, B., & Pagani, B. (2003). Spatial breakdown in spatial construction: Evidence from eye fixations in children with Williams syndrome. *Cognitive Psychology, 46*(3), 260–301.

Hollich, G., Golinkoff, R. M., & Hirsh-Pasek, K. (2007). Young children associate novel words with complex objects rather than salient parts. *Developmental Psychology, 43, 1051–1061.*

Horton, W. S., & Keysar, B. (1996). When do speakers take into account common ground? *Cognition, 59*(1), 91–117.

Hunt, E., & Agnoli, F. (1991). The Whorfian hypothesis: A cognitive psychology perspective. *Psychological Review, 98*(3), 377–389.

Hurewitz, F., Brown-Schmidt, S., Thorpe, K., et al. (2001). One frog, two frog, red frog, blue frog: Factors affecting children's syntactic choices in production and comprehension. *Journal of Psycholinguistic Research, 29*(6), 597–626.

Isaacs, E. A., & Clark, H. H. (1987). References in conversation between experts and novices. *Journal of Experimental Psychology: General, 116*(1), 26–37.

Ivanova, I., & Costa, A. (2008). Does bilingualism hamper lexical access in speech production? *Acta Psychologica, 127,* 277–288.

Izard, C. E. (2007). Basic emotions, natural kinds, emotion schemas, and a new paradigm. *Perspectives on Psychological Science, 2, 260–280.*

Jusczyk, P. W., Friederici, A. D., Wessels, J. M., et al. (1993). Infants' sensitivity to the sound patterns of native language words. *Journal of Memory and Language, 32*(3), 402–420.

Kantor, J. R. (1936). *An Objective Psychology of Grammar.* Bloomington, IN: Indiana University Press.

Konishi, H., Brezack, N., Golinkoff, R.M., & Hirsh-Pasek, K. (2019). Crossing to the other side: Language influences children's perception of event components. *Cognition, 192.*

Kuhl, P. K. (2000). A new view of language acquisition. *Proceedings of the National Academy of Sciences of the United States of America, 97, 11850–11857.*

Kuhl, P. K., Stevens, E., Hayashi, A., et al. (2006). Infants show a facilitation effect for native language phonetic perception between 6 and 12 months. *Developmental Science, 9,* F13–F21.

Kuhl, P. K., Tsao, F. M., & Liu, H. M. (2003). Foreign-language experience in infancy: effects of short-term exposure and social interaction on phonetic learning. *Proceedings of the National Academy of Sciences of the United States of America, 100*(15), 9096–9101.

Krauss, R. M., & Weinheimer, S. (1967). Effects of referent similarity and communication mode on verbal encoding. *Journal of Verbal Learning and Verbal Behavior, 6, 359–363.*

Landau, B., Smith, L. B., & Jones, S. (1992). Syntactic context and the shape bias in children's and adults' lexical learning. *Journal of Memory and Language, 31*(6), 807–825.

Lashley, K. S. (1951). The problem of serial order in behavior. In L. A. Jeffress (Ed.), *Cerebral Mechanisms in Behavior: The Hixon Symposium* (p. 112–146). Hoboken, NJ: Wiley.

Lehtonen, M., Soveri, A., Laine, A., et al. (2018). Is bilingualism associated with enhanced executive functioning in adults? A meta-analytic review. *Psychological Bulletin, 144*(4), 394–425.

Lenneberg, E. H. (1967). *Biological Foundations of Language.* New York: Wiley.

Levelt, W. J. M. (1989). *ACL-MIT Press series in natural-language processing. Speaking: From intention to articulation.* Cambridge, MA: The MIT Press.

Levinson, S. (2003). *Space in Language and Cognition: Explorations in cognitive diversity.* Cambridge: Cambridge University Press.

Levinson, S. C. (2016). Turn-taking in human communication—origins and implications for language processing. *Trends in Cognitive Sciences, 20, 6–14.*

Li, P., Abarbanell, L., Gleitman, L., & Papafragou, A. (2011). Spatial reasoning in Tenejapan Mayans. *Cognition, 120*(1), 33–53.

Lidz, J., & Gagliardi, A. (2015). How nature meets nurture: Universal grammar and statistical learning. *Annual Review of Linguistics, 1, 333–353.*

Lindquist, K. A., Barrett, L. F., Bliss-Moreau, E., & Russell, J. A. (2006). Language and the perception of emotion. *Emotion, 6, 125–138.*

Lindquist, K. A., Gendron, M., Barrett, L. F., & Dickerson, B. C. (2014). Emotion, but not affect perception, is impaired with semantic memory loss. *Emotion, 14, 375–387.*

Lindquist, K. A., MacCormack, J. K., & Shablack, H. (2015). The role of language in emotion: predictions from psychological constructionism. *Frontiers in psychology, 6, 444.*

Luntz, F (2007). *Words That Work: It's Not What You Say, it's What People Hear.* New York: Hyperion.

Majid, A., & Levinson, S. C. (2008). Language does provide support for basic tastes. [Commentary] *Behavioral and Brain Sciences, 31,* 86–87.

Marcus, G. F. (1993). Negative evidence in language acquisition. *Cognition, 46*(1), 53–85.

Markman, E. M. (1989). *Categorization and Naming in Children: Problems of induction.* Cambridge, MA: The MIT Press.

Markman, E. M. (1991). The whole-object, taxonomic, and mutual exclusivity assumptions as initial constraints on word meanings. In S. A. Gelman & J. P. Byrnes (Eds.), *Perspectives on Language and Thought: Interrelations in development* (pp. 72–106). Cambridge: Cambridge University Press.

Markman, E. M. (1992). Constraints on word learning: Speculations about their nature, origins, and domain specificity. In M. R. Gunnar & M. Maratsos (Eds.), *The Minnesota symposia on child psychology, Vol. 25. Modularity and constraints in language and cognition* (pp. 59–101). Mahwah, NJ: Lawrence Erlbaum Associates, Inc.

Markson, L., & Bloom, P. (1997). Evidence against a dedicated system for word learning in children. *Nature, 385*(6619), 813–815.

Mazuka, R., Jincho, N., & Oishi, H. (2009). Development of executive control and language processing. *Language and Linguistics Compass, 3,* 59–89.

Meyer, D. E., & Schvaneveldt, R. W. (1971). Facilitation in recognizing pairs of words: Evidence of a dependence between retrieval operations. *Journal of Experimental Psychology, 90*(2), 227–234.

Miller, G. A., & Gildea, P. M. (1987). How children learn words. *Scientific American, 257*(3), 94–99.

Miyawaki, K., Jenkins, J. J., Strange, W., et al. (1975). An effect of linguistic experience: The discrimination of (r) and (l) by native speakers of Japanese and English. *Perception & Psychophysics, 18*(5), 331–340.

Nichols, E. S., Wild, C. J., Stojanoski, B., et al. (2020). Bilingualism affords no general cognitive advantages: A population study of executive function in 11,000 people. *Psychological Science, 31*(5), 548–567.

Novick, J. M., Trueswell, J. C. & Thompson-Schill, S. L. (2005). Cognitive control and parsing: Reexamining the role of Broca's area in sentence comprehension. *Cognitive, Affective, & Behavioral Neuroscience, 5,* 263–281.

Parish, J., Hennon, E., Hirsh-Pasek, K., et al. (2007). Children with autism illuminate the role of social intention in word learning. *Child Development, 78,* 1265–1287.

Piantadosi, S. T. (2014). Zipf's word frequency law in natural language: A critical review and future directions. *Psychonomic Bulletin & Review, 21*(5), 1112–1130.

Piantadosi, S. T., Tily, H., & Gibson, E. (2012). The communicative function of ambiguity in language. *Cognition, 122,* 280–291.

Pinker, S. (1989). *Learnability and Cognition: The acquisition of argument structure.* Cambridge, MA: The MIT Press.

Pinker, S. (1994). *The Language Instinct.* New York: William Morrow and Company, Inc.

Pinker, S. (2015). *The Sense of Style: The thinking person's guide to writing in the 21st century.* New York: Penguin.

Polka, L., Jusczyk, P. J., & Rvachew, S. (1995). Methods for studying speech perception in infants and children. In W. Strange (Ed.) *Speech Perception and Linguistic Experience: Issues in cross-language speech research.* Timonium, MD: York Press.

Pozzan, L., & Trueswell, J. C. (2015). Revise and resubmit: Processing effects on grammar acquisition. *Cognitive Psychology, 80,* 73–108.

Price, C. J., & Devlin, J. T. (2011). The interactive account of ventral occipitotemporal contributions to reading. *Trends in Cognitive Sciences, 15*(6), 246–253.

Ransdell, S. E., & Fischler, I. (1987). Memory in a monolingual mode: When are bilinguals at a disadvantage? *Journal of Memory and Language, 26*(4), 392–405.

Ratcliff, R., & McKoon, G. (1988). A retrieval theory of priming in memory. *Psychological Review, 95*(3), 385–408.

Regier, T., Kay, P., & Khetarpal, N. (2007). Color naming reflects optimal partitions of color space. *Proceedings of the National Academy of Sciences, 104,* 1436–1441.

Ritzenthaler, R. E., & Peterson, F. A. (1954). Courtship whistling of the Mexican Kickapoo Indians. *American Anthropologist, 56,* 1088–1089.

Rolls, G. (2014). *Classic Case Studies in Psychology,* Third Edition. Hove, UK: Routledge.

Rubin, D. C. (1975). Within word structure in the tip-of-the-tongue phenomenon. *Journal of Verbal Learning & Verbal Behavior, 14,* 392–397.

Saffran, J. R., Aslin, R. N., & Newport, E. L. (1996). Statistical learning by 8-month-old infants. *Science, 274,* 1926–1928.

Saffran, J. R., Newport, E. L., & Aslin, R. N. (1996). Word segmentation: The role of distributional cues. *Journal of Memory and Language, 35,* 606–621.

Savage-Rumbaugh, E., Murphy, J., Sevcik, R., et al. (1993). Language comprehension in ape and child. *Monographs of the Society for Research in Child Development, 58*(3/4), i–252.

Savin, H. B. (1963). Word frequency effect and errors in the perception of speech. *Journal of the Acoustical Society of America, 35*(2), 200–206.

Senghas, A., & Coppola, M. (2001). Children creating language: How Nicaraguan sign language acquired a spatial grammar. *Psychological science, 12,* 323–328.

Senghas, A., Kita, S., & Özyürek, A. (2004). Children creating core properties of language: Evidence from an emerging sign language in Nicaragua. *Science, 305*(5691), 1779–1782.

Sherman, M. A. (1976). Adjectival negation and the comprehension of multiply negated sentences. *Journal of Verbal Learning and Verbal Behavior, 15,* 143–157.

Skinner, B. F. (1957). *Verbal Behavior.* New York: Appleton-Century-Crofts.

Slobin, D. I. (1966). Grammatical transformations and sentence comprehension in childhood and adulthood. *Journal of Verbal Learning & Verbal Behavior, 5*(3), 219–227.

Smith, L. B., Jones, S. S., & Landau, B. (1992). Count nouns, adjectives, and perceptual properties in children's novel word interpretations. *Developmental Psychology, 28*(2), 273–286.

Spelke, E. S. (2003). What makes us smart? Core knowledge and natural language. In D. Gentner & S. Goldin-Meadow (Eds.), *Language in Mind: Advances in the study of language and thought* (pp. 277–311). Cambridge, MA: The MIT Press.

Streeter, L. A. (1976). Language perception of 2-mo-old infants shows effects of both innate mechanisms and experience. *Nature, 259*(5538), 39–41.

Swingley, D. (2010). Fast mapping and slow mapping in children's word learning. *Language Learning and Development, 6,* 179–183.

Tabor, W., & Hutchins, S. (2004). Evidence for self-organized sentence processing: Digging-in effects. *Journal of Experimental Psychology: Learning, Memory, and Cognition, 30*(2), 431–450.

Taft, M. (1979). Lexical access via an orthographic code: The Basic Orthographic Syllabic Structure (BOSS). *Journal of Verbal Learning and Verbal Behavior, 18,* 21–39.

Tanenhaus, M. K., Spivey-Knowlton, M. J., Eberhard, K. M., & Sedivy, J. C. (1995). Integration of visual and linguistic information in spoken language comprehension. *Science, 268,* 1632–1634.

Terrace, H. S. (1980). More on monkey talk. Response to Patterson's rejoinder to Martin Gardner's review of Nim and Speaking of Apes. *New York Review of Books,* December 4, 1980, p. 59.

Tessler, M., & Nelson, K. (1994). Making memories: The influence of joint encoding on later recall by young children. *Consciousness and Cognition: An International Journal, 3*(3-4), 307–326.

Tomasello, M. (2003). *Constructing a Language: A usage-based theory of language acquisition.* Cambridge, MA: Harvard University Press.

Tomasello, M., & Farrar, M. J. (1986). Joint attention and early language. *Child Development, 57*(6), 1454–1463.

Tomasello, M., & Barton, M. E. (1994). Learning words in nonostensive contexts. *Developmental Psychology, 30*(5), 639–650.

Townsend, S., Rasmussen, M., Clutton-Brock, T., & Manswer, M. (2012). *Flexible alarm calling in meerkats: The role of the social environment and predation urgency. Behavioral Ecology, 23,* 1360–1364.

Truswell, R. (2017). Dendrophobia in bonobo comprehension of spoken English. *Mind & Language, 32,* 395–415.

Trueswell, J. C., Sekerina, I., Hill, N. M., & Logrip, M. L. (1999). The kindergarten-path effect: Studying on-line sentence processing in young children. *Cognition, 73*(2), 89–134.

Tversky, B., Kugelmass, S., & Winter, A. (1991). Crosscultural and developmental trends in graphic productions. *Cognitive Psychology, 23,* 515–557.

Vygotsky, L. (1962). Studies in communication. In E. Hanfmann & G. Vakar (Eds.), *Thought and Language.* Cambridge, MA: The MIT Press.

Wagner, M., & Watson, D. G. (2010). Experimental and theoretical advances in prosody: A review. *Language and Cognitive Processes, 25*(7–9), 905–945.

Warren, R. M. (1970). Restoration of missing speech sounds. *Science, 167,* 392–393.

Watson, D. G., Jacobs, C. L., & Buxó-Lugo, A. (2020). Prosody indexes both competence and performance. *Cognitive Science, 11*(3), e1522.

Weighall, A. R. (2008). The kindergarten path effect revisited: Children's use of context in processing structural ambiguities. *Journal of Experimental Child Psychology, 99,* 75–95.

Werker, J. F. (1995). Exploring developmental changes in cross-language speech perception. In L. R. Gleitman & M. Liberman (Eds.), *Language: An invitation to cognitive science* (pp. 87–106). Cambridge, MA: The MIT Press.

Werker, J. F., Gilbert, J. H., Humphrey, K., & Tees, R. C. (1981). Developmental aspects of cross-language speech perception. *Child Development, 52*(1), 349–355.

Whorf, B. L. (1956). *Language, Thought, and Reality: Selected writings of Benjamin Lee Whorf.* New York: Wiley.

Winawer, J., Witthoft, N., Frank, M. C., et al. (2007). Russian blues reveal effects of language on color discrimination. *Proceedings of the National Academy of Sciences of the United States of America, 104*(19), 7780–7785.

Wolff, B., & Holmes, K. (2010). Linguistic relativity. *WIREs Cognitive Science, 2*(3), 253–265.

Woodward, A. L., Markman, E. M., & Fitzsimmons, C. M. (1994). Rapid word learning in 13- and 18-month-olds. *Developmental Psychology, 30*(4), 553–566.

Woodard, K., Pozzan, L., & Trueswell, J. C. (2016). Taking your own path: Individual differences in executive function and language processing skills in child learners. *Journal of Experimental Child Psychology, 141,* 187–209.

Wundt, W. (1900). *Die Sprache* [Language]. Leipzig: Verlag won Wilhelm Engelmann.

Zelazo, P. D., & Frye, D. (1998). Cognitive complexity and control. The development of executive function in childhood. *Current Directions in Psychological Science, 7,* 121–126.

Zipf, G. (1936). *The Psychobiology of Language.* London, UK: Routledge.

Chapter 9

Alter, A. L., & Oppenheimer, D. M. (2006). Predicting short-term stock fluctuations by using processing fluency. *Proceedings of the National Academy of Sciences of the United States of America, 103*(24), 9369–9372.

Ariely, D. (2008). *Predictably Irrational: The Hidden Forces That Shape Our Decisions.* New York: HarperCollins.

Arkes, H. R., & Ayton, P. (1999). The sunk cost and concorde effects: Are humans less rational than lower animals? *Psychological Bulletin, 125*(5), 591–600.

Balleine, B. W., Delgado, M. R., & Hikosaka, O. (2007). The role of the dorsal striatum in reward and decision-making. *The Journal of Neuroscience, 27*(31), 8161–8165.

Bechara, A. (1997). Deciding advantageously before knowing the advantageous strategy. *Science, 275*(5304), 1293–1295.

Bechara, A. (2005). Decision making, impulse control and loss of willpower to resist drugs: A neurocognitive perspective. *Nature Neuroscience, 8*(11), 1458–1463.

Bechara, A., Damasio, A. R., Damasio, H., & Anderson, S. W. (1994). Insensitivity to future consequences following damage to human prefrontal cortex. *Cognition, 50*(1–3), 7–15.

Bernoulli, D. (1738/1954). Exposition of a new theory on the measurement of risk. *Econometrica, 22*, 22–36.

Camerer, C., Loewenstein, G., & Prelec, D. (2005). Neuroeconomics: How neuroscience can inform economics. *Journal of Economic Literature, 43*(1), 9–64.

Chen, M. K., Lakshminarayanan, V., & Santos, L. R. (2006). How basic are behavioral biases? Evidence from capuchin monkey trading behavior. *Journal of Political Economy, 114*(3), 517–537.

Choi, J. J., Laibson, D., & Madrian, B. C. (2004). Plan design and 401(k) savings outcomes. *National Tax Journal, 57*, 275–298.

Davidson, R. J. (2000). Dysfunction in the neural circuitry of emotion regulation: A possible prelude to violence. *Science, 289*(5479), 591–594.

Dawkins, R., & Carlisle, T. R. (1976). Parental investment, mate desertion and a fallacy. *Nature, 262*(5564), 131–133.

Detweiler, J. B., Bedell, B. T., Salovey, P., et al. (1999). Message framing and sunscreen use: Gain-framed messages motivate beach-goers. *Health Psychology, 18*(2), 189–196.

Dijksterhuis, A., Bos, M. W., Nordgren, L. F., & van Baaren, R. B. (2006). On making the right choice: the deliberation-without-attention effect. *Science, 311*(5763), 1005–1007.

Elwyn, G., Edwards, A., Eccles, M., & Rovner, D. (2001). Decision analysis in patient care. *Lancet, 358*(9281), 571–574.

Gaissmaier, W., & Marewski, J. N. (2011). Forecasting elections with mere recognition from small, lousy samples: A comparison of collective recognition, wisdom of crowds, and representative polls. *Judgment and Decision Making, 6*(1), 73–88.

Gigerenzer, G., & Gaissmaier, W. (2011). Heuristic decision making. *Annual Review of Psychology, 62*, 451–482.

Gigerenzer, G., & Goldstein, D. G. (1996). Reasoning the fast and frugal way: Models of bounded rationality. *Psychological Review, 103*(4), 650–669.

Gilovich, T., Vallone, R., & Tversky, A. (1985). The hot hand in basketball: On the misperception of random sequences. *Cognitive Psychology, 17*(3), 295–314.

Green, L., & Mehr, D. R. (1997). What alters physicians' decisions to admit to the coronary care unit? *Journal of Family Practice, 45*(3), 219–226.

Hauser, J. R., Ding, M., & Gaskin, S. P. (2009). Non-compensatory (and compensatory) models of consideration-set decisions. *Proceedings of the Sawtooth Software Conference.*

Hertwig, R., Gigerenzer, G., & Hoffrage, U. (1997). The reiteration effect in hindsight bias. *Psychological Review, 104*(1), 194–202.

Hoyer, W. D., & Brown, S. P. (1990). Effects of brand awareness on choice for a common, repeat-purchase product. *Journal of Consumer Research, 17*, 141–148.

HRS Health Resources & Services Administration, U. S. Department of Health and Human Services, U. S. Government Information on Organ Donation and Transplantation. Last Rewiewed: April 2021.

Hsu, M., Bhatt, M., Adolphs, R., et al. (2005). Neural systems responding to degrees of uncertainty in human decision-making. *Science, 310*(5754), 1680–1683.

Jacoby, L. L., & Dallas, M. (1981). On the relationship between autobiographical memory and perceptual learning. *Journal of Experimental Psychology: General, 110*(3), 306–340.

Jacoby, L. L., Woloshyn, V., & Kelley, C. (1989). Becoming famous without being recognized: Unconscious influences of memory produced by dividing attention. *Journal of Experimental Psychology: General, 118*(2), 115–125.

Johnson, E. J., & Goldstein, D. G. (2003). Do defaults save lives? *Science, 302*, 1338–1339.

Kahneman, D., Knetsch, J. L., & Thaler, R. (n.d.). Fairness as a constraint on profit seeking: Entitlements in the market. *American Economic Review, 76*, 728–741.

Kahneman, D., & Tversky, A. (1979). Prospect theory: An analysis of decision under risk. *Econometrica*, Vol. 47, pp. 263–291.

Kahneman, D. (2003). A perspective on judgment and choice: Mapping bounded rationality. *The American Psychologist, 58*(9), 697–720.

Kahneman, D. (2011). *Thinking, Fast and Slow.* New York, NY: Farrar, Straus, and Giroux.

Kahneman, D., Knetsch, J. L., & Thaler, R. H. (1990). Experimental tests of the endowment effect and the coase theorem. *Journal of Political Economy, 98*(6), 1325–1348.

Kahneman, D., & Tversky, A. (1972). Subjective probability: A judgment of representativeness. *Cognitive Psychology, 3*(3), 430–454.

Kahneman, D., & Tversky, A. (1973). On the psychology of prediction. *Psychological Review, 80*(4), 237–251.

Kahneman, D., & Tversky, A. (1984). Choices, values, and frames. *American Psychologist, 39*(4), 341–350.

Knetsch, J. L., & Sinden, J. A. (1984). Willingness to pay and compensation demanded: Experimental evidence of an unexpected disparity in measures of value. *Quarterly Journal of Economics, 99*, 507–521.

Knutson, B., Rick, S., Wimmer, G. E., Prelec, D., & Loewenstein, G. (2007). Neural predictors of purchases. *Neuron, 53*(1), 147–156.

Levin, A. (2012). Green tip: Trayless dining. Retrieved from http://fesmag.com/features/foodservice-issues/10237-trayless-dining

Levy, I., Snell, J., Nelson, A. J., et al. (2010). Neural representation of subjective value under risk and ambiguity. *Journal of Neurophysiology, 103*(2), 1036–1047.

Madrian, B. C., & Shea, D. F. (2001). The power of suggestion: Inertia in 401(k) participation and savings behavior. *The Quarterly Journal of Economics, 116*(4), 1149–1187.

McCammon, I., & Hägeli, P. (2007). An evaluation of rule-based decision tools for travel in avalanche terrain. *Cold Regions Science and Technology, 47*(1–2), 193–206.

McNiel, B. J., Pauker, S. G., Sox, H. C., & Tversky, A. (1982). On the elicitation of preferences for alternative therapies. *New England Journal of Medicine, 306*(21), 1259–1262.

The Nielsen Company (US), LLC.

O'Doherty, J., Winston, J., Critchley, H., et al. (2003). Beauty in a smile: The role of medial orbitofrontal cortex in facial attractiveness. *Neuropsychologia, 41*(2), 147–155.

Paulus, M. P., Rogalsky, C., Simmons, A., et al. (2003). Increased activation in the right insula during risk-taking decision making is related to harm avoidance and neuroticism. *NeuroImage, 19*(4), 1439–1448.

Peters, E., & Slovic, P. (2000). The springs of action: Affective and analytical information processing in choice. *Personality and Social Psychology Bulletin, 26*(12), 1465–1475.

Petrie, M., & Halliday, T. (1994). Experimental and natural changes in the peacock's (*Pavo cristatus*) train can affect mating success. *Behavioral Ecology and Sociobiology, 35*(3), 213–217.

Phelps, E. A., Lempert, K. M., & Sokol-Hessner, P. (2014). Emotion and decision making: Multiple modulatory neural circuits. *Annual Review of Neuroscience, 37*, 263–287.

Plassmann, H., O'Doherty, J., & Rangel, A. (2007). Orbitofrontal cortex encodes willingness to pay in everyday economic transactions. *The Journal of Neuroscience, 27*(37), 9984–9988.

Plassmann, H., O'Doherty, J., Shiv, B., & Rangel, A. (2008). Marketing actions can modulate neural representations of experienced pleasantness. *Proceedings of the National Academy of Sciences of the United States of America, 105*(3), 1050–1054.

Pohl, R. F. (2006). Empirical tests of the recognition heuristic. *Journal of Behavioral Decision Making, 19*(3), 251–271.

Rahman, S. (1999). Specific cognitive deficits in mild frontal variant frontotemporal dementia. *Brain, 122*(8), 1469–1493.

Rangel, A., Camerer, C., & Montague, P. R. (2008). A framework for studying the neurobiology of value-based decision making. *Nature Reviews. Neuroscience, 9*(7), 545–556.

Rao, A. R., & Monroe, K. B. (1989). The effect of price, brand name, and store name on buyers' perceptions of product quality: An integrative review. *Journal of Marketing Research, 26*, 351–357.

Ropeik, D., & Holmes, N. (2003). Never bitten, twice shy: The real dangers of summer. *New York Times*, August 9, 2003.

http://www.nytimes.com/2003/08/09/opinion/09OPAR.html.

Ross, M., & Sicoly, F. (1979). Egocentric biases in availability and attribution. *Journal of Personality and Social Psychology, 37*(3), 322–336.

Rothman, A. J., & Salovey, P. (1997). Shaping perceptions to motivate healthy behavior: The role of message framing. *Psychological Bulletin, 121*(1), 3–19.

Schwartz, B., Ward, A., Monterosso, J., et al. (2002). Maximizing versus satisficing: Happiness is a matter of choice. *Journal of Personality and Social Psychology, 83*(5), 1178–1197.

Serwe, S., and Frings, C. (2006). Who will win Wimbledon? The recognition heuristic in predicting sports events. *Journal of Behavior and Decision Making, 19*(4), 321–332.

Shiv, B., Loewenstein, G., & Bechara, A. (2005). The dark side of emotion in decision-making: When individuals with decreased emotional reactions make more advantageous decisions. *Cognitive Brain Research, 23*(1), 85–92.

Simon, H. A. (1979). Rational decision making in business organizations. *American Economic Review, 69*, 493–513.

Staw, B. M., & Hoang, H. (1995). Sunk costs in the NBA: Why draft order affects playing time and survival in professional basketball. *Administrative Science Quarterly, 40*(3), 474.

Thaler, R. (1980). Toward a positive theory of consumer choice. *Journal of Economic Behavior & Organization, 1*(1), 39–60.

Tversky, A., & Kahneman, D. (1974). Judgment under uncertainty: heuristics and biases. Biases in judgments reveal some heuristics of thinking under uncertainty. *Science, 185*, 1124–1131.

Tversky, A., & Kahneman, D. (1981). The framing of decisions and the psychology of choice. *Science, 211*(4481), 453–458.

Tversky, A., & Kahneman, D. (1973). Availability: A heuristic for judging frequency and probability. *Cognitive Psychology, 5*(2), 207–232.

Tversky, A., & Kahneman, D. (1983). Extensional versus intuitive reasoning: The conjunction fallacy in probability judgment. *Psychological Review, 90*(4), 293–315.

Tversky, A., & Kahneman, D. (1992). Advances in prospect theory: Cumulative representation of uncertainty. *Journal of Risk and Uncertainty, 5*(4), 297–323.

U.S. Department of Health & Human Services. (2015). Chris Domine: Getting a second chance, and running with it. Retrieved from http://www.organdonor.gov/lifestories/chris-kidney-recipient.html

Wallis, J. D. (2007). Orbitofrontal cortex and its contribution to decision-making. *Annual Review of Neuroscience, 30*, 31–56.

Wilson, T. D., Lisle, D. J., Schooler, J. W., et al. (1993). Introspecting about reasons can reduce post-choice satisfaction. *Personality and Social Psychology Bulletin, 19*, 331–339.

Wisdom, J., Downs, J. S., & Loewenstein, G. (2010). Promoting healthy choices: Information versus convenience. *American Economic Journal: Applied Economics, 2*(2), 164–178.

Zajonc, R. B. (1968). Attitudinal effects of mere exposure. *Journal of Personality and Social Psychology, 9*(2, Pt.2), 1–27.

Chapter 10

Ahn, W.-K., Kim, N. S., Lassaline, M. E., & Dennis, M. J. (2000). Causal status as a determinant of feature centrality. *Cognitive Psychology, 41*(4), 361–416.

Ahn, W.-K., Kalish, C. W., Medin, D. L., & Gelman, S. A. (1995). The role of covariation versus mechanism information in causal attribution. *Cognition, 54*(3), 299–352.

Amabile, T. M. (1982). Children's artistic creativity: Detrimental effects of competition in a field setting. *Personality and Social Psychology Bulletin, 8*(3), 573–578.

Amabile, T. M. (1987). The motivation to be creative. In *Frontiers of Creativity Research: Beyond the Basics*. S. Isaksen (Ed.). Buffalo, NY: Bearly, Ltd.

Amabile, T. M. (1998). How to kill creativity. *Harvard Business Review, 76*(5).

Amabile, T. M., & Gryskiewicz, N. D. (1989). The creative environment scales: Work environment inventory. *Creativity Research Journal, 2*(4), 231–253.

Axelrod, R., & Hamilton, W. D. (1981). The evolution of cooperation. *Science, 211*(4489), 1390–1396.

Baron-Cohen, S., Leslie, A. M., & Frith, U. (1985). Does the autistic child have a "theory of mind"? *Cognition, 21*(1), 37–46.

Bassok, M., & Novick, L. R. (2012). Problem solving. In K. J. Holyoak & R. G. Morrison (Eds.), *The Oxford Handbook of Thinking and Reasoning*. New York: Oxford University Press.

Baumeister, R. F., Bratslavsky, E., Muraven, M., & Tice, D. M. (1998). Ego depletion: Is the active self a limited resource? *Journal of Personality and Social Psychology, 74*(5), 1252–1265.

Beaty, R. R., Benedek, M., Silvia, P. J., & Schacter, D. L. (2016). Creative cognition and brain network dynamics. *Trends in Cognitive Sciences, 20*(2), 87–95.

Bransford, J. D., Brown, A. L., & Cocking, R. R. (2000). *How People Learn: Brain, Mind, Experience, and School*. Washington, D.C.: National Academy Press.

Casey, B. J. (2014). Beyond simple models of self-control to circuit-based accounts of adolescent behavior. *Annual Review of Psychology, 66*, 295–319.

Chapman, L. J. (1967). Illusory correlation in observational report. *Journal of Verbal Learning and Verbal Behavior, 6*, 151–155.

Chase, W. G., & Simon, H. A. (1973). Perception in chess. *Cognitive Psychology, 4*(1), 55–81.

Chater, N., Tenenbaum, J. B., & Yuille, A. (2006). Probabilistic models of cognition: Conceptual foundations. *Trends in Cognitive Sciences, 10*(7), 287–291.

Cheng, P. W., & Holyoak, K. J. (1985). Pragmatic reasoning schemas. *Cognitive Psychology, 17*(4), 391–416.

Chi, M. T. H., Feltovich, P. J., & Glaser, R. (1981). Categorization and representation of physics problems by experts and novices. *Cognitive Science, 5*(2), 121–152.

Cohen, A. O., & Casey, B. J. (2014). Rewiring juvenile justice: The intersection of developmental neuroscience and legal policy. *Trends in Cognitive Sciences, 18*(2), 63–65.

Cushman, F., & Young, L. (2011). Patterns of moral judgment derive from nonmoral psychological representations. *Cognitive Science, 35*, 1052–1075.

Dahl, R. E. (2001). Affect regulation, brain development, and behavioral/emotional health in adolescence. *CNS Spectrums, 6*(1), 60–72.

Davies, J. (2002). *Visual abstraction in analogical problem solving: A dissertation proposal*. Georgia Institute of Technology.

de Groot, A. (1965). *Thought and Choice in Chess*. The Hague: Mouton.

Diedrich, J., Benedek, M., Jauk, E., & Neubauer, A. C. (2015). Are creative ideas novel and useful? *Psychology of Aesthetics, Creativity, and the Arts, 9*(1), 35–40.

Duncker, K. (1945). On problem solving. *Psychological Monographs, 58*, i–113.

Ericsson, K. A., & Charness, N. (1994). Expert performance: Its structure and acquisition. *American Psychologist, 49*(8), 725–747.

Evans, J. S. B. T. (2013). Reasoning. In D. Reisberg (Ed.), *The Oxford Handbook of Cognitive Psychology*. New York: Oxford University Press.

Evans, J. S. B. T., Handley, S. J., & Harper, C. N. J. (2001). Necessity, possibility and belief: A study of syllogistic reasoning. *Quarterly Journal of Experimental Psychology Section A: Human Experimental Psychology, 54A*(3), 935–958.

Feeney, A., & Heit, E. (2011). Properties of the diversity effect in category-based inductive reasoning. *Thinking and Reasoning, 17*(2), 156–181.

Fehr, E., & Fischbacher, U. (2004). Social norms and human cooperation. *Trends in Cognitive Sciences, 8*(4), 185–190.

Fenker, D. B., Waldmann, M. R., & Holyoak, K. J. (2005). Accessing causal relations in semantic memory. *Memory and Cognition, 33*, 1036–1046.

Fiddick, L., Cosmides, L., & Tooby, J. (2000). No interpretation without representation: The role of domain-specific representations and inferences in the Wason selection task. *Cognition, 77*(1), 1–79.

Finke, R. A., Ward, T. B., & Smith, S. M. (1992). *Creative Cognition: Theory, Research, and Applications*. Cambridge, MA: The MIT Press.

Fridja, N. H., & de Groot, A. D. (1982). *Otto Selz: His contribution to psychology*. The Hague: Mouton.

Gallagher, H. L., & Frith, C. D. (2003). Functional imaging of 'theory of mind.' *Trends in Cognitive Sciences, 7*(2), 77–83.

Gardner, H. (1983). *Frames of Mind: The Theory of Multiple Intelligences*. New York: Basic Books.

Gauthier, I., Skudlarski, P., Gore, J. C., & Anderson, A. W. (2000). Expertise for cars and birds recruits brain areas involved in face recognition. *Nature Neuroscience, 3*(2), 191–197.

Gelman, S. A., & Markman, E. M. (1986). Categories and induction in young children. *Cognition, 23*(3), 183–209.

Getzels, J. W. (1975). Problem-finding and the inventiveness of solutions. *The Journal of Creative Behavior, 9*(1), 12–18.

Getzels, J. W., & Csikszentmihalyi, M. (1972). The creative artist as an explorer. In J. McVicker Hunt (Ed.), *Human Intelligence*. Oxford: Transaction Books. 182–192.

Getzels, J. W., & Csikszentmihalyi, M. (1976). *The Creative Vision: A Longitudinal Study of Problem Finding in Art*. New York: John Wiley & Sons.

Gick, M. L., & Holyoak, K. J. (1980). Analogical problem solving. *Cognitive Psychology, 12*(3), 306–355.

Gigerenzer, G., & Edwards, A. (2003). Simple tools for understanding risks: From innumeracy to insight. *British Medical Journal, 327*(7417), 741–744.

Gigerenzer, G., & Hug, K. (1992). Domain-specific reasoning: Social contracts, cheating, and perspective change. *Cognition, 43*(2), 127–171.

Gigerenzer, G. (2002). *Calculated Risks: How to Know When Numbers Deceive You*. New York: Simon and Schuster.

Gigerenzer, G., & Hoffrage, U. (1995). How to improve Bayesian reasoning without instruction: Frequency formats. *Psychological Review, 102*(4), 684–704.

Giordano, L. A., Bickel, W. K., Loewenstein, G., et al. (2002). Mild opioid deprivation increases the degree that opioid-dependent outpatients discount delayed heroin and money. *Psychopharmacology, 163*(2), 174–182.

Gobet, F., Lane, P. C. R., Croker, S., et al. (2001). Chunking mechanisms in human learning. *Trends in Cognitive Sciences, 5*, 236–243.

Gopnik, A., Sobel, D. M., Danks, D., et al. (2004). A theory of causal learning in children: Causal maps and bayes nets. *Psychological Review, 111*(1), 3–32.

Guildford, J. P. (1950). Creativity. *American Psychologist, 5*(9), 444–454.

Hayes, B. K., & Heit, E. (2013). Induction. In D. Reisberg (Ed.), *The Oxford Handbook of Cognitive Psychology*. New York: Oxford University Press.

Holyoak, K. J., & Cheng, P. W. (2011). Causal learning and inference as a rational process: The new synthesis. *Annual Review of Psychology, 62*, 135–163.

Insel, T. R., & Young, L. J. (2001). The neurobiology of attachment. *Nature Reviews. Neuroscience, 2*(2), 129–136.

Jarrard, R. D. (2001). Scientific Methods. [E-book]. Available: https://www.emotionalcompetency.com/sci/sm_all.pdf. 236p. Accessed May 24, 2021.

Joireman, J., Balliet, D., Sprott, D., et al. (2008). Consideration of future consequences, ego-depletion, and self-control: Support for distinguishing between CFC-Immediate and CFC-Future sub-scales. *Personality and Individual Differences, 45*(1), 15–21.

Jung, R. E., Mead, B. S., Carrasco, J., & Flores, R. A. (2013). The structure of creative cognition in the human brain. *Frontiers in Human Neuroscience, 7*, 330.

Kaufman, S. B. (2014). The controlled chaos of creativity. Scientific American (blog). June 25, 2014, https://blogs.scientificamerican.com/beautiful-minds/the-controlled-chaos-of-creativity/.

Kim, K. H. (2006). Can we trust creativity tests? A review of the Torrance tests of creative thinking (TTCT). *Creativity Research Journal, 18*(1), 3–14.

Kim, N. S., & Keil, F. C. (2003). From symptoms to causes: Diversity effects in diagnostic reasoning. *Memory and Cognition, 31*(1), 155–165.

Kosfeld, M., Heinrichs, M., Zak, P. J., et al. (2005). Oxytocin increases trust in humans. *Nature, 435*(7042), 673–676.

Leslie, A. M., & Keeble, S. (1987). Do six-month-old infants perceive causality? *Cognition, 25*(3), 265–288.

Lien, Y., & Cheng, P. W. (2000). Distinguishing genuine from spurious causes: A coherence hypothesis. *Cognitive Psychology, 40*(2), 87–137.

López, A., Gelman, S. A., Gutheil, G., & Smith, E. E. (1992). The development of category-based induction. *Child Development, 63*(5), 1070–1090.

Lord, C. G., Ross, L., & Lepper, M. R. (1979). Biased assimilation and attitude polarization: The effects of prior theories on subsequently considered evidence. *Journal of Personality and Social Psychology, 37*(11), 2098–2109.

Maier, N. R. F. (1930). Reasoning in humans. I. On direction. *Journal of Comparative Psychology, 10*, 15–43.

Mayer, R. E. (2013). Problem solving. In D. Reisberg (Ed.), *The Oxford Handbook of Cognitive Psychology*. New York: Oxford University Press.

McCabe, K., Houser, D., Ryan, L., et al. (2001). A functional imaging study of cooperation in two-person reciprocal exchange. *Proceedings of the National Academy of Sciences of the United States of America, 98*(20), 11832–11835.

Mednick, S. (1962). The associative basis of the creative process. *Psychological Review, 69*(3), 220–232.

Mednick, S. (1968). The remote associates test. *The Journal of Creative Behavior, 2*, 213–214.

Metcalfe, J., & Wiebe, D. (1987). Intuition in insight and noninsight problem solving. *Memory & Cognition, 15*(3), 238–246.

Michotte, A. (1963). *The Perception of Causality*. London: Routledge.

Mischel, W., Shoda, Y., & Rodriguez, M. I. (1989). Delay of gratification in children. *Science, 244*, 933–938.

Mischel, W. (2014). *The Marshmallow Test: Mastering self-control*. New York: Little, Brown and Co.

Murphy, R. (n.d.). 10 most superstitious athletes. Retrieved July 15, 2018, from Men's Journal website: https://www.mensjournal.com/sports/10-most-superstitious-athletes/

Murray, H. A. (1938). *Explorations in Personality*. New York: Oxford University Press.

Newell, A., & Simon, H. A. (1972). *Human Problem Solving*. Englewood Cliffs, NJ: Prentice-Hall.

Newell, B. R., & Pitman, A. J. (2010). The psychology of global warming. *Bulletin of the American Meteorological Society, 91*(8), 1003–1014.

Nickerson, R. S. (1998). Confirmation bias: A ubiquitous phenomenon in many guises. *Review of General Psychology, 2*(2), 175–220.

Nunes, T., Schliemann, A. D., & Carraher, D. W. (1993). *Street Mathematics and School Mathematics*. Cambridge: Cambridge University Press.

Osherson, D. N., Wilkie, O., Smith, E. E., et al. (1990). Category-based induction. *Psychological Review, 97*(2), 185–200.

Pearl, J. (2011). *Causality: Models, Reasoning, and Inference, Second Edition*. Cambridge: Cambridge University Press.

Pink, D. H. (2006). *A Whole New Mind: Why Right-Brainers will Rule the Future*. New York: Riverhead Books.

Proctor, D., Williamson, R. A., de Waal, F. B. M., & Brosnan, S. F. (2013). Chimpanzees play the ultimatum game. *Proceedings of the National Academy of Sciences of the United States of America, 110*(6), 2070–2075.

Redelmeier, D. A., & Tversky, A. (1996). On the belief that arthritis pain is related to the weather. *Proceedings of the National Academy of Sciences of the United States of America, 93*, 2895–2896.

Rhodes, M. (1961/1987). An analysis of creativity. *The Phi Delta Kappan, 42*, 305–310.

Rilling, J. K., Gutman, D. A., Zeh, T. R., et al. (2002). A neural basis for social cooperation. *Neuron, 35*(2), 395–405.

Rips, L. J. (1975). Inductive judgments about natural categories. *Journal of Verbal Learning and Verbal Behavior, 14*(6), 665–681.

Robbins, P., & Aydede, M. (2008). *The Cambridge Handbook of Situated Cognition*. Cambridge: Cambridge University Press.

Roese, N. J. (1997). Counterfactual thinking. *Psychological Bulletin, 121*(1), 133–148.

Runco, M. A. (2004). Creativity. *Annual Review of Psychology, 55*, 657–687.

Runco, M. A., & Jaeger, G. J. (2012). The standard definition of creativity. *Creativity Research Journal, 24*(1), 92–96.

Sally, D., & Hill, E. (2006). The development of interpersonal strategy: Autism, theory-of-mind, cooperation and fairness. *Journal of Economic Psychology, 27*(1), 73–97.

Samanez-Larkin, G. R., & Knutson, B. (2015). Decision making in the ageing brain: Changes in affective and motivational circuits. *Nature Reviews. Neuroscience, 16*(5), 278–289.

Sanfey, A. G., Rilling, J. K., Aronson, J. A., et al. (2003). The neural basis of economic decision-making in the Ultimatum Game. *Science, 300*(5626), 1755–1758.

Schellenberg, E. G. (2004). Music lessons enhance IQ. *Psychological Science, 15*(8), 511–514.

Scholl, B. J., & Tremoulet, P. D. (2000). Perceptual causality and animacy. *Trends in Cognitive Sciences, 4*, 299–309.

Silver, N. (2012). *The Signal and the Noise: Why So Many Predictions Fail—but Some Don't*. New York: Penguin Books.

Singley, M. K., & Anderson, J. R. (1989). *The Transfer of Cognitive Skill*. Cambridge, MA: Harvard University Press.

Sloman, S. A. (1993). Feature-based induction. *Cognitive Psychology, 25*(2), 231–280.

Sloman, S. A., & Lagnado, D. (2015). Causality in thought. *Annual Review of Psychology, 66*, 223–247.

Sloman, S. A., & Lagnado, D. A. (2005). Do we "do"? *Cognitive Science, 29*(1), 5–39.

Spellman, B. A., & Mandel, D. R. (2006). Psychology of causal reasoning. In *Encyclopedia of Cognitive Science*. Hoboken, NJ: John Wiley & Sons, Ltd.

Steinberg, L. (2008). A social neuroscience perspective on adolescent risk-taking. *Developmental Review, 28*(1), 78–106.

Steyvers, M., Tenenbaum, J. B., Wagenmakers, E.-J., & Blum, B. (2003). Inferring causal networks from observations and interventions. *Cognitive Science, 27*(3), 453–489.

Takagishi, H., Kameshima, S., Schug, J., Koizumi, M., & Yamagishi, T. (2010). Theory of mind enhances preference for fairness. *Journal of Experimental Child Psychology, 105*(1–2), 130–137.

Tenenbaum, J. B., Griffiths, T. L., & Kemp, C. (2006). Theory-based Bayesian models of inductive learning and reasoning. *Trends in Cognitive Sciences, 10*(7), 309–318.

Torrange, E. P. (1966). Torrance tests of creative thinking. Norms-technical manual. Research edition. Verbal tests, forms A and B. Figural tests, forms A and B. Princeton, NJ: Personnel Press.

Waldmann, M. R., & Hagmayer, Y. (2013). Causal Reasoning. In D. Reisberg (Ed.), *Oxford Handbook of Cognitive Psychology*. New York: Oxford University Press.

Wason, P. C. (1968). Reasoning about a rule. *The Quarterly Journal of Experimental Psychology, 20*(3), 273–281.

Wertheimer, M. (1959). *Productive Thinking*. New York: Harper.

Whitmarsh, L. (2008). What's in a name? Commonalities and differences in public understanding of "climate change" and "global warming." *Public Understanding of Science, 18*(4), 401–420.

Wilson, B. A. (2010). *Fundations, Nonsense Word Lists: Level 3, unit 1*. Wilson Language Training: Oxford, MA. Retrieved July 25, 2018, from http://bhm.link75.org/common/pages/DisplayFile.aspx?itemId=802187

Witt, L. A., & Beorkrem, M. N. (1989). Climate for creative productivity as a predictor of research usefulness and organizational effectiveness in an R&D organization. *Creativity Research Journal, 2*(1–2), 30–40.

Yuille, A., & Kersten, D. (2006). Vision as Bayesian inference: Analysis by synthesis? *Trends in Cognitive Sciences, 10*(7), 301–308.

Zak, P. J., Stanton, A. A., & Ahmadi, S. (2007). Oxytocin increases generosity in humans. *PLOS ONE, 2*(11), e1128.

Zhang, H.-B., Dai, H.-C., Lai, H.-X., & Wang, W.-T. (2017). U.S. withdrawal from the Paris Agreement: Reasons, impacts, and China's response. *Advances in Climate Change Research, 8*(4), 220–225.

Chapter 11

Anderson, J. R. (1990). *The Adaptive Character of Thought*. Hillsdale, NJ: Lawrence Erlbaum Associates, Inc.

Au, J., Sheehan, E., Tsai, N., et al. (2015). Improving fluid intelligence with training on working memory: A meta-analysis. *Psychonomic Bulletin and Review, 22*(2), 366–377.

Bahník, Š., & Vranka, M. A. (2017). Growth mindset is not associated with scholastic aptitude in a large sample of university applicants. *Personality and Individual Differences, 117*, 139–143.

Baillargeon, R. (1987). Object permanence in 3 1/2- and 4 1/2-month-old infants. *Developmental Psychology, 23*(5), 655–664.

Barrett, G. V., & Depinet, R. L. (1991). A reconsideration of testing for competence rather than for intelligence. *American Psychologist, 46*, 1012–1024.

Barsalou, L. W. (1983). Ad hoc categories. *Memory & Cognition, 11*(3), 211–227.

Barsalou, L. W. (1999). Perceptual symbol systems. *Behavioral and Brain Sciences, 22*(4), 577–609.

Barsalou, L. W. (2008). Grounded cognition. In *Annual Review of Psychology, 59*, 617–645.

Binet, A., & Simon, T. (1916). *New methods for the diagnosis of the intellectual level of subnormals. (L'Année Psych., 1905, pp. 191-244).* In A. Binet, T. Simon & E. S. Kite (Trans.), *The development of intelligence in children (The Binet-Simon Scale)* (pp. 37–90). Philadelphia: Williams & Wilkins Co.

Blackwell, L. S., Trzesniewski, K. H., & Dweck, C. S. (2007). Implicit theories of intelligence predict achievement across an adolescent transition: a longitudinal study and an intervention. *Child Development, 78*(1), 246–263.

Breedlove, S. M. (2015). *Principles of Psychology*. Sunderland, MA: Oxford University Press/Sinauer.

Brody, N. (2003). Construct validation of the Sternberg Triarchic abilities test: Comment and reanalysis. *Intelligence, 31*(4), 319–329.

Brown, R. (1958). How shall a thing be called? *Psychological Review, 65*(1), 14–21.

Caramazza, A., & Mahon, B. Z. (2003). The organization of conceptual knowledge: The evidence from category-specific semantic deficits. *Trends in Cognitive Sciences, 7*(8), 354–361.

Caramazza, A., & Shelton, J. R. (1998). Domain-specific knowledge systems in the brain: The animate-inanimate distinction. *Journal of Cognitive Neuroscience, 10*(1), 1–34.

Carpenter, P. A., Just, M. A., & Shell, P. (1990). What one intelligence test measures: A theoretical account of the processing in the Raven progressive matrices test. *Psychological Review, 97*(3), 404–431.

Carroll, J. B. (1993). *Human Cognitive Abilities: A Survey Of Factor-Analytic Studies*. Cambridge: Cambridge University Press.

Cattell, R. B. (1943). The description of personality: Basic traits resolved into clusters. *The Journal of Abnormal and Social Psychology, 38*(4), 476–506.

Cattell, R. B. (1971). *Abilities: Their Structure, Growth, And Action*. Boston: Houghton Mifflin.

Ceci, S. J. (1991). How much does schooling influence general intelligence and its cognitive components? A reassessment of the evidence. *Developmental Psychology, 27*(5), 703–722.

Chabris, C. F., Hebert, B. M., Benjamin, D. J., et al. (2012). Most reported genetic associations with general intelligence are probably false positives. *Psychological Science, 23*(11), 1314–1323.

Chao, L. L., Haxby, J. V., & Martin, A. (1999). Attribute-based neural substrates in temporal cortex for perceiving and knowing about objects. *Nature Neuroscience, 2*(10), 913–919.

Chen, J.-Q. (2004). Theory of multiple intelligences: Is it a scientific theory? *Teachers College Record, 106*, 17–23.

Collins, A. M., & Quillian, M. R. (1969). Retrieval time from semantic memory. *Journal of Verbal Learning and Verbal Behavior, 8*(2), 240–247.

Colom, R., Román, F. J., Abad, F. J., et al. (2013). Adaptive n-back training does not improve fluid intelligence at the construct level: Gains on individual tests suggest that training may enhance visuospatial processing. *Intelligence, 41*(5), 712–727.

Conway, A. R. A., Kane, M. J., & Engle, R. W. (2003). Working memory capacity and its relation to general intelligence. *Trends in Cognitive Sciences, 7*(12), 547–552.

Cooper, H., Nye, B., Charlton, K., et al. (1996). The effects of summer vacation on achievement test scores: A narrative and meta-analytic review. *Review of Educational Research, 66*(3), 227–268.

Cronbach, L. J., & Snow, R. E. (1977). *Aptitudes And Instructional Methods: A handbook for research on interactions*. Oxford: Irvington.

Deary, I. J. (2012). Intelligence. *Annual Review of Psychology, 63*, 453–482.

Deary, I. J., & Der, G. (2005). Reaction time explains IQ's association with death. *Psychological Science, 16*(1), 64–69.

DeLoache, J. S. (1987). Rapid change in the symbolic functioning of very young children. *Science, 238*(4833), 1556–1557.

DeLoache, J. S., Miller, K. F., & Rosengren, K. S. (1997). The credible shrinking room: Very young children's performance with symbolic and nonsymbolic relations. *Psychological Science, 8*(4), 308–313.

Dewar, K. M., & Xu, F. (2010). Induction, overhypothesis, and the origin of abstract knowledge: Evidence from 9-month-old infants. *Psychological Science, 21*(12), 1871–1877.

Duckworth, A. L., & Seligman, M. E. P. (2005). Self-discipline outdoes IQ in predicting academic performance of adolescents. *Psychological Science, 16*(12), 939–944.

Duncan, J. (2000). A neural basis for general intelligence. *Science, 289*(5478), 457–460.

Dweck, C. S. (2006). *Mindset: The new psychology of success*. New York: Random House.

Dweck, C. S. (2015). *Growth. British Journal of Educational Psychology, 85*, 242–245.

Engle, R. W. (2002). Working memory capacity as executive attention. *Current Directions in Psychological Science, 11*(1), 19–23.

Engle, R. W., Cantor, J., & Carullo, J. J. (1992). Individual differences in working memory and comprehension: A test of four hypotheses. *Journal of Experimental Psychology. Learning, Memory, and Cognition, 18*(5), 972–992.

Federal Trade Commission. (2016). Lumosity to pay $2 million to settle FTC deceptive advertising charges for its "brain training" program. Retrieved December 31, 2019, from https://www.ftc.gov/news-events/press-releases/2016/01/lumosity-pay-2-million-settle-ftc-deceptive-advertising-charges

Fei, X., & Carey, S. (1996). Infants' metaphysics: The case of numerical identity. *Cognitive Psychology, 30*(2), 111–153.

Feigenson, L., Dehaene, S., & Spelke, E. (2004). Core systems of number. *Trends in Cognitive Sciences, 8*(7), 307–314.

Finn, E. S., Shen, X., Scheinost, D., et al. (2015). Functional connectome fingerprinting: Identifying individuals using patterns of brain connectivity. *Nature Neuroscience, 18*(11), 1664–1671.

Gardner, H. (1983). *Frames of Mind: The theory of multiple intelligences.* New York: Basic Books.

Gardner, H. (1999). *Intelligence Reframed: Multiple intelligences for the 21st century.* New York: Basic Books.

Gelman, S. A. (2007). *The Essential Child: Origins of essentialism in everyday thought.* New York: Oxford University Press.

Gelman, S. A., & Markman, E. M. (1986). Categories and induction in young children. *Cognition, 23*(3), 183–209.

Goren, C. C., Sarty, M., & Wu, P. Y. K. (1975). Visual following and pattern discrimination of face like stimuli by newborn infants. *Pediatrics, 56*(4), 544–549.

Gottfredson, L. S., & Deary, I. J. (2004). Intelligence predicts health and longevity, but why? *Current Directions in Psychological Science, 13*(1), 1–4.

Graner, J., Oakes, T. R., French, L. M., & Riedy, G. (2013). Functional MRI in the investigation of blast-related traumatic brain injury. *Frontiers in Neurology, 4*, 16.

Gray, J. R., Chabris, C. F., & Braver, T. S. (2003). Neural mechanisms of general fluid intelligence. *Nature Neuroscience, 6*(3), 316–322.

Hamlin, J. K., Wynn, K., & Bloom, P. (2007). Social evaluation by preverbal infants. *Nature, 450*(7169), 557–559.

Harrison, T. L., Shipstead, Z., Hicks, K. L., et al. (2013). Working memory training may increase working memory capacity but not fluid intelligence. *Psychological Science, 24*(12), 2409–2419.

Haxby, J. V, Gobbini, M. I., Furey, M. L., et al. (2001). Distributed and overlapping representations of faces and objects in ventral temporal cortex. *Science, 293*(5539), 2425–2430.

Ho, Y.-C., Cheung, M.-C., & Chan, A. S. (2003). Music training improves verbal but not visual memory: Cross-sectional and longitudinal explorations in children. *Neuropsychology, 17*(3), 439–450.

Hughes, M., & Donaldson, M. (1979). The use of hiding games for studying the coordination of viewpoints. *Educational Review, 31*(2), 133–140.

Hyde, K. L., Lerch, J., & Norton, A., et al. (2009). Musical training shapes structural brain development. *The Journal of Neuroscience, 29*(10), 3019–3025.

Inhelder, B., & Piaget, J. (1958). *The Growth of Logical Thinking: From childhood to adolescence.* (A. Parsons & S. Milgram, Trans.). New York: Basic Books.

Ishai, A., Ungerleider, L. G., & Haxby, J. V. (2000). Distributed neural systems for the generation of visual images. *Neuron, 28*(3), 979–990.

Jaeggi, S. M., Buschkuehl, M., Jonides, J., & Perrig, W. J. (2008). Improving fluid intelligence with training on working memory. *Proceedings of the National Academy of Sciences of the United States of America, 105*(19), 6829–6833.

Jaeggi, S. M., Buschkuehl, M., Jonides, J., & Shah, P. (2011). Short- and long-term benefits of cognitive training. *Proceedings of the National Academy of Sciences of the United States of America, 108*(25), 10081–10086.

Jensen, A. R. (1998). *The g Factor: The science of mental ability.* Westport, CT: Praeger Publishers/Greenwood Publishing Group.

Just, M. A., & Carpenter, P. A. (1992). A capacity theory of comprehension: Individual differences in working memory. *Psychological Review, 99*(1), 122–149.

Keil, F. C. (2013). *Developmental Psychology.* New York: W.W. Norton & Company.

Kelly, D. J., Quinn, P. C., Slater, A. M., et al. (2007). The other-race effect develops during infancy: Evidence of perceptual narrowing. *Psychological Science, 18*(12), 1084–1089.

Kelly, D. J., Quinn, P. C., Slater, A. M., et al. (2005). Three-month-olds, but not newborns, prefer own-race faces. *Developmental Science, 8*(6), F31–F36.

Kim, I. K., & Spelke, E. S. (1992). Infants' sensitivity to effects of gravity on visible object motion. *Journal of Experimental Psychology: Human Perception and Performance, 18*(2), 385–393.

Koopman, P. R., & Ames, E. W. (1968). Infants' preferences for facial arrangements: A failure to replicate. *Child Development, 39*(2), 481–487.

Kuhn, D. (1989). Children and adults as intuitive scientists. *Psychological Review, 96*(4), 674–689.

Kuhn, D., & Brannock, J. (1977). Development of the isolation of variables scheme in experimental and "natural experiment" contexts. *Developmental Psychology, 13*(1), 9–14.

Kyllonen, P. C., & Christal, R. E. (1990). Reasoning ability is (little more than) working-memory capacity?! *Intelligence, 14*(4), 389–433.

Langlois, J. H., & Roggman, L. A. (1990). Attractive faces are only average. *Psychological Science, 1*(2), 115–121.

Langlois, J. H., Roggman, L. A., Casey, R. J., et al. (1987). Infant preferences for attractive faces: Rudiments of a stereotype? *Developmental Psychology, 23*(3), 363–369.

Lindley, R. H., & Smith, W. R. (1992). Coding tests as measures of IQ: Cognition or motivation? *Personality and Individual Differences, 13*(1), 25–29.

Lindsay, P. H., & Norman, D. A. (1972). *Human Information Processing: An Introduction to Psychology*. New York: Academic Press, 142.

Lubinski, D. (2004). Introduction to the special section on cognitive abilities: 100 years after Spearman's (1904) "'General intelligence,' objectively determined and measured." *Journal of Personality and Social Psychology, 86*(1), 96–111.

Malt, B. C., & Smith, E. E. (1984). Correlated properties in natural categories. *Journal of Verbal Learning & Verbal Behavior, 23*(2), 250–269.

Mandler, J. M., & McDonough, L. (1993). Concept formation in infancy. *Cognitive Development, 8*(3), 291–318.

Markman, A. B., & Rein, J. R. (2013). The nature of mental concepts. In D. Reisberg (Ed.), *The Oxford Handbook of Cognitive Psychology*. New York: Oxford University Press.

Martin, A. (2007). The representation of object concepts in the brain. In *Annual Review of Psychology, 58*, 25–45.

Martin, A., Haxby, J. V., Lalonde, F. M., et al. (1995). Discrete cortical regions associated with knowledge of color and knowledge of action. *Science, 270*(5233), 102–105.

Martin, A., Wiggs, C. L., Ungerleider, L. G., & Haxby, J. V. (1996). Neural correlates of category-specific knowledge. *Nature, 379*(6566), 649–652.

Mayer, J. D., & Salovey, P. (1997). What is emotional intelligence? In P. Salovey & D. J. Sluyter (Eds.), *Emotional Development and Emotional Intelligence: Educational Implications*. New York: Basic Books. 3–34.

McClelland, J. L., & Rumelhart, D. E. (1981). An interactive activation model of context effects in letter perception: I. An account of basic findings. *Psychological Review, 88*(5), 375–407.

McClelland, J. L., Rumelhart, D. E., & Hinton, G. E. (1986). The appeal of parallel distributed processing. In D. E. Rumelhart, J. L. McClelland and the PDP Research Group (Eds.), *Parallel Distributed Processing: Explorations in the Microstructure of Cognition*, Vol. 1. Cambridge, MA: MIT Press, 3–40.

McGarrigle, J., & Donaldson, M. (1974). Conservation accidents. *Cognition, 3*(4), 341–350.

Medin, D. L., & Schaffer, M. M. (1978). Context theory of classification learning. *Psychological Review, 85*(3), 207–238.

Miller, L. T., & Vernon, P. A. (1992). The general factor in short-term memory, intelligence, and reaction time. *Intelligence, 16*(1), 5–29.

Mitchell, T. M., Shinkareva, S. V., Carlson, A., et al. (2008). Predicting human brain activity associated with the meanings of nouns. *Science, 320*(5880), 1191–1195.

Moreno, S., Bialystok, E., Barac, R., et al. (2011). Short-term music training enhances verbal intelligence and executive function. *Psychological Science, 22*(11), 1425–1433.

Moscovitch, M., Winocur, G., & Behrmann, M. (1997). What is special about face recognition? Nineteen experiments on a person with visual object agnosia and dyslexia but normal face recognition. *Journal of Cognitive Neuroscience, 9*(5), 555–604.

Neisser, U., Boodoo, G., Bouchard Jr., T. J., et al. (1996). Intelligence: Knowns and unknowns. *American Psychologist, 51*(2), 77–101.

Nisbett, R. E., Aronson, J., Blair, C., et al. (2012). Intelligence: New findings and theoretical developments. *American Psychologist, 67*(2), 130-159.

Nosofsky, R. M. (1987). Attention and learning processes in the identification and categorization of integral stimuli. *Journal of Experimental Psychology: Learning, Memory, and Cognition, 13*, 87–108.

Oakes, L. M., & Cohen, L. B. (1990). Infant perception of a causal event. *Cognitive Development, 5*(2), 193–207.

Osherson, D. N., Wilkie, O., Smith, E. E., et al. (1990). Category-based induction. *Psychological Review, 97*(2), 185–200.

Owen, A. M., Hampshire, A., Grahn, J. A., et al. (2010). Putting brain training to the test. *Nature, 465*(7299), 775–778.

Piaget, J., & Inhelder, B. (1956). *The Child's Conception of Space*. London: Routledge & Kegan Paul.

Plomin, R. (1990). The role of inheritance in behavior. *Science, 248*(4952), 183–188.

Posner, M. I., & Keele, S. W. (1968). On the genesis of abstract ideas. *Journal of Experimental Psychology, 77*, 353–363.

Posner, M. I., Boies, S. J., Eichelman, W. H., & Taylor, R. L. (1969). Retention of visual and name codes of single letters. *Journal of Experimental Psychology, 79*, 1–16.

Posner, M. I., Goldsmith, R., & Welton Jr., K. E. (1967). Perceived distance and the classification of distorted patterns. *Journal of Experimental Psychology, 73*(1), 28–38.

Purves, D., Brannon, E. M., Cabeza, R., et al. (2008). *Principles of Cognitive Neuroscience*. Sunderland, MA: Oxford University Press/Sinauer.

Purves, D., LaBar, K. S., Platt, M. L., et al. (2012). *Principles of Cognitive Neuroscience*, 2nd Edition. Sunderland, MA: Oxford University Press/Sinauer.

Raven, J. (2000). The Raven's progressive matrices: Change and stability over culture and time. *Cognitive Psychology, 41*(1), 1–48.

Rosch, E. H. (1973). Natural categories. *Cognitive Psychology, 4*(3), 328–350.

Rosch, E., & Mervis, C. B. (1975). Family resemblances: Studies in the internal structure of categories. *Cognitive Psychology, 7*(4), 573–605.

Rosch, E., Mervis, C. B., Gray, W. D., et al. (1976). Basic objects in natural categories. *Cognitive Psychology, 8*(3), 382–439.

Rumelhart, D. E., McClelland, J. L., & PDP Research Group. (1988). *Parallel Distributed Processing: Explanations in the micro structure of cognition*, Vol. 1. Cambridge, MA: The MIT Press.

Ryan, J. J., Sattler, J. M., & Lopez, S. J. (2000). Age effects on Wechsler Adult Intelligence Scale-III subtests. *Archives of Clinical Neuropsychology, 15*, 311–317.

Sala, G., & Gobet, F. (2020). Cognitive and academic benefits of music training in children: A multilevel meta-analysis. *Memory & Cognition, 48*(8), 1429–1441.

Salovey, P., & Grewal, D. (2005). The science of emotional intelligence. *Current Directions in Psychological Science, 14*(6), 281–285.

Schellenberg, E. G. (2004). Music lessons enhance IQ. *Psychological Science, 15*(8), 511–514.

Sheppard, L. D., & Vernon, P. A. (2008). Intelligence and speed of information-processing: A review of 50 years of research. *Personality and Individual Differences, 44*(3), 535–551.

Simons, D. J., Boot, W. R., Charness, N., et al. (2016). Do "brain-training" programs work? *Psychological Science in the Public Interest, 17*(3), 103–186.

Slater, A., Von der Schulenburg, C., Brown, E., et al. (1998). Newborn infants prefer attractive faces. *Infant Behavior and Development, 21*(2), 345–354.

Smith, E. E., & Medin, D. L. (1981). *Categories and Concepts.* Cambridge, MA: Harvard University Press.

Smith, E. E., Shoben, E. J., & Rips, L. J. (1974). Structure and process in semantic memory: A featural model for semantic decisions. *Psychological Review, 81*(3), 214–241.

Spearman, C. (1904). "General intelligence," objectively determined and measured. *The American Journal of Psychology, 15*(2), 201–293.

Spelke, E. S., & Kinzler, K. D. (2007). Core knowledge. *Developmental Science, 10*(1), 89–96.

Spelke, E. S., Katz, G., Purcell, S. E., et al. (1994). Early knowledge of object motion: Continuity and inertia. *Cognition, 51*(2), 131–176.

Steele, C.M. (1997). A threat in the air: How stereotypes shape intellectual identity and performance. *American Psychologist, 52*, 613-629.

Sternberg, R. J. (1984). Toward a triarchic theory of human intelligence. *Behavioral and Brain Sciences, 7*(2), 269–315.

Sternberg, R. J., & Detterman, D. K. (1986). *What is Intelligence? Contemporary viewpoints on its nature and definition.* Westport, CT: Praeger Publishers/Greenwood Publishing Group.

Stevenson, H., & Stigler, J. W. (1992). *Learning Gap: Why Our Schools Are Failing And What We Can Learn From Japanese And Chinese Education.* New York: Summit Books.

Thurstone, L. L. (1938). Primary mental abilities. *Psychometric Monographs, 1*, ix–121.

Tigner, R. B., & Tigner, S. S. (2000). Triarchic theories of intelligence: Aristotle and Sternberg. *History of Psychology, 3*, 168–176.

Vernon, P. A., & Kantor, L. (1986). Reaction time correlations with intelligence test scores obtained under either timed or untimed conditions. *Intelligence, 10*(4),

Vernon, P. A., & Weese, S. E. (1993). Predicting intelligence with multiple speed of information-processing tests. *Personality and Individual Differences, 14*(3),

Warrington, E. K., & Mccarthy, R. A. (1987). Categories of knowledge: Further fractionations and an attempted integration. *Brain, 110*(5), 1273–1296.

Warrington, E. K., & Shallice, T. (1984). Category specific semantic impairments. *Brain, 107*(3), 829–853.

Wechsler, D. (2008). *Wechsler Adult Intelligence Scale*, 4th Edition. San Antonio, TX: Pearson Assessment.

Wechsler, D. (2014). *Wechsler Intelligence Scale for Children*, 4th Edition. San Antonio, TX: Pearson Assessment.

Wechsler, D. (1939). *The Measurement of Adult Intelligence.* Baltimore: The William and Wilkins Company.

Whalley, L. J., & Deary, I. J. (2001). Longitudinal cohort study of childhood IQ and survival up to age 76. *BMJ (Clinical Research Ed.), 322*(7290), 819.

Wittgenstein, L. (1953). *Philosophical Investigations.* Hoboken, NJ: Wiley-Blackwell.

Woodward, A. L. (1998). Infants selectively encode the goal object of an actor's reach. *Cognition, 69*(1), 1–34.

Woolley, A. W., Chabris, C. F., Pentland, A., et al. (2010). Evidence for a collective intelligence factor in the performance of human groups. *Science, 330*(6004), 686 –688.

Wynn, K. (1992). Addition and subtraction by human infants. *Nature, 358*(6389), 749–750.

Chapter 12

Aboud, F. E. (1988). *Children and Prejudice.* New York: Basil Blackwell.

Agerström, J., & Rooth, D.-O. (2011). The role of automatic obesity stereotypes in real hiring discrimination. *Journal of Applied Psychology, 96*(4), 790–805.

Allport, G. W. (1954). *The Nature of Prejudice.* Boston: Addison-Wesley.

Ambady, N., Hallahan, M., & Conner, B. (1999). Accuracy of judgments of sexual orientation from thin slices of behavior. *Journal of Personality and Social Psychology, 77*(3), 538–547.

Ambady, N., & Rosenthal, R. (1993). Half a minute: Predicting teacher evaluations from thin slices of nonverbal behavior and physical attractiveness. *Journal of Personality and Social Psychology, 64*(3), 431–441.

Amodio, D. M., & Cikara, M. (2021). The social neuroscience of prejudice. *Annual Review of Psychology, 72*, 439–469.

Amodio, D. M., Harmon-Jones, E., Devine, P. G., et al. (2004). Neural signals for the detection of unintentional race bias. *Psychological Science, 15*(2), 88–93.

Amodio, D. M. & Swencionis, J. K. (2018). Proactive control of implicit bias: A theoretical model and implications for behavior change. *Journal of Personality and Social Psychology, 115*, 255–275.

Arcuri, L., Castelli, L., Galdi, S., et al. (2008). Predicting the vote: Implicit attitudes as predictors of the future behavior of the decided and undecided voters. *Political Psychology, 29*, 369–387.

Avenanti, A., Sirigu, A. & Aglioti, S. M. (2010). Racial bias reduces empathic sensorimotor resonance with other-race pain. *Current Biology, 20*, 1018–1022.

Azevedo, R. T., Macaluso, E., Avenanti, A., et al. (2013). Their pain is not our pain: Brain and autonomic correlates of empathic resonance with the pain of same and different race individuals. *Human Brain Mapping, 34*, 3168–3181.

Bail, C. A., Argyle, L. P., Brown, T. W., et al. (2018). Exposure to opposing views on social media can increase political polarization. *Proceedings of the National Academy of Sciences, 115*, 9216–9221.

Banaji, M. R., & Hardin, C. D. (1996). Automatic stereotyping. *Psychological Science, 7*(3), 136–141.

Bargh, J. A. (1994). The four horsemen of automaticity: Awareness, intention, efficiency, and control in social cognition. In R. S. Wyer, Jr. & T. K. Srull (Eds.), *Handbook of Social Cognition: Basic processes; Applications* (pp. 1–40). Mahwah, NJ: Lawrence Erlbaum Associates, Inc.

Bargh, J. A., & Williams, E. L. (2006). The automaticity of social life. *Current Directions in Psychological Science, 15*(1), 1–4.

Baron-Cohen, S., Leslie, A. M., & Frith, U. (1985). Does the autistic child have a "theory of mind"? *Cognition, 21*(1), 37–46.

Batson, C. D. (2009). These things called empathy: Eight related but distinct phenomena. In J. Decety & W.J. Ickes (Eds.), *The Social Neuroscience of Empathy* (pp. 3–15). Cambridge, MA: The MIT Press.

Batson, C. D., & Ahmad, N. Y. (2009). Using empathy to improve intergroup attitudes and relations, *Social Issues and Policy Review, 3*, 141–177.

Berry, D. S., & McArthur, L. Z. (1985). Some components and consequences of a babyface. *Journal of Personality and Social Psychology, 48*(2), 312–323.

Berry, D. S., & Zebrowitz-McArthur, L. (1988). What's in a face?: Facial maturity and the attribution of legal responsibility. *Personality and Social Psychology Bulletin, 14*(1), 23–33.

Bickart, K. C., Wright, C. I., Dautoff, R. J., et al. (2011). Amygdala volume and social network size in humans. *Nature Neuroscience, 14*(2), 163–164.

Biernat, M. (1991). Gender stereotypes and the relationship between masculinity and femininity: A developmental analysis. *Journal of Personality and Social Psychology, 61*(3), 351–365.

Billig, M. (1985), Prejudice, categorization and particularization: From a perceptual to a rhetorical approach. *European Journal of Social Psychology, 15*, 79–103.

Blair, I. V. (2002). The malleability of automatic stereotypes and prejudice. *Personality and Social Psychology Review, 6*(3), 242–261.

Blanton, H., Jaccard, J., Klick, J., et al. (2009). Strong claims and weak evidence: Reassessing the predictive validity of the IAT. *Journal of Applied Psychology, 94*(3), 567–582.

Bonanno, G. A. & Burton, C. L. (2013). Regulatory flexibility: An individual differences perspective on coping and emotion regulation. *Perspectives on Psychological Science, 8*, 591–612.

Bradbard, M. R., Martin, C. L., Endsley, R. C., & Halverson, C. F. (1986). Influence of sex stereotypes on children's exploration and memory: A competence versus performance distinction. *Developmental Psychology, 22*(4), 481–486.

Breedlove, S. M. & Watson, N. V. (2019). *Behavioral Neuroscience*, 9th Edition. Sunderland, MA: Oxford University Press/Sinauer.

Brewer, M. B., & Lui, L. N. (1989). The primacy of age and sex in the structure of person categories. *Social Cognition, 7*(3), 262–274.

Cacioppo, J. T. & Cacioppo, S. (2014). Social relationships and health: The toxic effects of perceived social isolation. *Social and Personality Psychology Compass, 8*, 58–72.

Cadogan, G. (2015). Black and blue. In J. Freeman (Ed.), Freeman's: *Arrival: The Best New Writing on Arrival*. New York: Grove Atlantic.

Cameron, C. D., Hutcherson, C. A., Ferguson, A. M., et al. (2019). Empathy is hard work: People choose to avoid empathy because of its cognitive costs. *Journal of Experimental Psychology: General, 148*(6), 962–976.

Campbell, D. T. (1958). Common fate, similarity, and other indices of the status of aggregates of persons as social entities. *Behavioral Science, 3*, 14–25.

Castelli, F., Happé, F., Frith, U., & Frith, C. (2000). Movement and mind: A functional imaging study of perception and interpretation of complex intentional movement patterns. *NeuroImage, 12*, 314–325.

Chambers, D. W. (1983). Stereotypic images of the scientist: The Draw-A-Scientist test. *Science Education, 67*, 255–265.

Cikara, M. Botvinick, M. M., & Fiske, S. T. (2011). Us versus them: Social identity shapes neural responses to intergroup competition and harm. *Psychological Science, 22*, 306–313.

Cikara, M., Bruneau, E. G., & Saxe, R. R. (2017). Us and them: Intergroup failures of empathy. *Current Directions in Psychological Science, 20*, 149–153.

Cikara, M. & Fiske, S. T. (2012). Stereotypes and schadenfreude: Affective and physiological markers of pleasure at outgroup misfortunes. *Social Psychological and Personality Science, 3*, 63–71.

Combs, D. J. Y., Powell, C. A. J., Schurtz, D. R., & Smith, R. H. (2009). Politics, *schadenfreude*, and ingroup identification: The sometimes happy thing about a poor economy and death. *Journal of Experimental Social Psychology, 45*, 635–646.

Contreras, J. M., Banaji, M. R., & Mitchell, J. P. (2012). Dissociable neural correlates of stereotypes and other forms of semantic knowledge. *Social Cognitive and Affective Neuroscience, 7*(7), 764–770.

Correll, J., Park, B., Judd, C. M., & Wittenbrink, B. (2002). The police officer's dilemma: Using ethnicity to disambiguate potentially threatening individuals. *Journal of Personality and Social Psychology, 83*(6), 1314–1329.

Cosmides, L. (1989). The logic of social exchange: Has natural selection shaped how humans reason? Studies with the Wason selection task. *Cognition, 31*(3), 187–276.

Cosmides, L., & Tooby, J. (1992). Cognitive adaptations for social exchange. In J. H. Barkow, L. Cosmides, & J. Tooby (Eds.), *The Adapted Mind: Evolutionary psychology and the generation of culture* (pp. 163–228). New York: Oxford University Press.

Crockett, M. J. (2013). Models of morality. *Trends in Cognitive Sciences, 17*(8), 363–366.

Cuddy, A. J. C., Rock, M. S., & Norton, M. I. (2007). Aid in the Aftermath of Hurricane Katrina: Inferences of Secondary Emotions and Intergroup Helping. *Group Processes & Intergroup Relations, 10*(1), 107–118. https://doi.org/10.1177/1368430207071344

Cushman, F. (2013). Action, outcome, and value: A dual-system framework for morality. *Personality and Social Psychology Review, 17*(3), 273–292.

Dapretto, M., Davies, M. S., Pfeifer, J. H., et al. (2006). Understanding emotions in others: Mirror neuron dysfunction in children with autism spectrum disorders. *Nature Neuroscience, 9,* 28–30.

Dasgupta, N., & Greenwald, A. G. (2001). On the malleability of automatic attitudes: Combating automatic prejudice with images of admired and disliked individuals. *Journal of Personality and Social Psychology, 81*(5), 800–814.

Decety, J., & Jackson, P. L. (2004). The functional architecture of human empathy. *Behavioral and Cognitive Neuroscience Reviews, 3,* 71–100.

Deveney, C. M., & Pizzagalli, D. A. (2008). The cognitive consequences of emotion regulation: An ERP investigation. *Psychophysiology, 45*(3), 435–444.

Devine, P. G. (1989). Stereotypes and prejudice: Their automatic and controlled components. *Journal of Personality and Social Psychology, 56*(1), 5–18.

Dimberg, U., Thunberg, M., & Elmehed, K. (2000). Unconscious facial reactions to emotional facial expressions. *Psychological Science, 11,* 86–89.

Dion, K., Berscheid, E., & Walster, E. (1972). What is beautiful is good. *Journal of Personality and Social Psychology, 24*(3), 285–290.

Dovidio, J. F., Evans, N., & Tyler, R. B. (1986). Racial stereotypes: The contents of their cognitive representations. *Journal of Experimental Social Psychology, 22*(1), 22–37.

Dunbar, R. I. M. (1993). Coevolution of neocortical size, group size and language in humans. *Behavioral and Brain Sciences, 16*(4), 681–735.

Dunbar, R. I. M. (1998). The social brain hypothesis. *Evolutionary Anthropology, 6,* 178–190.

Dunbar, R. I. M. (2014). The social brain: Psychological underpinnings and implications for the structure of organizations. *Current Directions in Psychological Science, 23*(2), 109–114.

Ecker, U. K., Lewandowsky, S., Swire, B., & Chang, D. (2011). Correcting false information in memory: manipulating the strength of misinformation encoding and its retraction. *Psychonomic Bulletin & Review, 18*(3), 570–578.

Ehrlich, H. J. (1973). *The Social Psychology of Prejudice: A systematic theoretical review and propositional inventory of the American social psychological study of prejudice.* New York: John Wiley & Sons.

Eisenberger, N. I. (2012). The pain of social disconnection: Examining the shared neural underpinnings of physical and social pain. *Nature Reviews Neuroscience, 13,* 421–434.

Eisenberger, N. I., Lieberman, M. D., & Williams, K. D. (2003). Does rejection hurt? An fMRI study of social exclusion. *Science, 302,* 290–292.

Epley, N., Akalis, S., Waytz, A., & Cacioppo, J. T. (2008). Creating social connection through inferential reproduction: Loneliness and perceived agency in gadgets, gods, and greyhounds. *Psychological Science, 19,* 114–120.

Epley, N., Waytz, A., Akalis, S., & Cacioppo, J. T. (2008). When we need a human: Motivational determinants of anthropomorphism. *Social Cognition, 26,* 143–155.

Fazio, R. H. (1990). Multiple processes by which attitudes guide behavior: The MODE model as an integrative framework. In M. Zanna (Ed.), *Advances in Experimental Social Psychology* (pp. 75–109). San Diego: Academic Press.

Fazio, R. H., Jackson, J. R., Dunton, B. C., & Williams, C. J. (1995). Variability in automatic activation as an unobtrusive measure of racial attitudes: A bona fide pipeline? *Journal of Personality and Social Psychology, 69*(6), 1013–1027.

Fiske, S. T. (2018). Stereotype content: Warmth and competence endure. *Current Directions in Psychological Science, 27,* 67–73.

Fiske, S. T., Cuddy, A. J., Glick, P., & Xu, J. (2002). A model of (often mixed) stereotype content: Competence and warmth respectively follow from perceived status and competition. *Journal of Personality and Social Psychology, 82,* 878–902.

Fiske, S. T., Lin, M., & Neuberg, S. L. (1999). The continuum model: Ten years later. In S. Chaiken & Y. Trope (Eds.), *Dual-Process Theories in Social Psychology* (pp. 231–254). New York: Guilford Press.

Fiske, S. T., & Neuberg S. L. (1990). A continuum of impression formation, from category-based to individuating processes. In M. P. Zanna (Ed.), *Advances in Experimental Social Psychology* (pp. 1–74). New York: Academic Press.

Fiske, S. T. & Taylor, S. E. (2017). *Social Cognition: From Brains to Culture,* 3rd Edition. LondoN: Sage Publications.

Forscher, P. S., Lai, C. K., Axt, J. R., et al. (2019). A meta-analysis of procedures to change implicit measures. *Journal of Personality and Social Psychology, 117*(3), 522–559.

Friedman, T. L. (2018). The American Civil War, Part II. *The New York Times,* October 2, 2018. https://www.nytimes.com/2018/10/02/opinion/the-american-civil-war-part-ii.html

Frith, U., & Frith, C. (2001). The biological basis of social interaction. *Current Directions in Psychological Science, 10*(5), 151–155.

Gaertner, S. L., & Dovidio, J. F. (2000). *Reducing Intergroup Bias: The common ingroup identity model*. London: Psychology Press.

Galdi, S., Arcuri, L., & Gawronski, B. (2008). Automatic mental associations predict future choices of undecided decision-makers. *Science, 321,* 1100–1102.

Gilbert, D. T., & Hixon, J. G. (1991). The trouble of thinking: Activation and application of stereotypic beliefs. *Journal of Personality and Social Psychology, 60*(4), 509–517.

Gorn, G. J., Jiang, Y., & Johar, G. V. (2008). Babyfaces, trait inferences, and company evaluations in a public relations crisis. *Journal of Consumer Research, 35,* 36–49.

Gray, H. M., Gray, K., & Wegner, D. M. (2007). Dimensions of mind perception. *Science, 315*(5812), 619.

Gray, K., Young, L., & Waytz, A. (2012). Mind perception is the essence of morality. *Psychological Inquiry, 23*(2), 101–124.

Green, A. R., Carney, D. R., Pallin, D. J., et al. (2007). The presence of implicit bias in physicians and its prediction of thrombolysis decisions for black and white patients. *Journal of General Internal Medicine. 22,* 1231–1238.

Greene, J. D., Sommerville, R. B., Nystrom, L. E., et al. (2001). An fMRI investigation of emotional engagement in moral judgment. *Science, 293*(5537), 2105–2108.

Greenwald, A. G., Banaji, M. R., & Nosek, B. A. (2015). Statistically small effects of the implicit association test can have societally large effects. *Journal of Personality & Social Psychology, 108*(4), 553–561.

Greenwald, A. G., McGhee, D. E., & Schwartz, J. L. K. (1998). Measuring individual differences in implicit cognition: The implicit association test. *Journal of Personality and Social Psychology, 74*(6), 1464–1480.

Gross, J. J. (2001). Emotion regulation in adulthood: Timing is everything. *Current Directions in Psychological Science, 10*(6), 214–219.

Gross, J. J. (2002). Emotion regulation: affective, cognitive, and social consequences. *Psychophysiology, 39,* 281–291.

Gross, J. J., & John, O. P. (2003). Individual differences in two emotion regulation processes: Implications for affect, relationships, and well-being. *Journal of Personality and Social Psychology, 85*(2), 348–362.

Gutsell, J. N., & Inzlicht, M. (2010). Empathy constrained: Prejudice predicts reduced mental simulation of actions during observation of outgroups. *Journal of Experimental Social Psychology, 46*(5), 841–845.

Hackel, L. M., Looser, C. E., & Van Bavel, J. J. (2014). Group membership alters the threshold for mind perception: The role of social identity, collective identification, and intergroup threat. *Journal of Experimental Social Psychology, 52,* 15–23.

Hagá, S., Olson, K. R., & Garcia-Marques, L. (2018). The bias blind spot across childhood. *Social Cognition, 36*(6), 671–708.

Haidt, J. (2001). The emotional dog and its rational tail: A social intuitionist approach to moral judgment. *Psychological Review, 108*(4), 814–834.

Hamilton, D. L. (1981). Stereotyping and intergroup behavior: Some thoughts on the cognitive approach. In D.

L. Hamilton (Ed.), *Cognitive Processes in Stereotyping and Intergroup Behavior* (pp. 333–353). Hillsdale, NJ: Erlbaum.

Harris, L. T., & Fiske, S. T. (2006). Dehumanizing the Lowest of the Low: Neuroimaging Responses to Extreme Out-Groups. *Psychological Science, 17*(10), 847–853.

Harris, L. T., & Fiske, S. T. (2007). Social groups that elicit disgust are differentially processed in mPFC. *Social Cognitive and Affective Neuroscience, 2*(1), 45–51.

Harris, L. T., & Fiske, S. T. (2011). Dehumanized perception: A psychological means to facilitate atrocities, torture, and genocide? *Zeitschrift fur Psychologie, 219*(3), 175–181.

Harris, L. T., McClure, S. M., van den Bos, W., et al. (2007). Regions of the MPFC differentially tuned to social and nonsocial affective evaluation. *Cognitive, Affective & Behavioral Neuroscience, 7*(4), 309–316.

Hehman, E., Mania, E. W., & Gaertner, S. L. (2010). Where the division lies: Common ingroup identity moderates the cross-race facial-recognition effect. *Journal of Experimental Social Psychology, 46*(2), 445–448.

Heider, F., & Simmel, M. (1944). An experimental study of apparent behavior. *The American Journal of Psychology, 57,* 243–259.

Hein, G., Silani, G., Preuschoff, K., et al. (2010). Neural responses to ingroup and outgroup members' suffering predict individual differences in costly helping. *Neuron, 68,* 149–160.

Inzlicht, M., & Gutsell, J. N. (2007). Running on empty: Neural signals for self-control failure. *Psychological Science, 18*(11), 933–937.

Ito, T. A., Willadsen-Jensen, E., & Correll, J. (2007). Social neuroscience and social perception: New perspectives on categorization, prejudice, and stereotyping. In E. Harmon-Jones & P. Winkielman (Eds.), *Social Neuroscience: Integrating biological and psychological explanations of social behavior* (pp. 401–421). New York: Guilford Press.

John, O. P., & Gross, J. J. (2004). Healthy and unhealthy emotion regulation: Personality processes, individual differences, and life span development. *Journal of Personality, 72,* 1301–1334.

Johnson, H. M., & Seifert, C. M. (1994). Sources of the continued influence effect: When misinformation in memory affects later inferences. *Journal of Experimental Psychology: Learning, Memory, and Cognition, 20,* 1420–1436

Jussim, L. & Harber, K. D. (2005). Teacher expectations and self-fulfilling prophecies: knowns and unknowns, resolved and unresolved controversies. *Personality and Social Psychology Review, 9,* 131–155.

Kanai, R., Bahrami, B., Roylance, R., & Rees, G. (2012). Online social network size is reflected in human brain structure. *Proceedings. Biological sciences, 279*(1732), 1327–1334.

Kanwisher, N., McDermott, J., & Chun, M. M. (1997). The fusiform face area: A module in human extrastriate cortex specialized for face perception. *The Journal of Neuroscience, 17*(11), 4302–4311.

Kaplan, J., Gimbel, S. & Harris, S. (2016). Neural correlates of maintaining one's political beliefs in the face of counterevidence. *Scientific Reports, 6,* 39589.

Krieglmeyer, R., & Sherman, J. W. (2012). Disentangling stereotype activation and stereotype application in the stereotype misperception task. *Journal of Personality and Social Psychology, 103*(2), 205–224.

Kuhn, D., Nash, S. C., & Brucken, L. (1978). Sex role concepts of two- and three-year-olds. *Child Development, 49,* 445–451.

Kunda, Z. (1990). The case for motivated reasoning. *Psychological Bulletin, 108*(3), 480–498.

Kunda, Z., & Sinclair, L. (1999). Motivated reasoning with stereotypes: Activation, application, and inhibition. *Psychological Inquiry, 10*(1), 12–22.

Leach, C. W. & Spears, R. (2009). Dejection at in-group defeat and schadenfreude toward second- and third-party out-groups. *Emotion, 9,* 659–665.

Lewandowsky, S., Ecker, U. K., Seifert, C. M., et al. (2012). Misinformation and its correction: Continued influence and successful debiasing. *Psychological Science in the Public Interest, 13*(3), 106–131.

Lewin, K. (1939). Field theory and experiment in social psychology: Concepts and methods. *American Journal of Sociology, 44,* 868–896.

Lindenfors, P., Wartel, A., & Lind, J. (2021). 'Dunbar's number' deconstructed. *Biology letters, 17*(5), 20210158.

Lord, C. G., Ross, L., & Lepper, M. R. (1979). Biased assimilation and attitude polarization: The effects of prior theories on subsequently considered evidence. *Journal of Personality and Social Psychology, 37*(11), 2098–2109.

Lowery, B. S., Hardin, C. D., & Sinclair, S. (2001). Social influence effects on automatic racial prejudice. *Journal of Personality and Social Psychology, 81*(5), 842–855.

Maccoby, E. E., & Jacklin, C. N. (1987). Gender segregation in childhood. In H. W. Reese (Ed.), *Advances in Child Development and Behavior, Vol. 20* (p. 239–287). New York: Academic Press.

Malhotra, D. & Liyanage, S. (2005). Long-term effects of peace workshops in protracted conflicts. *Journal of Conflict Resolution, 49,* 908–924.

Malpass, R. S. & Kravitz, J. (1969). Recognition for faces of own and other race. *Journal of Personality and Social Psychology, 13,* 330–334.

Manktelow, K. I., & Evans, J. S. (1979). Facilitation of reasoning by realism: Effect or non-effect? *British Journal of Psychology, 70*(4), 477–488.

Masten, C. L., Gillen-O'Neel, C., & Brown, C. S. (2010). Children's intergroup empathic processing: The roles of novel ingroup identification, situational distress, and social anxiety. *Journal of Experimental Child Psychology, 106,* 115–128.

Meissner, C. A. & Brigham, J. C. (2001). Thirty years of investigating the own-race bias in memory for faces: A meta-analysis review. *Psychology, Public Policy, and Law, 7,* 3–35.

Mill, J. S. (1869). *The Subjection of Women.* London: Longmans, Green, Reader and Dyer.

Miller, D. I., Nolla, K. M., Eagly, A. H., & Uttal, D. H. (2018). The development of children's gender-science stereotypes: A meta-analysis of 5 decades of U.S. draw-a-scientist studies. *Child Development, 89*(6), 1943–1955.

Mitchel, A., Gottfried, J., Kiley, J., & Matsa, K. E. (2014). *Political Polarization and Media Habits.* Pew Research Center. Washington, D.C. https://www.journalism. org/2014/10/21/political-polarization-media-habits/.

Mitchell, J. P., Heatherton, T. F., & Macrae, C. N. (2002). Distinct neural systems subserve person and object knowledge. *Proceedings of the National Academy of Sciences of the United States of America, 99*(23), 15238–15243.

Mitchell, J. P., Nosek, B. A., & Banaji, M. R. (2003). Contextual variations in implicit evaluation. *Journal of Experimental Psychology: General, 132*(3), 455–469.

Moser, J. S., Most, S. B. & Simons, R. F. (2010). Increasing negative emotions by reappraisal enhances subsequent cognitive control: A combined behavioral and electrophysiological study. *Cognitive, Affective, & Behavioral Neuroscience, 10,* 195–207.

Mosleh, M., Pennycook, G., Arechar, A. A., & Rand, D. G. (2021). Cognitive reflection correlates with behavior on Twitter. *Nature communications, 12*(1), 921.

Moss-Racusin, C. A., Dovidio, J. F., Brescoll, V. L., et al. (2012). Science faculty's subtle gender biases favor male students. *Proceedings of the National Academy of Sciences of the United States of America, 109*(41), 16474–16479.

Most, S. B., Sorber, A. V., & Cunningham, J. G. (2007). Auditory Stroop reveals implicit gender associations in adults and children. *Journal of Experimental Social Psychology, 43*(2), 287–294.

Neisser, U. (1976). *Cognition and Reality: Principles and implications of cognitive psychology.* New York: W. H. Freeman/Times Books/Henry Holt & Co.

Nisbett, R. E., & Wilson, T. D. (1977). Telling more than we can know: Verbal reports on mental processes. *Psychological Review, 84*(3), 231–259.

Nock, M. K., & Banaji, M. R. (2007). Assessment of self-injurious thoughts using a behavioral test. *American Journal of Psychiatry, 164,* 820–823.

Nock, M. K., & Banaji, M. R. (2007). Prediction of suicide ideation and attempts among adolescents using a brief performance-based test. *Journal of Consulting and Clinical Psychology, 75,* 707–715.

Nyhan, B., & Reifler, J. (2010). When corrections fail: The persistence of political misperceptions. *Political Behavior, 32*(2), 303–330.

O'Brien, M., & Huston, A. C. (1985). Development of sex-typed play behavior in toddlers. *Developmental Psychology, 21*(5), 866–871.

Ochsner, K. N., & Gross, J. J. (2005). The cognitive control of emotion. *Trends in Cognitive Sciences, 9,* 242–249.

Ochsner, K. N., Silvers, J. A., & Buhle, J. T. (2012). Functional imaging studies of emotion regulation: a synthetic review and evolving model of the cognitive control of emotion. *Annals of the New York Academy of Sciences, 1251*, E1–E24.

Olsson, A., Ebert, J. P., Banaji, M. R., and Phelps, E. A. (2005). The r*ole of social groups in the persistence of learned fear. Science, 309*, 785–787.

Oswald, F. L., Mitchell, G., Blanton, H., et al. (2013). Predicting ethnic and racial discrimination: A meta-analysis of IAT criterion studies. *Journal of Personality and Social Psychology, 105*(2), 171–192.

Paluck, E. L., (2009). Reducing intergroup prejudice and conflict using the media: A field experiment in Rwanda. *Journal of Personality and Social Psychology, 96*, 574–587.

Payne, B. K. (2001). Prejudice and perception: The role of automatic and controlled processes in misperceiving a weapon. *Journal of Personality and Social Psychology, 81*(2), 181–192.

Pennycook, G., Epstein, Z., Mosleh, M., et al. (2021). Shifting attention to accuracy can reduce misinformation online. *Nature, 592*(7855), 590–595.

Pennycook, G., & Rand, D. G. (2019). Lazy, not biased: Susceptibility to partisan fake news is better explained by lack of reasoning than by motivated reasoning. *Cognition, 188*, 39–50.

Perrett, D. I., Burt, D. M., Penton-Voak, I. S., et al. (1999). Symmetry and human facial attractiveness. *Evolution and Human Behavior, 20*, 295–307.

Peters, W. (1985). *A Class Divided*. Consortium of Public Television Stations, Yale University, & PBS Video. Washington, DC: PBS Video.

Pitcher, D., & Ungerleider, L. G. (2021). Evidence for a third visual pathway specialized for social perception. *Trends in Cognitive Sciences, 25*(2), 100–110.

Premack, D., and Woodruff, G. (1978). Does the chimpanzee have a theory of mind? *Behavioral & Brain Sciences, 1*, 515–526.

Preston, S. D., & de Waal, F. B. M. (2002). Empathy: Its ultimate and proximate bases. *Behavioral and Brain Sciences, 25*, 1–72.

Pronin, E., Lin, D. Y., & Ross, L. (2002). The bias blind spot: Perceptions of bias in self versus others. *Personality and Social Psychology Bulletin, 28*(3), 369–381.

Redlawsk, D. P., Civettini, A. J. W., & Emmerson, K. M. (2010). The affective tipping point: Do motivated reasoners ever "get it"? *Political Psychology, 31*, 563–593.

Richeson, J. A., & Ambady, N. (2003). Effects of situational power on automatic racial prejudice. *Journal of Experimental Social Psychology, 39*(2), 177–183.

Richeson, J. A., Baird, A. A., Gordon, H. L., et al. (2003). An fMRI investigation of the impact of interracial contact on executive function. *Nature Neuroscience, 6*, 1323–1328.

Richeson, J. A., & Shelton, J. N. (2003). When prejudice does not pay: Effects of interracial contact on executive function. *Psychological Science, 14*(3), 287–290.

Rizzolatti, G., & Craighero, L. (2004). The mirror-neuron system. *Annual Review of Neuroscience, 27*, 169–192

Rosenthal, R. (1974). *On the Social Psychology of the Self-Fulfilling Prophecy: Further evidence for Pygmalion effects and their mediating mechanisms*. New York: MSS Modular.

Rosenthal, R. & Jacobson, L. (1968). *Pygmalion in the Classroom: Teacher expectations and student intellectual development*. New York: Holt.

Ross, L., Greene, D., & House, P. (1977). The "false consensus effect": An egocentric bias in social perception and attribution processes. *Journal of Experimental Social Psychology, 13*, 279–301.

Saxe, R., & Kanwisher, N. (2003). People thinking about thinking people: The role of the temporo-parietal junction in "theory of mind". *NeuroImage, 19*, 1835–1842.

Saxe, R., Xiao, D., Kovács, G., et al. (2004). A region of right posterior superior temporal sulcus responds to observed intentional actions. *Neuropsychologia, 42*, 1435–1446.

Schmeichel, B. J. (2007). Attention control, memory updating, and emotion regulation temporarily reduce the capacity for executive control. *Journal of Experimental Psychology: General, 136*(2), 241–255.

Scholl, B. J., & Tremoulet, P. D. (2000). Perceptual causality and animacy. *Trends in Cognitive Sciences, 4*, 299–309.

Shamosh, N. A., & Gray, J. R. (2007). The relation between fluid intelligence and self-regulatory depletion. *Cognition and Emotion, 21*(8), 1833–1843.

Smith, R. H., Powell, C. A. J., Combs, D. J. Y., & Schurtz, D. R. (2009). Exploring the when and why of Schadenfreude. *Social and Personality Psychology Compass, 3*, 530–546.

Stiller, J., & Dunbar, R. I. M. (2007). Perspective-taking and memory capacity predict social network size. *Social Networks, 29*(1), 93–104.

Tajfel, H. (1970). Experiments in intergroup discrimination. *Scientific American, 223*, 96–102.

Tajfel, H. (1981). *Human Groups and Social Categories: Studies in social psychology*. Cambridge: Cambridge University Press.

Tajfel, H., Billig, M. G., Bundy, R. P., & Flament, C. (1971). Social categorization and intergroup behaviour. *European Journal of Social Psychology, 1*(2), 149–178.

Takahashi, H., Kato, M., Matsuura, M., et al. (2009). When your gain is my pain and your pain is my gain: Neural correlates of envy and Schadenfreude. *Science, 323*, 937–939.

Tavernise, S., & Oppel Jr., R.A. (2020). Spit on, yelled at, attacked: Chinese-Americans fear for their safety. *The New York Times*, March 23, 2020. https://www.nytimes.com/2020/03/23/us/chinese-coronavirus-racist-attacks.html

Teachman, B. A., Smith-Janik, S. B., & Saporito, J. (2007). Information processing biases and panic disorder: Relationships among cognitive and symptom measures. *Behaviour Research and Therapy, 45*, 1791–1811.

Telzer, E. H., van Hoorn, J., Rogers, C. R., & Do, K. T. (2018). Social influence on positive youth development: A developmental neuroscience perspective. *Advances in Child Development and Behavior, 54*, 215–258.

Thush, C., & Wiers, R. W. (2007). Explicit and implicit alcohol-related cognitions and the prediction of future drinking in adolescents. *Addictive Behaviors, 32*, 1367–1383.

Todorov, A., Mandisodza, A. N., Goren, A., & Hall, C. C. (2005). Inferences of competence from faces predict election outcomes. *Science, 308*, 1623–1626.

Troje, N. F. (2002). Decomposing biological motion: A framework for analysis and synthesis of human gait patterns. *Journal of Vision, 2*(5), 371–387.

Turner, J. C., Hogg, M. A., Oakes, P. J., et al. (1987). *Rediscovering the social group: A self-categorization theory.* Oxford: Basil Blackwell.

Unkelbach, C., Forgas, J. P., & Denson, T. F. (2008). The turban effect: The influence of Muslim headgear and induced affect on aggressive responses in the shooter bias paradigm. *Journal of Experimental Social Psychology, 44*(5), 1409–1413.

Van Bavel, J. J., & Cunningham, W. A. (2010). A social neuroscience approach to self and social categorisation: A new look at an old issue. *European Review of Social Psychology, 21*(1), 237–284.

Van Bavel, J. J., Packer, D. J., & Cunningham, W. A. (2008). The neural substrates of in-group bias: a functional magnetic resonance imaging investigation. *Psychological Science, 19*, 1131–1139.

Wason, P. C. (1968). Reasoning about a rule. *Quarterly Journal of Experimental Psychology, 20*, 273–281.

Waytz, A. & Epley, N. (2012). Social connection enables dehumanization. *Journal of Experimental Social Psychology, 48*, 70–76.

Wegner, D. M., Schneider, D. J., Carter, S. R., & White, T. L. (1987). Paradoxical effects of thought suppression. *Journal of Personality and Social Psychology, 53*(1), 5–13.

Westen, D., Blagov, P. S., Harenski, K., et al. (2006). Neural bases of motivated reasoning: An fMRI study of emotional constraints on partisan political judgment in the 2004 U.S. presidential election. *Journal of Cognitive Neuroscience, 18*, 1947–1958.

Wilkes, A. L., & Leatherbarrow, M. (1988). Editing episodic memory following the identification of error. *The Quarterly Journal of Experimental Psychology A: Human Experimental Psychology, 40A*(2), 361–387.

Willis, J., & Todorov, A. (2006). First impressions: making up your mind after a 100-ms exposure to a face. *Psychological Science, 17*, 592–598.

Wood, T., & Porter, E. (2019). The elusive Backfire Effect: Mass attitudes' steadfast factual adherence. *Political Behavior, 41*, 135–163.

Xu, X., Zuo, X., Wang, X., & Han, S. (2009). Do you feel my pain? Racial group membership modulates empathic neural responses. *The Journal of Neuroscience, 29*, 8525–8529.

Zebrowitz, L. A., & McDonald, S. M. (1991). The impact of litigants' baby-facedness and attractiveness on adjudications in small claims courts. *Law and Human Behavior, 15*(6), 603–623.

Index

Page numbers followed by "f" and "t" indicate figures and tables.

About the Book

Editors: Jessica Fiorillo and Joan Kalkut
Project Editor: Linnea Duley
Development Editor: Lauren Mine
Permissions Supervisor: Michele Beckta
Copy Editor: Elizabeth Pierson
Production Manager: Joan Gemme
Photo Researcher: Mark Siddall
Book Design and Production: Donna DiCarlo
Cover Design: Donna DiCarlo
Illustration Program: Dragonfly Media Group
Indexer: Samantha Miller
Cover and Book Manufacturer: LSC Communications